Musical Networks

Musical Networks
Parallel Distributed Perception and Performance

EDITED BY NIALL GRIFFITH AND PETER M. TODD

Bradford Books
The MIT Press
Cambridge, Massachusetts
London, England

This book was set in Plantin on the Monotype "Prism Plus" PostScript Imagesetter by Asco Trade Typesetting Ltd., Hong Kong.

Printed and bound in the United States of America.

Library of Congress Cataloging-in-Publication Data

Musical networks : parallel distributed perception and performance /
   edited by Niall Griffith and Peter M. Todd.
      p.   cm.
   "A Bradford book."
   Includes bibliographical references.
   ISBN 0-262-07181-9 (hardcover : alk. paper)
   1. Musical perception. 2. Cognition. 3. Connectionism.
I. Griffith, Niall. II. Todd, Peter M.
ML3838.M955   1999
781'.11—DC21   98-25671
                                                          CIP
                                                          MN

Contents

Preface

Some 50,000 years ago, our Neanderthal ancestors may have created the first arti-facts—bone flutes—to help produce tonal music (Wilford, 1996). About a decade ago, Rumelhart and McClelland (1986) first widely introduced a new set of com-putational tools—parallel distributed processing (PDP) models of human cogni-tion—that could help us further understand the musical legacy of the past 50 millennia. Five years later, the first book on the musical uses of these new compu-tational tools was published (Todd & Loy, 1991), and now, after a similarly short period of time, we present the current volume with the hope of summarizing the latest work in this field.

What *is* this field? The authors of the chapters in this volume, while coming from a variety of disciplines, all aim at greater understanding of the processes by which we make and listen to music. These processes are all assumed to be implemented in cognitive and perceptual mechanisms, operating on different representations of music in our brains and bodies. To learn more about the processes and repre-sentations involved in music perception, production, comprehension, and compo-sition, the researchers gathered here make computer models based on 'brain-style computation' to see if we can accurately capture human musical behaviour in an artificial system. The extent to which we succeed reflects our level of understanding of the musical phenomena involved. The models all use some form of PDP, pat-terned after the way that the multitudes of interconnected neurons in the brain process information. These so-called 'connectionist' or neural network computer models allow investigation of processes, such as learning and generalization, and forms of representation, such as non-symbolic distributions of activity, that were difficult or impossible to study in earlier psychological models. Hence, the 'musical networks' in this book are all intended to help us explore and learn more about the ways our minds—and brains—behave when perceiving and thinking musically.

Most of the articles collected here come from a special issue of the journal *Connection Science* that we edited on the topic of music and creativity. We have added recent articles on connectionist approaches to musical behaviour that have appeared in other journals as well, and new chapters written specifically for this volume, to make our coverage of the current state of the field as complete as pos-sible. The research presented spans a broad spectrum of musical activity, from the perception of pitch, tonality, meter, and rhythm, to memory and processing of melodic structure, to the creative processes underlying composition and harmoni-zation. As such, we think that there is much of interest in these chapters for readers studying and working in a wide range of cognitive science fields, including percep-tion, psychology, neuroscience, artificial intelligence, music, and anthropology. We now present a brief overview of the material covered in the four sections of this book, followed by an indication of what we could not yet include, and where we would like to see the field progress.

Pitch and Tonality

Beginning the section on connectionist models of pitch and tonality, Ian Taylor and Mike Greenhough ask how we recognize musical pitches irrespective of the instrument that is playing them. The similarities between the timbres of different instruments make this a difficult pattern-matching problem that requires a mechanism capable of fine overtone-series discrimination. Taylor and Greenhough use a supervised ARTMAP network model for this purpose. Supervised learning requires a specific training signal from the environment that is synchronized with the inputs being learned—in this case, a 'teacher' of some sort, for example, visual feedback, indicating 'this note is from a trumpet' or 'that's a marimba'. But how this mapping or grounding between two such streams of information is achieved is as yet relatively unexplored. We still need to understand more about the cues used to derive the teaching signals when we learn to distinguish instruments or other sound sources.

This work leads naturally to questions about the relationship between pitch recognition and instrument recognition. Both exhibit forms of auditory perceptual invariance important to a listener. Recognizing an instrument irrespective of the pitch it is playing and recognizing a pitch irrespective of the instrument playing that pitch are perhaps complementary. Their relationship is an interesting area for further research, with strong links to speech perception and speaker identification.

Another form of perceptual/cognitive invariance is the ability to recognize tonal centre and pitch function. Here the invariance involved is the recognition of the coherence of a set of pitches and the function of each pitch within the set. Niall Griffith's model suggests that this process can be modelled partially as a mechanism that tracks the use made of pitches and intervals over time. Although the sets of pitches used in different keys overlap, their frequency of occurrence, and of the intervals between them, allow the context and function of pitches to be identified. The model is applied to fragments of Western music. In moving to embrace other, non-Western systems of tonality, models such as this one will encounter the largely unexplored relationships between tonality and other musical dimensions, such as rhythm and phrasing. The significance of these relationships has often been sidelined by forms of musical analysis that tend to emphasize the separation of tonal from rhythmic structure.

Pitch production is the flip side of pitch perception. Rounding out the section on pitch and tonality, Michael Casey discusses a model that maps a desired pitch to a violin string position that produces that pitch, using the clever connectionist techniques of forward modelling and distal teaching. Knowing how to produce a particular pitch is closely related to knowing *what* produced a particular pitch, and so this modelling approach can be applied to the problem of pitch-invariant instrument recognition as well, as Casey has explored in further work (see the general bibliography at the end of this volume).

Rhythm and Meter

The process of rhythmic entrainment, when music listeners and performers keep in time by perceiving and following a 'beat', is so natural to us that many people are often unaware that they are tapping or swaying along to a piece of music. Despite this apparent instinctive simplicity, though, the issues surrounding how a nervous system recognizes and produces rhythms are complex, and models of these phenomena must tackle difficult constraints such as real-time adjustment and response. Edward Large and John Kolen have modelled the process of rhythmic entrainment using an oscillatory *integrate and fire* connectionist unit that learns to adjust its oscillations to coincide with beats of varying periodicities in a rhythmic stream. This ability is a necessary skill for any musical accompanist, whether human or artificial, trying to synchronize with fellow performers.

The issues surrounding rhythmic entrainment—adjusting to perceived time-based behaviour—and metric quantization—trying to map perceived time intervals onto a small set of musically relevant durations—are closely related. Both involve predicting what will happen based on the evidence of the length and periodicity of previous events. Stephen Smoliar addresses the second set of issues in his review of the metrical quantization model of Peter Desain and Henkjan Honing that appeared in *Music and Connectionism* in 1991. It is interesting to compare the discussion of this model with the Large and Kolen model of entrainment. Desain and Honing respond to Smoliar's challenges in an update of their own work, furthering the lively debate on this musically important topic.

Melodic Memory, Structure, and Completion

Before we can begin to put perceived pitch and rhythm together into a heard melody, we must be able to track sequences of notes in the auditory environment and associate them temporally. The perceptual construction of separate successive sounds into coherent sequential streams is a problem of great interest in the broader field of auditory scene analysis (Bregman, 1990). In a specifically musical context, pitch-streaming mechanisms allow us to distinguish between different voices and instruments in a piece, and between melody and (harmonic) ground. Stephen Grossberg's chapter describes a model of pitch streaming comprising a series of processes realized using adaptive resonance theory (ART). The model extracts pitches by assembling spectral components and then allocates each successive pitch to a stream through inter-stream competition. Priming and inhibition between layers ensure that subsequent inputs are allocated correctly. Grossberg discusses his model in relation to various auditory illusions and outlines its future development.

Pitch streaming is closely related to the question of how we hear the transitions between pitches. Robert Gjerdingen describes a model of the apparent continuity between successive discrete pitches, generalizing to auditory events the approach of Rudd and Grossberg's model of apparent motion in vision. The essential intuition in this model is that when a note is sounded its activation also affects similar "nearby" pitches. This neighbourhood of activation decays and shifts over time rather than disappearing suddenly. The activation of one pitch bridging to the next pitch thus forms a perception (or illusion?) of continuity. This model of musical apparent motion is also interesting because it relates the script of discrete notes specified on a score to a putative perceptual process. Issues involving such relationships have been discussed by Nicholas Cook (1994), who argues that phrases rather than pitches are the *atoms* of our musical perception.

Of course, it is not sensible to deny an important musical role to individual notes—it is clear, for instance, that we can memorize melodies on a note-by-note basis. But how do we remember the order of pitches and durations in a melody so that we can later reproduce them correctly? Several different approaches to this problem are possible, and in this section we include the first of four chapters to tackle these issues (the other three being in the next section on compositional processes). Michael Page's chapter describes a model of how we learn a hierarchical reduction of pitch sequences. His SONNET model is an extension of Grossberg and Cohen's masking field paradigm. The architecture is an unsupervised mechanism that learns to aggregate a melody into a hierarchy of phrases. Its inputs are an invariant scale representation of pitch. Thus the events it deals with are simple tokens abstracted from any relationship to other musical descriptors (such as duration or intensity), making the problem of learning the order of these events all the more difficult. It will be interesting to see how models of this kind develop to accommodate rhythm, metrical accent, and dynamics, which may actually make the learning task easier.

The memorization of a sequence of notes allows us to reproduce what we have heard. What we *think* of these sequences is another matter. What constitutes a good melody preoccupies many people, from composers to consumers. One principle thought to be involved in aesthetic judgements of melody is that of how we view change: there should be enough change to maintain interest, but not so much that it breaks continuity. Bruce Katz describes a model of aesthetic judgements of melody that is based on measures of unity in diversity. These measures come, in Katz's model, from the activation dynamics of a competitive learning system classifying melodic sequences. This model predicts the observed prominence of stepwise movement in aesthetically pleasing melodies. Katz's chapter again draws our attention to the relationship between representation and process in musical behaviour, and the different ways that this relationship can be organized. It is interesting to compare the kinds of perceptual and categorical continuity being modelled here, using a representation of melody that embraces pitch, rhythm, and interval, with the form of perceptual continuity that emerges from the processes of Gjerdingen's model of apparent motion.

Composition

From the problem of short-term serial order involved in learning simple melodies, we proceed to the problem of creating long-term temporal structure in new musical compositions—something that (good) human composers are adept at, but which has so far eluded artificial systems. In considering this problem, Michael Mozer takes a very different approach to the representation of structure and order from that of Michael Page. Mozer's goal is to use temporal dependencies and phrase structure learned from a set of selected melodies in the composition of novel melodies. To do this, Mozer has developed a sequential memory embodied in a modified simple recurrent network (SRN) architecture called CONCERT. This architecture construes the learned phrase structure not as a hierarchy of chunks, but in terms of dependencies between states in the internal representation developed by the SRN over time. Mozer uses varying time delay constants over the SRN's context units to capture longer-term dependencies than are typically learned by recurrent network designs. The capacities of the network are computationally impressive, yet Mozer concludes that its compositions have some way to go before receiving popular acclaim. The main reason for this seems to be that the structures and relationships assumed to underlie the pleasing form of long musical sequences are very difficult to capture in terms of simple long-term temporal dependencies between notes.

Another compositional skill related to the memorization and production of melodies is a composer's ability to arrange a tune—that is, to compose an appropriate harmony for it. Using harmony to hold a piece of music together over a period of time requires, as in composition, that memorized musical structure and expectation can be referenced and accessed over a variety of time scales. Matthew Bellgard and C.P. Tsang describe how Boltzmann machines can be used to model the generation of choral harmonies as a process of contextual pattern completion. Boltzmann machines with overlapping perceptual domains can harmonize successive measures of a melody and thereby produce smooth harmonies over longer periods of time.

The ability to recognize that two melodies are similar, and the ability to produce similar-sounding variations of a given piece are also central to composition and improvisation. Considering these abilities raises two issues: the usual question of how the structure of musical events is to be remembered, and a new puzzle of how to introduce novelty into new productions based upon what we have remembered. Edward Large, Caroline Palmer, and Jordan Pollack describe a mechanism based upon recursive auto-associative memory (RAAM) networks that identifies structurally important elements in musical passages. These are defined as the most stable and frequently occurring elements over a set of composed variations of the original passage. Creating a reduced representation of a sequence of events is dealt with here quite differently from the chunking in SONNET, or the sequential dependencies of CONCERT. In this case, the emphasis is on the selective encoding of significant elements.

Modelling how we remember and recall melodies or multi-voiced music is explored in this volume from a variety of perspectives: temporal dependencies (Mozer), chunking (Page), representation reduction (Large *et al.*), and pattern completion (Bellgard and Tsang). Each approach tackles a particular aspect of serial memory, reflecting the complexity of this concept. Comparison of these different approaches to the same problem—remembering the *important* aspects of a piece of music—indicates both how successful we can be in modelling specific aspects of musical representation and how far we are from providing a complete, unified account of musical memory that covers both veridical (note-by-note) and schematic (higher-level-structure) memory.

Having learned and remembered a piece of music, a composer can draw inspiration from it for compositions—but how? As we have seen, connectionist composition systems typically involve learning, and new compositions are based on musical ideas picked up from old melodic examples. The process of evolution is similarly adept at creating new ideas from old parts, and a few researchers have started to incorporate evolutionary methods into synthetic composition systems as well. Peter Todd and Gregory Werner review these efforts and propose ways in which learning and evolution can be combined to good effect in the composition of novel melodies. In the only non-musical chapter in the book, Shumeet Baluja, Dean Pomerleau, and Todd Jochem apply this union of learning and evolutionary methods to the task of creating interesting new visual images. First, they employ a neural network to learn the visual aesthetic preferences of a human user who rates a selection of images. Then, they allow that network to express its learned preferences in a process of interactive evolution, during which successive generations of images are created from the most-preferred images of the previous generation. After many generations of such selection and reproduction, images that the human user also finds interesting and pleasing are often produced.

Finally, Garrison Cottrell presents perhaps the most speculative piece in this volume, on a novel interface for musical performance. This interface uses a neural network to learn the mapping from musical intentions to appropriate sound output. While some work remains to be done on this system, its implications for the future of musical performance are profound.

Future Directions?

What else lies ahead in the area of musical networks? The models presented here are all quite specific: In each, a mechanism is conceived to perform a particular transduction, memorization, extraction, production, or completion on a stream of musical information. One of the most important next steps must be to start building upwards, combining these individual blocks of understanding into models that capture the relationships between different aspects of musicality. We know that musical cognition involves these interrelations, but our understanding of what these relationships are, how they are encoded, and how they affect musical activity is still incomplete. Dynamic process models, embodied in artificial neural networks, provide powerful experimental paradigms in which such ideas can be tested.

In building models that operate across and between musical domains, we will have to confront the nature of the processes within each domain. Are these processes unique to each domain, or are there general mechanisms involved? For example, the representations and mechanisms thought to be appropriate to pitch and rhythm seem to be quite distinct. If this is so, what is it about their separate mechanisms and representations that facilitates their conjoint encoding and processing? Is melody grounded in rhythm, or vice versa? What is the evolutionary relationship between prosody, rhythm, and melody? Are the mechanisms that we think of as specifically designed to manipulate one form of representation applicable to other domains? To continue the pitch and rhythm example, isolated sounds, rhythmic events, and continuous streams are all points along a time line of increasing frequency. Can we speculate that the mechanisms that categorize pitch are similar to those that recognize metric and rhythmic structure, but with each set of mechanisms focused over a different temporal span? What would such mechanisms consist of? Again, we believe that connectionist models are a useful tool with which to explore these issues.

We also wish to see extended the range of musical domains that connectionist modellers (and others) explore. As just mentioned, we can imagine a single dimension of increasing temporal scale through pitch, to rhythm, to melody, and on to whole compositions. The models we present in this volume have addressed issues at many of the points on this scale, but other points remain largely uncharted.

Beginning with the shorter time scale, we hope to see more investigations of network models of musical signal processing, which have been rare so far (but see our bibliography for some related references). Given the great interest in networks for signal processing in other domains, from speech to time series, this lack in the musical realm is surprising. At this time scale in particular, neurologically plausible network models of the actual neuron-level information processing going on inside the brain are also much needed. A deeper understanding of neurological processes can only enrich our current psychological and functional models based on the observation of musical behaviour. While our conscious experience of music is synthetic, many of the neurological processes that facilitate it are localized (Wallin, 1991). Models that are at present architecturally and functionally unified should therefore develop to accommodate architectural diversity.

At the intermediate time scales that most of our models already fall within, there are still some musical application areas of neural networks awaiting colonization. In particular, we envision connectionist systems for a variety of useful real-world musical applications. For instance, the pattern recognition and generalization abilities of neural networks make them desirable for adaptive performance interfaces, such as interactive real-time performance-gesture recognizers that can follow the movements of conductors or dancers. Music and sound databases could use neural network front-ends to allow adaptive, intelligent sound retrieval based on a user's rough input ('find me a song that goes something like this', or 'give me the sound nearest to this *squawk*'). Compositional systems that can improvise and play along with a user in real-time would also be an attractive step ahead. And the ability of networks to map between different musical representations will allow for systems that can read visual music scores (for performance or digital encoding), and others that can 'listen' to auditory input and segment it by instrument, pitch, or duration, on the way to creating an automatic score transcription.

Over longer time scales, we propose models of the *social* networks through which musical cultures develop. Given a population of music-learning and performing individuals, how can we understand the processes by which their cultural body of music (or collection of musical 'memes' as Dawkins, 1976, would describe it) grows and evolves over time? Here there are many issues concerning the relationship between the individual and the collective group, and the nature of the models that can (and should) be realized using connectionist materials. At what resolution do cultural learning and development take place, and at what resolution should we model them? Is it most useful to equate a network model with a whole society (with a 'unit' in a network standing for an individual person, who receives musical input from other units representing other people), or with an individual (with a different network inside each individual's head, learning pieces of the culture and creating and communicating new pieces in turn)? Different models (and modellers) with different goals in mind should investigate these various possibilities.

Finally, over the longest time scales we need to consider evolution of a different sort: the evolution of the musical behaviour mechanisms themselves, and their relationship to other evolved capacities. How and why did psychological mechanisms for song production and song perception evolve? In different species, these musical abilities may have served different functions; in birds versus humans, for instance, were they for territory identification, courtship, or individual recognition? In humans, might song have evolved from pre-existing speech prosody mechanisms, or vice versa? What new representations arose to bring musical capacities under the control of our conscious attention and intention? What is music's relationship to our understanding and articulation of change and causation, perhaps the deepest link it has with language? Such questions about the original functions of the evolved abilities underlying our musical behaviour could have a profound impact on how we view and model that behaviour. While the papers by Todd and Werner and Baluja and colleagues give some hints as to how neural network models might help us investigate such questions, the techniques to be used in these explorations, and the questions themselves, need much further elaboration.

More immediately, we must also broaden our perspective, not only temporally, but also spatially, to consider music beyond our Western tradition. Computational musicology has taken so many analytical views from Western musical analysis and theory that we are grounded in a terminology that diminishes other possible arrangements between, for instance, rhythm and tonality. It seems worthwhile to ask what a computational cognitive musicology applicable to all cultures and embracing all aspects of music would look like, and how connectionist models can contribute to that research program. Understanding how so many musics can reside in the human mind must surely be as significant as understanding the processes associated with a single cultural manifestation. Part of the answer will come from making connections between the models we have developed so far. Understanding music does not lie in exploring any process or mechanism in isolation, but in fathoming the interplay between them, part of the game of sound and movement we seem to enjoy playing so frequently and enduringly. It is this challenge that we hope will be commenced in the next collection of musical connectionism.

Musical Connectionist Publications

The quantity and diversity of research into neural network modelling of music is increasing all the time. Not all of it gains as prominent dissemination as it deserves. To help alleviate the problem of isolated work in this area, we have compiled a list of publications applying neural network models to music that we hope is largely complete. We include this bibliography at the end of the book. Apologies to those that we are still unaware of. Thanks to Leigh Smith whose web page provided a number of late additions.

Acknowledgements

Editing a book is not achieved in isolation. Without the encouragement of Noel Sharkey, the special issue of *Connection Science*, 6(2 & 3) (1994) on music and creativity would never have started, and without those involved at Carfax Publishing, particularly Deborah Myson-Etherington, it would never have been completed. Many thanks are also due to all the reviewers and the authors for their hard work and patience with the rounds of reading and revision. The publishers of *Music Perception* and *Cognitive Science* kindly gave permission to include the additional chapters by Robert Gjerdingen and by Edward Large, Caroline Palmer, and Jordan Pollack. The support of Kathleen Caruso, Jerry Weinstein, and Harry and Betty Stanton at Bradford Books/MIT Press was invaluable when the long distance run seemed in danger of extending to infinity. We were greatly saddened by the news of Harry Stanton's death as our book was going to press, and we dedicate this volume to his memory. Finally, last but not least, most thanks to our families for laying down a good beat, filling in the harmonies, and giving us the rests for this project to be accomplished.

NIALL GRIFFITH
University of Limerick, Ireland

PETER M. TODD
*Max Planck Institute for
Human Development, Berlin,
Germany*

References

Bregman, A.S. (1990) *Auditory Scene Analysis.* Cambridge, MA: MIT Press.

Cook, N. (1994) Perception: A perspective from music theory. In R. Aiello & J. Sloboda (Eds.), *Musical Perceptions* (pp. 64–95). New York: Oxford University Press.

Dawkins, R. (1976) *The Selfish Gene.* New York: Oxford University Press. (New edition, 1989.)

Rumelhart, D.E., & McClelland, J.L. (Eds.) (1986) *Parallel Distributed Processing: Explorations in the Microstructure of Cognition.* Cambridge, MA: MIT Press/Bradford Books.

Todd, P.M., & Loy, D.G. (Eds.) (1991) *Music and Connectionism.* Cambridge, MA: MIT Press.

Wallin, N.L. (1991) *Biomusicology: Neurophysiological, Neuropsychological, and Evolutionary Perspectives on the Origins and Purposes of Music.* Stuyvesant, NY: Pendragon Press.

Wilford, J.N. (1996) Playing of flute may have graced Neanderthal fire. *New York Times,* October 29, 1996, pp. C1, C7.

Part I
Pitch and Tonality

Modelling Pitch Perception with Adaptive Resonance Theory Artificial Neural Networks

IAN TAYLOR & MIKE GREENHOUGH

Most modern pitch-perception theories incorporate a pattern-recognition scheme to extract pitch. Typically, this involves matching the signal to be classified against a harmonic-series template for each pitch to find the one with the best fit. Although often successful, such approaches tend to lack generality and may well fail when faced with signals with much depleted or inharmonic components. Here, an alternative method is described, which uses an adaptive resonance theory (ART) artificial neural network (ANN). By training this with a large number of spectrally diverse input signals, we can construct more robust pitch-templates which can be continually updated without having to re-code knowledge already acquired by the ANN. The input signal is Fourier-transformed to produce an amplitude spectrum. A mapping scheme then transforms this to a distribution of amplitude within 'semitone bins'. This pattern is then presented to an ARTMAP ANN consisting of an ART2 and ART1 unsupervised ANN linked by a map field. The system was trained with pitches ranging over three octaves (C_3 to C_6) on a variety of instruments and developed a desirable insensitivity to phase, timbre and loudness when classifying.

KEYWORDS: ART, ARTMAP, pitch perception, pattern recognition.

1. Introduction

This paper describes a computer system that models aspects of human pitch perception using an adaptive resonance theory (ART) artificial neural network (ANN). ART was introduced in order to analyze how brain networks can learn about a changing world in real time in a rapid but stable fashion. Here, ART will be used to self-organize musical pitch by using a supervised ANN called ARTMAP (Carpenter *et al.*, 1991a).

Section 2 briefly describes the auditory system and outlines the various pitch-perception theories. Section 3 describes an ART system we have developed that is capable of determining pitch on a wide variety of musical instruments. Section 4 presents experiments that were undertaken using this system.

2. Aspects of Musical Pitch

Sound waves are conducted via the outer and middle ears to the basilar membrane

This article appeared originally in *Connection Science*, 1994, **6**, 135–154, and is reprinted with permission.

in the inner ear (cochlea). This membrane varies in mechanical structure along its length in such a way that a signal component of a particular frequency will cause a particular place on it to vibrate maximally. An array of neurons along the length of the membrane is thus able to convey a rough frequency analysis to the brain via the auditory nerve. Historically, therefore, pitch-perception was explained in terms of simple spectral cues by the 'place' theory (Helmholtz, 1863).

However, it was found that the pitch of complex periodic sounds corresponds to the fundamental frequency, independently of the presence or absence of energy in the sound spectrum at this frequency. Consequently, the 'periodicity' theory (Schouten, 1940) was introduced, which explained perception of sounds in terms of the timing of nerve impulses. Later still, the inadequacy of these cochlea-based explanations for pitch perception of complex tones was revealed by musical intelligibility tests (Houtsma & Goldstein, 1972) which demonstrated that the pitch of complex tones made up of a random number of harmonics can be heard equally well whether the subject is presented with them monotically (all in one ear) or dichotically (different harmonics sent to each ear). Therefore, neither energy at the fundamental frequency nor fundamental periodicities in the cochlea output are necessary for a subject to determine the pitch of a periodic sound. This implies that some pitch processing takes place at a higher level than the cochlea. Following this discovery, three pattern-recognition theories were published that attempted to explain how the brain learned to extract pitch from complex sounds.

2.1. Pattern-recognition Theories

De Boer (1956) suggested how a template model could predict the pitch of both harmonic and inharmonic sounds. He argued that the brain, through wide contact with harmonic stimuli, could be specifically tuned to such harmonic patterns. Thus, an inharmonic stimulus could be classified by matching the best-fitting harmonic template. For example, consider three components 1000, 1200 and 1400 Hz, frequency-shifted by 50 Hz to give 1050, 1250 and 1450 Hz. The reported resulting pitch sensation for this set of harmonics is 208 Hz. Similarly, using de Boer's harmonic template-matching scheme, the best-fitting pitch would also be 208 Hz, where 1050, 1250 and 1450 Hz are the closest-fitting harmonics to the 5th, 6th and 7th harmonics of 208 Hz, i.e. 1040, 1248 and 1456 Hz.

The optimum-processor theory (Goldstein, 1973), the virtual-pitch theory (Terhardt, 1972) and the pattern-transformation theory (Wightman, 1973) are all quantified elaborations on de Boer's ideas. Perhaps the most closely related theory is the optimum-processor theory which explicitly incorporates these ideas. Goldstein includes a hypothetical neural network called the 'optimum-processor', which finds the best-fitting harmonic template for the spectral patterns supplied by its peripheral frequency analyzer. The fundamental frequency is obtained in a maximum-likelihood way by calculating the number of harmonics which match the stored harmonic template for each pitch and then choosing the winner. The winning harmonic template corresponds to the perceived pitch.

Terhardt, in his virtual-pitch theory, distinguishes between two kinds of pitch mode: spectral pitch (the pitch of a pure tone) and virtual pitch (the pitch of a complex tone). The pitch percept governed by these two modes is described, respectively, by the spectral-pitch pattern and the virtual-pitch pattern. The spectral-pitch pattern is constructed by spectral analysis, extraction of tonal components, evaluation of masking effects and weighting according to the principle of spectral

Figure 1. Visual analogy of virtual pitch. The visual system perceives contours which are not physically present (Terhardt, 1974).

dominance. The virtual-pitch pattern is then obtained from the spectral-pitch pattern by subharmonic-coincidence assessment.

Terhardt considers virtual pitch to be an attribute which is a product of auditory Gestalt perception. The virtual pitch can be generated only if a learning process has been undergone previously. In vision, Gestalt perception invokes the law of closure to explain how we often supply missing information to 'close a figure' (see Figure 1). Terhardt (1974) argues that, "merely from the fact that, in vision, 'contours' may be perceived which are not present one can conclude that, in hearing, 'tones' may be perceptible which are not present, either."

Wightman presents a mathematical model of human pitch perception called the pattern-transformation model of pitch. It was inspired by what appears to be a close similarity between pitch perception and other classic pattern-recognition problems. In his analogy between pitch and character recognition, he describes characters as having a certain characteristic about them, regardless of size, orientation, type style etc. For example the letter C as it is seen here, has its C-ness in common with other Cs, whether it is written by hand, printed in a newspaper or anywhere else. Even though the letter style can vary greatly it is still recognized as the letter C. Wightman argues that in music this is also true, e.g. middle C has the same pitch regardless of the instrument which produces it. Hence, he concluded that the perception of pitch is a pattern-recognition problem.

In the pattern-transformation model, pitch recognition is regarded as a sequence of transformations, which produce different so-called 'patterns of neural activity'. A limited-resolution spectrum (called a peripheral activity pattern), similar to that produced in the cochlea, is created from the input stimuli. This is then Fourier transformed to compute the autocorrelation function, resulting in a phase-invariant pattern. The final stage of the model incorporates the pitch extractor, which although not explicitly described, is performed by a pattern-matching algorithm.

The three models described here have been demonstrated to be closely related mathematically (de Boer, 1977). In his paper, de Boer demonstrated that under certain conditions, Goldstein's optimum-processor theory can give the same pitch predictions as both Wightman's pattern-transformation theory and Terhardt's virtual-pitch theory. If the spread of a single-frequency component is substantial, Goldstein's theory is equivalent to Wightman's theory, and if the spread is zero it predicts the same pitches as Terhardt's theory.

2.2. Implementations of Pattern-recognition Theories

Implementations have been published of Terhardt's virtual-pitch theory (Terhardt *et al.*, 1982) and Goldstein's central processor theory (Duifhuis *et al.*, 1982).

Terhardt *et al.* (1982) present an algorithm which effectively reproduces the virtual-pitch theory mechanisms for determining pitch. They use a fast Fourier transform (FFT) to calculate the power spectrum of the sampled signal. This is then analyzed in order to extract the tonal components of importance to the pitch-determining process, which effectively cleans up the spectrum so that just high-intensity frequency components remain. Evaluation of masking effects follows, resulting in the discarding of irrelevant frequency components and the frequency-shifting of others. Weighting functions are then applied which control the extent to which tonal components contribute towards the pitch-extraction process. The subsequent spectral-pitch pattern is then processed by a method of subharmonic summation to extract the virtual pitch.

The implementation of Goldstein's optimum-processor theory (Duifhuis *et al.*, 1982) is often called the 'DWS pitch meter' (Scheffers, 1983). This has three stages of operation. In the first stage, a 128-point FFT is computed, producing a spectrum of the acoustic signal. A 'component-finder' algorithm then finds the relevant frequency components and then by interpolation pinpoints the actual frequency positions more precisely. The third stage consists of an optimum-processor scheme which estimates the fundamental frequency whose template optimally fits the set of resolved frequency components.

An elaboration of the DWS meter, a year later (Scheffers, 1983), included a better approximation of auditory frequency analysis and a modification to the 'best-fitting fundamental' procedure. Scheffers reported that errors induced by the absence of low harmonics were significantly reduced and noted that their model produced the same results that were originally predicted by Goldstein in 1973.

Terhardt's subharmonic-summation pitch-extracting scheme has been used in a large number of other computer implementations. Hermes (1988) presented an alternative method of computing the summation by applying a series of logarithmic frequency shifts to the amplitude spectrum and adding component amplitudes together to produce the subharmonic sum spectrum. Many speech-processing algorithms also use types of subharmonic summation, e.g. Schroeder (1968), Noll, (1970) and Martin (1982). A number of frequency-tracking algorithms also use variations on the subharmonic summation scheme, e.g. Piszczalski and Galler (1982) and Brown (1991, 1992).

However, these implementations generally involve complex algorithms whose success is often qualified by the need to set parameters, in an *ad hoc* fashion, so that the results fit empirical data from psychoacoustic experiments. In this paper, we propose an alternative system which uses an ART neural network called ARTMAP to classify the pitch of an acoustic signal from a Fourier spectrum of harmonics. In effect, such a network can fit psychoacoustic data itself by associating input signals with desired output states.

2.3. The Use of ANNs for Pitch Classification

ANNs offer an attractive and alternative approach to pitch-determination by attempting to improve on the widely used harmonic-ideal template (i.e. the harmonic series) matched against the input data to find the pitch template with the closest fit. Although such methods work well in general, there are musical instruments which do not readily fit into the harmonic-ideal category, e.g. those which produce a much depleted or inharmonic set of spectral components. Such spectrally ambiguous patterns may well confuse systems which use simple comparisons of this kind. Of course, such algorithms may be extended to cater for a greater variety of instruments which do not fit the harmonic ideal; but the process is by no means a simple one, involving further pitch analysis and re-coding of the computer implementations.

ANNs, on the other hand, offer an original way of constructing a more robust harmonic template. This is achieved by training the ANN with a wide variety of spectrally different patterns, so that the information relevant to the pitch-determining process can be extracted. Through this interaction with a large variety of pitches taken from different musical instruments the ANN can learn to become insensitive to spectral shape and hence timbre when determining pitch. There are two ways in which the conventional pitch-template pattern can be improved:

(1) by training an ANN with various spectral examples for a single pitch and then using this information to predict the harmonic template for any pitch;
(2) by training the ANN with various spectral examples taken from a wide variety of different pitches.

The second approach was chosen as likely to be the more thorough. This decision was somewhat intuitive, inspired by the considerable variation in spectral patterns of different fundamental frequency. We did not directly test the first approach experimentally. Previous results (Taylor & Greenhough, 1993) demonstrate that the second training scheme can indeed out-perform template matching and subharmonic summation.

3. Outline for an Adaptive Resonance Theory System

The model can be divided into three stages as illustrated in Figure 2. The first stage performs a Fourier transform on the sampled waveform to produce an amplitude spectrum. The second stage maps this representation to an array of 'semitone bins'. Finally, this is presented to an ARTMAP network which learns to extract the pitch from the signals. It is essential to the learning process that the network acquires an insensitivity to other factors such as spectral shape (and hence timbre) and overall amplitude (and hence loudness). All stages, including the ANN simulation, were written by us using Objective-C on a NeXT Workstation. The next three sections describe these stages in more detail.

3.1. Sampling and Spectrum Analysis

The NeXT Workstation's on-board sampling chip was used for the acquisition of the pitch examples. This chip has a 12-bit dynamic range and has a fixed sampling

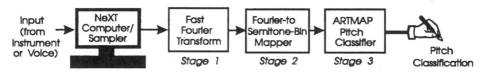

Figure 2. The adaptive resonance theory system. A Fourier transform is performed on the input waveform to produce an amplitude spectrum. This is mapped to a 'semitone-bin' distribution which is then fed into the ART neural network architecture called ARTMAP, which learns to extract pitch.

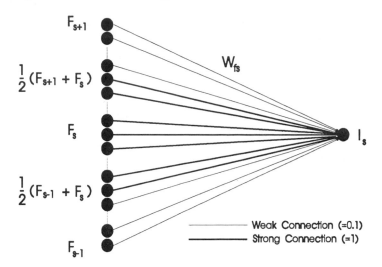

Figure 3. The mapping scheme from a Fourier spectrum to a distribution of 'semitone bins'. There are strong connections for frequencies within $\pm\frac{1}{4}$-tone (approximately, $\pm\frac{1}{2}(F_s - F_{s-1})$) of the semitone frequency and weaker ones within $\pm\frac{1}{2}$-tone.

rate of 8012.8 Hz, called the 'CODEC converter rate'. We found that this was sufficient for the current work but a more sophisticated chip, ideally with a sampling rate of 44.1 kHz and a 16-bit dynamic range, should be used in a working application. The CODEC converter rate, according to Nyquist's theorem, can resolve frequencies up to about 4000 Hz. (Although the human ear can detect frequencies up to around 20 kHz, any spectral energy above 4000 Hz is likely to have little effect on the pitch-determination process (see, for example, Ritsma (1962).) A FFT algorithm was then applied to 1024 samples, producing an amplitude spectrum of the sampled data. The resulting frequency spacing of 7.825 Hz (8012.8/1024) represents a somewhat limited resolution, but this was not a problem in the context of these experiments.

3.2. *Mapping from the Fourier Spectrum to a 'Semitone Bin' Representation*

Groups of frequency components lying within bandwidths of a semitone are mapped to individual 'semitone bins' of a representative intensity. Thus, the Fourier spectrum is transformed into a distribution of intensity over the semitones of the chromatic scale. However, to do this one has to take into account that a bandwidth of a semitone, in Hz, varies with the centre frequency. For example, the semitone bandwidth around the frequency point $G\sharp_2$ is 7 Hz while that around C_8 is 242 Hz. We must, however, ensure the same intensity level in these two semitone bins, if the activation levels are the same.

The mapping scheme used here has strongly weighted connections to the area within a bandwidth of a semitone around the semitone's centre frequency and weaker connections outside this area up until the neighbouring semitone's centre frequency (Figure 3). These weaker connections enable the network to be more robust when presented with a mistuned note or harmonic. Figure 4 summarizes the actual operations which are performed to produce the required mappings. The

$$I_s = Max(I_f * W_{fs})$$

where

$$W_{fs} = \begin{cases} 1 & if & \tfrac{1}{2}(F_s + F_{s-1}) \le f \le \tfrac{1}{2}(F_s + F_{s+1}) \\ 0.1 & if & F_{s-1} \le f < \tfrac{1}{2}(F_s + F_{s-1}) \\ 0.1 & if & \tfrac{1}{2}(F_s + F_{s+1}) < f \le F_{s+1} \\ 1 & if & F_{s+1} < f < F_{s-1} \end{cases}$$

and

F_s	is the centre frequency of semitone s
I_f	is the intensity at node f in the Fourier spectrum
I_s	is the intensity assigned at node s of the semitone-bin distribution
W_{fs}	is the connection weight between node f and node s

Figure 4. Operations used to map frequency components in the Fourier spectrum to a semitone-bin distribution.

restriction to just three octaves of a diatonic scale was a consequence of there being a considerable variety of network architectures to investigate with only limited processing power. A much finer-grained input mapping is possible and would allow, for example, an exploration of the subtle pitch-shifts observed with groups of inharmonically related frequency components.

The input, therefore, to the ANN is 60 input nodes representing the 60 chromatic semitone bins in the range C_3 to B_7, i.e. 131 Hz to 3951 Hz (see Figure 5). The ANN's output layer is used to represent the pitch names of the C-major scale in the range C_3 to C_6 (i.e. 131 Hz to 1047 Hz) and therefore consists of 22 nodes (see Figure 6).

Input patterns and corresponding expected output patterns are presented to the ARTMAP network in pairs. The goal of the network is to associate each input pattern with its appropriate output pattern by adjusting its weights (i.e. by learning). The network in this experiment has a training and a testing phase. In the training phase the network learns the training patterns presented to it, while in the testing phase it is asked to classify patterns which it has not seen before. Optimally, the ARTMAP network should learn all the training patterns and also classify all the test

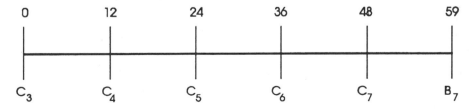

Figure 5. The input-layer representation for the ARTMAP ANN.

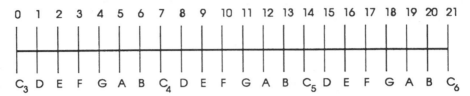

Figure 6. The output-layer representation for the ARTMAP ANN.

patterns correctly by generalizing using knowledge it has learned in the training phase.

3.3. *The ART Architecture and Its Use in Pitch Classification*

ANNs are currently the subject of much theoretical and practical interest in a wide range of applications. One of the main motivations for the recent revival of computational models for biological networks is the apparent ease, speed and accuracy with which biological systems perform pattern recognition and other tasks. An ANN is a processing device, implemented either in software or hardware, whose design is inspired by the massively parallel structure and function of the human brain. It attempts to simulate this highly interconnected, parallel computational structure consisting of many relatively simple individual processing elements. Its memory comprises nodes, which are linked together by weighted connections. The nodes' activation levels and the strengths of the connections may be considered to be short-term memory and long-term memory respectively. Knowledge is not programmed into the system but is gradually acquired by the system through interaction with its environment.

The brain has been estimated to have between 10 and 500 billion neurons, or processing elements (Rumelhart & McClelland, 1986). According to one opinion (Stubbs, 1988), the neurons are arranged into approximately 1000 main modules, each having 500 neural networks consisting of 100 000 neurons. There are between 100 and several thousand axons (from other neurons), which connect to the dendrites of each neuron. Neurons either excite or inhibit neurons to which they are connected (Eccles law).

ANNs, on the other hand, typically consist of no more than a few hundred nodes (neurons). The ANN pitch-determination system described in this paper consists of just 304 neurons (60 input neurons, 22 output neurons and 200 + 22 neurons connecting to the input layer and the output layer, respectively), with 16 884 weighted connections. It should be emphasized therefore that, generally, ANNs are not implemented on the same scale as biological neural networks and that ANNs are not considered to be exact descriptions of mammalian brain neural networks. Rather, they take into account the essential features of the brain that make it such a good information processor.

In our system, we have used an ANN architecture called ARTMAP to perform pattern recognition on the semitone-bin distribution. The introduction of ART (Grossberg, 1976a, b) has led to the development of a number of ANN architectures including ART1, ART2, ART3 and ARTMAP ((Carpenter & Grossberg, 1987a, b, 1990) and (Carpenter *et al.*, 1991b)). ART networks differ in topology from most other ANNs by having a set of top-down weights as well as bottom-up ones. They also have the advantage over most others of an ability to solve the 'stability–

plasticity' dilemma, that is once the network has learned a set of arbitrary input patterns it can cope with learning additional patterns without destroying previous knowledge. Most other ANNs have to be retrained in order to learn additional input patterns.

ART1 self-organizes recognition codes for binary input patterns. ART2 does the same for binary and analogue input patterns, while ART3 is based on ART2 but includes a model of the chemical synapse that solves the memory-search problem of ART systems. ARTMAP is a supervised ANN which links together two ART modules (ART_a and ART_b) by means of an 'inter-ART associative memory', called a map field. ART_a and ART_b are both unsupervised ART modules (e.g. ART1, ART2, ART3, ART2-A etc.).

Our system consists of an ART2 and an ART1 ANN for the ART_a and ART_b modules, respectively. Vector $\mathbf{a}_p$ encodes the pitch information in the form of semitone bins and the vector $\mathbf{b}_p$ encodes its 'predictive consequence' which corresponds, in this case, to the conventional name of that pitch, e.g. A_4, C_3 etc. The next four sections describe the unsupervised ART_a and ART_b modules which were used in our system, followed by an experiment which demonstrates why the supervised learning scheme adopted was needed. Finally, details of the ARTMAP system are given.

3.3.1. ART1.

ART1 is an ANN which self-organizes, without supervision, a set of binary input vectors. Vectors which are similar enough to pass the so-called 'vigilance test' are clustered together to form categories (also known as exemplars or recognition codes). ART1 has been described as having similar properties to that of the single leader sequential clustering algorithm (Lippmann, 1987). Briefly, the leader algorithm selects the first input as the leader of the class. The next input is then compared to the first pattern and the distance is calculated between the vectors. If this distance is below a threshold (set beforehand), then this input is assigned to the first class, otherwise it forms a new class and consequently becomes the leader for that class. The algorithm continues in this fashion until all patterns have been assigned to a class. The number of classes produced by the leader algorithm depends on both the threshold value chosen and the distance measure used to compare input to class leaders.

The leader algorithm differs from ART1 in that it does not attempt to improve on its leading pattern for a class (i.e. the weight vector), which would make the system more tolerant to future input patterns. Thus, the classes produced by the leader algorithm can vary greatly depending on the input presentation order, whereas in ART1 this is not the case.

The ART1 ANN consists of an attentional subsystem comprising an input layer (the F_1 field) and an output layer (the F_2 field), fully interconnected by a set of bottom-up and top-down adaptive weights, and an orienting subsystem which incorporates the reset mechanism (Figure 7). The bottom-up weights constitutes ART1's long-term memory and the top-down weights store the learned expectations for each of the categories formed in the F_2 field. The top-down weights are crucial for recognition-code self-stabilization.

In brief, a binary input pattern is presented to the F_1 field. This pattern is then multiplied by the bottom-up weights in order to compute the F_2 field activation. A winning F_2 node is chosen from the F_2 field by lateral inhibition. The top-down weights from this winning node and the F_1 field pattern then take part in the

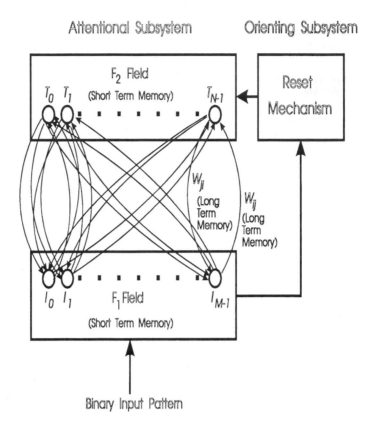

Figure 7. An ART1 ANN, consisting of an F_1 field (input layer), an F_2 field (output layer), a reset mechanism and two sets of fully connected weights (bottom-up and top-down).

vigilance test, to check whether the match between the input pattern and the stored expectation of the winning category is higher than the set vigilance level. If it is, then learning takes place by adapting the bottom-up and top-down weights for the winning F_2 node, in such a way as to make the correlation between these weights and the input pattern greater. If not, the winning F_2 node is reset (i.e. it is eliminated from competition) and the algorithm searches for another suitable category. Uncommitted nodes (i.e. those which have not had previous learning) will always accommodate the learning of a new pattern. The algorithm continues in this way until all input patterns have found suitable categories.

3.3.2. ART2. The ART2 ANN, like ART1, is self-organizing and unsupervised. It is the analogue counterpart of ART1, designed for the processing of analogue, as well as binary input patterns. ART2 attempts to pick out and enhance similar signals embedded in various noisy backgrounds. For this purpose, ART2's feature representation fields F_0 and F_1 include several pre-processing levels and gain-control systems (Figure 8).

ART2 is made up of two major components, common in the design of all ART systems, namely the attentional subsystem and the orienting subsystem. The

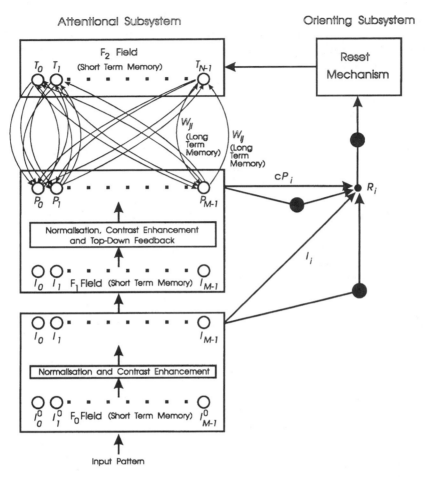

Figure 8. A simplified version of the ART2 ANN architecture consisting of an attentional subsystem, containing three fields, F_0, F_1 and F_2 and two sets of adaptive weights (bottom-up and top-down) and an orienting subsystem incorporating the reset mechanism. Large filled circles (gain-control nuclei) represent normalization operations carried out by the network.

attentional subsystem consists of two input representation fields F_0 and F_1 and a category representation field F_2, which are fully connected by a bottom-up and a top-down set of weights. As in ART1, the bottom-up weights represent the system's long-term memory and the top-down weights store the learned expectations for each F_2 category. The orienting subsystem interacts with the attentional subsystem to carry out an internally controlled search process.

In short, an analogue input vector is passed to the F_0 field. This pattern is normalized and then a threshold function is applied which sets to zero any part of the input pattern which falls below a set threshold value. This pattern is then renormalized to produce the input to the F_1 field. The F_1 field also incorporates normalization and threshold operations which are applied before the F_2 activation is calculated by a feed-forward multiplication of the output of the F_1 field and the bottom-up weights. The F_2 field then undergoes a process of lateral inhibition to find the F_2 node with the highest activity. A vigilance test then takes place to check whether the top-down learned expectation from the winning F_2 node matches the input pattern well enough. If it does, the F_1 calculations are iterated a number of times and then learning takes place between the F_1 field and the winning F_2 node. If not, the F_2 node is reset and another F_2 node is chosen. This repeats until the vigilance test has been passed, and then, either a committed node is found whose stored expectations match the input sufficiently, or an uncommitted node is chosen (to which learning can always take place).

3.3.3. Why supervised learning is needed. For our implementation, a supervised learning network was needed. We found that an optimum level of vigilance could not be found to give a satisfactory solution using the unsupervised ART networks. This is demonstrated in Figure 9. Here, an ART2 ANN was trained with 14 patterns, 7 examples of different spectral shapes taken from 7 different musical instruments for C_3 (patterns 0–6) and the same for C_4 (patterns 7–13). The instruments were, respectively, a tenor voice singing *la*, a tenor voice singing *me*, a contralto voice singing *la*, a steel-string guitar strummed *Sul Tasto* (by the neck), a steel-string guitar strummed *Sul Ponticello* (by the bridge), a French horn and a piano. Figure 9 shows how these patterns were clustered together at various levels of vigilance. For example, at vigilance level 0.98 input patterns 0, 1, 5, 6, 7, 8, 9, 10, 11, 12 and 13 were clustered to the F_2 category 0 and patterns 2, 3 and 4 were

	Vigilance	0.98	0.99	0.9975	0.998	0.999	0.9995	0.9998	0.99991	0.99995
Category										
0		0 1 5 6 7 8 9 10 11 12 13	0 1 5 6 7 8 9 10 12 13	0 1 5 6 7 12 13	0 1 5 7 12	0 1 7 12	0 7	0 7	0	0
1		2 3 4	2 3 4	2 3 4	2 3 4	2 3	1 5 8 9 10	1 6 8	1 9 10	1 9
2			11	8 9 10	6 8 9 10 13	4 5	2 3	2 3	2 3	2
3				11	11	6 8 9 10 13	4	4	4	3
4						11	6 12 13	5	5	4
5							11	9 10	6 8	5
6								11	7	6
7								12 13	11	7
8									12	8
9									13	10
10										11
11										12
12										13

Figure 9. The category representations made by the ART2 ANN for 14 input patterns (7 examples taken from different instruments for the note C_3 and the same for C_4) at 9 different levels of vigilance.

clustered to the F_2 node 1. The optimum level of vigilance would be one which separated the patterns from different octaves (e.g. the C_3s from the C_4s) while clustering together as much as possible patterns which are from the same octave. This would allow the network to distinguish between pitches of different octaves and also give some insensitivity to timbre of input patterns having the same pitch by picking out common features within the internal structures of such patterns.

It can be seen from Figure 9 that there was no level of vigilance which could separate the pitch examples from the two octaves. Even at high levels of vigilance (i.e. 0.99995), patterns 1 and 9 were clustered together (1 being the tenor voice example singing *me* of C_3 and 9 being the contralto voice example singing *la* of C_4) when all other patterns were associated with different output nodes. Thus, a more advanced network was needed to control the vigilance of the ART network so that it would cluster together only input patterns which have the same output state (i.e. have the same pitch). ARTMAP was able to perform such an operation. In an ARTMAP network the map field controls ART_a's vigilance parameter, as it associates pairs of vectors presented to ART_a and ART_b while reducing redundancy by clustering as many patterns presented to ART_a together as possible, within a base-rate vigilance, which have the same 'predictive consequence' at ART_b. The mechanisms of the ARTMAP network are described below.

3.3.4. ARTMAP. ARTMAP is a self-organizing, supervised ANN which consists of two unsupervised ART modules, ART_a and ART_b, and an inter-ART associative memory, called a map field (Figure 10). ART_a and ART_b are linked by fully connected adaptive connections between ART_a's F_2 layer and the map field, and

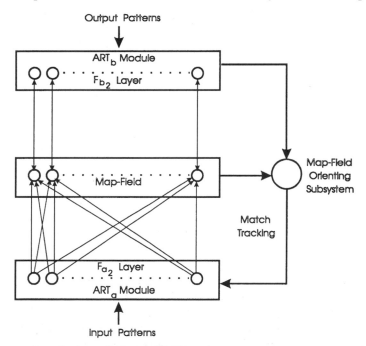

Figure 10. A predictive ART, or ARTMAP, system includes two ART modules linked by a map field. Internal control structures actively regulate learning and information flow. ART_a generally self-organizes input data (e.g. pitch information) and ART_b self-organizes desired output states (e.g. pitch names).

non-adaptive, bidirectional, one-to-one connections from the map field to ART_b's F_2 layer. The ART_b network self-organizes the 'predictive consequence' or 'desired output' patterns for each input pattern presented to ART_a.

Briefly, a pair of vectors $\mathbf{a}_p$ and $\mathbf{b}_p$ are presented to ART_a and ART_b simultaneously. The ART_a and the ART_b networks choose suitable output (F_2) categories for these vectors. The map field then checks to see if the ART_a's choice can correctly predict the choice at ART_b. If it can, then outstar learning between F_{a_2} and the map field takes place, i.e. learning takes place between the map-field node corresponding to the winning F_{b_2} node and the F_{a_2} pattern. Connections to all other F_{b_2} nodes are inhibited. If not, the map field increases ART_a's vigilance so that ART_a does not choose the same F_2 category again but searches on until a suitable F_{a_2} category is found. If there are no suitable categories ART_a chooses an uncommitted node, in which case learning can always take place.

4. Pitch Classification Experiments Using ARTMAP

4.1. Training the ARTMAP System

The supervised ARTMAP system consisting of an ART2, a map field and an ART1 ANN was trained to recognize pitches from four different musical instruments. Instruments that are bright or sharp sounding produce a spectrum with relatively strong higher harmonics, whereas instruments with a mellower tone tend to have a strong fundamental but weak higher harmonics. Figure 11 illustrates this by showing the amplitude spectrum of three different sound sources. Each instrument (or vocal) was asked to play (or sing) a note with a pitch of C_4. The top spectrum is that of a clarinet and contains a full spectrum of harmonics with varying amplitudes. The middle spectrum was taken from a vocal singing *la* and the bottom spectrum is taken from a vocal singing *me*. It can be seen that spectra vary greatly between different sound sources and therefore, to determine pitches on a variety of instruments, the network was required to learn features from a range of possible spectra for each pitch and thus become insensitive to spectral shape (and hence timbre) when classifying.

The network was trained with a total of 194 patterns, which were examples from a C-major scale between C_3 and C_6 on the four instruments. Samples were taken at various times (determined randomly) within the duration of the note. The training patterns were divided up as follows:

(1)   22 patterns (C_3–C_6) from a 'tubular-bells' sound on a commercial synthesizer.
(2)   22 patterns (C_3–C_6) from a 'strings' sound on a commercial synthesizer.
(3)   22 patterns taken from an upright piano recorded digitally via a (Toshiba EM-420) microphone placed in front of it (roughly at the place the pianist's head would be).
(4)   128 patterns taken from an electric guitar. More training patterns are needed for a guitar because the spectrum of a particular note varies with the string it is played on, and with where and how that string is plucked. These patterns can be divided into two sets, consisting, respectively, of examples played *Sul Tasto* and *Sul Ponticello*. Each of these sets consists of patterns taken from every note in the C-major scale between C_3 and C_6, played on all possible strings.

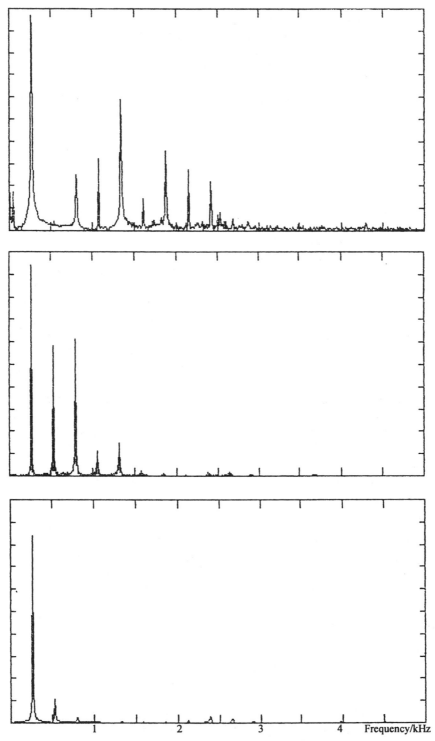

Figure 11. The amplitude spectrum of three different musical instruments for the note C4. The top spectrum is that of a clarinet, the middle spectrum was taken from a vocal singing *la* and the bottom spectrum is taken from a vocal singing *me*. It can be seen that spectra vary greatly between different sound sources.

Patterns were presented in ascending order of pitch for each of the first three cases. However, it was felt appropriate to present the many repeated notes from the different strings of the guitar in a quasi-random order. A slow learning rate was used to train the network with the 194 input patterns. 100 cycles were performed, which took about half an hour on a NeXT Workstation. The 194 patterns were clustered to 46 patterns at the F_{a_2} layer and then mapped to 22 nodes corresponding to the names of each pitch in the F_{b_2} layer. Thus, the ART_a network achieved a code compression of the input patterns of greater than 4 to 1.

4.2. The Test Data

The network was tested using 412 patterns. 194 of these were taken from the original training set but were sampled at different points in time, thus producing a spectrum which was in general rather different from the original training pattern. In some cases, e.g. tubular bells, the difference can be quite considerable.

The other test patterns consisted of:

(1) 108 patterns from the guitar. These included plucking the notes halfway between *Sul Tasto* and *Sul Ponticello* positions, playing each note *Sul Tasto* with vibrato, and playing each note *Sul Ponticello* with vibrato. Vibrato involves a frequency modulation of the order of a percent or so at a rate of a few hertz and is a common characteristic of musical tones. It is normally accompanied by amplitude modulation of a similar order of magnitude. Together they present a realistic challenge to a pitch-determining system.
(2) 22 tubular-bells patterns with each note played with clearly audible amplitude modulation.
(3) 22 notes from the strings sound played with amplitude modulation.
(4) 22 notes played softly, and 22 notes played with the sustain pedal depressed, on an acoustic piano.
(5) 22 notes played on the piano sound of a commercial synthesizer.

4.3. Results

Overall the ARTMAP network made mistakes in about 5% of cases. Around 70% of these mistakes, in turn, were 'octave' mistakes, by which we mean a classification by the network one octave above or below the correct pitch. For example, an octave mistake that arose with a soft-piano pattern was:

Correct classification B_3:

(1) B_4: intensity 796;
(2) B_3: intensity 795;
(3) G_3: intensity 693.

where (1) is first choice, (2) is second choice, etc. and the intensity (the measure of the network's certainty) is a score scaled to 1000. Here, it can be seen that there is ambiguity in the network's choice. Its preference for B_4 over B_3 is so slight as to be insignificant compared with statistical variations inherent in the method. The competition is particularly close in this example. However, it was generally the case that when the network did make a mistake the winning intensity was rather low in itself, or very close (within 50 out of 1000) to the correct classification. In the latter case the network could be adjusted to output a 'don't know'. This, however, would mildly impair its estimated accuracy in other respects as it sometimes made 'correct' classifications which could be considered ambiguous, e.g. from the strings sound:

Correct classification E₃:

(1) E₃: intensity 853;
(2) E₄: intensity 839;
(3) C₃: intensity 492.

Generally, in the ambiguous 'correct' classifications (about 4%) the runner-up was an octave away from the winner. Most of the 'correct' classifications, however, were clear cut:

Correct classification A₃:

(1) A₃: intensity 980;
(2) E₄: intensity 318;
(3) F₅: intensity 279.

The network made mistakes on only two of the data sets, namely the upright piano and the tubular-bells sets. Most of the piano mistakes were made when the note was hit softly. Inspecting the Fourier spectrum in each of these cases revealed that the harmonic components were of very low amplitude and partly obscured by low-level noise. Indeed, checking the quality of the recorded notes did reveal a rather poor signal-to-noise ratio.

The network made the remaining mistakes on the tubular-bells sound. The pitch of such sounds is in any case more difficult for listeners to determine, because the components are to some considerable degree inharmonic. The network classified 86% of test tubular-bells sounds correctly, which we regard as a reasonable performance. Increasing the number of training examples of this sound would probably improve this figure greatly. The network was able to classify all but one of the synthesized piano sounds correctly (over 95% accuracy). This is to be compared with the real piano sounds where only 86% accuracy was achieved. This is not surprising as synthesized sounds tend to vary less dramatically with how they are played, whereas the spectrum of an acoustic piano note is quite sensitive to, for example, the velocity of striking.

4.4. Conclusions

The ARTMAP network has proved capable of determining pitches with a high degree of reliability over a wide range. A significant proportion of the small number of mistakes made are readily explicable in terms of noise or spectral inharmonicity and could be largely eliminated by straightforward improvements in the quality and quantity of the training patterns. The 'octave' mistakes which predominate are particularly interesting and significant. Such mistakes are common amongst musically sophisticated human listeners and reflect the inherent similarity of tones whose fundamental frequencies can be expressed as a simple, whole-number ratio. Indeed, it could be argued that such similarity is the very foundation of western harmony.

The indications are that the capability of the system may be extended to a great variety of instruments. This would result in a generalized pitch determiner which exhibited a desirable insensitivity to the dynamic level and spectral shape of the input signal.

5. Recent and Future Work

The ARTMAP system described here was written as one program (object) in Objective C on a NeXT Workstation. Recently, by using object-oriented techniques, we have created different classes for each ART network, e.g. for ART1, ART2, ART2-A (Carpenter *et al.*, 1991b), S_ART (modification of ART2-A, developed by Taylor (1994)) and a map field, all of which can be dynamically created at run-time (Taylor & Greenhough, 1993). This allows more complicated networks to be built by simply instantiating the relevant classes needed for an application. A general ARTMAP network that can link any combination of the above networks together has also been constructed, allowing great flexibility when applying different ARTMAP topologies to particular applications. This has led to the use of ARTMAP in other music-pattern classification tasks such as coping with polyphonic acoustic signals (Taylor *et al.*, 1993).

Also recently, a comparison of performance of three different ANN architectures for pitch determination has been made. These include back-propagation, and two distinct ARTMAP architectures. Each ARTMAP architecture contains a different ART_a module, respectively, ART2-A, and S_ART.

Each ANN was trained with a total of 198 examples of pitched notes from the C-major scale on 10 different instruments in the range C_3 to C_6. Instruments were chosen to cover a wide variety of spectral shapes so that the network could pick out the characteristic features for each pitched note, and yet acquire an insensitivity to timbre. These instruments included soprano, contralto and tenor voices, saxophone and French horn, violin, acoustic guitar and sitar, piano and some examples of whistling.

In order to assess the system's robustness, the majority of testing examples were chosen from different instruments but some were taken from instruments from the training set and sung or played with vibrato. The test set altogether consisted of 443 patterns. The network was also tested on the 198 training patterns, and showed that it had learned all the pitch examples. Test-set instruments included alto and bass voices, classical, 12-string and electric guitar, recorder, clarinet, mandolin and steel drums, as well as some synthetic sounds (produced by computer) which consisted of a harmonic series without a fundamental. Other test examples were: soprano, contralto ($\times 2$) and tenor ($\times 2$) voices either sung with vibrato or taken from different singers, saxophone and violin with vibrato, and piano played softly.

For this experiment, the back-propagation network was investigated for a large number of input-parameter combinations to optimize it fully (2500 different conditions in all, taking the equivalent of about 12 days of Sun SPARC Station time). Each ART network was also optimized by first setting the optimum θ (threshold) value and then tweaking its vigilance level which in both cases took considerably less time than the back-propagation network (around 4 hours in the ART2-A's case and less than 30 minutes in S_ART's case).

It was found that the best back-propagation network achieved an absolute-pitch classification rate of 98.0% and a chroma-pitch classification rate (i.e. ignoring the octave) of 99.1%. In the same trial, the two ARTMAP networks achieved rates of

97.7% and 99.6% (for S_ART) and 98.2% and 99.8% (for ART2-A), respectively. It was also found that for these cases the back-propagation network took over 8 minutes (on a NeXT Workstation) to learn the training data. The ART2-A network took just over 2 minutes while the S_ART network took less than 20 seconds to learn the training data. It was also found that all ANNs performed better than straightforward pattern-matching against stored templates which achieved an absolute-pitch classification rate of 97.1% and a chroma-pitch classification rate of 98.2% (Taylor & Greenhough, 1993).

It is found that although the ANN-based ARTMAP pitch-determining system had to be trained, this is well worth while, since it only takes 2 minutes in the ART2-A's case (and just 20 seconds in S_ART's case) and results in a more robust pitch-classification ability. The use of the back-propagation ANN, however, would have to be offset against the training time and optimization problems if it is to be considered for use in a pitch-determining system.

Future work includes the tracking of vocal and instrumental solos in the presence of an accompaniment. This requires the ANN to reject everything in the source except the main melody. We believe that this can be accomplished by teaching the ANN what a particular instrument sounds like (i.e. its spectral characteristics and thus its timbre) for each pitch. The network can then 'listen' for recurrences of this sound in the music, and thus classify just the pitches of the instrument it has been trained for. Preliminary experiments with some musical instruments have shown that one particular ANN network (ARTMAP) can indeed be trained to perform such classifications. Such tracking systems may eventually find application in certain contemporary music performances involving the interaction of human players and computer systems, and perhaps in ethnomusicological studies where it is required to transcribe previously unnotated live or recorded music. The latter application may require the handling of a pitch continuum, in which case the input mapping system will need to be refined, as suggested in Section 3.2.

References

Brown, J.C. (1991) Musical frequency tracking using the methods of conventional and 'narrowed' autocorrelation. *The Journal of the Acoustical Society of America*, **89**, 2346–2354.

Brown, J.C. (1992) Musical fundamental frequency tracking using a pattern recognition method. *The Journal of the Acoustical Society of America*, **92**, 1394–1402.

Carpenter, G.A. & Grossberg, S. (1987a) A massively parallel architecture for a self-organizing neural pattern recognition machine. *Computer Vision, Graphics, and Image Processing*, **37**, 54–115.

Carpenter, G.A. & Grossberg, S. (1987b) ART2: Self-organization of stable category recognition codes for analog input patterns. *Applied Optics*, **26**, 4919–4930.

Carpenter, G.A. & Grossberg, S. (1990) ART3: Hierarchical search using chemical transmitters in self-organizing pattern recognition architectures. *Neural Networks*, **3**, 129–152.

Carpenter, G.A., Grossberg, S. & Reynolds, J.H. (1991a) ARTMAP: Supervised real-time learning and classification of nonstationary data by a self-organizing neural network. *Neural Networks*, **4**, 565–588.

Carpenter, G.A., Grossberg, S. & Rosen, D.B. (1991b) ART2-A: An adaptive resonance algorithm for rapid category learning and recognition. *Neural Networks*, **4**, 493–504.

De Boer (1956) *On the Residue in Hearing*. Unpublished doctoral dissertation. University of Amsterdam.

De Boer, E. (1977) Pitch theories unified. In E.F. Evans & J.P. Wilson (Eds), *Psychophysics and Physiology of Hearing*, pp. 323–334. London: Academic.

Duifhuis, H., Willems, L.F. & Sluyter, R.J. (1982) Measurement of pitch in speech: An implementation of Goldstein's theory of pitch perception. *The Journal of the Acoustical Society of America*, **71**, 1568–1580.

Goldstein, J.L. (1973) An optimum processor for the central formation of pitch of complex tones. *The Journal of the Acoustical Society of America*, **54**, 1496–1516.

Grossberg, S. (1976a) Adaptive pattern classification and universal recoding. I: Parallel development and coding of neural feature detectors. *Biological Cybernetics*, **23**, 121–134.

Grossberg, S. (1976b) Adaptive pattern classification and universal recoding, II: Feedback, expectation, olfaction, and illusions. *Biological Cybernetics*, **23**, 187–202.

Helmholtz, H.L.F. von (1863) *On the Sensations of Tone as a Physiological Basis for the Theory of Music.* Translated by A.J. Ellis from the 4th German edition, 1877, Leymans, London, 885 (reprinted, New York: Dover, 1954).

Hermes, D.J. (1988) Measurement of pitch by subharmonic summation. *The Journal of the Acoustical Society of America*, **83**, 257–264.

Houtsma, A.J.M. & Goldstein, J.L. (1972) The central origin of the pitch of complex tones: Evidence from musical interval recognition. *The Journal of the Acoustical Society of America*, **51**, 520–529.

Lippmann, R.P. (1987) An introduction to computing with neural nets, *IEEE ASSP Magazine*, **3**, 4–22.

Martin Ph. (1982) Comparison of pitch detection by cepstrum and spectral comb analysis. *Proceedings of IEEE International Conference on Acoustics, Speech and Signal Processing*, pp. 180–183. ICASSP-82.

Noll, A.M. (1970) Pitch determination of human speech by the harmonic product spectrum, the harmonic sum spectrum, and a maximum likelihood estimate. In the Microwave Institute (Eds), *Symposium on Computer Processing in Communication* **19**, 779–797, Polytechnic University of Brooklyn, New York.

Piszczalski, M. & Galler, B.F. (1982) A computer model of music recognition. In M. Clynes (Ed.), *Music, Mind and the Brain: The Neuropsychology of Music*, pp. 321–351. London: Plenum Press.

Ritsma, R.J. (1962) Existence region of the tonal residue, I. *The Journal of the Acoustical Society of America*, **34**, 1224–1229.

Rumelhart, D.E. & McClelland, J.L. (1986) *Parallel Distributed Processing, Explorations in the Microstructure of Cognition*, Vol. 1: Foundations. Cambridge, MA: MIT Press.

Scheffers, M.T.M. (1983) Simulation of auditory analysis of pitch: an elaboration on the DWS pitch meter. *The Journal of the Acoustical Society of America*, **74**, 1716–1725.

Schouten, J.F. (1940) The residue and the mechanism of hearing. *Proceedings Konikl. Ned. Akad. Wetenschap.* **43**, 991–999.

Schroeder, M.R. (1968) Period histogram and product spectrum: new methods for fundamental-frequency measurement. *The Journal of the Acoustical Society of America*, **43**, 829–834.

Stubbs, D. (1988) Neurocomputers, *M. D. Computing*, **5**, 14–24.

Taylor, I. (1994) *Artificial Neural Network Types for the Determination of Musical Pitch*. PhD thesis, University of Wales, College of Cardiff.

Taylor, I. & Greenhough, M. (1993) An object-oriented ARTMAP system for classifying pitch. *Proceedings of International Computer Music Conference*, pp. 244–247.

Taylor, I., Page, M. & Greenhough, M. (1993) Neural networks for processing musical signals and structures. *Acoustics Bulletin*, **18**, 5–9.

Terhardt, E. (1972) Zur Tonhoehenwahrnehmung von Klaengen II: ein Funktionsschema. *Acustica*, **26**, 187–199.

Terhardt, E. (1974) Pitch, consonance, and harmony. *The Journal of the Acoustical Society of America*, **55**, 1061–1069.

Terhardt, E., Stoll, G. & Seewann, M. (1982) Algorithm for extraction of pitch and pitch salience from complex tonal signals. *The Journal of the Acoustical Society of America*, **71**, 679–688.

Wightman, F.L. (1973) The pattern-transformation model of pitch. *The Journal of the Acoustical Society of America*, **54**, 407–416.

Development of Tonal Centres and Abstract Pitch as Categorizations of Pitch Use

NIALL GRIFFITH

Modelling how people establish a sense of tonality and encode pitch invariance are important elements of research into musical cognition. This paper describes simulations of processes that induce classifications of pitch and interval use from a set of nursery-rhyme melodies. The classifications are identified with keys and degrees of the scale. The extractive process has been implemented in various forms of shunting, adding and tracking memory, and ART2 networks, Kohonen feature maps and feedforward nets are used as classifiers, in modular combinations. In the model, stable tonal centres emerge as general categories of pitch use over the short to medium term, while degree categories emerge from classifying interval use over the longer term. The representations of degree reflect the similarity relations between degrees. Overall, this research is concerned with the problem of how to abstract representations of sequences in a way that is both resilient and adaptive. It uses various extractive processes cooperatively to derive consistent representations from sequences of pitches, and shows that by using information generated within one process it is possible to guide the development of another, in this case functional representation.

KEYWORDS: Music, induction, tonality, pitch use, interval use, sequence categorization, ART2, Kohonen feature maps, feedforward networks.

1. Introduction

The simulations described in this paper[1] are concerned with modelling the abstraction of profiles of pitch use from music, and how statistical representations may contribute to the development of musical tonality. Musical tonality is a complex phenomenon. While not wishing to discuss in detail all the processes that have been recognized as influencing tonal understanding, it is worthwhile to outline its four major aspects.

Firstly, there is a precedent stage of psychoacoustic transduction. It is unclear how the identities and relations emerging from this transduction influence other tonal processes. While psychoacoustics seems insufficient to account for tonality as a whole (Storr, 1992; Griffith, 1993a), it is obviously a necessary phenomenal basis (Terhardt, 1974; Patterson, 1986). The psychophysical transduction of sound is assumed to be a psychological constant, i.e. it has been acquired over evolutionary time-scales.

This article appeared originally in *Connection Science*, 1994, **6**, 155–175, and is reprinted with permission.

Secondly, there are processes involving a dialogue between social conventions, top-down schematic processes and psychoacoustic mechanisms. An example of this kind of process is the evolution of temperaments leading to the system of keys in western music. This involved an understanding of the mathematics underlying tuning, the development of keyboard instruments, and the wish to resolve aesthetic problems inherent in previous tunings. The historical development of scales and temperaments suggests a multiplicity of processes: some as precedent as gestalt grouping principles, others as tertiary as the formalization of the properties and implications of pitch sets. How these perceptual and conceptual processes interact is part of the ongoing research agenda for cognitive musicology.

Thirdly, there is the coincidence of tonal with non-tonal musical dimensions (Bregman, 1990; Handel, 1973). These are considered to include phrasing (Narmour, 1984; Page, 1993), rhythmic and metrical structures (Peretz & Kolinsky, 1993) and expressive timing (Shaffer *et al.*, 1985). The influence between tonality and these structures seems to some extent to be mutual. However, very little is known for certain about the operation of coincidence between musical dimensions, or how and when it takes place in auditory processing.

Fourthly, tonality involves functions that induce structure from the use that is made of pitches. These functions are concerned with structure that arises over time, i.e. they are sequential. Pitch use has three aspects: (1) the memorization of sequences, (2) the abstraction of the attributes of pitch use within sequences, (3) the compositional relations—in the general sense of putting together—between the first two aspects. The simulations reported focus on the second of these aspects, the abstraction of patterns of pitch use.

2. Computational Models of Key and Tonality

Over the last 30 or so years, various programs have been written with the aim of identifying, from a stream of pitch information, the key of a piece of music. Most of these have been concerned with the operation of a fully developed sense of key (Simon, 1968; Winograd, 1968; Longuet-Higgins & Steedman, 1970; Holtzmann, 1977; Ulrich, 1977; Krumhansl, 1990a; Huron & Parncutt, 1993). More recently, artificial neural networks (ANNs) have been used to model some of the processes involved in learning about musical structure via simulated exposure to pieces of music.

The idea that musical schemas emerge from broad perceptual processes, classifying structured sequences of sound, is prominent in the work of both Bharucha (Bharucha, 1987, 1991), who stresses the chordal structure of tonality, and Leman (Leman, 1990, 1992), who stresses the harmonic (overtone) structure of tonality. Francés (1988) argues that there is not enough information in melody by itself to serve as the basis for tonality. The simulations described below explore how much can be learned from a minimum of melodic information.

Leman's model (Leman, 1992) involves the temporal integration of the harmonic constituents of pitches, and is based on the virtual-pitch theory of Terhardt *et al.* (1982), and developed by Parncutt (1988). Pitch representations integrated over a few seconds are related to tonal centres previously developed from representations of chords. Tonal attribution is a function of the distance between the current integrated pitch representation and tonal centres. The model specifies no mechanism to account for the emergence of abstract pitch.

MUSACT (Bharucha, 1987) is a spreading activation model of chord and key relations. Layers of units representing pitches, chords and keys are connected to each other by virtue of membership, i.e. a pitch is only linked to those chords it is a member of. When a set of pitches is fed into the network, the connections propagate activation to chords and then to keys. Overall, the net settles into a vote for different chords and keys. MUSACT has been extended using competitive learning to simulate the acquisition of the chord and key schemas. The learning model proposes that chords are grouped in pools. The chords in a group are 'yoked' together for the purposes of learning. When a chord of a particular type, e.g. C major, is mapped to an uncommitted node in a group, the other nodes in the group are also adjusted so as to be predisposed to the same pattern of pitches at other points in the chromatic scale. Yoking chords in this way is necessary because there is nothing to suggest, for example, that the chord *c e g* (C major) is of the same type as *f a c* (F major). The learning mechanism incorporates the pitch transformations through the chromatic pitch set that relate chords of the same type built from different roots. By using this mechanism, MUSACT eschews the use of interval information. However, it is arguable that if it used interval information, then the chord pools could be developed in a simpler, and more general, way out of categorizations of the interval structure of chords. The issues that arise out of whether pitch relations are encoded by mechanisms of the type proposed in MUSACT, or whether pitch relations are previously encoded as intervals, allowing their subsequent use by other processes, is beyond the scope of this paper. The model described below proposes that intervals are encoded, and that this information is used to establish abstract pitch identity.

MUSACT models the construction of tonality as the integration of pitches into chords and scales. It specifies only a black-box 'gating' model of the abstraction of pitch into an invariant form such as the tonic *sol-fa*, or scale degrees. Although the tonic *sol-fa* is primarily an *aide-memoire*, and the system of degrees is primarily an analytical device, both describe an abstract, single octave scale. These abstract scales play an important role in learning and remembering music. MUSACT uses pitch class and key identities to gate pitch into a form where the tonic of a scale is always 0. An equivalent mechanism is described by Scarborough *et al.* (1989). How might such a mechanism be learned? It is difficult to see how to establish a direct phenomenal basis for abstract pitch in the overtone characteristics of pitches, as this does not vary by key—yet the abstract function, and scale position, of pitches and chords depends upon the key they are played within. However, differentiation does arise in a representation of how pitches are related to other pitches over a period of time. These relationships can be thought of either in terms of the statistics of the pitch transitions (Griffith, 1993a), or in terms of the statistics of the interval transitions associated with sets of pitches.

The model described below investigates constructive mechanisms that extract and classify the statistics associated with the use of pitch classes and their associated intervals. These mechanisms induce outlines of tonal structure representing diatonic centres and degrees of the scale.

3. Pitch Use and the Development of Tonality

The music used in the simulations is a set of nursery rhymes. These are represented by vectors that identify the pitch classes and intervals used in western music.

The tonality of pieces of music is often described in terms of subsets of pitches. In western music the diatonic scales are pre-eminent. Each diatonic major scale

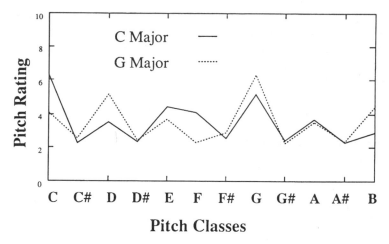

Pitch Classes

Figure 1. The prominence of pitches in the scales of C and G major. The figures were derived using the probe-tone method (Krumhansl, 1990a).

consists of seven pitches related by a pattern of tone (T) and semitone (S) intervals—T T S T T T S. Thinking about tonality as a set emphasizes that a piece in a particular key tends to use those pitches which are members of the scale identified with this key. Furthermore, different pitches are emphasized by being used more and less frequently. Figure 1 shows how the salience of pitches, from Krumhansl (1990a), differentiates the scales of C and G—which differ by only one pitch.

Although this description is specific to the western pitch system the underlying principle is more general. The emphasis of some pitches over others through repetition and return occurs in many musical systems, including Indian, Chinese and Japanese (May, 1980). Deutsch (1975, 1978) has argued that repetition aids memorization, and (Krumhansl, 1990b) has developed this kind of insight into a theory of tonal structure. The psychological experiments of Krumhansl (1990a) indicate a strong correlation between the measured salience of pitches in different scales, and the frequency of occurrence and accumulated duration of the pitch classes in pieces of music.

However, what is not clear is whether or not patterns of frequency of pitch occurrence that arise over pieces of music are distinct enough to allow the induction of categories underlying tonal structure, i.e. keys and degrees. The first set of simulations illustrate in a simple model that it is possible to track and classify the statistics associated with pitch use into tonal centres.

The frequency of pitch occurrence is a very general characterization of a pitch sequence. Underlying it there are local patterns, such as phrases, verses, etc., and the overall pitch profile arises from them. The repeated use of short pitch sequences forms contextual patterns that vary with the key. This is closely related to the function of a pitch as a degree of the scale (Butler & Brown, 1984; Butler, 1989), and also with its identity in abstract mnemonic scales.

There is a variety of opinions about the status of encodings of interval in tonal structure, for example, Krumhansl (1990b) and Butler and Brown (1984), and in melodic memory, for example, Dowling (1984, 1988). However, the close relationship between the two is well established. The representation of pitch use in terms of intervals allows comparison between pitch use in different keys.

The model focuses on the frequency of occurrence of pitches and intervals in diatonic major scales. As such, it can make no claim to be a complete model of tonal induction. It is a partial synthesis of insights in the work of Krumhansl, Butler and Brown and others (Krumhansl, 1990a; Butler & Brown, 1984; Brown, 1988; Butler, 1989).[2] More generally, tonality is conceived to arise from a diverse set of processes (Bharucha, 1987; Terhardt, 1984; Bregman, 1990; Balzano, 1980).

Several concerns have influenced the development of the model. Firstly, the idea that classification is an adaptive process, concerned with developing stable, consistent representations of aspects of experience. Secondly, that classification is focused at appropriate levels of granularity, both representationally and temporally, resulting in categorizations that are more or less general (Lakoff, 1987). Thirdly, that representations derived at one level of granularity may be used as a source of attentional focus by processes making other classifications. These characteristics— adaptive stability, appropriate categorical granularity and attentional structure—are all viewed as desirable properties. In particular the simulations are interested in how categorical processes which attend to different dimensions of pitch use, over different representational and temporal spans, can be used together.

The experiments to be described all use the same overall procedure. A stream of vectors representing the melodies of the nursery rhymes are tracked by a memory function. The content of the memory is then presented to an Adaptive Resonance Theory (ART) type of ANN classifier.

4. Inducing Key from Patterns of Pitch Use

The nursery rhymes used in the simulations are from three collections (Chesterman, 1935; Mitchel & Blyton, 1968; Anon, 1979). The training set consisted of 60 songs, the test set of a further 25. Each song was present in the training set transposed to all keys, giving in all 720 sequences in the training set and 300 in the test set. The songs' profiles of frequency of pitch occurrence were all highly correlated with the pitch salience profiles in Krumhansl (1990b).

In these first experiments, the songs are input to a self-organizing ART ANN classifier, ART2[3] (Carpenter & Grossberg, 1987). The model is outlined in Figure 2. Each sequence is represented by a succession of vectors, each of which identifies a pitch class. Three representations of pitch were compared.

The first representation, *FREQ*, is a simple identity vector of 12 elements. The identity of the pitch is indicated by the value of one element being 1. In the *DUR* representation, the value associated with a pitch reflects the length of the note. A crotchet is 1, quavers are 0.5, etc. The *SLI*, *timesliced* representation, involves the repetition of each *FREQ* vector a number of times to reflect its duration. Semi-quavers are presented twice, quavers four times, etc. A similar representation was used by Todd (1989).

The pattern of pitch use presented to the ART2 classifier is constructed in a *memory* (TRK), which tracks the number of occurrences of pitches in melodies. This memory is implemented in a network form as a process of slow learning, shown in Figure 3. The memory vector has elements equivalent to the input vector. At the start of each song the values in the memory are set to zero. The values developed within the memory during the passage of a song reflect the number of times different pitches occur. The memory is presented to the ART2 classifier at the end of each song.

Where values in the input vector **X** are between 0 and *n*, the learning in the

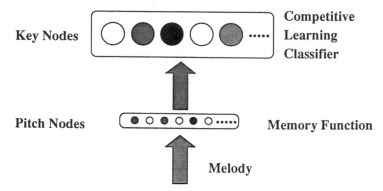

Figure 2. A model of the memorization and classification of pitch use in a simple memory model and competitive-learning classifier.

TRK memory is as follows, where $\mathbf{x}_i$ is the input value, $\mathbf{w}_i$ is the memory value, initialized to zero, and the response of the memory is determined by η:[4]

if $\mathbf{x}_i(t) > 0$: $\mathbf{w}_i(t + 1) = \mathbf{w}_i(t) + \eta(\mathbf{x}_i(t))(1 - \mathbf{w}_i(t))$

else   : $\mathbf{w}_i(t + 1) = \mathbf{w}_i(t)$

η^T rates of 0.005, 0.01, 0.05, 0.1 and 0.5 were used. In all simulations the network developed twelve nodes, each equivalent to a key. They were stable over the different η^T rates and emerge with ART2 vigilance (ρ) set between 0.91 and 0.97. The percentage of mappings to the home[5] key was 91.5–98.3%. After the network had been trained, it was tested with the developing memory, pitch by pitch. This showed a generalization of between 79% and 90.3%. Results for the *FREQ* representation were slightly better than for either the *DUR* or *SLI* representation.

In both the training and test set the end-of-song memory pattern for those songs lacking degree $\hat{3}$ and, or $\hat{4}$,[6] were irregularly misplaced. The accuracy of the

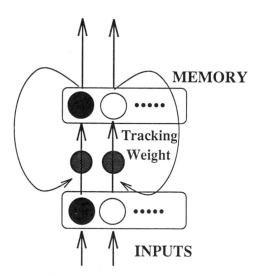

Figure 3. Simple memory function which tracks the frequency of occurrence of pitches in a sequence.

Table I. The typicality and attribution of four songs from the training and test set, using the FREQ representation at an η^T rate of 0.05

Set	Song	Typicality	Activation	Attribution (%)
Train	Bye Baby Bunting	0.6180	0.7850	2.75–22.2
Test	Little Bo Peep	0.6684	0.9107	100.0
Train	The Man With The Gun	0.8908	0.9469	50.98–74.51
Test	Ding Dong Bell	0.8452	0.9691	100.0

pitch-by-pitch mappings reflects how closely the TRK memory approximates the overall pattern of frequency of occurrence encoded in a key exemplar as a song progresses. The songs that are consistently misattributed when the memory is presented pitch by pitch often have atypical representations of degree $\hat{5}$ and some have degree $\hat{6}$ or $\hat{7}$ missing.

The typicality of each song was measured by correlating the frequency of occurrence of pitches in each song with the average frequency of occurrence of pitches in all songs. There is a high correlation—at the 0.001 level of significance—between end-of-song activation and song typicality for all representations and η^T rates. However, the correlation between the number of correct pitch-by-pitch attributions and typicality is generally insignificant at the <0.10 level for all η^T rates, as are the correlations between song length and song typicality, between end-of-song activations and song length, and between correct mappings and song length.

The pattern of attributions indicates variations in pitch use within songs. The pattern of frequency becomes more stable over time. The relationship between typicality, activation and number of attributions is shown in Table I for four songs. Two are typical in terms of the overall frequency of occurrence of their degrees, two are not. Two are well attributed, two are not. Because a song is not typical of a key does not mean that it is closer to another. The total activation for all the key nodes over time was calculated for the selected songs, and plotted in Figure 4. The final activations of the songs does not reflect how quickly the pattern of activation emerges.

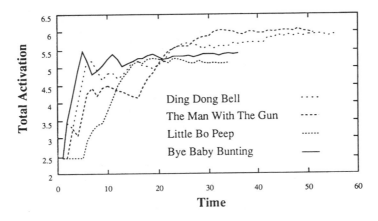

Figure 4. The total activations for *Bye Bye Baby Bunting* (atypical), *Little Bo Peep* (atypical), *The Man With The Gun*, (typical) and *Ding Dong Bell* (typical), *FREQ* simulation using an η^T of 0.05, plotted over time.

The networks were also tested with 27 pitch sequences, as described in Brown (1988). These sequences were designed to show that the pitches used in a sequence—the tonal content—are not enough to determine correct key attribution. Only 35% are correctly attributed at the end of sequence. 45% of attributions are to the adjacent key, and the rest—all of which are chromatic sequences—are to more distant keys. If these are excluded on the grounds that the network was trained on diatonic melodies, the correct attributions rise to 42% and the incorrect attributions are all, bar one, to the adjacent keys. The network's performance is better than was expected. However, the information available to the network is obviously not sufficient to ensure it makes the correct attributions.

Overall, the viability of inducing the form of pitch salience derived by Krumhansl (1990a), is supported by the simulations. However, presenting the TRK memory at the end of songs means that only developed memory patterns are paid attention. If the memory is presented to the classifier after each pitch has been incorporated in the memory, then the categories are less clear-cut. This reflects the undeveloped patterns tracked at the start of songs, which form nodes in their own right. It could be argued that as more coherent nodes develop, these impoverished nodes would eventually be pruned away, by some form of cognitive economy. An alternative argument is that the classification of the statistics of frequency of occurrence, at this level of generality, is likely to reflect an attentional mechanism that is concerned with relatively stable patterns of pitch use. It certainly seems feasible to construct a mechanism that will only present stable patterns for classification.

The derived key centres exhibit relations that are congruent with some of the topological relations described by Krumhansl (1990a). This reflects the nature of the vector representations derived, and the concomitant geometrical proximity of the exemplars for keys adjacent on the circle of fifths. Figure 5 shows an image of the surface of a Kohonen feature map (Kohonen, 1989) developed from a set of

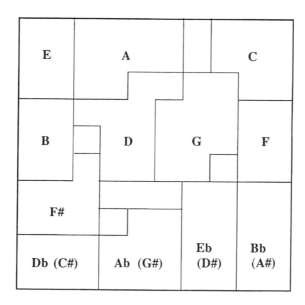

Figure 5. Distribution of key areas over a KFM using the exemplar weights developed in *FREQ* simulation using an η^T of 0.05. The KFM was a 10×10 surface, started with an initial update area of area 7×7 and a learning rate η^K of 0.3.

ART2 key exemplars. The key areas are discrete and each is adjacent to its neighbours in the circle of fifths.

5. Abstracting Pitch from Patterns of Interval Use

The encoding of abstract pitch (degree) is accepted as an important part of the mechanism that memorizes melodies. The work of Dowling (1984, 1988) indicates that melodic memory involves the encoding of abstract pitch and the pattern of intervals between pitches. These two components appear to be used with greater and lesser accuracy in different situations. The model that is outlined below investigates the relationship between the two by suggesting that it is possible to derive representations of abstract pitches as classifications of patterns of memorized interval use associated with pitches. The model assumes that the categorical interval between two pitches in the chromatic scale has been identified. It is a very similar model to that used to derive key centres from frequency of pitch occurrence. However, it differs in two ways. First, the statistics of the use of pitch classes are separated, so that the use of different pitches can be compared. Second, pitch use is specified in terms of the interval relationships between pitches. If pitch use is described directly in terms of other pitches its representation is limited by the positional specification of pitch within the input vector space[7]—and by implication within actual pitch space. Interval, on the other hand, represents pitch relations directly.

The model investigates whether different degrees of the scale are associated with different patterns of intervals, sufficiently distinct to delineate interval-based categories of pitch use. If they do, the representation will lend support to the intervallic model of pitch function advocated by Browne (1981) and Butler and Brown (1984). The model should reflect, for example, that the tonic $\hat{1}$ and the dominant $\hat{5}$ are functionally more similar than the tonic $\hat{1}$ and the leading tone $\hat{7}$. This kind of property is more interesting than the position or identity of the degree.

5.1. The Intervals of the Major Scale

In these simulations, intervals are identified in vectors in the same way as pitches—a vector position being associated with an interval. The sets of intervals within the diatonic major scale are described in Browne (1981), and are shown in Table II. The pattern of intervals associated with each degree of the scale is very similar, and will have limited discriminatory value.

However, as with the frequency of occurrence of pitches, the way in which the sets of intervals are used is quite different, as can be seen in Figure 6. The values plotted are calculated by summing the intervals that precede each pitch in the songs.

Table II. Intervals between the degrees of the major diatonic scale

Degree	$\hat{1}$	$\hat{2}$	$\hat{3}$	$\hat{4}$	$\hat{5}$	$\hat{6}$	$\hat{7}$
$\hat{1}$	U	M2	M3	P4	P5	M6	M7
$\hat{2}$	m7	U	M2	m3	P4	P5	M6
$\hat{3}$	m6	m7	U	m2	m3	P4	P5
$\hat{4}$	P5	M6	M7	U	M2	M3	T
$\hat{5}$	P4	P5	M6	m7	U	M2	M3
$\hat{6}$	m3	P4	P5	m6	m7	U	M2
$\hat{7}$	m2	m3	P4	T	m6	m7	U

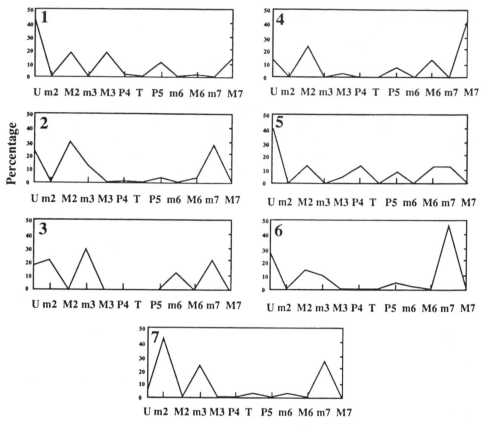

Figure 6. The percentage of intervals associated with the degrees of the scale in the training set.

The resulting counts of the different intervals associated with each pitch are then expressed as percentages. The overall pattern of interval use shows a marked preponderance of intervals between pitches that are near neighbours in the scale, as might be expected in a set of melodies. In the model the representation of the intervallic context of pitches is constructed in a set of memories similar to those used to extract frequency of pitch occurrence, except that twelve memories are used—one for each pitch.

5.2. An Outline Model of Pitch Abstraction

An outline of the model of pitch abstraction is shown in Figure 7. The functions within the model are bipartite. Firstly, a process of self-organizing, bottom-up statistical extraction, using ART2, classifies patterns constructed in echoic and tracking memory models. The memory patterns are consolidated in a set of discrete pitch-in-key representations guided by the key identified in the process described in Section 4. These pitch-in-key representations comprise the most general description of interval use associated with pitch. When they are classified the result is a set of nodes identified with degrees of the scale.

The second element of the model is concerned with acquiring associative

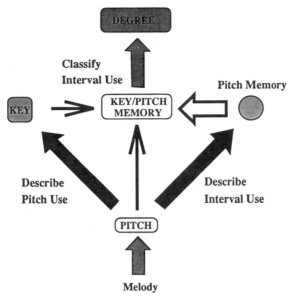

Figure 7. Outline of the model of pitch abstraction showing the relationship between processes classifying pitch use into keys and interval use into degrees.

mappings between pitch, key and degree. The degree identities, such as emerge from the self-organizing statistical extraction, are used as teaching patterns in a supervised learning model. Two kinds of association are learned. The first are the associative mappings often taken to epitomize the abstract system of degrees. This involves mappings between pitch, key and degree, to allow the recovery—from a combination of pairs of identities of the third identity. For example, if we know the identity of pitch and key, e.g. f♯ and G major, then we know the degree—$\hat{7}$. Conversely, if we know the key and degree, G major and $\hat{7}$, then we know the pitch, f♯ . Similarly, the identification of pitch and degree allows the extrapolation of key. The second kind of mapping is between the developing interval memories and degree identities. This mapping allows the identification of degree directly from developing interval memories, as a song progresses, and encodes intervallic patterns as tonal descriptors parallel to the identification of keys.

The self-organizing part of the model was implemented using four similar memory models, which derive representations of the intervallic context of each pitch class. The general form of the memory is shown at the bottom of Figures 8 and 10. It comprises two stages. The first stage traces the occurrence of intervals over all the pitch classes. This *echoic* (ECH) or trace memory is of the shunting (multiplicative), adding type (Grossberg, 1978), and is similar to that used by Gjerdingen (1990). The box in Figure 10 shows the trace values that might occur in such a memory using an η^E rate of 0.5, applied to the sequence $e \rightarrow b \rightarrow c \rightarrow a$. Here one memory type is described. The SAT memory is a shunting, adding, tracking memory. It is reset to zero at the start of each song. Where values in the input vector **X** are either 0 or 1, x_j is the input value and w_j is the echoic memory value, initialized to zero, and η^E is the memory rate:

if $\mathbf{x}_j(t) > 0$: $\mathbf{w}_j(t) = (\mathbf{w}_j\,(t-1) + (\eta^E\mathbf{x}_j(t)))$

else   : $\mathbf{w}_j(t) = \eta^E\mathbf{w}_j(t-1)$

The ECH memory models used are straightforward and are easily implemented. They are described in more detail in Griffith (1993b). They produce a trace of events in which the recency of each interval is reflected by a value between 0 and 1. The results they produce are very similar.

The second stage is a set of TRK memories, like that used to track the frequency of occurrence of pitch. One memory is dedicated to each pitch class and receives input from the initial ECH memory. The tracking memory is identical in all four models and is the same as that used in the model of key identification described in Section 4, except that the frequency of occurrence is tracked separately for the twelve pitch classes. Learning takes place in the TRK memory associated with a pitch *only* when that pitch occurs.

The two-stage memory computes two things. Firstly, the ECH memory produces a vector that reflects the recency of intervals. The actual values reflect the η^E rate and the configuration of the adding and shunting elements. Elements that are more prominent (recent) in the ECH memory have larger values. The second TRK memories are specific to pitch; the tracking only takes place in a pitch memory when that pitch occurs. This memory tracks the pattern of intervals in the ECH memory, emphasizing the intervals that are consistently prominent in a pitch's context by scaling up the tracking of the more recent intervals relative to older, lower-valued intervals.

As the TRK memory for a pitch is only activated when that pitch occurs, the intervals associated with less frequent pitches are tracked less often and the pattern that is tracked in the TRK memory is sensitive to the idiosyncracies of pitch use in particular songs. This problem is intrinsic to the pattern of events being represented in this way and cannot be resolved by setting the η^E memory rate of the initial ECH memory to a high value. If it is, the interval events will stay longer in the ECH memory, but the subsequent TRK memory-tracking representations become less differentiated. The lower the η^E rate the closer the contents of the TRK memory should approximate the frequency of occurrences of intervals associated with each pitch.

5.3. Topological Maps of Pitch-interval Use

The representations developed within the pitch memories were investigated initially using a Kohonen feature map (KFM) (Kohonen, 1989). These initial simulations looked specifically at how differentiated the representations developed in the two stage memories were. All four types of memory were used. The KFM used was a two-dimensional, 12 by 12 surface. The local update area was initialized to 11, and the learning rate, η^K, was 0.3. The set of experiments covered four memory types, three η^E rates—0.75, 0.5 and 0.25—and five η^T rates—0.005, 0.01, 0.05, 0.1 and 0.5—making a set of 60 simulations. The experiment is outlined in Figure 8.

The memories were presented at the end of a song. The pattern of interval use in a pitch memory at this point reflects the pattern of intervals associated with a particular pitch in a particular song and key. The degree identity associated with the pitch and the key, e.g. g in C major being degree $\hat{5}$, is used to tag the points plotted on the KFM. If the set of songs were homogeneous in their association of pitches and intervals, then we would expect the KFM to develop discrete areas associated with specific degrees. However, we have already seen in Figure 4 that, pitch by pitch, there is a variety of pitch use in the different songs. In fact, all the maps produced by these KFM simulations were highly fragmented (Figure 9), with

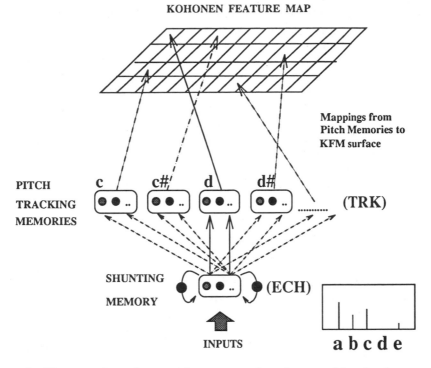

Figure 8. The mapping of composite memory functions tracking the frequency of occurrence of interval against pitches in a song on to a KFM.

much intermixing of different degrees. The specific pitch memories represent the variability of pitch use within songs more accurately, but this makes the patterns more diffuse, and abstraction more difficult.

.	.	7	3	3	.	.	.	.	5	.	.
.	5	.	.	3	.	.	.	.	.	.	.
5	.	.	.	.	.	.	.	1	5	.	.
5	5	.	3	.	3	.	4	.	.	.	1
4	.	.	.	.	.	2	.	2	.	4	6
4	.	.	.	7	.	.	2	5	5	2	5
4	4	.	.	7	.	.	5	6	.	3	.
5	1	1	1	.	3	.	.	.	.	.	5
3	1	1	1	.	3	.	.	.	.	.	.
.	.	.	.	3	3	.	.	3	6	6	.
.	.	2	.	3	.	.	6	.	.	.	.
.	2	.	6	7	2	1	1	.	6	.	4

Figure 9. KFM of interval representation of pitch. Simulation AST η^E 0.25 and η^T 0.005.

How well these pitch memories reflect the variation in pitch use found among the songs was assessed by comparing the contents of the memories with what was expected to be in them. The reference figures for intervallic context are those used to plot Figure 6, for the association of degrees and intervals. The mean vectors for all the memories of each degree are calculated and compared to these figures. The correlations for each degree are generally at the 0.001 level—a minority are significant at the 0.01 level. The range of correlations confirms that the performance of the memories is influenced by the setting of η^E in the initial tracking memory. The lowest η^E rate of 0.25 gives the highest correlations over all memory types, which confirms the characteristics of the memory functions. With a lower η^E rate, the ECH memory contains a shorter history and so the TRK memory approximates more closely the frequency of interval occurrence. The larger the η^E rate the more the TRK memory is tracking sets of values that reflect a sequence of intervals, and diverges from simply counting the associations between a pitch and its immediately prior intervals.

5.4. Integrating Patterns of Interval over Pitch and Key

The initial KFM simulation confirms that the variations in pitch use in different songs—represented as patterns of intervals—is too great to allow the emergence of

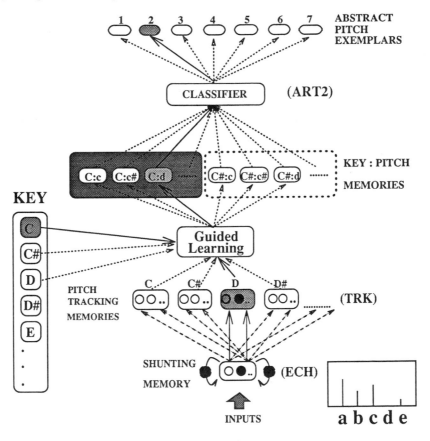

Figure 10. Outline of a model showing the classification of abstract pitch from patterns of interval use.

clear patterns of intervals that reflect the functional contexts of pitches identifiable with degrees. However, the network is not limited to learning the pitch representations active during a song, in isolation. The key of each song, identified in the process outlined in Section 4, is available to guide the attention of a further process learning pitch representations identified with a key.

Figure 10 outlines the simulation. The representations developed in the two-stage memories are tracked using the same slow learning as an ART2 network (Carpenter & Grossberg, 1987). This learning takes place in a layer of memories in which the recipient node is determined by the current key and pitch class.[8] The representations developed within these nodes can be used as the input to a self-organizing ART2 network for classification.

In these simulations the association of pitch and key is implemented, for convenience, by the use of indices. Another simulation established that this mapping can be acquired via a process of self-organizing classification. Vectors identifying pitch and key were concatenated to form pitch-in-key identities, e.g. c in C or c in F. By setting the vigilance in an ART2 network high, only identical pitch-in-key identity vectors are mapped to the same node. Each node identified in this way can be associated with a second set of memory weights to be used in learning pitch-in-key representations.

The integration of intervallic patterns over keys was simulated for the same set of η^T rates and η^E rates, as for the KFM experiments. Each interval was presented to the network and passed via the ECH memory into the TRK memory identified with the current pitch. Then using the identity of the pitch and key the contents of the TRK memory was learned by the appropriate pitch-in-key node. The weights for this node learn in the same way as used within the ART2 network. The result is that the pitch-in-key nodes develop representations that lie at the centre of the cluster of memory vectors mapped to them (Hinton, 1989). When these pitch-in-key representations are classified in a self-organizing ART2 network, seven clearly differentiated categories of interval use emerge, each populated with one degree of the scale only. The hierarchical similarity relations between the degree exemplars developed in this way are shown in Figure 11. The greatest similarities are between degrees $\hat{1}$, $\hat{5}$ and $\hat{4}$, with $\hat{1}$ and $\hat{5}$ being more similar to each other than $\hat{4}$ is to either.

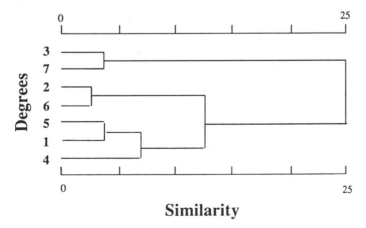

Similarity

Figure 11. Hierarchical cluster analysis of the abstract pitch exemplars developed within an ART 2 network classifying *AST* memories of interval use extracted over pitches and keys, η^E 0.25 and η^T0.005.

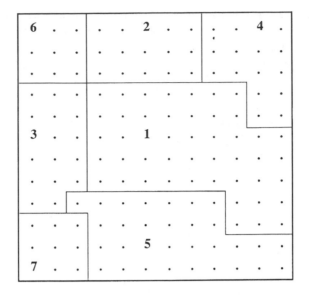

Figure 12. Mappings of interval representation of abstract pitch. Simulation illustrated is AST using η^E 0.25 and η^T 0.005.

Degrees $\hat{2}$, $\hat{6}$ occur as a pair quite close to the core trio, while $\hat{3}$ and $\hat{7}$ are more distant (Griffith, 1993b). This pattern conforms well to musical notions of functional similarities between degrees of the scale, but does not measure the importance of each degree in the scale. This is implicit in the relative size of the areas associated with each degree representation when these are mapped on a KFM (Figure 12).

The learning of the interval representations over pitch-in-key and the clear degree categories that emerge from classifying them leaves open the question of how well the pitch-by-pitch or end-of-song memories map to the degree categories. The fragmentary nature of the KFM maps learned from the end-of-song memories suggested that it would not be productive to look at the even shorter-term pitch-by-pitch memories. Consequently, the end-of-song memories for a selection of three η^E and η^T rates over the four memory types were taken and classified to the seven degree nodes. The results for the test set are broadly equivalent over the memories and parameter settings. The percentage of correct attributions was very low, 42–57%. The percentage of attributions to nodes of degrees a fifth above and below the correct degree identity is 16–23% and 9–13%, respectively, and 2–8% were not mapped to any of the exemplars at all. In this set of songs the use of the dominant $\hat{5}$ and subdominant $\hat{4}$ in some songs is very similar to that of the tonic $\hat{1}$. Overall, it confirms the variation in the data set and that this variation reflects functional similarity between degrees. It also implies that the model is incomplete. Another mechanism is required to enable the identification of degree directly from a developing interval memory. It is very easy to see shortcomings of this kind as commensurate with human performance. However, what characterizes human performance in this case is not clear. The current assessment is based upon a reading of the score by a trained musician. The significance of this appraisal in terms of the development of tonality is not clear, nor how to construct a meaningful psychological test of general human performance to compare with it.

5.5. *Mapping Key and Pitch and Interval Memories to Degree*

The abstract pitch representation formed within the model has several possible uses. It can be used as input to further networks—e.g. memorizing a melody or prototyping patterns of degree use. Similar representations have been used by Gjerdingen (1990) and Page (1993), and it was for this purpose that the model was originally conceived. Here, it is also used to acquire the associative mappings between *pitch & key → degree*; between *key & degree → pitch*, and from *pitch & degree → key*. These mappings were learned in a back-propagation network (Rumelhart *et al.*, 1986), but could have been achieved as easily with an ARTMAP architecture. The network consisted of 24 input units, 12 hidden units and 12 output units for degrees of the scale.[9] The η^B rate was 0.1 and the α rate used was 0.9.

The developing pitch-by-pitch and end-of-song memories were also mapped to degree, using a back-propagation net.[10] The reason for using a supervised network to learn the classification of interval memories to degree identity was to facilitate more accurate recovery of the degree identity from the memory patterns. The accuracy of this direct attribution in the ART2 network outlined in Section 5.4 is quite low. Also, the self-organizing process of degree induction is arguably rather indirect, with various stages and complexities. If the pitch-by-pitch or end-of-song memories can be mapped directly to a degree identity, this mapping can be used as a tonal descriptor parallel to the identification of key arrived at by tracking pitch frequency of occurrence (Butler & Brown, 1984).

The association between emerging memory patterns and degree identity was simulated for the extremes and central combinations of η^T and η^E rates over all the memory types. To do this, the developing memories were preserved either at the end of each song, or pitch-by-pitch, and then used as input to the back-propagation net. The target was the degree associated with the current pitch-in-key identity. The simulations were all run with the same resources and from the same initial conditions. The network consisted of 12 input and output and 18 hidden units, and used an η^B of 0.01 and an α of 0.9. The simulations were allowed to run for 1000 cycles. This approach was taken because it was found that over a range of resources and random initial conditions the network learned upwards of 90% of the patterns reasonably quickly, a further 5–7% were learned by cycle 1000, after which very few more were learned.[11] The networks learned the degree identity of 85–98% of the end-of-song memories. However, this percentage dropped to 53–74% generalization when the network was tested. The higher memory rates in both ECH and TRK memories produces the lowest figures. The network learns 58–93% of pitch-by-pitch memory mappings to degree. Again, the higher memory rates produce the poorest results. If they are discounted the networks learn 82–93% and generalize to 73–80% in the test set. The network trained on pitch-by-pitch patterns generalized to end-of-song patterns with between 89–93% and 70–76% success for the training and test sets respectively. Again, high ECH and TRK rates gave the lower results. At the lower and medium memory rates the results are consistently reasonable, but obviously open to improvement. It is possible that the process could take more account of qualifications of the memory by non-tonal factors such as duration or metrical or rhythmic factors.

5.6. *Conclusions*

The simulations described in this paper have modelled the induction of two aspects of tonal structure. Firstly, the acquisition of tonal centres equivalent to keys and, secondly, the abstraction of pitch function from patterns of interval use.

The first part of the model uses a tracking memory to extract a representation of the frequency of occurrence of pitches in nursery-rhyme melodies. The frequency of occurrence patterns is classified in an ART2 network and the result is a set of exemplars equivalent to keys. Subsequent testing showed that the exemplars are robust. The classification of patterns of frequency of pitch occurrence models one of a number of processes contributing towards tonal structure.

One of these processes is the emergence of the abstract pitch identities that seem to be used in the memorization of melodies. The model outlines a process of developmental boot-strapping. The diatonic identities that emerge from tracking pitch frequency of occurrence are used as an attentional mechanism to define the reference of a process inducing patterns of interval associated with pitches. An initial investigation using four types of composite trace and tracking memories mapped interval memories on to Kohonen feature maps. This showed a considerable diversity of patterns of interval across songs, and confirmed the need for an attentional mechanism to guide learning. The model shows how more stable patterns emerge when this attentional focus is used to integrate memories associated with pitches in keys. These stable patterns differentiate patterns of interval use very well, and are classified into discrete exemplars identified with the seven degrees of the major diatonic scale, across a range of memory types and tracking rates. Subsequently, pitch, key and degree identities were used to learn three-way mappings that provide the basis for encoding, transposition and retrieval of songs in any key. Also, the developing patterns of interval use were mapped to degree. The model outlines how a process of statistical extraction, implemented in an ANN mechanism (ART2) allows the construction, from pitch sequences, of categories that reflect important aspects of tonal structure. The model assumes categorical pitch classes and intervals have already been identified. It may be that some of the processes are better modelled in terms of more distributed representations of pitch and interval. This is a moot point, as is the general question of the relations between levels of representations, e.g. psychoacoustic and categorical. What the model has explored is whether the statistics of pitch and interval use over time are a good basis for identifying keys and degrees. The indication is that these statistics do allow the construction of stable representations of pitch use.

The model combines both unsupervised and supervised paradigms as elements of its overall function. The intention has been to use these different ANN paradigms in functionally appropriate ways. The model outlines an effective procedure that uses its own derived information to guide subsequent processes. Further, work will investigate improving the generalization of the pitch-by-pitch memory-to-degree mappings; using the degree mappings in conjunction with key identification; using the representations in a model of transposition between keys; using metrical and phrase-boundary information, as well as improving the functional involvement of pitch-duration information. The model also needs to be evaluated over a much wider set of songs using other types of scales.

It is clear from much of the experimental work over the last 30 years that tonality is a complex mechanism. It seems unlikely that it can be resolved to a single representational process. Rather it is likely that functions attending to different aspects and descriptors are used and their various implications resolved. In some situations, some indicators will predominate, in others where perhaps some information is degraded, other descriptors may be relied upon. The model described here has focused on how patterns of pitch and interval can be used to induce exemplars of tonal centres and abstract pitch. It is a first approximation of an inductive mechanism capable of learning the functionality of key and degree.

Acknowledgements

My thanks to the editor of *Connection Science*, Noel Sharkey, for organizing the reviews for this paper and to Peter Todd and the two reviewers for their comments.

Notes

1. The research presented in this paper is part of the author's doctoral research, supervised by Noel Sharkey and Henry Shaffer and funded by a SERC studentship.
2. This synthesis is discussed more fully in Griffith (1993b).
3. The implementation of ART2 used here was adapted from code originally written by Paulo Guadiano at Boston University. This code implemented the net illustrated in Figure 10 of Carpenter and Grossberg (1987).
4. Because a variety of memories and learning mechanisms are described in this paper the η rate used in each is superscripted with an identifier to avoid confusion, e.g. η^T is the η for the TRK memory, η^K is the η for the Kohonen feature map, etc.
5. As classification is unsupervised the idea of a correct mapping is not the same as for a supervised network. However, any node has an identifiable majority—for example if 91.5% of the instances mapped to a node n are identified with C-major, this node is taken to be the home node for this key.
6. The network has not identified degrees of the scale at this point. The use of degree names is a descriptive convenience, and also recognizes that all the songs are presented in all keys.
7. In the pitch vector the equivalence of pitches in different keys can only be recovered by rotating the vectors until the patterns coincide.
8. This layer consists of 84 nodes. If the tunes were not diatonically limited the number would be 144.
9. The simulation used 12 outputs to ensure compatibility with future simulations in which the data set may not be diatonically limited.
10. Again this could have been achieved by an ARTMAP network.
11. The criterion for determining that a pattern had been learned was the required output becoming the maximum value in the output vector—rather than being within a tolerated distance of the output.

References

Anon (1979) *The Nursery Rhyme Book*. London: Amsco Music Publishing.

Balzano, G. (1980) The group-theoretic description of 12-fold and microtonal pitch systems. *Computer Music Journal* **4**, 66–84.

Bharucha, J. (1987) Music cognition and perceptual facilitation: a connectionist framework. *Music Perception*, **5**, 1–30.

Bharucha, J. (1991) Pitch, harmony and neural nets: a psychological perspective. In P.M. Todd & D.G. Loy (Eds), *Music and Connectionism*, Cambridge. MA: MIT Press/Bradford Books.

Bregman, A. (1990) *Auditory Scene Analysis*. Cambridge, MA: MIT Press.

Brown, H. (1988) The interplay of set content and temporal context in a functional theory of tonality perception. *Music Perception*, **5**, 219–250.

Browne, R. (1981) Tonal implications of the diatonic set. *In Theory Only*, **5**, 3–21.

Butler, D. (1989) Describing the perception of tonality in music: A critique of the tonal hierarchy theory and a proposal for a theory of intervallic rivalry. *Music Perception*, **6**, 219–242.

Butler, D. & Brown, H. (1984) Tonal structure versus function: studies of the recognition of harmonic motion. *Music Perception*, **2**, 5–24.

Carpenter, G. & Grossberg, S. (1987) ART2: Self-organization of stable category recognition codes for analog input patterns. *Applied Optics*, **26**, 4919–4930.

Chesterman, L. (1935) *Music for the Nursery School*. London: Harrap.

Deutsch, D. (1975) Facilitation by repetition in recognition memory for tonal pitch. *Memory and Cognition*, **3**, 263–266.

Deutsch, D. (1978) Delayed pitch comparisons and the principle of proximity. *Perception and Psychophysics*, **23**, 227–230.

Dowling, W. (1984) Assimilation and tonal structure: comment on Castellano, Bharucha, and Krumhansl. *Journal of Experimental Psychology*, **113**, 417–420.

Dowling, W. (1988) Tonal structure and children's early learning of music. In J. Sloboda (Ed.), *Generative Processes in Music*. Oxford: Oxford University Press.

Francés, R. (1988) *La Perception de la Musique*. Hillsdale, NJ: Lawrence Erlbaum Associates. Originally Published 1954. Libraire Philosophique J. Vrin, Paris Translated by J.W. Dowling.

Gjerdingen, R. (1990) Categorisation of musical patterns by self-organizing neuronlike networks. *Music Perception*, **7**, 339–370.

Griffith, N. (1993a) *Modelling the Acquisition and Representation of Musical Tonality as a Function Of Pitch-use through Self-Organising Artificial Neural Networks*. Department of Computer Science, University of Exeter. Unpublished PhD thesis.

Griffith, N. (1993b) Representing the tonality of musical sequences using neural nets. *Proceedings of the First International Conference on Cognitive Musicology*, pp. 109–132, Jyväskylä, Finland.

Grossberg, S. (1978) Behavioral contrast in short term memory: serial binary memory models or parallel continuous memory models, *Journal of Mathematical Psychology*, **17**, 199–219.

Handel, S. (1973) Temporal segmentation of repeating auditory patterns. *Journal of Experimental Psychology*, **101**, 46–54.

Hinton, G.E. (1989) Connectionist learning procedures. *Artificial Intelligence*, **40**, 185–234.

Holtzmann, S.R. (1977) A program for key determination. *Interface*, **6**, 29–56.

Huron, D. & Parncutt, R. An improved key-tracking method encorporating pitch salience and echoing memory. *Psychomusicology* (in press).

Kohonen, T. (1989) *Self-organization and Associative Memory*. Berlin: Springer Verlag.

Krumhansl, C. (1990a) *Cognitive Foundations of Musical Pitch*. Oxford: Oxford University Press.

Krumhansl, C. (1990b) Tonal hierarchies and rare intervals in music cognition. *Music Perception*, **7**, 309–324.

Lakoff, G. (1987) *Women, Fire and Dangerous Things: What Categories Reveal about the Mind*. Chicago: University of Chicago Press.

Leman, M. (1990) *The Ontogenesis of Tonal Semantics: Results of a Computer Study*. Reports from the Seminar of Musicology SM-IPEM 18, Institute of Psychoacoustics and Electronic Music, University of Ghent.

Leman, M. (1992) The theory of tone semantics: concept, foundation, and application. *Minds and Machines*, **2**, 345–363.

Longuet-Higgins, H. & Steedman, M. (1970) On interpreting Bach. *Machine Intelligence*, **6**, 221–239.

May, E., (Ed.) (1980) *Musics of Many Cultures: An Introduction*. Los Angeles, CA: University of California Press.

Mitchel & Blyton (1968) *The Faber Book of Nursery Songs*. London: Faber.

Narmour, E. (1984) Toward an analytical symbology: The melodic, harmonic and durational functions of implication and realization. In M. Baroni & L. Callegari (Eds), *Musical Grammars and Computer Analysis*. Florence: Olschki.

Page, M.P.A. (1993) *Modelling Aspects of Music Perception using Self-Organizing Neural Networks*. PhD thesis, University of Wales College of Cardiff.

Parncutt, R. (1988) Revision of Terhardt's psychoacoustical model of the root(s) of a musical chord. *Music Perception*, **6**, 65–93.

Patterson, R. (1986) Spiral detection of periodicity and the spiral form of musical scales. *Psychology of Music*, **14**, 44–61.

Peretz, I. & Kolinsky, R. (1993) Boundaries of separability between melody and rhythm in music discrimination: a neuropsychological perspective. *The Quarterly Journal of Experimental Psychology*, **46A**, 301–325.

Rumelhart, D., Hinton, G. & Williams, R. (1986) Learning internal representations by error propagation. In D. Rumelhart & J. McClelland (Eds), *Parallel Distributed Processing: Explorations in the Microstructure of Cognition*, Vol. 1: Foundations. Cambridge, MA: MIT Press.

Scarborough, D., Miller, O. & Jones, J. (1989) Connectionist models for tonal analysis. *Computer Music Journal*, **13**, 49–55.

Shaffer, L., Clarke, E. & Todd, N. (1985) Meter and rhythm in piano playing. *Cognition*, **20**, 61–77.

Simon, H.A. (1968) Perception du pattern musical par auditeur. *Science de l'Art*, **V**, 28–34.

Storr, A. (1992) *Music and the Mind*. Glasgow: Harper Collins.

Terhardt, E. (1974) Pitch, consonance, and harmony. *The Journal of the Acoustical Society of America*, **55**, 1061–1069.

Terhardt, E. (1984) The concept of musical consonance: A link between music and psychoacoustics. *Music Perception*, **1**, 276–295.

Terhardt, E., Stoll, G. & Seewann, M. (1982) Algorithm for extraction of pitch and pitch salience from complex tonal signals. *The Journal of the Acoustical Society of America*, **71**, 679–688.

Todd, P. (1989) A connectionist approach to algorithmic composition. *Computer Music Journal*, **13**, 27–43.

Ulrich, W. (1977) The analysis and synthesis of jazz by computer. *Proceedings of the 5th IJCAI*, pp. 865–872.

Winograd, T. (1968) Linguistics and the computer analysis of tonal harmony. *Journal of Music Theory*, **12**, 2–49.

Understanding Musical Sound with Forward Models and Physical Models

MICHAEL A. CASEY

This research report describes an approach to parameter estimation for physical models of sound-generating systems using distal teachers and forward models (Jordan & Rumelhart, 1992; Jordan, 1990). The general problem is to find an inverse model of a sound-generating system that transforms sounds to action parameters; these parameters constitute a model-based description of the sound. We first show that a two-layer feedforward model is capable of performing inverse mappings for a simple physical model of a violin string. We refer to this learning strategy as direct inverse modeling; it requires an explicit teacher and it is only suitable for convex regions of the parameter space. A model of two strings was implemented that had non-convex regions in its parameter space. We show how the direct modeling strategy failed at the task of learning the inverse model in this case and that forward models can be used, in conjunction with distal teachers, to bias the learning of an inverse model so that non-convex regions are mapped to single-point solutions in the parameter space. Our results show that forward models are appropriate for learning to map sounds to parametric representations.

KEYWORDS: Distal learning, musical instruments, parameter estimation.

1. Introduction

When we listen to music, we perceive more than pitches, durations and a general sense of timbre; we also recover detailed gestural information, such as how hard an instrument is bowed, and even which part of the bow is on the string. As listeners, we correlate what we hear with our gestural understanding of the perceived sound model. The interpretation of gestural information is part of the experience of listening to music and, more generally, that of listening to any sound. Our understanding of musical instruments, for example, is a combination of implicit and explicit knowledge of their input and output behaviors. Musicians may correlate gestural information with musical signals on a much finer scale than lay listeners because they possess a more detailed understanding of musical instruments, from direct physical experience, and are thus able to parameterize according to their internalized instrumental models. Lay listeners, however, may map musical information in a more abstract manner, relating to sound models other than musical

This article appeared originally in *Connection Science*, 1994, **6**, 355–371, and is reprinted with permission.

instruments, voice for example, or perhaps not in terms of sound at all; however, such speculation is beyond the scope of this paper.

We present a general technique for recovering gestural information for sound models from audio signals. Our claim is that such information is part of the mechanism by which we learn to understand and recreate sounds. If we can parameterize a sound environment in terms of learned models of sound-generating systems, we have achieved a form of understanding. Our goal is to show that physically meaningful parameters can be recovered from audio signals if they closely fit a learned sound model. Although we develop our examples in terms of recovering physically parameterized data for a sound model, it is also possible that more abstract feature mappings could be learned, such as those described by Grey (1975). The learning paradigms presented below are suitable for parameterized mappings to many classes of sound model.

2. Direct Inverse Modeling

The obvious starting point for the problem of learning to map a sound to a parametric representation is to use the direct inverse modeling strategy. The model learns the inverse mapping by reversing an observed set of inputs and outputs for the instrument, producing a functional mapping between them; instead of a physical action producing a sound, we want the sound to produce the physical action.

An example of a direct solution to the inverse modeling problem is classical supervised learning. The learner is explicitly presented with a set of sound, action-parameter pairs observed from the physical model $\{y^\star, x^\star\}$ and is trained using an associative learning algorithm capable of non-linear mappings. Once trained, the learner has the ability to produce actions from sound intentions, with, it is hoped, good generalization. This technique is only suitable for modeling data that is convex in the region of the solution space that we are interested in (see Figure 1).

2.1. Direct Inverse Modeling of a Convex Solution Space

Solution regions and learnability are well-studied characteristics in the machine learning community (see, for example, Anthony & Biggs, 1992; Haussler, 1989; Minsky & Papert, 1969). A solution set X is said to be convex if and only if there exist three collinear points p, q, r such that, if $p \in X$ and $r \in X$, then $q \in X$; otherwise the region is non-convex (see Figure 2).

Figure 1. Direct inverse modeling. The direct inverse modeling strategy takes intentions as input and maps them to actions. This is the reverse function of a physical environment, which takes actions as input and maps them to an outcome. Supervised learning in a two-layer, feedforward network is an example of direct inverse modeling.

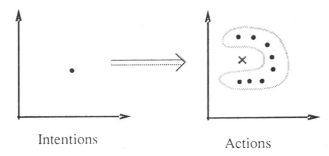

Intentions   Actions

Figure 2. Non-convexity of one-to-many mappings. The point on the left should be mapped inside the bounded region on the right, but the multiple solutions are averaged to the cross in the center of the graph. Since the cross lies outside of the solution region (the bounded area) the problem is non-convex.

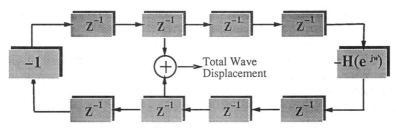

Figure 3. Digital waveguide model of a string. A single string can be modeled with a bidirectional delay line representing the right (top) and left (bottom) traveling components of the wave. The output of the string model is the sum of the two waves at a given output point. The two ends of the string reflect the wave back in the opposite direction. The dispersion, damping and resonance characteristics of the string can either be collected in a single filter, as in this diagram, or they can be distributed across separate filters.

As an illustration of modeling a convex solution space, we implemented an inverse model to learn to map a sound waveform, generated by a physical model of a single violin string, to the physical stop position on the string. This mapping was unique, and therefore convex, since for every sampled waveform that was produced using the physical model, there was only one stop-parameter value.

The violin string model was implemented using a discrete version of the wave equation efficiently computed using digital waveguides and linear time-invariant filters for damping, dispersion and resonance characteristics (Smith, 1992) (see Figure 3). The parameterization of the violin model is given in Table I.

The first experiment required only the D string of the violin. The length of the violin from the nut to the bridge was 0.32 m and the model was calibrated so that

Table I. String model parameters

Symbol	Description	Units
d	Initial string displacement	m
l	Total string length (nut to bridge)	m
c	String velocity	m s^{-1}
s	Stop position	m

the pitch class A4 was at 440.000 Hz, thus the open D string had a fundamental frequency of $f_0 = 293.665$ Hz. The speed of wave propagation in the string was determined by $c = \sqrt{K\!/\!\varepsilon}$) where K was the string tension and ε was the linear mass density of the string; for the D string the wave propagation speed was 187.9456 m s^{-1}.

The training set for the direct inverse model comprised a set of time-domain waveforms generated by the violin model $y^\star$ and a set of target parameters that produced the waveforms $x^\star$. The original waveforms were represented at 16-bit resolution with floating-point values in the range 0–1. We used the first 61 samples generated by the physical model as the representative set for each of the waveforms; this allowed frequencies as low as 293.665 Hz (D4) to be uniquely represented. The waveforms were generated at frequencies spaced a half-step apart along the D string, spanning two octaves starting in open position (0.32 m). The stop position for each of the waveforms was expressed as distance along the string.

The direct inverse model was implemented as a two-layer feedforward network with biases, utilizing the generalized delta rule as a learning algorithm (Rumelhart *et al.*, 1986). There were 61 linear input units, one for each sample of the sound intention $y^\star$, 20 logistic hidden units and a single linear output unit for the stop position. The training pairs were presented in random order with the entire set of data being presented in each epoch. We used an adaptive learning-rate strategy and included a momentum term for faster convergence.

Figure 4 shows the convergence of the parameter errors in the inverse model for

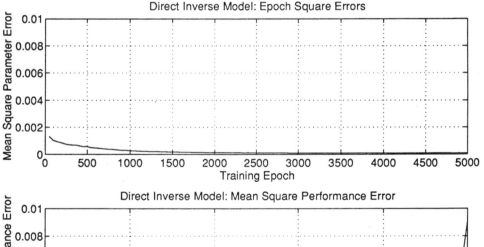

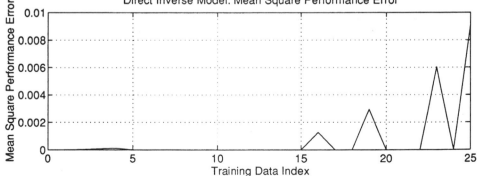

Figure 4. Convergence and mean errors of direct inverse model: convex data. The upper graph shows the convergence of the direct inverse model to the parameter error criterion ≤ 0.0001. The lower graph shows how the performance error is distributed across the training set. The mean-squared performance error was ≈ 5.6 bits.

5000 epochs of the training data, and the mean-squared performance error for each of the training patterns after the inverse model reached criterion. The parameter error is the difference between the target actions $x^\star$ and the output of the inverse model $\hat{x}$:

$$\mathcal{J}_{\text{param}} = 1/2\ (x^* - \hat{x})^{\text{T}}\ (x^* - \hat{x}) \tag{1}$$

The performance waveforms and the squared performance errors are shown in Figure 5. The performance outcome was computed by applying the outputs of the inverse model $\hat{x}$ to the inputs of the physical model. The performance error compares the input waveform $y^\star$ to the outcome waveform y:

$$\mathcal{J}_{\text{perf}} = 1/2\ (y^* - y)^{\text{T}}\ (y^* - y) \tag{2}$$

The mean-squared performance errors are given by

$$Perf_{\text{mse}} = \frac{1}{N} \sum_{i=1}^{N} \left(\frac{1}{M} \sum_{j=1}^{M} \left(y_j^{*(i)} - y_j^{(i)} \right) \right) \tag{3}$$

where N is the number of training patterns and M is the number of samples in the waveform.

The original waveforms had 16 bits of resolution; the mean-squared performance error of the direct inverse model after convergence to criterion was 7.8267×10^{-4}. The accuracy of the performance was given by $16 + \log_2 7.8267 \times 10^{-4} \approx 5.6$

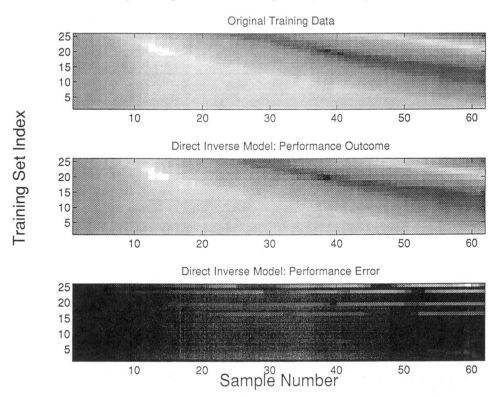

Figure 5. Performance outcome of direct inverse model: convex data. The upper two images show gray-scale plots of the waveforms for the convex training set and the direct inverse model's performance outcome; dark regions are small values. The lower image shows the performance squared error.

bits. This was the performance accuracy of the inverse model when trained to a mean square parameter accuracy of ≤0.0001. The accuracy of the direct inverse model of the convex data set was acceptable for our purposes. (The typical noise margin for digital recording ≈ 6 bits.)

The evaluation of the model in this manner was purely a matter of convenience for illustration purposes. If we were interested in developing a perceptual representation of auditory information, we would not use the error criterion cited above, which reflects the ability of the system to reconstruct the original data. For more sophisticated applications of inverse modeling for audio data, we would need to develop perceptual error measures, ensuring that the machine makes judgements that are perceptually valid in human terms (see Grey, 1975; Lee & Wessel, 1992).

2.2. Direct Inverse Modeling of a Non-convex Solution Space

By adding another degree of freedom to the violin string model, we made the task of learning the inverse model a much harder problem. In the next experiment, we added a second string; the learning task was to map a set of waveforms to parameters representing the string stop positions (as in the previous experiment) as well as a unit representing string selection, in this case the D string ($f_0 = 293.665$ Hz) and the A string ($f_0 = 440.000$ Hz). In the physical-model implementation, the fundamental pitch f_0 of each string in open position was determined by the speed of

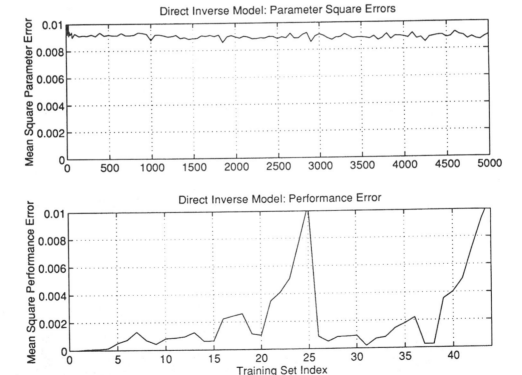

Figure 6. Convergence and mean errors of direct inverse model: non-convex data. The upper graph shows the mean-square parameter error for 5000 epochs of the non-convex training data. The inverse model failed to converge to a criterion of 0.0001 for this data. The lower plot shows the performance errors resulting from the parameters given by the direct inverse model. The mean-squared performance error was ≈7.3 bits.

propagation of the wave through the string, $c = \sqrt{K/\varepsilon}$. For the D string the speed of propagation was 187.9456 m s^{-1} and for the A string it was 281.6000 m s^{-1}.

The set of stop positions spanned two octaves for the D string (D3–D5) and an augmented eleventh for the A string (A4–D♯5) spaced at half-step intervals. The pitch ranges were determined by the resolution of the physical model since it was implemented as a digital waveguide with unit delays. The highest frequency for half-step resolution, without adding fractional delays to the model, is given by SR/n where SR is the sampling rate of the physical model and n is the number of delays used to model the string. The minimum number of delays required for a half-step resolution has to satisfy the inequality:

$$n \le 2 \left\lceil \frac{-1}{1 - 2^{\frac{1}{12}}} \right\rceil \tag{4}$$

This gave $n \le 34$ for the required half-step interval resolution. The sample rate was 44 100 Hz, thus the highest frequency was 1297.1 Hz, approximately D♯5.

There was considerable overlap in the training data because the waveforms from the string model for pitch classes A4–D5 on both strings were exactly equivalent. With this overlap the solution space was non-convex; thus, solutions that averaged the multiple parameter sets for each duplicated waveform were not valid.

To show how this applies to the problem of inverse modeling, we used the direct inverse modeling strategy of Section 2.1 on the non-convex training data. Figures 6 and 7 show the results obtained using the two-layer feedforward network de-

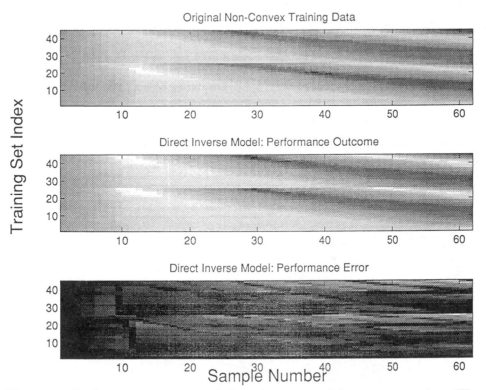

Figure 7. Performance outcome of direct inverse model: non-convex data. The upper two images show gray-scale plots of the waveforms for the non-convex training set and the direct inverse model's performance outcome; dark regions are small values. The lower image shows the performance squared error.

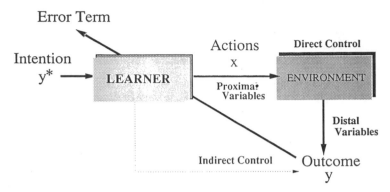

Figure 8. Distal learning. The distal learning paradigm uses errors collected at the output of the environment to drive the learning of the proximal variables. The learner's task is to find the set of action parameters that produce the intended outcome.

scribed above, with an extra output unit representing the choice of string. The model failed to converge to criterion over 5000 epochs, so the performance error was significant in some regions of the solution space. The mean-squared performance error was 0.0024; using the same calculation for the accuracy as for the convex data set, we got $\log_2 0.0024 + 16 \approx 7.3$ bits of error, which was significantly worse performance than for the convex data set.

These results show that direct inverse modeling using a two-layer feedforward network gave unsatisfactory results for non-convex training data. We improved on the accuracy of the inverse model by implementing a learning technique that was better suited to non-convex data sets.

3. Forward Models for Non-convex Data

A forward model is a learned approximation of the physical environment and it is used in series with an inverse model to form a composite learning system. This learning system is capable of solving the inverse mapping for non-convex regions of the solution space (Jordan, 1990; Jordan & Rumelhart, 1992). The training technique for the composite model is called distal learning and it is illustrated in Figure 8. The learner controls a distal outcome via a set of proximal variables which are inputs to a physical environment, in our case a physical model of two violin strings. The variable names and their functions for the composite system are outlined in Table II.

Table II. Simulation input and output variables

Symbol	Variable	Description
y^*	Intention (target outcome)	Sampled waveform
$\hat{y}$	Predicted outcome	Approximated waveform
y	Actual outcome	Waveform output from physical model
$\hat{x}$	Actions	Estimated action parameters
x^*	Target actions	Training action parameters

3.1. Training the Forward Model

The training set for the forward model comprised pairs of action parameters and sound outcomes. We used the same non-convex training set as for the direct inverse model but with the inputs and outputs reversed. Once learned, the forward model was able to approximate the input/output behavior of the physical model. The output of the forward model is called the predicted outcome $\hat{y}$ and the difference between the sound intention $y^\star$ and the predicted outcome $\hat{y}$ is the predicted performance error:

$$\mathcal{J}_{\text{pred}} = 1/2\ (y^* - \hat{y})^{\mathrm{T}}\ (y^* - \hat{y}) \tag{5}$$

We used this error for optimizing the forward model. As in the two previous experiments, the forward model was implemented as a two-layer feedforward network with two linear units for inputs, representing string selection and stop positions, 20 logistic hidden units and 61 output units corresponding to the sample estimates of the violin string models. The forward model was trained until the predicted performance error reached an accuracy of ≈ 6 bits (mean-squared predicted performance error ≤ 0.001). Figure 9 shows the convergence of the forward model to within the chosen threshold. The lower graph in Figure 9 shows the mean-squared predicted performance error for each of the training patterns. Figure 10 shows the predicted performance outcome for the forward model.

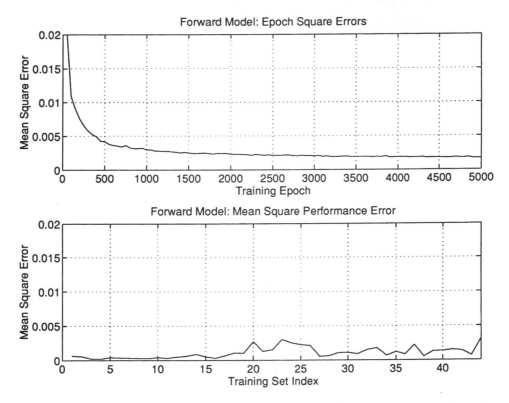

Figure 9. Convergence and mean errors of forward model. The upper graph shows the convergence of the forward model's mean-squared predicted performance error. The lower figure shows the mean-squared predicted performance error, ≈ 6 bits.

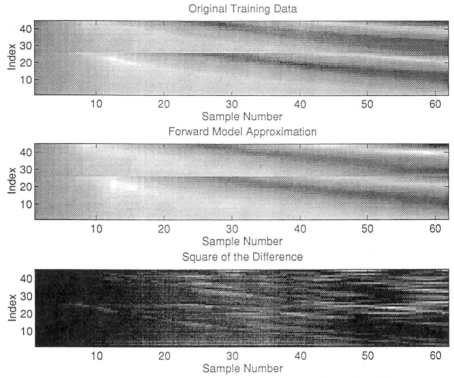

Figure 10. Predicted performance outcome of forward model. The upper two images show the waveforms for the training set and the forward model's approximation; i.e. the predicted performance. The lower image shows the predicted performance squared error.

3.2. Training the Inverse Model Using the Forward Model

Once the forward model was trained, we placed it in series with the inverse model to form a composite learning system of the type shown in Figure 11. Again, the inverse model was implemented as a two-layer feedforward network with 61 input units, 20 logistic hidden units and 2 output units. The composite model can also be thought of as a single four-layer feedforward network (see Figure 12). First the intention waveform $y^\star$ was given to the input units of the inverse model. The activations were fed forward, through the inverse model, to the forward model. The activations passed completely through the four layers of the network until values were obtained for the output of the forward model. We then recursively computed the deltas for each of the four layers and adjusted the weights of the inverse model, leaving the forward model unchanged since it had already converged to a satisfactory solution.

There are three approaches to training the inverse model using a forward model: training from random initial conditions, training from the direct inverse model's final condition and training with the predicted performance error of equation (5).

Training from random initial conditions is standard practice for many applications of connectionist networks. The strength of the connections are initialized to small ($|w| \le 0.1$) uniformly distributed values with zero mean. As the network

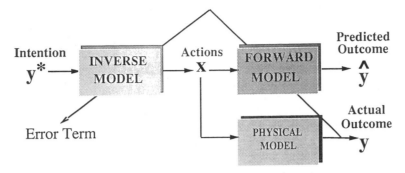

Figure 11. Composite learning scheme. A forward model is placed in series with the inverse model and in parallel with the physical environment. The performance errors are propagated back through the forward model to the inverse model but the forward model's weights are left unchanged. The entire composite system is designed to produce accurate actions by optimizing the outcome.

converges to a globally satisfactory solution, the weights get larger, representing a progressively higher-order fit to the training data. Initializing the network with small weights ensures that the model does not over-fit the data.

If we initialize the distal inverse model with the weights obtained from the direct inverse model the task of the composite learning system is made somewhat easier and we observe faster convergence than for random initial conditions. This technique works because the direct inverse model is good for convex regions of the solution space; if the inverse modeling problem has relatively small non-convex regions the difference between the direct inverse model and distal inverse model will be small.

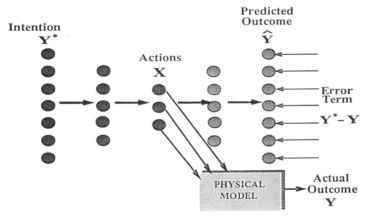

Figure 12. Connectionist implementation of composite learning scheme. The distal learning architecture is implemented as two feedforward networks placed in series; the first is the inverse model and the second is the forward model. The system can also be thought of as a single four-layer network. The forward model's outputs are replaced by the physical model's outputs so that the performance error is used for optimization. The outputs of the composite network occur in the middle since it is the actions that we want to obtain.

Table III. Training sets and error terms for the inverse models

	Forward model	Direct inverse model	Distal inverse model
Training set	Actions, outcomes $\{x^\star, y^\star\}$	Intentions, actions $\{y^\star, x^\star\}$	Intentions $\{y^\star, y\}$
Optimization error	Predicted performance error $1/2\ (y^\star - \hat{y})^{\mathrm{T}}(y^\star - \hat{y})$	Parameter error $1/2\ (x^\star - \hat{x})^{\mathrm{T}}(x^\star - \hat{x})$	Performance error $1/2\ (y^\star - y)^{\mathrm{T}}(y^\star - y)$

We used the performance error for optimization during learning with these models, see equation (2), which is different from the predicted performance error of equation (5).

However, we also obtained good results with faster convergence by using the predicted performance error; the difference was that the predicted performance error used the forward model's outputs as an error measure, so there was no need to present the action parameters to the physical model. An inverse model trained in this way is biased by the inaccuracies of the forward model, thus we switched to performance error optimization for the last few epochs of training. This technique is effective only if the forward model has converged to a good approximation of the physical model. We initialized the inverse model with the direct inverse model's

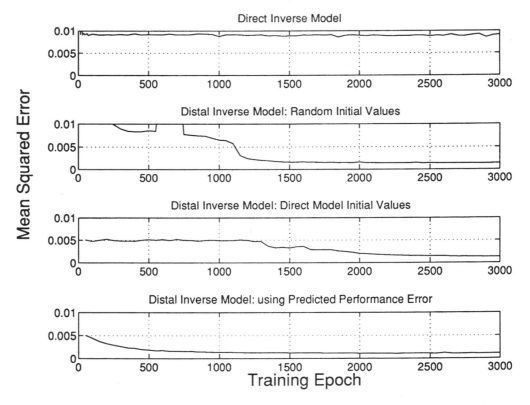

Figure 13. Convergence of the inverse models: non-convex data. Each of the four figures shows the evolution of the mean-squared error for 3000 epochs of the non-convex training set. The upper graph shows the mean-squared parameter error for the direct model, the remaining three graphs show the mean-squared performance error for the distal inverse models.

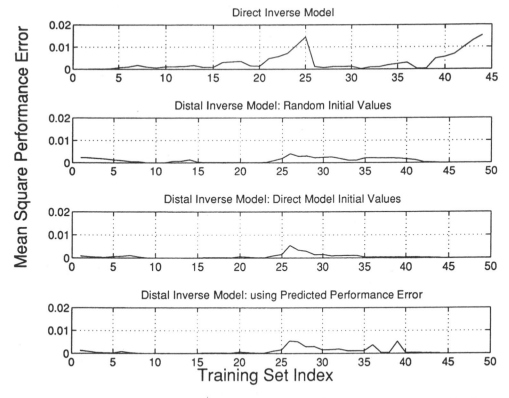

Figure 14. Mean performance of the inverse models: non-convex data. The four figures show the mean-squared performance errors of each of the direct inverse modeling strategies for all waveforms in the convex training set. The best performance was the distal inverse model initialized with the direct model's final state; the mean-squared error for this model was ≈5 bits.

final values. See Table III for a summary of the various error functions and training sets that were used for the above models.

Figures 13, 14 and 15 show the results of training the inverse model using the three forward-modeling strategies outlined above, as well as the results for the direct inverse modeling technique.

We can see from Figure 13 that the fastest convergence was given by the third of the non-direct techniques, which used the predicted performance error for most of the training epochs. After 3000 trials the three distal inverse models had converged to a solution that met the error criterion, the direct inverse model had not.

The mean-squared performance errors for the entire training set of the two-string violin model are shown in Figure 14. The performance errors, shown in Figure 15, are concentrated in smaller regions for the three distal inverse models than for the direct inverse model. The inverse model with the best overall performance was the distal inverse model trained from the direct inverse model's final values. The mean-squared performance error for this model was 5.1136×10^{-4}, which gives an accuracy of $\log_2 5.1136 \times 10^{-4} + 16 \approx 5$ bits. This is significantly better performance than for the direct inverse model and is well within the required criterion of 6 bits of error.

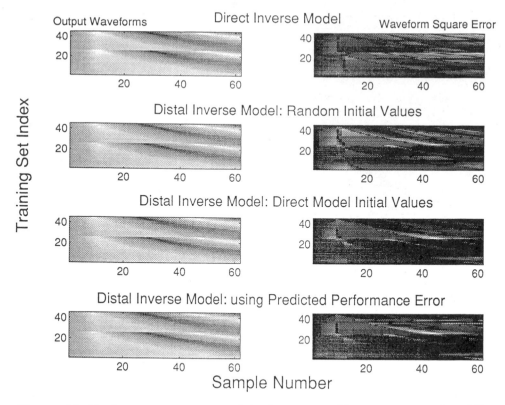

Figure 15. Performance outcomes of the inverse models: non-convex data. The images on the left show gray-scale plots of the output waveforms of the physical model, given the action parameters from each of the inverse models. The images on the right show the squared performance error; dark regions are small values.

4. Performance on Novel Data

In order to evaluate the generalization capabilities of each of the inverse modeling techniques, we constructed a novel data set comprising target sounds that required parameter values that were not in the original training set but that were generalized as a result of the learning. We produced a new set of waveforms using the D string on the violin with stop positions that were in quarter-tones with the training set. The frequencies available at a quarter-tone resolution were limited by

$$n \leq 2 \left\lceil \frac{-1}{1 - 2^{\frac{0.5}{12}}} \right\rceil \tag{6}$$

which gave $n = 69$. Therefore, $f_{max} = 44\,100/69 = 639.13$ Hz (D♯5). So we had to limit the testing set to 14 waveforms computed in the range D4–D♯5.

Figures 16 and 17 show the distribution of errors in the output of each of the inverse models. The inverse model with the best overall performance on the novel data was the model trained using the predicted performance error. The mean-squared performance error for this model was 1.5724×10^{-4} giving an error of $\log_2 1.5724 \times 10^{-4} + 16 \approx 3.4$ bits. The accuracy is better than for the original

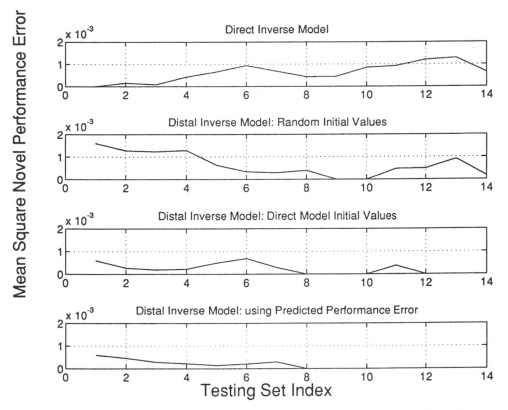

Figure 16. Mean performance of the inverse models: novel data. The four figures show the mean-squared performance error for each of the inverse models give novel data as input. The distal inverse model trained using the predicted performance error gave the best performance with an error of ≈3.4 bits.

training data because we were testing the model in a small range of the problem space, due to the limited frequency resolution of the physical model. The results show that the generalization capabilities of distal inverse models are good for the given problem domain.

5. Conclusions

In this paper, we have shown that inverse modeling techniques can be used to map representations of sound to physical parameters for sound-generating models. The inverse modeling strategy depends on the geometry of the solution space. If the solution region is convex, we can use a direct inverse-modeling strategy, such as back-propagation in a two-layer, feedforward network. However, non-convex solution regions require a more sophisticated approach to deriving the inverse model. One such approach is that of using distal teachers with forward models. We implemented such a system and obtained satisfactory results for recovering physical parameters for models of violin strings.

With careful implementation, the forward modeling strategy is general enough to be applied to many inverse modeling problems in the auditory domain. We are currently expanding the scope of the current research to include models of other

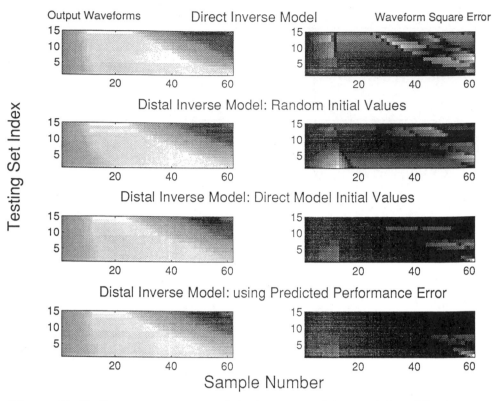

Figure 17. Performance outcomes of the inverse models: novel data. The images on the left show gray-scale plots of the output waveforms of the physical model given the action parameters of each of the inverse models in response to novel data. The images on the right show the squared performance error; dark regions are small values.

sounding systems, e.g. single-reed, brass and vocal-tract models. The outputs of these inverse models can be treated as features to which we can apply pattern-recognition techniques for source classification and gesture recognition. An example of this is to use parameters recovered from real musical performances to classify different playing styles or performance techniques, perhaps creating a machine-listening system that can understand the subtleties of musical performance.

Future work will include the development of distance functions for auditory data that take into account human perceptual factors. Time-domain representations are unsatisfactory for many applications of audio inverse modeling; there are many different time-domain representation of a signal that produce a single auditory percept. This is due, in large part, to the low salience of phase in the human auditory system. We have experimented with a constant-Q frequency representation which better represents the perceptual distance between auditory stimuli.

Acknowledgements

The author would like to acknowledge the help of Michael Jordan of the MIT Brain and Cognitive Sciences department during the early development of this work, Eric

Scheirer of the MIT Media Lab for his insightful comments during the revision process and Barry Vercoe of the MIT Media Lab for providing continual support for this research.

References

Anthony, M. & Biggs, N. (1992) Computational learning theory. In M. Anthony (Ed.), *Cambridge Tracts in Theoretical Computer Science*. Cambridge: Cambridge University Press.

Grey, J.M. (1975) *An exploration of musical timbre*. PhD Dissertation, Department of Psychology, Stanford University.

Haussler, D. (1989) Generalizing the PAC model: sample size bounds from metric dimension-based uniform convergence results. *Proceedings of the 30th Annual Symposium on Foundations of Computer Science*.

Jordan, M.I. (1990) Motor learning and the degrees of freedom problem. In M. Jeannerod (Ed.), *Attention and Performance*, XIII. Hillsdale, NJ: Erlbaum.

Jordan, M.I. & Rumelhart, D.E. (1992) Forward models: supervised learning with a distal teacher. *Cognitive Science*, **16**.

Lee, M. & Wessel, D. (1992) Connectionist models for real-time control of synthesis and compositional algorithms. *Proceedings of the International Computer Music Conference*. San Francisco, September.

Minsky, M.L. & Papert, S.A. (1969) *Perceptrons: An Introduction to Computational Geometry*. Cambridge, MA: MIT Press.

Rumelhart, D.E. Hinton, G.E. & Williams, R.J. (1986) Learning internal representations by error propagation. In D.E. Rumelhart & J.L. McClelland (Eds), *Parallel Distributed Processing: Explorations in the microstructure of cognition. Vol. 1: Foundations*, pp. 318–363. Cambridge, MA: MIT.

Smith, J.O. (1992) Physical modeling using digital waveguides. *Computer Music Journal*, **16**, 74–87.

Part II
Rhythm and Meter

Resonance and the Perception of Musical Meter

EDWARD W. LARGE & JOHN F. KOLEN

Many connectionist approaches to musical expectancy and music composition let the question of 'What next?' overshadow the equally important question of 'When next?'. One cannot escape the latter question, one of temporal structure, when considering the perception of musical meter. We view the perception of metrical structure as a dynamic process where the temporal organization of external musical events synchronizes, or entrains, a listener's internal processing mechanisms. This article introduces a novel connectionist unit, based upon a mathematical model of entrainment, capable of phase- and frequency-locking to periodic components of incoming rhythmic patterns. Networks of these units can self-organize temporally structured responses to rhythmic patterns. The resulting network behavior embodies the perception of metrical structure. The article concludes with a discussion of the implications of our approach for theories of metrical structure and musical expectancy.

KEYWORDS: Beat, meter, metrical structure, entrainment, phase-locking, beat-tracking, meter perception.

1. Introduction

> Embodied musical meaning is, in short, a product of expectation. . . . If this hypothesis is correct, then an analysis of the process of expectation is clearly a prerequisite for the understanding of how musical meaning, whether affective or aesthetic, arises in any particular instance (Meyer, 1956).

Meyer proposed that 'expectation' is the key to understanding human intellectual and emotional response to music. Through artful patterning of the acoustic environment, composers and performers evoke expectations in their listeners. They skilfully manipulate these expectations, satisfying some and frustrating others, to arouse both affective and intellectual responses. Meyer argued that this is the property of musical experience that enables artistic communication. Since his proposal, a number of theorists have adopted Meyer's basic point of view, each exploring various types of expectancy in music perception. Simon and Sumner (1968) provide an analysis of music perception as a sequence extrapolation task, one in which the listener attempts to predict what patterns will follow based on analysis of the current pattern context. Narmour's implication-realization theory (1990) focuses on the innate expectancies that arise in response to the basic

This article appeared originally in *Connection Science*, 1994, **6**, 177–208, and is reprinted with permission.

properties of individual melodic intervals and chains of melodic intervals. While these and other theoretical approaches differ in many important respects, one facet they share is a central concern with the musical question: 'What Next?'.[1]

Since time is the primary medium of musical communication, however, we cannot adequately characterize musical expectancy simply by considering *what* events a listener expects to occur. We must also take into account *when* a listener expects events to occur (Jones, 1981). In this regard, we find it useful to distinguish between sequence processing and temporal processing. In sequence processing, a system must predict the sequential ordering of future events ('What next?'). Thus, a sequence-processing system must collect, organize and use knowledge of sequential structure. On the other hand, a temporal processing system must predict when future events are likely to occur ('When next?') by exploiting knowledge of temporal structure.

Several connectionist models of music perception and production have focused on issues of sequential structure using discrete-time recurrent neural networks trained with back-propagation (Bharucha & Todd, 1989; Todd, 1991; Mozer, 1991). Such architectures deal well with sequential information. In music, however, temporal organization includes periodic structure on multiple time-scales and systematic expressive deviations from timing regularity. Simple discrete-time recurrent neural networks have difficulty capturing both forms of organization, thus hampering their application to complex, temporally structured sequences such as music and speech (Cottrell *et al.*, 1993; de Vries & Principe, 1992; Mozer, 1991; Mozer, 1993; Todd, 1991).

We believe that a more direct approach is called for. In order to address the problem of temporal structure in music, we focus on the perception of metrical structure: the perceived temporal structure of musical patterns that manifests itself phenomenologically as a sense of alternating strong and weak beats. Metrical structure provides listeners with a temporal framework upon which to build expectations for events. These expectations dramatically affect human perception, attention and memory for the complex event sequences found in music (Jones & Boltz, 1989; Palmer & Krumhansl, 1990; Povel & Essens, 1985). It has been proposed (Jones, 1976, 1987a; Jones & Boltz, 1989) that the perception of rhythm is a dynamic process in which the temporal organization of external musical events synchronizes, or entrains, a listener's internal rhythmic processes. Due to the absence of plausible mechanistic accounts, however, many implications of this theoretical position remain unclear. This article introduces a mathematical model of entrainment appropriate for modeling the perception of metrical structure. We present the model as a single abstract processing unit, amenable to connectionist implementation. This oscillatory unit phase- and frequency-locks to a single periodic component of a rhythmic pattern, embodying the notion of musical pulse, or beat. Models of meter perception will require interconnected networks of these units, whose self-organizing response to an incoming rhythmic pattern embodies a dynamic 'perception' of metrical structure. We will analyze the behavior of both individual units and collections of units with the goal of understanding how to construct such a network.

2. Connectionist Approaches to Musical Expectancy

One approach to the problem of modeling musical expectancy equates event expectation with time-series prediction (Dirst & Weigend, 1993). Connectionist approaches often employ recurrent networks (Elman, 1990; Jordan, 1986; Port,

1990) trained to predict the next event of a sequence, given a memory of past events. Bharucha and Todd (1989), for example, proposed a connectionist model of musical expectation to predict chords in a sequence using a recurrent neural network that stored previous sequence elements. These elements provided the necessary context to predict the next chord. This approach is appealing for a number of reasons. Firstly, recurrent networks are simple; they process sequences one event at a time and assume no complex control mechanism. Secondly, recurrent networks fix no *a priori* limit on the size of the context that is used for prediction. Finally, recurrent neural networks can also be used for musical composition. By connecting the network's output units to its input units, the network can generate novel sequences that reveal what it has learned about musical structure (Todd, 1991; Mozer, 1991).

Despite these incentives to implement general musical expectation engines using recurrent networks, certain problems arise in the processing of complex, temporally structured sequences such as music. Firstly, the ability of discrete-time recurrent neural networks to learn and/or make use of temporal context information appears to be limited (de Vries & Principe, 1992; Mozer, 1993). Specifically, recurrent networks have difficulty capturing relationships that span long temporal intervals, as well as relationships that involve very high-order statistics (Mozer, 1993). Unfortunately, these are the sorts of relationships that a model must capture in order to model musical expectancy or music composition adequately (Todd, 1991; Mozer, 1991). Secondly, recurrent networks generalize poorly to novel presentation rates, relying upon absolute rate information to recognize temporal patterns (Cottrell *et al.*, 1993). A network trained to recognize a melody played at 80 beats per minute, for example, may not recognize the same melody played at 90 beats per minute. McGraw *et al.* (1991) attempted to train various recurrent networks as simple 'beat detectors', but found that a network trained on one melody at three different tempos may not correctly respond to the same melody played at a fourth, intermediate tempo. The problems of temporal context and absolute rate dependence are symptoms of insensitivity to temporal structure. Musical rhythms display complex forms of temporal organization that listeners abstract and use to process complex musical event sequences. However, discrete-time recurrent neural networks fail to take advantage of this temporal information.

In this article, we focus on issues of temporal structure in music, although our results may pertain to the processing of other complex, temporally structured sequences as well. The remainder of this paper is organized as follows. In the next section, we outline the problem of temporal structure in music. We review music-theoretic notions of rhythm and meter, and some recent literature on human rhythm perception. We then discuss current connectionist models related to meter perception and highlight some problems with these models. We introduce the mathematical concepts that play an important role in our theory, and then propose a mathematical model of entrainment appropriate for modeling aspects of human rhythm perception. We present the model as a single abstract connectionist processing unit. We assume that it will be necessary to compose a network of these abstract oscillatory units to model the perception of meter. We provide analyses of the model, revealing implications for theories of meter perception. Finally, we return to the problems of recurrent neural networks, connectionist time-series prediction and musical expectancy in general.

3. Rhythm and Meter

In this section, we explore issues related to the temporal structure of music and the processing of rhythmic sequences. We review music-theoretic notions of rhythm, beat and meter, concentrating on recent cognitive proposals. We then review recent literature on human rhythm perception, highlighting the role of temporal structure in music perception. Finally, we discuss existing approaches to modeling beat tracking, entrainment and meter perception.

3.1. *Music-theoretic Perspective*

The term 'rhythm' refers to the general sense of movement in time that characterizes our experience of music (Apel, 1972). Rhythm often refers to the organization of events in time, such that they combine perceptually into groups or induce a sense of meter (Cooper & Meyer, 1960; Lerdahl & Jackendoff, 1983). In this sense, rhythm is not an objective property of music, it is an experience that has both objective and subjective components. The experience of rhythm arises from the interaction of the various materials of music—pitch, intensity, timbre and so forth—within the individual listener.

We will use the term 'rhythm' in a second, more restricted sense—to refer to an objective component of musical rhythm. When we speak of 'a rhythm' or 'a rhythmic pattern', we will mean the pattern of inter-onset durations associated with a music sequence (Dowling & Harwood, 1986; Jones, 1987b). In music, a rhythm has an associated pattern of phenomenal accents, which is the physical patterning of events in the musical stream such that some seem to be stressed relative to others (Lerdahl & Jackendoff, 1983). Phenomenal accent can be conferred upon an event by the manipulation of many possible physical variables, including duration, pitch and intensity.

By 'beat', we mean one of a series of perceived pulses marking subjectively equal units in the temporal continuum. Although the sense of beat is generally established and supported by objectively occurring musical events, beat is a subjective experience. Once a sense of beat has been established, it continues in the mind of the listener, even after the supporting stimulus has ceased. The experience of beat is necessary for the experience of meter (Cooper & Meyer, 1960). The term 'tempo' refers to the rate (beats per unit time) at which beats occur. In this paper, we will generally refer to the reciprocal measure, the 'beat period', or the span of time between consecutive beats.

'Meter', as it is traditionally defined, refers to the measurement of the number of beats between more or less regularly recurring accents (Apel, 1972; Cooper & Meyer, 1960). There are two important implications here. Firstly, in order for meter to exist, the listener must feel some beats to be accented relative to others. Accented beats are called 'strong', while unaccented beats are called 'weak'. Although phenomenal accents may correspond to strong and weak beats, metrical accent is subjective. Early research on the perception of rhythm indicated that even isochronous, unaccented pulse trains may elicit the experience of alternating strong and weak beats, a phenomenon called 'subjective rhythm'[2] (Bolton, 1894; Woodrow, 1909). Secondly, the experience of meter implies the existence of at least two recurrent periodicities, describable as two separate levels of beats with related beat periods. Integer ratios usually characterize the beat period relationship (2:1 or 3:1, for example), so that meter is said to describe a nested grouping of beats (Lerdahl & Jackendoff, 1983).

Metrical organization usually exists on multiple time-scales (Cooper & Meyer, 1960; Lerdahl & Jackendoff, 1983). Lerdahl and Jackendoff (1983) have proposed a construct that describes the temporal organization of a piece at all relevant metrical levels, called a metrical structure. The metrical structure of a piece can be transcribed as a grid (Figure 1). According to this notation, each horizontal row of dots represents a level of beats, and the relative spacing between dots of adjacent levels captures the relationship between the beat periods of adjacent levels of beats. A metrical structure describes one of the most important subjective components of rhythmic experience: the feeling of regularly recurring strong and weak beats called metrical accent (Lerdahl & Jackendoff, 1983). Points of metrical accent are captured, using a metrical grid, as temporal locations where the beats of many levels coincide. Points where many beats coincide are (subjectively) felt as stronger; points where few beats coincide are felt as weaker.

Lerdahl and Jackendoff's (1983) proposal describes certain aspects of music perception and cognition. A rhythm, with its pattern of phenomenal accent, functions as a perceptual 'input' to metrical accent. Although phenomenal accent information may be missing or ambiguous, moments of musical stress in the raw signal are thought to serve as cues from which the listener may extrapolate a regular pattern of metrical accents (Lerdahl & Jackendoff, 1983). Lerdahl and Jackendoff (1983) have proposed a generative theory for the perception of metrical structure that is expressed as two sets of rules. A set of well-formedness rules describes legal metrical structure hierarchies. These rules restrict metrical structures to strictly nested hierarchies with beat-period ratios of either 2:1 or 3:1. Next, a set of preference rules describes which legal metrical structure an experienced listener would actually perceive for a given rhythmic pattern. These rules are concerned mainly with the placement of strong beats, as determined by the alignment of beats at adjacent levels in the metrical structure hierarchy.

Theories of metrical structure, such as the generative theory we have just described, have some limitations. Firstly, the characterization of metrical structure as a hierarchical nesting of beats limits the scope of the theory. Only some music can be described in this way. Lerdahl and Jackendoff (1983) explicitly restrict their theory to western tonal music of the common practice period. Much non-western music, as well as contemporary western art music, jazz and popular music, make use of dissonant rhythmic structures (Yeston, 1976), known as 'polyrhythms'. A polyrhythmic relationship between two levels of beats is a relationship of beat-periods such that N beats at one level occupy the same amount of time as M beats at

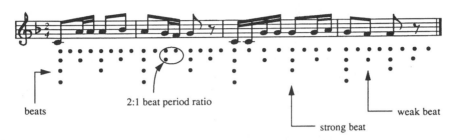

Figure 1. A metrical structure hierarchy (Lerdahl & Jackendoff, 1983). Each horizontal row of dots represents a level of beats, and the relative spacing between dots describes the relationship between the beat periods of adjacent levels. Points where beats of many levels align describe points of metrical accent.

the next level. 'Rational' ratios $N{:}M$, such that the integers N and M are relatively prime (3:2, 4:3, 5:4, and so forth), characterize polyrhythmic ratios. Hierarchical nestings do not adequately capture polyrhythmic structures, thus it is more general to think of metrical structures as being composed of layers, or 'strata', of beats at different time scales (Yeston, 1976).

A second limitation of current theories of meter is that they fall short of adequately explaining perception. Theories of metrical structure, as discussed above, apply to musical time as notated. It is well established, however, that musicians never perform rhythms in a perfectly regular, or mechanical, fashion. Instead, performers produce sound patterns that reveal both intentional and unintentional timing variability (Sloboda, 1983; Clarke, 1985; Shaffer *et al.*, 1985; Todd, 1985; Palmer, 1989; Drake & Palmer, 1993). Current theories of metrical structure do not explain how listeners are able to perceive meter in rhythms that performers actually play (unless the performer is a computer). As we shall see, this is no small problem.

In summary, theories of metrical structure attempt to describe the perceived temporal organization of rhythmic patterns. A metrical structure is composed of layers, or strata, of beats that align with the onset of musical events. Theories of metrical structure address issues related to the beat period ratio and the relative alignment between adjacent levels of beats. Theories that require the layering of beats to describe a strictly nested hierarchy, however, are limited in scope. In order to include the polyrhythmic structures common in many forms of music, more complex relationships between adjacent levels must be allowed. Finally, because traditional theories do not deal with the issue of timing variability in music performance, they stop short of explaining the perception of metrical structure. As we shall see below, recent psychological results implicate a class of mechanisms capable of linking traditional theories with the perception of metrical structure.

3.2. Psychological Perspective

Research into the human processing of complex, temporally structured sequences has provided some of the most intriguing results in the study of human perception and cognition. The temporal structure of sequences has been shown to affect dramatically human abilities to perceive, remember and reproduce serial patterns. Recent results support theoretical proposals that implicate an entrainment response as one of the basic processes of human rhythm perception. Here we review some of the relevant psychological results. In the next section, we will explore in more detail mechanistic accounts that have been proposed to account for the perception of metrical structure.

Abstract knowledge of metrical structure has been shown to affect memory for temporal information in auditory sequences. In one study, memory for pitch sequences was found to be dependent on a perceived temporal frame. Pitch structures that coincided with temporal structures enhanced recall, while pitch structures that conflicted with temporal structures negatively affected recall (Deutsch, 1980). In a related finding, memory confusions of temporal patterns in a discrimination task were found to be consistent with a music-theoretic metrical structure hierarchy (Palmer & Krumhansl, 1990). Other studies have demonstrated similar memory constraints, by showing that the reproducibility of rhythms is affected by the patterns of phenomenal accentuation in the to-be-reproduced rhythm. The evidence suggests that sequences of events that imply a metrical organization are easier to memorize and reproduce than sequences lacking such organization (Essens & Povel, 1985; Povel & Essens, 1985).

These and related findings are often cited as evidence that listeners represent and/or remember rhythms in terms of metrical structure hierarchies. Essens and Povel (1985) have hypothesized that in perceiving a temporal pattern, listeners induce an internal clock that is subsequently used as a measuring device to code the structure of a temporal pattern. Rhythmic sequences are encoded in memory with respect to this clock, so that patterns that correspond well with an induced clock (metrical patterns) can be represented using simpler memory codes, and are therefore easier to remember and reproduce. Jones (1976, 1987a) and Jones and Boltz (1989) offer a more comprehensive interpretation. They argue that the organization of perception, attention and memory is inherently rhythmical. Music (and other rhythmic stimuli) entrain listeners' perceptual 'rhythms', and these rhythms embody 'expectancies' for when in time future events are likely to occur. Expectancies in turn guide 'anticipatory pulses of attention' that facilitate perception of events that occur at expected points in time.

One source of evidence for the temporal expectancy hypothesis stems from studies that directly test listener attention rather than listener memory. These studies show that temporal pattern structure constrains the ability of subjects to attend to melodic sequences. For example, regularity of phenomenal accent placement has been shown to affect listeners' abilities to judge the temporal order of tones in a sequence (Jones *et al.*, 1981). Listeners are also better able to identify pitch changes in sequences when these changes occur at points of strong metrical accent (Jones *et al.*, 1982). Additional evidence suggests that listeners' implicit knowledge of meter (beyond immediate sensory context) contributes to the perception of temporal sequences. Listeners' goodness-of-fit judgements for events presented in metrical contexts were shown to be consistent with multi-leveled metrical structure hierarchies (Palmer & Krumhansl, 1990).

Another source of evidence for the temporal expectancy hypothesis comes from psychophysical studies of time perception. It appears that the temporal structure of auditory patterns actually affects humans' abilities to perceive time. For inter-onset durations corresponding roughly to musical time-scales, it can be shown that the ability to detect differences in temporal intervals approximately obeys Weber's law (Getty, 1975; Halpern & Darwin, 1982). That is, when subjects are asked to compare two intervals, the accuracy of their time-discrimination judgement is related to the base length of the interval they are asked to judge. Adherence to Weber's law breaks down under certain circumstances, however. Temporal difference judgements improve as the number of reference intervals increases (Schulze, 1989; Drake & Botte, 1993). It has also been shown that sensitivity to time changes in sequences is best for metrically regular sequences (Yee *et al.*, in press), and that sensitivity to tempo changes degrades with the regularity of the stimulus (Drake & Botte, 1993). Some researchers have suggested that these results indicate perceptual synchronization of the listener to a perceived beat (e.g. Schulze, 1989; Yee *et al.*, 1994).

In our view, the psychological literature offers strong support for the temporal expectancy hypothesis. In addition, the literature on motor coordination reveals a number of activities, including rhythmic hand movements and cascade juggling, to be consistent with mathematical laws governing coupled oscillations (e.g. Kelso & deGuzman, 1988; Schmidt *et al.*, 1991; Treffner & Turvey, 1993); (for a review of recent models, see Beek *et al.*, 1992). Shaffer (1981) has proposed that the

performance of two-handed polyrhythms in music may be described as the entrainment of clocks. However, the experimental literature often stops short of proposing
specific mechanisms of entrainment. In Section 2.3, we explore specific proposals
that have been made relating to the perception of metrical structure.

3.3. Connectionist Perspective

Metrical structure plays an important role in the organization of human perception.
However, mechanisms for the perception of metrical structure are still poorly
understood. Symbolic approaches relying on the parsing of temporal patterns have
been proposed (e.g. Longuet-Higgins & Lee, 1982; Scarborough et al., 1992), but
like the generative theories of metrical structure upon which they are based, they
fail to explain the perception of meter in musical performance. Entrainment, or
synchronization to a perceived beat, may provide some answers. Connectionists,
however, are only beginning to appreciate the power of this approach. We will
discuss a number of models related to the perception of metrical structure, including
previous connectionist approaches to entrainment, illustrating the problems entailed
by the design of entrainment mechanisms for the perception of complex musical
rhythms.

Scarborough et al. (1992) have described a model of meter perception called
BeatNet, based on a parallel constraint satisfaction paradigm. Conceptually, the
BeatNet network is a one-dimensional array of idealized low-frequency oscillators
with different beat-periods that operate to align their output 'ticks' with event
onsets, producing a metrical grid of the style proposed by Lerdahl and Jackendoff
(1983). A metrical structure emerges from local interactions between oscillators,
rather than from the global effect of rule-based analysis. An advantage of this
approach is that it handles the problem of metrical preferences through real-time
processing constraints, rather than by global evaluation of alternative constructs.
This approach cannot deal with timing variability, however, because of the simplifying assumption of 'idealized' oscillatory units.

According to Desain and Honing (1991), the problem of timing variability is
the key problem for mechanistic accounts of meter perception. From this point of
view, the relevant task is one of inferring, from the inter-onset intervals that the
performer 'creates', what inter-onset intervals the performer 'intended'—a process
called 'quantization'. Desain and Honing have developed a connectionist quantizer
to 'clean up' messy timing data so that the meter may be inferred. The quantizer
works to adjust durations so that every pair of durations is adjusted toward an
integer ratio, if it is already close to one. A disadvantage of this approach is that it
relies on a fixed input window, whose size may need to be adjusted depending on
the input (Desain & Honing, 1991). Recently, Desain (1992) extended this approach to present a theory of complex temporal expectancy.

An alternative approach to the problem of timing variability relies on a form of
entrainment called beat-tracking (Allen & Dannenberg, 1989; Dannenberg, 1984;
Dannenberg & Mont-Reynaud, 1987). This approach does not assume that the
beat-period is static, rather the length of a beat is adjusted throughout the performance as the performer speeds up or slows down. Results reported to date indicate
that this task is surprisingly difficult (Allen & Dannenberg, 1989). Longuet-Higgins
and Lee (1982) have modeled the perception of meter as the parsing of inter-onset
durations. Longuet-Higgins (1987) proposes a hybrid method that combines beat-
tracking with metrical structure parsing. The program uses a static tolerance

window, within which it will treat any onset as being 'on the beat'. Onsets which fall outside the window are interpreted as subdividing the beat (into groups of either two or three). This approach may solve some of the problems inherent in tracking a single level of beats, because separate mechanisms track separate levels of beats, reducing the potential for confusion.

Page (1993) acknowledges the problem that temporal structure poses for connectionist approaches to modeling music perception. He also suggests that entrainment may provide solutions to some of these problems, and proposes that a neural entrainment mechanism should operate analogously to a phase-locked loop, an electronic circuit commonly used in communications applications. We agree that entrainment mechanisms are important in addressing problems of temporal structure; however, the standard phase-locked loop is not acceptable. Page's (1993) simulations detail the difficulties associated with this approach. The standard phase-locked loop design assumes that the input signal is periodic. This assumption places limitations on the circuit's ability to deal with the complex rhythmic structures of music. Because the phase-locked loop reacts to every input event, it cannot extract a 'component periodicity' from a complex rhythmic pattern. Page attempts to deal with this problem by assuming that relevant periodicities are unambiguously marked in the signal via phenomenal accent information. In music, however, phenomenal accent information is often missing, ambiguous or even misleading (e.g. syncopation).

Other connectionists have proposed entrainment mechanisms for meter perception as well (Large & Kolen, 1993; McAuley, 1993, 1994). An important research problem is to determine an appropriate type of oscillator for modeling musical beat. To illustrate the relevant issues, we begin with a simple model that has been used as a model of single-cell oscillation in the nervous system, the integrate-and-fire oscillator (Glass & Mackey, 1988; Winfree, 1980). The simplest formulation of the integrate-and-fire model is shown in Figure 2. Activation increases (linearly) to a threshold, the unit 'fires', resets its activation to zero and the process begins again. As can be seen in Figure 2(a), the unit spontaneously oscillates with a period determined by the slope of the activation function and the height of the threshold. Figure 2(b) shows the unit phase-locking to a discrete periodic stimulus. Each discrete stimulus event temporarily lowers the unit's threshold so that the oscillator may fire and reset earlier than would otherwise be the case. Figure 2(b) also illustrates one problem with phase-tracking oscillators as models of musical beat. When the stimulus ceases, or when an onset is missing, the oscillator immediately reverts to its original period, as though no stimulus had ever been present. In other words, the oscillator has no memory of the previous rhythmic context. Torras (1985) proposed a scheme for frequency-tracking in a somewhat more complex integrate-and-fire model. In this formulation, an integrate-and-fire oscillator can phase-lock to a stimulus by adapting its threshold. This situation is shown for our simpler model in Figure 2(c). McAuley (1993) proposed that a Kohonen map of Torras oscillators could memorize, categorize and reproduce musical rhythms.

Integrate-and-fire units have their own set of problems in the domain of meter perception. For example, the discontinuity in the activation function constrains the oscillator to adjust its period only by speeding up (McAuley, 1994). We have proposed a continuous model (presented below, in a revised form) to avoid this problem, as well as the problems exhibited by phase-locked loop models (Large & Kolen, 1993). McAuley (1994) recently compared the performance of four different oscillatory units including two integrate-and-fire models, our earlier model (Large

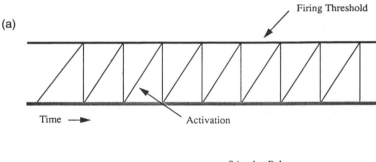

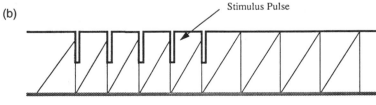

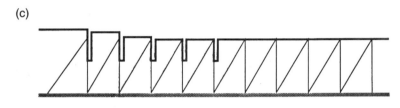

Figure 2. A periodic signal and the response of an integrate-and-fire oscillator. (a) The oscillator in the absence of stimulation. When activation reaches the threshold, the oscillator 'fires'. The period of the resulting oscillation is determined by the slope of the activation function and the height of the firing threshold. (b) Phase-tracking. Discrete periodic stimulus affects the oscillator by lowering its firing threshold. The oscillator comes into phase and frequency lock with the periodic stimulus. The effect is temporary, however. When the stimulus is removed, the oscillator reverts to its intrinsic period. (c) Frequency-tracking. By adjusting its firing threshold in response to stimulus, the unit may achieve permanent or semi-permanent frequency lock. When the stimulus is removed, the oscillator continues to fire at the stimulus period.

& Kolen, 1993) and a simplification of this model. McAuley (1994) prefers the simpler model, although in our view this simplification creates problems similar to those found in phase-locked loop models; both require strong assumptions about phenomenal accentuation to display appropriate behavior.

In summary, modeling the perception of metrical structure is difficult, in large measure because of problems arising from timing variability in musical performance. Entrainment remains an interesting possibility, despite the inadequacies of straight-forward approaches to entrainment such as phase-locked loop models. Entrainment models must have the ability to 'pick' component periodicities out of a complex rhythmic pattern in spite of missing, ambiguous or misleading phenomenal accent information. An entrainment model that provides such a capability would have important implications for theories of musical meter. We propose such a model below.

4. Mathematical Considerations

Musical rhythms afford the perception of a particular type of temporal organization called metrical structure. Both psychological evidence and connectionist analyses suggest that entrainment might serve as a useful tool in modeling this perception. The mathematics of entrainment describes many natural systems, and one of the goals of this paper is to add the perception of musical rhythm to this list. In this section, we briefly summarize some important mathematical concepts relevant to theories of entrainment and introduce the principles underlying our proposal. As we shall demonstrate, entrainment provides properties that map quite nicely on to the task of rhythm perception.

The swinging of a pendulum, the ticking of a metronome and the firing of a neural pace-maker cell are examples of oscillations. Oscillations are periodic events—events that cycle, or repeat, after some specific interval of time, called the period of the oscillation. Let us assume that the beginning of each cycle is identified by a discrete marker, and define the phase at this marker to be 0. Let us further assume that each cycle of the oscillation has intrinsic period T_0. We then define the phase at any time $0 < t < T_0$ to be $\phi = t/T_0$. As we define it here, phase lies between 0 and 1. Two oscillations are synchronized when they regularly come into phase, or begin their cycles together. A process by which two or more oscillators achieve synchronization is called entrainment. Entrainment occurs because a coupling between two or more oscillations causes them to synchronize. Coupling allows one oscillator to perturb another by altering its phase, its intrinsic period, or both.

One important type of entrainment is phase-locking. Phase-locking phenomena have been of interest in the connectionist community for some time, especially since the discovery of oscillations and synchronization behavior in the cat visual cortex (Eckhorn *et al.*, 1989; Gray *et al.*, 1989). It has been proposed that the oscillations of neurons in the cat visual cortex phase-lock to establish relations between features in different parts of the visual field (Gray *et al.*, 1989). It has further been suggested that the brain could be using synchronized oscillations as a general method of solving the binding problem (von der Malsberg & Schneider, 1986). Phase-locking may add an extra degree of freedom to neural network models, so that a number of different entities may be represented simultaneously using the same set of units, each by a different phase in an oscillatory cycle.

Our use of oscillatory units differs from that proposed in the literature on connectionist feature binding. Firstly, rather than using coupled oscillations to describe a neural strategy for performing an implementation-level operation such as feature binding, we will use synchronization to describe how the brain may execute the relatively high-level cognitive function of meter perception. Consequently, the oscillatory units we propose will represent higher levels of neural abstraction than individual neurons. Secondly, we will be interested in dynamics that are more complex than 1:1 phase-locking. Therefore, we will need to take a moment to introduce the analytical tools used in subsequent sections.

Researchers since Poincaré have described entrainment phenomena using the mathematics of non-linearly coupled oscillators. The method we describe here assumes that the constituent processes are oscillatory, and the oscillations may be linear or non-linear. However, the coupling between the oscillators may exhibit various types of non-linearities. The Poincaré map, or circle map, summarizes the long-term dynamics of a system of two oscillators. Consider the following mapping:

$$\phi_{i+1} = \phi_i + \frac{p}{q} + b \sin (2\pi\phi_i)$$

This equation is a model circle map, called the sine circle map, that describes the dynamics of a system of two oscillators, a driving and a driven oscillator. The parameter q is the period of the driving oscillator, p is the period of the driven oscillator and $b \sin (2\pi\phi_i)$ is a non-linear coupling term that describes the perturbations delivered to the period of the driven oscillator by coupling to the driver. ϕ_i is the phase of the driving oscillator at which the driven oscillator fires on iteration i. When $b = 0$ (no coupling), the behavior of the system is summarized by the ratio p/q, the so-called 'bare winding number'. So, for example, if $p = 1$ and $q = 2$, the driven oscillator fires twice for each time the driver fires. As coupling strength, b, increases, another ratio, $N:M$, the so-called 'dressed winding number', describes the long-term dynamics of the system. In the dressed winding number, N is the period of the driven oscillator under the influence of coupling and M is the period of the driver. If the coupling strength is high enough, even as p/q is perturbed away from 1/2, the system will still lock in a 1:2 relationship, because each time the driven oscillator fires, its phase is perturbed slightly by the coupling to the driving oscillator.

This locking behavior is highly structured. The dynamics of coupled systems like the sine circle map can be summarized in a regime diagram. Figure 3(a) shows a regime diagram for the sine circle map. The x-axis is the bare winding number, p/q, and the y-axis is coupling strength, b. The regime diagram identifies stable phase-locked states, also called attractors, mode locks or resonances (Treffner & Turvey, 1993), for particular coupling strengths and driven/driver period ratios. The parameter regions that correspond to stable phase-locked states are known as Arnol'd tongues (Glass & Mackey, 1988; Schroeder, 1991). From this diagram, we can see, for example, that for a bare winding number of 0.52, if coupling strength is high enough, the system will still phase-lock in a 1:2 relationship. We have labeled each tongue with a ratio corresponding to its locking mode. The width of each 'tongue' reflects the stability of the corresponding mode lock for a given coupling strength, i.e. its sensitivity to noise in the p/q ratio. For example, Figure 3 shows that, for a fixed coupling strength, 1:1 entrainment is more stable than 1:2 entrainment, which is more stable than 2:3 entrainment, and so forth. Depending upon the coupling strength, it can be shown that entrainment is possible at any frequency ratio, $N:M$, where N and M are relatively prime integers (Glass & Mackey, 1988). The regime diagram is not arbitrarily organized. Rather, its structure can be summarized by a mathematical construct known as the Farey tree (Figure 3(b)). The Farey tree enumerates all rational ratios according to the stability of the corresponding mode lock in the coupled system. Its branching structure corresponds the structure of the Arnol'd tongues of the sine circle map, as well as to known bifurcation routes in other mathematical and natural systems (Schroeder, 1991).

In phase-tracking systems, the frequency of the driven oscillator is altered because its phase is perturbed in every cycle. When the effect of the driving oscillator is removed, even for one cycle, the driven oscillator reverts to its intrinsic period. When the driver returns, a number of cycles may be required to re-establish phase lock. This behavior is unacceptable for the present purposes. In musical rhythms, events do not necessarily occur on every beat. Thus, musical beat cannot be

(a)

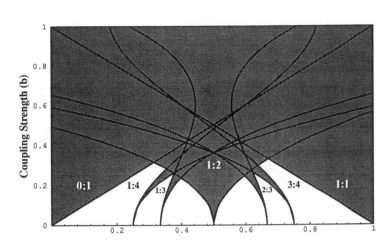

Bare Winding Number (p/q)

(b)

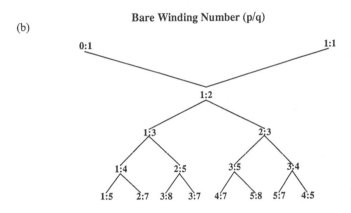

Figure 3. Entrainment. (a) A regime diagram. The dynamics of a system of coupled oscillators may be summarized in a regime diagram. The parameter regions that correspond to mode-locked states are known as Arnol'd tongues (shaded). The width of each resonance tongue reflects the stability of the corresponding mode lock. For example, 1:1 entrainment is more stable than 1:2 entrainment, is more stable than 3:2 entrainment, and so forth. (b) The Farey tree. The Farey tree is a mathematical object that summarizes the structure of the regime diagram. It provides an enumeration of all rational ratios according to the stability of the corresponding mode-lock in the coupled system. Its branching structure corresponds to known bifurcation routes in both mathematical and natural systems.

adequately modeled simply as phase-tracking entrainment. In order to model beat, the oscillator must somehow identify and 'remember' the beat period. One way to do this is to allow frequency-tracking. Frequency-tracking entrainment occurs when coupling allows the driving signal to perturb the intrinsic period of the driven oscillator. A frequency-tracking oscillator can model musical beat because when the driving signal is removed, the oscillator continues at the driver's frequency, 'expecting' the driver's eventual return.

In the model of musical beat that we propose, the driving signal (a rhythmic pattern) perturbs both the phase and the intrinsic period of the driven oscillator, causing a (relatively) permanent change to the oscillator's behavior. In addition, the oscillator will adjust its phase and period only at certain points in the rhythmic pattern, effectively isolating a single periodic component of the incoming rhythm. With these assumptions, it will be possible to model the perception of metrical structure as a self-organizing process. What looks like a single macroscopic temporal pattern, a metrical structure, may emerge as the collective consequence of mutual entrainment among many constituent processes. We propose a network of oscillators of various native periods that entrain simultaneously to the periodic components of a rhythmic signal at different time-scales, and to the outputs of one another. We will use regime diagrams to analyze the mode-locking behavior of individual units, and we will examine the response of a system of units to an improvised musical performance, revealing the implications of this proposal for the perception of metrical structure.

5. An Entrainment Model

In this section, we present a model of entrainment that is suitable for explaining aspects of the perception of metrical structure. First, we develop the basic oscillatory unit, a unit capable of locking on to and tracking a single periodic component of a driving rhythm, to embody the musical concept of beat. Next, we analyze the dynamics of the unit using regime diagrams in order to understand its response to periodic stimulation. Finally, we examine aspects of the ability of a system of oscillators to self-organize a response to rhythmic patterns, embodying a dynamic 'perception' of metrical structure. We discuss how our approach deals with problems that we have identified for theories of metrical structure. Finally, we address issues of neural implementation.

5.1. The Basic Oscillatory Unit

The basic unit has periodic output, and adjusts both its phase and period so that during stimulation the unit's output pulses become phase- and frequency-locked to a stimulus. The stimulus consists of a series of discrete pulses, $s(t)$, corresponding to the onset of individual events (e.g. notes). Event onsets may be derived from an acoustic representation of signal intensity (Marr, 1982; Todd, 1994) or, alternatively, onsets may be extracted from a list of MIDI events. In this article, we assume that $s(t) = 1$ at the onset of an event, and 0 at other times.

The activation function of the unit is periodic:

$$a(t) = \cos \frac{2\pi}{p} (t - t_0) - 1 \tag{1}$$

where t is time, p is the period of the oscillation and $t - t_0$ (mod p) is the phase. The output of the unit is given by

$$o(t) = 1 + \tanh (\gamma a(t)) \tag{2}$$

where γ is the output gain. Figures 4(a) and (b) show the output of the unit, in the absence of input, as a function of time. Output strength is maximum ($o(t) = 1$) at the beginning of each cycle (i.e. phase is 0), quickly falls to zero for the body of the cycle, then begins to rise again to a maximum as the cycle comes to a close.

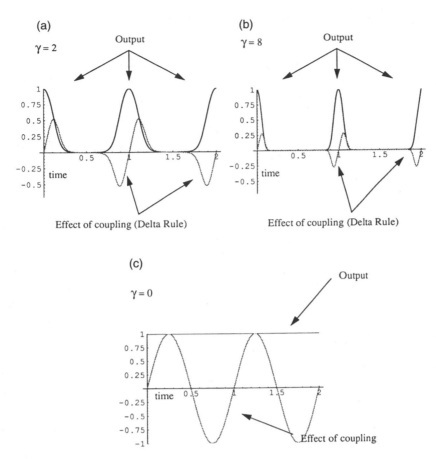

Figure 4. Schematics for the phase- and frequency-locking oscillator for different values of γ. The dark curves represent the output of the oscillator. The light curves summarize the effect of coupling on the phase and period of the driven oscillator. As gamma increases, the temporal receptive field shrinks. (a) $\gamma = 2$; (b) $\gamma = 8$; (c) $\gamma = 0$.

Output is only non-zero for a relatively small portion of the cycle, which we refer to as an output pulse. An output pulse defines a temporal receptive field for the unit, a region of temporal expectancy. After a unit has entrained to an input pattern, its output pulse marks a window of time during which it 'expects' to see a stimulus pulse. As the unit entrains to stimulus pulses, it responds (i.e. adjusts its phase and period) only to pulses that occur within this temporal expectancy region; it ignores stimulus pulses that occur outside of this region. The parameter γ, the output gain, determines the width of this field. When γ is small, as shown in Figure 4(a), the region is wide and temporal expectancy is relatively unfocused. When γ is large, as shown in Figure 4(b), the region is narrow and temporal expectation is highly focused.

The unit entrains to the stimulus using a modified gradient descent procedure. That is, the unit adjusts its phase and period in such a way as to minimize an error function that measures the difference between when the unit maximally expects event onsets to occur, and when onsets actually do occur. Changes to phase and period are proportional to the partial derivative of the error function with respect to t_0 and p, respectively. We define the following error function:

$$E(t) = s(t) \ (1 - o(t)) \tag{3}$$

$E(t)$ has a non-zero value only when a stimulus is present ($s(t) = 1$), and single minimum value when the output strength is maximum ($o(t) = 1$). Therefore, minimization of the error function for both phase and period in response to a periodic input signal implies that the unit will act to align its points of maximum expectancy with the discrete-event onsets in the signal.

To implement phase-tracking behavior, we minimize the error function by gradient descent on t_0. This yields the following delta rule for phase:

$$\Delta t_0 = - \eta_1 \ s(t)p \ \text{sech}^2 \ \gamma a(t) \sin \frac{2\pi}{p} (t - t_0) \tag{4}$$

where η_1 is the coupling strength (similar to b in the sine circle map), incorporating constants from the actual derivative of the error function. The factor p has been added to the 'true' delta rule as a convenience. This has a scaling effect, so that this delta rule yields the same proportional phase adjustment regardless of the actual period of the oscillator. The light curves of Figures 4(a) and (b) show the shape of this curve, summarizing the effect of the delta rule in relation to the oscillator output. A stimulus pulse that occurs within the unit's expectancy region, but before the maximum of the output function, causes a negative phase shift, because $\Delta t_0 < 0$. A stimulus pulse after the maximum of the output function causes a positive phase shift, because $\Delta t_0 > 0$. Thus, this delta rule provides a non-linear coupling term implementing phase-locking entrainment. When $\gamma = 0$, as shown in Figure 4(c), $\text{sech}^2 \ \gamma a(t) = 1$, and the delta rule becomes the sine function. This is a significant special case because in this case the unit's phase-locking dynamics will become equivalent to those of the sine circle map. We will discuss this in more detail in the next section.

The preceding equations implement phase-tracking through a modified gradient descent strategy. We achieve frequency-tracking behavior using a similar strategy. For frequency-tracking, however, it is useful to limit the period of the oscillator to a fixed range between $p_{\min}$ and $p_{\max}$. One way to do this is to introduce a frequency control parameter, Ω, according to the following relationship:

$$p = p_{\min} + 0.5 \ (p_{\max} - p_{\min}) \ (1 + \tanh \Omega) \tag{5}$$

When $\Omega = 0$, then p takes on a value halfway between $p_{\min}$ and $p_{\max}$, and we refer to this as the resting period of the oscillator ($p = p_{\min} + p_{\max})/2$. Because Ω determines p, we minimize the error function by gradient descent on Ω to implement frequency-tracking behavior. The change of Ω is proportional to the partial derivative of the error function with respect to Ω, which yields the following delta rule:

$$\Delta \Omega = - \eta_2 s(t) \ \text{sech}^2 \ \gamma a(t) \sin \frac{2\pi}{p} (t - t_0) \frac{\partial p}{\partial \Omega} \tag{6}$$

where η_2 is the coupling strength for frequency-tracking. Like the phase-tracking rule, this rule does not implement 'true' gradient descent; we have taken some liberties to ensure quick, stable convergence over a range of frequencies. Note also that this delta rule is similar to the delta rule for phase-tracking, except for the term $\partial p/\partial \Omega$. Because of the similarity between the two delta rules, the shape of the light curves of Figures 4(a) and (b) also summarize the effect of the frequency-tracking delta rule. A stimulus pulse that occurs within the unit's receptive field, but before

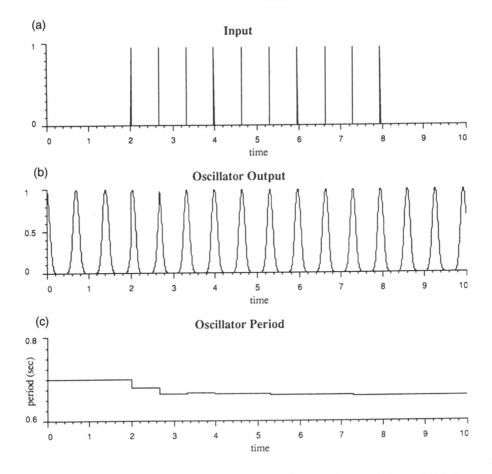

Figure 5. An oscillator responding to periodic stimulation at 660 ms. Initially, the oscillator's period is 700 ms. After a few stimulus cycles, the oscillator adjusts its period to 660 ms. (a) periodic stimulus; (b) oscillator response; (c) oscillator period.

the maximum of the output function, causes the unit to shorten its period, because $\Delta\Omega < 0$, whereas a stimulus pulse after the maximum of the output function causes the unit to lengthen its period, because $\Delta\Omega > 0$.

Figure 5 shows the output behavior of a unit with $p_{min} = 600$ ms, $p_{max} = 800$ ms, $\gamma = 8$, $\eta_1 = 0.2$ and $\eta_2 = 4.0$ exposed to a stimulus with a period of 660 ms. The oscillator initially fires at its resting period, $p = 700$ ms. In response to input, it adjusts its phase and period so that it becomes synchronized to the stimulus within a few cycles. When the stimulus is removed, the oscillation continues with a period of 660 ms. As described above, the oscillation at this new period may be said to embody an 'expectation' for events at these particular future times.

In summary, this single oscillatory unit synchronizes its output pulses to a periodic train of discrete-event onsets. Each output pulse instantiates a temporal receptive field for the oscillatory unit—a window of time during which the unit 'expects' to see a stimulus pulse. The unit responds to stimulus pulses that occur within this field by adjusting its phase and period, and ignores stimulus pulses that occur outside this field. The width of the receptive field can be adjusted by changing the unit's output gain. We have shown that the unit can entrain 1:1 to a simple periodic train of event onsets within its frequency range. A metrical structure, however, consists of levels of beats with different periods. To model the perception of metrical structure, we envision a network of units with different frequency ranges. Therefore, we must understand how the unit responds to periodic stimulation outside its frequency range. We address this issue by examining a regime diagram for the model. Next, we must understand how the unit will respond under conditions of complex rhythmic stimulation: is the unit capable of isolating and responding to a single periodic component of a complex rhythmic stimulus?

5.2. Response of Single Units to Periodic Stimulation

If the unit is to be used within a network for self-organizing a perception of metrical structure, it will be exposed to stimulus frequencies that lie outside of its response range. Therefore, we must understand how the unit responds to periodic stimulation outside of this range. We can address this issue by examining a regime diagram for the model. This analysis will be useful in understanding how the unit will respond to any periodic driving stimulus, whether that stimulus arises from an external signal or from the output of another oscillator in a network. Thus, the analysis will provide insight into several key aspects of our proposal for modeling the perception of metrical structure.

In order to understand the unit's response to periodic stimulation, we can formulate a circle map that summarizes the phase-locking behavior of the oscillator in response to a periodic signal. We assume that the driving signal has period q, and p is the resting period of the driven oscillator. We then use the delta rule to derive a non-linear coupling term, which gives the following circle map:

$$\phi_{i+1} = \phi_i + \frac{q}{p} - \eta_1 \operatorname{sech}^2 \gamma (\cos 2\pi\phi_i - 1) \sin 2\pi\phi_i \tag{7}$$

where η_1 is the coupling strength for phase-tracking, and ϕ_i represents the phase of the driven oscillation at which the driver fires on iteration i. This equation reveals the relationship between this circle map and the sine circle map, because when $\gamma = 0$, $\operatorname{sech}^2 \gamma (\cos 2\pi\phi_i - 1) = 1$.

To create a regime diagram, rather than solving the model equations to determine analytically the boundaries of phase-locked states (as in Figure 3(a)), we repeatedly iterate this difference equation for different initial values of q/p and η_1, beginning with $\phi_0 = 0$ (i.e. we assume that the oscillators initially fire together). This allows us to calculate the number of cycles that it takes for the system to converge on stable phase-locked states, which is useful since time-to-convergence is an important factor in real-time processing.

Iteration of the equation yields the regime diagrams of Figure 6. Figures 6(a)–(c) show stable phase-locking modes for rational ratios, q/p such that $p \leq 8$. Darker regions correspond to regions of faster convergence. Each individual picture corresponds to a different value of γ. Figure 6(a), the regime diagram for our model with $\gamma = 0$, again shows the relationship between this circle map and the sine circle map (compare Figure 6(a) with Figure 3(a)). Figures 6(b) and (c) show entrainment zones for $\gamma = 2$ and $\gamma = 8$, respectively. As the diagrams show, the effect of increasing γ, thereby shrinking the oscillator's temporal receptive field, is to shrink the zones of 0:1 and 1:1 entrainment while widening the regions corresponding to more complex ratios. This allows the oscillator to acquire stable phase-locks in complex ratios with the stimulus more easily.

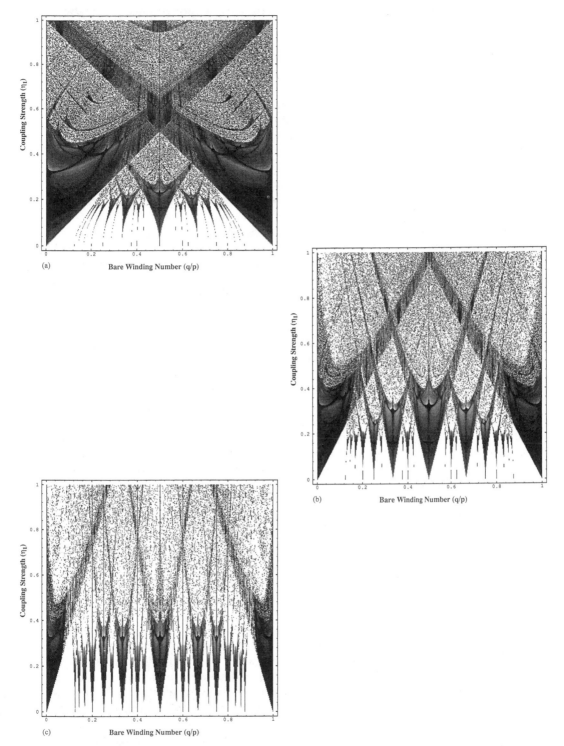

Figure 6. Regime diagrams summarizing phase-locking behavior for various values of γ. Darker regions correspond to parameter values that yield faster phase-locking. White regions are regions of quasi-periodic response. (a) γ = 0; (b) γ = 2; (c) γ = 8.

Regime diagrams for the frequency-tracking version of the oscillator can also be developed. We add the equation:

$$\Omega_{i+1} = \Omega_i + \frac{q}{p_i} - \eta_2 \, \text{sech}^2 \, \gamma(\cos 2\pi\phi_i - \gamma) \sin 2\pi\phi_i \frac{dp}{d\Omega} \qquad (8)$$

and recalculate p_i according to equation (5) at each iteration. Figure 7 shows the frequency-tracking resonance tongues. For easy comparison with Figure 6, we added equation (8) to the model keeping η_2 fixed at a value of 2.5, and varied η_1 (in equation (7)) along the y-axis. Figures 7(a)–(c) show resonance tongues for $\gamma = 0$, 2 and 8, respectively. The entrainment regions for the frequency-tracking oscillator are larger than the corresponding regions for phase-locking alone. Frequency-tracking causes widening of the resonance tongues. Therefore, not only does frequency-tracking act as a sort of memory, but it enhances the stability of the oscillator's response in the presence of timing deviations.

The regime diagrams above detail the behavior of our oscillatory unit in response to periodic stimulation. In so doing, the analysis summarizes key implications of our single unit model for resonance-based theories of metrical structure. Firstly, regime diagrams will capture the content of resonance theories regarding the well-formedness of metrical structures. Rather than formulate a set of rules summarizing allowable beat period ratios, we may specify the connectivity of a network and a set of parameters to each unit, and let the system dynamics enumerate allowable beat-period ratios. In principle any ratio of relatively prime integers may describe the relationship between two levels of beats. Thus, this approach affords a wider scope than conventional theories of metrical structure, incorporating not only integer ratios (such as 2:1 and 3:1), but also polyrhythmic ratios. Secondly, the width of each resonance tongue describes the stability of each beat period ratio in the face of timing variability. Therefore, the regime diagram provides an enumeration of allowable beat period ratios by sensitivity to timing variability. One implication of this observation is that in practice the number of mode-locks systems can achieve will be limited, preventing extravagant theoretical claims regarding the perception of polyrhythmic structure. This brings us to the issue of timing variability. The style of the above analysis raises the possibility that this entrainment theory may allow the formulation of theories of meter perception that adequately handle timing variability in musical performance. It also suggests that the units may be able to isolate effectively individual periodic components of complex rhythmic patterns. These and other empirical issues are examined in the following section.

5.3. Rhythmic Stimulation

As we have just seen, the response of a single unit to a simple periodic stimulus is quite complex. The response to a rhythmic performance will be even more complex. Therefore, rather than jumping to the complexity of a network of oscillators, we examine the behavior of individual units in more detail. In this section, we expose an unconnected system of oscillators to a performed musical rhythm, in order to address the response of individual units to complex temporal patterns. We demonstrate how individual units can isolate and track component periodicities in a complex rhythm, and also show how units realize natural metric preferences. We also address the problem of timing variability. Finally, the output of a system of multiple units may be interpreted as a perception of metrical structure. In fact, we

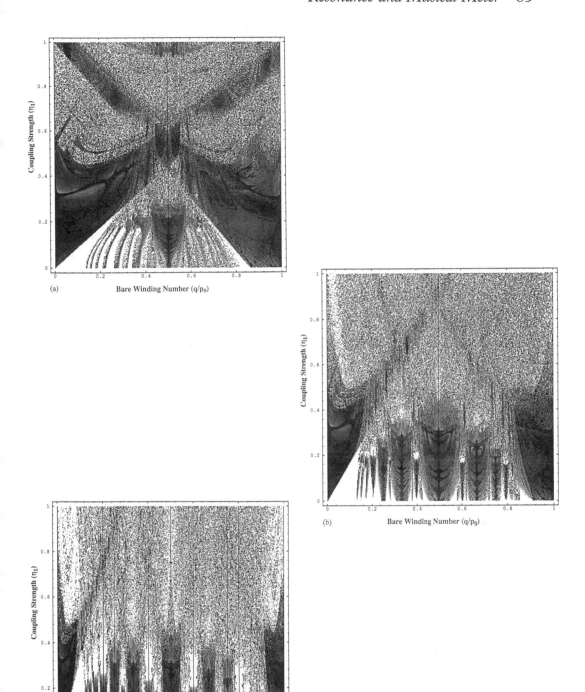

Figure 7. Regime diagrams summarizing phase-locking behavior for various values of γ, with frequency-tracking turned on (compare with Figure 6). Frequency-tracking strength is fixed at $\eta_2 = 2.5$. (a) $\gamma = 0$; (b) $\gamma = 2$; (c) $\gamma = 8$.

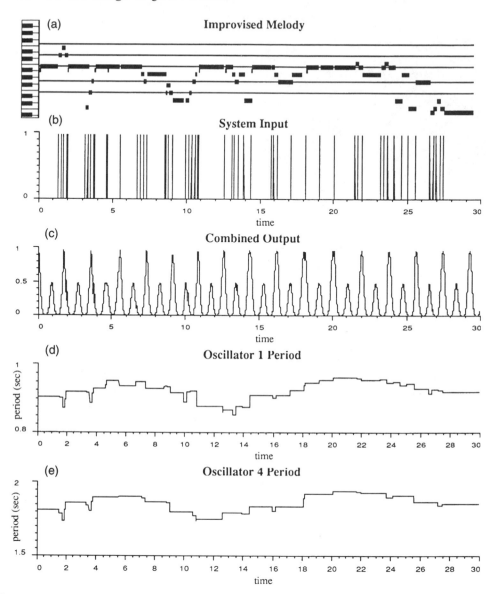

Figure 8. Two oscillators responding to an improvised melody: (a) piano roll notation for the melody; (b) input to the oscillators; (c) weighted sum of the oscillators' output; (d) oscillator 1's period tracking curve; (e) oscillator 4's period tracking curve.

will observe a system of unconnected units behaving quite reasonably in response to complex rhythmic stimulation.

We exposed a system of oscillators to one of the musical performances collected in an earlier study of musical improvisation (Large *et al.*, in press). This performance was collected on a computer-monitored Yamaha Disklavier acoustic upright piano. Optical sensors and solenoids in the piano allowed precise recording and playback without affecting the touch or sound of the acoustic instrument. The pitch, timing and hammer velocity values (correlated with intensity) for each note event were recorded. The pianist performed and recorded an original melody, as presented in musical notation, five times. With the musical notation remaining in place, the pianist was then asked to play five 'simple' improvisations. All performances were of a single-line melody only; the subject was instructed not to play harmonic accompaniment. The recording yielded a list of MIDI events, from which we extracted note-on times to use as input to our model. Figure 8(a) gives the performance in piano-roll notation, and Figure 8(b) shows the input, $s(t)$, to the system of oscillators. Our metrical interpretation of this performance, in the form of a transcription, is given in Figure 9.

For this study, we composed a system of oscillators with different frequency ranges. Such systems are useful for self-organizing metrical responses to rhythmic stimuli (Large & Kolen, 1993). We set each oscillator's period range according to the rule $p_{max} = \frac{4}{3}p_{min}$. We then spaced oscillators such that the relationship between the resting period of one oscillator and the next was given by $p_{i+1} = 2^{3\sqrt{p_i}}$. This relationship, in conjunction with the frequency range of each oscillator, provides for slight overlap in resonant frequency ranges between oscillators. We composed a system of two 'octaves' of oscillators, six in all. The minimum period of the entire system was 600 ms, and the maximum was 2560 ms. For each oscillator, we set $\eta_1 = 0.159$, $\eta_2 = 3.1416$.

We exposed the entire bank of oscillators to the performance, and each oscillator responded independently to the discrete-event onsets. We assumed that the initial onset of the performance phase-reset all oscillators. Two of the six oscillators (oscillators 1 and 4) acquired stable mode-locks for this performance, the remaining oscillators never stabilized. Figure 8(c) shows the output of these two oscillators, combined according to the rule $[o_1(t) + o_4(t)]/2$. Figures 8(d) and (e) show the period of these two oscillators, respectively, as they track the expressive timing of the performance.

This single example provides much insight into the behavior of individual oscillators in response to musical rhythms. It also provides insight into the issues involved in using such units to build a network for meter perception. First, each of these oscillators is isolating a periodic component of the complex rhythm without any phenomenal accent information. The global response, as can be seen from the combined output of the two units in Figure 8(c), shows that a stable metrical interpretation of the input rhythm emerges rather quickly, with strong and weak beats clearly observable. According to our metrical interpretation of this performance (see Figure 9), these two oscillators are correctly responding to the metrical structure at the quarter-note and half-note levels. Also, as Figures 8(d) and (e) show, the oscillators are tracking the performance over rather large changes in tempo.

To understand how this happens, let us first examine how the units respond to timing variation in performance. Note that by the middle section of the performance ($14 < t < 17$), unit 1 has locked into a periodic component of the rhythm, and is

Figure 9. Transcription of the improvised melody from Figure 8. Grace notes are not transcribed.

maintaining a relatively stable tempo. The next few onsets signal an audible *ritardando* in the performance. At each of these onsets the unit fires a bit early. The effect of the input in each case is to cause a slight positive phase shift, and a slight lengthening of the unit's period. The units can be seen to follow the systematic timing deviations that occur in this musical performance.

Next, we examine how individual units isolate periodic components in complex rhythmic patterns. We also see how this process instantiates metrical preferences for individual units, which manifest themselves as the alignment between adjacent levels of beats. We are interested in understanding which onset of a group is interpreted by each unit to mark the beat at its beat period level. We can gain some insight by examining Figure 10, which shows a close-up for units 1 and 4 as they

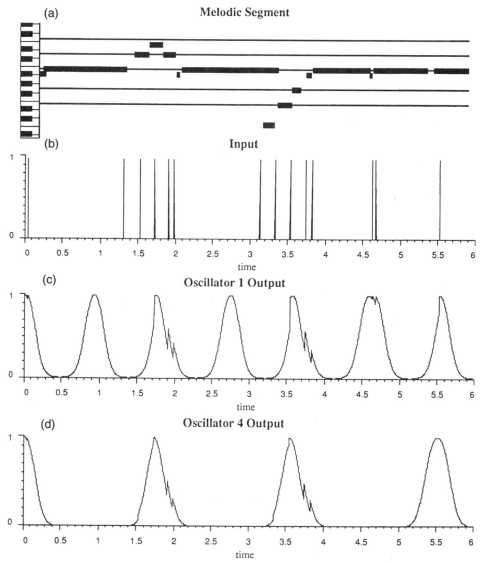

Figure 10. A close-up of two oscillators' response to the first few seconds of an improvised performance: (a) piano roll notation of the melody; (b) input to the oscillators; (c) oscillator 1's output; (d) oscillator 4's output.

respond individually in the early seconds of the performance. The panel for each unit shows the individual output pulses. Consider responses to the group of onsets between $t = 1$ and $t = 2$. The second onset (at $t \cong 1.5$) is ignored by unit 1, because it does not fall within the unit's expectancy region. The same onset, however, causes a slight negative phase and period adjustment in unit 4 (see also Figure 8(e) at $t \cong 1.5$). The third onset (at $t \cong 1.7$) causes unit 1 to make a rather large adjustment and unit 4 to make another small adjustment, eliciting coincident output pulses from both units. We interpret this onset as marking the second half of the 4/4 measure (see Figure 9), therefore both oscillators are responding correctly. However, the two onsets immediately following do cause some adjustment in both units. The response is still in flux.

Interestingly, both units respond almost identically to the next group of onsets, between times $t = 3$ and $t = 4$. This time, however, they respond maximally to the 'wrong' onset (the third of the group). The fourth and fifth onsets actually mark the onset of the second measure according to our interpretation. These onsets do have some effect on both oscillators. However, it is the next two onsets (not counting the grace note accompanying the first onset) that clearly establish the beat at the quarter-note level. At this point, both oscillators lock into the rhythm, responding correctly to the remainder of the performance with little difficulty.

It is difficult to extract precise rules to explain individual unit preferences. However, there are some general observations that can be made. First, each unit's choice is brought about by a subtle interplay between the unit's point of maximum expectancy (in the current cycle), the spacing of event onsets around this point, the width of the unit's expectancy region (determined by γ, the output gain), and the absolute amount of adjustment made to phase and period in response to each onset (determined by the coupling strengths, η_1 and η_2).

Assuming fairly high coupling strengths, as we used in the above example, consider a group of event onsets that surrounds a unit's point of maximum expectancy, such that the unit 'expects' that an event somewhere between the first and last event of the group will mark the beat. If the spacing of the surrounding onsets is greater than the width of the unit's expectancy region, then the unit will simply ignore the surrounding events. However, as we squeeze the onsets closer together, encroaching on the unit's expectancy region, the unit will begin to respond to these onsets. If the onsets are very close together, the unit will continue to respond until reaching the end of the group. Thus, each unit tends to favor the end of a group of events, where 'end of the group' is defined in relation to the width of the unit's expectancy region. Additionally, places where a number of events occur in rapid succession (grace notes above, or chords for example) act as points of greater 'gravity' for all units, because they have additional impact via the delta rules.

This analysis has illustrated several important aspects of our proposal. Firstly, the individual oscillatory units we propose can successfully pick out and lock on to periodic components of complex rhythmic patterns without making any assumptions about the structure of phenomenal accent patterns in the stimulus. This distinguishes our model from attempts to model musical beat using traditional phase-locked loop circuits. Secondly, the way in which units with different native periods accomplish this task effectively implements metrical preferences. Metrical preferences manifest themselves as the alignment, or relative phase, between adjacent levels of beats. This system of unconnected units correctly interpreted two levels of metrical structure for a complex performed rhythm, without any attempt to implement metrical well-formedness constraints. We assume that, in general, it will be necessary to implement well-formedness constraints using interactions among oscillators. However, results such as this suggest that the structure of rhythmic patterns, even for very complex performances, may contain more information than had previously been thought. Finally, this example demonstrates the proposed oscillatory units handling systematic timing deviations throughout a rhythmically free improvised performance. These results suggest that theories of metrical structure based on such models of entrainment may provide more complete theoretical accounts of metrical structure perception than have previously been offered.

5.4. Implementation Issues

We have described our model as a single abstract processing unit, in order to focus attention on the adequacy of the proposal for modeling the human response to musical rhythm. However, the issues surrounding implementation deserve some attention. Page (1993), in his proposal of an oscillatory connectionist network for tracking musical beats, recruits a relatively large network of traditional connectionist units into a neural implementation of a standard phase-locked loop. The heart of the network is a gated pace-maker circuit (Carpenter & Grossberg, 1983). Page then implements a type II phase detector and a low-pass filter using networks of connectionist processing units, to provide an error signal that controls adjustments of phase and period in the gated pacemaker. It seems likely that the oscillatory unit that we have proposed above could yield to a similar implementation strategy using a large network of simpler connectionist units with appropriate dynamics.

It is not clear, however, that a complex implementation strategy such as Page's (1993) is necessary. Consider that synchronization behavior has been proposed by other connectionist modelers to explain how the brain solves problems of binding. Often, a network of two units produces the oscillatory behavior of interest, and synchronization arises given simple couplings (e.g. Wang, 1993). Such proposals have received considerable physiological support, especially since the discovery of oscillations and synchronization in the cat visual cortex (Eckhorn *et al.*, 1989; Gray *et al.*, 1989). McAuley (1993, 1994), who has proposed entrainment models for the perception of rhythm, has suggested that behaviors relevant to this task, including frequency-tracking, may be found at the single neuron level. While we welcome this possibility, we do have some reservations. We have proposed a functional approach, not an implementation-level strategy. We have proposed oscillatory units to describe how the brain may execute the relatively high-level cognitive function of meter perception. Therefore we assume that our abstract, functional units represent higher levels of abstraction than individual neurons. Further, consider that the behaviors we have identified as necessary for rhythm perception may be implemented using large networks of simpler oscillatory elements. For these reasons, we suggest that the behavior of these abstract units may be plausibly regarded as the emergent behavior of a wide range of possible brain structures from simple neuronal substructures to large networks of oscillatory neurons.

6. General Discussion

The primary goal of our proposal has been to understand the implications of entrainment for theories of metrical structure and musical expectancy. To this end, we have proposed an abstract oscillatory unit that may be composed into networks for modeling the perception of metrical structure. The unit may synchronize its periodic output pulses with an incoming rhythmic pattern. The unit responds to event onsets that occur within its temporal receptive field by adjusting its phase and period, and ignores stimulus pulses that occur outside this field. The width of the receptive field can be adjusted using a parameter called output gain. This enables the unit to isolate single periodic components of complex rhythms.

Analysis of the behavior of a single unit in response to periodic stimulation reveals complex dynamics. In principle, the unit may mode-lock to a periodic stimulus in any one of an infinite number of rational ratios. Tuning the unit's temporal receptive field has the effect of adjusting the relative stability of mode-locking regions. Large temporal receptive fields result in a preference for simple ratios while finely tuned regions allow more complex ratios. These properties have important implications for entrainment theories of metrical structure. Regime diagrams will summarize the content of such theories regarding the well-formedness of metrical structures. The Farey tree enumerates the possible relationships between two levels of beats, while the corresponding regime diagram describes the stability of resulting metrical relationships.

The phase- and frequency-locking behavior of individual units implicitly describes a set of metrical preferences—a set of preferred phase relationships between two levels of beats in a metrical structure, relative to the structure of the incoming rhythm. Such preferences may be best understood in terms of the characteristic response of an individual unit to a complex rhythmic pattern. Ultimately, in a network, the influence of other units may mediate individual unit preferences, and subsets of units will respond to an afferent rhythmic pattern as a whole. We have also demonstrated that entrainment provides a robust approach to the perception of meter in musical performance. This allows us to account for the perception of meter in the face of timing variability. Thus, the model embodies a dynamic solution to the 'quantization problem' (Desain & Honing, 1991). Finally, we demonstrated a system of oscillatory units correctly tracking two metrical levels in an improvised melodic performance. The rhythm of the improvised melody was complex, yet the simple system behaved quite reasonably. This indicates that our proposal may provide the basis for more comprehensive, robust and parsimonious theories of the perception of metrical structure.

6.1. Future Work

The primary goal of this article has been to understand the implications of entrainment for theories of musical meter. We have stopped short of proposing a theory of musical meter. Before attempting to construct such a theory, we would need to resolve at least two issues. The first is the issue of phenomenal accent. We have seen how a tightly grouped set of onsets (a chord, or a melody note with an accompanying grace note) may impact the preference of individual units. The model, as it now stands, does not specify how other types of phenomenal accent (e.g. intensity, or large pitch leaps) may affect individual unit preferences regarding which events are interpreted as marking the beat. One possibility calls for a real-valued representation of event onsets, $s(t)$, to carry accent information. Because of the formulation of the delta rules, events with greater accent would cause greater phase and period adjustments. Although this technique appears promising, it does not provide a theory of accent such as Todd's (1994) 'rhythmogram' model.

The second issue that stands between our entrainment mechanism and a theory of musical meter is the issue of network construction. In this article, we have concentrated on the behavior of individual units independently responding to afferent rhythms. Yet one would expect individual units within a network to interact, responding to the outputs of other units in the network. The important question is: Could a stable response emerge from such a network subjected to a musical event sequence? Our analysis of the single unit case suggests that subsets of units in a loosely coupled network could self-organize a coherent response to an afferent rhythm. In addition, the interaction would instantiate metrical well-formedness constraints. The major challenge facing this approach is to determine the nature of the interaction. We leave the issues of network construction and phenomenal accent unresolved, and we regard these as important areas for future exploration. We believe that an understanding of mechanisms of entrainment will result in theories of meter perception that are wider in scope, and more parsimonious, than those that have previously been offered. Entrainment and self-organization provide expressive power and useful physicalist constraints unavailable within more general-purpose theoretical frameworks. At the same time, these principles offer greater robustness to deal with the problems associated with the perception of actual musical performances.

6.2. *Implications for Connectionist Approaches to Expectancy*

At the outset of this article, we pointed to two limitations of recurrent neural network approaches to musical expectancy. The first problem was the representation of temporal context. Mozer (1993) and deVries and Principe (1992) have suggested that an exponential recency gradient, inherent in most network architectures, limits the ability of recurrent networks to represent temporal context. The most recent items presented to the network carry more weight than previous inputs, inhibiting the network's ability to capture global structure. Other connectionist approaches have addressed this issue by using a system of short-term memory delays to explicitly capture temporal context (Lang *et al.*, 1990; Unnikrishnan *et al.*, 1991; Bodenhausen & Waibel, 1991; deVries & Principe, 1992); (for a review, see Mozer, 1993). Delays may be hard-wired or learned during batch training, but during processing they remain fixed. The problem with a fixed-memory delay solution for music processing should now be apparent. Music lacks fixed temporal structure. Musical signals display complex forms of temporal organization including expressive timing deviations and periodic structure on multiple time-scales.

The second problem with recurrent neural network approaches to music expectancy was their inability to generalize to novel rates of presentation. Cottrell *et al.* (1993) have attempted to solve this problem by implementing a strategy for rate-invariant sequence recognition. They first trained a recurrent network to predict a target input signal presented at some 'normal' rate. A typical recurrent network would be able to track the target signal at this rate, but would lose the signal at other rates. Cottrell *et al.* augmented their network to control its own processing rate by adapting time constants and processing delays. Using prediction error, the recurrent network adapted its processing rate to match the rate of the current signal, much as a phase-locked loop varies its internal frequency to match the phase of an incoming signal. This approach appears to yield plausible explanations for some aspects of perception, including the perception of music. It is not a general solution to the problem of rate invariance in music, however, because it applies only to learned sequences.

Each approach described above addresses individual aspects of temporal sequence recognition and prediction, and leaves others unattended. Resonance-based approaches provide an alternative that combines the strengths of the above-mentioned proposals, while solving some remaining problems. The combined output of a system of oscillators, as shown in Figure 8(c), can provide complex temporal control (i.e. pulses of attention) to affect the further processing of a musical sequence. A resonance-based system could adapt its processing rate according to the structure of the signal, without memorizing the signal in advance. Memory delays, implemented as resonance-based components, could likewise adapt to the rate of the incoming signal. In addition, the structure of memory itself could adapt to reflect the temporal organization (e.g. the metrical structure) of the incoming signal. Thus, we feel that resonance mechanisms offer a particularly novel route toward understanding musical expectancy.

7. Conclusions

Lashley (1951) identified the problem of serial order ". . . the logical and orderly arrangement of thought and action" as a central problem for psychologists, neurobiologists, and all those who ultimately wish to describe the phenomena of mind in terms of the mathematical and physical sciences. Lashley realized that the problem was not merely one of sequence processing. The temporal structure of human perception and action implies that the temporal structure of neural computation is extraordinarily complex (Lashley, 1951). In this regard, the study of music is invaluable to the understanding of neural computation. Music, unlike natural language, forces us to deal with all aspects of time: time is so fundamental to music that it cannot be conveniently and convincingly abstracted away. It may even be that composers and performers shape the temporal structure of music to reflect and to explore natural modes of temporal organization in the human nervous system.

For inherently temporal tasks, such as perception and motor coordination, we agree that resonance provides a more useful metaphor than general-purpose computation (Gibson, 1966, 1979; Treffner & Turvey, 1993). According to this view, the brain may be treated as a special-purpose device, capable of temporarily adapting its function to specific perception–action situations (Kelso & deGuzman, 1988). In perception, the nervous system may adapt endogenous modes of temporal organization to external rhythmic patterns, controlling attention and memory (Jones, 1976). Other connectionists have noted the fundamental consonance of such dynamical systems approaches with modern connectionist cognitive modeling (e.g. van Gelder & Port, in press). Ours is an attempt to bring the two closer together to overcome the limitations of current connectionist models. We have found music perception to be a fertile testing ground for this approach. Our current proposal attempts to explain the mechanisms underlying temporal adaptation in the human response to musical rhythms. We believe that this approach will lead to more robust and parsimonious theories of musical meter and musical expectancy.

Acknowledgements

This research was partially supported by the Ohio State University Presidential Fellowship to the first author, by NIMH grant 1R29-MH45764 to Caroline Palmer in support of the first author, and by ONR Grant N00014-92-J115 to Jordan B. Pollack in support of the second author. The authors would like to thank Mari Jones for many helpful discussions, and for comments on earlier drafts of this paper. We would also like to thank Caroline Palmer, Jordan Pollack, Timothy Walker, Kevin Lenzo, Flip Phillips, Shannon Campbell and Gregory Saunders for helpful comments and discussions. Thanks also to two anonymous reviewers for providing thoughtful and thorough comments on an earlier draft of the paper.

Notes

1. *What Next* is also the name of a computer program that models musical expectancy (Larson, 1993).
2. The term 'subjective rhythm' is a misnomer according to modern terminology. According to conventional modern usage, this phenomenon would be called 'subjective meter'.

References

Allen, P.E. & Dannenberg, R.B. (1989) Tracking musical beats in real time. *Proceedings of the 1990 International Computer Music Conference*, Computer Music Association.

Apel, W. (1972) *Harvard Dictionary of Music* (2nd edn). Cambridge, MA: Belknap Press of Harvard University Press.

Beek, P.J., Peper, C.E. & van Wieringen, P.C.W. (1992) Frequency locking, frequency modulation, and bifurcations in dynamic movement systems. In G.E. Stelmach and J. Requin (Eds), *Tutorials in Motor Behavior II*. Amsterdam: Elsevier.

Bharucha, J.J. & Todd, P.M. (1989) Modeling the perception of tonal structure with neural nets. *Computer Music Journal*, **13**, 44–53.

Bodenhausen, U. & Waibel, A. (1991) The Tempo 2 algorithm: adjusting time delays by supervised learning. In R.P. Lippmann, J. Moody, & D.S. Touretsky (Eds), *Advances in Neural Information Processing Systems*, 3. San Mateo, CA: Morgan Kaufman.

Bolton, T.L. (1894) Rhythm. *American Journal of Psychology*, **6**, 145–238.

Carpenter, G.A. & Grossberg, S. (1983) A neural theory of circadian rhythms: the gated pacemaker. *Biological Cybernetics*, **48**, 35–59.

Clarke, E. (1985) Structure and expression in rhythmic performance. In P. Howell, I. Cross & R. West (Eds), *Musical Structure and Cognition*. London: Academic Press.

Cooper, G. & Meyer, L.B. (1960) *The Rhythmic Structure of Music*. Chicago: University of Chicago Press.

Cottrell, G.W., Nguyen, M. & Tsung, F. (1993) Tau Net: the way to do is to be. *Proceedings of the Fifteenth Annual Conference of the Cognitive Science Society*. Hillsdale, NJ: Erlbaum Press.

Dannenberg, R.B. (1984) An on-line algorithm for real-time accompaniment. *Proceedings of the 1984 International Computer Music Conference*. Computer Music Association.

Dannenberg, R.B. & Mont-Reynaud, B. (1987) Following an improvisation in real time. *Proceedings of the 1987 International Computer Music Conference*. Computer Music Association.

Desain, P. (1992) A (de)composable theory of rhythm perception. *Music Perception*, **9**, 101–116.

Desain, P. & Honing, H. (1991) The quantization of musical time: a connectionist approach. In P.M. Todd & D.G. Loy (Eds), *Music and Connectionism*, pp. 150–160. Cambridge, MA: MIT Press.

de Vries, B. & Principe, J.C. (1992) The gamma model—a new neural net model for temporal processing. *Neural Networks*, **5**, 565–576.

Deutsch, D. (1980) The processing of structured and unstructured tonal sequences. *Perception and Psychophysics*, **28**, 381–389.

Dirst, M. & Weigend, A.S. (1993) Baroque forecasting: On completing J.S. Bach's last fugue. In A. Weigend & N. Gershenfeld (Eds), *Predicting the Future and Understanding the Past*, pp. 151–172. Reading, MA: Addison-Wesley.

Dowling, W.J. & Harwood, D.L. (1986) *Music Cognition*. San Diego: Academic Press.

Drake, C. & Botte, M. (1993) Tempo sensitivity in auditory sequences: evidence for a multiple-look model. *Perception and Psychophysics*, **54**, 277–286.

Drake, C. & Palmer, C. (1993) Accent structures in music performance. *Music Perception*, **10**, 343–378.

Eckhorn, R., Reitboeck, H.J., Arndt, M. & Dicke, P. (1989) Feature linking via stimulus evoked oscillations: Experimental results from cat visual cortex and functional implications from a network model. *Proceedings of the International Joint Conference on Neural Networks*. Washington.

Elman, J. (1990) Finding structure in time. *Cognitive Science*, **14**, 179–211.

Essens, P.J. & Povel, D. (1985) Metrical and nonmetrical representation of temporal patterns. *Perception and Psychophysics*, **37**, 1–7.

Getty, D.J. (1975) Discrimination of short temporal intervals: a comparison of two models. *Perception & Psychophysics*, **18**, 1–8.

Gibson, J.J. (1966) *The Senses Considered as Perceptual Systems*. Boston: Houghton Mifflin.

Gibson, J.J. (1979) *The Ecological Approach to Visual Perception*. Boston: Houghton Mifflin.

Glass, L. & Mackey, M.C. (1988) *From Clocks to Chaos: The Rhythms of Life*. Princeton, NJ: Princeton University Press.

Gray, C.M., Konig, P., Engel, A.K. & Singer, W. (1989) Oscillatory responses in cat visual cortex exhibit inter-columnar synchronization which reflects global stimulus properties. *Nature*, **338**, 334–337.

Halpern, A.R. & Darwin, C. (1982) Duration discrimination in a series of rhythmic events. *Perception & Psychophysics*, **31**, 86–89.

Jones, M.R. (1976) Time, our lost dimension: toward a new theory of perception, attention, and memory. *Psychological Review*, **83**, 323–335.

Jones, M.R. (1981) Music as a stimulus for psychological motion: Part I: Some determinants of expectancies. *Psychomusicology*, **1**, 34–51.

Jones, M.R. (1987a) Dynamic pattern structure in music: recent theory and research. *Perception & Psychophysics*, **41**, 621–634.

Jones, M.R. (1987b) Perspective on musical time. In A. Gabrielsson (Ed.), *Action and Perception in Rhythm and Music*, pp. 153–175. Stockholm: The Royal Swedish Academy of Music.

Jones, M.R. & Boltz, M. (1989) Dynamic attending and responses to time. *Psychological Review*, **96**, 459–491.

Jones, M.R., Kidd, G. & Wetzel, R. (1981) Evidence for rhythmic attention. *Journal of Experimental Psychology: Human Perception & Performance*, **7**, 1059–1073.

Jones, M.R., Boltz, M. & Kidd, G. (1982) Controlled attending as a function of melodic and temporal context. *Journal of Experimental Psychology: Human Perception & Performance*, **7**, 211–218.

Jordan, M. (1986) *Serial order*. Technical Report 8604, Institute for Cognitive Science, University of California at San Diego, La Jolla, CA.

Kelso, J.A.S. & deGuzman, G.C. (1988) Order in time: how the cooperation between the hands informs the design of the brain. In H. Haken (Ed.), *Natural and Synergetic Computers*, pp. 44–57. Berlin: Springer-Verlag.

Lang, K., Waibel, A.H. & Hinton, G.E. (1990) A time-delay neural network architecture for isolated word recognition. *Neural Networks*, **3**, 23–44.

Large, E.W. & Kolen, J.F. (1993) *A Dynamical Model of the Perception of Metrical Structure*. Presented at Society for Music Perception and Cognition. Philadelphia, June.

Large, E.W., Palmer, C. & Pollack, J.B. Reduced memory representation for music. *Cognitive Science* (in press).

Larson, S. (1993) Modeling melodic expectation: Using three 'musical forces' to predict melodic continuations. *Proceedings of the Fifteenth Annual Conference of the Cognitive Science Society*. Hillsdale, NJ: Erlbaum Press.

Lashley, K. (1951) The problem of serial order in behavior. In Jeffress (Ed.), *Cerebral Mechanisms in Behavior*. NY: Wiley.

Lerdahl, E. & Jackendoff, R. (1983) *A Generative Theory of Tonal Music*. Cambridge, MA: MIT Press.

Longuet-Higgins, H.C. (1987) *Mental Processes*. Cambridge: MIT Press.

Longuet-Higgins, H.C. & Lee, C.S. (1982) The perception of musical rhythms. *Perception*, **11**, 115–128.

McAuley, J.D. (1993) *Learning to Perceive and Produce Rhythmic Patterns in an Artificial Neural Network*. Technical Report, Department of Computer Science, Indiana University.

McAuley, J.D. (1994) Finding metrical structure in time. In M.C. Mozer, P. Smolensky, D.S. Touretsky, J.L. Elman & A.S. Weigend (Eds), *Proceedings of the 1993 Connectionist Models Summer School*. Hillsdale, NJ: Erlbaum Associates.

McGraw, G., Montante, R. & Chalmers, D. (1991) *Rap-master Network: Exploring Temporal Pattern Recognition with Recurrent Networks*. Technical Report No. 336. Computer Science Department, Indiana University.

Marr, D. (1982) *Vision*. New York: W.H. Freeman.

Meyer, L. (1956) *Emotion and Meaning in Music*. Chicago: University of Chicago Press.

Mozer, M.C. (1991) Connectionist music composition based on melodic, stylistic and psychophysical constraints. In P.M. Todd & D.G. Loy (Eds), *Music and Connectionism*, pp. 195–211. Cambridge, MA: MIT Press.

Mozer, M.C. (1993) Neural net architectures for temporal sequence processing. In A. Weigend & N. Gershenfeld (Eds), *Predicting the Future and Understanding the Past*, pp. 243–264. Reading, MA: Addison-Wesley.

Narmour, E. (1990) *The Analysis and Cognition of Basic Melodic Structures: The Implication-realization Model.* Chicago: University of Chicago Press.

Page, M.P.A. (1993) *Modelling Aspects of Music Perception Using Self-organizing Neural Networks.* Unpublished doctoral dissertation, University of Cardiff.

Palmer, C. & Krumhansl, C.L. (1990) Mental representations of musical meter. *Journal of Experimental Psychology: Human Perception & Performance,* **16,** 728–741.

Port, R.F. (1990) Representation and recognition of temporal patterns. *Connection Science,* **2,** 151–176.

Povel, D. & Essens, P.J. (1985) Perception of temporal patterns. *Music Perception,* **2,** 411–440.

Scarborough, D.L., Miller, P. & Jones, J.A. (1992) On the perception of meter. In M. Balaban, K. Ebcioglu & O. Laske (Eds), *Understanding Music with AI: Perspectives in Music Cognition,* pp. 427–447. Cambridge, MA: MIT Press.

Schmidt, R.C., Beek, P.J., Treffner, P.J. & Turvey, M.T. (1991) Dynamical substructure of coordinated rhythmic movements. *Journal of Experimental Psychology: Human Perception & Performance,* **17,** 635–651.

Schroeder, M. (1991) *Fractals, Chaos, Power Laws.* New York: Freeman.

Schulze, H.H. (1989) The perception of temporal deviations in isochronic patterns. *Perception & Psychophysics,* **45,** 291–296.

Shaffer, L.H. (1981) Performances of Chopin, Bach, and Bartok: studies in motor programming. *Cognitive Psychology,* **13,** 326–376.

Simon, H.A. & Sumner, R.K. (1968) Pattern in music. In B. Kleinmuntz (Ed.), *Formal Representation of Human Thought.* New York: Wiley.

Sloboda, J.A. (1983) The communication of musical meter in piano performance. *Quarterly Journal of Experimental Psychology,* **35,** 377–396.

Todd, N.P.M. (1985) A model of expressive timing in tonal music. *Music Perception,* **3,** 33–59.

Todd, N.P.M. (1994) The auditory primal sketch: a multi-scale model of rhythmic grouping. *Journal of New Music Research,* **23,** 25–69.

Todd, P.M. (1991) A connectionist approach to algorithmic composition. In P.M. Todd & D.G. Loy (Eds), *Music and Connectionism,* pp. 173–194. Cambridge, MA: MIT Press.

Torras, C. (1985) *Temporal Pattern Learning in Neural Models.* Berlin: Springer-Verlag.

Treffner, P.J. & Turvey, M.T. (1993) Resonance constraints on rhythmic movement. *Journal of Experimental Psychology: Humant Perception & Performance,* **19,** 1221–1237.

Unnikrishnan, K.P., Hopfield, J.J. & Tank, D.W. (1991) Connected-digit speaker-dependent speech recognition using a neural network with time-delayed connections. *IEEE Transactions on Signal Processing,* **39,** 698–713.

van Gelder, T. & Port, R. (forthcoming) Introduction. In T. van Gelder & R. Port (Eds), *Mind as Motion.* Cambridge, MA: MIT Press.

von der Malsberg, C. & Schneider, W. (1986) A neural cocktail-party processor. *Biological Cybernetics,* **54,** 29–40.

Wang, D. (1993) Pattern recognition: neural networks in perspective. *IEEE Expert,* **8,** 52–60.

Winfree, A.T. (1980) *The Geometry of Biological Time.* New York: Springer-Verlag.

Woodrow, H. (1909) A quantitative study of rhythm. *Archives of Psychology,* **14,** 1–66.

Yee, W., Holleran, S. & Jones, M.R. (1994) Sensitivity to event timing in regular and irregular sequences: influences of musical skill. *Journal of Experimental Psychology: Human Perception & Performance* **55,** 1–11.

Yeston, M. (1976) *The Stratification of Musical Rhythm.* New Haven: Yale University Press.

Modelling Musical Perception: A Critical View

STEPHEN W. SMOLIAR

This is a study of two attempts to develop quantitative models of timing in music performance, one based on connectionism and the other involving the autocorrelation function. The former is concerned with the 'quantization problem' of interpreting durations of time from a musical performance as note shapes which represent duration in music notation. The latter is an attempt to represent what makes such performances 'expressive'. These models were derived by Peter Desain, but there is a paucity of validating data in the published literature. Attempts to collect additional data have revealed significant shortcomings in both models, as well as methodological flaws. The most important problem is that the attempt to solve the quantization problem lacks any representation of high-level structure. As a result, if the music itself tends to be based on relatively irregular rhythmic patterns, the connectionist model can distort even a metronome-perfect performance, rather than recognizing the correct temporal patterns. Attempts are made to explain how these shortcomings may have arisen.

KEYWORDS: Musical expression, autocorrelation.

1. Introduction

Peter Desain's thesis, entitled 'Structure and Expressive Timing in Music Performance', addresses two topics: the detection of metric beats in a performance and the ways in which a performance becomes 'expressive' through departure from a perfectly rigid spacing of those beats. The first of these topics focuses on the design of a connectionist model developed in response to a critical analysis of a meter detection program by Christopher Longuet-Higgins (Longuet-Higgins, 1976). The second is concerned with exploiting the use of the autocorrelation function in the analysis of timing data. Thus, in both cases the focus is on attempts to derive mathematical models of particular aspects of music behaviour. Reprints of papers presenting results of both studies have been collected in a book entitled *Music, Mind and Machine: Studies in Computer Music, Music Cognition and Artificial Intelligence* (Desain & Honing, 1992a).

While this is a bold title, 'music cognition' faces a serious problem in grounding its results in actual music behaviour (Sloboda, 1985). Therefore, although it is impressive to see a researcher approach this topic with apparent signs of mathematical rigour, it may be necessary to be somewhat sceptical about accepting the

This article appeared originally in *Connection Science*, 1994, **6**, 209–222, and is reprinted with permission.

experimental results at face value. (Most problematic is the fact that there just are not enough published results to justify many of Desain's claims.) This is a report of personal attempts to collect further data to either reproduce those results or collect other results which would support the same conclusions. What follows is thus a synthesis of those experiences which have been documented by Desain and his colleagues with the author's own 'follow-up' experiences. Since all these experiences have to do with the analysis and interpretation of music, several specific examples in music notation will be given.

2. Reviewing the Models

2.1. The Analysis of Musical Rhythm

2.1.1. The quantization problem.   One of the more interesting tasks in computer music has always been the development of a program 'which will transcribe a live performance of a classical melody into the equivalent of standard musical notation' (Longuet-Higgins, 1976). Some of the most substantial pioneering research on this problem was conducted by Longuet-Higgins in the early 1970s. He began by dividing the problem into two subproblems concerned with the perception of rhythm and tonality, respectively. The latter problem involves determining what the key signature should be and what accidentals should be assigned to the notes which require them. The former problem requires determining which shapes, corresponding to duration values, should be assigned to each note.

While Longuet-Higgins restricted his attention to melody, he was able to demonstrate some impressive results. When he reported these results in 1976 (Longuet-Higgins, 1976), he discussed his algorithm using the old 'shave and a haircut' melodic cliché (Figure 1). However, at the end of the paper, he provided two examples from the English horn solo which opens the first scene of the third act of Richard Wagner's *Tristan und Isolde*—the sort of exercise which many humans would find quite challenging. These results demonstrated that Longuet-Higgins' program was no mere toy.

Unfortunately, the system never really caught on in the music community. Interest in computers in 1976 was still quite low, particularly since computers were beyond the budgets of most practising musicians; and interest in artificial intelligence was even lower. To make matters worse, Longuet-Higgins had coded his program in POP2, whose popularity was even less than that of artificial intelligence. By the time musicians were more disposed to think seriously about computers and artificial intelligence, Longuet-Higgins' work had been all but forgotten.

Desain, however, not only remembered Longuet-Higgins but found him inspirational. He decided to focus his attention on the rhythmic side of Longuet-Higgins' results—the problem of interpreting temporal intervals on a continuous scale as discrete symbols representing different values of musical duration. He began with a thorough study of Longuet-Higgins' source code in an attempt to develop a theory to explain why it performed the way it did. At the same time, given that POP2 is no longer a particularly active language, he reimplemented the system in COMMON LISP.

Figure 1. Longuet-Higgins' first rhythmic test.

The most important conclusion from this effort was that there was really less theory in Longuet-Higgins' code than met the eye (Desain, 1992b). Indeed, some portions of the code exhibited rather eccentric behaviour which could not be interpreted as 'musical knowledge'. Furthermore, the operation of the program itself was dependent on the proper setting of several parameters; so one could not view it as a simple system which accepted a performance as input and generated duration notation as output. Thus, as far as Desain was concerned, this 'quantization problem' of inferring rhythms expressed in the symbols of music notation from the continuum of durational values of actual performances was far from solved.

2.1.2. A connectionist approach. By the time Desain was completing his study of Longuet-Higgins' system, not only artificial intelligence but also connectionism were becoming 'in' among musicians with a taste for challenging research (Todd & Loy, 1991). Together with his colleague, Henkjan Honing, Desain decided to see if connectionism would provide a more satisfactory handle on the quantization problem than Longuet-Higgins' symbolic approach had (Desain *et al.*, 1992). Not only were they concerned with replacing what theory there was at the foundation of Longuet-Higgins' code with a new set of principles, but also Desain wanted to develop systematic techniques to compare their alternative system with that of Longuet-Higgins (Desain, 1992a).

Unfortunately, the resulting comparison leaves much to be desired, particularly in matters of objectivity. One quickly discovers that the dice have been loaded on the connectionist side; and the 'loyal opposition' tends to get misrepresented. For example, another symbolic approach was pursued at Stanford University (Chafe *et al.*, 1989), but Desain dismisses that system with a grossly inaccurate generalization about the technology of rule-based systems (Desain, 1992a):

> Because of its design as an unordered collection of rules it is, like all rule based systems, impossible to characterize its behavior in non-operational terms.

Such a statement makes it clear that Desain is not very familiar with the nuts and bolts of artificial intelligence practice, an observation which is reinforced when he tries to contrast the Longuet-Higgins system as being 'knowledge-based', while the connectionist one is 'knowledge-free'.

2.1.3. Comparing the symbolic and connectionist solutions
(1) *The reported comparison.* Ultimately, Desain's primary grounds for comparison have to do with the theoretical infrastructure of the two systems. Given that he had already made his point about the weakness of this infrastructure in the Longuet-Higgins system, it is not surprising to see how well the connectionist system shines. Indeed, some of the implications of these results will be discussed in Section 2.1.4 as they could well have significant impact on the study of music theory. However, practice sometimes deserves as much attention as theory. Longuet-Higgins subjected his system to a seemingly impressive acid test, so it is worth asking if the Desain–Honing connectionist system is up to the same calibre.

Thus far, there has been only one published account of experimental data used to compare the performances of the two systems (Desain & Honing, 1992b); and this paper considers only one example. It is rather complex, although it would probably not pose any problems for an average undergraduate music major (Figure

Figure 2. Rhythmic test example.

2). However, it is difficult to assess the results of this test without a better understanding of the actual input and output. The input seems straightforward—durations from a recorded performance rounded to four significant digits: (1.177 0.592 0.288 0.337 0.436 0.337 0.387 0.600 0.634 0.296 0.280 0.296 0.346 1.193). Note that the fourth and sixth notes were performed with the same duration but correspond to different notated interpretations. This is probably the most challenging problem which the two algorithms must be able to solve.

Longuet-Higgins' algorithm works by taking one of these values as a baseline, interpreting its duration to be 1, and representing all computed durations as rational multiples of this baseline. The default value is that of the first duration, and Desain and Honing ran their test with this assumption. Longuet-Higgins also provides a tolerance parameter; any duration less than this value is ignored. Longuet-Higgins' default value is 0.10; for their test run, Desain and Honing set it to 0.15. The output is easy to interpret: (1 ½ ¼ ¼ ⅓ ⅓ ⅓ ½ ½ ¼ ¼ ¼ ¼ 1). The initial and final quarter-notes are interpreted as the unit duration. All eighth-notes have half that duration, sixteenth-notes have a quarter of the duration, and triplet eighth-notes have a third of the duration. The fourth note is correctly interpreted as a sixteenth-note, while the sixth note, which occupies the same 'clock time', is correctly interpreted as a triplet eighth.

The connectionist algorithm iteratively alters the input values, 'steering' the ratios between successive durations towards simple integer ratios (Desain *et al.*, 1992). The rate of change is controlled by two exponent parameters called 'peak' and 'decay'. Desain and Honing ran the test of this algorithm with their default values for these parameters, 5 and −1, respectively. The other parameter is the number of iterations of change which are applied, having a default value of 20. What this means is that their algorithm is basically trying to 'round off' the initial values, where the goal is not revisions of those values with fewer significant digits but results which exhibit simple integer ratios. In this case, they present their results rounded to only two significant digits: (1.2 0.6 0.3 0.3 0.4 0.4 0.4 0.6 0.6 0.3 0.3 0.3 0.3 1.2). Notice that most of these values may be achieved by simply rounding the input data to two significant digits: 1.177 maps to 1.2, 0.592 maps to 0.6, 0.288 maps to 0.3, etc. Nevertheless, 0.337 does get mapped to different values for its two instances: 0.3 when it appears as the fourth note, and 0.4 when it appears as the sixth. Therefore, the algorithm really is doing more than a simple round-off.

(2) *What was not reported.* It is very easy to interpret this output, even if it does not use a notation as 'quantized' as Longuet-Higgins' rational numbers; but is it so readable because the initial value happens to be 'steered' towards a number readily divided by both two and three? Suppose, for the sake of argument, that the input had been normalized by a multiplicative factor to adjust the first duration to 1.0. In this case the input values, again rounded to four significant digits, would be the following: (1.000 0.503 0.245 0.286 0.370 0.286 0.329 0.510 0.539 0.251 0.238 0.251 0.294 1.014). Running the same algorithm on this input and again rounding

the output to two significant digits yields a much less satisfactory result: (1.0 0.5 0.3 0.3 0.3 0.3 0.3 0.5 0.5 0.3 0.2 0.3 0.3 1.0).

The problem is immediately apparent: this representation does not really allow for a sensible interpretation of 0.3 and 0.2. The algorithm has not performed any differently. It still 'steers' all values towards simple ratios which correspond to Longuet-Higgins' fractions: 0.5, 0.25 and 0.33. Unfortunately, presenting these results with only two significant digits forces 0.25 and 0.33 both to round to 0.3, losing the ability to distinguish sixteenth-notes from triplet eighths. Furthermore, if the computed real numbers are actually closely distributed around 0.25, some will round up to 0.3 while others round down to 0.2. We see this in the representation of the last four sixteenth-notes, the tenth, eleventh, twelfth and thirteenth numbers in the output (0.3 0.2 0.3 0.3). These results are sufficiently confusing to defy any useful interpretation! In other words, one of the reasons why the connectionist results look as nice as they do is that the input is actually conducive to their looking that way. If the input values are less 'amenable', choosing an appropriate number of significant digits and interpreting the results may be far more problematic.

This may seem like a rather ponderous attempt to beat down a relatively simple demonstration with an idiosyncratic property of rounding errors, but it is more than that. Desain calls the task which he and Longuet-Higgins attempted a 'quantization problem'. Actually, it is a classification problem, assigning duration values to a set of categories determined by the expressiveness of music notation. By representing his output as rational numbers, Longuet-Higgins made the resulting categorization of each input value perfectly clear. Ultimately, any rational number can be represented in music notation (although many demand constructs used by few composers other than Karlheinz Stockhausen). A representation in decimal digits (no matter how many significant digits are presented), on the other hand, does not explicitly provide a classification. That task is left to the intuition of the user, who has to interpret those results. This is easy enough with the example used by Desain and Honing as a basis for comparison, and it is obvious that the solution to normalizing the input is to allow another significant digit in the output. However, how representative is this example; and how many significant digits will be required for another, arbitrarily selected, example?

The lesson here is not that rounding is as much of a problem as it has ever been but that this particular example is just not sufficiently representative for a study of this quantization/classification problem. Even if the bias towards such a simple output display was unintentionally introduced, at least one example is necessary which is less susceptible to such biases. Furthermore, that example should reflect more realistic circumstances of music performance than a single, well-crafted, exercise for ear training. Longuet-Higgins tested his system on two excerpts from *Tristan und Isolde*, but even these apparently more 'realistic' cases may be subject to similar questions of bias: were the excerpts selected for the sake of brevity or because they happened to work? Another problem of bias is that the performer who provided the data for Longuet-Higgins was required to preface his performance with one measure's worth of beats to set the tempo (Longuet-Higgins, 1976). Such an initial action might well influence the performer to play the music sufficiently rhythmically that it would give the system an easier time than might be expected under more musical conditions.

(3) *Testing the symbolic approach with 'real' music.* This discussion will concentrate on the first Wagner excerpt which Longuet-Higgins used as a test case (Figure 3).

Figure 3. Longuet-Higgins' first *Tristan* test.

(We shall see shortly that this sample is not a serendipitous choice which happened to work nicely.) However, the experimental data were taken from a performance of the entire solo from which these measures were excerpted. This performance was provided by a professional English horn player.[1] To avoid the problem of having to perform audio processing on a recorded performance, he played the solo on a MIDI keyboard with the same rhythmic expressiveness he would apply to his English horn performance. (This is basically the same approach which Longuet-Higgins used, although he did not have the luxury of MIDI technology.[2]) A file of this MIDI performance was then used as input to the code for both symbolic and connectionist algorithms which was reproduced in Desain and Honing (1992b). Finally, a rhythmically 'perfect' interpretation of the notation derived by the Finale 2.0 score entry system (Pogue, 1989) was used as a control case.

In all fairness, this performance would probably be problematic for many humans trying to transcribe it. Passages notated as triplets were actually performed as duplet rhythms—an eighth-note followed by two sixteenths, rather than three triplet eighths. Similarly, many of the sustained notes are held rather freely, even though they have explicit duration values. Indeed, this is probably a pretty bad example for testing transcription. About the only way one would be likely to get it right would be if one had memorized the score in advance. The performer had assumed that Wagner wanted a relatively free interpretation and that the notation is merely an approximation to that free expression.

These data may thus be viewed as the *aqua regia* of acid tests, so it should come as no surprise that Longuet-Higgins' algorithm does not manage very well. The duration of a 'blip' from an erroneous note had a floating-point value of 0.0167, and the duration of the grace note in the seventh measure is 0.2063. Overlooking these brief quantities, the duration of the shortest 'real' note is 0.2646; so the tolerance parameter was set to 0.25. If one uses the default parameter which selects the first note as a baseline, then the interpretation goes very wrong after the first two notes. However, given that a performer is likely to take some liberty in sustaining that first half-note, its duration does not make for a particularly secure baseline. If the algorithm is run with the first quarter-note (the eighteenth duration value) as the baseline, results improve, although not particularly spectacularly. Figure 4 is a translation of the output back into music notation. Since there was one faulty note in the performance of this excerpt, there were 33 duration values in the input, of which sixteen were correctly interpreted—not a particularly impressive score.

There are at least two major conclusions one can draw from these results. One is that the algorithm is not very good for free improvisations. Once it loses the beat, it has no way of recovering it. This is due in part to the fact that once rhythmic values have been assigned, they cannot be revised. All reasoning concentrates on

Figure 4. Transcription of Longuet-Higgins' output.

the relationship of each note to its predecessors. This then leads to the second conclusion, which is that the algorithm only reasons about notes, rather than measures. Longuet-Higgins' experiments with tonality involved an attempt to infer the key signature of the music being performed, but no such analogous reasoning is applied to duration to deduce that, for example, this particular excerpt has four quarter-note beats to a measure. If the algorithm had the ability to determine that certain notes 'made more sense' if they were aligned with the measures (such as the pattern in the fifth measure of Figure 3 which is repeated), it would probably make fewer errors in which a duration is off by an eighth or sixteenth beat. Ironically, this rather critical flaw in the logic of Longuet-Higgins' system was not discussed by Desain (1992b).

(4) *Testing the connectionist approach with the same data.*   One potential advantage of the connectionist algorithm is that it allows for a more global interpretation of the data. In contrast to the Longuet-Higgins approach, rhythmic interpretations are initially assigned to all durations and then updated by iterative refinement. Unfortunately, since the input in this case consisted of actual intervals of elapsed time, calculated by dividing durations in MIDI beats by a 'metronome marking' of 480 beats per second (included in the MIDI file), the resulting numbers were far less conducive to simple divisions by two and three than were those of the example provided by Desain and Honing. As a result the output of the connectionist algorithm, expressed in units of seconds as LISP floating-point numbers rounded to five significant digits, seemed relatively indecipherable at first blush (Figure 5).

```
(

1.9742 2.8090 0.6204 1.8285 0.6448 1.9084 0.5228 0.4564 0.5739 1.6851

0.6360 2.2734 2.6275 0.4912 0.2666 0.2627 1.7700 1.0638 0.4171 0.2897

0.2942 1.7761 1.1921 0.4496 0.0167 0.3204 0.3351 1.9895 0.2073 2.3746

2.8420 7.7158 2.6670

)
```

Figure 5. Connectionist output of *Tristan* performance.

(

1.8558 2.6405 0.5831 1.7188 0.6061 1.7939 0.4915 0.4290 0.5395 1.5840

0.5978 2.1371 2.4699 0.4617 0.2506 0.2469 1.6638 1.0000 0.3921 0.2723

0.2765 1.6696 1.1206 0.4226 0.0157 0.3012 0.3150 1.8701 0.1948 2.2321

2.6715 7.2528 2.5070

)

Figure 6. Normalized connectionist output of *Tristan* performance.

The problem with this output is that these 'rounded' values of elapsed time in seconds hardly constitute a 'quantization' of continuous values into discrete symbols representing intended musical durations. Nevertheless, if the objective of the algorithm was to seek out simple ratios among these durations, a display of those ratios might be more meaningful. Given that the eighteenth note from this example is a quarter-note, the list makes a bit more sense if all entries are divided by the 'rounded' duration of that particular note (Figure 6).

At this point, we can squint at these numbers and ask if they really reflect quantizations of the original values. For example, how justified are we in interpreting 1.8558 as an approximation to 2.0, which is how the half-note should be represented? What are we to make of the variations in the values for the three sets of triplets?

0.4617   0.2506   0.2469

0.3921   0.2723   0.2765

0.4226   0.3012   0.3150

Can these really all be interpreted as durations which require the same notation?

A better way to consider these numbers is in terms of their departure from those values which actually do correspond to the notation. One may represent the 'answer sheet' for this particular problem as in Figure 7. (The grace note has been assigned

(

2.0000 2.5000 0.5000 1.5000 0.5000 1.5000 0.5000 0.5000 0.5000 1.5000

0.5000 2.0000 2.0000 0.3333 0.3333 0.3333 2.0000 1.0000 0.3333 0.3333

0.3333 2.0000 1.0000 0.3333 0.0000 0.3333 0.3333 2.0000 0.0000 2.0000

2.0000 5.0000 2.0000

)

Figure 7. *Tristan* performance 'answer sheet'.

(

```
+0.1442  -0.1404  -0.0831  -0.2188  -0.1061  -0.2939  +0.0085  +0.0710  -0.0395

-0.0840  -0.0978  -0.1371  -0.4699  -0.1283  +0.0828  +0.0864  +0.3362  +0.0000

-0.0587  +0.0610  +0.0568  +0.3304  -0.1206  -0.0893  -0.0157  +0.0321  +0.0183

+0.1299  -0.1948  -0.2321  -0.6715  -2.2528  -0.5070
```

)

Figure 8. Differences from 'answer sheet'.

a value of 0.0, as has the very brief erroneous 'blip' in the performance; and the triplets are the result of computing (/1.0 3.0).) We may now inspect the list of differences between the entries in the connectionist result list and this 'answer' list (Figure 8).

In terms of a 'score', these results are a significant improvement over those of Longuet-Higgins. Only six of these error values correspond to a duration greater than that of a triplet eighth-note. In other words the algorithm seems to have 'made sense of' many of the liberties taken by the performer.

However, just how informative are these numbers when it comes to trying to interpret the results in terms of music notation? The list of differences establishes that 1.8558 is, indeed, 'close enough' to the 'actual answer', 2.0; but it is even closer to 1.75. Why not interpret it as a double-dotted quarter-note, a piece of notation just as valid as the half-note tied to an eighth-note which Wagner uses? The only way we can determine whether or not the connectionist algorithm 'got it right' is if we already know what 'right' is! This really does not solve the classification problem which Longuet-Higgins set out to tackle.[3]

(5) *Testing with the control data.*   It is also worth observing that the Longuet-Higgins algorithm performed much better on the control version. Indeed, when it was run on the entire solo passage, rather than just the initial excerpt, it made only one mistake: it interpreted the final dotted eighth-note followed by a sixteenth as a triplet quarter followed by a triplet eighth.[4] The connectionist algorithm, on the other hand, was run only on the excerpt since it runs so slowly on a serial machine.

(

```
2.2763  2.7658  0.5781  1.7578  0.5761  1.7298  0.5781  0.5736  0.5767  1.7290

0.5745  2.2338  2.0252  0.3307  0.3350  0.3325  2.0021  1.0000  0.3335  0.3278

0.3292  2.0033  1.1192  0.3727  0.3732  0.3731  2.4027  2.4351  2.5035  5.9673

2.1969
```

)

Figure 9. Connectionist output of *Tristan* control.

Presenting all durations relative to that same duration of the first quarter-note in the passage yields quite discouraging results (Figure 9). The most glaring errors are the three half-notes in measures 7 and 8 (the third, fourth and fifth numbers from the end of the list), whose durations are closer to that of a half-note tied to an eighth-note; and the following quarter-note tied to a whole-note comes out as a half-note tied to a whole-note.

This control example demonstrates again that the connectionist approach is not as 'global' as one might think. Ultimately, it deals with the same limited note-to-note relations that are addressed by the Longuet-Higgins algorithm; and, in this case at least, it actually deals with them more poorly. Thus, the connectionist algorithm is no better in reasoning about measures than Longuet-Higgins' system is; but while Longuet-Higgins only seems to run afoul of performances which are too free in interpreting the notation, the connectionist approach can be thrown by metrically perfect performances which happen to involve rather unorthodox rhythmic patterns. (A new technique, based on rms error minimization (Pressing & Lawrence, 1993), appears to show greater promise in its ability to reason about what measures are and how they affect the interpretation of note durations.)

2.1.4. Interpreting the results.   In terms of the understanding of rhythmic perception, however, the connectionist approach, in spite of its currently inadequate performance, may actually turn out to be the more valuable source of insight. If Desain's comparison of his system with that of Longuet-Higgins exhibits a certain amount of distortion and bias, there is still much to be gained from the way in which he analyzes the behaviour of both systems. This analysis is based on two constructs, called, respectively, the rhythm space and the expectancy space (Desain, 1992a).

The rhythm space is an attempt to map the relationship between actual temporal durations and their quantifications. This relationship is visualized as a plot in N-dimensional space, where the number of dimensions corresponds to the number of successive duration values being quantized. Unfortunately, Desain never analyzes anything more sophisticated than two-dimensional plots. This rather limited scope of interpretation may be a key reason why his connectionist algorithm still performs so poorly: if interpreting a test case like the *Tristan* excerpt requires an understanding of how the algorithm behaves on a larger scale than note-to-note relations, such two-dimensional plots cannot reveal the effect of this larger scale. Nevertheless, these modest results definitely point the way towards a more thorough analysis.

Taken at their surface appearance, these results demonstrate how the input space can be partitioned into regions, all points of which are mapped to the same interpretation. While, on the one hand, the regions defined by the connectionist algorithm are much more continuous than those of Longuet-Higgins' system (which exhibits anomalous points which do not map the same as all surrounding neighbours), the Longuet-Higgins approach shows a tendency towards interpretations using simpler notation constructs. Thus, Occam's razor may have had a significant influence on the implicit control structure of Longuet-Higgins' system, even if this was not immediately apparent in Desain's analysis of his code (Desain, 1992b). Nevertheless, one cannot learn very much from only two successive temporal intervals (or conclude very much, if one is to go by current system performance); so the impact of rhythm spaces on the interpretation of the behaviour of both systems will require further, and far more thorough, analysis.

The expectancy space, as its name implies, is an attempt to represent the fact that, on the basis of past input, both systems have 'predisposed' preferences for the interpretation of the next duration value. Such predispositions may have their origins in, for example, the 'laws of organization' of Gestalt theory (Hochberg, 1987). For example, the 'law of good continuation' would imply that the strongest expectancy of a succession of even beats of the same duration would be more beats of the same duration. Simple multiples or divisions of that duration would have lesser, but not negligible, expectancies, while other durations would be negligible.

The advantage which this analysis has over rhythm spaces is that Desain has derived a technique for mapping the expectancy based on the past history of an entire rhythmic phrase, as opposed to the most recent two or three durations. He performs this analysis on both his own and Longuet-Higgins' systems. The most significant difference between the two analyses is that Longuet-Higgins' expectancy space is discrete, while Desain's is continuous. Nevertheless, the qualitative expectancies of the two systems are reasonably similar.

Desain's work on expectancy spaces may, however, be more valuable than its application to the quantization problem. There has long been an interest in applying the laws of organization of Gestalt theory to music perception. Leonard Meyer (1973) has written extensively on the subject and attempted to support his arguments with various examples of musical analysis. Ultimately, however, Meyer's analyses tend to reinforce Julian Hochberg's assessment of the Gestalt laws of organization—that they "remain subjective demonstrations of unknown reliability" (Hochberg, 1987). Desain's approach appears to rest on much more objective foundations, and that objectivity may ultimately prove useful when the time comes to try to assess the predictions made by his theory against the observations of either human subjects or computer models of such subjects.

2.2. Expressive Performance

The other issue of perception which Desain has investigated, this time with colleague Siebe de Vos, concerns those aspects of a musical performance which cause it to be perceived as 'expressive' (Desain & de Vos, 1992). This work is concerned with applying autocorrelation to timing data of actual performances. The motivation for this approach is that 'musical expression' is based on a variation of regularities implicit in the structure of the music being performed. Thus, analysis of the music must precede its expressive performance, which then serves to highlight the regularities detected by analytical reasoning.

This immediately poses a paradox. Autocorrelation is basically a technique concerned with detecting regularities in time series. However, such regularities have more to do with the analysis of a musical composition prior to performance than they have to do with the performance itself. Expression is often implemented by departures from regularity which call the attention of the listener to key moments in the musical structure. Thus, Desain may have taken off on the wrong foot in attempting to make a case for autocorrelation as a tool.

He has further compounded the problem by choosing a musical example which may not be particularly appropriate: the C major prelude from the first volume of Johann Sebastian Bach's *Well Tempered Clavier*. The reason this choice of music is awkward is that it is composed as a perfectly uniform sequence of events: from the very beginning until the final sustained chord, every duration interval has exactly the same notation—one sixteenth-note. Thus, from a point of view of analysis, autocorrelation has no information to provide. If applied to a metronome-perfect

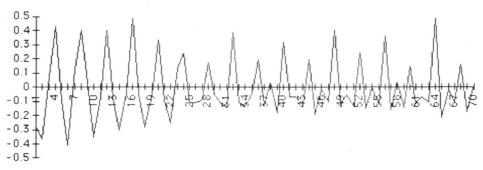

Figure 10. Autocorrelation of a Bach performance.

performance, it will yield flat values of 1.0 at any point in the score over any lag interval.

Suppose the performance is not metronome-perfect (i.e. 'expressive'); what, then, can the autocorrelation function say? Unfortunately, the answer to this question depends on how the performer chooses to be expressive. Figure 10 is an example which comes very close to reproducing the results presented in Desain and de Vos (1992). As in Desain and de Vos (1992), the data are taken from bar 31 of a performance of the Bach prelude. The horizontal axis is labelled in note events, with sixteen notes to a measure. The vertical axis gives the value of the autocorrelation function. This value represents the correlation of the passage beginning at bar 31 with preceding events, based strictly on the durations of those events. Thus, the value of the function at event 16 is the correlation of the passage at bar 31 with the passage at bar 30. The autocorrelation function is computed over a window whose size is proportional to the distance between the two events, where the proportionality factor is 4.

The data for Figure 10 were taken from a performance by a professional piano teacher.[5] The peaks indicate strong correlations at the distances of whole, half and quarter measures. Thus, while every measure is evenly divided into sixteen six-teenth-notes, there is a clear attempt to emphasize grouping these notes into clusters of four, grouping those groups into clusters of two, and grouping those groups into clusters of two. The results further reveal a slight tendency to emphasize the measure-level groupings with some decrease of emphasis at the half measure and a bit less at the quarter measure. To some extent, this constitutes a relatively 'approved' approach to phrasing this music.

However, it would be a great mistake to assume that this particular performance is, in any way, definitive. Figure 11 provides the same data for another performance of the same music by the same performer. In this case, there is more attention to pulse at the *eighth* measure level, and the balance of emphasis is quite different. Thus, any performer is likely to apply different approaches to rhythmic shaping in different readings of the same music.

Nevertheless, autocorrelation seems to be a useful way to detect evenness of pulse, even if the level of that pulse tends to vary. Unfortunately, not all 'musical' performances place priority on such evenness. Figure 12 illustrates the autocorrelation data for a third performance by the same pianist, this one with a much freer approach to rhythm and phrasing. In this case the autocorrelation function reveals a few peaks, many of which are relatively negligible; and there is little revealed about how the performer has chosen to shape this particular reading.

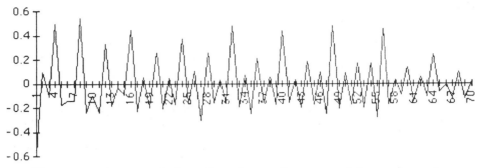

Figure 11. Autocorrelation of another performance of the same music.

The conclusion, then, is that this study of autocorrelation has been based on insufficient data (only a single performance) which may not be particularly representative (because the *a priori* evenness of Bach's music makes it a poor example of music which tends to be phrased expressively). Furthermore, it may be resting on faulty assumptions about the role of regularity of data. There is a confusion of analysis and performance in Desain's approach which may ultimately defeat the value of statistical techniques such as autocorrelation. Finally, and, perhaps, most importantly, there is the question of whether timing data can be studied in isolation. At the very least, loudness contributes as much to expressive performance as does timing; and often the interaction between these two factors is more important than either considered in isolation.

3. Conclusions

To the extent that much of 'music cognition' seems to prefer weak philosophy to concrete results (Smoliar, 1990), Desain's attempt to apply mathematical rigour to the study of mental processes associated with 'music behaviour' and the modelling of those processes by a machine is nothing if not admirable. While this paper has chosen to focus on methodological flaws in his work, these flaws serve to point out just how subtle and elusive the problems he has chosen to examine are. For all its faults, this work is still an important contribution to artificial intelligence as a study of several aspects of human behaviour which have received comparatively little serious attention. Nevertheless, the faults should serve to illustrate vividly just how far we are from 'closing the book' on this area of inquiry. Hopefully, they will help to point the way to the next round of equally rigorous investigations.

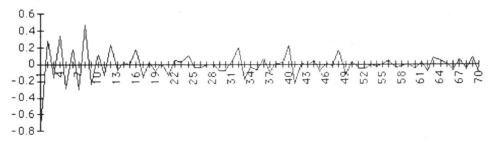

Figure 12. Autocorrelation of a third performance of the same music.

Notes

1. Harold Smoliar, English Horn, Pittsburgh Symphony Orchestra.
2. This approach may still be methodologically flawed. No matter how hard the performer may try to reproduce a wind performance at the keyboard, there is still the problem that he lacks the sense of 'breath' which would influence his English horn performance. Nevertheless, this seemed to be an acceptable approximation of 'real-world' data upon which these 'competing' algorithms could be tested.
3. Another way to resolve this problem would be to examine the trajectory of each result value through successive iterations. This could indicate whether 1.8558 was 'headed towards' 2.0 or 1.75. It could also indicate whether or not a sufficient number of iterations had been performed. However, it is also an output which looks even less 'quantized' and requires even more interpretation from the user.
4. Because of its sequential logic, the Longuet-Higgins algorithm yields the same result for the excerpt as it does when the excerpt is embedded in the entire passage; therefore, it made no errors for this particular excerpt.
5. Janet Ang.

References

Chafe, C., Mont-Reynaud, B. & Rush, L. (1989) Toward an intelligent editor of digital audio: recognition of musical constructs. In C. Roads (Ed.), *The Music Machine*, Chapter 42, pp. 537–548. Cambridge, MA: The MIT Press.

Desain, P. (1992a) A connectionist and a traditional AI quantizer, symbolic versus sub-symbolic models of rhythm perception. In P. Desain & H. Honing (Eds), *Music, Mind and Machine: Studies in Computer Music, Music Cognition and Artificial Intelligence*, pp. 81–98. Amsterdam: Thesis Publishers.

Desain, P. (1992b) Parsing the parser: a case study in programming style. In P. Desain & H. Honing (Eds), *Music, Mind and Machine: Studies in Computer Music, Music Cognition and Artificial Intelligence*, pp. 251–304. Amsterdam: Thesis Publishers.

Desain, P. & de Vos, S. (1992) Autocorrelation and the study of musical expression. In P. Desain & H. Honing (Eds), *Music, Mind and Machine: Studies in Computer Music, Music Cognition and Artificial Intelligence*, pp. 117–122. Amsterdam: Thesis Publishers.

Desain, P. & Honing, H. (1992a) *Music, Mind and Machine: Studies in Computer Music, Music Cognition and Artificial Intelligence*. Amsterdam: Thesis Publishers.

Desain, P. & Honing, H. (1992b) The quantization problem: traditional and connectionist approaches. In P. Desain & H. Honing (Eds), *Music, Mind and Machine: Studies in Computer Music, Music Cognition and Artificial Intelligence*, pp. 43–58. Amsterdam: Thesis Publishers.

Desain, P., Honing, H. & de Rijk, K. (1992) The quantization of musical time: a connectionist approach. In P. Desain & H. Honing (Eds), *Music, Mind and Machine: Studies in Computer Music, Music Cognition and Artificial Intelligence*, pp. 59–78. Amsterdam: Thesis Publishers.

Hochberg, J. (1987) Gestalt theory. In R.L. Gregory (Ed.), *The Oxford Companion to the Mind*, pp. 288–291. New York: Oxford University Press.

Longuet-Higgins, H.C. (1976) Perception of melodies. *Nature*, **263**, 646–653.

Meyer, L.B. (1973) *Explaining Music: Essays and Explorations*. Berkeley, CA: University of California Press.

Pogue, D. (1989) *Learning Finale*. Bloomington, MN: Coda Music Software.

Pressing, J. & Lawrence, P. (1993) *Transcribe*: a comprehensive autotranscription program. *Proceedings of the 1993 International Computer Music Conference*, pp. 343–345. International Computer Music Association, Tokyo, Japan.

Sloboda, J.A. (1985) *The Musical Mind: The Cognitive Psychology of Music*. Oxford: Clarendon Press.

Smoliar, S.W. (1990) Book review: *Models of Musical Communication and Cognition. Artificial Intelligence*, **44**, 361–371.

Todd, P.M. & Loy, D.G. (1991) Preface. In P.M. Todd & D.G. Loy (Eds), *Music and Connectionism*, pp. ix–xi. Cambridge, MA: The MIT Press.

A Reply to S. W. Smoliar's 'Modelling Musical Perception: A Critical View'

PETER DESAIN & HENKJAN HONING

In 'Modelling Musical Perception: A Critical View', Stephen Smoliar (1994) presents a review of some of the work in *Music, Mind and Machine* by Peter Desain and Henkjan Honing (1992).[1] This publication, a collection of research papers exploring an interdisciplinary approach to the study of music cognition, is the result of a close collaboration, though Smoliar's critique mentions mostly Desain. For full reviews see Smoliar (1995) and Dannenberg (1995). This reply is an attempt to correct some of the errors and misrepresentations made in Smoliar's review.

The critical view concentrates first on the 'quantization problem'. Smoliar, in common with many others, uses the term to reflect only the extraction of a metrical score from a performance. But in general it is the process that separates the discrete (score) and continuous (expressive) components of musical time in a performed musical fragment. The programs of a connectionist model (p. 61) and a reimplementation of a symbolic musical parser (Longuet-Higgins, 1976) in Lisp (p. 253) were taken and used in a re-evaluation using new data (i.e. unpublished "real music"). In this enterprise, a number of serious mistakes were made, including the following:

The data consisted of a "professional English horn player" playing the English horn solo from Wagner's *Tristan und Isolde* on a MIDI keyboard, at a relatively slow tempo and freely using tempo rubato. Suspicious of this curious experimental setup, we obtained the original data (a MIDI file). In addition to the key-presses that were measured and used as input for the models, the file contained a large number of so-called 'aftertouch' messages. These represent key-pressure and are usually mapped to a loudness parameter of the synthesizer. This means that there is no guarantee that the perceptual onsets, as heard by the performer, occurred at the same time as the time of note onsets. Nonetheless, it is this pattern of onsets that the quantizer has to interpret (see Table I). Smoliar recognizes some of these problems when he states that the performance cannot even be transcribed by human listeners, yet he proceeds to criticize the model's performance based on this pathological input.

Furthermore, this data contains grace notes—short notes that are outside the metrical framework and essentially 'unquantizable'. The fragment also contained two errors, one of which was identified as a 'brief erroneous blip' and left in the data, while the other was simply removed. Some common data collection

This paper was written for this volume and appears here for the first time.

Table I. Performance data as used by Smoliar for his test
(interonset intervals in seconds)

1.975	2.808	0.621	1.821	0.648	1.896	0.525	0.452	0.573	1.698
0.642	2.281	2.648	0.489	0.275	0.265	1.764	1.063	0.414	0.290
0.302	1.765	1.189	0.448	0.017	0.317	0.347	1.982	0.206	2.360
2.857	7.693	2.671							

precautions for expressive timing research seem thus to have been ignored: use expert performers (playing their own instruments) and record repeated performances so as to distinguish between motor noise, errors, and the actual musical intention of the performer. Although human listeners do have the ability to process rhythmic and metric structure in the presence of, for instance, grace notes, the quantization model that we proposed was simply not designed to deal with these issues yet: it simply breaks down in these cases.

The quantizer network was never designed to quantize a long musical fragment in a single operation. While there is evidence that some of the context following a note can influence its rhythmic interpretation, a human listener does not need to wait until the end of the fragment before perceiving the rhythm, nor is it realistic in terms of memory capacity.[2] Having initially designed the network for short fragments, we worked to extend it into a process model in which the input data shifts through the network while being quantized (see page 75). Thus Smoliar is applying the original model in a way that was never intended by applying it to the whole performance at once.

The quantizer network slowly relaxes into a state in which many integer ratios between time durations are discovered, but there are of course also cells that represent noninteger ratios. They continue to 'pull' slightly on the time intervals, which is the cause of the inaccuracy still inherent in the output pattern (especially in long patterns with many active cells).

Mutual inhibition, and a strategy for letting good cells 'win' was not part of the original design.[3] However, an extension of this kind can easily cancel out the influence of cells that stay too far from perfect integer ratios and thus boost the accuracy of the model. The problem that the resulting numbers still have to be categorized and named in a symbolic way (having decided what a good base for notation would be) falls completely outside the intended realm of the model. This issue only arises because the quantization model is equated with a technical application as transcription system.

Regarding Longuet-Higgins' musical parser, this model's essence is that it constructs metrical trees on top of the performed notes. Smoliar's claim that it "only reasons about notes" is misleading. First, it does not reason: it searches for an appropriate metrical tree; and second, most of its work is above the level of notes. The metrical trees are constructed up to a metrical level that is given to the model as a parameter, be it a measure, the tactus, or the like. And, ironically, it is Smoliar himself who prevents the model from analyzing higher metrical levels by starting it off with this parameter set to the first note: a half-bar. The observation that "[the connectionist model] deals with the same limited note-to-note relations that are addressed in the Longuet-Higgins algorithm" is also inaccurate. We showed, for example, that the connectionist quantizer is context sensitive, just as was shown for humans in Clarke (1987) where different metrical contexts can yield a different quantization for the same material.

Contrary to what Smoliar stated, we found that Longuet-Higgins' musical parser works remarkably well. This, in part, can be attributed to some inexplicit inter-actions between the tempo-tracking decisions that are made at different metrical levels. This, for example, gives rise to an area of patterns captured as triplets that is neatly shifted from its regular position toward the unequal way in which performers often play those rhythmic figures. Thus, while the musical parser is not intended as a model of expression, it turns out that in its behavior it expects certain regularities in performance timing, undoubtedly because the algorithm was tested and refined extensively by Longuet-Higgins. We made this "hidden knowledge" explicit through the use of the kind of simple low-dimensional behavioral analysis that Smoliar criticizes. In fact, both the graphical representation of the parameter space and rhythm space proved an immensely valuable tool for analysis of the models—the parameter space shows the areas in which a model interprets rhythmic perfor-mances correctly (given that for a certain set it is known what 'correct' is) and the rhythm space shows the actual clustering behavior of the model in a space of all possible rhythms. It is unfortunate, but surely obvious, that to be able to print a graphical representation of these spaces in a book, one has to resort to a low-dimensional example. Interestingly, one of the low-dimensional representations turned out to be interpretable in terms of an expectancy of events still to happen in the future. It was elaborated into a cognitive model of rhythm perception (page 101), and subsequently into a beat induction model (Desain & Honing, 1994). It might well be that Longuet-Higgins' insight that quantization can best be done in the context of metric parsing is a very valuable one. This is the reason why we postponed further work on quantization until the research on beat and meter induction has matured.

Regarding our comments on another approach, namely the AI method used in the Stanford music transcription project, Smoliar raises doubts about our compe-tence. Contrary to what he suggests, we are only too familiar with the "nuts and bolts" of the practice of AI in which powerful ideas are implemented as a rule-based system. These systems often quickly reach their limits: they become 'brittle' and difficult to extend (or even understand) for their designers. Many of these projects were abandoned and, worse, the valuable work that went into formalizing the knowledge involved gets lost (see e.g. Winograd & Flores, 1986)—which was exactly what happened to the Stanford music transcription project.

Concerning our exploratory study of the use of autocorrelation for the analysis of timing data, Smoliar makes one mistake of interpretation after another. Because a uniform time series of tempo data captures the performance, not the rhythmic regularity in the score, it is a perfectly sound research question to study the extent to which autocorrelation methods can reveal periodic regularity in the expressive timing of the performance. Furthermore, because in a piece with an isochronous notated rhythm the series of interonset times is directly related (inversely propor-tional) to the tempo, no intervening data points have to be inferred, and a difficult problem (the tempo at a point in time where there is no event) can be avoided. This is why (among other reasons) the Bach *C-Major Prelude* is used so often in the literature of expressive timing and why the choice of this piece is not "awkward" at all. Smoliar's demonstration that different interpretations "unfortunately" give rise to different autocorrelation profiles, far from being a problem, is exactly what the method is intended to show: it distinguishes between different performance inter-pretations (though see page 122 for some problems and the limits of applicability of this method).

To end on a more general methodological note, Smoliar's critique demonstrates the advantages of publishing computational models and data so that they are open to immediate test. Had he published his own data in turn, his criticism would also have been open to falsification. We agree whole-heartedly with the principle that AI programs should be tested with multiple examples (page 73) and we agree that much remains to be done in the case of quantization models. Interestingly, even an algorithm that always produces a 'correct' output is not good enough: it does not validate the algorithm as a model of the cognitive process itself. If we want to make statements about the architecture of human cognition, we have to relate the architecture of the program to that of the human subject. This is still one of the major challenges of the computational modelling of music cognition.

Notes

1. All page numbers mentioned in this reply refer to this publication.
2. The model takes about n^2 cells for processing an input string of length n.
3. A recent version of the code is maintained at (URL): http://mars.let.uva.nl/honing/ABSTRACTS/DH-92-E.HTML

References

Clarke, E.F. (1987) Categorical rhythm perception: An ecological perspective. In A. Gabrielsson (Ed), *Action and Perception in Rhythm and Music*. Stockholm: Royal Swedish Academy of Music. No. 55, 19–33.

Dannenberg, R.B. (1995) Book review: Peter Desain and Henkjan Honing *Music, Mind and Machine: Studies in Computer Music, Music Cognition and Artificial Intelligence*. Music Perception, **12**(3), 365–367.

Desain, P., & Honing, H. (1992) *Music, Mind and Machine. Studies in Computer Music, Music Cognition and Artificial Intelligence*. Amsterdam: Thesis Publishers.

Desain, P., & Honing, H. (1994) Advanced issues in beat induction modeling: Syncopation, tempo and timing. In *Proceedings of the 1994 International Computer Music Conference*, pp. 92–94. San Francisco: International Computer Music Association.

Longuet-Higgins, H.C. (1976) The perception of melodies. *Nature*, **263**, 646–653. Reprinted in Longuet-Higgins (1987) *Mental Processes*. Cambridge, MA: MIT Press.

Smoliar, S.W. (1994) Modelling musical perception: A critical view. *Connection Science*, **6**(2 & 3), 209–222. (Reprinted in this volume.)

Smoliar, S.W. (1995) Book review: Peter Desain and Henkjan Honing *Music, Mind and Machine: Studies in Computer Music, Music Cognition and Artificial Intelligence*. Artificial Intelligence, **79**, 361–371.

Winograd, T., & Flores, F. (1986) *Understanding Computers and Cognition, a New Foundation for Design*. Norwood, NJ: Ablex Corp.

Part III
Melodic Memory, Structure, and Completion

Pitch-based Streaming in Auditory Perception

STEPHEN GROSSBERG

This article summarizes a neural model of how humans use pitch-based information to separate and attentively track multiple voices or instruments in distinct auditory streams, as in the cocktail party problem. The model incorporates concepts of top-down matching, attention, and resonance that have been used to analyse how humans can autonomously learn and stably remember large amounts of information in response to a rapidly changing environment. These adaptive resonance theory, or ART, concepts are joined to a spatial pitch network, or SPINET, model to form an ARTSTREAM model for pitch-based streaming. The ARTSTREAM model suggests that a resonance between spectral and pitch representations is necessary for a conscious auditory percept to occur. Examples from auditory perception in noise and context-sensitive speech perception are discussed, such as the auditory continuity illusion and phonemic restoration. The Gjerdingen analysis of apparent motion in music is shown to have a natural embedding within the ARTSTREAM model.

KEYWORDS: Streaming, pitch, harmonic sieve, neural network, adaptive resonance theory, music perception.

1. Auditory Streaming, Pitch Perception, and Music Perception

When we talk to a friend in a crowded noisy room, we can usually keep track of our conversation above the hubbub, even though the sounds emitted by the friendly voice partially overlap the sounds emitted by other speakers. How do we separate this jumbled mixture of sounds into distinct voices? This is often called the cocktail party problem. The same problem is solved whenever we listen to a symphony or other music wherein overlapping harmonic components are emitted by several instruments. If we could not separate the instruments or voices into distinct sources, or auditory streams, then we could not hear the music as music or intelligently recognize a speaker's sounds. A major cue for separating sounds into distinct sources is their pitch (Bregman, 1990). Thus, to understand how music is perceived, we need to understand how the pitch of a sound is determined and how different sources of sound are separated into distinct auditory streams.

A simple version of this competence is illustrated by the auditory continuity illusion (Miller & Licklider, 1950). This percept also calls attention to some remarkable properties of the events that lead to a conscious perception of music, or of any other sound. Suppose that a steady tone shuts off just as a broadband noise turns on. Suppose, moreover, that the noise shuts off just as the tone turns on once again

This paper was written for this volume and appears here for the first time.

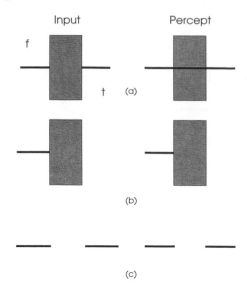

Figure 1. (a) Auditory continuity illusion: When a steady tone occurs both before and after a burst of noise, then under appropriate temporal and amplitude conditions, the tone is perceived to continue through the noise. (b) This does not occur if the noise is not followed by a tone. (c) Nor does it occur if two tones are separated by silence.

(see Figure 1a). When this happens under appropriate conditions, the tone seems to continue right through the noise, which seems to occur in a separate auditory 'stream'. This example suggests that the auditory system can actively extract those components of the noise that are consistent with the tone and use them to track the 'voice' of the tone right through the hubbub of the noise.

To appreciate how remarkable this property is, let us compare it with what happens when the tone does not turn on again for a second time, as in Figure 1b. Then the first tone does not seem to continue through the noise. It is perceived to stop before the noise. In Figure 1a, the second tone turns on only after the first tone and the subsequent noise turn off. How does the brain use the information about a future event, the second tone, to continue the first tone through the noise? Does this not seem to require that the brain can operate 'backwards in time' to alter its decision as to whether or not to continue a past tone through the noise based on future events?

The reality of this problem is emphasized by the third condition: If no noise occurs between two temporally disjoint tones, as in Figure 1c, then the tone is not heard across the silent interval. Instead, two temporally disjoint tones are heard. This fact raises the additional question: How does the brain use the noise to continue the tone through it?

Many philosophers and scientists have puzzled about this sort of problem. I will argue that the process whereby we consciously hear the first tone takes some time to unfold, so that by the time we hear it, the second tone has an opportunity to influence it. To make this argument, we need to ask, Why does conscious audition take so long to occur after the actual sound energy reaches our brain? Just as important, Why can the second tone influence the conscious percept so quickly, given that the first tone could not?

2. Phonemic Restoration, Attentive Matching, and Adaptive Resonance

I suggest that the neural mechanisms whereby auditory streaming is achieved are used, in specialized form, in other brain systems as well. Another example from the auditory system operates at a higher level of processing. It concerns how we understand speech. In this example, too, the process whereby conscious awareness occurs takes a long time, on the order of 100 ms or more. The phenomenon in question is called phonemic restoration (Samuel, 1981; Warren, 1984; Warren & Sherman, 1974). Suppose that a listener hears a noise followed immediately by the words 'eel is on the ...'. If this string of words is followed by the word 'orange', then 'noise-eel' sounds like 'peel'. If the word 'wagon' completes the sentence, then 'noise-eel' sounds like 'wheel'. If the final word is 'shoe', then 'noise-eel' sounds like 'heel'.

This example vividly shows that the bottom-up occurrence of the noise is not sufficient for us to hear it. Somehow the sound that we *expect* to hear based upon our previous language experiences influences what we do hear. Such an expectation takes time to influence the speech that we consciously hear. As in the auditory continuity illusion, the brain works 'backwards in time' to allow the meaning imparted by a later word to alter the sounds that we consciously perceive in an earlier word.

I suggest that this happens because, as the individual words occur, they are stored temporarily in a working memory. The working memory converts a temporal sequence of events into a spatial pattern of activation across the items that represent each word. A similar recoding enables musical phrases to be stored. As the items of the words are stored, they activate previously learned memories that attempt to categorize the stored sound stream into familiar language units at a higher processing level. Such learned categories encode abstract lists of items that may include the words themselves, their syllables, or even their phonemes (Cohen & Grossberg, 1986; Grossberg, 1984, 1987). Which list categories are chosen depends upon the temporal context in which all the sounds occur, whether they are the sounds of language or of music. The list category layer is designed to activate those groupings of working memory items that are most predictive in the context within which they appear.

The list categories, in turn, activate learned top-down expectations that are matched against the items stored in working memory to verify that the information expected from previous learning experiences is really there. This concept of bottom-up activation of learned categories by a working memory, followed by read-out of learned top-down expectations, is illustrated in Figure 2a.

What is the nature of this matching, or verification, process? Its properties have been clarified by experiments in which the spectral content of the noise was varied (Samuel, 1981). If the noise includes all the formants of the expected sound, then that is what the subject hears, and other spectral components of the noise are suppressed. If some formants of the expected sound are missing from the noise, then only a partial reconstruction is heard. If silence replaces the noise, then only silence is heard. The matching process thus cannot 'create something out of nothing'. It can select the expected features that are represented in the bottom-up signal and suppress the rest, as in Figure 2b.

The process whereby the top-down expectation selects some features while suppressing others helps to 'focus attention' upon information that matches our momentary expectations. By filtering out the flood of irrelevant sensory signals, expectations prevent these signals from destabilising previously learned memories (Carpenter & Grossberg, 1991; Grossberg, 1980, 1982).

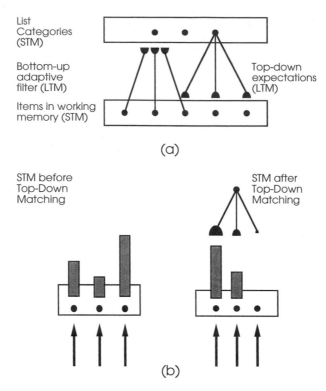

(a)

(b)

Figure 2. ART matching: (a) Auditory items activate short-term memory (STM) traces in a working memory, which send bottom-up signals toward a level at which list categories, or chunks, are activated in STM. These bottom-up signals are multiplied by learned long-term memory (LTM) traces that influence the competitive selection of the list categories that are stored in STM. The list categories, in turn, activate top-down expectation signals that are also read out of LTM. These expectations, or prototypes, are matched against the active STM pattern in working memory. (b) This matching process selects STM activations that are supported by contiguous LTM traces and suppresses those that are not.

What does all this have to do with our conscious percepts of speech and music? This can be seen by asking, If top-down expectations can select consistent bottom-up signals using attentional focus, then what keeps the attended bottom-up signals from reactivating their top-down expectations in a continuing cycle of bottom-up and top-down feedback? Nothing does! In fact, this reciprocal feedback process takes a while to equilibrate, and when it does, the bottom-up and top-down signals lock the activity patterns of the interacting levels into a resonant state that lasts much longer and is more energetic than any individual activation. I claim that only resonant states of the brain can achieve consciousness, and that the time needed for a bottom-up/top-down resonance to develop helps to explain why a conscious percept of an event takes so long to occur after its bottom-up input is delivered.

Adaptive resonance theory, or ART, is a cognitive theory that was introduced to explain how the brain continues to learn rapidly about the world throughout life without undergoing catastrophic forgetting (Carpenter & Grossberg, 1991, 1993; Grossberg, 1980, 1982, 1987). ART models how top-down expectations are learned and help to focus attention in the manner described above to ensure that learning can proceed in a stable fashion throughout life. A key result of ART is that only resonant states trigger the learning process—hence the name *adaptive* resonance—and all conscious states are resonant states. Thus the properties of conscious audition that we are discussing may be viewed as special cases of how each brain can effectively learn about its world.

The same types of properties may now be seen to hold in the auditory continuity illusion. The first main point is that bottom-up activation by the tone is not immediately perceived. A bottom-up/top-down resonance first needs to develop. This slower resonance time scale helps to explain why the tone continues to be heard even after the noise input begins. From here it is not hard to see how the second tone in Figure 1a can quickly access the already active tone resonance to keep it going through the percept of the noise, which also takes a while to develop. All the percepts are hereby shifted in time relative to the onset times of their inputs.

The type of top-down matching in the auditory continuity illusion is also similar to that in phonemic restoration. An active categorical representation of the tone, as in Figure 1a, can use its top-down expectation to select those frequency components in the noise that are compatible with it and to suppress the rest. The selected frequency components can then resonate with their category until the percept of the tone becomes conscious.

This summary clarifies some properties of the auditory continuity percept but also raises new questions as it does so. For example, what is the 'expectation' against which a sound, such as the tone, is matched? How do we hear the noise as a separate perceptual stream from the tone? In a more general cocktail party or concert hall situation, how do we hear multiple voices or instruments? What are the rules whereby multiple streams of sound are simultaneously heard, even as each stream selectively suppresses the spectral components that do not belong to its source using top-down expectations?

3. Pitch Cues for Streaming

Perhaps the most important cue for perceptual streaming is the pitch of a sound. Naturally occurring periodic sources often have harmonic frequency components at integer multiples of the fundamental frequency, F_0. The subjective experience of F_0 describes the sound's pitch. For example, when a speaker produces a vowel at a particular fundamental frequency, (e.g., 150 Hz), the vowel contains harmonics at integer multiples (e.g., 300, 450, 600 Hz, etc.), whose pattern of relative amplitudes corresponds to the vowel percept. Because such a set of related harmonics typically comes from the same sound source, a categorical representation of pitch can be used to group the corresponding harmonic components together.

Pitch-based grouping is used by listeners in both speech and music perception. For example, listeners can use F_0 to segregate multiple voices. Listeners' identification of two concurrent vowels increases as the difference in the two F_0 increases, and plateaus between .5 and 2 semitones (Scheffers, 1983). When the two F_0 are chosen an octave apart, identification is poor (Brokx & Noteboom, 1982; Chalika & Bregman, 1989). Because an octave corresponds to a doubling of frequency, half the harmonics for the two vowels will overlap. In addition, a speech formant may become segregated from the vowel in which it occurs when the formant has a different F_0 (Broadbent & Ladefoged, 1957; Gardner, Gaskill, & Darwin, 1989), and speech stimuli with discontinuous pitch contours tend to segregate at the discontinuities (Darwin & Bethell-Fox, 1977).

4. A Neural Model of Pitch Perception and Auditory Streaming

The present article summarizes a model of how humans perceive pitch-based auditory streams. This model includes a specialized filter that inputs to a grouping network. The filter is a *spatial pitch network*, or SPINET model, that models how the brain converts temporal streams of sound into spatial representations of pitch (Cohen, Grossberg, & Wyse, 1995). The grouping network is a specialized ART network that breaks sounds into separate streams based upon their pitch. The model wherein an ART streaming network is joined to a SPINET front end is called the ARTSTREAM model (Govindarajan, Grossberg, Wyse, & Cohen, 1994). This model was developed to simulate psychophysical data concerning how the brain achieves pitch-based separation and streaming of multiple acoustic sources.

First, the SPINET model will be introduced and its operations illustrated by a simulation of pitch perception. Then a circuit for ART matching and resonance will be described and incorporated into the ARTSTREAM model, whose operation will be illustrated by a simulation of streaming. Finally it will be suggested how the Gjerdingen (1994) analysis of streaming percepts in music, which was based upon the motion-perception model of Grossberg and Rudd (1989, 1992), can be incorporated into ARTSTREAM. Gjerdingen's analysis quantifies aspects of the analogy between visual and motion perception and auditory streaming that several authors have noted; see Bregman (1990) for a review. Other extensions of the ARTSTREAM model will also be discussed.

4.1. The SPINET Model

The SPINET model (Cohen, Grossberg, & Wyse, 1995) was developed to neurally instantiate ideas from the spectral pitch modeling literature and join them to neural network signal-processing designs to simulate a broader range of perceptual pitch data than in previous spectral models. Figure 3 shows the main processing stages of the SPINET model. A key goal of the model is to transform a spectral representation of an acoustic source into a spatial distribution of pitch strengths that could be incorporated into a larger network architecture, such as ARTSTREAM, for separating multiple sound sources in the environment. The SPINET model preprocesses sounds at Levels 1 to 5 to generate a spectral representation of sound across a spatial array of frequency-tuned cells at Level 6. The spatial interactions from the spectral representation of Level 6 to the pitch representation of Level 7 are critical for our analysis of pitch perception and streaming. These interactions show that SPINET is a type of pattern-matching model, a class that also includes the pitch models of Goldstein (1973) and Wightman (1973). Each possible pitch samples regions of the spectrum with a sampling period equal to the pitch frequency. That is, a region around nf_0, for integers n and fundamental frequency f_0, contributes to the strength of the pitch percept at frequency f_0. The weighting function for the region is Gaussian and symmetric in log frequency space (Figure 3), causing the resolution of the filter to scale with frequency.

In all, these interactions define a weighted 'harmonic sieve' whereby the strength of activation of a given pitch depends upon a weighted sum of narrow regions around the harmonics of the nominal pitch value, and higher harmonics contribute less to a pitch than lower ones (Duifhuis, Willems, & Sluyter, 1982; Goldstein, 1973; Scheffers, 1983; Terhardt, 1972). Suitably chosen harmonic weighting functions support computer simulations of pitch-perception data involving mistuned components (Moore, Glassberg, & Peters, 1985), shifted harmonics (Patterson &

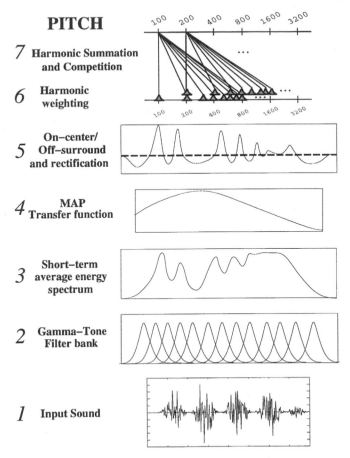

PITCH

7 **Harmonic Summation and Competition**

6 **Harmonic weighting**

5 **On–center/ Off–surround and rectification**

4 **MAP Transfer function**

3 **Short–term average energy spectrum**

2 **Gamma–Tone Filter bank**

1 **Input Sound**

Figure 3. SPINET model processing stages. See the Appendix for more details. (Reprinted with permission from Cohen, Grossberg, & Wyse [1995].)

Wightman, 1976; Schouten, Ritsma, & Cardozo, 1962), and various types of continuous spectra including rippled noise (Bilsen & Ritsma, 1970; Yost, Hill, & Perez-Falcon, 1978). The weighting functions also produce the dominance region (Plomp, 1967; Ritsma, 1967), octave shifts of pitch in response to ambiguous stimuli (Patterson & Wightman, 1976; Schouten, Ritsma, & Cardozo, 1962), and how they lead to a pitch region in response to the octave-spaced Shepard tone complexes and Deutsch tritones (Deutsch, 1992a, 1992b; Shepard, 1964) without the use of attentional mechanisms to limit pitch choices. The on-center off-surround network in the model (Level 5) helps to produce noise suppression, partial masking, and edge pitch (von Békésy, 1963). The model's peripheral filtering and short-term energy measurements (Levels 2–4) produce pitch estimates that are sensitive to certain component phase relationships (Ritsma & Engel, 1964; Moore, 1977).

Figure 4b compares an illustrative computer simulation with pitch data in Figure 4a concerning pitch shifts as a function of shifts in component harmonics. In particular, when harmonic components ($f_n = nf_0, n = 1, \ldots$) are all shifted by a constant amount, Δ, in frequency so that they maintain their spacing of f_0, ($f_n = nf_0 + \Delta, n = 1, \ldots$), the pitch shift in linear frequency is slower than that of the

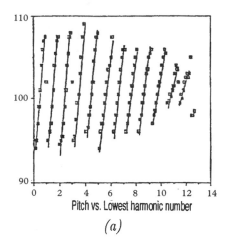
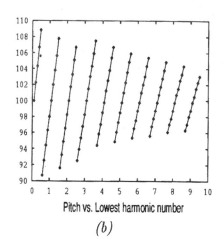

Pitch vs. Lowest harmonic number

(a)   *(b)*

Figure 4. Pitch shift in response to a complex of six components spaced by 100 Hz, as a function of the lowest component's harmonic number. (a) Data from Patterson and Wightman (1976). (b) Maximally activated pitch produced by the network model. See text for details. (Reprinted with permission from Cohen, Grossberg & Wyse [1995].)

components (Patterson & Wightman, 1976; Schouten, Ritsma, & Cardozo, 1962). The data exhibit an ambiguous pitch region at shift values of $\Delta = lf_0$, $l = .5$, $1.5, 2.5, \ldots$ where the most commonly perceived pitch jumps down to below the value of f_0. Figure 4a shows the pitch of components spaced by $f_0 = 100$ Hz as a function of the lowest component's harmonic number, l. When the shift value Δ is near a harmonic of f_0 ($\Delta = lf_0, l = 0, 1, 2, \ldots$), then the pitch is unambiguous and near 100 Hz.

The model simulates these data in Figure 4b in terms of the gradual reduction in the contribution a component makes to a pitch as it is mistuned, combined with the effect of filters whose widths are approximately constant in log coordinates for high frequencies (see Level 6 in Figure 3). As the components shift together in linear frequency away from harmonicity, the higher components move into the shallow skirts of the filters centered at harmonics of the original nominal pitch frequency much more slowly than do the lower components, thereby slowing the shift away from the original pitch. Moreover, as the lowest stimulus component increases in harmonic number, all components are moving through broader filters, so the slopes of the pitch shift become less steep, as can be seen in both the data and the model output in Figure 4.

As indicated above, other pitch data explanations of the SPINET model depend for their explanation upon properties of other model-processing levels. The full array of simulated data makes use of all these levels. A key hypothesis of the model in all these explanations is that the harmonic summation at Level 7 of Figure 3 filters each frequency spectrum through a harmonic sieve that transforms logarithmically scaled and Gaussian-weighted harmonic components into activations of pitch cells at the model's final layer. The harmonic sieve prevents spectral components that are not harmonically related to a prescribed pitch from activating the corresponding pitch node. It is assumed that the harmonic sieve gets adaptively tuned during development in response to harmonic preprocessing by peripheral acoustic mechanisms. This learning process is not explicitly modeled in SPINET,

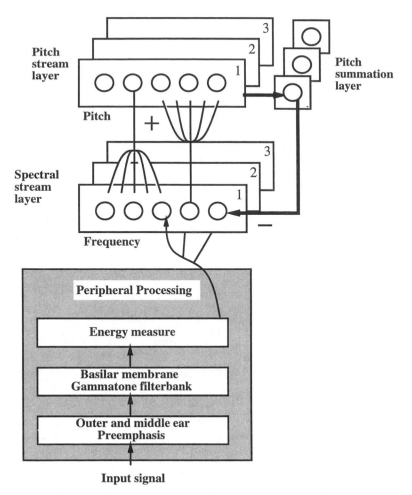

Figure 5. Block diagram of the ARTSTREAM auditory streaming model. Note the nonspecific top-down inhibitory signals from the pitch level to the spectral level that realize ART matching within the network. (Reprinted with permission from Govindarajan *et al.* [1994].)

but the use of ART matching and resonance mechanisms in the ARTSTREAM model clarifies how this learning process could occur.

4.2. ART Matching and Resonance in ARTSTREAM

In particular, the ARTSTREAM model incorporates all the stages of the SPINET model, as shown in Figure 5, but also elaborates them into multiple spectral and pitch layers that are capable of representing multiple streams of sound. As in the SPINET model, each of the bottom-up filters from spectral to pitch layers forms a harmonic sieve. In addition, there are top-down filters that also form harmonic sieves and satisfy ART matching constraints. This is how top-down signals can select those spectral components that are compatible with the chosen pitch node, while suppressing all other frequencies that may have initially activated that spectral stream layer.

These ART matching circuits satisfy the following constraints:

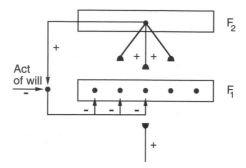

Figure 6. One way to realize the ART matching rule between two successive processing levels (a feature level F_1 and a category level F_2) using top-down activation of nonspecific inhibitory interneurons, as in Figure 5. In Figure 5, the feature level codes spectra and the category level codes pitches. In this circuit, an 'act of will' can shut off top-down inhibition, thereby enabling internally generated fantasy activities, such as hearing a familiar tune in your head, to occur. Several mathematically possible alternative ways are suggested in the Appendix of Carpenter and Grossberg (1987). See Grossberg (1995) for other applications of this rule in auditory and visual perception.

- *Bottom-up automatic activation.*   A cell, or node, can become active enough to generate output signals if it receives a large enough bottom-up input, other things being equal.
- *Top-down priming.*   A cell can become sensitized, or subliminally active, without generating output signals, if it receives only a large top-down expectation input. Such a top-down signal prepares, or primes, a cell to react more quickly and vigorously to subsequent bottom-up input that matches the top-down prime.
- *Match.*   A cell can become active if it receives large convergent bottom-up and top-down inputs. Such a matching process can generate enhanced activation as resonance takes hold.
- *Mismatch.*   A cell is suppressed even if it receives a large bottom-up input if it also receives only a small, or zero, top-down expectation input.

Figure 6 illustrates perhaps the simplest way that the ART matching rule can be realized. Figure 5 embeds this circuit into multiple copies of the spectral and pitch layers. By this scheme, bottom-up signals to the spectral stream level can excite their frequency-sensitive cells if top-down signals are not active. Top-down signals try to excite those spectral nodes that are consistent with the pitch node that activates them. By themselves, top-down signals fail to activate spectral nodes because the pitch node also activates a pitch summation layer that nonspecifically inhibits all spectral nodes in its stream. The nonspecific top-down inhibition hereby prevents the specific top-down excitation from supraliminally activating any spectral nodes. On the other hand, when excitatory bottom-up and top-down signals occur together, then those spectral nodes that receive both types of signals can be fully activated. All other nodes in that stream are inhibited, including spectral nodes that were previously activated by bottom-up signals but received no subsequent top-down pitch support. Attention hereby selectively activates consistent nodes while nonselectively inhibiting all other nodes in a stream. Because the top-down signals form a (fuzzy) harmonic sieve, only spectral components that are (nearly) harmonically related to the active pitch node can survive a top-down match.

4.3. Resonant Dynamics During Auditory Streaming

Resonant processing is used in the ARTSTREAM model to help explain separation of distinct voices or instruments into auditory streams, as in the auditory continuity illusion of Figure 1. In the ARTSTREAM model, sounds are grouped into streams at the spectral and pitch stream levels, as in Figure 5. After the auditory signals are preprocessed by SPINET mechanisms, the active spectral, or frequency, components are redundantly represented in multiple spectral streams. These streams are then filtered by bottom-up harmonic sieve signals that activate multiple representations of the sound's pitch at the pitch stream level. These pitch representations compete across streams to select a winner, which inhibits the redundant representations of the same pitch across streams. The winning pitch node also sends matching signals through its top-down harmonic sieve back to the spectral stream level. By the ART matching rule, the frequency components that are consistent with the winning pitch node are selected, and all others are suppressed. The selected frequency components reactivate their pitch node that, in turn, reads out selective top-down signals. In this way, a spectral-pitch resonance develops within the stream of the winning pitch node. The pitch layer hereby binds together the frequency components that correspond to a prescribed auditory source. The selected frequency components inhibit redundant representations of the same frequency across streams, thereby achieving a type of exclusive allocation (Bregman, 1990). In addition, all the frequency components that are suppressed by ART matching in the resonant spectral stream are freed to activate and resonate with a different pitch in a different stream, thereby realizing a type of old-plus-new heuristic (Bregman, 1990). The net result is multiple resonances, each selectively grouping together into pitches those frequencies that correspond to distinct auditory sources.

Figure 7 depicts in greater detail the balance of excitatory and inhibitory interactions within and between the spectral and pitch stream layers that enables multiple streams to capture their own frequency components and inhibit their redundant activation within other streams, while freeing other components to resonate in these streams.

Using the ARTSTREAM model, Govindarajan *et al.* (1994) have simulated a number of basic streaming percepts, including those in Figure 8. The percept summarized in Figure 8c is the auditory continuity illusion. It occurs, I contend, because the spectral stream resonance takes a while to develop that is commensurate to the duration of the subsequent noise. Once the tone resonance does develop, the second tone can quickly act through bottom-up signalling to support and maintain it throughout the duration of the noise. ART matching selects the tone from the noise, and the interstream competitive interactions enable the noise to be captured by different streams. Of course, for this to make sense, one needs to accept the fact that the tone resonance does not start to get consciously heard until well after the noise begins.

4.4. Simulation of the Auditory Continuity Illusion

Model dynamics are illustrated by a computer simulation of the auditory continuity illusion, whereby continuation of a tone occurs in noise, even though the tone is not

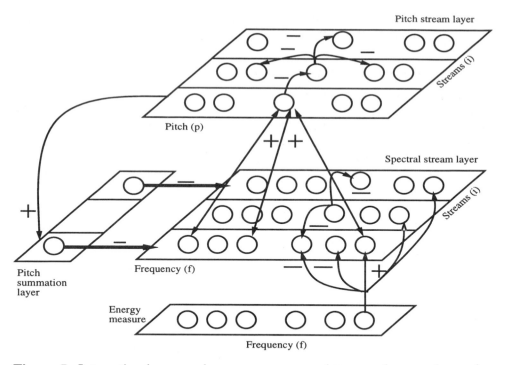

Figure 7. Interaction between the energy measure, the spectral stream layer, the pitch stream layer, and the pitch summation layer. The energy measure layer is fed forward in a frequency-specific one-to-many manner to each frequency-specific stream node in the spectral stream layer. This feed-forward activation is contrast enhanced. Competition occurs within the spectral stream layer across streams for each frequency so that a component is allocated to only one stream at a time. Each stream in the spectral stream layer activates its corresponding pitch stream in the pitch stream layer. Each pitch neuron receives excitation from its harmonics in the corresponding spectral stream. Because each pitch stream is a winner-take-all network, only one pitch can be active at any given time. Across streams in the pitch stream layer, asymmetric competition occurs for each pitch so that one stream is biased to win and the same pitch cannot be represented in another stream. The winning pitch neuron feeds back excitation to its harmonics in the corresponding spectral stream. The stream also receives nonspecific inhibition from the pitch summation layer, which sums up the activity at the pitch stream layer for that stream. This nonspecific inhibition helps to suppress those components that are not supported by the top-down excitation, which plays the role of a priming stimulus or expectation. (Reprinted with permission from Govindarajan *et al.* [1994].)

physically present in the noise (Miller & Licklider, 1950). In addition, for a tone-silence-tone stimulus (Figure 8b), the tone should not continue across the silence but should stop near the onset of silence. Figure 9 shows the simulated spectrogram and the resulting spectral layer and pitch layer activities for the tone-silence-tone stimulus for the selected stream (numbered 1) and for an unselected stream (numbered 2). The figures show that the first stream captures the tone but does not remain active in the silent interval. An acoustic percept is assumed to occur when there is a spectral-pitch resonance that supports activity in the spectral stream. Thus the tone is not perceived within the model to fill the silent interval. The same

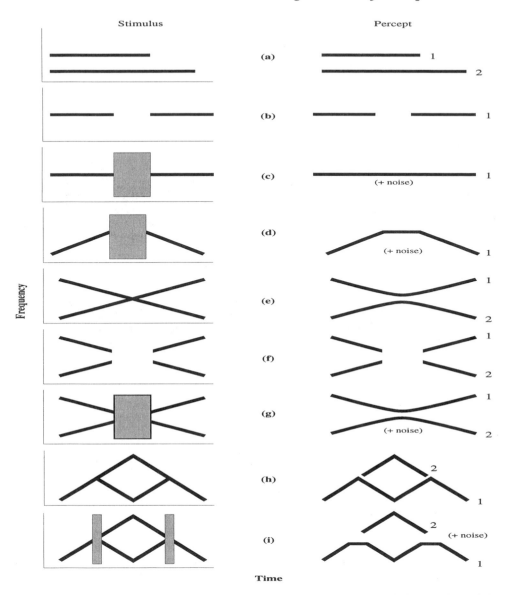

Figure 8. Illustrative stimuli and the listeners' percepts that ARTSTREAM model simulations emulate. The hashed boxes represent broadband noise. The stimuli consist of (a) two inharmonic tones, (b) tone-silence-tone, (c) tone-noise-tone, (d) a ramp or glide-noise-glide, (e) crossing glides, (f) crossing glides where the intersection point has been replaced by silence, (g) crossing glides where the intersection point has been replaced by noise, (h) Steiger diamond stimulus, and (i) Steiger diamond stimulus where bifurcation points have been replaced by noise. (Reprinted with permission from Govindarajan *et al.* [1994].)

stream then captures the tone after the silence as well. The second stream is not active because there are no other components to capture.

The simulation of the case where the silent interval is replaced by noise is illustrated by Figure 10, which shows the spectrogram and the resulting spectral and pitch layer activations of two streams. The first stream here captures the tone, and

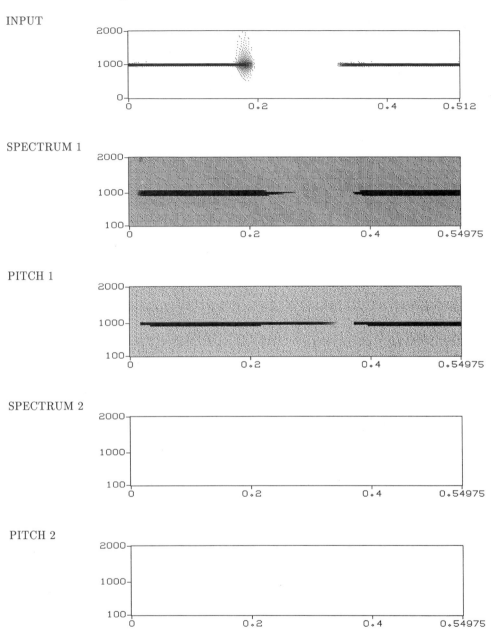

Figure 9. Computer simulation of the tone-silence-tone stimulus and percept. (Adapted with permission from Govindarajan *et al.* [1994].)

the resonance between the spectral and pitch layers continues through and past the noise interval. The noise is captured by the second stream. The use of more streams could possibly break up the noise into smaller groupings.

An extension of the ARTSTREAM model to include interactions between pitch cues and spatial location cues clarifies how acoustic sources that are placed at different angles with respect to the head can be separated into streams more easily than sources that are not. This interaction has also been used to suggest an explanation of the scale illusion of Deutsch (1975). In this percept, a downward scale

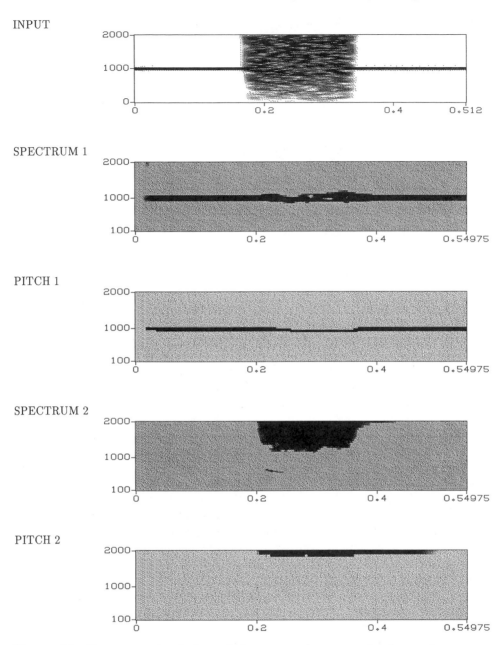

Figure 10. Computer simulation of the tone-noise-tone stimulus and percept. (Adapted with permission from Govindarajan *et al.* [1994].)

and an upward scale are played at the same time, except that every other tone in a given scale is presented to the opposite ear. Listeners group the scales based upon frequency proximity, so that the alternating ear of origin is not heard. Moreover, at the point where the scales intersect, a bounce percept is heard, so that each ear hears a rising and descending sequence of tones in one ear, and a descending and rising sequence in the other, rather than a complete scale. Thus, as in the Steiger (1980) percept of Figure 8h, grouping is dominated by frequency proximity. In all these cases, the stream resonances provide the coherence that allows distinct voices or instruments to be separated and tracked through a multiple-source environment.

4.5. Apparent Motion in Music?

The model is being further developed to emulate other streaming phenomena. For example, the existing model does not yet contain onset or offset mechanisms to help create more sharply synchronized resonant onsets and offsets. As a result, the spectral layer decays slowly at the offset of a tone. In addition, onset and offset cues can influence the segregation process itself. For example, the continuity illusion of hearing a tone in noise can be destroyed by decreasing or increasing the amplitude of the tone at the onset or offset of the noise (Bregman, 1990; Bregman & Dannenberg, 1977). Another set of data that needs further investigation demonstrates how the addition of harmonics can help overcome grouping by proximity. In particular, the addition of harmonics to one glide in a stimulus that consists of crossing ascending and descending glides can lead to a percept of crossing glides rather than of a bounce that separates them into V and inverted V percepts of pitch streaming (Bregman, 1990). Using analog, rather than winner-take-all, activations of pitch stream neurons helps to explain these cases by making the activity of pitch nodes covary with the number of harmonics that activate them.

Gjerdingen (1994; also in this volume) has exploited the similarities between apparent motion in vision and streaming in audition by applying the Grossberg and Rudd (1989, 1992) motion model to simulate a variety of streaming percepts that are found in music perception. His analysis takes as a point of departure the realization that "a great deal of the motion perceived in music is apparent rather than real. On the piano, for example, no continuous movement in frequency occurs between two sequentially sounded tones. Though a listener may perceive a movement from the first tone to the second, each tone merely begins and ends at its stationary position on the frequency continuum" (Gjerdingen, 1994, p. 335). Using the Grossberg-Rudd model, Gjerdingen has simulated properties of the van Noorden (1975) melodic-fission/temporal-coherence boundary, various Gestalt effects involving musical phrasing and rhythm, aspects of dynamic attending, and the Narmour (1990) categorical distinction between those musical intervals that imply a continuation and those that imply a reversal of direction.

In an apparent motion display, two successive flashes of light at different locations can cause a percept of continuous motion from the first flash to the second flash if their time delay and spatial separation fall within certain bounds (Kolers, 1972). A key mechanism that helps to simulate this percept in the Grossberg-Rudd model is Gaussian filtering of visual inputs across space followed by contrast-enhancing competition. If the input (flash) to one Gaussian wanes through time as the input (flash) to another waxes, then the sum of the Gaussian outputs has a maximum that moves continuously between the input locations if the Gaussians overlap sufficiently (Figure 11a). In other words, a travelling wave of activity moves continuously from one location to the other. The contrast-enhancing competition spatially localizes the maximum activity as it moves across space (Figure 11b). This Gaussian wave, or G-wave, has properties of apparent motion percepts in response to a variety of stimulus conditions.

In the acoustic domain, visual flashes are replaced by acoustic tones. Gaussian filtering of visual inputs across space followed by contrast-enhancing competition

LONG-RANGE INTERACTION

SHARP MOTION SIGNAL

$$R_i = \sum_j r_j G_{ji}$$

$$x_i^{(R)} = \begin{cases} 1 & \text{if } R_i > R_j, j \neq i \\ 0 & \text{otherwise} \end{cases}$$

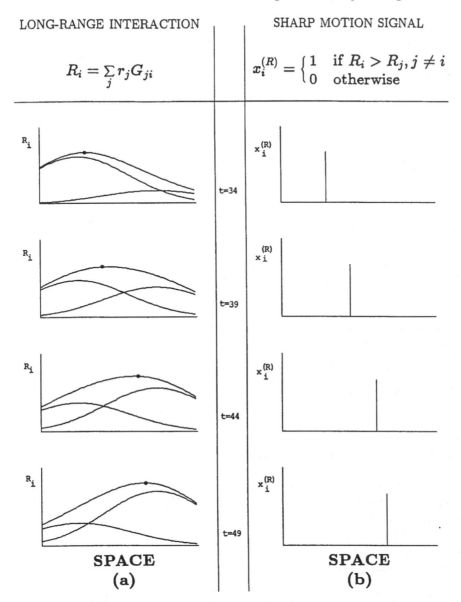

SPACE
(a)

SPACE
(b)

Figure 11. Simulation of an apparent motion G-wave. Each successively lower row depicts a later time. In (a), the two lower curves in each row depict the waning (leftward) and waxing (rightward) Gaussians through time. The upper curve depicts the sum of these Gaussians. Its maximum moves continuously from the location (on the left) of the first flash to the location (on the right) of the second flash. In (b), this maximum is plotted at successive times after the contrast-enhancing competition selects the node that receives the maximum total input. (Reprinted with permission from Grossberg and Rudd [1989].)

is replaced by Gaussian filtering of acoustic inputs across frequency followed by contrast-enhancing competition. For example, although an arpeggio is composed of temporally discrete tones, it leads to the perception of a continuous musical phrase, which Gjerdingen (1994) has compared with the properties of a G-wave. Such properties include the key fact that a G-wave can continuously link distinct tones whose relative timing is uniform but whose frequency separation is variable.

How do the Gaussian and contrast-enhancing properties needed to generate G-waves compare with properties of the ARTSTREAM model? Remarkably, these properties are already part of the spectral and pitch stream layers of the ARTSTREAM model; see equations (18) through (20) in the Appendix. Term E_{ip} there describes the Gaussian-distributed kernel $M_{f,kp}$ across frequency. Term I_{ip} describes contrast-enhancing competition. Thus the ARTSTREAM model, in its original form, already incorporates the key mechanisms for causing 'apparent motion' between successive tones. Within ARTSTREAM, these mechanisms are a manifestation of the need for harmonic grouping of frequency spectra into winning pitch representations.

Other relevant properties of the Grossberg-Rudd model are the use of transient cells that are sensitive to input onsets and offsets, and multiple spatial scales to cope with objects that move across space at variable speeds. In the acoustic domain, a movement across space at variable speeds is replaced by movement across frequencies with variable speed or spacing.

Michiro Negishi and I are now working to develop the ARTSTREM model further using the visual motion model of Chey, Grossberg, and Mingolla (1994, 1995) that builds upon the Grossberg-Rudd model. The Chey et al. model uses transient cells and multiple spatial scales to simulate human psychophysical data concerning the perceived speed and direction of moving objects. Analogous mechanisms in the ARTSTREAM model are helping to explain directionally selective auditory streaming percepts (e.g., Bregman, 1990; Steiger & Bregman, 1981) as well as properties of directionally sensitive auditory neurons (e.g., Wagner & Takahashi, 1992). All the properties simulated by Gjerdingen (1994) should also be achievable within this version of the ARTSTREAM model when the Gaussians, transient cells, and multiple scales are combined. These several developments should enable the ARTSTREAM model to simulate a broader variety of phenomena about musical phrasing and separation into multiple voices.

Finally, no learning presently exists in the ARTSTREAM model. An exploration of how an organism can learn during development to tune adaptively the harmonic sieves that abut its pitch stream representations remains to be developed. Previous analyses of learning by ART networks should provide helpful guideposts for these future studies, which may ultimately shed light on cultural differences in music perception.

Acknowledgements

This work is supported in part by the Air Force Office of Scientific Research (AFOSR F49620-92-J-0225), the Advanced Research Projects Agency (ONR N00014-92-J-4015), and the Office of Naval Research (ONR N00014-95-1-0409). The author wishes to thank Cynthia E. Bradford and Diana Meyers for their valuable assistance in the preparation of this manuscript.

References

Bilsen, F. & Ritsma, R. (1970) Some parameters influencing the perceptibility of pitch. *Journal of the Acoustical Society of America*, **47**, 469–475.

Bregman, A.S. (1990) *Auditory Scene Analysis: The Perceptual Organization of Sound*. Cambridge, MA: MIT Press.

Bregman, A.S. & Dannenbring, G. (1977) Auditory continuity and amplitude edges. *Canadian Journal of Psychology*, **31**, 151–159.

Broadbent, D.E. & Ladefoged, P. (1957) On the fusion of sounds reaching different sense organs. *Journal of the Acoustical Society of America*, **29**, 708–710.

Brokx, J.P.L. & Noteboom, S.G. (1982) Intonation and the perceptual separation of simultaneous voices. *Journal of Phonetics*, **10**, 23–26.

Carpenter, G.A. & Grossberg, S. (1987) A massively parallel architecture for a self-organizing neural pattern recognition machine. *Computer Vision, Graphics, and Image Processing*, **37**, 54–115.

Carpenter, G.A. & Grossberg, S. (1991) *Pattern Recognition by Self-Organizing Neural Networks*. Cambridge, MA: MIT Press.

Carpenter, G.A. & Grossberg, S. (1993) Normal and amnesic learning, recognition, and memory by a neural model of cortico-hippocampal interactions. *Trends in Neurosciences*, **16**, 131–137.

Chalika, M.H. & Bregman, A.S. (1989) The perceptual segregation of simultaneous auditory signals: Pulse train segregation and vowel segregation. *Perception and Psychophysics*, **46**, 487–497.

Chey, J., Grossberg, S. & Mingolla, E. (1994) *Neural Dynamics of Motion Processing and Speed Discrimination*. (Tech. Rep. No. CAS/CNS-TR-94-030). Boston University. Submitted for publication.

Chey, J., Grossberg, S. & Mingolla, E. (1995) *Neural Dynamics of Motion Speed and Directional Grouping: From Aperture Ambiguity to Plaid Coherence*. (Tech. Rep. No. CAS/CNS-TR-95-031). Boston University. Submitted for publication.

Cohen, M.A. & Grossberg, S. (1986) Neural dynamics of speech and language coding: Developmental programs, perceptual grouping, and competition for short term memory. *Human Neurobiology*, **5**, 1–22.

Cohen, M.A., Grossberg, S. & Wyse, L. (1995) A spectral network model of pitch perception. *Journal of the Acoustical Society of America*, **98**, 862–879.

Darwin, C.J. & Bethell-Fox, C.E. (1977) Pitch continuity and speech source attribution. *Journal of Experimental Psychology: Human Perception and Performance*, **3**, 665–672.

de Boer, E. & de Jongh, H.R. (1978) On cochlear encoding: Potentialities and limitations of the reverse correlation technique. *Journal of the Acoustical Society of America*, **63**, 115–135.

Deutsch, D. (1975) Two-channel listening to musical scales. *Journal of the Acoustical Society of America*, **57**, 1156–1160.

Deutsch, D. (1992a) Paradoxes of musical pitch. *Scientific American*, **264**, 88–95.

Deutsch, D. (1992b) Some new pitch paradoxes and their implications. *Philosophical Transactions of the Royal Society of London*, **336**, 391–397.

Duifhuis, H., Willems, L.F. & Sluyter, R. (1982) Measurement of pitch in speech: An implementation of Goldstein's theory of pitch perception. *Journal of the Acoustical Society of America*, **71**, 1568–1580.

Gardner, R.B., Gaskill, S.A. & Darwin, C.J. (1989) Perceptual grouping of formants with static and dynamic differences in fundamental frequency. *Journal of the Acoustical Society of America*, **85**, 1329–1337.

Gjerdingen, R.O. (1994) Apparent motion in music? *Music Perception*, **11**, 335–370.

Goldstein, J. (1973) An optimum processor theory for the central formation of the pitch of complex tones. *Journal of the Acoustical Society of America*, **54**, 1496–1515.

Govindarajan, K.K., Grossberg, S., Wyse, L.L. & Cohen, M.A. (1994) *A Neural Network Model of Auditory Scene Analysis and Source Segregation*. (Tech. Rep. No. CAS/CNS-TR-94-039). Boston University. Submitted for publication.

Grossberg, S. (1973) Contour enhancement, short-term memory, and constancies in reverberating neural networks. *Studies in Applied Mathematics*, **52**, 217–257.

Grossberg, S. (1980) How does a brain build a cognitive code? *Psychological Review*, **87**, 1–51.

Grossberg, S. (1982) *Studies of Mind and Brain*. Boston: Reidel Press.

Grossberg, S. (1984) Unitization, automaticity, temporal order, and word recognition. *Cognition and Brain Theory*, **7**, 263–283. (Reprinted in *Pattern Recognition by Self-Organizing Neural Networks*, by G.A. Carpenter & S. Grossberg, Eds., 1992, Cambridge, MA: MIT Press, pp. 593–614).

Grossberg, S. (1987) Competitive learning: From interactive activation to adaptive resonance. *Cognitive Science*, **11**, 23–63.

Grossberg, S. (1995) The attentive brain. *American Scientist*, **83**, 438–449.

Grossberg, S. & Rudd, M.E. (1989) A neural architecture for visual motion perception: Group and element apparent motion. *Neural Networks*, **2**, 421–450.

Grossberg, S. & Rudd, M.E. (1992) Cortical dynamics of visual motion perception: Short-range and long-range apparent motion. *Psychological Review*, **99**, 78–121.

Kolers, P.A. (1972) *Aspects of Motion Perception*. Elmsford, NY: Pergamon Press.

Miller, G.A. & Licklider, J.C.R. (1950) Intelligibility of interrupted speech. *Journal of the Acoustical Society of America*, **22**, 167–173.

Moore, B.C.J. (1977) Effects of relative phase of the components on the pitch of three-component complex tones. In E. Evans & J. Wilson (Eds.), *Psychophysics and Physiology of Hearing*. New York: Academic Press.

Moore, B.C.J., Glasberg, B.R. & Peters, R.W. (1985) Relative dominance of individual partials in determining the pitch of complex tones. *Journal of the Acoustical Society of America*, **77**, 1853–1860.

Narmour, E. (1990) *The Analysis and Cognition of Basic Melodic Structures: The Implication-Realization Model*. Chicago: University of Chicago Press.

Patterson, R. & Wightman, F. (1976) Residue pitch as a function of component spacing. *Journal of the Acoustical Society of America*, **59**, 1450–1459.

Plomp, R. (1967) Pitch of complex tones. *Journal of the Acoustical Society of America*, **41**, 1526–1533.

Ritsma, R. (1967) Frequencies dominant in the perception of the pitch of complex sounds. *Journal of the Acoustical Society of America*, **42**, 191–198.

Ritsma, R. & Engel, F. (1964) Pitch of frequency-modulated signals. *Journal of the Acoustical Society of America*, **36**, 1637–1644.

Samuel, A.G. (1981) Phonemic restoration: Insights from a new methodology. *Journal of Experimental Psychology: General*, **110**, 474–494.

Scheffers, M.T.M. (1983) *Sifting Vowels: Auditory Pitch Analysis and Sound Segregation*. Unpublished doctoral dissertation, Groningen University, The Netherlands.

Schouten, J., Ritsma, R. & Cardozo, B. (1962) Pitch of the residue. *Journal of the Acoustical Society of America*, **34**, 1418–1424.

Shepard, R. (1964) Circularity in judgments of relative pitch. *Journal of the Acoustical Society of America*, **36**, 2346–2353.

Steiger, H. (1980) *Some Informal Observations Concerning the Perceptual Organization of Patterns Containing Frequency Glides*. (Tech. Rep.). McGill University, Montreal.

Steiger, H. & Bregman, A.S. (1981) Capturing frequency components of glided tones: Frequency separation, orientation, and alignment. *Perception and Psychophysics*, **30**, 425–435.

Terhardt, E. (1972) Zur Tonhöhenwahrnehmung von Klängen. *Acustica*, **26**, 173–199.

van Noorden, L.P.A.S. (1975) *Temporal Coherence in the Perception of Tone Sequences*. Unpublished doctoral dissertation, Eindhoven University of Technology, The Netherlands.

von Békésy, G. (1963) Hearing theories and complex sound. *Journal of the Acoustical Society of America*, **35**, 588–601.

Wagner, H. & Takahashi, T. (1992) Influence of temporal cues on acoustic motion-direction sensitivity of auditory neurons in the owl. *Journal of Neurophysiology*, **68**, 2063–2076.

Warren, R.M. (1984) Perceptual restoration of obliterated sounds. *Psychological Bulletin*, **96**, 371–383.

Warren, R.M. & Sherman, G.L. (1974) Phonemic restoration based on subsequent context. *Perception and Psychophysics*, **16**, 150–156.

Wightman, F.L. (1973) The pattern-transformation model of pitch. *Journal of the Acoustical Society of America*, **54**, 407–416.

Yost, W., Hill, R. & Perez-Falcon, T. (1978) Pitch and pitch discrimination of broadband signals with rippled power spectra. *Journal of the Acoustical Society of America*, **63**, 1166–1173.

Appendix

The mathematical equations that define the ARTSTREAM model, including its embedded SPINET mechanisms, are now summarized to clarify how pitch-based streaming is achieved by it.

Outer and Middle Ear

The outer and middle ear act as a broad bandpass filter that linearly boosts frequencies between 100 to 5000 Hz. This is approximated by preemphasizing the signal using a difference equation:

$$y(t) = x(t) - A * x(t - \Delta t) \tag{1}$$

where A is the preemphasis parameter, and Δt is the sampling interval. In the simulations, A was set to 0.95, and $\Delta t = 0.125$ ms, corresponding to a sampling frequency of 8 kHz.

Cochlear Filterbank

The basilar membrane acts like a filterbank whose responses at a particular location act like a bandpass filter. This bandpass characteristic was modeled as a fourth-order gammatone (de Boer & de Jongh, 1978; Cohen, Grossberg, & Wyse, 1995) filter:

$$g_{f_0}(t) = \begin{cases} t^{n-1}e^{-2\pi t b(f_0)}\cos(2\pi f_0 t + \phi) & t > 0 \\ 0 & \text{otherwise} \end{cases} \tag{2}$$

Its frequency response is

$$G_{f_0}(f) = [1 + j(f - f_0)/b(f_0)]^n \tag{3}$$

where n is the order of the filter, f_0 is the center frequency of the filter, ϕ is a phase factor, and $b(f)$ is the gammatone filter's bandwidth parameter, corresponding to

$$b(f) = 1.02 * \text{ERB}(f) \tag{4}$$

The equivalent rectangular bandwidth (ERB) of a gammatone filter is the equivalent bandwidth that a rectangular filter would have if it passed the same power:

$$\text{ERB}(f) = 6.23e^{-6}f^2 + 93.39e^{-3}f + 28.52 \tag{5}$$

Sixty gammatone filters, which were equally spaced in ERB, were used to cover the range 100 Hz to 2000 Hz. The output of each gammatone filter was converted into an energy measure.

Energy Measure

The energy measure measures a short-time energy spectrum

$$e_f(t) = \frac{\Delta t}{W} \sum_{k=0}^{W/\Delta t} |g_f(t - k\Delta t)|^2 e^{-\alpha \Delta t k} \tag{6}$$

where $e_f(t)$ is the energy measure output of the gammatone filter $g_f(t)$ centered at frequency f at time t, W is the time window over which the energy measure is computed, and α represents the decay of the exponential window. In the simulations, $\alpha = 0.995$, and $W = 5$ ms. The output of the energy measure sends the same signal pattern to the multiple fields in the spectral stream layer.

Spectral Stream Layer

The spectral stream layer is a plane with one axis representing frequency and the other axis representing different auditory streams. Each frequency channel inputs the energy measure e_f in equation (6) to each spectral stream layer in a one-to-many manner, so that all streams in the spectral stream layer receive equal bottom-up excitation. After the spectral stream layer becomes activated, the different streams activate their corresonding pitch streams in the pitch stream layer. When a pitch is selected in a given stream, it feeds back excitation to its spectral harmonics and inhibits that pitch in other streams of the pitch stream layer. In addition, non-specific inhibition, via the pitch summation layer, helps to realize ART matching and thereby to suppress those spectral components that do not belong to the given pitch within its stream.

The following equation describes the dynamics of the spectral stream layer:

$$\frac{d}{dt} S_{if} = -AS_{if} + [B - S_{if}]E_{if} - [C + S_{if}]I_{if} \tag{7}$$

where

$$E_{if} = \sum_g D_{fg}s(e_g) + F \sum_p \sum_k M_{f,kp}g(P_{ip})h(k) \tag{8}$$

and

$$I_{if} = \sum_{g \neq f} E_{fg}s(e_g) + \mathcal{J} \sum_{k \neq i} \sum_g N_{fg}[S_{kg}]^+ + LT_i \tag{9}$$

In equation (7), S_{if} is the activity of the spectral stream layer neuron corresponding to the ith stream and frequency f. Equation (7) is a membrane, or shunting equation, with passive decay $(-AS_{if})$, excitation $([B - S_{if}]E_{if})$, and inhibition $(-[C + S_{if}]I_{if})$ terms. The total excitatory input is E_{if} and the total inhibitory input is I_{if}. The excitatory term $D_{fg}s(e_g)$ in equation (8) is the bottom-up excitatory input from the energy measure, which has been passed through a sigmoid signal function $s(x)$ to contrast-enhance its signal and to compress its dynamic range:

$$s(x) = \begin{cases} x^2/(N_s + x^2) & \text{if } x > 0 \\ 0 & \text{otherwise} \end{cases} \tag{10}$$

Similarly, $E_{fg}s(e_g)$ in equation (9) is the bottom-up inhibitory input from the energy measure, which has also been passed through a sigmoid $s(x)$. Both $D_{fg}s(e_g)$ and $E_{fg}s(e_g)$ thus input to each spectral stream layer a contrast-enhanced version of the energy measure. Signal $s(e_g)$ is distributed across frequencies by the kernels D_{fg} and E_{fg}, which are Gaussians that are centred at frequency f, have standard deviation parameters σ_D and σ_E, and scaling parameters D and E, respectively:

$$D_{fg} = DG(f, \sigma_D) = D \frac{1}{\sigma_D \sqrt{2\pi}} e^{-.5(f-g)^2/\sigma_D^2} \tag{11}$$

$$E_{fg} = EG(f, \sigma_E) = E \frac{1}{\sigma_E \sqrt{2\pi}} e^{-.5(f-g)^2/\sigma_E^2} \tag{12}$$

The on-center $D_{fg}s(e_g)$ and off-surround $E_{fg}s(e_g)$ inputs balance each other so that the spectral stream layer can respond sensitively, without saturation, to the pattern of $s(e_g)$ signals across frequency (Grossberg, 1973, 1982).

Term $F \sum_p \sum_k M_{f,kp}g(P_{ip})h(k)$ in equation (8) is the top-down harmonic sieve signal. It sums all the pitches p that have a harmonic kp near frequency f in the pitch stream layer that corresponds to stream i. In equation (8), P_{ip} is the activity that represents pitch p in stream i, and $g(x)$ is a sigmoid function:

$$g(x) = \begin{cases} x^2/(N_g + x^2) & \text{if } x > 0 \\ 0 & \text{otherwise} \end{cases} \tag{13}$$

$h(k)$ is the harmonic weighting function, which weights the lower harmonics more heavily than higher harmonics:

$$h(K) = \begin{cases} 1 - M_h \log_2(k) & \text{if } 0 < M_h \log_2(k) < 1 \\ 0 & \text{otherwise} \end{cases} \tag{14}$$

and $M_{f,kp}$ is a normalized Gaussian that represents the top-down harmonic sieve. If a harmonic is slightly mistuned, it will still be within the Gaussian and thus get partially reinforced. The width of the Gaussian dictates the tolerance for mistuning. Kernel $M_{f,kp}$ is centered at frequency f and has a standard deviation parameter, σ_M:

$$M_{f,kp} = G(f, \sigma_M) = \frac{1}{\sigma_M \sqrt{2\pi}} e^{-.5(f-kp)^2/\sigma_M^2} \tag{15}$$

Term $\mathcal{J} \sum_{k \neq i} \sum_g N_{fg} [S_{kg}]^+$ in equation (9) represents the competition across streams for a component, so that a harmonic will resonate within only one stream. This inhibition embodies the principle of 'exclusive allocation' (Bregman, 1990). Because a harmonic can be mistuned slightly, a Gaussian window N_{fg} exists within which the competition takes place. Kernel N_{fg} is centered at frequency f and has a standard deviation parameter, σ_N:

$$N_{fg} = G(f, \sigma_N) = \frac{1}{\sigma_N \sqrt{2\pi}} e^{-.5(f-g)^2/\sigma_N^2} \tag{16}$$

Term LT_i in equation (9) is the top-down inhibition from the pitch summation layer that nonspecifically inhibits all components in stream i. It hereby suppresses those nonharmonic components that are not reinforced by the top-down harmonic sieve excitation from the active pitch unit in the ith pitch stream layer. This is akin to the matching process that is used in ART.

In all the simulations of Govindarajan *et al.* (1994), the parameters were set to $A = 1$, $B = 1$, $C = 1$, $D = 500$, $E = 450$, $F = 3$, $\mathcal{J} = 1000$, $L = 5$, $M_h = .3$, $N = .01$, $N_s = 10000$, $N_g = .01$, $\sigma_D = .2$, $\sigma_E = 4$, $\sigma_M = .2$, and $\sigma_N = 1$.

Pitch Summation Layer

The pitch summation layer sums up the pitch activity at stream i and provides nonspecific inhibition LT_i to stream i's spectral stream layer in equations (7) to (9) so that only those harmonic components that correspond to the selected pitch node remain active. The activity T_i of the ith pitch summation layer obeys

$$\frac{d}{dt} T_i = -AT_i + [B - T_i] \sum_p g(P_{ip}) \tag{17}$$

where $g(x)$ is the sigmoid function described above. In the simulations, $A = 100$, $B = 100$.

Pitch Stream Layer

In the ARTSTREAM model, the spectral and pitch representations of the SPINET model are modified to allow multiple streams to cooperate and compete between pitch units within and across streams. The pitch strength activation P_{ip} of pitch p in stream i obeys a membrane equation:

$$\frac{d}{dt}P_{ip} = -AP_{ip} + [B - P_{ip}]E_{ip} - [C + P_{ip}]I_{ip} \tag{18}$$

where

$$E_{ip} = E \sum_{k} \sum_{f} M_{f,kp}[S_{if} - \Gamma]^{+}h(k) \tag{19}$$

and

$$I_{ip} = \mathcal{J} \sum_{p \neq q} H_{pq}g(P_{iq}) + L \sum_{k > i} g(P_{kp}) \tag{20}$$

Term $E \sum_{k} \sum_{f} M_{f,kp}[S_{if} - \Gamma]^{+}h(k)$ in equation (19) corresponds to the bottom-up harmonic sieve input. Kernel $M_{f,kp}$ in equation (19) Gaussianly filters signals from the spectral layer that have suprathreshold components near a harmonic kp of pitch p. This Gaussian kernel is further weighted by the harmonic weighting function $h(k)$. The harmonic weighting function $h(k)$ and the Gaussian $M_{f,kp}$ are the same as in the spectral layer (equations (14) and (15), respectively). Term $\mathcal{J} \sum_{p \neq q} H_{pq}g(P_{iq})$ in equation (20) allows pitches to compete within a stream. This off-surround competition across pitches within a stream converts each pitch stream into a winner-take-all network (Grossberg, 1973, 1982) wherein only one pitch tends to be active within each stream. For simplicity, kernel H_{pq} is defined to be one within a neighborhood around pitch unit j and zero otherwise, so that a stream can maintain a pitch even if the pitch fluctuates:

$$H_{pq} = \begin{cases} 1 & \text{if } |p - q| > \sigma_H \\ 0 & \text{otherwise} \end{cases} \tag{21}$$

Term $L \sum_{k > i} g(P_{kp})$ in equation (20) represents inhibition across streams for a given pitch, so that only one stream can activate a given pitch. This is a form of asymmetric inhibition, from higher to lower pitches, that prevents deadlock from occurring between two streams that are competing for a given pitch. This inhibition breaks the symmetry that arises from the fact that all pitch streams initially receive equal bottom-up excitation from the spectral layer. In all the simulations, the parameters were set to $A = 100$, $B = 1$, $C = 10$, $E = 5000$, $\mathcal{J} = 300$, $L = 2$, $\sigma_H = .2$, and $\Gamma = .005$.

Apparent Motion in Music?

ROBERT O. GJERDINGEN

A great deal of the motion perceived in music is apparent rather than real. On the piano, for example, no continuous movement in frequency occurs between two sequentially sounded tones. Though a listener may perceive a movement from the first tone to the second, each component frequency of each tone merely begins and ends at or very near its stationary position on the frequency continuum. Recent advances in the modeling of apparent-motion effects in vision provide a starting point for the modeling of the strong apparent-motion effects in music. An adaptation of the Grossberg-Rudd model of apparent motion in vision, when given input representing the strengths of pitch sensations positioned along a one-dimensional frequency continuum, can simulate important musical phenomena of auditory stream segregation, van Noorden's melodic-fission/temporal-coherence boundaries, various Gestalt effects, aspects of dynamic attending, and Narmour's predicted categorical distinction between musical intervals implying a continuation and those implying a reversal of direction.

KEYWORDS: Apparent motion, Grossberg & Rudd, artificial neural networks, musical motion, Gestalt pattern perception.

> I hear the melody and its accompaniment even when they are played by an old-fashioned clock where each tone is separate from the others. —Wertheimer, 1923

1. Introduction

A psychologist, recreating one of the classic demonstrations of Gestalt principles for a group of undergraduates, places a row of lights at the front of a lecture hall. After darkening the room, she briefly flashes the lights from left to right in rapid sequence. The students see not isolated flashes (the physical reality) but rather an integrated perception of motion from one flash to the next. On the other side of campus an organist, demonstrating the subject of a Bach fugue for a music-appreciation class, presses the series of keys that sound the organ's pipes in the proper sequence. The students hear not isolated, static frequencies (the physical reality) but rather an integrated perception of melody moving from one tone to the next. The psychologist's flashing lights produce a phenomenon known as apparent motion (Exner, 1875; Kolers, 1972; Körte, 1915; Wertheimer, 1912). Do the organist's sounding pipes produce the same phenomenon? Is the "striking parallel" (Bregman, 1990, p. 21) between apparent motion in vision and in music more than just a tempting analogy?

This article is a revised version of 'Apparent Motion in Music?', *Music Perception*, 1994, **11**, 335–370, reprinted with permission of the University of California Press.

In their everyday speech, musicians clearly take it for granted that music moves. Melodies 'go' here and there, instruments 'run' up and down scales, vibrato 'wobbles' around a central pitch, trills 'shake', chords 'leap' to higher or lower ranges, and so forth. The allied notion that tones leave behind a curvilinear trace of their motion has so deeply ingrained itself in musical discourse that, for example, 'melody' and 'melodic line' have become all but synonymous. Yet even if musicians—and listeners in general—concur in sensing motion in music, there is little agreement about the nature of the motion (Zuckerkandl, 1956). In viewing a classic visual demonstration of apparent motion, one can easily imagine an intermittently flashing light source that moves in normal three-dimensional space. In hearing the subject of a Bach fugue, however, it is not at all clear what is moving or where that motion takes place. So in the sense that a melody is not imagined as the product of an intermittently sounding, physically moving tone source, the analogy between apparent motion in vision and apparent motion in music breaks down.

If this often-mentioned analogy (Bregman, 1990; Miller & Heise, 1950; van Noorden, 1975; Wertheimer, 1923) does not rest on high-level ascriptions of source and meaning, then perhaps it is grounded instead on shared low-level, Gestalt-like grouping processes that yield smooth, continuous traces of motion from discontinuous inputs. This article will explore the conjecture that many motion percepts in music may be a product of the same type of neural circuitry proposed by Grossberg and Rudd (1989) to explain apparent-motion percepts in vision. The Grossberg-Rudd model is a massively parallel, multiplex, feed-forward neural-network system. Its nonlinear internal dynamics, though complicated in detail, nevertheless endow the behavior of the system as a whole with a measure of simplicity. In the following sections I will first present an overview of the Grossberg-Rudd model, stressing the emergent simplicity of its overall behavior, and then demonstrate how this motion-tracking system can account for various apparent-motion effects in music. These will include aspects of what more specialized studies have described as melodic fission (Miller & Heise, 1950), various Gestalt effects (Meyer, 1956), auditory stream segregation (Bregman & Campbell, 1971), temporal coherence (van Noorden, 1975), dynamic attending (Jones & Boltz, 1989), and the predicted categorical distinction between musical intervals implying a continuation and those implying a reversal of direction (Narmour, 1990).

2. The Basic Grossberg-Rudd Model

The stimuli that prompt the illusion of apparent motion are, as already illustrated, often discontinuous in both space and time. A motion-tracking system must thus be capable of smoothing out both spatial and temporal discontinuities if it is to reintegrate discrete stimuli into a continuous percept of motion. The neural-network architecture of Grossberg and Rudd (1989) accomplishes the requisite reintegrations through the agencies of specialized processing levels. These levels, though originally described solely in terms of the visual system, can be generalized as stages of information processing that deal with (1) input, (2) temporal reintegration, (3) spatial reintegration, and (4) motion analysis. Figure 1 shows these four processing levels in schematized form.

2.1. Level 1: Input

Level 1, when adapted for music input, approximates a one-dimensional continuum of virtual pitch sensations (Terhardt, 1974, 1984). That is, the model assumes

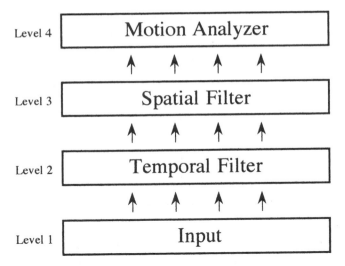

Figure 1. A schematization of four processing levels in the Grossberg-Rudd model of motion tracking.

that the auditory system, at some stage prior to the motion-tracking system, reduces the multiple signals produced by the many frequency components of a complex tone to a unitary signal of perceived pitch. That signal then excites only one point along the pitch continuum in the first level of the motion-tracking system. The assumption of pitch localization prior to motion analysis may, on the one hand, be an oversimplification, inasmuch as motion analysis probably contributes to pitch localization (Bregman, 1990). Moreover, the present model does not require pitch localization for the simulation of simple apparent-motion effects created by solo melodies or single bands of noise. On the other hand, more complex apparent-motion effects such as the tracking of individual melodic lines in a multivoice musical texture are difficult to explain without either the prior unitization of pitch sensations or some more inclusive model of the interaction of motion analysis with the determination of pitch and timbre. In any case, the computer simulations described below all assume a strict form of prior pitch determination in which a (simulated) musical tone excites, at any one moment, only one of 980 separate pitch positions in Level 1, each position representing a 5-cent (1/20th-of-a-semitone) interval of the four-octave range from C_2 to C_6. Thus the model has a very fine-grained response to simulated pitch sensations, much finer than even the most micro of microtones and independent of any culturally determined scale system.

2.2. *Level 2: Temporal Reintegration*

Level 2 receives signals from each and every Level 1 pitch position and processes them simultaneously on the basis of their individual amplitude envelopes. In the simplest case, Level 2 just smooths out rapid changes in signal intensities by averaging them over time (the special treatment of signal transients will be discussed later). Figure 2 illustrates how the output of the ith Level 2 processing unit alters the angular rise and fall of the ith Level 1 signal (assumed here to maintain the square-wave-like amplitude envelope of the simulated sound). This smoothing or temporal smudging can be modeled by various designs for neural dynamics. For

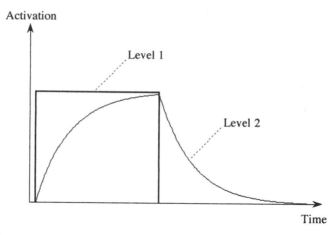

Figure 2. Output from Level 1 represents a simulated tone whose amplitude envelope has an instantaneous rise, a constant sustain, and an instantaneous decay. Level 2 smooths out rapid changes in Level 1 activations by averaging them over time.

the computer simulations described below, however, the actual time averages were calculated directly by numerical approximation (Euler's method) to the differential equation

$$d/dt\, x_i = -Ax_i + I_i \tag{1}$$

where x_i is the activation strength of the ith pitch location at Level 2, A is its decay rate ($A = 0.03125$ in the simulations), and I_i is the signal strength of the ith pitch location at Level 1.

As an abstract algorithm for updating a single Level 2 unit, equation (1) requires five operations. First, get the previous activation value x. Second, multiply that value times the decay factor A to get the amount that x will decay by the next time step. Third, subtract that decay from any new input I arriving from the corresponding Level 1 unit. Fourth, take this change in the value of x (symbolized by dx) and divide it by the change in time (symbolized by dt) representing the next time step. Fifth, add this positive or negative change in activation to the previous activation of x. Repeat these five operations for each new time step.

2.3. Level 3: Spatial Reintegration

If Level 2 can be said to diffuse discrete temporal events over a wider span of time, Level 3 diffuses discrete pitch events over a wider span of frequency (cf. Seibert & Waxman, 1989). Figure 3 depicts how a signal from the ith Level 2 unit diffuses across a broad log-frequency band of Level 3 units. The shape of that diffusion is assumed to approximate a Gaussian distribution (i.e. a standard bell curve) whose height varies in proportion to the strength of the received Level 2 signal and whose standard deviation is an arbitrary musical interval of width W. The spatial diffusion of Level 3, in conjunction with the temporal diffusion of Level 2, transforms a unitary Level 1 signal into a broadly distributed, smoothly rising and falling Level 3 response, as shown in Figure 4.

The activity of the ith processing unit in Level 1 has no effect on the activities of other units in the same level. The same is true of units within Level 2. In Level 3,

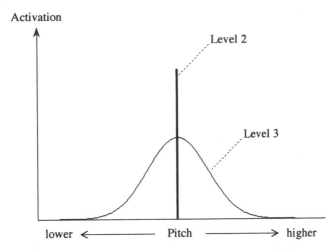

Figure 3. An output signal from the *i*th Level 2 unit diffuses across a broad pitch band of Level 3 units. The diffusion is assumed to approximate a Gaussian distribution.

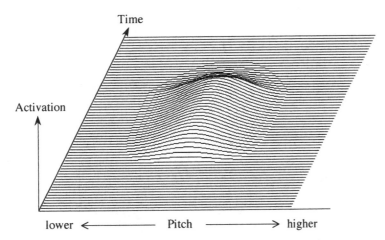

Figure 4. The spatial diffusion of Level 3, in conjunction with the temporal diffusion of Level 2, transforms a unitary Level 1 output signal into a broadly distributed, smoothly rising and falling Level 3 response.

however, the diffusion from one Level 2 signal often overlaps the diffusion from another Level 2 signal, producing a summed effect of both signals. For a given degree of diffusion, that is, for a given standard deviation of musical interval W, the Level 3 response to tones more than 2W apart in pitch differs markedly from that to tones less than 2W apart (Grossberg, 1977). Figure 5 illustrates the case of a melodic interval where the first tone is a simulated A_4 (440 Hz), the second tone is an octave higher at A_5 (880 Hz), and the value of W equals a minor third (chosen as a rough approximation of one critical bandwidth in this frequency range). Because the melodic interval of an octave ($= 4W$) far exceeds 2W, there is relatively little interaction between the two Gaussian distributions. Consequently the figure gives the visual impression of the sequential rise and fall of two distinct phenomena.

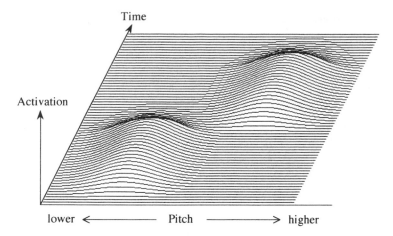

Figure 5. The response on the front left is to a simulated A_4 (440 Hz), the subsequent response on the back right to a simulated A_5 (880 Hz). Given a Level 2 to Level 3 signal diffusion resulting in Gaussian distributions whose standard deviations (W) equal a minor third, the melodic interval of an octave (= 4W) is greater than the critical distance of 2W. In consequence, there is little overlap between the two Gaussian distributions.

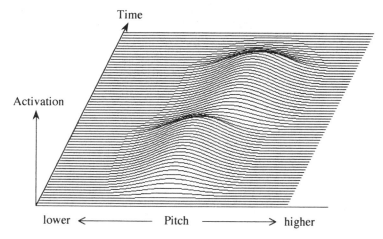

Figure 6. The response near the lower center left is to a simulated D_5, the subsequent response near the upper center right to a simulated F_5. With a value of W equal to a minor third, the melodic interval D_5-F_5 (= W) is less than the critical distance of 2W. In consequence, there is considerable overlap between the two responses.

Figure 6, by contrast, illustrates the case of a smaller melodic interval where the first tone is a simulated D_5, the second tone is a minor third higher at F_5, and W again equals a minor third. Because this melodic interval (= W) is less than 2W, there is considerable interaction between the two Gaussian distributions. The decay of D_5 overlaps the rise of F_5 to such an extent that the figure may be interpreted as presenting the apparent motion of a single undulating phenomenon that shifts to a higher pitch level between successive peaks of activation.

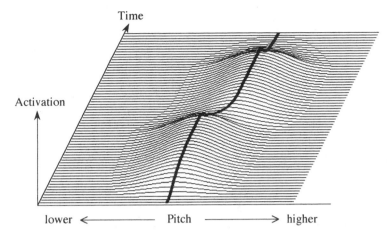

Figure 7. A heavy black line traces the moment-by-moment local maxima of the Level 3 activations shown previously in Figure 6. As the response to the first tone begins to decay and the response to the second, higher tone begins to rise, the trace of Level 3 maxima moves smoothly toward the right.

The calculation of Level 3's profile of activation presents a challenge due to the interaction of every Level 3 unit with every other Level 3 unit: 980 × 980, or just short of one million, interactions. The interactions, however, are only additive. Moreover, the bell-curved diffusion function need not be calculated one million times for each of a thousand time steps. Instead, it is possible to calculate the function once and then merely scale and translate it in reference to each Level 3 unit's activation and position. A simulated second of motion tracking may thus still require several billion computer operations, but the operations can be of a type that a digital computer performs most swiftly.

2.4. Level 4: Motion Analysis

Level 4 (and implicitly any higher level) must, in some fashion, analyze the activity at Level 3. At a minimum, such analysis must involve tracking the peaks of Level 3 activations as they move from one location to another. Thus Level 4 must thus somehow reverse the process that occurred from Level 2 to Level 3, where single points diffused into broad distributions. Lateral inhibition provides the essential neuronal process for accomplishing that task. In particular, if broad Level 3 distributions are transmitted to Level 4, and if there is strong lateral inhibition between Level 4 units, then maxima of Level 3 activations can translate at Level 4 into either narrower distributions or, in the limiting case, to single points of activation.

Figure 7 traces, with a heavy black line, the moment-by-moment local maxima of the Level 3 activations shown previously in Figure 6. Notice how, as the first pitch begins to decay and the second begins to rise, the trace of Level 3 maxima moves smoothly toward the right. Figure 8 eliminates the varying activation levels of this trace to show an idealized Level 4 analysis of Level 3 activity, what I will henceforth term a *motion trace*. The simulations described below produce this motion trace algorithmically through the identification of local maxima. A full implementation of lateral inhibition leads to problems of hysteresis that extend conceptually well beyond the scope of this article.

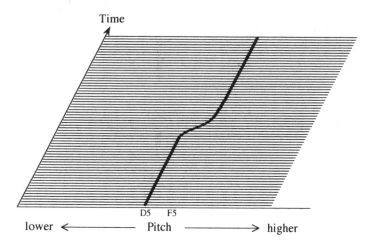

Figure 8. Eliminating the varying activation levels shown previously in Figure 7 creates an idealized Level 4 analysis of Level 3 activity, here termed a *motion trace*.

Further refinements in both the Grossberg-Rudd model and its predecessors (Burt & Sperling, 1981; Marr & Ullman, 1981; Seibert & Waxman, 1989) found their motivations in problems raised by special visual phenomena. For instance, whereas the above-described Level 2 responses to the intensities of flashing lights were sufficient to model the so-called beta or phi phenomena of apparent motion, the problem of simulating the shift from apparent group motion to apparent element motion in the Ternus display (Ternus 1926/1950) led Grossberg and Rudd to add to their model the agency of detectors sensitive to signal transients. Rather than review these refinements with respect to visual perception, I will instead attempt to show how the same refinements would grow out of problems posed by music perception.

3. Tracking Individual Voices in a Polyphonic Texture

Figure 9 presents both the musical notation of the final half measure of Bach's G-minor prelude from *The Well-tempered Clavier*, Book I (1722) and the motion traces that this excerpt generated (note the rotation of axes compared with Figure 8: Pitch is now the vertical axis and time the horizontal axis; only the traces for the upper three voices are shown because the trace for the missing bass voice is merely a straight line). Because Bach happened to keep all the voices separated from each other by intervals of a fifth or more (>2W) the basic model described above had no difficulty in producing four separate motion traces (cf. Huron, 1989). Had, however, Bach voiced this passage as shown in Figure 10, with the tenor D_3 transposed an octave higher to D_4, the motion-tracking model (even with a smaller W = major second) would no longer be able to distinguish between the tenor and alto voices. A musically trivial change would have a catastrophic effect on the model's analysis, which, as the figure shows, no longer conforms to the contour of the moving alto voice.

The problem could be resolved in part by switching attention to a still narrower W. Yet a W smaller than a semitone would be required to segregate C_4 and D_4 into distinct streams. More likely the problem lies in the model having responded just as strongly to the held portions of the long tones as it did to the musically more salient tones in the rapidly moving voice. To surmount this problem the model must have a means of responding preferentially to change rather than to stasis. As mentioned,

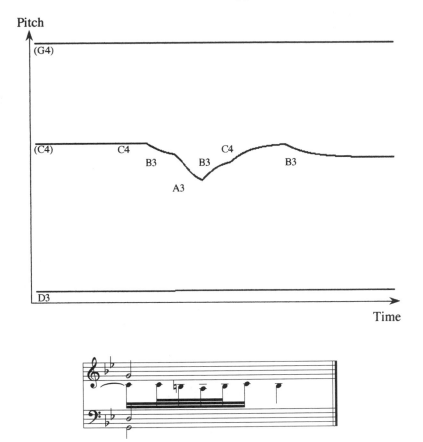

Figure 9. The musical notation of the final half measure of J.S. Bach's G-minor prelude from *The Well-tempered Clavier*, Book I (1722) and the motion traces generated by a simulation of this excerpt. As compared with Figure 8, the pitch and time axes have rotated: Here pitch is the vertical axis and time the horizontal axis. Traces are shown for the upper three voices only; the trace for the bass voice is, like the traces for the similarly stationary soprano and tenor (G_4 and D_3), merely a straight line.

such a means was introduced by Grossberg and Rudd (1989) in the form of detectors at Level 2 that respond to signal transients. For the computer simulations, the response of these transient detectors is given by approximation to the differential equation

$$d/dt\, x_i = -Bx_i + CF_i \tag{2}$$

where x_i is the activation strength of the ith pitch location at level two, B is its decay rate ($B = 0.03125$ in the simulations), F_i is the magnitude of the difference between the values of the ith input signal at times t and $t-1$, and C is a constant ($C = 0.03125$ in the simulations). Algorithmically, equation (2) is much the same as equation (1) except for the substitution of 'change in Level 1 input from the last time step' (CF) for 'Level 1 input' (I).

The signal then sent on to Level 3 is the *product* of the moment-by-moment outputs of equations (1) and (2). As shown in Figure 11, in response to the sudden

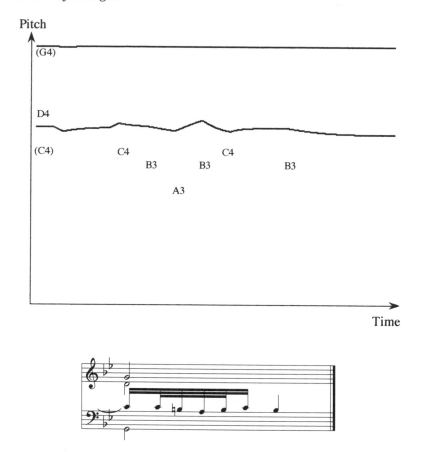

Figure 10. Introducing a musically trivial change in Bach's cadence—transposing the tenor D_3 (cf. Figure 9) an octave higher to D_4—has a catastrophic effect on the model's analysis. A confounding of the tenor and alto voices (even with a smaller W = major second) leads to a motion trace that bears little resemblance to the contour of the musically important alto voice.

onset of a steady-state tone, the gradual rise of the Level 2 sustained response is multiplicatively gated by the Level 2 transient response in such a way that the signal received at Level 3 approximates a curvilinear pulse. A strong pulse would also be sent to Level 3 should a tone end with a sudden and sharp offset. Indeed the instantaneous offset of a long sustained tone creates the strongest possible response (the product of a high sustained value and a high transient value).

Returning now to Bach's cadence, we can see in Figure 12 that, with the addition of transient detectors at Level 2, the model can successfully track the moving voice even when it remains in close proximity to one or more sustained tones.

4. Tracking Linear Processes: Scales and Arpeggios

A scale is the *locus classicus* of melodic motion. The above-described model can approximate a continuous motion trace for any common type of scale. Figure 13 presents the musical notation of an ascending C-major scale and the motion trace produced by the model as it processed that scale. In what may be more than a

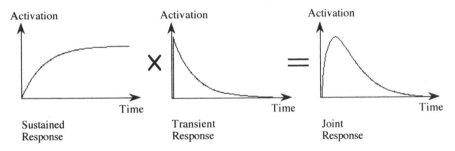

Figure 11. The addition of transient detectors to Level 2 gives the Grossberg-Rudd model a larger response to change than to stasis. For example, in response to the sudden onset of a steady-state tone, the gradual rise of the Level 2 sustained response is multiplicatively gated by the Level 2 transient response in such a way that the time course of the signals received at Level 3 approximates a curvilinear pulse. Such pulses will be sent to Level 3 whenever rapid changes occur in the strengths of signals entering Level 2.

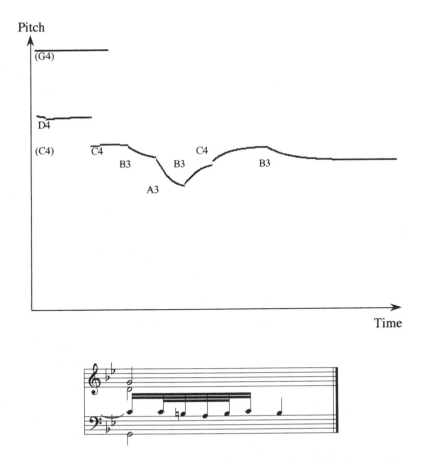

Figure 12. With the addition of transient detectors at Level 2, the model can successfully track the moving alto voice even when it remains in close proximity to the sustained D_4 in the transposed tenor.

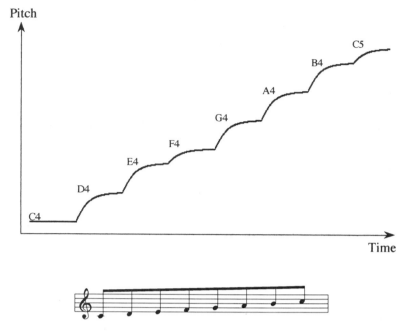

Figure 13. The musical notation of an ascending C-major scale and the motion trace produced by the model as it processed that scale. The visual appearance of the motion trace suggests the metaphor inherent in the musical term 'scale' (from the Italian *scala*, 'stairs').

fortuitous coincidence, the visual appearance of the motion trace suggests the metaphor inherent in the musical term *scale* (from the Italian *scala*: 'stairs').

The model is also capable of approximating a continuous motion trace for the most common types of arpeggios. Figure 14 presents the musical notation of an ascending C-major arpeggio and the motion trace produced by the model as it processed that arpeggio.

The musical notation of the arpeggio hints at a potential problem for a motion-tracking system: The intervals from tone to tone are not of uniform size. Indeed, the scales and arpeggios that music theorists describe as linear 'processes' (Meyer, 1956) are objectively nonlinear. A C-major scale contains two interval sizes even under equal temperament: whole tone (C_4-D_4, D_4-E_4, F_4-G_4, G_4-A_4, A_4-B_4) and semitone (E_4-F_4, B_4-C_5). And a C-major arpeggio contains three interval sizes: minor third (E_3-G_3), major third (C_3-E_3, C_4-E_4), and perfect fourth (G_3-C_4). Were a motion-tracking system limited to a uniform speed in traversing the pitch axis, the interval of a perfect fourth would take five times as long to traverse as the interval of a semitone. Yet musical practice and perception show no strong evidence of such distinctions in linear processes. On the contrary, the very notion of 'scale' or 'arpeggio' assumes isochronous performance as the default case, suggesting that a motion-tracking system must be capable of traversing unequal musical intervals in approximately equal times.

Grossberg (1977) provided a mathematical proof of how, for two sequentially activated Gaussian distributions whose origins are separated by less than 2W (two standard deviations), the maximum of their summed activations will traverse the halfway point of the interval between them in the same amount of time regardless of

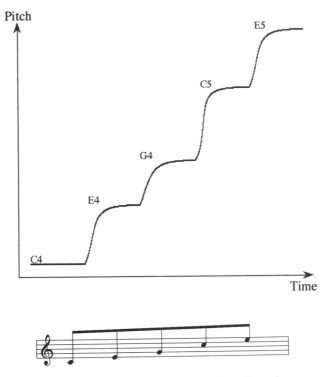

Figure 14. The musical notation of an ascending C-major arpeggio and the motion trace produced by the model as it processed that arpeggio. Although scales and arpeggios contain a series of unequal musical intervals, the motion traces traverse these unequal intervals in approximately equal times up to a distance of 2W.

the exact distance involved. Thus unequal musical intervals will be traversed in approximately equal times up to a distance of 2W. But what happens at distances beyond 2W?

Figure 15 presents the musical notation of an ascending linear process of alternating fifths and fourths. The motion-tracking model was able to connect the moves across the fourth (G_4-G_5 < 2W where W = minor third) but was unable to connect the moves across the fifths (C_4-G_4, C_5-C_5; >2W). As Miller and Heise (1950) said more than 40 years ago, "It is as if the listener's 'melodic tracking' could not follow a sudden change larger than a certain critical amount" (p. 637). On the one hand, this inability to connect the larger intervals is in keeping both with Meyer's characterization of large intervals as 'gaps' that imply a subsequent filling in (Meyer, 1973) and with Narmour's categorical distinction between intervals smaller than a tritone (= 2W) that commonly imply linear continuation and intervals larger than a tritone that commonly imply reversal of direction (Narmour, 1990). But on the other hand, the inability to connect large intervals is inconsistent with the musical effect of Figure 15. Listeners are quite capable of integrating an ascending sequence of fifths and fourths into a perceived linear process. Narmour himself recognizes this fact with a special category of 'retrospective process'. He claims, in effect, that after the first two intervals of Figure 15 a retrospective shift occurs in the listener's sense of how large is large (Narmour, 1990, pp. 273–277).

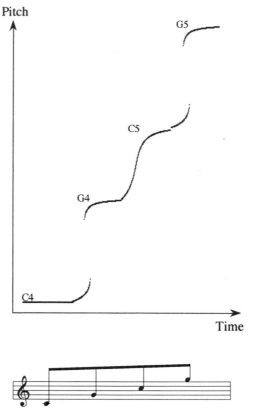

Figure 15. The musical notation of an ascending linear process of alternating fifths and fourths. The motion-tracking model was able to connect the moves across the fourth (G_4-$C_5 < 2W$ where W = minor third) but was unable to connect the moves across the fifths (C_4-G_4, C_5-G_5; $> 2W$).

If given a broader W, the present model could easily connect larger intervals. Yet how should the model determine when to shift the width of W? One obvious method would be to make W a variable controlled by the average width of recently occurring intervals. There are at least two major problems with this approach. First, large intervals are often registral gaps, not the beginnings of linear processes. By readjusting W for every large interval, the model would eliminate all of Meyer's registral gaps and all of Narmour's potential melodic reversals. Second, at an early stage the model would need to tag every tone as belonging to a particular polyphonic voice in order not to confuse the large intervals produced within a single voice with the large intervals produced between different voices. Yet how is the model to 'know', at an early stage, which voice is which, especially if all voices have the same timbre and frequently cross over each other (cf. Demske, 1993)? And in cases where a large interval in one voice coincides with smaller intervals in other voices, how would a single W be capable of accommodating the multiple sizes?

A more practical scheme for accommodating multiple interval sizes is for the motion-tracking system to have multiple copies of Levels 3 and 4 operating in parallel, each copy with a W of different width. Such a multiplex system—an obvious analog of Marr's description of the visual system with its multiple receptive-field and filter sizes (Marr, 1982)—allows a large interval to be simultaneously connected and disconnected in different parts of the model. Automatic processes of attention allocation and attention shifting, to be outlined below, could then contextually guide the overall interpretation of motion.

To summarize the treatment of linear processes, let me note that the basic model interprets common musical scales and arpeggios as connected motion traces resembling flights of stairs. Although the steps of these stairs are not equal distances apart, the model nevertheless traverses the distances in approximately equal times. For those linear processes with steps more than a tritone apart ($>2W$), the model can produce a shift of attention to a parallel copy of Levels 3 and 4 where W is wider. In particular, the motion-tracking model is assumed to be multiplex, with numerous Level 3 and 4 combinations whose values of W range from the very small to the very large, centering perhaps around a mean of about one critical bandwidth.

5. Multiplex Interpretations of an Ambiguous Melodic Figure

Figure 16 shows a short melody that can be perceived in several different ways. One can focus on the regular succession of eighth notes and consequently hear a widely oscillating seven-note series (G_4-G_5-A_4-E_5-C_5-B_5-C_5). One can focus on pitch proximity and consequently hear two converging melodic lines (ascending, G_4-A_4-C_5-B_4-C_5; descending, G_5-E_5-C_5-B_4-C_5). Or perhaps one can hear a little of both. For the motion-tracking model, a single choice of W necessarily forces a single interpretation of the melody. Setting W equal to a whole tone, for example, produces the motion analysis shown in Figure 17. While this analysis does a creditable job of following the two converging melodic lines it shows no hint of the oscillation between the alternating high and low tones. A much wider W could follow the note-to-note oscillation, but at the expense of the converging outer lines.

As mentioned earlier, a solution to this dilemma is to have multiple copies of Levels 3 and 4, each with a different size W (Grossberg & Rudd, 1989). The outputs of 15 such Level 3 and 4 combinations, with their Ws rising exponentially from a minimum width of one quarter tone to a maximum slightly in excess of a major sixth, are overlaid upon one another in Figure 18. At the smallest Ws, only the tones B_4 and C_5 were close enough to form a joint trace; all the other tones formed the separate, straight traces seen most clearly toward the right of the figure. At the medium size Ws, the tones of the two converging melodic lines formed stairlike traces of the type seen in Figure 17. And at the largest Ws, the alternating high and low tones formed the sinuous traces seen bouncing up and down toward the left of the figure.

Many of the traces just shown in Figure 18 are easily affected by subtle shadings in the simulated performance of the melody. Note, for instance, that the traces of ascending motion from A_4 directly to C_5 are considerably sparser and less coherent than either the traces from A_4 to E_5, or from E_5 to C_5. A shading of performance that makes A_4 more salient, E_5 less salient, or C_5 more salient will tend to strengthen the direct A_4-C_5 traces. Figures 19(a–d) compare the A_4-to-C_5 traces

Figure 16. A short melody with an ambiguous contour. One can attend to either a widely oscillating seven-note series (G_4-G_5-A_4-E_5-C_5-B_4-C_5) or two converging melodic lines (ascending, G_4-A_4-C_5-B_4-C_5; descending G_5-E_5-C_5-B_4-C_5).

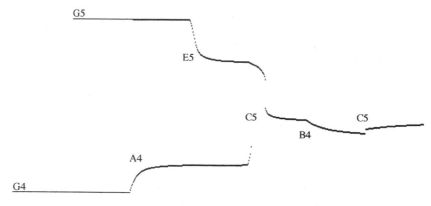

Figure 17. For the melody of Figure 16, a narrow W (= major second) results in motion traces of the two converging melodic lines but no trace of the oscillation between the alternating high and low tones. A much wider W could follow the note-to-note oscillation, but at the expense of the converging outer lines. A single value of W cannot accommodate both aspects of the melody.

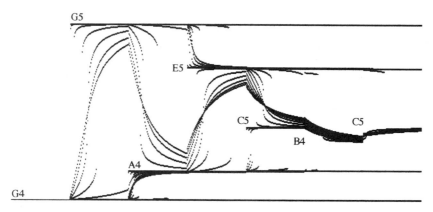

Figure 18. A multiplex version of the model, one with 15 copies of Levels 3 and 4, each with a unique size of W ranging from a quarter tone to over a major sixth, can produce motion traces that capture both aspects of the melody shown in Figure 16. For the medium size Ws, the tones of the two converging melodic lines formed stairlike traces of the type seen in Figure 17, while for the larger Ws, the alternating high and low tones formed the sinuous traces seen bouncing up and down toward the left of the figure. The horizontal lines represent the smallest size Ws, where all intervals except B_4-C_5 were more than the critical distance of 2W apart.

produced by three slightly differing performances. Figure 19(a) gives the baseline performance of Figure 18, where all simulated durations and amplitudes are uniform. Figure 19(b) shows the case of A_4 lengthened by one eighth of its duration, and E5 shortened by the same duration. Note that the A_4-C_5 traces (the steeply rising short traces indicted by the arrow) are more coherent and filled in than those in Figure 19(a). Figure 19(c) gives the case of equal durations but A_4 made a simulated 2.5 dB louder than the other tones. Again, the A_4-C_5 traces are improved. Figure 19(d) gives the combination of both durational shading (as in

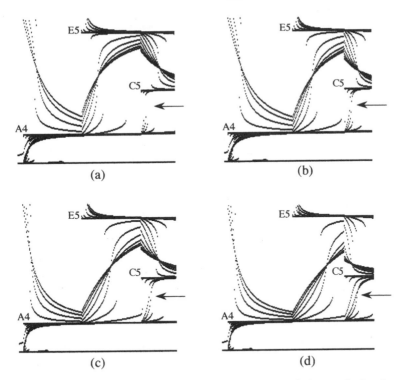

Figure 19. Highlight of four simulated performances of the melody shown previously in Figure 16. Arrows point to the direct A_4-C_5 traces resulting from (a) all tones having uniform duration and amplitude, (b) A_4 being lengthened by 12.5% and E_5 being shortened by the equivalent duration, (c) A_4 having a simulated 2.5-dB increase in amplitude, and (d) the combination of changes (b) and (c). Performance nuances can affect perceived melodic organization.

Figure 19(b)) and loudness shading (as in Figure 19(c)). Clearly the combination of both shadings greatly improves the A_4-C_5 traces.

A more global aspect of performance is set by the chosen tempo. As tempo increases (and durations decrease) the model begins to have difficulty connecting the traces between the most distant tones. Figure 20 compares the traces connecting the opening G_4-G_5 octaves at three different simulated tempos. At the left of the figure is the base tempo simulated in Figures 17–19, a tempo of x beats per minute. When, as at the middle of the figure, the tempo is doubled to $2x$ beats per minute (thereby halving durations) the G_4-G_5 traces begin to break up. A further doubling of tempo to $4x$ beats per minute, as at the right of the figure, increases the effect. And for each individual Level 3 and 4 combination (i.e. for a single W), the breaking up of the trace is more severe than the figure indicates, because the figure shows a composite of several superimposed traces. Of course, this breaking up of the ability to connect wide intervals at very fast tempos is exactly what has been repeatedly demonstrated in studies of 'trill thresholds' (Miller & Heise, 1950) and 'temporal coherence boundaries' (van Noorden, 1975).

Figures 17–20 give equal visual prominence to the traces produced by every Level 3 and 4 combination no matter how large or small the W. Such equanimity would not seem to conform to normal modes of Western music perception. In tracking the motion of voices in a Mozart string quartet, for instance, listeners

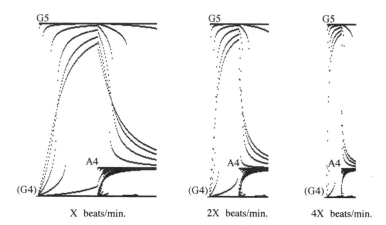

Figure 20. Highlights of three simulated performances of the opening octave leap in the melody shown previously in Figure 16. As the tempo increases, first doubling (2x beats/min.) and then quadrupling (4x beats/min.), the motion traces become progressively more tenuous. The ability of the model to connect wide musical intervals is thus tied to tempo, with slower tempos allowing wider connections.

would seem to pay much more attention to the normal interval sizes of scale steps and arpeggios than to tiny inflections of vibrato or potential one-and-a-half-octave leaps. Whether a product of nature, nurture, or immediate context, this allocation of attention might profitably be represented in the motion traces.

Figure 21 attempts such a representation by implementing two principles. The first is that the sizes of W should be normally distributed about a moderately sized central value, chosen here to be 2.5 semitones (musically, a so-called neutral third and psychoacoustically, near one critical bandwidth). The exact sizes of the 15 Ws displayed are (in semitones) 0.50, 1.00, 1.45, 1.95, 2.15, 2.30, 2.41, 2.50 (the central value), 2.59, 2.70, 2.85, 3.05, 3.55, 4.50, and 6.65.

The second principle is that the heaviest lines should correspond to the central values of W and that progressively lighter lines should correspond to Ws at progressively greater distances from the central value. Though this scheme is admittedly clumsy, it does seem to produce in Figure 21 a musically reasonable interpretation of the performance described above for Figure 19(d) (here the final C_5 is also emphasized with simulated dynamic stress). The heaviest traces highlight the important neighbor-note pattern of C_5-B_4-C_5 on which the two apparent voices converge; the next heaviest traces follow these converging voices, with this particular performance giving a slight edge to the ascending A_4-C_5 over the descending E_5-C_5; light traces show potential connections across the opening octave, with these oscillating traces becoming more coherent as the up-and-down intervals contract; and finally, the entire pattern of traces provides a visual record of the resolution of conflicting primary and secondary melodic patterns—what is initially ambiguous and highly implicative becomes unitary and closed.

6. The van Noorden Demonstration: Pitch Streaming

Van Noorden (1975) describes a striking interaction between a static and a mobile stream of pitch. His demonstration, one variation of which is schematized in Figure 22, generates its static stream by rapidly repeating a 1000-Hz tone: on, off, on, off,

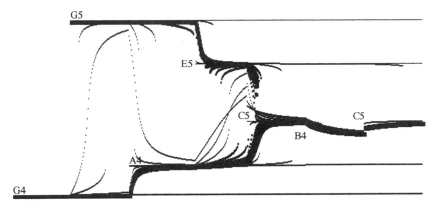

Figure 21. An alternative to Figure 17. Here sizes of W are normally distributed about a moderately sized central value: 2.5 semitones. The heaviest lines correspond to the central values of W and progressively lighter lines correspond to Ws at progressively greater distances from the central value.

Figure 22. A visual representation of the Gestalt law of good continuation also serves to schematize the static stream (white squares) and mobile stream (black squares) of van Noorden (1975).

ad infinitum. The demonstration generates its mobile stream by interposing, during the odd-numbered silences in the static stream, a different tone whose pitch rises slightly between every presentation.

As a visual image, Figure 22 closely resembles illustrations of the Gestalt law of good continuation: The diagonal line representing the mobile stream appears to pass smoothly through the horizontal line representing the static stream. Listeners, however, do not hear the mobile stream pass smoothly through the static stream. Rather, the static stream seems to capture the mobile stream when it nears 1000 Hz. Moreover, the rhythmic sense of evenness that had prevailed suddenly vanishes, to be replaced by what van Noorden terms a 'galloping rhythm' of three-tone groups: dum-di-dum, dum-di-dum. Only after the mobile stream's pitch has passed through and moved well away from 1000 Hz—even further away than the distance at which capture occurred—does the mobile stream seem to break free and reintegrate as a separate percept.

Though the change in rhythm during capture still awaits comprehensive explanation (and highlights a lacuna in the study of rhythmic perception), the motion-tracking model can simulate both the capture of the mobile stream by the static stream and the hysteresis effect that impedes the mobile stream from breaking free. Figure 23 presents the motion traces from a simulation of van Noorden's demonstration. The rapid repetition of the static stream generates the horizontal line at mid-figure. The mobile stream generates the stairlike diagonal that approaches, is captured by, and then escapes from the static stream. Note that during capture, the

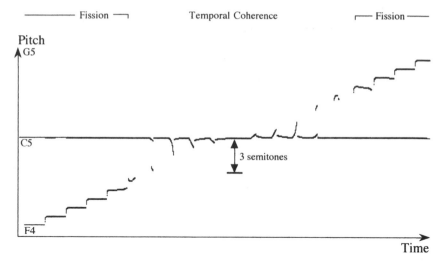

Figure 23. Motion traces from a simulation of van Noorden's demonstration (cf. Figure 22). The static stream generates the horizontal line at mid-figure. The mobile stream generates the stairlike diagonal that approaches, is capture by, and then escapes from the static stream. Note that during capture, the two streams interact to produce a periodic inflection of the static stream, first below and then above its central frequency. The inflections in the static stream correspond to the unstable 'di's' in the dum-di-dum galloping rhythmic groupings perceived during the period of temporal coherence.

two streams interact to produce a periodic inflection of the static stream, first below and then above its central frequency. This inflection of the central stream would seem to affect, in some unspecified way, the perceived rhythm. That is, the inflections in the static stream correspond to the unstable 'di's' in the perceived dum-di-dum galloping rhythmic groupings.

In this model, the hysteresis effect—the seeming reluctance of the static stream to release the mobile stream—is not the product of any unique property of the static stream, though its higher Level 3 activation is a contributing factor (higher because sustained responses to the rapidly repeating tones of the static stream decay only a third as long as those for the sparser tones of the mobile stream and thus, when multiplied by transient responses, generate stronger onset and offset responses). Instead, the two prime factors causing the hysteresis effect originate in the mobile stream itself.

The first can be metaphorically described as the 'trailing edge of the wave' created by the mobile stream. By 'trailing edge of the wave' I mean the residual Level 3 Gaussian distributions of previous tones in the mobile stream. Though the first tone of the mobile stream always produces a symmetrical Gaussian distribution at Level 3, when the first new (and higher) tone occurs, the combination of the two distributions becomes asymmetrical or skewed, with a sharper slope in the direction of the new tone and a more gradual slope trailing off toward the old tone. This asymmetry, which becomes more pronounced as more new and incrementally higher tones sound, is in itself sufficient to explain much of the hysteresis effect. That is, the interactions with the static stream will be asymmetrical as well, preserving segregation as the steep leading edge of the 'wave' approaches the central frequency and prolonging integration as the long trailing edge of the wave moves across and

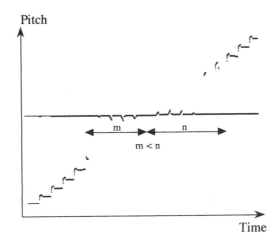

Pitch

m

n

m < n

Time

Figure 24. In the van Noorden demonstration, the distance from the breakup of the mobile stream to the crossing point (distance *m*) is often shorter than the distance from the crossing point to the reintegration of the mobile stream (distance *n*). The text suggests how this asymmetry may be caused by the dynamics of the mobile stream.

beyond the central frequency. As shown in Figure 24, where tones are shorter than those shown in Figure 23 and where a wider W is used, the hysteresis effect can become quite pronounced. As the figure points out, the distance from the perceived collapse of the mobile stream to the central crossing point (distance *m*) can be much shorter than the distance from that crossing point to where the mobile stream seems to become reconstituted (distance *n*).

The second factor that can contribute to a hysteresis effect is the specific dynamics of Level 2. As described earlier, the output of Level 2 is the product of a sustained response and a transient response. Should either response be very low, the product will be low. Very brief tones of the type used in van Noorden's demonstration may allow neither the sustained responses to rise very high nor the transient responses to decay very low. When these brief tones end, the product of the two responses may not compensate for the sudden loss of input from Level 1, with the result that at Level 3 there is a collapse of the 'leading edge of the wave'. As a result of such a collapse, the maximum of the 'wave' will move slightly backward toward the still decaying traces of earlier tones, an effect evident in Figure 24. Notice that the horizontal section of each stair step has fallen back to a position slightly lower in pitch than where each stair step began. The result is, again, that segregation is preserved as the mobile stream approaches the static stream, and that integration is prolonged as it moves through and beyond the static stream.

The just-mentioned tendency for a Level 3 maximum to shift slightly back toward previous maxima can, when stacatto-like tones are involved, result in unexpected side effects. For example, if each pitch in the mobile stream is repeated once before the next higher pitch sounds, under certain conditions the motion traces may indicate that the mobile stream moves up in pitch at *each* tone. As shown in Figure 25, the simulation suggests that certain incrementally ascending pairs of repeated stacatto pitches can form a sequence where, ambiguously, one may hear either repeated pairs of tones or a linear process where each tone appears at least slightly higher than the previous one.

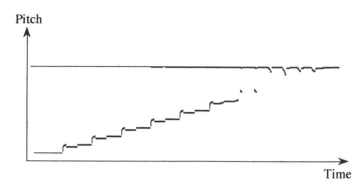

Figure 25. A variation on the van Noorden demonstration. Here each pitch in the mobile stream is repeated once before the next higher pitch sounds. The text suggests how listeners, given staccato tones rapidly represented, might perceive either ascending pairs of tones or an ascending series where *each* tone seems slightly higher than the previous tone.

Van Noorden's emphasis was on mapping the boundaries between the perception of fission (two separate streams) and temporal coherence (one composite stream). So clear to him was the effect of attentional set that he reported two boundaries: a fission boundary for subjects attending to separate streams and a temporal coherence boundary for subjects attending to a composite stream. The fission boundary was between one and three semitones and changed very little as the tempo of the tones slowed. The temporal coherence boundary, by contrast, began at a value comparable to the fission boundary but widened considerably as tempo slowed. Put somewhat more simply, it appears that capture of the mobile stream occurs inevitably at a narrow pitch interval no matter what the tempo, whereas the ability to follow the dum-di-dum, up-and-down movement of a composite stream depends strongly on how fast the tones are presented—slower rates allow for wider intervals of apparent motion.

I have already discussed how tempo affects the ability of the motion-tracking model to connect tones widely separated in pitch (see Figure 20). Thus for any given W, there is a threshold of tempo above which temporal coherence or the sense of one composite stream breaks down. For any given W, there is also a relatively narrow distance from the central pitch at which capture will take place, and this distance is only slightly affected by tempo. So the behavior of the motion-tracking model simulates both of van Noorden's boundaries.

Van Noorden (1975) points out that even beyond the temporal coherence boundary one can still hear a 'weak connection' between the alternating tones:

> It should not be thought that no interaction at all can be observed between the tones A and B in the region beyond the temporal coherence boundary, i.e. in the region of inevitable fission. In fact, an effect similar to temporal coherence can be observed here. In the tone sequence ABA, for example, a very weak connection can be heard between the tones A and B in the region. However, the tone B is still heard separately in the background, so that this is definitely a case of fission. At very large frequency jumps, this effect is no longer heard. We will not discuss it any further here.

From the perspective of the present motion-tracking model, van Noorden could be interpreted as describing the operation of multiple-scale Ws. For a given W—the W

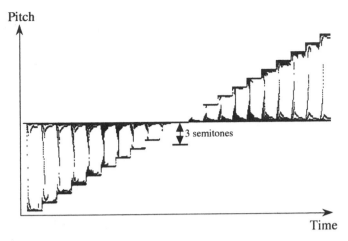

Figure 26. Superimposed traces of van Noorden's streaming demonstration as produced by 15 sizes of W ranging from a quarter tone to over a tritone. At a distance somewhat less than three semitones from the central pitch, the mobile stream collapses into the static stream even for the narrowest size of W. At a distance somewhat larger than a major sixth, the vertical connections between the two streams begin to break up.

that is the focus of a listener's attention—there will indeed be a temporal coherence boundary beyond which fission occurs. But for larger Ws, temporal coherence continues to function 'in the background'.

Figure 26 shows the superimposed traces of van Noorden's streaming demonstration as produced by 15 sizes of W ranging from a quarter tone to over a tritone (see above or Figure 21 for the exact sizes). The central line represents, of course, the static stream, and the ascending staircase represents the mobile stream. As the figure suggests, at a distance of somewhat less than three semitones from the central pitch the mobile stream is captured by the static stream even for the narrowest size of W. The figure also shows that at very large interval sizes—the intervals at the extreme left and right of the figure represent octaves—the vertical connections between the two streams begin to break up. Between these extremes of necessary stream segregation and necessary integration is, when the multiplex system is viewed as a whole, an area of considerable indeterminacy. Presumably, however, a listener focuses attention on a specific size of W, creating thereby an interesting mix of strongly categorical perception at the W in the attentional foreground and a more gradual, statistical perception of state transition at the Ws in the background.

As a general prediction of how attention is allocated in a multiplex motion-tracking system, let me suggest that attention flows to the W producing the strongest, most coherent motion traces. Considerations of this principle lead far beyond the confines of this article, but in the limited context of the van Noorden demonstration, it may be possible to specify some factors that would control such an allocation. First of all, in the case of fission or stream segregation, allocation will be driven by the height of the stair steps in the mobile stream. If each step rises only a small fraction of an octave, as was apparently the case in van Noorden's work and has definitely been true in replications of his work, then attention will flow to a small W, perhaps to a W of that approximate size. Given a step height of 1/10

octave and a W of 1/8 octave, capture of the mobile stream will occur near a distance 2W from the central pitch or, specifically, between 2.4 and 3.0 semitones
from the central pitch, a value largely independent of tempo and consistent with
van Noorden's results. By contrast, in the case of temporal coherence or stream
integration, attention can sequentially shift to larger and larger Ws as the oscillating
interval widens. The maximum possible W varies inversely with tempo, so the
temporal coherence boundary will widen as tempo slows. Again this is consistent
with van Noorden's results.

7. Trills

An important point of departure for van Noorden's work was the study of trill
perception by Miller and Heise (1950). They demonstrated that stream fission
increases when either the interval widens or the tempo increases. Of course the
relation between tempo, interval, and the ability of the motion-tracking system (for
a particular value of W) to connect two tones with a continuous, integrated trace
has already been discussed. Yet the framing of trill perception in terms of stream
fission of fusion has tended to create a binary opposition where, I would claim,
additional factors may be at work.

An additional factor that emerges from simulating the motion perception of trills
may be described as 'motion contraction' (Grossberg, 1977). The effect of motion
contraction is evident in Figure 27, where the up-and-down oscillation of the
motion trace progressively narrows as the speed of the trill increases. The extent
of motion contraction depends on the particular set of parameters for equations
(1) and (2) and on the amplitude envelopes of the alternating tones. The cause of
motion contraction is tied to the effective rate of decay for each tone. As the speed
of alternation of the two tones increases, each tone decays less before sounding
again. At extreme speeds the tones decay very little and the maxima of Level 3
activations produced by their joint distributions move toward the midpoint between
the two tones, the position these maxima would occupy if the two tones were played
simultaneously as a chord.

Trills, especially long trills of the type classical soloists use to signal the end of
a cadenza, often begin slowly and then accelerate to dizzying speed. A listener
can follow the alternating up-and-down motion up to a point where the percept

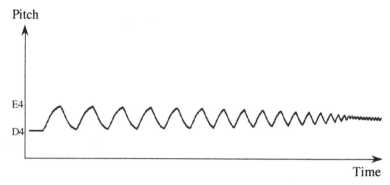

Figure 27. The motion trace of a simulated accelerating trill between D_4 and E_4.
Motion contraction is evident where the up-and-down oscillation of the motion
trace progressively narrows as the speed of the trill increases.

becomes that of something both madly active and securely stationary. This shift in perception may be illustrated in Figure 27 where, near the right of the figure, the previously gentle up-and-down motion rapidly collapses into a jittery line. Though stream fission explains the stationary aspect of the trill, it does not explain the percept of whirring activity. Motion contraction accounts for both aspects, because the motion trace continues to oscillate slightly even at extreme speeds of trilling. Of course, neither explanation excludes the other. Moreover, within a multiplex motion-tracking system, both fission and motion contraction can occur in different parts of the system.

8. Emergent Broader Streams: Parallel Voices and Outer-voice Salience

Since the Middle Ages, treatises on the art of writing counterpoint have consistently recommended making voices move in opposite directions, so-called 'contrary' motion. And just as consistently they have cautioned against making voices move in the same direction, so-called 'similar' or 'parallel' motion. From a modern perspective these admonitions speak to the tendency for voices with parallel motion paths to lose their autonomy and become melded into a joint (and perhaps fuzzier) percept (Huron, 1992; Wright, 1986).

Motion traces of voices moving in parallel are subject to the same effect noted when discussing motion contraction—the tendency for maxima of Level 3 activations to be located near the 'center of gravity' of the tones involved. For two equally salient voices, that location will be their midpoint. For three or more voices, that location may vary for each size W, but will be somewhere in the middle of the tones involved. Thus, if output from a motion-tracking system is correlated with output from systems sensitive to pitch locations, then voices moving in parallel present a situation where pitch locations and motion traces may not coincide.

An instance of three-note parallel chords can be found in the opening of the "Dance of the Reed Pipes" from Tchaikovsky's *Nutcracker* ballet. The motion trace (W = major second) in Figure 28 initially shows two streams: the melody and a combination of the two lower voices. The tracking of the notated melodic contour is to some extent fortuitous. That is, had Tchaikovsky slightly altered the seventh three-voice chord (G_4-A_4-E_5 in Figure 28) so as to retain the third-below-a-fourth spacing of the previous chords (A_4 changes to B_4, a modification barely noticeable to casual listeners), the upper motion trace would be drawn 'off the track' to follow the descending line of D_5-$C_{\sharp 5}$-B_4 rather than the melodic line of D_5-$C_{\sharp 5}$-E_5, as Figure 29 illustrates.

The D_5-$C_{\sharp 5}$-B_4 descending line suggested by Figure 29 is not easy to hear. A performance designed to bring it out would require the first flute to play its E_5 pianissimo and the second flute to play its B_4 fortissimo to overcome the strong tendency of the E_5 to be perceptually more salient. Explanations of this salience might appeal to special factors of register, masking, harmonic fusion, acculturation, saturation, and so forth. Yet musicians will attest that the highest and lowest voices in polyphonic textures—the 'outer' voices—are generally more salient no matter what the register, the harmony, or other factors. Student dictations of Bach Chorales, for example, while often quite accurate for the soprano and bass, rarely capture more than bits and pieces of the alto and tenor. The thesis presented here is that this salience of outer voices is, at least in part, an automatic product of lateral inhibition, resulting in what vision studies term edge or boundary enhancement.

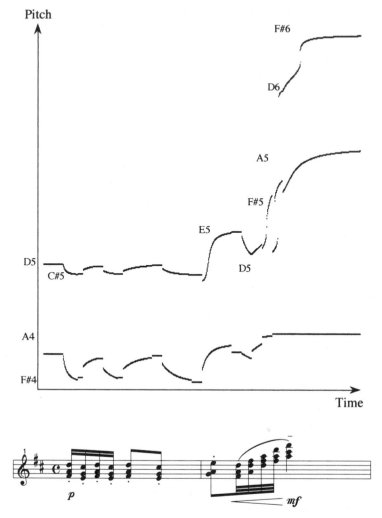

Figure 28. The opening of the "Dance of the Reed Pipes" from Tchaikovsky's *Nutcracker* ballet. The motion trace (W = major second) initially shows two streams: the melody and the combination of the two lower voices.

Let us take a four-voice, D-major chord, D_3-$F_{\sharp 4}$-A_4-D_5, and examine how a simple type of lateral inhibition occurring at or beyond the model's Level 4 can make the motion traces for outer voices more salient than those for the inner ones. The underlying rule is that the mutual inhibition between any two tones varies inversely (here a Gaussian function, though an asymmetrical function might conform better to data from masking studies) with the distance between them. Figure 30 illustrates how this rule would transform the relative salience of traces from four originally equivalued tones. The outer traces, those representing D_3 and D_5, become the strongest because whereas the inner traces are inhibited from both sides and at a close distance ($F_{\sharp 4}$-A_4 forms the smallest interval and thus mutual inhibition is strongest within that interval), the outer traces are inhibited from only one side and at larger distances.

The exact spacing of tones will determine the exact profile of imputted salience. For example, Figure 31 shows what musicians term an 'open' voicing of the chord

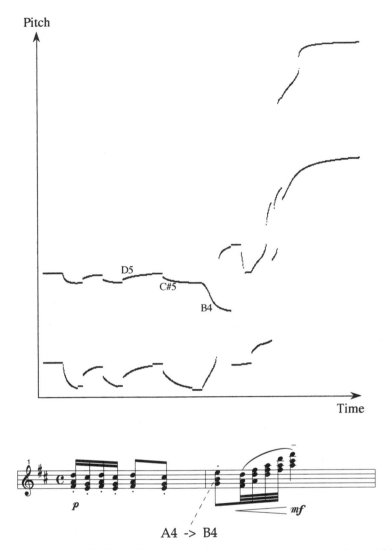

Figure 29. At the beginning of the second measure, a change in the middle tone from A_4 to B_4 (cf. Figure 28) draws the upper motion trace 'off the track' to follow the descending line of D_5-$C_{\sharp 5}$-B_4 rather than the melodic line of D_5-$C_{\sharp 5}$-E_5.

shown previously in Figure 30. Notice that the trace for the tenor voice (D_4) now is more salient than in Figure 30 because it has moved away from trace for the alto voice. The trace for the bass voice ($F_{\sharp 4}$), by contrast, is now somewhat less salient than in Figure 30 because it has moved up toward the other voices. Yet both outer traces remain more salient than their neighboring inner traces.

In conformity with the edge enhancement predicted by Figure 30, adjusting the signal strengths of the simulated tones in the *Nutcracker* example of Figure 29 eliminates the tendency for the motion to follow the descending D_5-$C_{\sharp 5}$-B_4 line (see Figure 32).

As a final example (Figure 33), I present 15 overlaid traces of the *Nutcracker* excerpt (sizes of W are distributed about a moderately sized central value of 2.5 semitones and displayed as previously detailed in Figure 21; each trace assumes

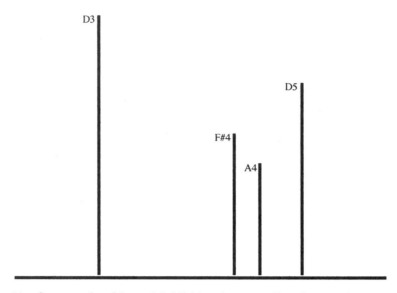

Figure 30. One result of lateral inhibition between Level 4 motion traces could be the increased salience of outer voices, analogous to edge enhancement in vision models. The figure shows how lateral inhibition suppresses traces inhibited from both sides ($F_{\sharp 4}$, A_4) more strongly than traces inhibited from only one side (D_3, D_5).

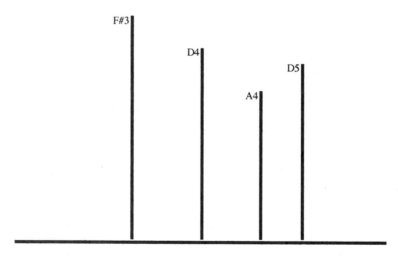

Figure 31. The particular voicing of chords can influence the extent of outer-voice edge enhancement. The figure shows how the traces exhibit a reduced effect of edge enhancement when they are more evenly spaced. Here, although the trace for the inner-voice D_4 is more salient than that for the outer-voice D_5, both outer traces remain more salient than their nearest inner-trace neighbors.

the edge enhancement just discussed). Only the very largest sizes of W can form coherent motion traces for the thirty-second notes that sweep up across the second measure.

This sudden ascent overwhelms the systems' ability to track an instrumental part with any accuracy. In place of a well-defined, stair-steplike arpeggio, the system

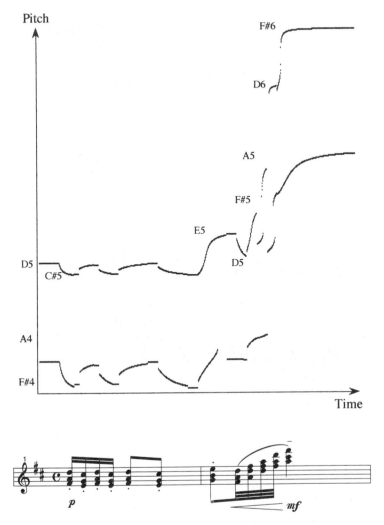

Figure 32. A second simulation of the music for Figure 29 incorporating a version of the edge-enhancement effects shown in Figures 30 and 31. The upper motion trace now follows the notated melody at the beginning of the second measure (cf. Figure 29). Outer-voice salience overcomes the lure of between-voice proximity.

produces a fan of fragmentary traces that unfold across almost two octaves of pitch. The effect on the motion-tracking system seems in keeping with the aesthetic effect of a sudden and exuberant expansion of activity that Tchaikovsky's music so charmingly creates.

9. Discussion

The above model of apparent-motion percepts in music can be applied to a large number of research problems in both the psychology of music and music theory. I have touched on only a few of these. This is not to say, however, that the model is mature or without important limitations. I did not, as mentioned earlier, attempt to integrate this motion model with a model of pitch perception, even though I suspect

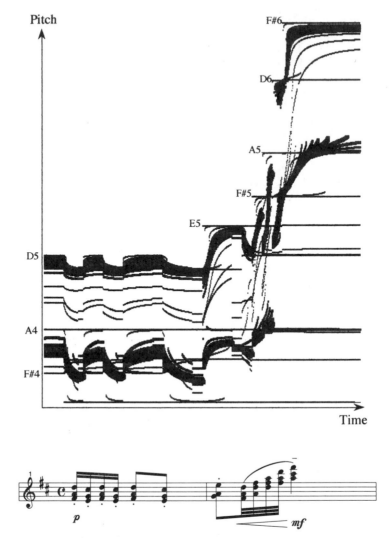

Figure 33. Fifteen superimposed motion traces from a multiplex simulation of the Tchaikovsky excerpt. Sizes of W range from a quarter tone to over a tritone. Only the very largest sizes of W produce coherent traces for the thirty-second-note arpeggio that concludes the excerpt.

the two domains are intimately related. And whereas the various motion traces shown in the above diagrams were determined algorithmically be simply calculation of local Level 3 maxima, the derivation of these traces through processes of lateral inhibition would be far from simple.

From the characteristic dynamics of similar competitive circuits one can predict at least four important effects of lateral inhibition at Level 4. (1) There would be a practical limit to the number of surviving maxima for each size of W. Thus even if there were, say, 20 melodic streams as input to the model, the system's output (for a given size W) could not produce coherent traces for more than perhaps 3 or 4 of those streams. (2) Streams that move in parallel motion will sum their effects on Level 3, with the result that parallel streams will emerge as dominant traces in the context of other, independent streams. Thus a musical shift from two independent voices to voices moving in parallel sixths, for example, would likely produce a shift of attention to the stronger, summed trace at a larger W. At the same time, limits to the contrast-enhancing abilities of real-time lateral inhibition could make the motion traces of wide parallel streams less focused than the streams for independently moving voices. (3) Lateral inhibition creates a type of inertia; that is, feedback loops and other resonances within a neural field can work to delay a change of state. Thus the several abrupt shifts of maxima shown in the above diagrams might, in a more elaborate simulation, be somewhat smoother and more continuous. And (4), the effects of lateral inhibition might work to focus attention on a size of W just larger than half the mean size of the intervals actually occurring in a particular piece of music. Broader sizes of W, with broader distributions of Level 3 activation will be more difficult for lateral inhibition to focus into sharply defined maxima, with the results that the more broadly defined maxima will have a lower mean activation level. Conversely, at sizes of W too small to connect typical melodic intervals, the high number of independent maxima (an octave scale, for example, could produce eight static maxima rather than one mobile maximum) will again result in a lower mean activation level. As a result, if attention within the motion-tracking system flows to those maxima with the highest levels of activation, those maxima should be found at a size of W just larger than half the size of recently processed musical intervals (the exception being for streams moving in parallel, where their summed activations could shift attention to a larger W). If these suppositions are correct, then attention would automatically direct itself to 'receptive field sizes' optimal for the music being heard.

For the sake of simplicity and replicability, all simulations were made assuming 'tones' with instantaneous onsets, unvarying sustains, and instantaneous offsets, as in Figure 2. As Figures 17–20 suggested, however, the fine points of musical performance can influence the interpretation of melodic structure. So the model was made with tonal and temporal resolution sufficient to allow for input derived from real performances. Most of the simulations presented here updated their calculations every (simulated) 10 msec and were performed, as mentioned earlier, with a tonal resolution of 1/20 of a semitone.

The motion-tracking system here described is assumed to be but one subsystem within the auditory system. Output from a motion-tracking subsystem might be used as input by other subsystems. Conversely, output from other subsystems might be used as input by the motion-tracking subsystem. Let me provide a few illustrative examples. First, some interaction seems evident between motion-tracking and rhythm-tracking subsystems in listeners' perceptions of the van Noorden demonstration. Were this not the case, it would be extremely difficult to explain the radical change in rhythmic perception that accompanies the shift from two perceived streams to one stream. Second, a warping of the pitch continuum of the motion-tracking subsystem by output from some type of tonality subsystem might explain certain effects of common pitch alphabets (Deutsch & Feroe, 1981; Simon & Sumner, 1968) on perceived motion, in particular the sense that the steps of a scale or arpeggio, though objectively of varying sizes, seem to be equidistantly spaced and 'adjacent'. And third, one subsystem might, so to speak, fill in the blanks left by other subsystems. The final flourish in the Tchaikovsky example (Figure 33) was almost uninterpretable in terms of the motion-tracking of individual flute parts. Yet because all the tones in the final flourish are members of a D-major chord, a harmony subsystem could, with little or no help from motion tracking, give a coherent interpretation of those fleeting thirty-second notes. By the same token, chords of the 'augmented sixth' (e.g. $A_{\flat4}$-C_5-$F_{\sharp5}$ resolving to G_4-B_4-G_5), which can be problematic for theories of harmony that emphasize root progressions, have often been defined instead by their motion. Sessions (1951) noted that "in some cases ... the pull of the voices is so much stronger and more perceptible than that of the root progression that the question of the latter seems purely academic" (p. 336). For such chords, as Prout (1903) said, "We must seek another explanation", which often takes the form of an appeal to the motion of the voices (s.v. 'Chords of the Augmented Sixth'). Apparently a clear understanding of what such chords *do* compensates for not knowing exactly what they *are*.

Although the analogy between apparent motion in vision and apparent motion in music is demonstrably weak when cast in terms of high-level cognition, it seems to gain considerable strength when cast in terms of low-level neural processes. Visual parameters such as stimulus contrast, size, luminance, duration, color, and figural organization (Kolers, 1972) have natural analogs in music (respectively, signal-to-noise ratio, bandwidth [or, assuming early pitch determination, chord spacing], amplitude, duration, timbre, and figural organization). Suitable timings for stimulus onset asynchronies and interstimulus intervals in visual apparent motion are comparable with timings for successive attacks and between-tone articulations in music. More than 70 years ago, Wertheimer (1923, p. 311) claimed that "quantitative comparisons can be made regarding the application of the same laws in regions—form, color, sound—heretofore treated as psychologically separate and heterogeneous". More recently, Bharucha (1987) has argued that generic forms of neural information processing, rather than specialized, exclusively musical forms, can account for data from a wide variety of psychological studies of music perception. The ease with which a neural model of apparent motion in vision can simulate complex examples of auditory stream segregation in music may lend support to both their contentions.

References

Bharucha, J.J. (1987) Music cognition and perceptual facilitation: A connectionist framework. *Music Perception*, 5, 1–30.

Bregman, A.S. (1990) *Auditory Scene Analysis: The Perceptual Organization of Sound*. Cambridge, MA: MIT Press.

Bregman, A.S. & Campbell, J. (1971) Primary auditory stream segregation and perception of order in rapid sequences of tone. *Journal of Experimental Psychology*, 89, 244–249.

Burt, P. & Sperling, G. (1981) Time, distance, and feature trade-offs in visual apparent motion. *Psychological Review*, 88, 171–195.

Demske, T. (1993) *Recognizing melodic motion in musical scores: Rules and contexts*. Unpublished doctoral dissertation, Department of Music, Yale University.

Deutsch, D. & Feroe, J. (1981) The internal representation of pitch sequences in tonal music. *Psychological Review*, 88, 503–522.

Exner, S. (1875) Über das Sehen von Bewegungen und die Theorie des zusammengesetzten Auges. *Sitzungsberichte: Akademie der Wissenschaften in Wien*, 72, 156–190.

Grossberg, S. (1977) Apparent motion. Unpublished manuscript.

Grossberg, S. & Rudd, M.E. (1989) A neural architecture for visual motion perception: Group and element apparent motion. *Neural Networks*, 2, 421–450.

Huron, D. (1989) Voice denumerability in polyphonic music of homogeneous timbres. *Music Perception*, 6, 361–382.

Huron, D. (1992) *A derivation of the rules of voice-leading from perceptual principles*. Paper presented at the Second International Conference on Music Perception and Cognition, Los Angeles, CA.

Jones, M.R. & Boltz, M. (1989) Dynamic attending and responses to time. *Psychological Review*, 96, 459–491.

Kolers, P.A. (1972) *Aspects of Motion Perception*. Oxford: Pergamon Press.

Körte, A. (1915) Kinematoskopische Untersuchungen. *Zeitschrift für Psychologie*, 72, 194–296.

Marr, D. (1982) *Vision*. San Francisco: Freeman.

Marr, D. & Ullman, S. (1981) Directional selectivity and its use in early visual processing. *Proceedings of the Royal Society of London (B)*, 211, 151–180.

Meyer, L.B. (1956) *Emotion and Meaning in Music*. Chicago: University of Chicago Press.

Meyer, L.B. (1973) *Explaining Music: Essays and Explorations*. Chicago: University of Chicago Press.

Miller, G.A. & Heise, G.A. (1950) The trill threshold. *Journal of the Acoustical Society of America*, 22, 637–638.

Narmour, E. (1990) *The Analysis and Cognition of Basic Melodic Structures: The Implication-Realization Model*. Chicago: University of Chicago Press.

Prout, E. (1903) *Harmony: Its Theory and Practice* (17th ed., rev.). London: Augener.

Seibert, M. & Waxman, A.M. (1989) Spreading activation layers, visual saccades, and invariant representations for neural pattern recognition systems. *Neural Networks*, 2, 9–27.

Sessions, R. (1951) *Harmonic Practice*. New York: Harcourt, Brace & World.

Simon, H.A. & Summer, R.K. (1968) Pattern in music. In B. Kleinmuntz (Ed.), *Formal Representation of Human Judgment* (pp. 219–250). New York: Wiley.

Terhardt, E. (1974) Pitch, consonance and harmony. *Journal of the Acoustical Society of America*, 55, 1061–1069.

Terhardt, E. (1984) The concept of musical consonance: A link between music and psychoacoustics. *Music Perception*, 1, 276–295.

Ternus, J. (1926) Experimentelle Untersuchungen über phänomenale Identität. *Psychologische Forschung*, 7, 81–136 [abstracted and trans. in part in W.D. Ellis (Ed.), *A Sourcebook of Gestalt Psychology*. New York: Humanities Press, 1950].

van Noorden, L. (1975) *Temporal Coherence in the Perception of Tone Sequences*. Eindhoven: Druk vam Voorschoten.

Wertheimer, M. (1912) Experimentelle Studien über das Sehen von Bewegung. *Zeitschrift für Psychologie*, 61, 161–265 [trans. in part in T. Shipley (Ed.), *Classics in Psychology*. New York: Philosophical Library, 1961].

Wertheimer, M. (1923) Untersuchungen zur Lehre von der Gestalt, II. *Psychologische Forschung*, 4, 301–350 [abstracted and trans. in part in W.D. Ellis (Ed.), *A Sourcebook of Gestalt Psychology*. New York: Humanities Press, 1950].

Wright, J.K. (1986) *Auditory object perception: Counterpoint in a new context*. Unpublished masters thesis, Faculty of Music, McGill University, Montreal.

Zuckerkandl, V. (1956) *Sound and Symbol: Music and the External World* (W. Trask, Trans.). New York: Pantheon Books.

Modelling the Perception of Musical Sequences with Self-organizing Neural Networks

MICHAEL P. A. PAGE

A brief review of studies into the psychology of melody perception leads to the conclusion that melodies are represented in long-term memory as sequences of specific items, either intervals or scale notes; the latter representation is preferred. Previous connectionist models of musical-sequence learning are discussed and criticized as models of perception. The Cohen–Grossberg masking field (Cohen & Grossberg, 1987) is described and it is shown how it can be used to generate melodic expectations when incorporated within an adaptive resonance architecture. An improved formulation, the SONNET 1 network (Nigrin, 1990, 1992), is described in detail and modifications are suggested. The network is tested on its ability to learn short melodic phrases taken from a set of simple melodies, before being applied to the learning of the melodies themselves. Mechanisms are suggested for sequence recognition and sequence recall. The advantages of this approach to sequence learning are discussed.

KEYWORDS: Music, sequence, expectation, self-organizing, neural network, masking-field, hierarchy.

1. Introduction

This article describes a connectionist model of the perception of musical sequences. For definiteness, attention will be directed to the perception of simple melodies, but the same approach can be applied to the perception of 'item sequences' in general, be they musical, such as chord sequences or rhythmic patterns, or non-musical, such as letter sequences. Much experimental work (e.g. White, 1960; Dowling & Fujitani, 1971; Deutsch, 1972; Dowling, 1972, 1978, 1986, 1991; Idson & Massaro, 1978; Kallman & Massaro, 1979; Dowling & Bartlett, 1981; Edworthy, 1985; Bartlett & Dowling, 1988) has been carried out in an attempt to establish the nature of the items, or elements, out of which a listener's mental representation of a melody is constructed: possibilities include the representation of a melody as a sequence of absolute pitches, as a sequence of relative pitches (scale notes), as a sequence of intervals, or as a contour (sequence of 'ups and downs' perhaps associated with a scale). This work is reviewed in Page (1993), with the conclusion that, while absolute pitch, scale and contour information seem to dominate recognition in the short term, long-term storage and subsequent recognition relies on

This article appeared originally in *Connection Science*, 1994, **6**, 223–246, and is reprinted with permission.

exact interval information. It is unclear whether the memory for such information comprises the storage of the intervals themselves, or rather the storage of scale notes, that is, pitches measured relative to a tonal centre. Indeed, Dowling (1986) suggests that both strategies are available, each to a degree dependent upon the listener's level of musical experience. As in the work of other connectionist modellers, the scale-note representation of melody will be adopted. Such a representation emphasizes the perceptual reality of the pitch event itself, rather than emphasizing the relationship between consecutive pitch events. This emphasis is more consistent with the model of melodic expectation developed later, in that this model assumes that expectations can be generated by a single pitch event, that is, at a stage before an interval can be defined. The scale-note representation has other advantages: it accounts better for the lack of cumulative errors in sequence reproductions, and it copes better with the fact that a given interval can give rise to different expectations depending on the scale notes by which it is bracketed.

A further observation can be made regarding musical sequences, namely that they are perceived as being 'chunked' into subsequences or phrases. The nature of this chunking has also been widely investigated. Restle (1970, 1972) and Restle and Brown (1970) apply hierarchical rule systems, originally developed to account for responses to serial patterns in the visual domain, to the analysis of one of Bach's two-part Inventions. In doing so, they foreshadow the work of Deutsch and Feroe (1981), who construct a model of what they term "the internal representation of pitch sequences in music". This latter model describes a melodic sequence with a sequence of operators, such as n (next) and p (previous), acting on a reference element, within a given alphabet of symbols. For instance, a rising F-major scale might be described as $\{\{(^\star,\ n^2,\ n^2,\ n,\ n^2,\ n^2,\ n^2,\ n); Cr\}F\}$, where the reference element F is substituted for the asterisk, and the operators act over the alphabet Cr, corresponding to the chromatic scale. An alternative coding for the same sequence would be $\{\{(^\star,\ 7n;\ M\}F\}$, where the alphabet M corresponds to the major scale. Hierarchical coding of extended sequences is accomplished by allowing each of the notes produced by a decoding at a given level to act as a reference element at a lower level. It is made clear that the alphabets themselves, as well as the operator sequences corresponding to specific melodies stored in memory, are learned by exposure to a particular 'musical environment'.

Deutsch and Feroe (1981) also discuss the means by which listeners infer a particular structure from the sequence of notes that they hear. Their explanation relies heavily on 'simple perceptual mechanisms' whereby, for instance, successive notes proximal in pitch might be supposed to belong to the same group. It is not made clear whether such grouping relies on genuinely primitive (innate) mechanisms (cf. Bregman, 1990), or whether pitch-proximal groups are favoured because of their prevalence in a given idiom. It seems likely that both nature and nurture have a role to play. Some more light is shed on this issue by experiments investigating the effect of phrasing on the recall of item sequences. Phrasing refers to the placing of pauses in a sequence, either by the lengthening of certain items or by the insertion of unfilled intervals. Deutsch (1980) showed that recall of extended sequences was best when the pause structure was consistent with the group structure (as defined by Deutsch and Feroe), that is, when pauses occurred at inter-group boundaries. Jones (1981) urges caution in the interpretation of Deutsch's results by pointing out that the latter's choice of stimuli did not control for alternative explanations based on contour and temporal contributions to the 'accent structure' of the stimulus. These caveats obviously do not call into question the experimental results themselves, but rather Deutsch's explanation of them solely in terms of her particular notion of grouping structure. Palmer and Krumhansl (1987a, b) explore further the independence or otherwise of pitch and temporal structures in their contributions to the determination of overall phrase structure. While the present paper refers principally to the perception of pitch phrases, Page (1993) shows how the same networks can be applied to the temporal domain.

Dowling (1973) shows that note pairs straddling a pause are less likely subsequently to be recalled than are within-group pairs, while Tan *et al.*, (1981) performed a similar experiment, but used a melodic/harmonic cadence, as opposed to a pause, to mark the phrase boundary. Their findings are particularly interesting in that they indicate a difference in performance between musically experienced and musically inexperienced subjects: the effect of the phrase boundary was more pronounced for experienced subjects who, furthermore, exhibited a sensitivity to the degree of closure associated with the various cadences used. Like Deutsch (1980), the authors often refer to the similarity of these results to those of experiments employing different types of stimuli, notably linguistic stimuli. These experiments include that of Bower and Springston (1970), who showed that pause structure interacted with group structure in the recall of letter sequences. The group structure in the 12-letter sequences resulted either from their consisting of four pronounceable, but meaningless, trigrams, as in the sequence *DATBECJAXPEL*, or from their consisting of meaningful trigrams, such as in *FBIPHDBBCPTO*. By highlighting the extensive similarities between such experiments and others employing musical stimuli, Deutsch and others apparently undermine the rule-based models described above. In particular, it is difficult to see how the rules and operators characteristic of such models could be applied to the letter sequences, with their subgroups defined by familiarity. It is, of course, possible that entirely different mechanisms underlie the convergent results of the two types of experiment, but this seems intuitively unlikely. A more likely explanation is that in melody perception, as in linguistic perception, the process of chunking into typical or familiar phrases plays an important part in the memory of extended sequences.

This view accords well with that of Oura (1991), who postulates a "reduced-pitch-pattern model for melodic processing" in which prototypes, that is archetypal melodic patterns, are stored in long-term memory and are used to aid in the learning of new melodies from the same idiom. Oura gives experimental support for this hypothesis as, indirectly, do Sloboda and Parker (1985), who tested the immediate recall of melodies, and who concluded that ". . . Musicians code harmonic relationships that seem less accessible to non-musicians. In both groups however there is evidence of a great amount of common processing. Subjects seem to share the pool of basic melodic and rhythmic building blocks. . . ."

The influence of learned prototypes also extends to the generation of melodic (and harmonic) expectations. Carlsen (1981) shows that melodic expectations are strongly influenced by a subject's cultural background and Schmuckler (1989, 1990) suggests that expectations are 'referent guided', that is, guided by underlying (culturally acquired) schemas, which he compares with Meyer's melodic processes (Meyer, 1973).

2. Previous Connectionist Models

Previous connectionist models of melodic-sequence learning, such as those proposed by Bharucha and Todd (1989), Todd (1989) and Mozer (1991), have, I believe, failed to take sufficient account of the phrased nature of melodies. Moreover, they employ networks, based on those of Jordan (1986) and Elman (1990), which are inappropriate as models of perception for several reasons:

(1)   The networks are not self-organizing, that is, their operation requires 'external' intervention. Much of the need for such intervention stems from the fact that these networks are adapted from standard feedforward networks for supervised learning, and therefore inherit, for instance, the need to be run in two distinct phases, namely a training phase and a testing, or performance, phase. The network dynamics are different for these two phases (particularly if teacher forcing is used), and intervention is necessary to specify which dynamics are in operation at a given time. The fact that the learning is supervised also implies a further distinction between phases. In the learning phase, the pattern corresponding to the next note in a sequence is deemed to be the output desired on presentation of the pattern corresponding to the current note and a 'decaying' context. If the pattern corresponding to the next note is available at the output, that note must already have occurred—this implies a time delay on the input. In the performance phase, during which expectations for the next note are generated, such a time delay would prevent those expectations from preceding the occurrence of the expected note.

(2)   The networks do not allow incremental learning. For instance, suppose a network is exposed to, and learns, five melodies. If we subsequently wish the same network to learn a further five melodies, we must train it with all ten melodies if we wish to ensure that the memory of the original five melodies is retained. This clearly casts considerable doubt on the ability of such networks to model melody learning *in vivo*.

(3)   The networks typically require many hundreds of epochs, that is, presentations of a given melody or set of melodies, before learning is achieved. For instance, Todd (1989) presented each of two melodies to his network over 5000 times, before they could both be learned. This was in spite of the fact that he went to considerable trouble to make each presentation analogous to the 'real-life' experience by faithfully varying event durations and so forth. The large number of presentations introduces a considerable disparity in the level of realism.

(4)   The networks are able to perform melody recall, when cued by the activation of the appropriate plan unit, but not, apparently, melody recognition. The lack of feedback to the plan units implies that there is no way to identify, or continue, a familiar melody when heard. This is clearly at odds with the trivial accomplishment of such tasks in reality.

(5)   The networks do not lend themselves to the formation of network hierarchies. Todd (1991) has suggested such a structure, but it requires that each input phrase be assigned a distinct plan unit in such a way that the correct sequence of plans can be extracted from the presentation of a melody. This plan sequence can then be used to train a higher-level network.

(6)   Finally, it is possible to criticize the 'back-propagation' learning rule, and in particular the variants required for training recurrent networks, as being 'far-fetched' (Crick, 1989) as a biological learning mechanism. Having said this, it is clear that it would be foolish to claim that the models proposed in this paper are detailed descriptions of those mechanisms that operate *in vivo*. Nonetheless, attention has been paid, during the development of these models,

to issues of self-organization, stability, locality, etc., and it is in these regards that they can be considered to exhibit greater plausibility than some competing models.

It should be noted that none of these criticisms necessarily denies the usefulness of this type of network for sequence learning; they merely suggest that such networks do not model well the equivalent perceptual process. There are, of course, other networks designed to process sequential input (e.g. Waibel *et al.*, 1989; Fahlman, 1991; Schmidhuber, 1991; Reiss & Taylor, 1991; Houghton, 1990; Kleinfeld, 1986; Wang & Arbib, 1990; etc.), though few of these have been applied to the modelling of music perception. All of them suffer from at least one of the weaknesses listed above. The next sections describe unsupervised networks for sequence learning, which avoid all of these problems.

3. Unsupervised Classification and the Masking Field

Self-organizing networks that perform unsupervised learning are well suited to the modelling of perceptual processes. Gjerdingen (1989, 1990) used ART2 networks (Carpenter & Grossberg, 1987) in the categorization of patterns derived from the early works of Mozart. The ART2 network essentially consists of two fields of cells: the lower field, F_1, stores a spatial pattern of activities; the upper field, F_2, classifies this pattern, the class (usually) being signalled by the sustained activation of only one of the F_2 cells. The classification performed by the network is both stable, in that learning of novel patterns does not obliterate previously acquired knowledge, and plastic, in that novel classes can always be learned, providing the capacity of the network is not exceeded. As Gjerdingen himself notes (Gjerdingen, 1991), the use of such a network to perform classification of patterns corresponding to item sequences necessitates a more complex structure for the classifying field, F_2, than that most often employed. He suggests the use of a masking field, developed by Cohen and Grossberg (1987) in an attempt to address the so-called 'temporal chunking problem'. This refers to the observation that sequences of items tend to be perceived in chunks (as described above), in spite of the fact that the individual items out of which those chunks are formed are necessarily at least as familiar, in terms of frequency of occurrence, as the chunks themselves.

The masking field, denoted F_m, is, like the ART F_2 field, an on-centre off-surround field of cells, that is, each cell sends excitatory input to itself and inhibitory input to all other cells in the field. A masking-field cell receives bottom-up input via weighted connections from an input or item field, F_i. The activities of the cells in F_i represent information relating to an item sequence: the non-zero activation of a given cell indicates that the corresponding item has occurred in the recent past, while the relative activation of cells indicates the order of item occurrence. For instance, the item sequence (1, 2, 3) might be represented by a pattern of activities such that $y_1 > y_2 > y_3$, where y_n represents the activity of the cell that responds to item *n*—this is further discussed later. Each masking-field cell is randomly connected to a small subset of the cells in F_i, for a given F_m cell this receptive field usually consists of four F_i cells or fewer. The size of a masking-field cell is defined as the number of F_i cells to which it is connected, that is, the magnitude of its receptive field. Larger masking-field cells 'dilute' their bottom-up input and therefore require a significant proportion of the cells in their receptive field to be active before they themselves can respond strongly. The magnitude of the inhibitory signal emanating from an F_m cell increases with that cell's size, while the weight of the inhibitory connection between two F_m cells is small for cells with distinct receptive fields, but increases with the overlap between receptive fields. Masking-field cells that share the same receptive field thus compete strongly.

The activities, x, of masking-field cells obey differential equations of the form

$$\frac{d}{dt} x_i = - Ax_i + (B - x_i) \, [I_i + f(x_i)] - (C + x_i) \sum_{m \neq i} g(x_m) \tag{1}$$

where x_i is the activation of the ith cell, such that $-C < x_i < B$, A is a decay parameter, I_i is the cell's bottom-up input, $f(x_i)$ is a self-excitation term and $\sum_{m \neq i} g(x_m)$ describes the inhibitory input from other cells in the field. The dynamic behaviour of the masking field is quite complex, but its design addresses the temporal chunking problem in the following way. When a single item cell is active, only F_m cells connected to that cell alone will be capable of responding strongly—larger F_m cells suffer from the dilution of their bottom-up input, as noted above. As more items activate at F_i, however, the larger cells connected to the set of active F_i cells are able to activate and, in doing so, mask (suppress) activation at other smaller cells, in spite of the fact that some of these smaller cells experience activity across the whole of their receptive fields. In this way, the presentation of a short item sequence, say (1, 2, 3), at F_1 will not, *a priori*, lead to the activation of three small cells at F_m, but rather will result in the activation of a single, larger F_m cell. The limit on the size of a given F_m cell's receptive field implies a corresponding maximum 'chunk size'—this is most often assumed to be four items (cf. Johnson, 1970).

The masking properties described above result from the structure of the masking field before any learning has taken place: there is an *a priori* bias towards the 'recognition' of chunks rather than individual items. Learning (pseudo-Hebbian and unsupervised) in the weighted connections linking the two fields can lead to subtle changes in the masking-field dynamics. To ensure the stability and plasticity required, such learning is most naturally carried out within an adaptive resonance architecture, in which the masking field replaces the field F_2. The construction of such a combined network is a non-trivial task: the design constraints involved are described in Gjerdingen (1992) and Page (1993). Both studies employed the resultant network in the processing of musical sequences: the former in the processing of harmonic sequences from the works of Handel; the latter in the generation of expectations resulting from the learning of simple nursery-rhyme melodies. Expectations for, in particular, the next note to occur following partial presentation of a melodic phrase were generated by considering the 'anticipatory' activation of large masking-field cells. For instance, suppose the sequence (1, 2, 3) has been presented frequently, so that a specific size-3 F_m cell has learned, by virtue of excitatory-weight adaptation, to respond to it strongly. On presentation of the partial sequence (1, 2), the size-3 cell will begin to activate prior to the completion of its learned phrase—the dilution of the input which, *a priori*, prevents activation of large cells in response to shorter sequences is offset somewhat by the strengthening of the bottom-up connections to the larger cell. The anticipatory activation of a large F_m cell leads to the priming of expected items via the top-down connections characteristic of an ART-type architecture. Thus, the network's expectations for future items can be 'read out' at F_i.

It is important to note the way in which this notion of expectation differs from that implied by the supervised-learning approach. The expectations discussed here result from the unsupervised learning of commonly occurring phrases. Bharucha (1991) correctly criticizes the inappropriate use of supervised learning and suggests that it be restricted to "tasks for which target vectors are both available and necessary", giving as an example the learning of musical sequences. The work described here suggests that target vectors, in the sense in which the term is employed within the supervised-learning paradigm, are not necessary for the learning of musical sequences, indicating, perhaps, that an unsupervised paradigm is to be preferred.

In fact, extensive simulation of the combined masking-field/ART network, described in Page (1993), shows that there are several fundamental problems with this particular structural formulation of the masking-field principles. These problems, many of which are associated with the ART-type reset events, become particularly evident when the network is operated in the high-vigilance regime needed to enable differentiation between similar phrases, such as the 'anagram' phrases (1,2,3,4) and (1,3,2,4). Moreover, the 'pre-wiring' of the F_i–F_m connections causes combinatorial explosion in the number of F_m cells required, which is evident even for apparently simple problems. In the light of these difficulties, subsequent work employed the SONNET 1 network developed by Nigrin (1990). This network is based on the same principles as those underlying the masking-field/ART combination but, nonetheless, offers considerable advantages—these will be highlighted in the detailed description that follows.

4. The SONNET 1 Network

4.1. Formal Description

The following description of the SONNET 1 network is based on that presented in Nigrin (1990, 1992), but necessarily omits much detail. It will chiefly be directed towards showing how the network can accomplish the learning of simple melodic sequences, and how this learning leads to the generation of the veridical expectations required for accurate recall of learned sequences.

A SONNET 1 network consists of two fields, an item field, denoted F_1, and a masking-type field, F_2. As before, the item field consists of a set of cells, each one of which responds to a distinct item, say a musical note. The F_1-cell activities, s, obey the differential equation

$$\frac{\mathrm{d}}{\mathrm{d}t} s_i = (B_1 - s_i)(v_1 s_i + I_i^{(1)}) - s_i \sum_{j \neq i} v_1 s_j \tag{2}$$

where B_1 is the maximum cell activation, $I_i^{(1)}$ is the cell's external input and v_1 is a constant. The parameters B_1, v_1 and $I_i^{(1)}$ can be varied, along with the time for which external input is applied, to produce a short-term memory (STM) field with an approximately constant ratio between the activations of cells corresponding to successive items in an isochronous sequence. This ratio was set approximately equal to 2 in Nigrin (1990) and in the work described here, so that the isochronously presented sequence (1,2,3,4) gives rise to a spatial pattern of F_1 activities such that $s_1 = 2s_2 = 4s_3 = 8s_4$. By enabling changes in F_1 activities to occur only during a fixed time-interval, t_c, after the onset of an item, the evolving spatial pattern can be made insensitive to the tempo in which the input-sequence is presented (providing t_c is less than the item inter-onset interval). Unfortunately, this measure also prevents different presentation rhythms from being reflected in the pattern at F_1. Page (1993) proposes that the output from an attentional beat-tracker be used to gate the changes in activation at F_1, rather than the onsets of actual items. Briefly, this enables activity changes for the time-interval, t_c, after the occurrence of each beat, regardless of whether an item occurs at that time point. Thus, for instance, the sequence $(1,2,3^2,4)$ (where the superscript indicates the item's duration in beats if it differs from one) is represented by an F_1 pattern in which $x_1 = 2x_2 = 4x_3 = 16x_4$, while tempo-invariance is preserved as long as the attentional mechanism tracks the beat reliably. The beat-based attentional modulation of activity changes is assumed to operate in the networks described here—a full description of a 'neural' beat-tracker, and its application to the modulation task as well as to the tempo-invariant coding of durational patterns, can be found in Page (1993). Clearly, the activation of cells corresponding to items early in the sequence cannot continue to grow without limit: when the total activation in F_1 reaches a given threshold, a reset event is triggered, which sets to zero the activities of those cells whose activation exceeds a certain value. This means of limiting the capacity of STM is further discussed below.

Unlike the Cohen–Grossberg masking field, the SONNET 1 network is initially homogeneous: F_1 is fully connected to F_2, and F_2 cells are of uniform size. The inhomogeneity that is characteristic of a masking field emerges in response to the input environment, thus avoiding the combinatorial explosion in the number of F_2 cells, described earlier. A crucial aspect of the network's behaviour involves the calculation of the bottom-up input, b, to an F_2 cell. This is given by

$$b_i = I_i^+ I_i^\times \tag{3}$$

where

$$I_i^+ = \sum_{j \in F_1} S_{ji}\, z_{ji}^+ \tag{4}$$

$$I_i^\times = \max_{j \in T_i} (\Pi\, I_{ji}^\times, K_8) \tag{5}$$

$$I_{ji}^\times = K_1 + K_2 \min \left(1, \frac{S_{ji}}{Z_{ji}}\right) \tag{6}$$

$$Z_{ji} = \frac{z_{ji}^+}{\left(\sum_{k \in T_i} (z_{ki}^+)^2\right)^{1/2}} \tag{7}$$

$$S_{ji} = \begin{cases} \dfrac{s_j}{\left(\sum_{k \in T_i} (s_k)^2\right)^{1/2}}, & \text{if } j \in T_i \\[3ex] \dfrac{s_j}{\left(\sum_{k \in F_1} (s_k)^2\right)^{1/2}}, & \text{otherwise} \end{cases} \tag{8}$$

where s_j is the activity of the jth F_1 cell, z_{ji}^+ is the excitatory weight from the jth F_1 cell to the ith F_2 cell, T_i is the set of indices corresponding to the set of F_1 cells to which the ith F_2 cell is 'significantly' connected (see later) and b_i represents the bottom-up input to the ith F_2 cell assembly, χ_i. The cell assembly χ_i comprises the set of cells b_i, c_i, d_i and e_i, the same symbol being used both for the name and for the activation of a given cell. A diagram of the network connectivity is given in Figure 1; filled squares represent adaptable weights.

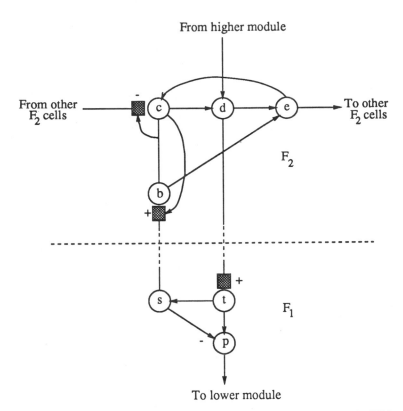

From higher module

From other
F_2 cells

To other
F_2 cells

F_2

F_1

To lower module

Figure 1. The network connectivity (adapted from Nigrin, 1990). This shows the arrangement of cells in both F_1 and F_2 cell assemblies. Changes in cell activations and intervening connection-weights are globally modulated by a beat-tracking attentional signal (not shown).

All parameters of the form K_n are constants and the subscripts are chosen so as to be compatible with the description given in Nigrin (1990). The term I_i^+ is the usual weighted activation term, that is, the inner product of the normalized input and the weight vector. The term I_i^x compares how well the current normalized input pattern matches the cell's weight vector (itself normalized over the set T_i)—Nigrin refers to this as the 'confidence' of the F_2 cell. The use of I^x ensures that even small changes in the input pattern, in particular those resulting from items towards the end of a sequence, can make a significant difference to the bottom-up input to a given cell. It should be noted that, in order to ensure that signals are available at all network 'localities' at which they are used, while minimizing the number of inter-cell connections required, Nigrin suggests that two signals, for example I^+ and I^x, can be multiplexed on the same 'channel'. Nigrin's scheme is assumed to operate in the networks described here.

The bottom-up weights are modified using the following differential equation:

$$\frac{\mathrm{d}}{\mathrm{d}t} z_{ji}^+ = \varepsilon_1 \varepsilon_2 \, r_{ji} \, c_i \, [-L_i z_{ji}^+ + S_{ji} \, c_i] \tag{9}$$

where $\varepsilon_1 \varepsilon_2$ is the learning rate. The bottom-up weight vector to a given F_2 cell becomes 'parallel' to the current input vector at a rate dependent on the activity,

c_i, of that cell. The term c_i also multiplies the input term, S_{ji}, causing "the maximum value of the weights to depend on the value of c_i". This is important in ensuring that a given input pattern will not be learned by an F_2 cell if there already exists an F_2 cell which has learned a sufficiently similar input pattern—'sufficient similarity' is measured, as in ART networks, relative to a vigilance parameter. In short, a cell which has previously learned a given input pattern will inhibit the activation of other cells on presentation of that input pattern (and similar patterns)—this keeps the activations, c, of such cells low and thus prevents them from fully learning the input pattern. The term L_i is set to zero at F_2 cells whose bottom-up weight vector, is small, and to a constant, L, otherwise. In addition, when sufficient learning has taken place at a given F_2 cell, such that $I_i^+ \geq 1.0$, all learning at that cell is stopped to ensure stability. A cell assembly at which the weights are thus frozen is referred to as being committed. The way in which the term r_{ji} regulates the learning process is described in detail in Nigrin (1990, 1992). It allows the network to learn, for instance, two distinct but similar patterns, rather than a single amalgam pattern, even when they are presented in alternation.

The set T_i was earlier described as the set of indices corresponding to the set of F_1 cells to which the ith F_2 cell is significantly connected. To be more accurate, the set T_i is the set of indices corresponding to the set of F_1 cells which tend to have a significant activation at times when c_i is also high. The set T_i is specified by

$$j \in T_i \text{ iff } K_3 \, w_{ji} \geq w_{0i} \tag{10}$$

where w_{0i} is the largest secondary weight w_{ji} to χ_i. The secondary weights, w_{ji}, are given by

$$\frac{\mathrm{d}}{\mathrm{d}t} w_{ji} = \begin{cases} \varepsilon_1 \, \varepsilon_2 \, r_{ji} \, c_i \, [-L_i \, w_{ji} + c_i], & \text{if } K_4 \, S_{ji} > S_{0i} \\ \\ \varepsilon_1 \, \varepsilon_2 \, r_{ji} \, c_i \, [-L_i \, w_{ji}], & \text{otherwise} \end{cases} \tag{11}$$

although Page (1993) suggests that the learning modulator, r_{ji}, should best be omitted. S_{0i} is the largest value of S_{ji} seen by the ith F_2 cell. The set T_i must be specified so that the calculation of $I_i^\times$ depends only on the activity of those F_1 cells which are active in χ_i's classified or near-classified pattern. In addition, information pertaining to the set T_i is used in the calculation of S_{ji}, Z_{ji} and r_{ji}. The evolution of the set T_i shows how the bottom-up connectivity pattern characteristic of a masking field, whereby each F_2 cell is connected only to a subset of the F_1 cells, can emerge from a network that is initially fully connected.

The activity of the cell c_i at F_2 is given by

$$\frac{\mathrm{d}}{\mathrm{d}t} c_i = \varepsilon_1 \left[-Ac_i + \frac{B_2 - c_i}{D_i} (v_2 \, b_i + e_i) - \frac{c_i}{D_i} v_3 \, Q_i \right] \tag{12}$$

where A is a decay constant, B_2 is the cell's maximum activity and v_2 and v_3 are constants. The parameter ε_1 allows the time axis to be scaled. Q_i represents the total lateral inhibitory input to the ith F_2 cell, and is given by

$$Q_i = \begin{cases} \sum_{j \neq i} e_j \, z_{ji}^-, & \text{if } x_i \text{ is committed or } (\sum_{j \neq i} e_j \, z_{ji}^- < K_7 \, e_i^{\text{big}}) \\ \\ K_7 \, e_i^{\text{big}}, & \text{otherwise} \end{cases} \tag{13}$$

where e_i^{big} is the largest current signal from any uncommitted e cell. Note that the total inhibition to an uncommitted cell is limited to allow uncommitted cells to begin to learn patterns even if the patterns, or patterns similar to them, are already classified. The value D_i is called the dilution parameter and it corresponds to the size of the ith F_2 cell. Changes in D_i are given by

$$\frac{d}{dt} D_i = \begin{cases} 0, & \text{if } x_i \text{ is committed} \\ \varepsilon_1 \varepsilon_2 \varepsilon_3 \, c_i \, (-D_i + I_i^\times), & \text{otherwise} \end{cases} \qquad (14)$$

D_i thus tracks the value of $I_i^\times$. The activations of the other F_2 cells are given by

$$d_i = \min(c_i, 1.0) \qquad (15)$$

$$e_i = b_i(d_i)^2 \qquad (16)$$

Uncommitted F_2 cells are prevented from learning to classify patterns that are already classified, by virtue of the fact that their activity remains low due to lateral inhibition from the relevant committed cell. The lateral inhibitory weight, z_{ji}^- from e_j to c_i, is modified as follows:

$$\frac{d}{dt} z_{ji}^- = \begin{cases} \varepsilon_1 \varepsilon_2 \varepsilon_3 \, c_i \, (-z_{ji}^- + 1), & \text{if } (\rho_i \leq I_j^\times) \text{ or both cells are committed} \\ \varepsilon_1 \varepsilon_2 \varepsilon_3 \, c_i \, (-z_{ji}^- - 1), & \text{if } (\rho_i > I_j^\times) \text{ and } (z_{ji}^- > 0) \\ 0, & \text{otherwise} \end{cases} \qquad (17)$$

where ε_3 is typically greater than 1, allowing the lateral inhibitory weights to vary faster than the bottom-up excitatory weights, and where

$$\rho_i = \begin{cases} (I_i^\times)^p, & \text{if } I_i^\times \geq 1 \\ (I_i^\times)^{(1/p)}, & \text{otherwise} \end{cases} \qquad (18)$$

This allows uncommitted cells, which have begun to classify a given pattern, to become 'uninhibited' by cells which have already learned, or are learning, sufficiently different patterns. The variable ρ is the vigilance parameter, which specifies how different the new pattern must be from previously classified patterns to allow it to be classified by an F_2 cell of its own. This vigilance parameter is thus similar in function to that found in ART networks, in that it specifies the 'breadth' of the categories formed; the mechanism differs, however, in that it does not make use of a reset signal—this allows SONNET 1 to avoid many of the problems associated with reset, alluded to earlier. Additionally, the inhibitory connections between committed cells whose sets T do not overlap, are set to, and frozen at, zero.

There also exist feedback (top-down) weights, z_{ij}^f, which are initially set to zero and whose subsequent variation is given by

$$\frac{d}{dt} z_{ij}^f = \varepsilon_1 \varepsilon_2 \, (d_i)^2 \, (-z_{ij}^f + S_j \, d_i) \qquad (19)$$

where z_{ij}^f is the feedback weight from χ_i to s_j and $S_j = s_j / \Sigma_{k \in F_1} s_k$. Thus, the feedback weights from χ_i become parallel to χ_i's classified pattern. A number of additional constraints (Nigrin, 1990, 1992) ensure stability.

Classified phrases (patterns) can be 'chunked out' of STM. Classification is assumed to occur if the activity c_i of a committed F_2 cell continuously exceeds a high threshold, K_{11}, for a time K_{12}, where $K_{12} \approx 2t_c$. The fact that c_i must maintain a high level of activity during the presentation of subsequent items prevents the network from, for instance, erroneously classifying the phrase (1,2,3) during presentation of the phrase (1,2,3,4), when both phrases are represented, or are required to be represented, at F_2. On classification, the activity, c, of the relevant F_2 cell is set to zero. In Nigrin (1990), the fact that a particular phrase (pattern) has been classified is communicated to the relevant F_1 cells by the large, sudden drop in feedback to these cells, which results from the resetting of the classifying F_2 cell; when an F_1 cell receives such a drop in feedback, its own activity is reset. Page (1993) favours the use of a direct reset signal to the relevant F_1 cells. Either process eliminates 'classified' items from STM, while allowing cells representing unclassified items to remain active.

A final point must be made, before the results of network simulations are described. The short-term memory field, F_1, configured as detailed above, is unable to represent sequences containing item repetitions, for example the sequence (1,2,1,3). Nigrin (1990) proposes a solution which entails considerable additional complexity. Briefly, multiple (M) distinct F_1 cells are assigned to respond to a given item, with the constraint that no more than one of them can be receiving external input, $I^{(1)}$, at any given time. In particular, F_1 cells which are already active when a relevant item occurs, will not receive additional external input as a result of that event. This formulation requires multiple (M) connections between each pair of cells (one from F_1 the other from F_2). These multiple links are themselves linked by inhibitory connections, so that only one of the F_1–F_2 links between a given pair of cells is active at any given time. Page (1993) suggests a computationally efficient way of simulating the effect of this connectivity pattern.

4.2. Simulations

The SONNET 1 network, with the modifications described above and extended so as to be capable of dealing with repeated items, was simulated on a NeXT Workstation. A specifically designed graphical interface enabled the changing of any of the network parameters at run-time and provided animated plots of certain cell activities. To illustrate the network's performance, it was tested with input sequences derived from simple nursery-rhyme melodies. The twelve melodies that were used are shown in Table I.

Table I. The melodies used in simulations: numbers indicate scale notes (1 = *do*, etc.); superscripts indicate note durations (in beats), when different from one

Melody	Data
1	5 4 5 1 2 4 5 1 5 4 5 1 2 4 5 1
2	1 3 2 4 3 4 2 1 1 3 2 4 3 4 2 1
3	3 2 1^2 3 2 1^2 5 4 3^2 5 4 3^2 1 7 1 5 1 7 1 5 1 7 1 5 3 2 1^2
4	1 5 6 5 4 3 2 1 5 4 3 2 5 4 3 2 1 5 6 5 4 3 2 1
5	1 1 5 1 2 2 7 5 1 1 5 1 2 5 1^2
6	1 2 3 1 1 2 3 1 1 2 3 1 6 2 3 1
7	1 3 5 5 4 2 3 1 1 3 5 5 4 2 3 1
8	5 5 3 1 2 2 7 5 5 5 3 1 6 7 1^2 3 4 3 1 2 2 7 5 3 4 3 1 6 7 1^2
9	1 5 6 5 4 3 2 1 1 7 6 5 1 5 3 1
10	1 3 2 1 3 5 4 3 6 5 4 3 1 3 2 1
11	5 3 4 2 1 3 5^2 5 3 4 2 1 5 1^2
12	1 2 3 1 1 2 3 1 3 4 5^2 3 4 5^2 5 5 3 1 5 5 3 1 1 5 1^2 1 5 1^2

Table II. The phrases found in the melody set

Phrase	No. of occurrences	Phrase	No. of occurrences
1,1,5,1	2	3,4,2,1	2
1,2,3,1	5	3,4,3,1	2
1,3,2,1	2	3,4,5^2	2
1,3,2,4	2	3,5,4,3	1
1,3,5^2	1	4,2,3,1	2
1,3,5,5	2	4,3,2,1	3
1,5,1^2	3	5,3,4,2	2
1,5,3,1	1	5,4,3^2	2
1,5,6,5	3	5,4,3,2	2
1,7,1,5	3	5,4,5,1	2
1,7,6,5	1	5,5,3,1	4
2,2,7,5	3	6,2,3,1	1
2,4,5,1	2	6,5,4,3	1
2,5,1^2	1	6,7,1^2	2
3,2,1^2	3		

Each number corresponds to one of the seven scale-notes in the diatonic scale, *do–ti*. A superscript refers to the duration (in beats) of a note, with the absence of a superscript denoting a duration of one. Underlining indicates that the note comes from an adjacent octave, although octave equivalence is assumed here. The melodies have been simplified from the originals,[1] so as to remove trills and other embellishments. The notes that remain represent the 'structural notes' (cf. Oura, 1991) of the melody. This process of simplification can be thought of as being carried out by the beat-tracking attentional mechanism discussed earlier, in that only on-beat notes are considered structural and thereby passed as inputs to F_1. The spacing of the numbers for a given melody signifies the phrases into which each is most naturally divided. This division reflects metrical factors as well as factors relating to each melody's verbal accompaniment—the way in which this 'external' information can be employed will be discussed later. The complete set of phrases found in the melody set is shown in Table II.

The object of these simulations was firstly to show that a SONNET 1 network could learn, under various presentation conditions, each of the phrases in the input set, and, secondly, to show that once these phrases had been learned, the network could generate 'plausible' expectations when presented with incomplete phrases. Before describing the presentation conditions, here are the details of some additional modifications that were made to the network after initial trials.

The first modification involved the short-term memory, F_1. Initially, activation and weight changes, at F_1 and F_2, were enabled over the same time period, t_c, after the occurrence of a beat. This meant that the full pattern representing a given sequence was only evident at the very end of the attentional pulse resulting from the beat accompanying the onset of its final note. This was undesirable, particularly when the generation of expectations was considered. To address this problem, activation changes at F_1 were enabled for a shorter time than were weight changes and activation changes at F_2. The only assumption is that the attentional signal affects each field differently. The parameters at F_1 were adjusted to ensure that the ratio between activities corresponding to successive items, remained approximately equal to 2 for an isochronously presented sequence.

The second modification involved a change in the way $I^\times$ was calculated for committed (or near-committed) cells. Again, this resulted from consideration of the network's ability to generate expectations after phrase learning. To illustrate the potential problem, assume that $\chi_{1,2,3,4}$ has learned to represent the sequence (1,2,3,4) and $\chi_{1,2,5,3}$ the sequence (1,2,5,3). On presentation of the sequence (1,2,3), the inputs to each cell are: $I^+_{1,2,3,4} = 0.99$, $I^+_{1,2,5,3} = 0.97$, $I^\times_{1,2,3,4} = I^\times_{1,2,5,3} = 4.0$. Thus $b_{1,2,3,4} = 3.96$ and $b_{1,2,5,3} = 3.88$. The small difference in the bottom-up input to each of the cells is at odds with the observation that one of them represents a legitimate superset of the current input, while the other does not. In order to remedy this situation, a simple modification was made so that $I^\times$, for all cells whose bottom-up weight vector exceeded a certain length (in the region of 0.7), was calculated thus:

$$I_i^\times = \max_{j \in T_i} (\Pi\ I_{ji}^\times, K_8) \tag{20}$$

$$I_{ji}^\times = K_1 + K_2 \min\left(\frac{Z_{ji}}{S_{ji}}, \frac{S_{ji}}{Z_{ji}}\right) \tag{21}$$

Using this formula, the inputs for the case described above would become $I^\times_{1,2,3,4} = 4.0$ and $I^\times_{1,2,5,3} = 2.5$, which correspond more clearly with the appropriateness of each cell.

In the first test of the extended SONNET 1's performance, a network with 7 F_1 cells and 65 F_2 cells was presented with each of the 29 distinct melodic phrases in an incremental learning regime. This regime consisted of the presentation of each phrase as many times as was necessary for an F_2 cell to become committed to classifying that phrase, before proceeding to the presentation of the next phrase. The presentation of a given phrase is accomplished in essentially the same manner as that detailed in Nigrin (1990). Initially, the activation of all cells is set to zero. Then, for each item in the input sequence in turn, the bottom-up input signal to the corresponding F_1 cell is turned on for a given time period. During this time, changes in all network activations and synaptic weights are enabled. For the case in which a note is prolonged over more than one beat, network changes are enabled for a correspondingly increased time period, with the difference that during this extra period there are no bottom-up input signals to F_1—this indicates that the network changes are enabled at such times by the attentional signal in the absence of actual note events. After the presentation of the last sequence item, network changes are further enabled for a number of beats, until the F_1 overload reset event sets the activities of all cells to zero again. Parameters were set so that F_1 overload occurred after a total time equivalent to approximately 7 beats. It should be emphasized that there is no external interference in the network dynamics—the network's behaviour is fully summarized by the differential equations given above.[2]

The full set of 29 different phrases was presented in this way for five random orderings, the network weights being initialized randomly before each of the five orderings. On each occasion, all phrases were learned in a small number of presentations, typically less than 5 (note that this figure depends on the choice of learning rate, ε_2, which was set to 6.0 in all the simulations reported here). Moreover, in each case no F_2 cell became spuriously committed, that is committed, for instance, to a pattern representing a subset of one of the input phrases, or to an amalgam of two different phrase patterns. The network thus accomplishes ideal learning of the input set, and it is by this criterion that the success of a given simulation is to be judged.

The network's performance with this task is encouraging. The input set, while only consisting of 29 distinct phrases, contains many phrases which are similar to each other—in particular, there are many anagram phrases, such as (4,3,2,1,), (4,2,3,1), (3,4,2,1) and (1,3,2,4). Additionally, the fact that SONNET 1's inhomogeneity emerges in response to a given input set, rather than being hard-wired, permits the ratio of the number of F_2 cells with which ideal learning can be achieved, to the number of distinct input patterns, to remain small. In this case, this ratio was a little over 2.

Ideal learning was also achieved for a much more challenging presentation regime, namely a cyclic regime. This involved repeatedly presenting all the phrases in the input set (once again in a random ordering), so that consecutive presentations of any given phrase were separated by presentation of each of the other phrases. Although 70–80% of the input phrases were learned within the first 20 presentations of the complete set, many more presentations (in the region of 80) were required before every single phrase was learned. Due to the prohibitive run-times associated with a cyclic presentation regime, these results describe only two complete runs, and should therefore be treated accordingly.

The third presentation regime involved the incremental presentation of each melody: a melody was presented until all its constituent phrases were learned, then the next melody was presented. The presentation of a melody is accomplished without any indication of the likely phrase boundaries. This regime can be considered to be intermediate between the two regimes detailed above: in the incremental regime, only one phrase is being learned at any given time; in the cyclic regime, all the phrases are (initially) being learned. For the third regime, a small number of new phrases are being learned at a given time. Ideal learning, typically requiring fewer than five presentations of each melody, was once again achieved, although this success relied on two factors. Firstly, for the current input set, which consists only of four-item phrases and three-item phrases with a lengthened final note, it was possible to set the F_1 overload threshold and the threshold above which F_1 cells are reset when overload occurs, so that overload always leads to the resetting of only those notes previous to the most recent phrase boundary. This was convenient in that it suppressed the learning of across-phrase groupings—such parameter settings might not be possible for a more varied input set. Secondly, confusion can arise if, for instance, the phrase (5,4,3) is learned before the phrase (5,4,3,2). Although the chunking out of the shorter phrase is delayed to allow the longer phrase to be learned, chunking out can still occur before F_1 overload—this leaves the item 2 stranded in STM, where it can be inappropriately associated with the subsequent phrase. Both of these potential problems concern the problem of 'bootstrapping', the process of sequence segmentation using the pitch-sequence information alone. In studying a similar bootstrapping problem in the segmentation of phonemic sequences (e.g. spoken language), Cutler and Norris (1988) suggest that stress patterns are important in providing preliminary information. It is therefore at least possible that the metrical aspects of a given melody afford similar clues, which discourage the learning of across-phrase groupings. This is reminiscent of the work of Jones and colleagues (e.g. Jones, 1987), who discuss the separate contributions made by pitch, duration and meter to the overall accent structure of a piece. Possible mechanisms for this 'inter-modal' effect are the subject of further work.

4.3. The Generation of Expectations

Once a SONNET 1 network has learned, within whatever regime, a given set of input patterns, in this case corresponding to short melodic phrases, we can probe it with incomplete phrases to discover whether plausible expectations can be elicited. Expectations are generated by a process similar to that described earlier. Active F_2 cells send top-down signals to F_1; when these signals arrive at currently inactive F_1 cells, they are taken to constitute expectations for the occurrence of the corresponding items. Items corresponding to those inactive F_1 cells which receive most top-down input are, accordingly, most expected. The aim was to generate veridical expectations, ultimately enabling the accurate recall of entire sequences, but Page (1993) found that this necessitated a number of modifications to the network algorithm. The principal problem was that of interference: for instance, on presentation of the (sub)phrase (5,4,3), the F_2 cell $\chi_{6,5,4,3}$ activates somewhat, leading to the inappropriate expectation of a 6.

To address this problem, Page (1993) proposes that the set, P, of F_2 cells that are able to generate top-down signals be restricted in various ways. Firstly, he suggests that only committed F_2 cells should be in the set P—this is intuitively reasonable, since expectations will only correspond to phrases that have occurred sufficiently frequently to be learned at F_2. Further restriction of the set P requires the calculation of two new variables, W^+ and $W^\times$, for each F_2 cell. They are defined thus:

$$W_i^+ = \sum_{j \in T_i} W_{ji}^+ \tag{22}$$

$$W_{ji}^+ = \begin{cases} 1, & \text{if } K_4 S_{ji} > S_{0i} \text{ and } S_{0i} > 0 \\ 0, & \text{otherwise} \end{cases} \tag{23}$$

$$W_{ji}^\times = \max_{j \in T_i} (\Pi \ W_{ji}^\times, K_8) \tag{24}$$

$$W_{ji}^\times = \begin{cases} K_1 + K_2, & \text{if } K_4 \ S_{ji} > S_{0i} \text{ and } S_{0i} > 0 \\ K_1, & \text{otherwise} \end{cases} \tag{25}$$

where S_{0i} is defined as before. The variables W^+ and $W^\times$ are calculated, using the secondary weights, in a way that is entirely analogous to the calculation of I^+ and $I^\times$. Thus, even though new variables are being introduced, no novel mechanism is introduced to account for their calculation. For a given F_2 cell, the value of W^+ represents the number of F_1 cells that are in the set T_i and that have significant activation; the value of $W^\times$ represents the highest value of $I^\times$ that a cell can be expected to have as a result of the currently active F_1 pattern.

The newly defined variables can now be used in restricting the set P to those F_2 cells which are 'on target'. A cell which is on target is defined as one whose learned pattern is entirely consistent with all, or part, of the current F_1 pattern. Thus, if the input pattern represents the sequence (1,2,3), then the F_2 cell $\chi_{1,2,3,4}$ is on target, while the cell $\chi_{1,3,2,4}$ is not. Likewise, for the input pattern representing the sequence (5,4,3), the cells $\chi_{5,4,3}$ and $\chi_{5,4,3,2}$ are on target, whereas the cell $\chi_{6,5,4,3}$ is not. We can ascertain those cells which are on target by comparing the values of $I^\times$ and $W^\times$ at a cell. Since $W^\times$ represents the highest value of $I^\times$ that can be expected at a given F_2 cell given the current input pattern, a cell can be deemed to be on target if the actual value of I^x is not significantly lower than this. The comparison between I^x and W^x uses information entirely local to the cell.

There remains the problem of unwarranted expectations that can occur, for instance, in response to the sequence (1,2,3,4), if there exist committed F_2 cells $\chi_{1,2,3,4}$ and $\chi_{3,4,5}$ Using the definition above, both cells will be considered on target, leading to the expectation of a 5, in spite of the apparent completion of a phrase. We can overcome this problem by comparing the values of W^+ for the two cells. In the circumstances described, $W^+_{1,2,3,4} = 4$ while $W^+_{1,2,3,4} = 2$. Thus, in order to define properly the set P, we conclude that a cell not only has to be committed and on target, but that it also must satisfy

$$W^+ > K_{16}\, W^+_{max} \tag{26}$$

where W^+_{max} is the maximum value of W^+ found at an on-target cell. This comparison of W^+ requires the distribution of this information across F_2, and thus some additional network structure; the comparison is not susceptible to noise, however, since W^+ is quantized, that is, it is able to take only integer values. This allows latitude in the setting of the constant K_{16}.

Finally, in generating veridical expectations, we wish the network to provide expectations of possible continuations without regard to the number of distinct learned phrases with which those expectations are consistent (since there is no reason to believe that this information necessarily reflects the probability of a given transition). The top-down feedback signal, t_j, received by the jth F_1 cell, is not, therefore, calculated by

$$t_j = \sum_{i \in F_2} d_i\, z^f_{ij} \tag{27}$$

but rather by

$$t_j = \max_{i \in P} (d_i\, z^f_{ij}) \tag{28}$$

Thus, instead of summing the priming signals from individual F_2 cells, t_j is defined as the maximum top-down feedback signal experienced at a given F_1 cell.

Having defined the set P and modified the calculation of t_j, an extended SONNET 1 network that had previously learned the set of input phrases was probed with the relevant one-, two- and three-note probe sequences. The expectations elicited are shown in Tables III–V: for each probe sequence, the expected items are indicated, the figures in parentheses denoting the corresponding expectation strengths. Attention should be paid to the relative expectations for various items, since the absolute values can be scaled arbitrarily.

Table III. Expectations elicited from one-note probes (note that no phrase begins with a '7')

Probe	Expectations					
1	3(0.023)	5(0.021)	1(0.010)	2(0.006)	7(0.006)	6(0.003)
2	5(0.023)	1(0.011)	4(0.006)	2(0.006)	7(0.003)	—
3	2(0.023)	4(0.021)	1(0.011)	5(0.010)	3(0.003)	—
4	2(0.006)	3(0.005)	1(0.001)	—	—	—
5	4(0.023)	3(0.011)	5(0.006)	2(0.001)	1(0.001)	—
6	7(0.023)	1(0.011)	5(0.006)	2(0.006)	3(0.003)	4(0.003)

Table IV. Expectations elicited from two-note probes

Probe	Expectations				
1,1	5(0.014)	1(0.006)	—	—	—
1,2	3(0.013)	1(0.006)	—	—	—
1,3	5(0.054)	2(0.015)	1(0.007)	5(0.006)	4(0.006)
1,5	1(0.051)	3(0.015)	6(0.015)	5(0.007)	—
1,7	1(0.014)	6(0.014)	5(0.006)	—	—
2,2	7(0.014)	5(0.006)	—	—	—
2,4	5(0.014)	1(0.007)	—	—	—
2,5	1(0.054)	—	—	—	—
3,2	1(0.054)	—	—	—	—
3,4	5(0.050)	2(0.014)	3(0.014)	1(0.007)	—
3,5	4(0.015)	3(0.007)	—	—	—
4,2	3(0.014)	1(0.006)	—	—	—
4,3	2(0.014)	1(0.007)	—	—	—
5,3	4(0.015)	2(0.007)	—	—	—
5,4	3(0.055)	5(0.014)	1(0.007)	2(0.006)	—
5,5	3(0.015)	1(0.007)	—	—	—
6,2	3(0.014)	1(0.007)	—	—	—
6,5	4(0.014)	3(0.007)	—	—	—
6,7	1(0.054)	—	—	—	—

The performance is good: for each of the probe sequences, the network's expectations correspond exactly with those suggested by inspection of the complete phrase set. Note that ambiguity is represented by approximately equal expectations for two or more notes. In addition, full presentation of a learned phrase resulted in zero expectation in all cases, apart from presentation of the phrase (5,4,3), which elicited an expectation for the item '2'. A larger context is necessary in order to

Table V. Expectations elicited from three-note probes

Probe	Expectations	
1,1,5	1(0.025)	—
1,2,3	1(0.019)	—
1,3,2	1(0.025)	4(0.023)
1,3,5	5(0.018)	—
1,5,3	1(0.023)	—
1,5,6	5(0.026)	—
1,7,1	5(0.024)	—
1,7,6	5(0.024)	—
2,2,7	5(0.025)	—
2,4,5	1(0.027)	—
3,4,2	1(0.026)	—
3,4,3	1(0.025)	—
3,5,4	3(0.026)	—
4,2,3	1(0.025)	—
4,3,2	1(0.025)	—
5,3,4	2(0.026)	—
5,4,3	2(0.017)	—
5,4,5	1(0.025)	—
5,5,3	1(0.027)	—
6,2,3	1(0.026)	—
6,5,4	3(0.026)	—

determine the circumstances under which this expectation is justified (see later). It should be noted that in the situation in which two cells, one representing a three-note phrase, the other a four-note phrase, are both on target in response to a one- or two-note probe, the expectations generated by the cell representing the three-note phrase will dominate those generated by the cell representing the four-note phrase—this is consistent with the fact that a greater proportion of the three-note phrase is present at F_1. The next section shows how this effect can be overcome, as it must be in certain circumstances, by the introduction of hierarchical expectations.

4.4. *Network Hierarchies and Hierarchical Expectations*

If the network is to be capable of producing unambiguous veridical expectations corresponding, for instance, to specific learned melodies, it is necessary to supply a means by which additional context can be influential. To illustrate the point, in the context of a particular melody, we will want the probe sequence (1,3) to elicit a stronger expectation for a 2 than for a 5. This is the reverse of the situation found in the absence of additional context.

Additional context information can be made available by the provision of a hierarchy of network modules, each containing an F_1 and an F_2 field. The hierarchy is constructed so that the classification of a note phrase at the F_2 field in the relevant module leads to the activation of a phrase item at the F_1 field in the module immediately above. This upper module thus learns familiar phrase sequences. The tempo-invariance described earlier allows the same set of parameters to be used for each module, regardless of its position in the hierarchy. To illustrate how the hierarchy can affect note expectations, suppose that, in addition to a module that has learned our input phrase set, there is also a module immediately above that has learned the single phrase sequence ((1,5,6,5), (4,3,2,1)). On presentation of that sequence, therefore, the activity of $\chi_{1,5,6,5}$ will grow steadily until it dominates other activities at the F_2 field of the lower module. At some point after the presentation of its associated phrase is complete (typically after the presentation of the 3), $\chi_{1,5,6,5}$ and the relevant F_1 cells will be reset (chunking out) and a phrase item will be forwarded to the F_1 field of the upper module. The occurrence of the phrase item (1,5,6,5) will lead to the expectation, within that module, for the phrase item (4,3,2,1). The top-down priming signal received by the relevant upper-module F_1 cell is transmitted back down the hierarchy to the corresponding lower-module F_2 cell assembly, where it has three effects. Firstly, it boosts the cell's activity d, which both enhances that cell's ability to compete for activation and boosts the top-down signal that it emits to F_1: remember that the boost in the top-down signal emitted by the primed F_2 cell will only be manifested if that cell is in the set P. Secondly, it boosts the value of $I^\times$ at that cell, which allows it to reach its classification threshold more quickly. Thirdly, it substantially decreases the time K_{12} for which the F_2 cell's activity c must continuously exceed the threshold K_{11} before chunking out can occur. This enables expectations to be elicited even for phrase-initiating items. By modulating the strength of the inter-module top-down signal, we can ensure that the hierarchical expectations have the desired effect on the note-level expectations. Nigrin (1990) describes, in general terms, the means by which a hierarchy can be constructed; Page (1993) suggests a specific mechanism and shows how object-oriented programming techniques can be employed in efficient simulation of hierarchical networks.

Table VI. Expectations produced during recall of melody 9

Melody 9: 1 5 6 5 4 3 2 1 1̲ 7 6 5 1̲ 5 3 1

F_1 Pattern	Expectations				
—	1(0.260)	5(0.131)	6(0.063)	5(0.030)	—
1	5(0.143)	6(0.069)	5(0.033)	3(0.023)	1(0.010)
1,5	6(0.093)	1(0.048)	5(0.044)	3(0.015)	—
1,5,6	5(0.084)	—	—	—	—
—	4(0.239)	3(0.119)	2(0.057)	1(0.027)	—
4	3(0.130)	2(0.063)	1(0.030)	—	—
4,3	2(0.086)	1(0.040)	—	—	—
4,3,2	1(0.078)	—	—	—	—
—	1(0.254)	7(0.122)	6(0.058)	5(0.027)	—
1	7(0.134)	6(0.063)	5(0.030)	3(0.022)	1(0.010)
1,7	6(0.084)	5(0.039)	1(0.012)	—	—
1,7,6	5(0.074)	—	—	—	—
—	1(0.263)	5(0.127)	3(0.061)	1(0.029)	—
1	5(0.140)	3(0.067)	1(0.032)	2(0.006)	7(0.006)
1,5	3(0.091)	1(0.047)	6(0.014)	5(0.007)	—
1,5,3	1(0.083)	—	—	—	—
—	—	—	—	—	—

4.5. Recognition and Recall

We are now in a position to detail the processes underlying sequence recognition and recall. A sequence is learned by first being chunked into phrases, then further into phrases of phrases, etc., at successive hierarchical levels. At some hierarchical level, a given learned sequence will be represented by a single F_2 cell, which can be thought of as that sequence's plan cell. This plan cell will be strongly activated only by the presentation of its associated sequence: such activation constitutes recognition of the sequence. Moreover, activation of the plan cell, either by partial presentation of the sequence, or by some 'external' means, will give rise to a series of expectations which will enable sequence recall. Page (1993) describes how expected items can be recalled, not only in the correct order, but also in the correct rhythm. The process involves a parallel network hierarchy at which the rhythmic sequence has been learned. The external activation of a plan cell can be thought of as resulting from additional information which can identify the melody in the absence of pitch events, for example, the melody's title.

Simulations have demonstrated the effectiveness of this mechanism: a two-module hierarchical network was taught all phrases, and all phrase phrases, derived from the set of melodies described earlier (actually the longer melodies require a three-module network if all melodies are to be represented by a single plan cell). Table VI shows the expectations that were generated when the plan cell corresponding to melody 9 was activated externally; the most expected note is assumed to be performed at each step. Perfect recall of all the melodies was accomplished in this way.

5. Summary

The connectionist model of sequence learning described here addresses each of the criticisms that were earlier levelled at alternative models.

(1) It is entirely self-organizing—a network's behaviour is described by a set of differential equations, which allow it to respond continuously to an environment in such a way as to learn regularities in that environment without any external interference in its operation. There is no distinction equivalent to that between the training and testing phases of alternative networks. No arbitrary time delays are required and the network is able to run in virtual time.

(2) Learning in the network is both stable and plastic. Novel patterns can be learned at any time and, once learned, will be retained in memory regardless of subsequent exposure.

(3) The stability of the network is maintained across a wide variety of learning rates, enabling patterns to be learned in only a small number of presentations.

(4) The network is able to perform recognition and recall of familiar sequences, and the availability of context information is appropriately modelled as a top-down process.

(5) The network deals naturally with sequences which possess a hierarchical structure. In fact, in order to learn an extended sequence, the network must impose a hierarchical chunking structure. The inability to learn an extended sequence without breaking it into phrases (and phrase phrases, etc.) is a consequence of the limited capacity of short-term memory.

(6) All the inter-cell interactions postulated in the model rely solely on locally available information. The cells themselves are simple and their behaviour can be modelled with differential equations corresponding to 'standard' neural models. All weight-learning is unsupervised and likewise employs only locally available information.

The idea that melodies are chunked on the basis of phrase familiarity rather than on the basis of, for instance, their correspondence with a parsimonious rule system suggests a more unified approach to the study of sequence perception in general. In particular, unlike the rule-based approaches described earlier, the masking-field/SON-NET approach can be easily extended to the study of the perception of linguistic sequences; indeed, it was for this purpose that the models were originally developed.

The phrasing effects noted earlier are also modelled well by the extended SONNET 1 network. The placement of a pause within an otherwise familiar phrase will affect the resulting STM pattern so as to disrupt the recognition (and subsequent chunking out) of that phrase; the placement of a pause between phrases will have no such deleterious effect, and will in fact aid in the chunking process. The experiments demonstrating poor recall for across-group phrases can also be related to chunking out: if a phrase is chunked out shortly after its completion, then the across-phrase group formed by its latter notes and the first notes of the next phrase will never find itself represented in STM and will, accordingly, be difficult to recall. The observation that those subjects with most musical experience perform less well when asked to recall across-phrase groupings particularly when the phrase structure is clearly delineated by a strong cadence, might indicate the relative facility with which they chunk out the first phrase. It should be emphasized that no quantitative analysis of this effect has yet been attempted.

The fact that expectations are seen as resulting from partial activation of cells that represent learned phrases accords well with Bregman's (1990) description of the role of sequential schemas:

> Each schema incorporates information about one particular regularity in our environment . . . we think that schemas become active when they detect, in the incoming sense

data, the particular pattern they deal with. Because many of the patterns schemas look for extend over time, when part of the evidence is present and the schema is activated, it can prepare the perceptual process for the remainder of the pattern.

Nigrin (1993) has extended the SONNET framework considerably beyond SON-NET 1, and further work is necessary to investigate the advantages that his extensions might confer on the current model of musical sequence perception. Nonetheless, it has been demonstrated here that the development of models based on unsupervised, self-organizing neural networks can benefit greatly from the consideration of specific problems from the field of music psychology.

Notes

1. The original rhymes are *Boys and Girls, Rock-a-bye Baby, Three Blind Mice, Twinkle, Twinkle Little Star, Here We Go Round the Mulberry Bush, Pop Goes the Weasel, Can You See (the Little Ducks Play), Polly, Put the Kettle On, I'm a Little Teapot, Incy, Wincy Spider, Little Bird* and *Frère Jacques* respectively.
2. The parameter settings used in the simulations reported here were: $K_1 = 0.5$, $K_2 = 1.5$, $K_3 = 1.6$, $K_4 = 12$, $K_7 = 50$, $K_8 = 0.1$, $K_{11} = 1$, $K_{12} = 0.3$, $\varepsilon_1 = 1$, $\varepsilon_2 = 6$, $\varepsilon_3 = 10$, $L = 1$, $B_1 = 50$, $B_2 = 2$, $v_1 = 0.075$, $v_2 = 3$, $v_3 = 12$, $A = 1$, $I^{(1)} = 0.007$ and $q = 2$.

Acknowledgements

This work was performed as part of a PhD supported by a grant from the UK Science and Engineering Research Council. I am grateful to Mike Greenhough, Al Nigrin and Bob Gjerdingen for their invaluable assistance during the course of the work, and to two anonymous reviewers for their comments on an earlier draft.

References

Bartlett, J.C. & Dowling, W.J. (1988) Scale structure and similarity of melodies. *Music Perception*, **5**, 285–314.
Bharucha, J.J. (1991) Pitch, harmony and neural nets: a psychological perspective. In P.M. Todd & D. Gareth Loy (Eds), *Music and Connectionism*, pp. 84–99. Cambridge, MA: MIT Press.
Bharucha, J.J. & Todd, P.M. (1989) Modeling the perception of tonal structure with neural nets. *Computer Music Journal*, **13**, 44–53.
Bower, G.H. & Springston, F. (1970) Pauses as recoding points in letter series. *Journal of Experimental Psychology*, **83**, 421–430.
Bregman, A.S. (1990) *Auditory Scene Analysis*. Cambridge, MA: MIT Press.
Carlsen, J.C. (1981) Some factors which influence melodic expectancy. *Psychomusicology*, **1**, 12–29.
Carpenter, G.A. & Grossberg, S. (1987) ART2: self-organization of stable category recognition codes for analog input patterns. *Applied Optics*, **26**, 4919–4930.
Cohen, M.A. & Grossberg, S. (1987) Masking fields: A massively parallel neural architecture for learning, recognizing, and predicting multiple groupings of patterned data. *Applied Optics*, **26**, 1866–1891.
Crick, F. (1989) The recent excitement about neural networks. *Nature*, **337**, 129–132.
Cutler, A. & Norris, D. (1988) The Rôle of strong syllables in segmentation for lexical access. *Journal of Experimental Psychology: Human Perception and Performance*, **14**, 113–121.
Deutsch, D. (1972) Octave generalization and tune recognition. *Perception and Psychophysics*, **11**, 411–412.
Deutsch, D. (1980) The processing of structured and unstructured tonal sequences. *Perception and Psychophysics*, **28**, 381–389.
Deutsch, D. & Feroe, J. (1981) The internal representation of pitch sequences in tonal music. *Psychological Review*, **88**, 503–522.
Dowling, W.J. (1972) Recognition of melodic transformations: Inversion, retrograde, and retrograde inversion. *Perception and Psychophysics*, **12**, 417–421.

Dowling, W.J. (1973) Rhythmic groups and subjective chunks in memory for melodies. *Perception and Psychophysics*, 14, 37–40.

Dowling, W.J. (1978) Scale and contour: two components of a theory of memory for melodies. *Psychological Review*, 85, 341–354.

Dowling, W.J. (1986) Context effects on melody recognition: scale-step versus interval representations. *Music Perception*, 3, 281–296.

Dowling, W.J. (1991) Tonal strength and melody recognition after long and short delays. *Perception and Psychophysics*, 50, 305–313.

Dowling, W.J. & Bartlett, J.C. (1981) The importance of interval information in long-term memory for melodies. *Psychomusicology*, 1, 30–49.

Dowling, W.J. & Fujitani, D.S. (1971) Contour, interval and pitch recognition in memory for melodies. *The Journal of the Acoustical Society of America*, 49, 524–531.

Edworthy, J. (1985) Melodic contour and musical structure. In P. Howell, I. Cross & R. West (Eds), *Musical Structure and Cognition*, pp. 169–188. London: Academic Press.

Elman, J.L. (1990) Finding structure in time. *Cognitive Science*, 14, 179–211.

Fahlman, S.E. (1991) *The Recurrent Cascade-correlation Architecture*. Technical Report CMU-CS-91-100. Carnegie Mellon University, School of Computer Science.

Gjerdingen, R.O. (1989) Using connectionist models to explore complex musical patterns. *Computer Music Journal*, 13, 1989.

Gjerdingen, R.O. (1990) Categorization of musical patterns by self-organizing neuronlike networks. *Music Perception*, 7, 339–370.

Gjerdingen, R.O. (1991) Addendum to: Using connectionist models to explore complex musical patterns. In P.M. Todd & D. Gareth Loy (Eds), *Music and Connectionism*, pp. 147–149. Cambridge, MA: MIT Press.

Gjerdingen, R.O. (1992) Learning syntactically significant temporal patterns of chords: a masking field embedded in an ART3 architecture. *Neural Networks*, 5, 551–564.

Houghton, G. (1990) The problem of serial order: A neural network model of sequence learning and recall. In R. Dale, C. Mellish & M. Zock (Eds), *Current Research in Natural Language Generation*, pp. 287–319. London: Academic Press.

Idson, W.I. & Massaro, D.W. (1978) A bidimensional model of pitch in the recognition of melodies. *Perception and Psychophysics*, 24, 551–565.

Johnson, N.F. (1970) The rôle of chunking and organization in the process of recall. In G.H. Bower (Ed.), *Psychology of Learning and Motivation*. New York: Academic Press.

Jones, M.R. (1981) A tutorial on some issues and methods in serial pattern research. *Perception and Psychophysics*, 30, 492–504.

Jones, M.R. (1987) Dynamic pattern structure in music: recent theory and research. *Perception and Psychophysics*, 41, 621–634.

Jordan, M.I. (1986) Attractor dynamics and parallelism in a connectionist sequential machine. *Proceedings of the Eighth Annual Conference of the Cognitive Science Society*, Hillsdale, N.J.

Kallman, H.J. & Massaro, D.W. (1979) Tone chroma is functional in melody recognition. *Perception and Psychophysics*, 26, 32–36.

Kleinfeld, D. (1986) Sequential state generation by model neural networks. *Proceedings of the National Academy of Sciences, USA*, 83, 9469–9473.

Meyer, L. (1973) *Explaining Music*. Berkeley: University of California Press.

Mozer, M.C. (1991) Connectionist music composition based on melodic, stylistic, and psychophysical constraints. In P.M. Todd & D. Gareth Loy (Eds), *Music and Connectionism*, pp. 195–212. Cambridge, MA: MIT Press.

Nigrin, A.L. (1990) *The Stable Learning of Temporal Patterns with an Adaptive Resonance Circuit*. Unpublished doctoral dissertation, Duke University.

Nigrin, A.L. (1992, submitted for publication) SONNET 1: a self-organizing masking field that forms stable category codes.

Nigrin, A.L. (1993) *Neural Networks for Pattern Recognition*. Cambridge, MA: MIT Press.

Oura, Y. (1991) Constructing a representation of a melody: Transforming melodic segments into reduced pitch patterns operated on by modifiers. *Music Perception*, 9, 251–266.

Page, M.P.A. (1993) *Modelling Aspects of Music Perception Using Self-organizing Neural Networks*. Unpublished doctoral dissertation, University of Wales.

Palmer, C. & Krumhansl, C.L. (1987a) Independent temporal and pitch structures in determination of musical phrases. *Journal of Experimental Psychology: Human Perception and Performance*, 13, 116–126.

Palmer, C. & Krumhansl, C.L. (1987b) Pitch and temporal contributions to musical phrase perception: Effects of harmony, performance timing, and familiarity. *Perception and Psychophysics*, 41, 505–518.

Reiss, M. & Taylor, J.G. (1991) Storing temporal sequences. *Neural Networks*, **4**, 773–787.

Restle, F. (1970) Theory of serial pattern learning: structural trees. *Psychological Review*, 77, 481–495.

Restle, F. (1972) Serial patterns: the rôle of phrasing. *Journal of Experimental Psychology*, **92**, 385–390.

Restle, F. & Brown, E.R. (1970) Serial pattern learning. *Journal of Experimental Psychology*, **83**, 120–125.

Schmidhuber, J. (1991) *Neural Sequence Chunkers*. Technical Report FKI-148-91. Universität München, Institut für Informatik, Technische.

Schmuckler, M.A. (1989) Expectation in music: Investigation of melodic and harmonic processes. *Music Perception*, 7, 109–150.

Schmuckler, M.A. (1990) The performance of global expectations. *Psychomusicology*, **9**, 122–147.

Sloboda, J.A. & Parker, D.H.H. (1985) Immediate recall of melodies. In P. Howell, I. Cross & R. West (Eds), *Musical Structure and Cognition*, pp. 143–167. London: Academic Press.

Tan, N., Aiello, R. & Bever, T.G. (1981) Harmonic structure as a determinant of melodic organization. *Memory and Cognition*, **9**, 533–539.

Todd, P.M. (1989) A connectionist approach to algorithmic composition. *Computer Music Journal*, **13**, 27–43.

Todd, P.M. (1991) Addendum to: A connectionist approach to algorithmic composition. In P.M. Todd & D. Gareth Loy (Eds), *Music and Connectionism*, pp. 190–194. Cambridge, MA: MIT Press.

Waibel, A.H., Hanazawa, T., Hinton, G., Shikano, K. & Lang, K.J. (1989) Phoneme recognition using time-delay neural networks. *IEEE Transactions on Acoustics, Speech and Signal Processing*, **37**, 328–339.

Wang, D. & Arbib, M.A. (1990) Complex temporal sequence learning. *Proceedings of the IEEE*, **78**, 1536–1543.

White, B.W. (1960) Recognition of distorted melodies. *American Journal of Psychology*, **73**, 100–107.

An Ear for Melody

BRUCE F. KATZ

A method for the evaluation of melody is presented. The method is based on a connectionist operationalization of the aesthetic ideal of unity in diversity. It is demonstrated that one can determine the degree of unity in diversity of a stimulus by measuring the mean activation levels of a competitive network. This measure is then used to show why stepwise motion is favoured in melodies, and why there tends to be a family resemblance between successive melodic groups. Four sets of simulations were then run to further test the model. In the first, it was shown that the model predicts that positive affect is an inverted U-shaped curve as a function of melodic complexity, in accord with human data. The second treats affect and exposure; the model predicts that exposure to a melody will increase affective response to it, but that this quantity will fall off with over-exposure. In the third set of simulations, it is shown that there is positive affective transfer within a musical genre, but relatively little transfer between genres. Finally, it is shown that degraded good melodies induce a decrease in the model's evaluation function. Difficulties with the model are then discussed, and it is suggested that these problems may be addressed by altering the network dynamics but by preserving the affective measure.

KEYWORDS: Neural networks, music, aesthetics.

1. Introduction

The primary motivation for listening to music is for the pleasurable experience it provides. Musical science could discover everything worth while about the strictly cognitive aspects of musical processing, but unless it revealed why good music produces positive affect, one would be left feeling short-changed. The danger arises because of the natural generalization from other aspects of cognitive science. For example, the qualitative state that accompanies the creation of an analogy may be dismissed as epiphenomenal to this problem-solving activity. But the question of musical affect cannot be dismissed (cf. Searle, 1991), because unless this issue is addressed, it will never be understood why most people spend at least a few hours a week and others devote their lives to detecting or creating pressure variations in the air.

Sloboda (1985) has speculated that musical drive may have evolved because music plays a mnemonic role. In pre-literate times, putting items to music was an important method of remembering them. According to this view, the musical drive

This article appeared originally in *Connection Science*, 1994, **6**, 299–324, and is reprinted with permission.

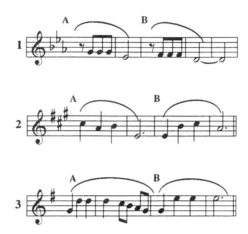

Figure 1. The first two phrases from three sample melodies, Beethoven's *Fifth Symphony*, *Chimes* and *Lavender's Blue*. In each case, the first and second phrases share important features.

remains as a side-effect of cognitive development, although writing has largely replaced its primary function. There are at least three problems with this explanation. First, it divorces music from other art forms, such as visual art, dance, architecture, etc., unless these also have mnemonic origins, which seems unlikely. Next, it suggests that the musical drive will eventually fade away, as it now serves no useful purpose, and this seems equally unlikely. Finally, it suggests that simple music that is easy to memorize will be preferred; in fact, as will be discussed later, there is a tendency to enjoy music that is neither too simple nor too complex.

This paper will take an alternative approach in explaining musical affect. The starting point for the derivation of this explanation is the observation that theme and variation is a universal feature of music that cuts across all cultures and all time periods. Consider the three musical snippets in Figure 1. In the first, the start of Beethoven's *Fifth Symphony*, the second phrase is simply a non-modulating transposition of the first. In the second example, *Chimes*, the second phrase contains the same notes as the first phrase, in a different order. In the third melody, *Lavender's Blue*, the second phrase is a contraction of the first. Theme and variation is also a ubiquitous feature of the larger-scale structure of music, influencing the relationship between groups of phrases, and, in longer pieces, the relationship between successive movements.

One explanation as to why music conforms to this pattern is that theme and variation is an instantiation of the general aesthetic principle of unity in diversity. Diversity is provided by the variations which recapitulate the theme by permuting or altering it. Unity is provided by the underlying invariant structure common to the theme and its variations. The principle of unity in diversity graces the writing of such diverse philosophers as Leibnitz, Mendelssohn and Hegel (Berlyne, 1971), and its fulfillment has long been held as the source of pleasure in art. Thus, one advantage of invoking this principle is that it relates musical affect to a theory of general aesthetic pleasure. Without the ability to measure the degree of unity, however, this principle cannot be used in a computational system. Subject-independent formulae such as $M = O * C$ (Eysenck, 1942), where M is a measure of pleasingness, O is the degree of order or unity in the stimulus, and C is the complexity or diversity of the stimulus, while providing a computational basis for aesthetics, are ultimately inadequate. The reason for this is that the degree of unity is always relative to a particular observer's ability to unify the relevant stimuli; thus, any method to measure this quantity must be embedded within a model of cognition.

The objective of this paper is to demonstrate that a connectionist measure of positive affect, based on unity in diversity, makes predictions that are broadly consistent with human data when applied to melody. The measure operates within a system whose sole aim is classification. Thus, it will be shown that musical affect is a side-effect of musical pattern recognition. The next section details the derivation of the measure of affect. The section following describes a system for classifying notes and groups of notes. Simulation results are then presented, and related to human affective data. The paper concludes with a discussion of the deficiencies of the model, and how they may be remedied.

2. Affect and the Activation

This section will demonstrate why it is sufficient to measure activation to measure the degree of unity in diversity in a competitive neural network. The ideas presented here are an elaboration of Martindale's (1984) work. I have demonstrated the generality of the affect measure in visual scene processing (Katz, 1992), in humour (Katz, 1993c), and within a musical context, in melody (Katz, 1993b) and harmony (Katz, 1993a). It has also been used to show why certain chord transitions are more common than others (Katz, 1993d).

The affect measure can be derived by observing the effects of varying stimuli on activation of a hypothetical network. For the purposes of this discussion, two general assumptions, applying to a broad class of networks, are made. First, it is assumed that the more diverse the stimulus, the more units there are that will potentially respond to the differing elements of the stimulus. Second, it is assumed that perceived unity is a reflection of the simultaneous activity of the units representing the elements of the stimulus. As an example of a unification process in the brain, consider three lines of equal length scattered at random on a large blank page, one parallel with the bottom edge, one at an angle of 45° and one at an angle of 135°. If they are sufficiently far apart, then only one line can capture one's attention at a time, and therefore only one angled line detector is active. If, however, they are brought together into an equilateral triangle, then they are seen as a unified whole, and three detectors will be mutually active. Presumably, the unification occurs due to the proximity of the lines, possibly with some added top-down help from a triangle detector which sends descending excitatory activation to the angled line detectors.

The effect on the total activity of a hypothetical network is now considered for the four possible cases of low and high diversity, and low and high unity.

(1) *Low diversity, low unity.* Low diversity will result in the need for relatively few active units to represent the stimulus. In addition, the lack of perceived unity between the elements of the stimulus will lead to even lower simultaneous activation of the units, and thus to very low total activation in the network.

(2) *High diversity, low unity.* Many units will be competing to represent the diverse aspects of the stimulus. However, the system's inability to unify these aspects will mean that only a small subset will be active at any one time. Thus, there is relatively low activation in this case also.

(3) *Low diversity, high unity.* The aspects of the stimulus will be perceived as parts of a whole, and thus simultaneously maintained. The low diversity of the stimulus, however, will mean that there are relatively few such units, and thus low total activation will also result.

(4) *High diversity, high unity.* Relatively large numbers of units will be needed to represent the diversity of the stimulus. Unity between the elements of the stimulus will be achieved if the system is able to keep these units simultaneously active. Thus, relatively high activation results.

It is therefore sufficient to measure the total activation of the network to measure the extent to which there is unity in diversity. For the purposes of this paper, two primary means of achieving high activation, and therefore unity in diversity, will be considered. The first, and simplest, concerns the degree to which the network responds to a given stimulus. Consider a network that has formed an unsupervised, distributed representation of a set of stimuli. This network will, in general, respond to a stimulus to the extent that it has been exposed to the stimulus in the past. This follows from the fact that unsupervised learning techniques, including the one to be described below, are variants of associative coupling rules. Thus, greater exposure to a stimulus means stronger weights between the input units and the classification units, and in the case of a distributed representation of the stimulus, greater total activity among the units in the representation.

The second means of achieving high activation derives from the ability of a stimulus to maintain partially the memory of its predecessor. This is the case in the scenario presented in the three panels in Figure 2. In panel 1, unit A, which along with B is a member of a winner-take-all subnetwork, has won the competition. It has received two units of activation to B's one (each weight is assumed to be of unit strength, each darkened unit to be at a level of unit activation, and each transparent unit to have no activation strength). In panel 2, the input to the network has changed, representing a new stimulus to be processed by the winner-take-all subnetwork. In this case, unit B receives two units of activation to A's one. However, A continues to receive some activation from unit b, and also from its recurrent connection. This will keep A partially active until it is fully suppressed by inhibitory activity received from unit B. This occurs in panel 3, when the network has fully relaxed.

This scenario results in an activation boost, i.e. a temporary increase in the activity in the winner-take-all-network because of the simultaneous activity of A and

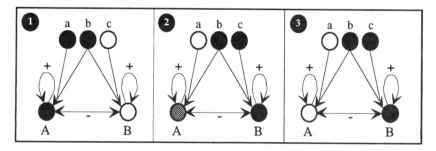

Figure 2. The network dynamics of the activation boost. In panel 1, unit A has won a prior competition. In panel 2, B is winning the new competition, but A is partially maintained for a short time by shared feature b, and its excitatory recurrent connection. Eventually, in panel 3, B fully wins the new competition.

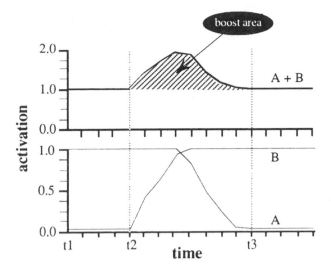

Figure 3. The graph of the activation boost. The bottom graph shows the activation trace for units A and B. The top graph shows the sum of these traces. The activation boost is the result of simultaneous activity of the units between times *t2* and *t3*. The hatched area shows the integral of the boost.

B in panel 2. This can be seen in the top graph in Figure 3, which shows the total activation of the units A and B. The activation traces for these units are shown separately in the bottom graph. The integral of the boost (the shaded area in Figure 3) is proportional to the amount of activation that the losing unit, A, receives. This means that the greater the support for a unit encoding an old stimulus, the greater the activation boost, and the greater the unity achieved between the old and new stimuli. This does not necessarily imply, however, that the greater the overlap between successive stimuli, the greater the resultant boost. As will be discussed below, too much similarity between the stimuli will result in their being placed in the same category, or, in the case of a distributed representation, in highly similar categories.

In summary, there are two primary factors affecting the activation level of a layer of units, the amount of activation that is passed through to these units, and the manner in which successive stimuli are triggered. The next section describes a melodic classification model in which these principles apply.

3. The Model

An overview of the model can be seen in Figure 4. The transducer layer and the note layer comprise a note-recognition system. Note recognition is simulated by approximating the operation of the inner ear as a series of bandpass filters. The operation of this system, and the origin of the activation boost in stepwise transitions, is described in the next section. The note-recognition system, along with units that extract rhythm and interval information, feeds into the low-order group layer, which consists of a set of competitive clusters. The purpose of this layer is to produce an unsupervised classification of notes that belong in the same note group. The term 'group' is being used here in a similar manner to that in Lerdahl and Jackendoff (1983), i.e. a set of sequential notes that appear to the listener to belong

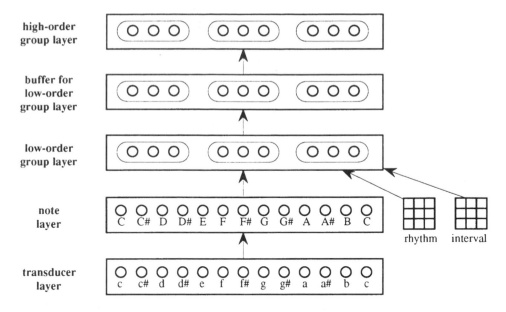

Figure 4. An overview of the model. The transducer layer and the note layer comprise a note-recognition system. The low-order group layer consists of a set of competitive clusters which classify note groups, based on the state of the note layer, and information in the rhythm and interval units. This classification is buffered in the following layer, so that the high-order group layer can classify groups of the low-order groups.

together. The low-order group layer is then buffered by the next layer, which provides the input for a high-order group layer. This layer produces an unsupervised classification of the low-order groups; thus, units in this layer respond to groups of groups. The operation of the group layers and the origin of the activation boost in these layers is described after the note-recognition system is detailed.

3.1. Note Recognition

The purpose of this section is to describe a note-recognition system that is consistent with a number of facts relating to the qualitative experience associated with stepwise melodic movement, and is also consistent with the operation of the ear. Sound is first encountered by the outer ear, which transmits focused air-pressure variations to the middle ear. The middle ear acts as an impedance matcher between the outer ear and the cochlea. There are two sets of hair cells in the cochlea, the outer hair cells which are believed to act as an automatic gain control, and the inner hair cells, arranged in order of frequency response along the cochlear spiral. The inner hair cells project to the cochlear nuclear structures, which ultimately project, in turn, via a number of intervening structures, to the auditory cortex.

The inner hair cells do not respond to a single frequency only, but act as linear bandpass filters centred on a characteristic frequency to which they respond with greatest activity. It is possible to profile this filter with a rectangular function centred on this frequency, although a more accurate picture can be obtained by the use of the rounded-exponential (Roex) function (Patterson & Moore, 1986)

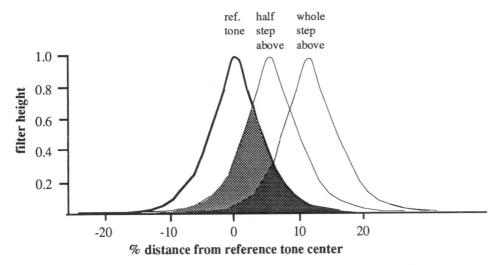

Figure 5. Roex filters ($Q = 10$, $\rho = 40$) for a reference tone, and two tones a semitone and whole tone above. There is a 49% overlap between the semitone and the reference tone, and a 19% overlap between the whole tone above and the reference tone. Note shown is the small, 7% overlap between a tone a minor third above and the reference tone.

$$R(g) = (1 + \rho g)e^{-\rho g} \tag{1}$$

where g is the normalized distance from the characteristic centre frequency f_0,

$$g = |f - f_0|/f_0 \tag{2}$$

and ρ is a passband parameter related to the more usual bandpass measure Q by the formula

$$Q = \rho/4 \tag{3}$$

Sano and Jenkins (1991) give Q as 10 for $f_0 > 500$ Hz, although estimates vary between authors. Q also varies with f_0, the intensity of the signal, age and degree of hearing loss, and is subject to individual differences (Buser & Imbert, 1992); in addition, the filter profile may be asymmetrical. Figure 5 shows three Roex filters with $Q = 10$ for fibres centred on a reference tone (assuming the tone is a pure sine wave, i.e. only one frequency is present), a tone a half-step above the reference tone, and a tone a whole step above the reference tone (this translates into approximately a 6% and 12% change in frequency, respectively).

The crucial fact for the purpose of this model is the overlap between the filters. There is a 49% overlap, relative to the area of the filter as a whole, between a reference tone and a tone a half-step above, and a 19% overlap between the reference tone and a tone a whole step above. There is also a small 7% overlap between the reference tone and a tone a minor third above, not shown in the figure.

In order to respond best in a noisy environment, a note-recognition system will, ideally, integrate the action of all relevant fibres. That is, a unit responsible for detecting the presence of a note at a given frequency should receive input not only from the fibre centred on this frequency, but all fibres that fire when this frequency is present. This will be all the fibres within the breadth of the filter. The network

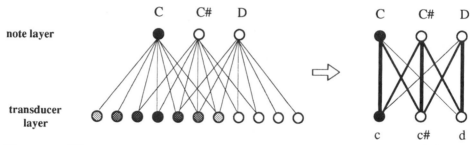

Figure 6. The model of note recognition. In the network on the left, note units receive input from all transducers that fire when the note pitch is present. If it is assumed that the stimuli contain only pitches corresponding to chromatic notes, then the equivalent network on the right can be used.

on the left of Figure 6 shows such an arrangement when the network is recognizing a stimulus centred on the pitch for c (only a representative set of transducer units are shown for simplicity). Transducer units respond in proportion to distance from this pitch, and the note unit is connected to all transducer units that fire when the pitch is present. This arrangement is also the basis of Sano and Jenkins' (1991) model, although their approach, unlike the one here, is equivalent to using a rectangular filter with all fibres within the filter providing an equal contribution. The current model makes the more realistic assumption that the input from the fibres follows the profile in Figure 5. Like the Sano and Jenkins model, however, this paper will not treat note recognition of complex timbres.

If the stimuli presented to the network are confined to the notes of the chromatic scale, then it is possible to replace a model which explicitly represents the filtering operation of each hair cell with the simplified model shown on the right of Figure 6. The operation of many transducer units are replaced by single weights equal to the net effect of these units. In order to be consistent with the network on the left of the figure, weights project not only to the note unit directly above, but also to adjacent notes. In the simulations below, the magnitude of these cross-weights will be estimated from the degree of overlap seen in Figure 5. Not shown in the diagram are inhibitory connections between units in the note layer needed to prevent simultaneous firing, at relaxation, of two adjacent notes when only one is triggered. The values of these parameters will be presented in the simulation section.

Examination of the model in Figure 6 reveals that similar dynamics to that of Figure 2 will be produced if a note is followed by another note a step apart. That is, an activation boost will be produced because of the overlapping support for the two units. This implies, by the arguments given above, that stepwise progression will induce positive affect.[1] The model is consistent with the following three facts.

(1) The most common way of resolving a dissonance is by stepwise movement. I have suggested (Katz, 1993a) that any weakening of the harmony by the dissonance is offset by the positive affect associated with the stepwise movement.

(2) The rapid alternation between two notes in stepwise relation results in a perceived blending of these notes. In the model, rapid alternation between such notes results in a prolonged activation boost, with the units encoding the notes

never fully dropping to nil activation before they are triggered again. This may cause the blending effect, and in addition, positive affect, resulting in this device being the most common means of ornamentation.

(3) Stepwise transitions are found with high frequency in melodies. It is possible to write a good melody with almost all steps, and very few leaps. Jeffries' (1974) analysis of popular song found a much higher number of minor and major second intervals than chance would predict.

The last fact is the most important for the purposes of this paper. The model in Figure 6 does not show, however, why other intervals are differentially favoured (e.g. the third and fifth intervals also occur in melodies greater than chance would predict); a modification to the model to account for this is proposed in the discussion section.

3.2. Group Recognition Model

The prior section described a model which suggests why stepwise movement is common in melodies. Melodies are not perceived, however, solely as a sequence of unrelated notes. Rather, additional structure is present due to phrasing mechanisms. The purpose of this section is to construct a system that shows that resemblance between melodic groups is another source of positive affect.

The three two-phrase melodies in Figure 1 are now reconsidered in the light of the current theory of affect. In each case, phrase A and phrase B share crucial features. In the first melody, the second phrase is a non-modulating sequence of the first. That is, the second phrase preserves the interval relationships of the first, except for the last interval, which is slightly different because of the constraints of remaining within the key. The rhythm is also preserved here. In the second melody the rhythm is also repeated in the second phrase. These two phrases also achieve unity by repeating the same notes in a different order. Finally, in the third melody, a phrase is followed by a contracted version, with the slight twist that the d in the first phrase becomes an e in the second.

Within two successive melodic groups, the effect just illustrated may be thought of as a type of question-and-answer mechanism, although the effect over larger structures is generally referred to as theme followed by variation. This effect is so ubiquitous both within the small-scale and large-scale structure of music that it hardly bears comment. The key question for the purpose of this paper is the reason for this ubiquity.

The proposed answer follows from the current model for the generation of positive effect. Assume that there is a mechanism for parsing the melody into groups. Further, assume that the representation of the melody is such that it is able to capture the features which allow successive groups to be perceived as variations on one another. Finally, assume that there exists an unsupervised, competitive-type learning mechanism capable of producing categorizations of the melodic groups. Then, if a melodic group B follows another group A, and B shares features with A as captured by the representation, then an activation boost will result in the competitive layer. The boost will occur because the unit categorizing group A continues to receive activation after group B is detected, thus yielding similar dynamics to that seen in Figure 3.

The following sections describe each of the three prerequisites for these dynamics: a sectioning of the melody into groups, a representation that captures the similarities between groups, and an unsupervised, competitive categorization mechanism.

3.2.1. Melodic grouping.   The smallest unit of musical communication, above the individual note level, is the musical group. The group may be equivalent to the phrase marking, although it is sometimes advisable to divide a phrase into two or more groupings. Grouping may also be performed hierarchically, with a higher-order group consisting of a group of groups. Lerdahl and Jackendoff (1983) describe a list of rules for parsing a melody into groups. Their rules are of two types: those that determine whether groups are well formed, and preference rules indicating where the likely boundaries between groups should occur. The former rules are directed to ensuring that groups have at least two members, and that group boundaries do not overlap. The latter rules, inspired by Gestalt principles, are meant to mimic human perceptual preferences. Thus, boundaries are formed whenever there is a relatively large gap between successive notes, whether this is a gap in pitch height, or a gap in time. They also discuss rules such as parallelism, whereby repeated structure, or a structure repeated with variation, is seen as an independent group.

It may be possible to translate these grouping mechanisms to a connectionist framework, e.g. I suggest (Katz, 1993b) that perceptual gaps may be detected when the cosine of the angle between successive neural states is sufficiently large. For the purposes of this paper, however, no computational mechanism of grouping will be suggested. Rather, in the case of existing melodies, group boundaries will be inserted as they were intended by the composer. For the relatively simple melodies in this paper, these boundaries can easily be determined by noting the phrase markings. Higher-order groupings, in which a group of groups forms a perceptual unit, are also determined by higher-order phrase markings, if these are present, or by following Lerdahl and Jackendoff's parallelism principle. For example, a melody of the form ABAC, where A, B and C are groups, would be divided into two parallel meta-groups, AB and AC. In the stochastically generated music in this study, which do not come with phrase markings, group boundaries are artificially inserted at regular intervals in the music; this applies to both high-order and low-order group boundaries and is described further in the section on complexity and affect.

3.2.2. Representation.   Figure 7 shows the representation used in the current model. It consists of three sets of units representing pitch, rhythm and interval information. The first set of units encodes pitch information; for the purpose of simplicity, only pitch height is represented. The current model takes the same approach as Gjerdingen (1991) in that pitch units fade exponentially in time. For example, Figure 7 shows the state of the network after processing the last note, e, of the first phrase in *Chimes*. The other notes in the phrase, a, b and c♯ are active proportionally to the recency of their presentation. The purpose of this fade mechanism is to ensure that the categorization scheme can take into account all the notes in the group.

The other alternative is to use a set of pitch units for each note in the group. While this approach better models some cases, such as repeated notes, it requires many more units (in this case, four times the number of pitch units). Moreover, it runs counter to one of the goals of the representation, which is to capture the perceived similarities between groups. In the case of *Chimes*, the notes of the two

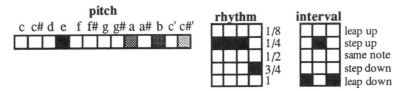

Figure 7. The representation of a group. Shown in the diagram is the state of the network after processing the first phrase in *Chimes*. The representation consists of three sets of units, pitch units, rhythm units and interval units.

groups are identical, but presented in different order. The similarity between these two groups is a direct consequence of the fade mechanism. The fade mechanism is applied to units in the transducer layer, which feeds into the note-recognition layer, as previously described. It does not affect the fact that stepwise transitions will result in higher activation levels in the note layer than transitions by leap.

The second set of units encodes rhythmic information. In this case, using a similar fade mechanism would presume that the same note lengths presented in different order are perceived as similar; this is not typically the way rhythmic variation is achieved. One method of achieving variation is for some, but not all, notes, to share rhythmic values between successive groups. This is the case in melody 3 in Figure 1, in which the rhythm is identical until the fourth note of both phrases. The representation in Figure 7 captures this by allotting one set of rhythmic units for each note of the phrase. Active units in the figure reflect the state after the network has processed the first phrase of *Chimes*, i.e. after three quarter-notes have been followed by a three-quarter note. In the actual network used in the simulations, there are more units vertically, to handle more rhythmic values such as sixteenth notes, and more units horizontally, to handle groups of greater than four notes.

Interval information is presented in the same way as rhythmic information for similar reasons. Two groups that have the same intervals presented in different order are not perceived as that similar; it is more usual to preserve all or some of the intervals between groups to suggest unity between them. Unlike the rhythmic representation, the interval representation does not have a slot for every possible value; rather, only five possibilities are present: leap down, step down, same note, step up and leap up. A leap is considered to be anything greater than or equal to a minor third. In the first group in *Chimes*, a leap down is followed by a step up followed by another leap down; this is reflected in the state of the interval units in Figure 7.

There are two reasons for restricting the range of values. First, Davies and Jennings (1977) have shown that subjects, when attempting to recall melodies, show poor memory for exact intervals. One possible explanation of this result is that melodies are not represented as sequences of precise interval changes. The second reason is to permit groups that have the same general contour but not the exact interval structure to be perceived as having intervallic identity; this is typically the case with non-modulating sequences, for example. To capture the full capacity of the untrained ear, it may be necessary to augment the representation with further distinctions, such as that between a small leap and a large leap, although the suggested representation is sufficient for the purposes of the simulations below.

3.2.3. Categorization.   This section will describe an unsupervised learning scheme that produces classifications of melodic groups and is consistent with the affective principles outlined previously. An ART-like (Grossberg, 1980) mechanism was chosen in order to control the degree to which a group must be similar to another group if it is to be placed in the same category. Learning occurs only at the detection of a group boundary, permitting the network to acquire categories that correspond to psychologically significant sets of stimuli. Learning for each group consists of choosing a unit in a competitive, winner-take-all cluster of units, and adjusting the weights to and from this unit.

Assume that G is the vector that represents the state of the input when the boundary is detected; G consists of the concatenation of vectors representing note, rhythm and interval information. Adaptation to the presence of G occurs in two stages. First, the winning unit in the competitive cluster is determined. The j which yields the maximum of the quantity

$$\cos \theta(G, W_j(fb)) = (G \cdot W_j(fb))/(|G| \; |W_j(fb)|) \tag{4}$$

is determined, where the $W_j(fb)$ are the feedback weights from cluster unit j to the layer containing G. If this maximum quantity is greater than a vigilance parameter ρ, then this is the winner. Otherwise, an uncommitted unit in the cluster in chosen. Uncommitted units are those with all feedback weights still set to their initial value of 0; upon being chosen as a winner an uncommitted units gets its weights set to G.

Feedforward weights from unit i in the input layer to winning unit j are determined by

$$W_{ij}(ff)(t + 1) = \lambda \hat{g}_i + (1 - \lambda) w_{ij}(ff)(t) \tag{5}$$

where λ is the learning rate, and the

$$\hat{g}_i = g_i |G| \tag{6}$$

are the normalized elements of G. This normalization, in conjunction with the fact that the input vector G is normalized before relaxation, ensures that the boost dynamics are independent of the length of the group. If λ is sufficiently small, then equations (5) and (6) guarantee that the feedforward weights to a cluster unit collapse to the average of the normalized inputs from all input vectors G that have this unit as winner; this fact will be used to create a fast-learning scheme for many of the simulations described below.

If two successive groups share features, then an activation boost will result because the dynamics are qualitatively similar to that of Figure 2. That is, the shared active units in the second group will continue to support partially the cluster units for the first group after the second group is presented. This effect is most cleanly produced if activation is gated to the group layers only when group boundaries are detected; thus, this procedure is followed in the simulations.

Another procedure followed in the simulations is to form a distributed representation in the group layer in order to capture the degree of similarity of groups for further classification by a higher-order group layer. A single cluster of units in the group layer will put two groups in either the same category or different categories, depending on the value of the vigilance parameter ρ. Suppose, however, that a number of competitive clusters were present, each with a unique ρ. For example, suppose there were nine clusters, with vigilance parameters of 0.1, 0.2, 0.3, . . ., 0.9. Also suppose two groups were presented to a new network, such that the cosine of the angle between the groups was 0.58. The presentation of the first group will cause the features of this group to be connected to one unit in each cluster. Features of the second group will become connected only to those clusters for which the cosine of the angle is greater than the vigilance, i.e. 0.1 to 0.5. Thus, the two groups, which are roughly half alike, will have representations with roughly half the units in common.

In this case, however, the high-order group layer would 'see' an almost identical picture responding to the low-order group layer, as it would if it responded to the note layer directly (see Figure 4). In the former case, the groups would appear to have a degree of similarity of 5/9, and in the latter, 58%. Thus, the quasi-linear transformation performed by the low-order group layer would serve no significant purpose, i.e. the two group layers could be reduced to a single layer computing the same effective function. This is analogous to the fact that an extra hidden layer adds no classification power to a network unless the units in that layer are non-linear (Jordan, 1986).

Therefore, for the purposes of the simulations below, ρ ranges from 0.5 to 0.8. Starting at 0.5 requires that there be a significant amount of similarity between two exemplars before they share any cluster units in common. The parameter ρ stops at 0.8 because above this value it is difficult to get a winner-take-all network to produce a single winner if the successive groups are highly similar. The threshold could be raised to prevent multiple winners for clusters with high vigilance, but then each cluster would possess unique boost dynamics; this paper has opted for a single threshold so that these dynamics remain constant.

The model does not reduce to the claim that positive affect is proportional to the degree of similarity between two successive groups. The reason for this can be seen in the graph in Figure 8, which shows mean activation as a function of overlap between two successive categories. Two cases are presented, the first in which a single cluster is present, with $\rho = 0.65$, and the second, in which seven clusters are present, with ρ ranging from 0.5 to 0.8, in steps of 0.05, as in the simulations below.

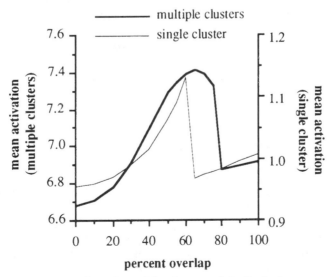

Figure 8. Activation as a function of the degree of similarity between two successive melodic groups. Shown are graphs for a single cluster with a single vigilance and multiple clusters with varying vigilance values.

In both cases, activation is an inverted U-shaped curve as a function of overlap. In the single-cluster case, as the similarity between the successive groups increases, the greater the support for the unit classifying the first group by the active note layer units for the second group, and therefore the greater the activation boost. If the groups are too similar, however, they share the same winning unit. Therefore, there is no transition from one unit to the next, and thus there is no activation boost. In the multiple cluster case, as the groups become more similar, more winners in the clusters will be the same, and there will thus be less activation boosts contributing to the overall boost. Multiple clusters form a smoother inverted U than a single cluster. There is a slight rise in both curves above the point at which no transitions take place in the clusters because of a greater initial triggering of the cluster units. The shape of the curve remains primarily an inverted U, however.[2] This will prove important in the simulations relating affect to musical complexity.

In addition to categorizing melodic groups, the network also categorizes the groups themselves in an attempt to discover higher-order structure in the music. A buffer layer stores the results of all categorizations until a higher-order boundary is detected, and these results are passed on to a higher-order group layer, operating in a similar fashion to the low-order group layer (see Figure 4). The buffer is necessary because the winner-take-all networks in the lower-order group layer will allow only one unit to be active per cluster at relaxation. If a melodic group A is followed by a group B, and a higher-boundary is then detected, one would like to form a higher-order category that responds to the presence of both A and B. The units classifying these groups must be buffered before presentation to the next classification layer, so as not to lose the fact that the units encoding A were initially active. Gjerdingen (1991) uses the same method to accomplish similar purposes.

4. Simulation Results

Four sets of simulations are described in this section. The first set compares the network's performance on melodies of varying complexity with human performance. The second set treats the relation between familiarity and affect. The third shows that the model predicts that there should be positive affective transfer between similar melodies. The final set describes how the network reacts to degraded forms of good melodies.

In all the simulations, spread of activation is governed by

$$o_i = S \left(\Sigma w_{ij} O_j \right) \tag{7}$$

where o_i is the output activation of unit i, w_{ij} is the weight between i and j, and S is the sigmoid transfer function

$$S(x) = 1/(1 + e^{-(x-\theta)/T}) \tag{8}$$

For all units, the threshold θ is set to 0.75, and the temperature T to 0.1.

Weights between the pitch layer and the note layer are in accordance with the degree of overlap pictured in Figure 6. The connection between a pitch unit and its corresponding unit in the note layer is just above the threshold θ, at 0.8; the connection between a pitch unit and the two units in the note layer a half-step above and below is 49% of this value, the connection between a pitch unit and the two units in the note layer a whole step above and below is 16% of this value, and the connection between a pitch unit and the two units in the note layer a minor third above and below is 7% of this value. Contrast enhancement in the note layer is achieved by creating a small recurrent excitatory connection from units to themselves, and small inhibitory connections from units to their near neighbours. The net effect of this arrangement is to produce an activation boost between successive notes inversely proportional to the size of the interval between the notes.

As mentioned in the previous section, the group layers consist of sets of competitive clusters rather than a single cluster to form a distributed representation of the layer it is classifying. For the purposes of the current simulations, seven clusters were used, with ρ varying from 0.5 to 0.8; this applies to both the low-order group layer and the high-order group layer. The clusters in both these layers consist of winner-take-all networks with recurrent excitatory connections from units to themselves of 0.5, and inhibitory connections of −0.25 to all other units in the cluster.

4.1. Complexity and Affect

Positive affect has been shown to be an inverted U-shaped function of musical complexity in computer-generated melodies (Vitz, 1966). Complexity is changed by varying the range over which a stochastically based generator can choose the elements of the music. As this range is increased, ratings by both musically trained and musically untrained subjects of the complexity of the melody increases; however, the pleasingness of the melody falls off above a certain complexity value. The inverted U has also been found in untrained subjects' judgements of real melodies where complexity was measured by subjects' ratings of these melodies, and also by a more objective measure of complexity (Stevens & Latimer, 1991).

In order to simulate this basic result, melodies with 16 notes were generated; each of these notes was chosen by a random process over the set of chromatic notes in a given range. For example, if the range was 5, each note would be chosen from the set c, c♯, d, d♯, e and f. A Gaussian distribution, centred on the middle note, was used. Note length was chosen from among the set of eighth, quarter and half-notes; this set did not vary. Melodies were divided into four groups of four notes each. These four low-order groups were then placed into two higher-order groups, containing two low-order groups each. Thus, each low-order group consisted of four notes, and each high-order groups eight notes. None of the results presented here depend on this artificial parsing; I describe (Katz, 1993b) a similar experiment in which a more natural parsing method is used that yields qualitatively similar results.

Figure 9 shows the network's response to melodies generated over a variety of note ranges. Each data point in this graph represents the average result over 25 trial melodies. A fast training routine which sets weights to units in the group layers to the mean of all input vectors which trigger the particular unit was used; this produces the same end result as repeated presentations of the melody to the network with λ sufficiently low in equation (5). The activation values are obtained by rerunning the melody through the network after this training phase. As in all simulations. in this paper, mean activation over the entire presentation of the melody, as measured in the note layer, and the group layers, is assumed to be proportional to the worth of the melody; the higher this number, the greater the mean boost area. In all three layers, an inverted U is obtained. The inverted U in the note layer is the result of the preference for stepwise movement. If the range is too low, then too many notes are repeated, either in direct succession, or with a note or two intervening. This lessens the chance for activation boosts due to

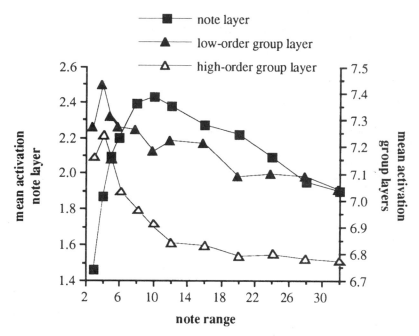

Figure 9. Mean activation as a function of the note range of artificially generated melodies. Inverted Us are found in the mean activation of the note layer, and in each of the group layers.

successive notes in a stepwise relation. If the range is too large, then the number of stepwise intervals also falls because of the increased incidence of leaps, thus lowering the overall activation in the note layer. The peak activation occurs when the range is neither too large nor too small.

The group layers also show inverted Us (although these may be more properly called inverted Vs). The greater the note range, the less similar successive groups are likely to be. This fact, in conjunction with the fact that mean activation in the group layers as a function of similarity is an inverted-U shaped curve, as seen in Figure 8, is sufficient to explain these results. Perhaps as significant as predicting the existence of the inverted-Us, the model highlights a fundamental problem in stochastic music generation, namely, the lack of large-scale structure (Todd, 1991). The graphs in Figure 9 show that higher-order unity can only be achieved by severely limiting the range of notes. When the group layers reach their maximum value, at a range of three notes, the note layer is well below its maximum value. This contrasts with real melodies (two examples are presented in the degradation experiments, below), which achieve group unity by explicit means such as transposition. This unifying device, for example, may be used irrespective of the degree of diversity at the note level.

4.2. Familiarity and Affect

There is a large degree of consensus that familiarity, at least over the short run, breeds content (Martindale *et al.*, 1988), contrary to the popular saying. Over-exposure to any stimulus, however, will generally lower affect. Anyone who purchases recorded music is familiar with the general affective response curve to a particular piece. Over a set of initial hearings, a good piece transforms from a relatively disjointed set of notes to a coherent set of themes and variations. There is a corresponding increase in positive affective response to the music. If, however, the piece is over-played, especially without interposing other music, there will be a decrease in affective response, and eventually the piece drops out of one's listening schedule.

The ascending affective phase corresponds to the discovery of thematic content of the music. It has been shown that subjects are more sensitive to themes with increasing repetition (Pollard-Gott, 1983). The latter stage, in which over-exposure decreases enjoyment, has also been studied. Stevens and Latimer (1991) found that subjects rated simple music lower after repetitive presentation of the melodies; they found no change in more complex music, although only six repetitions were used. With a higher degree of repetition, it may be possible to show decrease in positive affect with complex music also.

It seems natural to conjecture, then, given these findings, that positive affect is an inverted U-shaped curve as a function of repetition number, although there are as yet no studies that confirm this conjecture over the entire U. The rise in positive affect over a small number of repetitions, and the corresponding increase in sensitivity to thematic aspects of the music, follows directly from the adaptive characteristics of the current model. With repeated presentations, the weights to units in the group layer align themselves with the input vectors that have this unit as a winner. This increases the activation to these units upon future presentations of the same melody.

To explain decreased affective response to over-exposure requires an explicit habituation mechanism. It is also necessary that this mechanism involve long-term effects (i.e. weight-based) rather than short-term (i.e. activation-based) as one would expect that habituation may affect response hours or days after the original over-exposure. The simplest possible habituation mechanism which reduces response to non-novel stimuli is Kohonen's (1984) anti-Hebbian rule

$$\Delta w_{ij} = -\eta o_i o_j \tag{9}$$

which forms an inhibitory connection between units that tend to be simultaneously active. This rule is applied in the model to inter-cluster units in the group layer. There is already a strong inhibitory connection between units in the same cluster and thus there is no need to invoke this rule for these cases. Figure 10 shows the result of applying the rule to the first three clusters in the group layer, with vigilances of 0.5, 0.55 and 0.60 respectively. The winning unit for each cluster, after processing a group of notes, is shown in black. Inhibitory connections form between every combination of mutually active units, following equation (9). These connections,

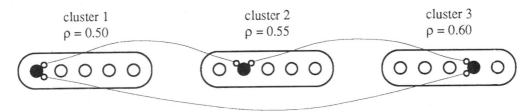

Figure 10. The formation of inhibitory connections between mutually active units in different clusters.

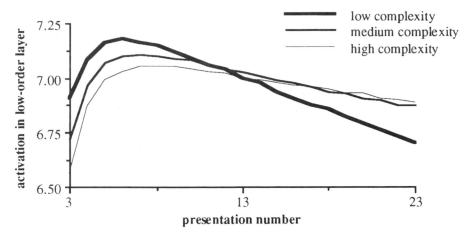

Figure 11. Activation as a function of the number of presentations for low, medium and highly complex melodies. All melody types exhibit an inverted U; the slope of the decline phase is steeper for less complex melodies.

when sufficiently large, will suppress the activity in this layer when the same group of notes is presented to the network.

Figure 11 shows activation in the low-order group layer as a function of the number of repetitions of 16-note melodies with parsing equivalent to the previous simulations. Three types of melodies were tested: low, medium and high complexity over a range of 4, 8 and 16 notes, respectively. The learning rate λ in equation (5) was set to 0.5, and the habituation rate in equation (9) was 0.001; each curve represents the average profile over 25 trials. Activation is reported for the low-order groups only; habituation in this simulation does not apply to the note layer, and the high-order groups give similar results.

All three types of melodies exhibit the predicted inverted U. The rise in activation over the initial set of presentations occurs because of the increased input to the group layer. The fall in activation is due to increased inhibitory connections in the group layer. Of equal importance to the inverted Us is the different results between the complexity levels. The steepness of decline is inversely proportional to the degree of complexity. The simpler the melody, the more likely it is that the melodic groups share the same set of winning units, and therefore the degree of habituation will be greater because these units will be active more often. This result is consistent with findings reported in Stevens and Latimer (1991), and also possesses some intuitive appeal. One is more likely to habituate to a simple popular tune than a Bach fugue, for example.

Stevens and Latimer also found, not surprisingly, that interposing other melodies between the successive repetitions of a melody will lower the habituation to that melody. This effect can be accommodated by assuming a dehabituating factor in equation (9), i.e. this rule becomes

$$\Delta w_{ij} = -\eta o_i o_j + \gamma \tag{10}$$

where γ is a positive term $<\eta$. This permits the inhibitory weight between two units to migrate back to 0 when the units are not simultaneously active.

Figure 12 shows the decline in activation from the peak to the final activation for low, medium and highly complex melodies. Two conditions are tested; in both,

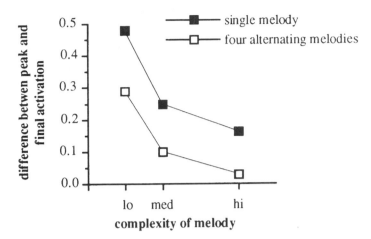

Figure 12. The decline in activation in the low-order group layer for single repeated melodies and four alternating melodies from the maximum after approximately six presentations to the state 20 presentations later.

η was set to 0.001 and γ to 0.0001. In the first, a single melody is successively presented without intervention, as in the previous simulation. In the new condition, a melody A is followed by three different melodies B, C and D with the same complexity, before A is then represented. The graphs in Figure 12 show the decline in activation in the low-order group layer from the peak value after approximately six presentations to the value obtained 20 presentations later. The decline in activation is less when the melodies are alternated, for melodies of all complexities. This is consistent with the human data which show less habituation when the subject is presented with a more varied set of melodies.

4.3. The Effect of Exposure to a Musical Genre

The previous section demonstrated that the model predicts that repeated exposure to a melody first results in increased appreciation of that melody, but eventually will lead to habituation to the melody. Of equal interest is the effect of exposure to similar melodies on judged liking of a melody. One would predict that enculturation to a musical genre would lead to greater appreciation of new music in that genre. For example, Chinese music initially sounds strange to western ears. Repeated exposure, however, will reduce the foreignness of the music, and will facilitate appreciation of other melodies of this type, even if these melodies have not been part of the exposure set.

In order to test this enculturation hypothesis within the current model, four sets of melodies were studied, Jamaican, Spiritual, Irish and Chinese. Four melodies were randomly chosen from each of four songbooks *Folk Songs of Jamaica* (Murray, 1952), *Spirituals* (Forster, 1955), (*Ireland the Songs*, 1993) and *Dragon Boat* (Chew, 1986).[3] Thus, these simulations involved a total of 16 melodies. All of the melodies were transposed to the same key so that similarities, such as ending a phrase on the tonic of the key, could be captured.

Each melody was studied under two conditions. The first was the effect of prior exposure to melodies outside the given melody's genre. This condition was carried out for each of the three other genres. For example, a given Jamaican melody would

Table I. Mean increase in activation for melodic styles as a function of prior exposure

Training set	Test set			
	Jamaican	Spiritual	Irish	Chinese
Jamaican	**0.39**	0.04	0.04	0.07
Spiritual	0.02	**0.09**	0.03	0.06
Irish	0.03	0.05	**0.17**	0.05
Chinese	0.05	0.06	0.05	**0.26**

be tested after the network was trained on the spirituals, it would be tested after training on the Irish melodies, and it would be tested after training on the Chinese melodies. The second condition was the effect of prior exposure to melodies within the genre. In this latter condition, the training set consisted of the other three melodies in the genre, but not the given melody itself.

Training in both conditions consisted of exposing the melodies in the training set to the network twice with a learning rate $\lambda = 0.5$ in equation (5). Testing consisted of exposing the test melody to the network once with the same learning rate and measuring the mean activation in the low-order group layer, after the network has been exposed to the relevant training set. The mean activation in the low-order group layer was also measured when the test melody was presented, but no prior training melodies were presented to the network. In order to gauge the effect of the training set, the difference between these two quantities was obtained.

Table I presents the results of these simulations. Each figure represents the mean increase in mean activation for all melodies within the genre, in the given condition. For example, on average, a Jamaican test melody will have an increase in activation of 0.39 if the network is first exposed to the other Jamaican melodies. In contrast, training on the Irish melodies leads to an average increase of 0.03 only. In general, intra-genre facilitation is much higher than inter-genre facilitation, as indicated by the fact that the figures along the diagonal (in bold) are higher than any figure in a given column. This is true for all columns, although the strength of the effect ranges from a relatively large one in the case of the Jamaican melodies, to a relatively weak one in the case of the spirituals.

The primary reason for positive transfer within a genre is the similarity between groups in different songs within the genre. Consider the first two phrases in two of the Chinese melodies, *Building Song* and *Kangding Love Song*, in Figure 13. Although they look markedly different to the eye, the network (and the ear) detects a number of points of similarity between these melodies, both from Sichuan Province. First, the third and fourth notes in both phrases are repeated notes. Next, the final interval is a downward stepwise movement from an eighth-note to a quarter-note. Finally, both phrases end on the second degree of the scale. Because the fade mechanism in the transducer layer carries over to the note layer, the final and most active note of a group is the most important for the purposes of categorization; this enhances the similarity between the two phrases.

Prior exposure to a melody will increase response to another, similar melody in much the same way that repeated exposure to the same melody increases response, as shown in the previous section. To the extent that melodies share the same winning units in the group layer, training on a similar melody will increase activity in this layer because of the Hebbian nature of unsupervised learning. In the case of

Figure 13. Selected phrases from two Chinese melodies.

a repeated melody, the winning units are identical from one trial to the next, whereas different but similar melodies will share only a subset of winning units (typically in only one or two of the clusters, for similar groups, in these simulations). This implies that the positive transfer from a melody to itself is faster than from another similar melody within the same genre, but also that negative transfer, due to habituation, will also be faster in the case of identical melodies. Thus, in addition to demonstrating that intra-genre affective transfer is greater than inter-genre transfer, as desired, the model makes testable predictions about the rate of positive and negative transfer between melodies as a function of similarity.

4.4. Degradation of Good Melodies

Ideally, the parameters in the model could be calibrated so that model's responses to real melodies would mirror mean human response to the same melodies. The model could then be tested by seeing if its response to melodies that it has not seen also match human response. There is an indirect alternative to this lengthy procedure that provides some indication that the model correctly judges real melodies. This involves taking melodies that can generally be agreed to provide a high degree of positive affect, and showing that the model rates these highly. One can then also show that the model's response to degraded versions of these melodies decreases with the degree of degradation. If one then makes the assumption that subjects' affective response will also be less to a stochastically degraded version of a good melody, then the argument for agreement between the model's judgement and that

Figure 14. The two melodies in the degradation simulations: (1) *Polly Put the Kettle On* and (2) *Greensleeves*.

of human subjects can be further strengthened. The justification for this assumption is that it is extremely unlikely that changing notes at random in a well-liked melody could improve that melody. Furthermore, as more of the melody is altered, and it approaches a purely random sequence of notes, affective judgement of the melody should decline in a monotonic fashion.

Two melodies were tested by this method: *Polly Put the Kettle On* and *Greensleeves*, as shown in Figure 14. The melodies were degraded by replacing a set number of randomly chosen notes with a random note in the pitch range between the highest and lowest note in the song, conforming to the key of the melody. Note durations of the chosen notes were also changed; a duration value was randomly chosen in the range between the shortest and longest note in the tune. The first, 25-note, melody is of the form AA'AB. Results for this melody can be seen in the left-hand graph in Figure 15. The initial mean activation values for note, low-order group, and high-order group layers are 2.23, 7.57 and 7.45, respectively. The note-layer value is not quite as high as the maximum value (over all note ranges) for the stochastically generated music, but both group layers are considerably above any of melodies generated by stochastic means. It should not be surprising that the melody does not outperform stochastic music in every layer, as it is likely that a melody with relatively high values for all layers, and therefore possessing global as well as local unity, will be perceived as better than a melody that does well in a single layer only. In this case, low-order group unity is achieved primarily by the second phrase repeating the first phrase a fourth lower, and higher-order unity by the repetition of the first phrase. There is an approximately linear decline in the note layer as the melody is degraded. The group layers, and especially the high-order group layer, display a more marked sensitivity to the change of relatively few notes.

Similar results are obtained for the first four phrases (37 notes) of *Greensleeves*, the second melody in Figure 14. The initial undegraded values for this melody are 2.62, 7.26 and 7.40 for the note layers, low-order group layers and high-order group layer, respectively. The note layer value is well above any stochastic melody, reflecting the flowing quality of this melody due to frequent stepwise transitions. The low-order group value is near the top of the range for the stochastic melodies, and the higher-order value is well above the maximum, reflecting the ABAC structure. As in the first melody, the note layer displays a near-linear monotonic decline. The group layers, and especially the high-order group layer, are very sensitive to the alteration of a few notes. The reason for the greater initial decline in the low-order group layer in both melodies is that changing a single note changes the note pitch, and the note duration, but also affects two intervals, both before and after the note. Any changes in the low-order group layer are then magnified in the higher-order layer. That is, because of the non-linear transformation by the low-order group layer of the note layer, it does not take a great deal of change to convert an ABAC melody to an ABCD melody, thus adversely affecting high-order unity.

5. Discussion

The previous set of simulations demonstrates that the model captures at least some aspects of what a melody needs in order to be enjoyed. This section discusses additions to the model that may align it better with human affective response. Three sets of issues will be treated: defects in the representational properties of the model, problems related to lack of learned expectations, and issues relating to the idea that good melodies involve a sense of closure.

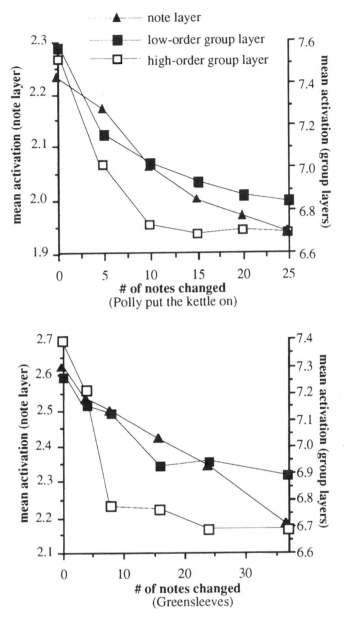

Figure 15. Evaluation of two melodies as a function of the degree of degradation of the melodies. In both melodies, and for all layers, the model's evaluation of the melody declines as they are degraded.

One representational problem involves pitch. It has been shown why stepwise transitions lead to greater activation in the note layer than transitions by leap. This, however, ignores the fact that there are some leaps which are also quite common, such as thirds, fifths and octaves. One solution to this difficulty is to include harmonics in the pitch representation for a given note. An activation boost would then result when harmonics overlap, as in the drop of a fifth. Problems with the pitch representation mean that the network underestimates the importance of making a melody conform to a key. Simulations showed that, all things being equal, melodies in a certain key exhibited higher group-layer scores, due to the greater unity between groups, but lower note-layer scores. The harmonic-based representation may help this latter score, although a full treatment of key and of the question of why melodies tend not to be written in a chromatic mode will probably go beyond this change.

Defects in the representation of rhythm cause the network to miss some unifying devices in natural melodies. For example, it is sometimes the case that a dotted pair consisting of a three-sixteenth-note followed by a sixteenth-note in one group corresponds to a quarter-note in the same position in the next group. The network has no way of knowing that the latter is a variation on the former; moreover, the extra note in the first group will mean that the following notes between the two groups will be misaligned. One solution to this difficulty is to change the rhythmic representation so that it also includes absolute time when comparing note durations.

Problems with the interval representation have already been alluded to; by including only five types of intervals, the network ends up lumping small leaps and large leaps in the same category. This may miss unifying devices based on the degree of leap. Representational changes to account for this and pitch and rhythmic problems will change the way in which the network responds to melody, but have no direct influence on the affective measure.

The current theory is essentially structural. A seemingly contrasting view is offered by Meyer (1956), who has stated that the basis of musical affect is the inhibition of a tendency to respond; thus, musical affect involves a play on musical expectations. One possible way of reconciling Meyer's principle with the affective measure presented here can be found in a neurally inspired theory of humour based on misdirection (Katz, 1993c). The joke context points in a certain direction, but the punchline supports an alternative, but plausible meaning. This results in the units underlying two concepts being jointly supported, and causes an activation boost. It may be possible to map this mechanism on to the melody model. For example, the first three repeated gs of Beethoven's Fifth Symphony (melody 1 in Figure 1) create the implication that the fourth note will also be a g. Instead the melody drops to e♭. If implications can be acquired within the model, then it may be possible to show that the g is partially primed by the notes that proceed it, and that this activation continues for a short time after the e has sounded, resulting in an activation boost.

Melodies often evoke a sense of a journey by starting off in secure territory, wandering around into uncharted areas, and then eventually returning to the original safe haven. The overall unity provided by this is not captured by the current model. However, assuming that implications within a given melody can be explicitly formed, it may be possible to show that the final resting place acts as a support system for the other aspects of the melody. For example, consider a melody of the form ABACA. Excitatory interconnections between A and the other groups in the melody will be formed by their juxtaposition. The presentation of the last A group will then serve to support any latent memories of the other groups, resulting in a final strong activation boost.

Thus, there is a need, in addition to the model's vertical adaptive component, for a horizontal adaptive component explicitly modelling the implication of a given melody (cf. Bharucha & Todd, 1991). It would be a mistake, however, to try to reduce the affective measure itself to an adaptive mechanism. The large size and irregularity of the search space makes it unlikely that a brute force inductive technique, trained on examples of good and bad melodies, will have much chance of success. Moreover, this approach is not psychologically realistic. Although people are influenced by the judgements of others in their taste in music, in general, music does not come pre-labelled; evaluation is based on one's internal, affective response to the music. Developing an ear for melody will depend on understanding the basis for this response; this paper has argued that this can be accomplished by a connectionist operationalization of the principle of unity in diversity.

Acknowledgement

The author would like to thank Marcy Dorfman for her help in the preparation of this manuscript.

Notes

1. The model explains positive affect associated with successive stepwise movement, but does not in itself explain why the simultaneous sounding of two notes at a sufficiently small interval is generally not pleasant. It may be possible to show, however, that the frequency beating which results lowers the overall input to the network, thus lowering affect.
2. Although the note-recognition model described here is hard-wired and not adaptive, it may be possible to use a similar sort of reasoning to explain why microtone transitions are not favoured. That is, if the note-recognition system derives from a similar unsupervised learning method, then an inverted U-shaped curve as a function of note similarity will result. This implies that small microtone transitions will not lead to greater affect than semitone transitions because it is too far to the right of the U. Or, in cognitive terms, although there will be high perceived unity between the successive notes, there will be insufficient diversity.
3. The randomly chosen melodies were as follows. Jamaican: *Linstead Market, Wata Come a Me Y'eye, Ribber Ben Come Dung* and *Las Kean Fine*; Spiritual: *Gimme Dat Ol'-time Religion, Jesus is the Ruler of my Life, Po' Mourners Got a Home at Last* and *Nobody Knows de Trouble I See*; Irish: *Fiddler's Green, Paddy's Green Shamrock Shore, Saint Patrick Was a Gentleman* and *The Little Old Cabin on the Hill*; Chinese: *The Wagon Driver, Shepherd's Song, Kangding Love Song* and *Building Song*.

References

Barucha, J.J. & Todd, P.M. (1991) Modelling the perception of tonal structure with neural nets. In P.M. Todd & D.G. Loy (Eds), *Music and Connectionism*. Cambridge, MA: MIT Press.

Berlyne, D.E. (1971) *Aesthetics and Psychobiology*. New York: Appleton-Crofts.

Buser, P. & Imbert, M. (1992) *Audition*. Cambridge, MA: MIT Press.

Chew, G.S. (1986) *Dragon Boat: 20 Chinese folk songs for voices and instruments*. London: Chester Music.

Davies, J.B. & Jennings, J. (1977) The reproduction of familiar melodies and the perception of tonal sequences. *Journal of the Acoustical Society of America*, **61**, 534–541.

Forster, W. (1955) *Spirituals*. Munich: Nymphenburger Verlagshandlung.

Gjerdingen, R.O. (1991) Using connectionist models to explore complex musical patterns. In P.M. Todd & D.G. Loy (Eds), *Music and Connectionism*. Cambridge, MA: MIT Press.

Grossberg, S. (1980) How does the brain build a cognitive code? *Psychological Review*, **87**, 1–51.

Ireland the Songs (1993) Dublin: Walton Manufacturing.

Jeffries, T.B. (1974) Relationship of interval frequency count to ratings of melodic intervals. *Journal of Experimental Psychology*, **102**, 903–905.

Jordan, M.I. (1986) An introduction to linear algebra in parallel distributed processing. In D.E. Rumelhart & James L. McClelland (Eds), *Parallel Distributed Processing*, Vol. 1. Cambridge, MA: MIT Press.

Katz, B. (1992) On the beauty of nature. *Proceedings of the International Conference on Artificial Neural Networks*, pp. 1321–1324.

Katz, B. (1993a) Musical resolution and musical pleasure. *Proceedings of the Conference on Artificial Intelligence and Simulation of Behaviour*.

Katz, B. (1993b) Musical pleasure through the unification of melodic sequences. *Proceedings of the Fifteenth Annual Conference of the Cognitive Science Society*, pp. 611–616.

Katz, B. (1993c) A neural resolution of the incongruity and incongruity-resolution theories of humour. *Connection Science*, 5, 59–75.

Katz, B. (1993d) Positive Affect and Structural Unity in Chord Transitions. In *Proceedings of IJCNN '93*.

Kohonen, T. (1984) *Self-organization and Associative Memory*. Berlin: Springer-Verlag.

Lerdahl, F. & Jackendoff, R. (1983) *A Generative Theory of Tonal Music*. Cambridge: MIT Press.

Martindale, C. (1984) The pleasures of thought: a theory of cognitive hedonics. *Journal of Mind and Behavior*, 5, 49–80.

Martindale, C., Moore, K. & West, A. (1988) Relationship of preference judgements to typicality, novelty, and mere exposure. *Empirical Studies of the Arts*, 6, 79–96.

Meyer, L.B. (1956) *Emotion and Meaning in Music*. Chicago: University of Chicago Press.

Murray, T. (1952) *Folk Songs of Jamaica*. London: Oxford University Press.

Patterson, R.D. & Moore, B.C.J. (1986) Auditory filters and excitation patterns as representations of frequency resolution. In B.C.J. Moore (Ed.), *Frequency Selectivity in Hearing*. London: Academic Press.

Pollard-Gott, L. (1983) Emergence of thematic concepts in repeated listening to music. *Cognitive Psychology*, 15, 66–94.

Sano, H. & Jenkins, B.K. (1991) A neural network model for pitch perception. In P.M. Todd & D.G. Loy (Eds), *Music and Connectionism*. Cambridge, MA: MIT Press.

Searle, J.A. (1991) The rediscovery of mind. Cambridge, MA: MIT Press.

Sloboda, J.A. (1985) *The Musical Mind: the Cognitive Psychology of Music*. Oxford: Oxford University Press.

Stevens, C. & Latimer, C. (1991) Judgements of complexity and pleasingness in music: the effect of structure, repetition, and training. *Australian Journal of Psychology*, 43, 17–22.

Todd, P.M. (1991). A connectionist approach to algorithmic composition. In P.M. Todd & D.G. Loy (Eds), *Music and Connectionism*. Cambridge: MIT Press.

Vitz, P.C. (1966) Affect as a function of stimulus variation. *Journal of Experimental Psychology*, 2, 84–88.

Part IV
Composition

Neural Network Music Composition by Prediction: Exploring the Benefits of Psychoacoustic Constraints and Multi-scale Processing

MICHAEL C. MOZER

In algorithmic music composition, a simple technique involves selecting notes sequentially according to a transition table that specifies the probability of the next note as a function of the previous context. An extension of this transition-table approach is described, using a recurrent autopredictive connectionist network called CONCERT. CONCERT is trained on a set of pieces with the aim of extracting stylistic regularities. CONCERT can then be used to compose new pieces. A central ingredient of CONCERT is the incorporation of psychologically grounded representations of pitch, duration and harmonic structure. CONCERT was tested on sets of examples artificially generated according to simple rules and was shown to learn the underlying structure, even where other approaches failed. In larger experiments, CONCERT was trained on sets of J. S. Bach pieces and traditional European folk melodies and was then allowed to compose novel melodies. Although the compositions are occasionally pleasant, and are preferred over compositions generated by a third-order transition table, the compositions suffer from a lack of global coherence. To overcome this limitation, several methods are explored to permit CONCERT to induce structure at both fine and coarse scales. In experiments with a training set of waltzes, these methods yielded limited success, but the overall results cast doubt on the promise of note-by-note prediction for composition.

KEYWORDS: Music composition, neural networks, recurrent networks, psychoacoustic representation, multi-scale processing.

1. Introduction

In creating music, composers bring to bear a wealth of knowledge of musical conventions. Some of this knowledge is based on the experience of the individual, some is culture specific, and perhaps some is universal. No matter what the source, this knowledge acts to constrain the composition process, specifying, for example, the musical pitches that form a scale, the pitch or chord progressions that are agreeable, and stylistic conventions like the division of a symphony into movements and the AABB form of a gavotte. If we hope to build automatic composition systems that create agreeable tunes, it will be necessary to incorporate knowledge of musical conventions into the systems. The difficulty is in deriving this knowledge in an

This article appeared originally in *Connection Science*, 1994, **6**, 247–280, and is reprinted with permission.

explicit form: even human composers are unaware of many of the constraints under which they operate (Loy, 1991).

In this article, a connectionist network that composes melodies with harmonic accompaniment is described. The network is called CONCERT, an acronym for *con*nectionist *c*omposer of *er*udite *t*unes. (The 'er' may also be read as *er*ratic or *er*satz, depending on what the listener thinks of its creations.) Musical knowledge is incorporated into CONCERT via two routes. First, CONCERT is trained on a set of sample melodies from which it extracts regularities of note and phrase progressions; these are melodic and stylistic constraints. Second, representations of pitch, duration and harmonic structure that are based on psychological studies of human perception have been built into CONCERT. These representations, and an associated theory of generalization proposed by Shepard (1987), provide CONCERT with a basis for judging the similarity among notes, for selecting a response, and for restricting the set of alternatives that can be considered at any time. The representations thus provide CONCERT with psychoacoustic constraints.

The experiments reported here are with single-voice melodies, some with harmonic accompaniment in the form of chord progressions. The melodies range from 10-note sequences to complete pieces containing roughly 150 notes. A complete composition system should describe each note by a variety of properties—pitch, duration, phrasing, accent—along with more global properties such as tempo and dynamics. In the experiments reported here, the problem has been stripped down somewhat, with each melody described simply as a sequence of pitch–duration–chord triples. The burden of the present work has been to determine the extent to which CONCERT can discover the structure in a set of training examples.

Before the details of CONCERT are discussed a description is given of a traditional approach to algorithmic music composition using Markov transition tables, the limitations of this approach, and how these limitations may be overcome in principle using connectionist learning techniques.

2. Transition Table Approaches to Algorithmic Music Composition

A simple but interesting technique in algorithmic music composition is to select notes sequentially according to a transition table that specifies the probability of the next note as a function of the current note (Dodge & Jerse, 1985; Jones, 1981; Lorrain, 1980). For example, the transition probabilities depicted in Table I constrain the next pitch to be one step up or down the C-major scale from the current pitch. Generating a sequence according to this probability distribution therefore results in a musical random walk. Transition tables may be hand-constructed according to certain criteria, as in Table I, or they may be set up to embody

Table I. Transition probability from current pitch to the next

Next pitch	Current pitch						
	C	D	E	F	G	A	B
C	0	0.5	0	0	0	0	0.5
D	0.5	0	0.5	0	0	0	0
E	0	0.5	0	0.5	0	0	0
F	0	0	0.5	0	0.5	0	0
G	0	0	0	0.5	0	0.5	0
A	0	0	0	0	0.5	0	0.5
B	0.5	0	0	0	0	0.5	0

a particular musical style. In the latter case, statistics are collected over a set of examples (hereafter, the training set) and the transition-table entries are defined to be the transition probabilities in these examples.

The transition table is a statistical description of the training set. In most cases, the transition table will lose information about the training set. To illustrate, consider the two sequences ABC and EFG. The transition table constructed from these examples will indicate that A goes to B with probability 1, B to C with probability 1, and so forth. Consequently, given the first note of each sequence, the table can be used to recover the complete sequence. However, with two sequences like BAC and DAE, the transition table can only say that following an A either an E or a C occurs, each with a 50% likelihood. Thus, the table cannot be used to reconstruct the examples unambiguously.

Clearly, in melodies of any complexity, musical structure cannot be fully described by the pairwise statistics. To capture additional structure, the transition table can be generalized from a two-dimensional array to n dimensions. In the n-dimensional table, often referred to as a table of order $n - 1$, the probability of the next note is indicated as a function of the previous $n - 1$ notes. By increasing the number of previous notes taken into consideration, the table becomes more context sensitive, and therefore serves as a more faithful representation of the training set.[1] Unfortunately, extending the transition table in this manner gives rise to two problems. First, the size of the table explodes exponentially with the amount of context and rapidly becomes unmanageable. With, say, 50 alternative pitches, 10 alternative durations and a third-order transition table—modest sizes on all counts—7.5 billion entries are required. Second, a table representing the high-order structure masks the tremendous amount of low-order structure present. To elaborate, consider the sequence

A F G B F G C F G D F G♯ E F G

One would need to construct a third-order table to represent this sequence faithfully. Such a table would indicate that, for example, the sequence GBF is always followed by G. However, there are first-order regularities in the sequence that a third-order table does not make explicit, namely the fact that an F is almost always followed by a G. The third-order table is thus unable to predict what will follow, say, AAF, although a first-order table would sensibly predict G. There is a trade-off between the ability to represent the training set faithfully, which usually requires a high-order table, and the ability to generalize in novel contexts, which profits from a low-order table. What one would really like is a scheme by which only the relevant high-order structure is represented (Lewis, 1991).

Kohonen (1989) and Kohonen *et al.*, (1991) have proposed exactly such a scheme. The scheme is a symbolic algorithm that, given a training set of examples, produces a collection of rules—a context-sensitive grammar—sufficient for reproducing most or all of the structure inherent in the set. These rules are of the form *context* → *next_note*, where *context* is a string of one or more notes, and *next_note* is the next note implied by the context. Because the context length can vary from one rule to the next, the algorithm allows for varying amounts of generality and specificity in the rules. The algorithm attempts to produce deterministic rules—rules that always apply in the given context. Thus, the algorithm will not discover the regularity F → G in the above sequence because it is not absolute. One could conceivably extend the algorithm to generate simple rules like F → G along with exceptions (e.g. DF → G♯), but the symbolic nature of the algorithm still leaves it poorly equipped to deal with statistical properties of the data. Such an ability is not critical if the algorithm's goal is to construct a set of rules from which the training set can be exactly reconstructed. However, if one views music composition as an intrinsically random process, it is inappropriate to model every detail of the training set. Instead, the goal ought to be to capture the most important—i.e. statistically regular—structural properties of the training set.

Both the transition-table approach and Kohonen's musical grammar suffer from two further drawbacks. First, both algorithms are designed so that a particular note, n, cannot be used to predict note $n + i$ unless all intervening notes, $n + 1, \ldots, n + i - 1$, are also considered. In general, one would expect that the most useful predictor of a note is the immediately preceding note, but cases exist where notes $n, \ldots, n + k$ are more useful predictors of note $n + i$ than notes $n + k + 1, \ldots, n + i - 1$ (e.g. a melody in which high-pitch and low-pitch phrases alternate, as in the solo violin partitas of J. S. Bach). The second, and perhaps more serious, drawback is that a symbolic representation of notes does not facilitate generalization from one musical context to perceptually similar contexts. For instance, the congruity of octaves is not encoded, nor is the abstract notion of intervals such as a 'minor third'.

Connectionist learning algorithms offer the potential of overcoming the various limitations of transition-table approaches and Kohonen musical grammars. Connectionist algorithms are able to discover relevant structure and statistical regularities in sequences (e.g. Elman, 1990; Mozer, 1989). Indeed, connectionist algorithms can be viewed as an extension of the transition-table approach, a point also noted by Dolson (1989). Just as the transition-table approach uses a training set to calculate the probability of the next note in a sequence as a function of the previous notes, so does the network to be described, CONCERT. The connectionist approach, however, is far more flexible in principle: the form of the transition function can permit the consideration of varying amounts of context, the consideration of non-contiguous context, and the combination of low-order and high-order regularities.

The connectionist approach also promises better generalization through the use of distributed representations (Hinton et al., 1986). In a local representation, where each note is represented by a discrete symbol, the sort of statistical contingencies that can be discovered are among notes. However, in a distributed representation, where each note is represented by a set of continuous feature values, the sort of contingencies that can be discovered are among features. To the extent that two notes share features, featural regularities discovered for one note may transfer to the other note.

3. Note-by-note Composition

The Markov transition table and the Kohonen algorithm both use a note-by-note technique in which notes are produced sequentially and linearly, from the start of a piece to the end, each note depending on the preceding context. Todd (1989) and Bharucha and Todd (1989) first explored this technique in a connectionist framework. Since then, it has been adopted by many other connectionist researchers (e.g. Stevens & Wiles, 1993). CONCERT also uses the note-by-note technique; it differs from earlier work primarily in that it uses an assortment of state-of-the-art connectionist tricks to achieve a sophisticated implementation of the technique (e.g. back-propagation through time, probabilistic interpretation of the network outputs, a maximum likelihood training criterion, representational considerations) and tests the technique on a variety of relatively large-scale problems. By using a powerful architecture and learning algorithm, the goal of the research is to see how far the note-by-note technique can be pushed. Previous research has been fairly uncritical in accepting and examining a network's performance; the simple fact that a network creates novel output tends to be interpreted as success. In this work, CONCERT's performance on simple, well-structured sequences is evaluated according to an objective criterion, and on complex musical examples according to the ears of experienced human listeners.

Despite the research effort expended on note-by-note composition, it might seem an unlikely technique to succeed. Music has a rich, hierarchical structure, from the level of notes within a theme, to themes within a phrase, to phrases within a movement, to movements within a symphony. One might well be skeptical that a sequential, linear composer could keep track of multiple levels of structure. In principle, however, the connectionist approach can; the present work is a test of whether it can do so in practice.

This type of linear technique has shown surprising and interesting results for natural-language processing. Elman (1990, 1993) has trained sequential networks on strings of letters or words and has found that the networks could infer grammatical and semantic structure, even recursive structure. However, this work has focused primarily on the sentence level; one can hardly imagine that it would scale up to handle, say, semantic structure of paragraphs or short stories. Fortunately, music is unlike natural language in several simplifying respects: the set of atomic elements is finite, relatively small and unambiguous, and psychoacoustic and stylistic regularities abound. Consequently, constraints among elements are stronger. Thus, it seems *a priori* plausible that at least several levels of structure might be inferrable by a linear technique for music.

4. The CONCERT Architecture

CONCERT is a recurrent network architecture that learns to behave as an autopredictor (Elman, 1990). A melody is presented to it, one note at a time, and its task at each point in time is to predict the next note in the melody. Using a training procedure described below, CONCERT's connection strengths are adjusted so that it can perform this task correctly for a set of training examples. Each example consists of a sequence of notes. The current note in the sequence is represented in the input layer of CONCERT, and the prediction of the next note is represented in the output layer. The input and output layers both represent three aspects of a note: its pitch, its duration and its harmonic chord accompaniment. As Figure 1 indicates, the next note is encoded in two different ways: the next-note-distributed (or NND) layer contains CONCERT's internal representation of the note—divided into three pools of units, forming distributed representations of pitch, duration and harmony—while the next-note-local (or NNL) layer contains one unit for each alternative pitch, duration and chord. The representation of a note in the NND layer, as well as in the input layer, is based on psychophysical studies, described further below. For now, it should suffice to say that this representation is distributed, i.e. a note is indicated by a pattern of activity across the units. Because such patterns of activity can be quite difficult to interpret, the NNL layer provides an alternative, explicit representation of the possibilities.

The context layer can represent relevant aspects of the input history, that is, the temporal context in which a prediction is made. When a new note is presented in

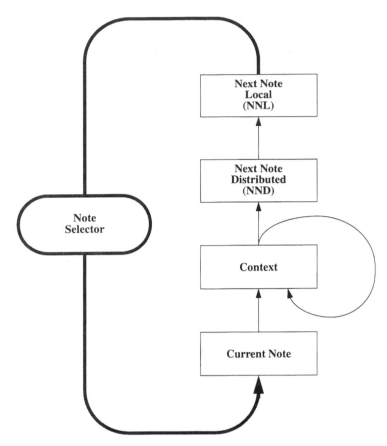

Figure 1. The CONCERT architecture. Rectangles indicate a layer of units, directed lines indicate full connectivity from one layer to another. The selection process is external to CONCERT and is used to choose among the alternatives proposed by the network during composition.

the input layer, the activity pattern currently in the context layer is integrated with the new note to form a new context representation. In general terms

$$\mathbf{c}(n) = f(\mathbf{c}(n-1), \mathbf{x}(n))$$

Where $\mathbf{x}(n)$ is a vector representing the nth note in the input sequence, $\mathbf{c}(n)$ is the context activity pattern following processing of input note n—which I refer to as step n—and f is a member of the class of functions that can be implemented by the connectionist hardware. At the start of each sequence the context layer is cleared, i.e. $\mathbf{c}(0) = 0$.

CONCERT could readily be wired up to behave as a kth order transition table. In this case, the function f is defined to implement a k-element stack in the context layer. This stack would hold on to notes $n - k + 1$ through n. The connections from the context layer to the output layer would then have to be set up to realize a look-up table in which each combination of previous notes maps to the appropriate probability distribution over the next note. However, the architecture is more general than a transition table because f is not limited to implementing a stack and the mapping from the context layer to the output need not be an arbitrary look-up table. From myriad possibilities, the training procedure attempts to find a set of connections that are adequate for performing the next-note prediction task. This involves determining which aspects of the input sequence are relevant for making future predictions and constructing the function f appropriately. Subsequently, the context layer will retain only task-relevant information. This contrasts with Todd's (1989) work on connectionist composition in which the recurrent context connections are pre-wired and fixed, which makes the nature of the information Todd's model retains independent of the examples on which it is trained.

Once CONCERT has been trained, it can be run in composition mode to create new pieces. This involves first seeding CONCERT with a short sequence of notes, perhaps the initial notes of one of the training examples. From this point on, the output of CONCERT can be fed back to the input, allowing CONCERT to continue generating notes without further external input. Generally, the output of CONCERT does not specify a single note with absolute certainty; instead, the output is a probability distribution over the set of candidates. It is thus necessary to select a particular note in accordance with this distribution. This is the role of the selection process depicted in Figure 1.

4.1. Unit Activation Rules

The activation rule for the context units is

$$c_i(n) = s\left[\sum_j w_{ij} x_j(n) + \sum_j v_{ij} c_j(n-1)\right] \tag{1}$$

where $c_i(n)$ is the activity of context unit i at step n, $x_j(n)$ is the activity of input unit j at step n, w_{ij} is the connection strength from unit j of the input to unit i of the context layer, v_{ij} is the connection strength from unit j to unit i within the context layer, and s is the standard logistic activation function rescaled to the range $[-1,1]$. Units in the NND layer follow a similar rule:

$$nnd_i(n) = s\left[\sum_j u_{ij} c_j(n)\right]$$

where $nnd_i(n)$ is the activity of NND unit i at step n and u_{ij} is the strength of connection from context unit j to NND unit i.

The NND and NNL representations can be broken into three component vectors, corresponding to pitch, duration and chord representations. The transformation from the NND pitch representation to the NNL pitch representation is described here; the transformation for the duration and chord representations is similar. The pitch transformation is achieved by first computing the distance between the NND pitch representation $\mathbf{nndp}(n)$, and the target (distributed) representation of each pitch i, $\mathbf{p}_i$:

$$d_i = \|\mathbf{nndp}(n) - \mathbf{p}_i\|$$

where $\|\cdot\|$ denotes the L_2 vector norm. This distance is an indication of how well the NND representation matches a particular pitch. The activation of the NNL unit corresponding to pitch i, $nnlp_i$, increases as the distance decreases:

$$nnlp_i(n) = \frac{e^{-d_i}}{\sum_j e^{-d_j}}$$

This normalized exponential transform was first proposed by Bridle (1990) and Rumelhart (in press). It produces an activity pattern over the NNL units in which each unit has activity in the range [0,1] and the activity of all units sums to 1. Consequently, the NNL activity pattern can be interpreted as a probability distribution—in this case, the probability that the next note has a particular pitch. An analogous transformation is performed to determine the activity of NNL units that represent note duration and accompanying chord. The distance measure and the exponential function have their basis in psychological theory (Shepard, 1987), a point that is elaborated on shortly.

4.2. Training Procedure

CONCERT is trained using a variation of the back-propagation algorithm (Rumelhart et al., 1986) which adjusts the connection strengths within CONCERT so that the network can perform the next-note prediction task for a set of training examples. The algorithm requires first defining a measure of the network's performance—of how good a job the network does at predicting each note in each of the training examples. Commonly, a squared difference measure of error is used:

$$E_{lms} = \sum_{q,\,n,\,j} (nnlp_j(n,\,q) - \delta(j,\,P(n,\,q)))^2 + \sum_{q,\,n,\,j} (nnld_j(n,\,q) - \delta(j,\,D(n,\,q)))^2$$
$$+ \sum_{q,\,n,\,j} (nnlc_j(n,\,q) - \delta(j,\,C(n,\,q)))^2$$

where q is an index over pieces in the training set, n is an index over notes within a piece, and j is an index over pitch, duration or chord units in the NNL layer; $P(n, q)$, $D(n, q)$, $C(n, q)$ are the indices of the target pitch, duration and chord for note n of piece q; $\delta(a,b) = 1$ if $a = b$ or 0 otherwise. This measure is minimized when the outputs of the units corresponding to the correct predictions are 1 and the outputs of all other units are 0.

Another performance measure is sensible in the context of output units that have a probabilistic interpretation (Bridle, 1990; Rumelhart, in press). Because each NNL unit's output represents the probabilistic expectation of a pitch, performance depends on predicting the appropriate notes with high probability. This suggests the likelihood performance measure

$$L = \prod_{q,n} nnlp_{P(n,\,q)}(n,\,q) \; nnld_{D(n,\,q)}(n,\,q) \; nnlc_{C(n,\,q)}(n,\,q)$$

which is the joint probability of making the correct prediction for all notes of all pieces.[2] A log-likelihood criterion

$$E = -\log L = -\sum_{q,n} \log nnlp_{P(n,\,q)}(n,\,q) + \log nnld_{D(n,\,q)}(n,\,q) + \log nnlc_{C(n,\,q)}(n,\,q)$$

is used instead because it is easier to work with, and has the same extrema as L.

Back-propagation specifies how the weights in the network should be changed to reduce E. This involves computing the gradient of E with respect to the weights in the network: $\partial E/\partial \mathbf{W}$, $\partial E/\partial \mathbf{V}$, and $\partial E/\partial \mathbf{U}$. The first step in this process is computing the gradient with respect to the activity of units in the NND layer, and then propagating this gradient back to the weights in layers below. For the NND pitch units

$$\frac{\partial E}{\partial \mathbf{nndp}(n,\,q)} = \left[\frac{\mathbf{nndp}(n,\,q) - \mathbf{p}_{P(n,\,q)}}{d_{P(n,\,q)}} - \sum_i nnlp_i(n,\,q)\, \frac{\mathbf{nndp}(n,\,q) - \mathbf{p}_i}{d_i} \right]$$

Back-propagation still cannot be used to train CONCERT directly, because CON-CERT contains recurrent connections and the algorithm applies only to feedforward networks. Several variations of the algorithm have been proposed for dealing with recurrent networks (Williams & Zipser, in press). Here, we use the 'back-propagation through time' (BPTT) procedure of Rumelhart *et al.* (1986), which transforms a recurrent network into an equivalent feedforward network.[3] This training procedure computes the true gradient of the objective function with respect to the various network weights. This means that if an input note at step *l* has any predictive utility at some later time *n*, then in principle the algorithm should adjust the connections so that note *l* is maintained in the network's memory. Contingencies over time should be discovered when they exist. There is a weaker version of BPTT that passes error back only a fixed number of steps (e.g. the training procedure used by Elman (1990)), which in principle makes contingencies across longer time spans more difficult to maintain and discover. CONCERT has been furnished with the most powerful connectionist recurrent-network learning procedure in order to endow it with the best possible chance of success.

5. Representing Musical Elements

Following this description of CONCERT's architecture, dynamics and training procedure, the issue of representing a musical piece arises. A piece is defined as a sequence of elements, each of which is characterized by a melody pitch, a melody duration and a harmonic chord accompaniment. The pitch and duration specify the notes of the melody, each of which is accompanied by a chord (or silence). This encoding synchronizes the melody and the harmony. Although chord changes generally occur at a slower rate than changes in the melody line, this is encoded simply by repeating chords for each note of the melody until the chord changes. The three elements—pitch, duration and chord representation—are discussed in turn.

5.1. Pitch Representation

To accommodate a variety of music, CONCERT needs the ability to represent a range of about four octaves. Using standard musical notation, these pitches are labeled as follows: C1, D1, . . ., B1, C2, D2, . . . B2, C3, . . . C5, where C1 is the lowest pitch and C5 the highest. Sharps and flats are denoted with ♯ and ♭, respectively, e.g. C♯3 and G♭2. Within an octave, there are twelve chromatic steps; the range C1–C5 thus includes 49 pitches.

Perhaps the simplest representation of pitch is to have one unit for each possibility. The pitch C1 would be represented by the activity vector $[1\ 0\ 0 \ldots]^T$, C♯1 by the vector $[0\ 1\ 0 \ldots]^T$, and so forth. An alternative would be to represent pitch by a single unit whose activity was proportional to the frequency of the pitch. One might argue that the choice of a pitch representation is not critical because back-propagation can, in principle, discover an alternative representation well suited to the task (Hinton, 1987). In practice, however, researchers have found that the choice of external representation is a critical determinant of the network's ultimate performance (e.g. Denker *et al.*, 1987; Mozer, 1987). Quite simply, the more task-appropriate information that is built into the network, the easier the job the learning algorithm has.

Laden and Keefe (1989) advocate the approach of including as much information as possible from psychoacoustics into the design of networks for music perception and cognition. They have developed a model of chord classification that categorizes triads as major, minor or diminished chords. Classification performance is superior with the use of a representation that explicitly encodes harmonics of the fundamental pitches.

In accord with this approach, and because CONCERT is being asked to make predictions about melodies that people have composed or to generate melodies that people perceive as pleasant, CONCERT has been furnished with a psychologically motivated representation of pitch. This means that notes that people judge to be similar should have similar representations in the network, indicating that the representation in the head matches the representation in the network. The local representation scheme proposed earlier clearly does not meet this criterion. In the local representation, every pair of pitches is equally similar (using either the distance or angle between vectors as a measure of similarity), yet people perceive pairs of notes like C1 and C#1 to be more similar than, say, C1 and A4. Other obvious representations of pitch do not meet the criterion either. For example, a direct encoding of frequency does not capture the similarity that people hear between octaves.

Shepard (1982) has studied the similarity of pitches by asking people to judge the perceived similarity of pairs of pitches. He has proposed a theory of generalization (Shepard, 1987) in which the perceived similarity of two items decreases exponentially with the distance between them in an internal or 'psychological' representational space.[4] For the internal representation of pitch, Shepard has proposed a five-dimensional space, depicted in Figure 2. In this space, each pitch specifies a point along the pitch height (or PH) dimension, an (x,y) coordinate on the chroma circle (or CC) and an (x,y) coordinate on the circle of fifths (or CF). We will refer to this representation as PHCCCF, after its three components. The PH component specifies the logarithm of the frequency of a pitch; this logarithmic transform places tonal half-steps at equal spacing from one another along the PH axis. In the CC, neighboring pitches are a tonal half-step apart. In the CF, the perfect fifth of a pitch is the next pitch immediately counterclockwise.[5] The proximity of two pitches in the five-dimensional PHCCCF space can be determined simply by computing the Euclidean distance between their representations.

Shepard presents detailed arguments for the psychological validity of the PHCCCF representation. Let us briefly look at some of its benefits. Consider first the PH and CC components. In this three-dimensional subspace, pitches form a helix in which the winding of the helix is due to the CC and the height is due to the PH. As pitches proceed up the chromatic scale, they wind up the helix. Pitches exactly one octave apart are directly above one another on the helix; that is, they have the same locus on the CC but different values of PH. For this reason, octaves have similar representations. Depending on how the PH component is scaled relative to the CC (i.e. how elongated the helix is), pitches like C1 and C2 may even be closer in the representational space than pitches like C1 and B1, even though C1 is closer to B1 in frequency.

The CF endows the representation with other desirable properties. First, the circle localizes the tones in a musical key. Any seven adjacent tones correspond to a particular key. For instance, the tones of the C-major and A-minor diatonic

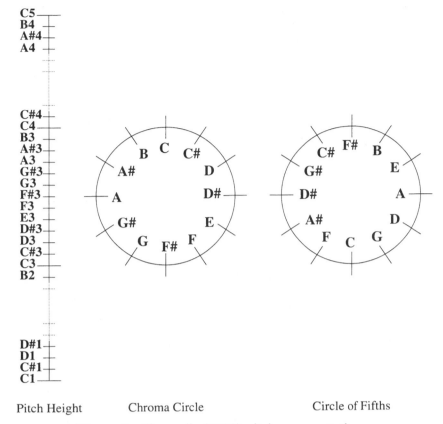

Pitch Height   Chroma Circle   Circle of Fifths

Figure 2. Shepard's (1982) pitch representation.

scales—C, D, E, F, G, A and B—are grouped together on the CF. The most common pentatonic keys are similarly localized. Second, and perhaps more critical, the CF can explain the subjective equality of the intervals of the diatonic scale. To elaborate, Shepard points out that people tend to hear the successive steps of the major scale as equivalent, although with respect to log frequency, some of the intervals are only half as large as others. For example, in C major, the E–F and B–C steps are half tones apart (minor seconds) while all others are a whole tone apart (major seconds). The combination of the PH and the CF permits a representation in which the distance between all major and minor seconds is the same. This is achieved by using a scale ratio of approximately 3:1 for the CC relative to the CF.

One desirable property of the overall PHCCCF representation is that distances between pitches are invariant under transposition. Consider any two pitches, say, D2 and G#4. Transposing the pitches preserves the distance between them in the PHCCCF representation. Thus, the distance from D2 to G#4 is the same as from E2 to A#4, from D1 to G#3, and so forth. See Bharucha (1991) for a further discussion of the psychological issues involved in the representation of musical pitch.

The relative importance of the PH, CC and CF components can be varied by adjusting the diameters of the CC and the CF. For example, if the two circles have the same diameter, then, in terms of the CC and CF components, the distance between C and G is the same as the distance between C and B. This is because B is one notch from the C on the CC and five notches on the CF, while the G is five notches away on the CC and one on the CF. However, if the diameter of the CC is increased, then C is closer to B than to G (based on the distance in the four-dimensional CC and CF subspace); if the diameter is decreased, C is closer to G than to B. If the diameters of both circles are decreased relative to the PH scale, then pitch frequency becomes the most important determinant of similarity. Shepard argues that the weighting of the various components depends on the particular musical task and the listener's expertise. Based on Shepard's evidence, a reasonable representation for expert musicians is to weigh the CF and CC components equally, and to set the diameter of the CC and CF components equal to the distance of one octave in PH. This is the scale shown in Figure 2.

The final issue to discuss is how the PHCCCF representation translates into an activity vector over a set of connectionist units. A straightforward scheme is to use five units, one for pitch height and two pairs to encode the (x, y) coordinates of the pitch on the two circles.[6]

One problem with this scheme is that, if the units have the usual sigmoidal activation function, equal spacing of tones in pitch height or on the circles in unit activity space is not preserved in unit net input space. This means that context units attempting to activate NND units do not reap the full benefit of the representation (e.g. transposition invariance). A second problem with the simple five-unit scheme is that each unit encodes a coordinate value directly; there are seven discrete values for the x- and y-coordinates of the circles, 49 for the pitch height. Consequently, minor perturbations of the activity vector could lead to misinterpretations.

Due to these problems, an alternative representation of the CC and CF components has been adopted. The representation involves six binary-valued units to represent a tone on each circle; the representation for CC tones is shown in Table II. This representation preserves the essential distance relationships among tones on the CC: the distance between two tones is monotonically related to the angle between the tones. Because each unit has to encode only two distinct values, the representation is less sensitive to noise than is one in which each unit encodes a coordinate of the circle.

Unfortunately, there is no similar scheme that can be used to encode PH in a Boolean space of reasonably low dimensionality that preserves intrinsic distance relationships. Consequently, a single linear unit has been used for PH. Although this means that the PH unit can take on 49 distinct values, it is not critical that the unit represent a value with great accuracy. The PH unit essentially conveys

Table II. Representation of tones on the CC

Tone	Representation					
C	−1	−1	−1	−1	−1	−1
C♯	−1	−1	−1	−1	−1	+1
D	−1	−1	−1	−1	+1	+1
D♯	−1	−1	−1	+1	+1	+1
E	−1	−1	+1	+1	+1	+1
F	−1	+1	+1	+1	+1	+1
F♯	+1	+1	+1	+1	+1	+1
G	+1	+1	+1	+1	+1	−1
G♯	+1	+1	+1	+1	−1	−1
A	+1	+1	+1	−1	−1	−1
A♯	+1	+1	−1	−1	−1	−1
B	+1	−1	−1	−1	−1	−1

Table III. PHCCCF representation for selected pitches

Pitch	PH	CC						CF					
C1	−9.978	+1	+1	+1	−1	−1	−1	−1	−1	−1	+1	+1	+1
F♯1	−7.349	−1	−1	−1	+1	+1	+1	+1	+1	+1	−1	−1	−1
G2	−2.041	−1	−1	−1	−1	+1	+1	−1	−1	−1	−1	+1	+1
C3	0	+1	+1	+1	−1	−1	−1	−1	−1	−1	+1	+1	+1
D♯3	1.225	+1	+1	+1	+1	+1	+1	+1	+1	+1	+1	+1	+1
E3	1.633	−1	+1	+1	+1	+1	+1	+1	−1	−1	−1	−1	−1
A4	8.573	−1	−1	−1	−1	−1	−1	−1	−1	−1	−1	−1	−1
C5	9.798	+1	+1	+1	−1	−1	−1	−1	−1	−1	+1	+1	+1
Rest	0	+1	−1	+1	−1	+1	−1	+1	−1	+1	−1	+1	−1

information about the octave; information about the pitch within an octave can be gleaned from the values on the other dimensions. Consequently, a precise response of the PH unit is not crucial. Its activity is scaled to range from −9.798 for C1 to +9.798 for C5. This scaling achieves the desired property previously described that the distance in the CC or CF component between pitches on opposite sides of the circle equals the distance between pitches one octave apart in the PH component.[7]

The PHCCCF representation consists of 13 units altogether. Sample activity patterns for some pitches are shown in Table III. Rests (silence) are assigned a unique code, listed in the last row of the table, that is maximally different from all pitches. The end of a piece is coded by a series of rests.

As with any distributed representation, there are limitations as to how many and which pitches can be represented simultaneously. The issue arises because the NND layer needs to be able to encode a set of alternatives, not just a single pitch. If, say, A1, D2 and E2 are equally likely as the next note, the NND layer must indicate all three possibilities. To do so, it must produce an activity vector that is nearer to p_{A1}, p_{D2} and p_{E2} than to other possibilities. The point in PHCCCF space that is simultaneously closest to the three pitches is simply the average vector, $(p_{A1} + p_{D2} + p_{E2})/3$. Table IV shows the pitches nearest to the average vector. As hoped for, A1, D2 and E2 are the nearest three. This is not always the case, though. Table V shows the pitches nearest to the average vector which represents the set {A1, D2, D♯2}. This illustrates the fact that certain clusters of pitches are more compact in the PHCCCF space than others. The PHCCCF representation not only introduces a similarity structure over the pitches, but also a limit on the combinations of pitches

Table IV. Distance from representation of {A1,D2,E2} to nearest 10 pitches

Rank	Pitch	Distance
1	D2	2.528
2	E2	2.779
3	A1	3.399
4	B1	3.859
5	C2	4.130
6	C♯2	4.422
7	A2	4.422
8	E1	4.441
9	G1	4.497
10	G2	4.497

Table V. Distance from representation of {A1, D2, D♯2} to nearest 10 pitches

Rank	Pitch	Distance
1	D2	2.373
2	C2	3.277
3	E2	3.538
4	C♯2	3.654
5	B1	3.714
6	D♯2	3.774
7	A1	3.946
8	F2	4.057
9	A♯1	4.146
10	G1	4.323

that can be considered simultaneously. Arbitrary limitations are a bad thing in general, but here the limitations are theoretically motivated.

One serious shortcoming of the PHCCCF representation is that it is based on the similarity between pairs of pitches presented in isolation. Listeners of music do not process individual notes in isolation; notes appear in a musical context which suggests a musical key which in turn contributes to an interpretation of the note. Some psychologically motivated work has considered the effects of context or musical key on pitch representation (Krumhansl, 1990; Krumhansl & Kessler, 1982; Longuet-Higgins, 1976, 1979). CONCERT could perhaps be improved by incorporating the ideas in this work. Fortunately, it does not require discarding the PHCCCF representation altogether, because the PHCCCF representation shares many properties in common with the representations suggested by Krumhansl and Kessler and by Longuet-Higgins.

5.2. Duration Representation

Although considerable psychological research has been directed toward the problem of how people perceive duration in the context of a rhythm (e.g. Fraisse, 1982; Jones & Boltz, 1989; Pressing, 1983), there appears to be no psychological theory of representation of individual note durations comparable to Shepard's work on pitch. Shepard suggests that there ought to be a representation of duration analogous to the PHCCCF representation, although no details are discussed in his work. The representation of duration built into CONCERT attempts to follow this suggestion.

The representation is based on the division of each beat (quarter-note) into twelfths. A quarter-note thus has a duration of 12/12, an eighth-note 6/12, an eighth-note triplet 4/12, and so forth (Figure 3). Using this characterization of note durations, a five-dimensional space can be constructed, consisting of three components (Figure 4). In this representation, each duration specifies a point along the duration height dimension, an (x, y) coordinate on the 1/3 beat circle and an (x, y) coordinate on the 1/4 beat circle. The duration height is proportional to the logarithm of the duration. This logarithmic transformation follows the general psychophysical law (Fechner's law) relating stimulus intensity to perceived sensation. The point on the $1/n$ beat circle is the duration after subtracting out the greatest integer multiple of $1/n$. For example, the duration 18/12 is represented by the point 2/12 on the 1/3 beat circle and the point 0/12 on the 1/4 beat circle. The two circles

Figure 3. The characterization of note durations in terms of twelfths of a beat. The fractions shown correspond to the duration of a single note of a given type.

result in similar representations for related durations. For example, eighth-notes and quarter-notes (the former half the duration of the latter) share the same value on the 1/4 beat circle; eighth-note triplets and quarter-note triplets share the same value on the 1/3 beat circle; and quarter-notes and half-notes share the same values on both the 1/4 and 1/3 beat circles.

This five-dimensional space is encoded directly by five units in CONCERT. It was not necessary to map the 1/3 or 1/4 beat circle into a higher-dimensional binary space, as was done for the CC and the CF (Table II), because the beat circles are sparsely populated. Only two or three values need to be distinguished along the x and y-dimensions of each circle, which is well within the capacity of a single unit.

Several alternative approaches to rhythm representation are worthy of mention. A straightforward approach is to represent time implicitly by presenting each pitch on the input layer for a number of time steps proportional to the duration. Thus, a half-note might appear for 24 time steps, a quarter-note for 12, an eighth-note for 6. Todd (1989) followed an approach of this sort, although he did not quantize time so finely. He included an additional unit to indicate whether a pitch was articulated or tied to the previous pitch. This allowed for the distinction between, say, two successive quarter-notes of the same pitch and a single half-note. The drawback of this implicit representation of duration is that time must be sliced into

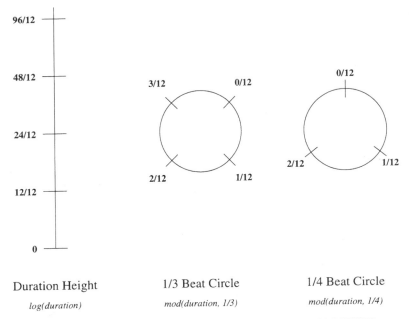

Figure 4. The duration representation used in CONCERT.

fairly small intervals to allow for a complete range of alternative durations, and as a result, the number of steps in a piece of music becomes quite large. This makes it difficult to learn contingencies among notes. For instance, if four successive quarter-notes are presented, to make an association between the first and the fourth, a minimum of 24 input steps must be bridged.

One might also consider a representation in which a note's duration is encoded with respect to the role it plays within a rhythmic pattern. This requires the explicit representation of larger rhythmic patterns. This approach seems quite promising, although it moves away from the note-by-note prediction paradigm that this work examines.

5.3. *Chord Representation*

The chord representation is based on Laden and Keefe's (1989) proposal for a psychoacoustically grounded distributed representation. Firstly, the Laden and Keefe proposal will be summarized and then it will be explained how it was modified for CONCERT.

The chords used here are in root position and are composed of three or four component pitches; some examples are shown in Table VI. Consider each pitch separately. In wind instruments, bowed string instruments and singing voices, a particular pitch will produce a harmonic spectrum consisting of the fundamental pitch (e.g. for C3, 440 Hz), and harmonics that are integer multiples of the fundamental (880 Hz, 1320 Hz, 1760 Hz and 2200 Hz). Laden and Keefe projected the continuous pitch frequency to the nearest pitch class of the chromatic scale, e.g. 440 to C3, 880 to C4, 1320 to G3, 1760 to C5 and 2200 to E5, where the projections to G3 and E5 are approximate. Using an encoding in which there is an element for each pure pitch class, a pitch was represented by activating the fundamental and the first four harmonics. The representation of a chord consisted of the superimposition of the representations of the component pitches. To allow for the range C3–C7, 49 elements are required. In Laden and Keefe's work, a neural network with this input representation better learns to classify chords as major, minor or diminished than a network with an acoustically neutral input representation.

Several modifications of this representation were made for CONCERT. The octave information was dropped, reducing the dimensionality of the representation from 49 to 12. The strength of representation of harmonics was exponentially weighted by their harmonic number; the fundamental was encoded with an activity of 1.0, the first harmonic with an activity of 0.5, the second harmonic with an activity of 0.25, and so forth. Activities were rescaled from a 0-to-1 range to a −1-to-1 range. Finally, an additional element was added to the representation based on a psychoacoustic study of perceived chord similarity. Krumhansl *et al.* (1982)

Table VI. Elements of chords

Chord	Component pitches			
C major	C3	E3	G3	
C minor	C3	E♭3	G3	
C augmented	C3	E3	G♯3	
C diminished	C3	E♭3	G♭3	
C7	C3	E3	G3	B♭3

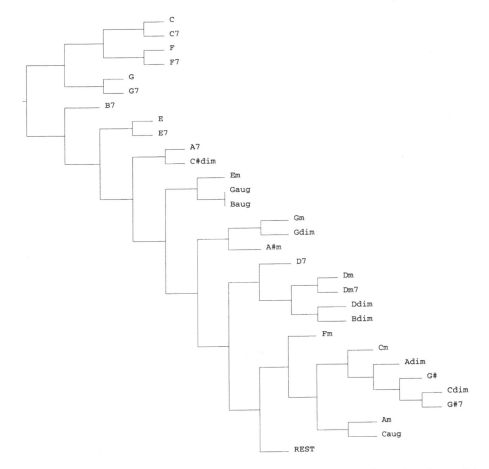

Figure 5. Hierarchical clustering of the representations of various chords used in simulation studies.

found that people tended to judge the tonic, subdominant and dominant chords (i.e. C, F and G in the key of C) as being quite similar. This similarity was not present in the Laden and Keefe representation. Hence, an additional element was added to force these chords closer together. The element had value +1.5 for these three chords (as well as C7, F7 and G7), −1.5 for all other chords. Hierarchical clustering shows some of the similarity structure of the 13-dimensional representation (Figure 5).

6. Basic Simulation Results

Many decisions had to be made in constructing CONCERT. In pilot simulation experiments, various aspects of CONCERT were explored, including variants in the representations, such as using two units to represent the circles in the PHCCCF representation instead of six; alternative error measures, such as the mean-squared error; and the necessity of the NNL layer. Empirical comparisons supported the architecture and representations described earlier.

One potential pitfall in the research area of connectionist music composition is the uncritical acceptance of a network's performance. It is absolutely essential that a network be evaluated according to some objective criterion. One cannot judge the enterprise to be a success simply because the network is creating novel output. Even random note sequences played through a synthesizer sound interesting to many listeners. Thus an examination of CONCERT's performance was begun by testing CONCERT on simple artificial pitch sequences, with the aim of verifying that it can discover the structure known to be present. In these sequences, there was no variation in duration and harmony; consequently, the duration and chord components of the input and output were ignored.

6.1. Extending a C-major Diatonic Scale

To start with a simple experiment, CONCERT was trained on a single sequence consisting of three octaves of a C-major diatonic scale: C1 D1 E1 F1 . . . B3. The target at each step was the next pitch in the scale: D1 E1 F1 G1 . . . C4. CONCERT is said to have learned the sequence when, at each step, the activity of the NNL unit representing the target at that step is more active than any other NNL unit. In 10 replications of the simulation with different random initial weights, 15 context units, a learning rate of 0.005 and no momentum, CONCERT learned the sequence in about 30 passes. Following training, CONCERT was tested on four octaves of the scale. CONCERT correctly extended its predictions to the fourth octave, except that in 4 of the 10 replications, the final note, C5, was transposed down an octave. Table VII shows the CONCERT's output for two octaves of the scale. Octave 3 was part of the training sequence, but octave 4 was not. Activities of the three most active NNL pitch units are shown. Because the activities can be interpreted as probabilities, one can see that the target is selected with high confidence.

CONCERT was able to learn the training set with as few as two context units, although surprisingly, generalization performance tended to improve as the number of context units was increased. CONCERT was also able to generalize from a two-octave training sequence, but it often transposed pitches down an octave.

6.2. Learning the Structure of Diatonic Scales

In this simulation, CONCERT was trained on a set of diatonic scales in various keys over a one-octave range, e.g. D1 E1 F#1 G1 A1 B1 C#2 D2. Thirty-seven such

Table VII. Performance on octaves 3 and 4 of C-major diatonic scale

Input pitch			Output unit activities			
C3	D3	0.961	C3	0.017	E3	0.014
D3	E3	0.972	D3	0.012	F3	0.007
E3	F3	0.982	D#3	0.008	G3	0.006
F3	G3	0.963	F3	0.015	A3	0.010
G3	A3	0.961	G3	0.024	B3	0.012
A3	B3	0.972	A3	0.025	C4	0.002
B3	C4	0.979	A#3	0.010	C#4	0.005
C4	D4	0.939	C4	0.040	E4	0.009
D4	E4	0.968	D4	0.018	F4	0.006
E4	F4	0.971	D#4	0.016	E4	0.005
F4	G4	0.931	F4	0.037	F#4	0.015
G4	A4	0.938	G4	0.044	B4	0.007
A4	B4	0.915	A4	0.080	A#4	0.003
B4	C5	0.946	A#4	0.040	B4	0.011

scales can be made using pitches in the C1–C5 range. The training set consisted of 28 scales—roughly 75% of the corpus—selected at random, and the test set consisted of the remaining 9. In 10 replications of the simulation using 20 context units, CONCERT mastered the training set in approximately 55 passes. Generalization performance was tested by presenting the scales in the test set one pitch at a time and examining CONCERT's prediction. This is not the same as running CONCERT in composition mode because CONCERT's output was not fed back to the input; instead, the input was a predetermined sequence. Of the 63 pitches to be predicted in the test set, CONCERT achieved remarkable performance: 98.4% correct. The few errors were caused by transposing pitches one full octave or one tonal half-step.

To compare CONCERT with a transition-table approach, a second-order transition table was built from the training set data and its performance measured on the test set. The transition-table prediction (i.e. the pitch with highest probability) was correct only 26.6% of the time. The transition table is somewhat of a straw man for this task: a transition table that is based on absolute pitches is simply unable to generalize correctly. Even if the transition table encoded relative pitches, a third-order table would be required to master the environment. Kohonen's musical grammar faces the same difficulties as a transition table.

A version of CONCERT was tested using a local pitch representation in the input and NND layers instead of the PHCCCF representation. The local representation had 49 pitch units, one per tone. Although the NND and NNL layers may seem somewhat redundant with a local pitch representation, the architecture was not changed to avoid confounding the comparison between representations with other possible factors. Testing the network in the manner described above, generalization performance with the local representation and 20 context units was only 54.4%. Experiments with smaller and larger numbers of context units resulted in no better performance.

6.3. *Learning Random Walk Sequences*

In this simulation, 10-element sequences were generated according to a simple rule: the first pitch was selected at random, and then successive pitches were either one step up or down the C-major scale from the previous pitch, the direction chosen at random. The pitch transitions can easily be described by a transition table, as illustrated in Table I. CONCERT, with 15 context units, was trained for 50 passes through a set of 100 such sequences. If CONCERT has correctly inferred the underlying rule, its predictions should reflect the plausible alternatives at each point in a sequence. To test this, a set of 100 novel random walk sequences was presented. After each note n of a sequence, CONCERT's performance was evaluated by matching the top two predictions—the two pitches with highest activity—against the actual note $n + 1$ of the sequence. If note $n + 1$ was not one of the top two predictions, the prediction was considered to be erroneous. In 10 replications of the simulation, the mean performance was 99.95% correct. Thus, CONCERT was clearly able to infer the structure present in the patterns. CONCERT performed equally well, if not better, on random walks in which chromatic steps (up or down a tonal half step) were taken. CONCERT with a local representation of pitch achieved 100% generalization performance.

6.4. Learning Interspersed Random Walk Sequences

The sequences in this simulation were generated by interspersing the elements of two simple random walk sequences. Each interspersed sequence had the following form: $a_1, b_1, a_2, b_2, \ldots, a_5, b_5$, where a_1 and b_1 are randomly selected pitches, a_{i+1} is one step up or down from a_i on the C-major scale, and likewise for b_{i+1} and b_i. Each sequence consisted of 10 pitches. CONCERT, with 25 context units, was trained on 50 passes through a set of 200 examples and was then tested on an additional 100. In contrast to the simple random walk sequences, it is impossible to predict the second pitch in the interspersed sequences (b_1) from the first (a_1). Thus, this prediction was ignored for the purpose of evaluating CONCERT's performance. CONCERT achieved a performance of 94.8% correct. Excluding errors that resulted from octave transpositions, performance improves to 95.5% correct. CONCERT with a local pitch representation achieves a slightly better performance of 96.4%.

To capture the structure in this environment, a transition-table approach would need to consider at least the previous two pitches. However, such a transition table is not likely to generalize well because, if it is to be assured of predicting a note at step n correctly, it must observe the note at step $n - 2$ in the context of every possible note at step $n - 1$. Hence, a second-order transition table was constructed from CONCERT's training set. Using a testing criterion analogous to that used to evaluate CONCERT, the transition table achieved a performance level on the test set of only 67.1% correct. Kohonen's musical grammar would face the same difficulty as the transition table in this environment.

6.5. Learning AABA Phrase Patterns

The melodies in this simulation were formed by generating two phrases, call them A and B, and concatenating the phrases in an AABA pattern. The A and B phrases consisted of five-note ascending chromatic scales, the first pitch selected at random. The complete melody then consisted of 21 elements—four phrases of five notes followed by a rest marker—an example of which is

F#2 G2 G#2 A2 A#2 F#2 G2 G#2 A2 A#2 C4 C#4 D4 D#4 E4 F#2 G2 G#2 A2 A#2 REST.

These melodies are simple examples of sequences that have both fine and coarse structure. The fine structure is derived from the relations among pitches within a phrase, the coarse structure is derived from the relations among phrases. This pattern set was designed to examine how well CONCERT could cope with multiple levels of structure and long-term dependencies, of the sort that is found (albeit to a much greater extent) in real music.

CONCERT was tested with 35 context units. The training set consisted of 200 examples and the test set another 100 examples. Ten replications of the simulation were run for 300 passes through the training set.

Because of the way that the sequences were organized, certain pitches could be predicted based on local context, whereas other pitches required a more global memory of the sequence. In particular, the second to fifth pitches within a phrase could be predicted based on knowledge of the immediately preceding pitch. To predict the first pitch in the repeated A phrases and to predict the rest at the end of a sequence, more global information is necessary. Thus, the analysis was split to distinguish between pitches that required only local structure and pitches that required more global structure. Generalization performance was 97.3% correct for the local components, but only 58.4% for the global components.

6.6. Discussion

Through the use of simple, structured training sequences, it is possible to evaluate the performance of CONCERT. The initial results from CONCERT are encouraging. CONCERT is able to learn structure in short sequences with strong regularities, such as a C-major scale and a random walk in pitch. Two examples of structure were presented that CONCERT can learn but that cannot be captured by a simple transition table or by Kohonen's musical grammar. One example involved diatonic scales in various keys, the other involved interspersed random walks.

CONCERT clearly benefits from its psychologically grounded representation of pitch. In the task of extending the C-major scale, CONCERT with a local pitch representation would simply fail. In the task of learning the structure of diatonic scales, CONCERT's generalization performance drops by nearly 50% when a local representation is substituted for the PHCCCF representation. The PHCCCF representation is not always a clear win: generalization performance on random walk sequences improves slightly with a local representation. However, this result is not inconsistent with the claim that the PHCCCF representation assists CONCERT in learning structure present in human-composed melodies. The reason is that random walk sequences are hardly based on the sort of musical conventions that gave rise to the PHCCCF representation, and hence the representation is unlikely to be beneficial. In contrast, musical scales are at the heart of many musical conventions; it makes sense that scale-learning profits from the PHCCCF representation. Human-composed melodies should fare similarly. Beyond its ability to capture aspects of human pitch perception, the PHCCCF representation has the advantage over a local representation of reducing the number of free parameters in the network. This can be an important factor in determining network generalization performance.

The result from the AABA-phrase experiment is disturbing, but not entirely surprising. Consider the difficulty of correctly predicting the first note of the third repetition of the A phrase. The listener must remember not only the first note of the A phrase, but also that the previous phrase has just ended (that five consecutive notes ascending the chromatic scale were immediately preceding) and that the current phrase is not the second or fourth one of the piece (i.e. that the next note starts the A phrase). Minimally, this requires a memory that extends back 11 notes. Moreover, most of the intervening information is irrelevant.

7. Capturing Higher-order Musical Organization

In principle, CONCERT trained with back-propagation should be capable of discovering arbitrary contingencies in temporal sequences, such as the global structure in the AABA phrases. In practice, however, many researchers have found that back-propagation is not sufficiently powerful, especially for contingencies that span long temporal intervals and that involve high-order statistics. For example, if a network is trained on sequences in which one event predicts another, the relationship is not hard to learn if the two events are separated by only a few unrelated intervening events, but as the number of intervening events grows, a point is quickly reached where the relationship cannot be learned (Mozer, 1989, 1992, 1993; Schmidhuber, 1992). Bengio *et al.* (1994) present theoretical arguments for inherent limitations of learning in recurrent networks.

This poses a serious limitation on the use of back-propagation to induce musical structure in a note-by-note prediction paradigm because important structure can be found at long time-scales as well as short. A musical piece is more than a linear string of notes. Minimally, a piece should be characterized as a set of musical phrases, each of which is composed of a sequence of notes. Within a phrase, local structure can probably be captured by a transition table, e.g. the fact that the next note is likely to be close in pitch to the current, or that if the past few notes have been in ascending order, the next note is likely to follow this pattern. Across phrases, however, a more global view of the organization is necessary.

The difficult problem of learning coarse as well as fine structure has been addressed recently by connectionist researchers (Mozer, 1992; Mozer & Das, 1993; Myers, 1990; Ring, 1992; Schmidhuber, 1992; Schmidhuber *et al.*, 1993). The basic idea in many of these approaches involves building a reduced description (Hinton, 1988) of the sequence that makes global aspects more explicit or more readily detectable. In the case of the AABA structure, this might involve taking the sequence of notes composing A and redescribing them simply as 'A'. Based on this reduced description, recognizing the phrase structure AABA would involve little more than recognizing the sequence AABA. By constructing the reduced description, the problem of detecting global structure has been turned into the simpler problem of detecting local structure.

The challenge of this approach is to devise an appropriate reduced description. I describe here the simple scheme in Mozer (1992) as a modest step toward a solution. This scheme constructs a reduced description that is a bird's eye view of the musical piece, sacrificing a representation of individual notes for the overall contour of the piece. Imagine playing back a song on a tape recorder at double the regular speed. The notes are to some extent blended together and indistinguishable. However, events at a coarser time-scale become more explicit, such as a general ascending trend in pitch or a repeated progression of notes. Figure 6 illustrates the idea. The curve in Figure 6(a), depicting a sequence of individual pitches, has been smoothed and compressed to produce the graph in Figure 6(b). Mathematically, 'smoothed and compressed' means that the waveform has been low-pass filtered and sampled at a lower rate. The result is a waveform in which the alternating upwards and downwards flow is unmistakable.

Multiple views of the sequence can be realized in CONCERT using context units that operate with different time constants. With a simple modification to the context unit activation rule (equation (1))

$$c_i(n) = \tau_i c_i(n-1) + (1 - \tau_i) \, s\left[\sum_j w_{ij} x_j(n) + \sum_j v_{ij} c_j(n-1) \right] \qquad (2)$$

where each context unit i has an associated time constant, τ_i, that ranges from 0 to 1 and determines the responsiveness of the unit—the rate at which its activity changes. With $\tau_i = 0$, the activation rule reduces to equation (1) and the unit can sharply change its response based on a new input. With large τ_i, the unit is sluggish, holding on to much of its previous value and thereby averaging the response to the net input over time. At the extreme of $\tau_i = 1$, the second term drops out and the

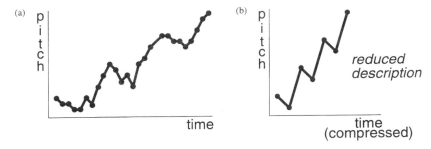

Figure 6. (a) A sequence of individual notes. The vertical axis indicates the pitch, the horizontal axis the time. Each point corresponds to a particular note. (b) A smoothed, compact view of the sequence.

unit's activity becomes fixed. Thus, large τ_i smooth out the response of a context unit over time. This is one property of the waveform in Figure 6(b) relative to the waveform in Figure 6(a).

The other property, the compactness of the waveform, is also achieved by a large τ_i, although somewhat indirectly. The key benefit of the compact waveform in Figure 6(b) is that it allows a longer period of time to be viewed in a single glance, thereby explicating contingencies occurring during this interval. Equation (2) also facilitates the learning of contingencies over longer periods of time. To see why this is the case, consider the relation between the error derivative with respect to the context units at step n, $\partial E/\partial \mathbf{c}(n)$, and the error back-propagated to the previous step, $n - 1$. One contribution to $\partial E/\partial c_i(n - 1)$, from the first term in equation (2), is

$$\frac{\partial E}{\partial c_i(n)} \frac{\partial}{\partial c_i(n - 1)} [\tau_i c_i(n - 1)] = \tau_i \frac{\partial E}{\partial c_i(n)}$$

This means that when τ_i is large, most of the error signal in context unit i at note n is carried back to note $n - 1$. Thus, the back-propagated error signal can make contact with points further back in time, facilitating the learning of more global structure in the input sequence.

Several comments regarding this approach are now given:

- Figure 6 is inaccurate in that it represents a filtering of the raw input sequence. The idea proposed here actually involves a filtering of the transformed input (i.e. the representation in the context layer). Regardless, the basic intuition applies in either case.

- Time constants have been incorporated into the activation rules of other connectionist architectures. Most pertinent is Bharucha and Todd's (1989) use of fixed time constants to implement an exponentially decaying memory of input context. McClelland's (1979) cascade model makes use of time constants in a feedforward network. The continuous-time networks of Pearlmutter (1989) and Pineda (1987) are based on a differential equation update rule, of which Equation (2) is a discrete-time version. Mozer (1989) proposed an architecture for sequence recognition that included linear-integrator units. However, none of this work has exploited time constants to control the temporal responsivity of individual units.

- Although Figure 6 depicts only two time-scales, context units can operate at many different time-scales, with smaller values of τ_i specializing the units to be sensitive to local properties of the sequence and larger values specializing the units to be sensitive to more global properties. One obvious possibility is to use back-propagation to determine the appropriate values of τ_i; however, my suspicion is that there are many local optima blocking the path to the best τ_i.
- This approach specializes each context unit for a particular time-scale. Nonetheless, it allows for interactions between representations at different time-scales, as each context unit receives input from all others. Thus, CONCERT can in principle learn to encode relationships between structure at different scales.
- Equation (2) suggests one particular type of reduced description, consisting of a smoothed and compressed representation of the context unit response over time. This is a simple-minded reduced description; ideally, one would like the reduced description to characterize meaningful 'chunks' or events in the input sequence. This idea is expanded later in the article.

7.1. AABA Phrase Patterns Revisited

In the experiment with AABA phrase patterns described earlier, the CONCERT architecture contained 35 context units, all with $\tau = 0$. In this experiment, called the reduced description (or RD) version, 30 context units had $\tau = 0$ and 5 had $\tau = 0.8$. The experiment was otherwise identical. Table VIII compares the generalization performance of the original and RD networks, for predictions involving local and global structure. Performance involving global structure was significantly better for the RD version ($F(1, 9) = 179.8$, $p < 0.001$), but there was only a marginally reliable difference for performance involving local structure ($F(1, 9) = 3.82$, $p = 0.08$). The global structure can be further broken down to prediction of the end of the sequence and prediction of the first pitch of the repeated A phrases. In both cases, the performance improvement for the RD version was significant: 88.0% versus 52.9% for the end of sequence ($F(1, 9) = 220$, $p < 0.001$); 69.4% versus 61.2% for the first pitch ($F(1, 9) = 77.6$, $p < 0.001$).

Experiments with different values of τ in the range 0.7–0.95 yielded qualitatively similar results, as did experiments in which the A and B phrases were formed by random walks in the key of C. Overall, modest improvements in performance are observed, yet the global structure is never learned as well as the local, and it is clear that CONCERT's capabilities are no match for those of people in this simple domain.

8. Larger Simulation Experiments

In the next three sections, simulations are described that use real music as training data, and the reduced description technique described in the previous section is used.

Table VIII. Performance on AABA phrases

Structure	Original net (%)	RD net (%)
Local	97.3	96.7
Global	58.4	75.6

Table IX. Bach training examples

Piece	Number of notes
Minuet in G major (no. 1)	126
Minuet in G major (no. 2)	166
Minuet in D minor	70
Minuet in A minor	84
Minuet in C minor	80
March in G major	153
March in D major	122
March in Eb major	190
Musette in D major	128
Little prelude in C major	121

8.1. Composing Melodies in the Style of Bach

The melody lines of 10 simple pieces by J. S. Bach were used to train CONCERT (Table IX). The set of pieces is not particularly coherent; it includes a variety of musical styles. The primary thing that the pieces have in common is their composer. The original pieces had several voices, but the melody generally appeared in the treble voice. Importantly, to naïve listeners, the extracted melodies sounded pleasant and coherent without the accompaniment.

In the training data, each piece was terminated with a sequence of three rests. This allowed CONCERT to learn not only the notes within a piece but also when the end of the piece was reached. Further, each major piece was transposed to the key of C major and each minor piece to the key of A minor. This was done to facilitate learning because the pitch representation does not take into account the notion of musical key; hopefully, a more sophisticated pitch representation would avoid the necessity of this step.

Two fixed input units were included in this simulation. One indicated whether the piece was in a major versus minor key, another whether the piece was in 3/4 meter versus 2/4 or 4/4. These inputs did not change value for a given piece. To keep CONCERT on beat, an additional input unit was active for notes that were on the downbeat of each measure. If a note was tied from one measure to the next, it was treated as two events; this ensured that each downbeat would correspond to a distinct input event.[8]

Learning the examples involves predicting a total of 1260 notes altogether. CONCERT was trained with 40 hidden units, 35 with $\tau = 0$ and 5 with $\tau = 0.8$, for 3000 passes through the training set. The learning rate was gradually lowered from 0.0004 to 0.0002. By the completion of training, CONCERT could correctly predict about 95% of the pitches and 95% of the durations. Attempts were made to train CONCERT with a greater proportion of RD context units and with greater τ values, but training performance suffered.

New pieces were created by presenting the first four notes of one of the training examples to seed CONCERT, and then allowing CONCERT to run in composition mode. Selection was made independently for the pitch and duration of each note, according to their respective probability distributions, with the additional constraint that durations were ruled invalid if the resulting note crossed measure boundaries (this was allowed only when the component of the duration representation indicating a tied note was active). Two examples of compositions produced by CONCERT are shown in Figure 7. CONCERT specifies the end of a composition by producing

Figure 7. Two sample compositions produced by CONCERT based on the Bach training set.

a sequence of rests. The compositions rapidly diverge from the training example used as seed, due to the probabilistic note selection process, although some compositions occasionally contain brief excerpts from the training examples.

Compositions were also generated based on the Bach examples using a transition-table approach. Two third-order transition tables were built from the training data, one for durations and one for pitches. (Combining the two in a single table is not feasible because the resulting table is too large—over 110 million cells—and is too sparse to be useful.) Twelve musically untrained listeners were asked to state their preference for the CONCERT compositions or the transition-table compositions. Two representative examples of each technique were played. Order of presentation was counterbalanced across listeners. All twelve chose CONCERT, some with ambivalence, others with a strong preference. Listeners commented that the CONCERT compositions were more coherent and had a more consistent beat. The final cadences of the CONCERT composition were also noted as superior, no doubt because at this point in the piece CONCERT did actually consider more than third-order structure.

Figure 8. A sample composition produced by CONCERT based on a training set of traditional European folk melodies.

8.2. Composing Melodies in the Style of European Folk Tunes

In a second experiment, CONCERT was trained on a set of 25 traditional European folk melodies (included in *Der Fluiten Luschof* of J. van Eyck). The pieces were somewhat shorter than the Bach examples, having an average of 74 notes per piece. All pieces were in the key of C major and had 4/4 meter. Because of the uniform mode and meter of the pieces, there was no need to represent these features explicitly on the input, as was done for the Bach examples.

CONCERT was trained with 50 hidden units, 45 with $\tau = 0$ and 5 with $\tau = 0.8$, for about 2000 passes through the training set. By the completion of training, CONCERT could correctly predict 93% of the pitches and 90% of the durations in the training set. Compositions using the trained network sounded reasonable, occasionally having more appeal than the training examples. Figure 8 shows a sample composition.

8.3. Explicit Training on Higher-order Structure: The Waltz Experiment

The two experiments with real musical data were a mixed success. Although clearly superior to a third-order transition table, CONCERT failed to produce music with high-order structure. One cannot claim a qualitative difference between the CONCERT and transition-table compositions.

The above experiments utilized only five RD context units. One might conjecture that higher-level structure might be learned better with more RD units.

However, even with no RD units, CONCERT achieved a training performance of 95%; replacing ordinary context units with RD units did not improve, and generally harmed, training performance. The problem appears to be that the prediction task can be performed very well using only local structure.

To encourage the consideration of structure on a longer time-scale, a final experiment introduced harmonic accompaniment to the melody line. The training examples were a set of 25 waltzes by various composers, collected in a 'Fakebook' with a rhythmically simplified melody line and accompanying chord progressions. The change in chords occurred at a slower rate than the change in notes of the melody: in the training set, the average duration of a melody note was 1.4 beats, while the average duration between chord changes was 5.9 beats. Consequently, one might hope that in order to learn the structure of the chord progression, it would be necessary to span longer periods of time, and, hence, it would be necessary for CONCERT to extract higher-level structure from the pieces.

Each note in the input was accompanied by the current chord. Chord duration was not explicitly represented; the duration of a chord was simply the sum of the durations of the consecutive notes that were associated with the chord.

Figure 9 shows two compositions produced by CONCERT based on the waltz data set. There was little evidence in the compositions that significant global structure was learned.

8.4. Discussion

While CONCERT performs well on simple, structured, artificial sequences, the prognosis looks bleaker for natural music. One critic described CONCERT's creations as "compositions only their mother could love". To summarize more delicately, few listeners would be fooled into believing that the pieces had been composed by a human. While the local contours made sense, the pieces were not musically coherent, lacking thematic structure and having minimal phrase structure and rhythmic organization.

It appears that the CONCERT architecture and training procedure do not scale well as the length of the pieces grows and as the amount of higher-order structure increases. This comes as no surprise to some: learning the structure of music through a note-by-note analysis is formally the same task as learning to read and understand English from a letter-by-letter analysis of text. Nonetheless, many researchers are pursuing a linear note-by-note approach to music analysis and composition. This is not entirely naïve, as connectionist algorithms are in principle capable of discovering the multiple levels of structure in music. However, the experiments reported here show no cause for optimism in practice, despite the use of state-of-the-art connectionist architectures and training algorithms, and attempts to encourage CONCERT to learn global structure.

The present results clearly signal difficulty in using sequential networks to match transition probability distributions of arbitrary order. Even more sophisticated approaches are clearly needed. Several directions are mentioned that one might consider in the domain of music analysis and composition.

- *Multiple recurrent hidden layers.* The current CONCERT architecture is limited in that the update rule for the context layer is a squashed linear mapping. That is, the new context is a linear function of the old context and current input, passed through a squashing function. To give CONCERT more flexibility in

Figure 9. Two compositions produced by CONCERT based on a training set of waltzes. For both compositions, CONCERT was given the same initial three measures, but the compositions rapidly diverged.

the update rule, one might consider multiple hidden layers in the recurrent loop (for related work, see Cottrell & Tsung, 1993; Tsung & Cottrell, 1993).

- *Alternative approaches to remembering the past.*   There are many connectionist approaches to constructing a memory of past events for the purpose of predicting the future (Mozer, 1993; Principe *et al.*, 1994). CONCERT with the RD units would be considered a TIS-exponential architecture according to Mozer's taxonomy. Another promising approach might be to include a small buffer in the input and/or context layers to hold a history of recent activities, allowing local temporal structure to be learned without wasting the resources of the recurrent connections.

- *Cascaded sequential networks.*   Burr and Miyata (1993) and Todd (1991) have proposed cascaded sequential networks for the purpose of representing hierarchically organized structure. Gjerdingen (1992) has suggested a related approach using a hierarchy of masking fields in an ART 3 architecture. The basic idea is for lower levels of the hierarchy to encode fine structure and higher levels to encode coarser structure. While only small-scale tests of this idea have been performed, it seems promising and worth pursuing.

- *Chunking architectures.*   In the cascaded sequential networks described above, the network designers specify in advance the hierarchical decomposition of a linear sequence. Todd (1991) assumes that an explicit decomposition is included as part of the training process. Burr and Miyata (1993) assume that successively higher levels operate on fixed, slower time-scales: the lowest level net is updated once a beat, the next net once every three beats, the next net every twelve beats, and so forth. Rather than providing the system with a hierarchical decomposition, one would really like the system to discover the decomposition itself. Ideally, each level of the hierarchy should encode meaningful 'chunks' or events in the sequence—the nature of a chunk being determined by the statistics of the environment—and the next higher level should operate on these chunks. Schmidhuber *et al.* (1993) describe an architecture of this sort in which the higher level analyzes only components of the input that cannot be interpreted by the lower level, yielding an automatic decomposition of sequences. This architecture has not been tested on musical sequences. Mozer and Das (1993) present an explicit chunking mechanism that has the capability of creating new symbols to represent an abstraction of a sequence of input elements. The mechanism operates on the generated symbols just as it does on the input elements, allowing it to chunk the chunks recursively. The creation of new symbols achieves a reduced description that is more flexible than the time-constant method proposed in this article. The time-constant method attempts to derive global statistics, whereas the chunking mechanism derives only local statistics, but does so over abstractions of the input. We are presently exploring how the chunking mechanism performs on musical sequences.

- *Explicit representation of structure.*   In the final simulation study, CONCERT was trained to predict harmonic accompaniment, which naturally operates at a coarser time-scale than the melody itself. The hope was that by including this coarser structure as an explicit component of the task, CONCERT would be forced to learn it. One can push this idea further and include structure at even coarser time-scales, e.g. the sort of description that musicologists might use to characterize or analyze a piece, such as phrase boundaries, themes, inversions, key modulations. Given training data annotated with these descriptions, CONCERT would have the opportunity to learn global structure explicitly.

- *Staged training.*   Music appears to have a tremendous amount of local structure that can mask the presence of global structure. The evidence for this comes from the fact that CONCERT performed very well on training sets even without paying attention to global structure. One might get around this problem by staging training in CONCERT, first training RD units with large time constants, and then gradually introducing units with smaller (and zero) time constants in the course of training. This would force CONCERT to examine the more global structure from the start.

- *Representations of musical elements in context.*   In the current work, the encoding of pitch, duration and harmony is independent of the temporal context in which the elements are embedded. This is clearly wrong from a psychological perspective: in music, as in every domain of cognition, context and expectations affect the interpretation of perceptual elements. A truer cognitive architecture would allow interactions between the processes that determine the encoding and the processes—modeled in CONCERT—that generate expectancies (see Bharucha (1987, 1991) for a relaxation model that has this general flavor). Another way of embodying this interaction is to consider the representation of musical elements in a musical context. The representations of pitch and chords in CONCERT are based on psychoacoustic studies that consider only pairwise similarities. Psychological studies of pitch and harmony in a musical context (e.g. Krumhansl, 1990; Krumhansl & Kessler, 1982; Longuet-Higgins, 1976, 1979) could potentially be of value in incorporating the preceding input history into the network's representations. Similarly, structured representations of rhythm (e.g. Lerdahl & Jackendoff, 1983; McAuley, 1993) might help to impose higher-level organization on the input sequences.

Acknowledgements

This research was supported by NSF Presidential Young Investigator award IRI-9058450 and grant 90-21 from the James S. McDonnell Foundation. My thanks to Paul Smolensky, Peter Todd, Debbie Breen, Yoshiro Miyata and two anonymous reviewers for helpful comments regarding this work, to Darren Hardy and Hal Eden for technical assistance, and to staff, faculty and students of the computer science department for serving as subjects in informal preference experiments.

Notes

1. Following Smolensky (1988), the phrase 'faithful representation' is used to mean that the represented items can be accurately reconstructed from the representation. A faithful transition-table representation of a set of examples would be one that, given the first few notes of any example, could unambiguously determine the remainder of the example.
2. Of course, this interpretation assumes independence of the predictions, which is certainly not true in CONCERT. However, Bridle (1990) provides another justification, somewhat less intuitive, for this performance measure in terms of an information-theoretic criterion.
3. An unforgivable pun: Rob Goldstone suggested calling CONCERT's training procedure 'Bach propagation'.
4. This is one justification for the exponential function in the NNL layer.
5. The perfect fifth is a musically significant interval. The frequency ratio of a note to its perfect fifth is 2:3, just as the frequency ratio of a note to its octave is 1:2.
6. The reader may wonder why points on a circle need to be represented in a two-dimensional space. After all, the points lie on a 1-D continuum, albeit embedded in a 2-D space. Without such an embedding, however, distance relationships between points cannot be preserved. If the circle is cut

and flattened into a 1-D continuum, formerly adjacent points on opposite sides of the cut will end up far apart.

7. Although a PH scale factor of 9.798 was used for the target NND representation, p_i, a PH scale factor of 1.0 was used for the input representation. This was based on empirical studies of what scale factors yielded the best performance. The primary reason that a PH scale factor other than 1.0 on the inputs causes difficulties is that the resulting error surface is poorly conditioned when different units have different activity ranges (Widrow & Stearns, 1985).

8. To maintain information about note ties, an additional component of the duration representation signaled whether a note was tied from the previous.

References

Bengio, Y., Simard, P. & Frasconi, P. (1993) Learning long-term dependencies with gradient descent is difficult. *IEEE Transactions on Neural Networks.* **5**, 157–161.

Bharucha, J.J. (1987) MUSACT: a connectionist model of musical harmony. In *Proceedings of the Ninth Annual Conference of the Cognitive Science Society*, pp. 508–517. Hillsdale, NJ: Erlbaum.

Bharucha, J.J. (1991) Pitch, harmony, and neural nets: a psychological perspective. In P.M. Todd & D.G. Loy (Eds), *Music and Connectionism*, pp. 84–99. Cambridge, MA: MIT Press/Bradford Books.

Bharucha, J.J. & Todd, P.M. (1989) Modeling the perception of tonal structure with neural nets. *Computer Music Journal*, 44–53.

Bridle, J. (1990) Training stochastic model recognition algorithms as networks can lead to maximum mutual information estimation of parameters. In D.S. Touretzky (Ed.), *Advances in Neural Information Processing Systems 2*, pp. 211–217. San Mateo, CA: Morgan Kaufmann.

Burr, D. & Miyata, Y. (1993) Hierarchical recurrent networks for learning musical structure. In C. Kamm, G. Kuhn, B. Yoon, S.Y. Kung & R. Chellappa (Eds), *Neural Networks for Signal Processing III*. Piscataway, NJ: IEEE.

Cottrell, G.W. & Tsung, F.-S. (1993) Learning simple arithmetic procedures. *Connection Science*, **5**, 37–58.

Denker, J., Schwartz, D., Wittner, B., Solla, S., Howard, R., Jackel, L. & Hopfield, J. (1987) Automatic learning, rule extraction, and generalization. *Complex Systems*, **1**, 877–922.

Dodge, C. & Jerse, T.A. (1985) *Computer Music: Synthesis, Composition, and Performance*. New York: Shirmer Books.

Dolson, M. (1989) Machine Tongues XII: neural networks. *Computer Music Journal*, **13**, 28–40.

Elman, J.L. (1990) Finding structure in time. *Cognitive Science*, **14**, 179–212.

Elman, J.L. (1993) Learning and development in neural networks: the importance of starting small. *Cognition*, **48**, 71.

Fraisse, P. (1982) Rhythm and tempo. In D. Deutsch (Ed.), *The Psychology of Music*, pp. 149–180. New York: Academic Press.

Gjerdingen, R.O. (1992) Learning syntactically significant temporal patterns of chords: a masking field embedded in an ART3 architecture. *Neural Networks*, **5**, 551–564.

Hinton, G. (1987) Learning distributed representations of concepts. In *Proceedings of the Eighth Annual Conference of the Cognitive Science Society*, pp. 1–12. Hillsdale, NJ: Erlbaum.

Hinton, G.E. (1988) Representing part-whole hierarchies in connectionist networks. *Proceedings of the Eighth Annual Conference of the Cognitive Science Society*, pp. 48–54.

Hinton, G.E., McClelland, J.L. & Rumelhart, D.E. (1986) Distributed representations. In D.E. Rumelhart & J.L. McClelland (Eds), *Parallel Distributed Processing: Explorations in the Microstructure of Cognition*. Vol. I: *Foundations*, pp. 77–109. Cambridge, MA: MIT Press/Bradford Books.

Jones, K. (1981) Compositional applications of stochastic processes. *Computer Music Journal*, **5**, 45–61.

Jones, M.R. & Boltz, M. (1989) Dynamic attending and responses to time. *Psychological Review*, **96**, 459–491.

Kohonen, T. (1989) A self-learning musical grammar, or "Associative memory of the second kind". In *Proceedings of the 1989 International Joint Conference on Neural Networks*, pp. 1–5.

Kohonen, T., Laine, P., Tiits, K. & Torkkola, K. (1991) A nonheuristic automatic composing method. In P.M. Todd & D.G. Loy (Eds), *Music and Connectionism*, pp. 229–242. Cambridge, MA: MIT Press/Bradford Books.

Krumhansl, C.L. (1990) *Cognitive Foundations of Musical Pitch*. New York: Oxford University Press.

Krumhansl, C.L. & Kessler, E.J. (1982) Tracing the dynamic changes in perceived tonal organization in a spatial representation of musical keys. *Psychological Review*, **89**, 334–368.

Krumhansl, C.L., Bharucha, J.J. & Kessler, E.J. (1982) Perceived harmonic structure of chords in three related musical keys. *Journal of Experimental Psychology: Human Perception and Performance*, **8**, 24–36.

Laden, B. & Keefe, D.H. (1989) The representation of pitch in a neural net model of chord classification. *Computer Music Journal*, **13**, 12–26.

Lerdahl, F. & Jackendoff, R. (1983) *A Generative Theory of Tonal Music*. Cambridge, MA: MIT Press.

Lewis, J.P. (1991) Creation by refinement and the problem of algorithmic music composition. In P.M. Todd & D.G. Loy (Eds), *Music and Connectionism*, pp. 212–228. Cambridge, MA: MIT Press/Bradford Books.

Longuet-Higgins, H.C. (1976) Perception of melodies. *Nature*, **263**, 646–653.

Longuet-Higgins, H.C. (1979) The perception of music (Review Lecture). *Proceedings of the Royal Society of London*, **205B**, 307–332.

Lorrain, D. (1980) A panoply of stochastic 'cannons'. *Computer Music Journal*, **3**, 48–55.

Loy, D.G. (1991) Connectionism and musiconomy. In P.M. Todd & D.G. Loy (Eds), *Music and Connectionism*, pp. 20–36. Cambridge, MA: MIT Press/Bradford Books.

McAuley, J.D. (1993) Finding metrical structure in time. In M.C. Mozer, P. Smolensky, D.S. Touretzky, J.E. Elman & A.S. Weigend (Eds), *Proceedings of the 1993 Connectionist Models Summer School*, pp. 219–227. Hillsdale, NJ: Erlbaum Associates.

McClelland, J.L. (1979) On the time relations of mental processes: an examination of systems of processes in cascade. *Psychological Review*, **86**, 287–330.

Mozer, M.C. (1987) RAMBOT: a connectionist expert system that learns by example. In M. Caudill & C. Butler (Eds), *Proceedings of the IEEE First Annual International Conference on Neural Networks*, pp. 693–700. San Diego, CA: IEEE Publishing Services.

Mozer, M.C. (1989) A focused back-propagation algorithm for temporal pattern recognition. *Complex Systems*, **3**, 349–381.

Mozer, M.C. (1992) The induction of multiscale temporal structure. In J.E. Moody, S.J. Hanson & R.P. Lippman (Eds), *Advances in Neural Information Processing Systems IV*, pp. 275–282. San Mateo, CA: Morgan Kaufmann.

Mozer, M.C. (1993) Neural network architectures for temporal pattern processing. In A. Weigend & N. Gershenfeld (Eds), *Time Series Prediction: Forecasting the Future and Understanding the Past*, pp. 243–264. Redwood City, CA: Addison-Wesley Publishing.

Mozer, M.C. & Das, S. (1993) A connectionist symbol manipulator that induces the structure of context-free languages. In S.J. Hanson, J.D. Cowan & C.L. Giles (Eds), *Advances in Neural Information Processing Systems V*, pp. 863–870. San Mateo, CA: Morgan Kaufmann.

Myers, C. (1990) *Learning with Delayed Reinforcement Through Attention-driven Buffering*. Technical Report. London: Neural Systems Engineering Group, Department of Electrical Engineering, Imperial College of Science, Technology, and Medicine.

Pearlmutter, B.A. (1989) Learning state space trajectories in recurrent neural networks. *Neural Computation*, **1**, 263–269.

Pineda, F. (1987) Generalization of back propagation to recurrent neural networks. *Physical Review Letters*, **19**, 2229–2232.

Pressing, J. (1983) Cognitive isomorphisms between pitch and rhythm in world musics: West Africa, the Balkans, and Western tonality. *Studies in Music*, **17**, 38–61.

Principe, J.C., Hsu, H.-H. & Kuo, J.-M. (1994) Analysis of short-term neural memory structures for nonlinear prediction. In J.D. Cowan, G. Tesauro & J. Alspector (Eds), *Advances in Neural Information Processing Systems VI*. San Mateo, CA: Morgan Kaufmann Publishers.

Ring, M. (1993) Learning sequential tasks by incrementally adding higher orders. In C.L. Giles, S.J. Hanson & J.D. Cowan (Eds), *Advances in Neural Information Processing Systems V*, pp. 115–122. San Mateo, CA: Morgan Kaufmann.

Rumelhart, D.E. (in press) Connectionist processing and learning as statistical inference. In Y. Chauvin & D.E. Rumelhart (Eds), *Backpropagation: Theory, Architectures, and Applications*. Hillsdale, NJ: Erlbaum.

Rumelhart, D.E., Hinton, G.E. & Williams, R.J. (1986) Learning internal representations by error propagation. In D.E. Rumelhart & J.L. McClelland (Eds), *Parallel Distributed Processing: Explorations in the Microstructure of Cognition. Vol. I: Foundations*, pp. 318–362. Cambridge, MA: MIT Press/Bradford Books.

Schmidhuber, J. (1992) Learning unambiguous reduced sequence descriptions. In J.E. Moody, S.J. Hanson & R.P. Lippman (Eds), *Advances in Neural Information Processing Systems IV*, pp. 291–298. San Mateo, CA: Morgan Kaufmann.

Schmidhuber, J.H., Mozer, M.C. & Prelinger, D. (1993) Continuous history compression. In H. Huening, S. Neuhauser, M. Raus & W. Ritschel (Eds), *Proceedings of the International Workshop on Neural Networks, RWTH Aachen*, pp. 87–95. Augustinus.

Shepard, R.N. (1982) Geometrical approximations to the structure of musical pitch. *Psychological Review*, **89**, 305–333.

Shepard, R.N. (1987) Toward a universal law of generalization for psychological science. *Science*, **237**, 1317–1323.

Smolensky, P. (1988) On the proper treatment of connectionism. *Behavioral & Brain Sciences*, **11**, 1–74.

Stevens, C. & Wiles, J. (1993) Representations of tonal music: a case study in the development of temporal relationships. In M.C. Mozer, P. Smolensky, D.S. Touretzky, J.E. Elman & A.S. Weigend (Eds), *Proceedings of the 1993 Connectionist Models Summer School*, pp. 228–235. Hillsdale, NJ: Erlbaum Associates.

Todd, P.M. (1989) A connectionist approach to algorithmic composition. *Computer Music Journal*, **13**, 27–43.

Todd, P.M. (1991) A connectionist approach to algorithmic composition. In P.M. Todd & D.G. Loy (Eds), *Music and Connectionism*, pp. 173–194. Cambridge, MA: MIT Press/Bradford Books.

Tsung, F.-S. & Cottrell, G.W. (1993) *Phase-space Learning in Recurrent Networks*. Technical Report CS93–285. La Jolla, CA: Department of Computer Science and Engineering, University of California, San Diego.

Widrow, B. & Stearns, S.D. (1985) *Adaptive Signal Processing*. Englewood Cliffs, NJ: Prentice-Hall.

Williams, R.J. & Zipser, D. (in press) Gradient-based learning algorithms for recurrent connectionist networks. In Y. Chauvin & D.E. Rumelhart (Eds), *Backpropagation: Theory, Architectures, and Applications*. Hillsdale, NJ: Erlbaum.

Harmonizing Music the Boltzmann Way

MATTHEW I. BELLGARD & C. P. TSANG

Music harmonization has long been recognized as a highly intellectual process. Musicologists have studied music pieces by great composers and formulated a number of symbolic rules. However, these rules usually form only a set of heuristics and may not be absolutely precise. In this paper, we demonstrate how to train a Boltzmann machine to capture these syntactic rules and use it to construct an effective Boltzmann machine (EBM) to harmonize some unseen pieces. We have also incorporated ways to apply absolute constraints to the completion process. Our experiments demonstrate that using an EBM, 'good' harmonies can be non-deterministically synthesized along with a relative measure of their quality.

KEYWORDS: Boltzmann machine, music harmonization, music composition, machine learning.

1. Introduction

The period between the 17th and 18th centuries saw the emergence and development of tonal harmony in western music. The underlying principles of tonal harmony may be found in chorale harmonization, which is also known as four-part writing. Chorale harmonization is considered a highly intellectual, time-consuming task and to produce a notable harmonization requires a wealth of knowledge and experience on the part of the composer (Piston, 1978; Siegmeister, 1966).

The formalization of four-part writing generally involves an analysis of musical pieces by musicologists. They formulate this process in terms of rules, heuristics and symbolic descriptions of the abstraction. However, as with most arts, the original composers did not write down the rules governing their works and the musicological analysis has been performed long after their demise. As a result, these analyses cannot be confirmed as entirely correct. The derived rules are only as good as both the analysis and the expressiveness of the symbolic representation employed. Existing computer harmonization systems have been generally designed by utilizing this human knowledge to search for an appropriate combination of musical notes. As a consequence, symbolic artificial intelligence (AI) systems cannot entirely

This article appeared originally in *Connection Science*, 1994, **6**, 281–297, and is reprinted with permission.

capture the musical style of a human composer. The quality of the harmonies synthesized by these systems has fallen short in comparison to those produced by experienced human composers.

Given the advances in machine learning in recent years, it is desirable to apply its learning techniques to music harmony in an attempt to build a system that learns to harmonize unseen melodies as well as to distinguish between different musical styles. However, symbolic rule-learning mechanisms are unsuitable for imprecise and noisy processes, like music harmonization. Alternatively, the choice of artificial neural network (ANN) methodologies appears to be a natural one (Hild *et al.*, 1991; Kohonen, 1989; Mozer, 1991; Todd, 1989). HARMONET (Hild *et al.*, 1991) is an example of a neural system for chorale harmonization. However, a major limitation of this system is its reliance on a feedforward neural architecture. As a result, HARMONET's harmonization process assumes a sequential operation, where it harmonizes a chorale melody from left to right, in a deterministic manner.

With the intention of building a machine-learning music harmonization system, we have designed a learning system based on the Boltzmann machine (BM) (Aarts & Korst, 1988; Hinton & Sejnowski, 1986). We use a BM to learn the local contexts of a set of chorales and use our effective Boltzmann machine (EBM) (Bellgard & Tsang, 1992; Tsang & Bellgard, 1990) to harmonize music via completion (Kohonen, 1978; Hertz *et al.*, 1991). We have demonstrated that our system can learn a particular harmonization style from learned local contexts which are subsequently used to harmonize new melodies. This harmonization process is non-deterministic and may produce different results on different runs due to the EBM's stochastic nature. There is a correspondence between the quality of the harmonization and the energy value of the EBM. The energy value can be used to identify wrongly harmonized notes within a piece.

In this paper, we describe various design issues affecting the EBM and also describe the process of incorporating external constraints in the EBM. These external constraints are vital to the success of the EBM as a harmonization system. We describe and discuss a set of experiments that highlight the appropriateness of the EBM to chorale harmonization.

2. Background

2.1. Chorale Harmonization

A chorale comprises four voices: soprano, alto, tenor and bass. It is performed either by singing voices or by instruments. Chorale harmonization involves writing the alto, tenor and bass parts for a given soprano melody. A chorale may be viewed as a sequence of four-note chords where each note in the chord corresponds to a part. Melodic notes are grouped into phrases and a cadence indicates the end of a phrase.

A musical style may be abstracted as a set of rules, restrictions or guidelines that should be observed by a composer so that the harmony remains within the confines of the style. These syntactic procedures include restrictions on chordal progressions as well as guidelines for appropriate choices of parts. For example, in the Baroque style (Kerman, 1978), parallel fifths and parallel octaves are disallowed, and voice leading is taken into consideration (Piston, 1978). The chorales that are of interest for the current work are those chorales composed in the Baroque period (17th and 18th centuries) (Dorffel, 1950).

The process of harmonization as described by Walter Piston (Piston, 1978 p. 152) states:

> True harmonisation, then, means a consideration of the alternatives in available chords, the reasoned selection of one of these alternatives, and the tasteful arrangement of the texture of the added parts with due regard for consistency of style.

A student learning the harmonization process would discover from the many treatises on music harmony (Denny, 1961; Piston, 1978; Siegmeister, 1966; Prout, 1903; Tunley, 1990) that chorales may be harmonized in one or in a combination of three methods. Firstly, a chorale may be viewed as a sequence of chords where chord choices are made on their 'mutual connectibility' from chord to chord (Piston, 1978). The bass part is a consequence of the chord and does not possess its own melodic shape. This is contrasted with the second method, which initially considers the soprano and the bass parts, furnishing the bass part with its own melodic identity (Piston, 1978; Siegmeister, 1966; Tunley, 1990). The inner parts are subsequently added. The final method requires a memorization of groups of chords that are commonly recurring formulae or harmonic words (Piston, 1978; Tunley 1990). Equipped with an understanding of the above methods as well as the general laws of four-part writing procedures, the student would be able not only to analyze the works of great composers, but also harmonize new chorale melodies.

To date, there has been no definitive formalization of the harmonization process. Learning or capturing the salient features of another composer's style is not clearly defined, as the implementation of four-part writing is invariably unique to a composer. For instance, students eventually develop their own unique harmonization styles. Although musical analysis may articulate certain universal principles of well-known western musical styles, proceduralization of the process is a problematical issue. There is also difficulty in prescribing heuristic and less understood elements of a musical style (Gjerdingen, 1991; Loy, 1991). Thus, many informal, yet important aspects of harmonization are neglected. There have been a number of attempts to formalize this process using (Schenkerian) structural analysis (Oswald 1973) and linguistic models such as generative grammars (Lerdahl & Jakendoff, 1983; Winograd, 1968). All these models do involve, however, the human analytical process.

2.2. AI/Music Research and Chorale Harmonization

The difficulties faced by musicologists have not been a deterrent for the development of prescriptive, knowledge-based systems. CHORAL (Ebcioglu, 1988) is a rule-based system for harmonizing chorales in the style of J. S. Bach. The system captures musical knowledge from multiple viewpoints which observe: chord skeleton, individual melodic lines of the different voices and Schenkerian voice leading within the descant and bass. Tsang and Aitken (1991) developed a harmonizing system using constraint logic programming (CLP). The rules of harmonization were defined in terms of numerical constraints.

Apart from the issues outlined above, these systems typically suffer from two other problems. Firstly, the search space is enormous, exponentially increasing depending on the size of the melody (to be harmonized), the number of rules encoded in the system as well as the complexity of the rules. Secondly, it is left to the researcher or a musician to decide when to terminate the search and evaluate the quality of the harmonies synthesized.

2.2.1. Neural network approaches. With the difficulties of articulating harmonization knowledge explicitly, research in ANNs and music is currently receiving a great deal of attention (Bellgard & Tsang, 1992; Hild *et al.*, 1991; Mozer, 1991; Todd, 1989; Todd & Loy, 1991). ANNs do not require the explication of rules as they have the ability to learn internal representations from a given set of examples. It is desirable that these internal representations capture the relevant concepts (Geman *et al.*, 1992). ANNs have been used to generate monophonic melodies in a particular style (Todd, 1989; Mozer, 1991; Kohonen, 1989).

The HARMONET system. The HARMONET system (Hild *et al.*, 1991) is a hybrid system combining both neural networks and symbolic methods to harmonize chorale melodies in the style of J. S. Bach. The music representation employed captures musically relevant symbolic information and also encodes look-ahead knowledge. Because the system operates in a linear fashion, harmonizing a melody (note by note) from start to finish, the look-ahead information is used in order to direct the harmony to an appropriate cadence. A feedforward neural network, employing the back-propagation learning algorithm (Rumelhart *et al.* 1986), is used to learn the harmonic skeleton (musically relevant information) of a set of example chorales. At the harmonization stage, the net will make predictions of the chord and bass part of a particular note in the melody using a fixed-length local context. Once the harmonic skeleton is determined by the neural network, symbolic algorithms are used to fill in the inner voices and also to insert passing notes. The symbolic algorithms ensure that constraints particular to the style are not violated. Such constraints are the prevention of parallel fifths and parallel octaves.

Analysis of some of the harmonies synthesized by HARMONET revealed that they contained parallel fifths and parallel octaves. For example, there are parallel octaves in the first and fifth bars of HARMONET's harmonization of *Christus, der ist mein Leben*, and there is a parallel fifth in the third bar of *Happy Birthday* (Hild *et al.*, 1991). An instance of a parallel octave appearing in the first bar of *Christus, der ist mein Leben* is reproduced in Figure 1.

However, the symbolic algorithms incorporated in HARMONET were intended to prevent parallel fifths and parallel octaves from occurring in the harmony. This apparent contradiction is due to the hierarchical nature of HARMONET. Once HARMONET has decided on the harmonic skeleton using the neural network, the results from this process are then processed by the symbolic algorithms to fill in the inner parts. It is not possible to revise the harmonic skeleton once it is passed to

Parallel Octaves

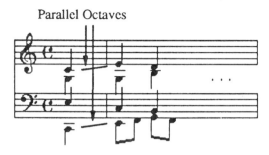

Figure 1. The first few chords of *Christus der ist mein Leben*, harmonized by the HARMONET system reproduced from Hild *et al.* (1991). The arrows point to the parallel octave from the first chord to the second: C in the 4th octave moves to E in the 4th octave (soprano part) and at the same time C in the 2nd octave moves to E in the 2nd octave (bass part).

the next stage. Thus, an inappropriate selection of notes for the harmonic skeleton will lead to violations or inappropriate chords as the symbolic algorithms fill in the inner parts. A good example of this is the piece, *Nicht so traurig, Nicht so sehr* (Hild *et al.*, 1991), where the inner parts progress abruptly through the harmonization. That is, the interval between consecutive pitches for both inner parts changes by relatively large amounts. This is unusual for chorales in the style of J. S. Bach. The output of the neural network in HARMONET is deterministic, thus only one harmonic skeleton is produced for a given melody.

2.3. Motivations for Current Work

2.3.1. Completion, chorale harmonization and constraint satisfaction.   Pattern completion is the process by which a partial specification of information is completed (Hertz *et al.*, 1991; Kohonen, 1987). Although feedforward networks are unable to perform this task, Hopfield and Boltzmann machine networks (Hinton & Sejnowski, 1986) can. Typically, if the information is binary encoded, then a partial specification of a binary pattern is clamped (Hinton & Sejnowski, 1986) to the completion device, which is then expected to 'fill-in' the missing bits of the pattern. The completion is constrained by both the partial input as well as what has been learnt by the completion device.

The chorale harmonization process may be viewed as the satisfaction of interdependent constraints via some completion process. The melody may be viewed as a partial input that must be completed, and the completion device (the composer) will 'fill-in' the other parts. During the completion of the melody, there are stylistic constraints as well as constraints imposed by the chorale melody. For example, for a given melody, a composer's choice of a particular cadence would constrain the choice of harmonies for notes immediately preceding the cadence. An experienced human composer would observe all the harmony constraints, those which are well defined and can be articulated into precise, left-to-right syntactic rules (prescriptive rules which can be easily implemented by knowledge-based systems) and those which cannot. As mentioned in Section 2.1, the completion process is unique to a composer.

2.3.2. Learning to harmonize using an effective Boltzmann machine.   We propose a constraint satisfaction, completion-based learning system named an EBM for music harmony. A BM is trained on the local contexts (training set) of a set of chorales and an EBM is constructed from the BM to harmonize new melodies in a similar style. The local contexts learnt by the BM will resemble the constraints of the harmonization process. By using the EBM construction, a melody of any length may be harmonized. Unlike HARMONET, the EBM's completion process is not directed. Thus, implicational constraints may hold in any direction. Because the system is non-deterministic, more than one harmony may be synthesized for a given melody. An energy measure is associated with each synthesized completion (each harmony). This measure may be used to indicate the quality of the harmony.

In summary, if it is required to complete a soprano melody, the EBM behaves as a harmonizing system. If no partial input is provided, the EBM behaves as a compositional system and, finally, if the complete piece is given as input the EBM may behave as an analysis system.

3. The Effective Boltzmann Machine

A description of the EBM may be found elsewhere (Bellgard & Tsang, 1992; Tsang & Bellgard, 1990) and hence only an overview will be given here. In the following sections, we briefly describe the music representation employed, how to learn the local contexts of the chorales and how to construct the EBM to synthesize harmonies for given chorale melodies.

3.1. Music Representation

In this music application, we use the pitch-height model (Barucha, 1991; Todd, 1989) to represent musical pitch. Each pitch is represented by a binary input/output (IO) unit. IO units are the visible units in the BM and EBM architecture. These IO units may be clamped or unclamped. Clamped IO units will act as inputs to the system as their values do not change during completion. A scale is a collection of all possible pitches. Each pitch is represented in the BM and the EBM by one IO unit. When the IO unit is activated to '1', the pitch associated with the unit is sounded, and vice versa. An event is an instance of a scale with some pitches sounded. In our particular application, each scale consists of 35 pitch units, two phrase control units and one spacer unit: a total of 38 IO units. As shown in Figure 2(a), the first 35 units correspond to a range of pitches from G in the second octave (G2) to F in the fifth octave (F5). The next two units in a scale represent start and end phrases respectively. *Start/end* phrase units are necessary to ensure that the system will recognize cadences at the end of a phrase, otherwise a cadence chordal progression could be placed anywhere in the phrase. The last unit indicates a spacer event (a '1' in this unit for an event implies that all other units in this event are set to '0'). The need for this unit will be detailed below. Figure 2(b) is a shorthand representation of a scale. All chorales are normalized to the same key before learning or completion commences.

The chorales used in the training set are taken from *Choralbuch* (Dorffel, 1950) which is used by musicians to study tonal harmony. As input to the system, each event describes a chord in a chorale. Hence, each event will have at most four pitch units clamped to '1' and the rest of the units clamped to '0'. Note that this is a very strong constraint, as in any four-part chorale there simply cannot be more than four voices sounding at any one time. We also make an assumption that each event is of the same duration. This length has the same length as the minimum length chord in all the chorales. Thus, chords held for twice this length in the chorale will be treated as two events in the system. Passing notes are omitted but there is no reason why they cannot be learned by this system at a later stage.

(a)   (b)

Figure 2. (a) A diagrammatical representation of a scale. There are 38 units corresponding to IO units in both the BM and EBM formalism. The first 35 units correspond to pitches from G2 to F5. The next two units correspond to the start/end phrase units. The last unit indicates spacer events which are placed between chorales. (b) A shorthand representation of a scale to be used in subsequent diagrams.

3.1.1. Error control codes and the pitch-height representation.   It was discovered that a serious problem of conflicting contexts can arise in using the EBM for this music application (Bellgard & Tsang, 1992). To highlight the problem, let us assume that an EBM must harmonize a melody (a partial sequence) and that the partial sequence contains local contexts that are not contained in the training set. That is, the melody is not similar to any of the chorale melodies used in the training set. Completion of this sequence, using the EBM, will result in conflicts by the learned local contexts (the trained BM) as to how the partial sequence should be completed. As a result, the EBM synthesizes ill-formed sequences. Ill-formed sequences are those which contain events that do not have the right number of voices. For example, if the EBM produced a harmony for a given melody but there were voices missing from some chords or there were more than four voices in each chord, then this would constitute an ill-formed sequence.

To overcome this problem, two pieces of information are required. We need to know when an event is ill-formed, and when it happens, the EBM must attempt to correct the ill-formed event. The first piece of information relates to the representation of the events (discussed in this section) and the second relates to the incorporation of external constraints on the EBM to ensure well-formed events are synthesized (discussed later). The correction ability will depend on the information acquired during the learning stage. Is the pitch-height representation a sufficient encoding in order to convey this information?

Results from coding theory may be utilized to determine the appropriate representation. If the events in sequences are encoded using an error-control code (Farrell, 1979), then it will be possible to detect ill-formed events. The error-control code used in the EBM is a simple redundant code (Farrell, 1979). The redundant code encodes sequences by a fixed-length binary code (tuple) containing a fixed number of bits with the value '1' in each code (parity). For four-part writing, the pitch-height model may be viewed as a redundant code. The tuple length in this case is 35 (the number of bits to represent an event) with a 4-bit parity (four voices for each chord). The information for determining ill-formed and well-formed events is readily available. We describe how ill-formed events are resolved in Section 4.2.1.

3.2. Learning the Local Contexts in Chorales

At this stage, a single BM is used to learn the local contexts of the chorales using the BM learning algorithm (Aarts & Korst, 1988; Hinton & Sejnowski, 1986). The BM topology consists of two sets of units: visible (IO) units and hidden units. There are bidirectional connections between the two sets of units and there are no lateral connections between units in the same set. Figure 3 describes a BM made up of three scales in the IO layer and a hidden layer. Each hidden unit is connected via a symmetric weight (represented collectively by W) to each unit in the IO layer.

The BM is governed by an energy function E. The energy E of the BM is defined to be the summation of the weighted connections of pairs of units that are activated:

$$E = -\sum_i \sum_j W_{ij}\, s_i\, s_j$$

where s_i and s_j represent the state of the units in the BM and the W_{ij} corresponds to the set of symmetric weights, where W_{ij} connects unit i to unit j.

Unit updates are made in relation to this energy function. The energy of a particular unit (known as the energy gap ΔE_s) is determined by a difference in the

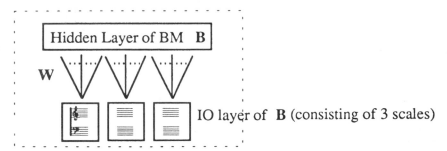

Figure 3. A BM *B* made up of three scales in the IO layer and a set of hidden units. There are connections between the two layers represented by *W*. *B* is used to learn the local contexts of a set of chorales.

global energy of the system when that unit is either '1' or '0', and is given by

$$\Delta E_{s_i} = \sum_{j \neq i} W_{ij}\, s_j$$

In conjunction with the simulated annealing algorithm (Aarts & Korst, 1988; Kirkpatrick *et al.*, 1983) the unit is stochastically updated according to the following probability acceptance criterion:

$$P_{s_i} = \frac{1}{1 + e^{-\Delta E_{s_i}/T}}$$

The BM attempts to minimize global energy where the larger the energy gap for a particular unit, the more likely it will be activated to '1' (Aarts & Korst, 1988; Hinton & Sejnowski, 1986). There is a positive correlation between the energy gap of a unit and its probability of being activated. For this reason, the energy of the system and the energy gap of all units may be used as a relative measure of the degree of confidence the BM places in its completions.

It is important to note that the definition of the energy gap is derived from the attempt to minimize the energy of the system. Thus, the larger the unit's energy gap, the more likely it will be activated in order to minimize energy of the entire system.

To obtain the local contexts of a set of chorales, it is helpful to view the chorale as a sequence of events. The training patterns from the chorales are obtained from a sliding window consisting of *M* scales. The window is initially set to the first *M* events of the chorale. What the window can see is taken as a training pattern. The window then slides to the right, one event at a time. This process continues until all local contexts are obtained from the chorales.

When learning more than one chorale, the sliding window does not overlap over chorales. This is achieved by placing *M*–1 spacer events (spacer events are those with all units clamped to '0' except the last bit in the event, which is set to '1') between each chorale. This set of binary patterns constitutes the training set. The standard BM learning algorithm (Hinton & Sejnowski, 1986) is used to obtain a set of weights that characterizes the patterns in the training set. At the completion stage, the BM relaxes to one of the stored patterns non-deterministically, using simulated annealing (Aarts & Korst, 1988; Kirkpatrick *et al.*, 1983). In other words, it is performing completion of a partially specified input. This trained BM is used to construct an EBM of arbitrary length.

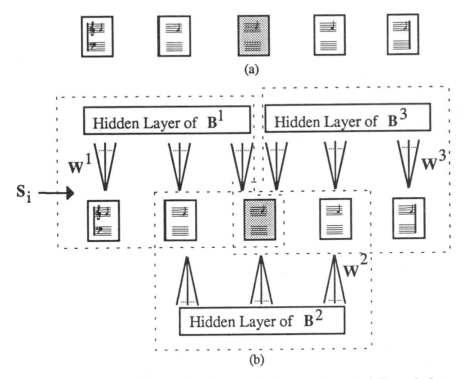

Figure 4. (a) A melody to be harmonized, consisting of five pitches and represented as five scales with one unit in each scale set to '1' corresponding to the pitch. (b) An example of an EBM constructed from the BM in Figure 3, completing a harmony for the melody in (a). The BM in Figure 3 is replicated three times. Each B^i has identical weights W^i and the same number of hidden units. All events appear in at least one copy of the BM B. For example, the 3rd event, which is shaded, appears in each B^i in a different location in the IO layer of each B^i.

3.3. Completion of an Arbitrary-length Melody

Given a BM which has learnt the local contexts of some chorales, a melody S of length L may be harmonized using the EBM. This melody will contain L events with one unit in each event, set to '1', corresponding to the pitch in the melody for that event. The units in S represent the IO layer of the EBM. An example melody S is shown in Figure 4(a). The units in the events of S may be clamped or unclamped. If they are unclamped, they are initially assigned '0' or '1' randomly.

An EBM may be constructed as shown schematically in Figure 4(b) to harmonize the melody in Figure 4(a). Assuming that the BM with a window size of $M = 3$, shown in Figure 3, is used to learn the local contexts of the chorales, then this machine is replicated and placed over S. There will be $L - M + 1$ copies of the BM. In Figure 4(b), each machine is enclosed by the dotted lines. An event in S will correspond to a specific event in one or more individual BMs.

We enforce the constraint that the events in the IO layer of an individual BM are no longer independent of the events in the IO layer of another BM. The events in the IO layer of each individual BM are constrained to take on the values of the events in the IO layer of the EBM (i.e. the events in S). This implies that during the completion process, the individual BMs cannot be individually annealed. The completion process is performed with respect to S. That is, the entire system (not the individual BMs) is subjected to the relaxation process to produce a solution (to synthesize a harmony). As may be seen in Figure 4(b), unit updates in S (as the system is relaxed) take into account the information arriving from neighbouring contexts (from more than one individual BM) and the whole sequence S is completed at the same time. As the system is slowly relaxed to a solution, the unclamped units along with the hidden units will be updated such that the energy function governing the system is minimized and a harmony produced. The energy gap of a unit in S is the summation of the energy gaps of units in the respective individual machines and its value is positively related to the consensus of the respective individual machines. Further details may be obtained from our earlier papers (Bellgard & Tsang, 1992; Tsang & Bellgard, 1990).

4. Experimentation

In this section, we present four different experiments. Five chorales with a total of 11 phrases, taken from *Choralbuch* (Dorffel, 1950), were chosen for the training set. The BM was chosen with a window size of $M = 5$ and there were 80 training patterns and 70 hidden units. It took about 25 minutes for each learning sweep of the training set on a Sun SPARC 2 processor. Our results are based on a training of approximately 400 sweeps. The experiment in Section 4.3 details a harmony that is produced with a window size of $M = 3$ using the same five chorales.

4.1. Completion of a Chorale in Training Set

In this experiment, the soprano melody of one of the chorales in the training set was clamped in the IO layer of the EBM. Hence, the soprano melody is the partial input into the EBM. Figure 5 shows the score produced after the EBM is annealed. This score is identical to the original score used in the training set. This demonstrates that a completely correct recognition can be achieved by the EBM. Completion took approximately 2 minutes on a Sun SPARC 2 processor.

This completion involved selecting 12 correct patterns (local contexts) from the 80 stored in the BM. Other experiments were also conducted. For example, the bass line of the above piece was clamped to the IO layer of the EBM, which was then annealed. The same chorale was synthesized. That is, given the bass part, the EBM filled in the tenor, alto and soprano parts. In another experiment, the first three and the last three chords of the above chorale were clamped and the EBM filled in the rest of the piece.

These experiments demonstrate long-range effects by the EBM. For instance,

Figure 5. *Es ist genug, so nimm, Herr* chorale. Given just the part of soprano, EBM produced exactly the same harmony as the original chorale.

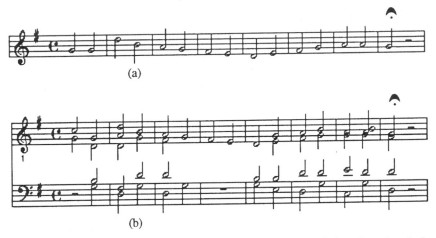

Figure 6. (a) The soprano melody of the first phrase of the chorale, *Lobe den Herren, den machtigen Konig.* (b) Harmony to the melody in Figure 6(a), produced by EBM. It can be seen that some events are not harmonized, while other events do not have exactly four parts.

the soprano melody provided sufficient context to recall the entire chorale. On the other hand, clamping the first and last three chords also provided sufficient context to complete the entire chorale.

4.2. Completion of Chorale Melody that Is Not in the Training Set

Using a chorale which is not in the training set, *Lobe den Herren, den machtigen Konig*, we clamped the soprano part of the first phrase of this chorale, shown in Figure 6(a), to the IO layer in the EBM. Figure 6(b) shows the score produced after the EBM is annealed. It can be seen that the EBM did not produce a correct harmony to every note in the melody. In fact, it is apparent that when given a new melody not in the training set, the EBM has no concept of how many notes to produce for each event. It also does not have any information telling it not to provide notes above the melody line. In addition to this, from the chorales provided to it in the training set, the EBM is unable to ensure that there should not be notes within two semitones below the melody. It is evident that we need to overcome these problems if we wish to obtain harmonies that are correct for this musical style.

4.2.1. Effects of absolute constraints.
There are certain implicit rules that must be enforced by any composer (both human and artificial) to ensure a syntactically correct harmony. We have called these rules absolute constraints (ACs). Given a soprano melody, the system must not produce a harmony with notes above this melody line. Secondly, there must only be at most four notes for each event corresponding to the four different parts (voices). Finally, for this style of music, there must not be a note in the harmony within two semitones of the note in the melody.

Implicit in the nature of the system, the first and the third ACs can be easily satisfied by clamping the respective units to '0' in the IO layer before EBM is annealed. That is, all units above the soprano melody note and the two units below the melody note in each event are turned off.

Figure 7. Harmony to the melody in Figure 6(a) by the EBM with the inclusion of the absolute constraints.

For the second AC, where we must enforce at most four units on in each event, we introduce an encouragement/discouragement function. The function makes use of the pitch height (or error-control encoding, see Section 3.1). This function, at each temperature before the last few annealing temperatures, encourages the best T units in each event (we have taken T to be 10 in our experiments). This encouragement takes the form of an increment of energy E. The best T units have their energy gap incremented by E before they are annealed again. Towards the final annealing temperatures, we encourage only the best three units by E, and discourage the other seven units by a multiple of E before annealing the units again. Figure 7 is a harmony of the same melody shown in Figure 6(a) but this time it is annealed with the encouragement function. It can be seen that the harmony produced is almost entirely correct except for the third and ninth events which, for this style, are incorrect chords. Apart from these two chords, as judged by a trained musician, this harmony is of comparable quality to the style it is mimicking.

4.2.2. Start/end phrase units.   From our experimentation we discovered that the cadence point was not placed correctly when completing simply the events from a given melody. This is because there is no way to determine the start and the end of a phrase. Thus, start/end phrase units were included in the representation to ensure that a cadence chordal progression was completed at the end of a phrase. For example, when considering a phrase melody consisting of 15 events, each of the events would have one pitch unit activated (and clamped) to '1'. The rest of the pitch units in all events would be set to '0'. The first/last event would have the start/end phrase unit activated to '1' respectively. For events 2–14, the start and end phrase units would be clamped to '0'.

Although the cadence chordal progressions are prevented from appearing within the phrase, they cannot be forced to appear at the end of the phrase. Considering the above example, if the window size was $M = 5$, the context of event 1 and event 15 are only constrained by one BM window, while the contexts from event 5 to 11 are constrained by five staggered BM windows.

Because each of the events containing the activated start/end phrase units are constrained by one BM window, the events containing the activated start/end phrase units do not contribute sufficient information to their respective context. This implies that a cadence chordal progression may not necessarily be completed at the end of the phrase.

The above problem can be resolved by adding (if the window size was $M = 5$) four spacer events (see Section 3.1) before and after the phrase to be completed. In this way, all events in the phrase melody will appear in five BM windows each

Figure 8. The chorale melody shown in Figure 6(a) harmonized by an EBM constructed from a BM using a window size of $M = 3$. The BM was trained on the same set of chorales from *Choralbuch* (Dorffel, 1950) which were used to train the BM with a window size of $M = 5$.

(spacer events are added at both the learning and the completion stages). The harmony in Figure 7 was completed with spacer events.

4.3. Effects of a Different Window Size

In this experiment, we construct an EBM using a different BM, which used a window size of $M = 3$ to learn the local contexts of the same set of chorales taken from *Choralbuch* (Dorffel, 1950). This EBM (which incorporates absolute constraints) is used to harmonize the chorale melody in Figure 6(a). One of the harmonies produced by this EBM is shown in Figure 8. As is evident upon listening to this harmony, its quality is not as high as the harmony produced from a window $M = 5$, shown in Figure 7. Like the harmony in Figure 7, the third and ninth events are incorrect for this style of music. In addition, however, the bass part from the 4th to the 6th chords jumps abruptly, the fifth chord is not resolved properly to the 6th chord and there is an overlapping part from the 14th to the 15th chord. The harmony is of low quality as judged by a trained musician.

In comparison with the harmony in Figure 7, the poor quality of the harmony in Figure 8 would indicate that a window size of $M = 3$ is not a sufficiently large enough context to ensure a smooth progression from one chord to the next. Other experiments that we have conducted seem to confirm this.

4.4. Using the Energy Gap to Determine the Validity of the Harmony Produced by EBM

Despite the incorporation of ACs, it is still possible that the harmony synthesized for a particular event is not entirely appropriate. This is acceptable, since we have based our results on just five chorales and there are many contexts, as well as many chords, not present in the training set which have not been learnt. The system is currently unable to produce a correct harmony when it encounters these particular contexts.

We would like to have some indication of the validity of the harmony produced. We can achieve this by reporting the energy gap of each event of the completion that the EBM settled to. This is given by the sum of the energy gaps for the activated units in each event. Figure 9 shows five different harmonies produced by the EBM. The soprano part was taken from the chorale, *Nun lob, mein Seel, den Herren*, which is not part of the training set. Along with the score is the energy gap of each event. The BM trained with a window size of $M = 5$ was used in the construction.

As shown by Figure 9, events which the EBM is confident of, will have higher-energy gap values. For example, the first event and the last few events of each phrase in Figure 9 have a high energy. The harmony for Figure 9(d) is almost correct except for chord five. The corresponding energy graph reflects an error by the reduction in energy for this chord. The harmony in Figure 9(e) is totally correct if we are not too strict on overlapping parts. Once again, because of the nature of the system, the problem of overlapping parts may be overcome by clamping the relevant units in each event to '0' before the system is relaxed.

However, for events which the EBM is not so confident about, lower energy gaps are produced. In Figure 9(a), event 2 has the wrong note doubled, if we assume that the tenor and bass part both sound a B in the third octave, and event three is a wrong chord. This is reflected in the low energy gaps of events 2 and 3. In Figure 9(b), there are parallel octaves from event 5 to 6, which is reflected in the low energy gap of event 5. In Figure 9(c), the second event uses the chord I in its second inversion. This chord was never used in the training set, hence the low energy value for this event.

5. Conclusion

We have presented an application of the EBM to four-part chorale harmonization. We have demonstrated that an EBM can synthesize good harmonies after being trained on only a few chorales. We describe the harmonization process as a non-deterministic completion process where a melody, presented to the EBM for harmonization, is the partial input and may be of any length. The completion process is not sequential, completing the harmony, step by step, from left to right, and it is not solely dependent on local information of the previous step. The EBM will attempt to satisfy all constraints on the system simultaneously from the start of the completion process. In this way the completion process takes on a global perspective of the entire melody, as the EBM attempts to minimize the energy of the entire system.

The pitch-height representation behaves as an error-control code which enables the detection of ill-formed events and the correction ability is obtained from the learning stage. If appropriate local contexts are learnt by the BM, then the EBM is equipped with the necessary information to correct ill-formed events. The encouragement/discouragement function will bias the EBM (in its search for a solution) to a more correct one.

It was shown that as a consequence of the musical representation employed in the EBM, when harmonizing a soprano melody, the system is unaware that pitches should not be sounded above a melody pitch and that there should only be four pitches sounded in each chord. We have termed these constraints on four-part writing as absolute because it is imperative that they be observed during harmonization. To overcome these deficiencies in the EBM, we introduced methods for incorporating external (absolute) constraints (ACs) on the system. They are introduced into the stochastic approximation of the system as a selection bias and, depending on the particular AC incorporated, they do not necessarily possess the rigidity of a symbolic rule. For instance, the encouragement/discouragement function, which encourages the activation of four pitches in each chord of the chorale, is flexible enough to encourage only three pitches in a particular chord. This is the situation when two parts in a particular chord sound the same pitch.

It was demonstrated that the EBM approximates some long-range dependencies. Given just the melody of a chorale used in the training set, the EBM is able to

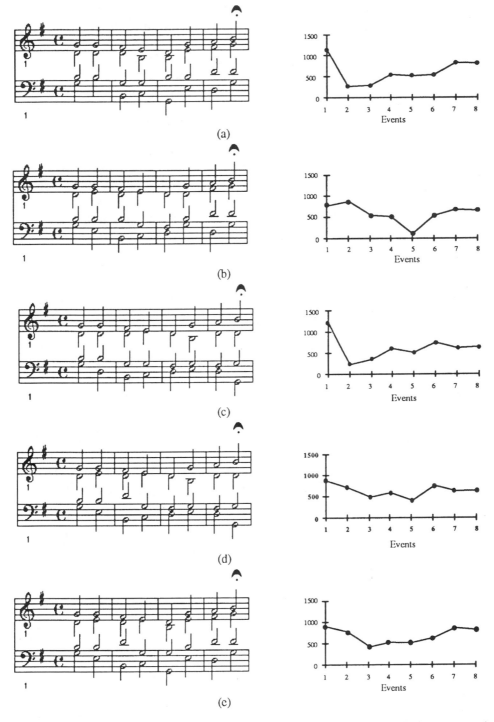

Figure 9. Different harmonies to the same melody produced by the EBM. Plotted beside each harmony is a plot of the energy gap of each event in that harmony. High energy values correspond to EBM's certainty of the harmony for that event, while low values of energy correspond to EBM's uncertainty of the harmony to produce for that event.

complete the rest of the chorale. In another experiment, only the first three and the last three chords of the same chorale were clamped, and the EBM completed the rest of the chorale. There are, of course, other long-range dependencies in music harmony that are not captured with the current system. However, it is envisaged they can be ascertained via a variation on the training method as well as with the incorporation of other ACs. We are currently investigating this important area.

We have shown that the EBM is able to relate the energy gap of events to the quality of the harmony. In the above experiments, a BM was trained with only five chorales. Thus, the EBM's judgements on synthesized harmonies are restricted to patterns found within the training set. Events completed by the EBM with relatively low energy levels correspond to harmonies that did not appear in any of the learned contexts obtained from the training set. In the experiments in this paper, only five chorales were used in the training set; however, a larger training set would equip the EBM with a greater repertoire. We are currently testing this situation and the initial results confirm this. While the computational requirement for this simulation is still too expensive for the harmonization of large musical works, there remains substantial scope for improvement. In particular, we are currently investigating the use of a deterministic BM (Hinton, 1989) to speed up this simulation.

From a music standpoint, this research is of great significance, because we have demonstrated that complex harmonization rules can be learnt by our EBM solely from examples of local contexts. It is significant that we can capture these contexts without requiring any musicological analysis and using only a simple pitch representation. The inherent nature of the EBM formalism to behave as a completion device is complementary to the simple musical representation employed. These properties of the EBM make it well suited to music harmonization. There are numerous avenues for this research. We are currently investigating how the EBM may be used to compare musical styles, and we are interested in listening to harmonies synthesized by an EBM which uses a BM trained on chorales in more than one key. Of course, training a BM on chorales from more than one musical style may enable the EBM to harmonize melodies in ways never before imagined.

This paper has concentrated on learning the harmonies for the chorales and has ignored meter and rhythm. Although meter and rhythm may be omitted from analysis for the Baroque style of music, it cannot be ignored in other styles, such as music from the Romantic Period (Kerman, 1978). Ways of incorporating rhythm and meter into the EBM formalism would broaden its potential application in this area.

Although we are applying the EBM to music harmony, its application is certainly not restricted to music. We believe that this method can be used for any complex sequences. We are currently applying the system to learning vowel harmony in natural language with success. The EBM cannot only inductively capture contexts, but can also incorporate known absolute constraints in the induction process. This opens up the possibility that domain knowledge can be incorporated within the neural network framework.

Acknowledgements

We would like to acknowledge the assistance of the following people: Professor David Tunley and Ralph Wilson from the School of Music Department at The University of Western Australia, and Peter Dodd, Leigh Smith and Mark Messenger of the Department of Computer Science, UWA.

References

Aarts, E. & Korst, J. (1988) *Simulated Annealing and Boltzmann Machines*. New York: Wiley.

Barucha, J.J. (1991) Pitch, Harmony, and Neural Nets: A Psychological Perspective. In P.M. Todd & D.G. Loy (Eds), *Music and Connectionism*. Cambridge, MA: MIT Press.

Barucha, J.J. & Todd, P.M. (1989) Modelling the perception of tonal structure with neural networks, *Computer Music Journal*, **13**, 44–53.

Bellgard, M.I. & Tsang, C.P. (1992) Harmonizing music using a network of Boltzmann machines. *Proceedings of Fifth International Conference of Artificial Neural Networks and their Application (Neuro-Nimes '92)*, EC2, pp. 321–332.

Denny, J. (1961) *The Oxford School Harmony Course*. London: Oxford University Press.

Dorffel, A. (1950) *CHORALBUCH*. New York: C.F. Peters Corporation.

Ebcioglu, K. (1988) An expert system for harmonizing four-part chorals. *Computer Music Journal*, **12**, 43–51.

Farrell, P.G. (1979) A survey of error-control codes. In G. Longo (Ed.), *Algebraic Coding Theory and Applications*. New York: Spinger-Verlag.

Geman, S., Bienenstock, E. & Doursat, R. (1992) Neural networks and the bias/variance dilemma. *Neural Computation*, **4**, 1–58.

Gjerdingen, R.O. (1991) Using connectionist model to explore complex musical patterns. In P.M. Todd & D.G. Loy (Eds), *Music and Connectionism*. Cambridge, MA: MIT Press.

Hertz, J., Krogh, A. & Palmer, R. G. (1991) *Introduction to Theoty of Neural Computation, A Lecture Notes Volume in the Santa Fe Institute Studies in the Sciences of Complexity*. Reading, MA: Addison-Wesley.

Hild, H., Feulner, J. & Menzel, W. (1991) HARMONET: a neural net for harmonizing chorals in the style of J.S. Bach, appearing in *Advances in Neural Information Processing*, **4**,

Hinton, G.E. (1989) Connectionist learning procedures. *Artificial Intelligence* No. 40, 185–234.

Hinton, G.E. & Sejnowski, T.J. (1986) Learning and relearning in Boltzmann machines, In D.E. Rumelhart & J.L. McClelland (Eds), *Parallel Distributed Processing*, Vol. 1. Cambridge, MA: MIT Press.

Kerman, J. (1980) *Listen*. New York: Worth Publishers Inc.

Kirkpatrick, S., Gelatt, C.D. Jr. & Vecchi, M.P. (1983) Optimization by simulated annealing, *Science*, **220**, 671–680.

Kohonen, T. (1987) *Content-addressable Memories*, 2nd edn. Germany: Springer Verlag.

Kohonen, T. (1989) A self-learning grammar, or associative memory of the second kind. *Proceedings of the International Joint Conference on Neural Networks*.

Lerdahl, F. & Jackendoff, R. (1983) *A Generative Theory of Tonal Music*. Cambridge, MA: MIT Press.

Loy, D.G. (1991) Connectionism and musiconomy. In P.M. Todd & D.G. Loy (Eds), *Music and Connectionism*. Cambridge, MA: MIT Press.

Mozer, M.C. (1991) Connectionist music composition based on melodic and stylistic constraints. In R.P. Lippmann, J.E. Moody & D.S. Touretzky (Eds), *Advances in Neural Information Processing*, 3, pp. 789–796. Los Altos, CA: Morgan Kaufmann.

Oswald, J. (Ed.) (1973) *Harmony: Schenkerian Analysis*. Translated by E. Mann. Cambridge, MA: MIT Press.

Piston, W. (1978) *Harmony*, 4th edn. revised and expanded by Mark DeVeto. London: Norton.

Prout, E. (1903) *Harmony: Its Theory and Practice*, Augener's Edition, No. 9182. London: Augener & Co.

Rumelhart, D.E., Hinton, G.E. & Williams, R.J. (1986) Learning internal representations by error propagation. In D.E. Rumelhart & J.L. McClelland (Eds), *Parallel Distributed Processing*, Vol. 1. Cambridge, MA: MIT Press.

Siegmeister, E. (1966) *Harmony and Melody*, Vols I & II. California: Wadsworth.

Todd, P. (1989) A connectionist approach to algorithmic composition. *Computer Music Journal*, **13**,

Todd, P.M. & Loy, D.G. (Eds) (1991) *Music and Connectionism*. Cambridge, MA: MIT Press.

Tsang, C.P. & Aitken, M. (1991) Harmonizing music as a discipline in constraint logic programming. *Proceedings of the International Computer Music Conference* (ICMC-91), pp. 61–64.

Tsang, C.P. & Bellgard, M.I. (1990) Sequence generation using a network of Boltzmann machines. *Proceedings of the 4th Australian Joint Conference on Artificial Intelligence* (AI '90), C.P. Tsang (Ed.), pp. 224–233. World Scientific.

Tunley, D. (1990) *Harmony in Action: A Practical Course in Tonal Harmony*. London: Faber Music.

Winograd, T. (1968) Linguistics and the computer analysis of tonal harmony. *Journal of Music Theory*, **12**, 2–49.

Reduced Memory Representations for Music

EDWARD W. LARGE, CAROLINE PALMER & JORDAN B. POLLACK

We address the problem of musical variation (listeners' identification of different musical sequences as variations) and its implications for mental representations of music. According to reductionist theories, listeners judge the structural importance of musical events while forming mental representations. These judgments may result from the production of reduced memory representations that retain only the musical gist. In a study of improvised music performance, pianists produced variations on melodies. Analyses of the musical events retained across variations provided support for the reductionist account of structural importance. A neural network trained to produce reduced memory representations for the same melodies represented structurally important events more efficiently than others. Agreement among the musicians' improvisations, the network model, and music-theoretic predictions suggests that perceived constancy across musical variation is a natural result of a reductionist mechanism for producing memory representations.

KEYWORDS: Music cognition, improvisation, neural networks, learning, musical structure.

1. Introduction

A common observation about musical experience is that some musical sequences are heard as variations of others. The tendency of listeners to hear musical variation has been exploited by composers and performers of various cultures and styles for centuries. Examples from Western music include 'theme and variations' forms of classical and romantic music, and the improvisational forms of modern jazz. This problem is not specific to music; the problem of perceptual constancy in the face of physical variation is central to cognitive science. This problem has interested many researchers in the field of music cognition because the invariance of musical identity that characterizes the listener's experience is perceived across a wide range of differences in the surface content of the music (Dowling & Harwood, 1986; Lerdahl & Jackendoff, 1983; Schenker, 1979; Serafine, Glassman, & Overbeeke, 1989; Sloboda, 1985). To explain phenomena such as musical variation, most theorists rely on structural descriptions of musical sequences. Depending on the musical dimension(s) under consideration, the nature of the description will vary, but each relies on some abstract system of knowledge representing the underlying regularities of a particular musical style or culture. Through experience with a musical

This article is a revised version of 'Reduced Memory Representations for Music', *Cognitive Science*, 1995, **19**, 53–96, reprinted with permission from Ablex Publishing Corp.

A.

B.

A.

B.

Figure 1. A. Two original melodies, *Hush Little Baby* (top), and *Mary Had a Little Lamb* (bottom). B. Improvisations on each tune, from Experiment 1.

style, listeners are thought to internalize characteristic patterns of rhythm, melody, harmony, and so forth, which are used to integrate and organize musical sequences and afford experiences such as musical variation.

The problem that musical variation presents to theorists is best illustrated by an example. Consider the melodies of Figure 1. The melodies labeled A are the children's tunes *Hush Little Baby* (top), and *Mary Had a Little Lamb* (bottom). The melodies labeled B are improvisations on these tunes, performed by pianists in an experiment described in this article. Most listeners readily identify the B melodies as 'variations' of the A melodies: Listeners believe that the B melodies share an identity with the original melodies. However, one's listening to these examples or inspecting the musical notation will reveal that at the surface level these two sequences differ along a number of dimensions, including pitch content, melodic contour, and rhythm. Where is the similarity between these sequences? One possibility is that as listeners produce internal representations for musical sequences, they implicitly evaluate the structural importance of events. Thus, certain events may be more important than others in determining the relationships that listeners hear between the melodies and variations of Figure 1. The evaluation of relative importance allows listeners to create reduced descriptions of musical sequences that retain the gist of the sequences and at the same time reduce demands on memory. Other theorists have made similar proposals, which we refer to as reductionist theories of music comprehension (Deutsch & Feroe, 1981; Lerdahl & Jackendoff, 1983; Schenker, 1979). Reductionist theories propose to explain musical variation by positing a similarity of the underlying structures in related melodies.

This explanation for musical variation, that listeners produce reduced memory descriptions for musical sequences, poses three major challenges for theories of music cognition. The first is the problem of knowledge specification. Reductionist theories posit that an experienced listener assigns to a musical sequence a relative importance structure that is based on previously acquired information: information that is not necessarily present in the individual musical sequences. Therefore, the notion of reduction requires that listeners implicitly use style- and culture-specific musical knowledge in creating reduced descriptions. This type of structural description is extracted from the input with the aid of general knowledge about the roles that events play in a particular musical idiom and is thought to reflect the statistical regularities of the particular musical culture or style in question (cf. Knopoff & Hutchinson, 1978; Palmer & Krumhansl, 1990). A great deal of effort has gone into the explicit identification of the musical knowledge required for listeners to produce reduced descriptions of musical sequences (Lerdahl & Jackendoff, 1983; Schenker, 1979). However, no mechanism has been proposed that specifies what form such knowledge might take or how this knowledge is put to use.

A second major problem is that of empirical validation. Do listeners hear musical sequences in terms of a hierarchical structure of relative importance? Some empirical support for this claim has begun to emerge in the literature. Earlier studies have examined the role of relative importance in perceptual phenomena such as judgments of musical completion and stability (Palmer & Krumhansl, 1987a,b), and judgments of similarity (Serafine *et al.*, 1989). However, little research has investigated the role of structural importance in musical performance tasks such as improvisation, in which performers are required to create musical variations.

Finally, a third major challenge remains for reductionist accounts of music comprehension: the specification of learning mechanisms. The fact that reduced descriptions require culture- and style-specific musical knowledge implies that a complete theory of musical reduction will also have a significant learning component. Krumhansl (1990) argues that listeners abstract and internalize underlying regularities through experience with musical patterns. These cognitive representations give rise to expectations and affect the stability of memory (Krumhansl, 1979; Krumhansl, Bharucha & Castellano, 1982). Jones (1981) argues that listeners abstract and store 'ideal prototypes' of musical styles that lead to musical expectations. Unexpected events in music create interest but are more difficult to recall (Jones, Boltz & Kidd, 1982). However, little work has addressed the mechanisms by which listeners may learn the musical regularities or prototypes that are necessary for the identification of the underlying structure of specific musical sequences.

In this article, we discuss the problem of musical variation and its implications for the mental representation of musical sequences. In particular, we address each of these three challenges posed for reductionist theories. We propose a mechanism that is capable of producing reduced memory representations for music, based on sequences that are first parsed into constituent data structures. We then model the reduced descriptions using recursive distributed representations (Pollack, 1988, 1990), a connectionist formalism that allows us to represent symbolic data structures as patterns of activation in connectionist networks. We also describe an empirical study in which we collect and analyze musicians' improvised variations on three melodies. We compare the improvisations with predictions of structural importance based on reductionist accounts. The evidence from improvisational music performance addresses the validity of reductionist claims and their relationship to the problem of musical variation. It also provides us with empirical data to compare with the performance of the connectionist mechanism for producing reduced memory representations. Finally, we describe a computational experiment in which a neural network is trained to produce recursive distributed representations for the same three melodies used in the improvisation study. The network model demonstrates a form of learning, providing an example of how listeners may acquire intuitive knowledge through passive exposure to music that allows them to construct reduced memory representations for musical sequences. We test the network's ability to generalize: to produce reduced descriptions for a musical variation of a known melody, and for a completely novel musical sequence. An examination of the reduced descriptions reveals that the representations differentially weight musical events in terms of their relative importance, thus emphasizing some aspects of the musical content over others. Finally, we compare these results with the empirical study to address whether the network's differential weightings agree with the relative importance of events inferred from the improvisational music performances.

2. Theories of Memory for Music

As Dowling and Harwood (1986) have observed, the role of memory in listening to a piece of music is not unlike the role of memory in listening to a conversation. To understand what is being said at any given moment, one need not have perfect recall of the conversation up to that point; what is important is the overall meaning or gist of the previous conversation. Listening to a piece of music is similar in at least one important way. For even moderately complex pieces, most listeners do not literally remember every detail; instead, they understand a complex piece by a process of abstraction and organization, remembering its musical 'gist'. Psychologists studying patterned sequence learning in the 1950s and 1960s made similar observations regarding individuals' abilities to perceive and memorize patterns in time. Two main theoretical proposals were advanced to explain the psychological findings: recoding theories, and rule-formation theories. The concept of information recoding, first introduced by Miller (1956), suggested that subjects presented with to-be-remembered sequences can reduce the amount of information to be retained by recoding, or chunking, subsets of more than one item into a single memory code. Researchers such as Estes (1972), Vitz and Todd (1969), and Garner and Gotwald (1968) argued that subjects assign codes to the subgroups of a sequence to reduce demands on memory, and these codes can be recalled and decoded on a later occasion to reconstruct the entire sequence. The principles proposed for grouping elements to produce codes were often perceptual; for example, Vitz and Todd (1969) suggested that runs of perceptually similar elements are cast into memory codes. However, the recoding view has been criticized for its reliance on perceptual regularities and for its inability to explain subjects' abilities to predict upcoming events in patterned sequences.

In contrast to recoding theories, rule-formation theories emphasized individuals' use of ordered vocabularies, or alphabets, and rules that apply to alphabetic properties. Several researchers (Jones, 1974; Restle, 1970; Simon & Kotovsky, 1963) proposed that subjects abstract serial relations and, using rule-based transformations such as repeat, transpose, complement, and reflection, generate cognitive data structures. The use of such transformations was thought to account for subjects' abilities to represent and predict unfolding serial patterns. Simon and Sumner (1968) proposed that listening to music could similarly be modeled as a process of pattern induction and sequence extrapolation, using alphabets and rule-based transformations such as *same* (repeat) and *next* (next element in the alphabet).

Both recoding and rule-formation theories, however, fail to explain the extraction of invariant identification in musical variation. To handle this and other challenges posed by musical experience, reductionist theories of music cognition posit cognitive representations that identify the structural importance of musical events (Deutsch & Feroe, 1981; Lerdahl & Jackendoff, 1983; Schenker, 1979). One of the most comprehensive of the reductionist theories is Lerdahl and Jackendoff's (1983) generative theory of tonal music. The theory takes as its goal the description of the musical intuitions of listeners experienced with Western tonal music. This is accomplished using a combination of music-theoretic analyses, of which *metrical structure* and *time-span reduction* are the most relevant for our purposes.

The primary function of metrical structure analysis is to describe the sense of alternating strong and weak pulses that characterizes musical experience, called *metrical accent*. A metrical structure consists of beats: psychological pulses marking equally spaced points in time.[1] Stronger and weaker pulses form nested levels of beats. The larger the metrical level of the beat marking a temporal location, the stronger that beat location, as shown by the dots in Figure 2 for the melody *Hush Little Baby*. A second function of metrical structure is to mark the onsets of temporal chunks that, in combination with grouping rules, divide a musical sequence into rhythmic units called *time-spans*. The resulting *time-span segmentation* divides a piece into nested time-spans. It captures aspects of the piece's rhythmic structure, providing a constituent structure description for the entire musical piece, as shown by the brackets in Figure 2.

A time-span segmentation forms the input to a time-span reduction analysis, which organizes musical events into a structure that reflects a strict hierarchy of relative importance. Within each time-span a single most important event, called the *head* of the time-span, is identified. All other events in the time-span are heard as subordinate to this event. The time-span reduction assigns relative importance to each event according to rules that consider metrical accent in addition to melodic, harmonic, and structural factors. Thus, time-span reduction provides a unification of musical factors and predictions regarding which events listeners will perceive to be most important. Figure 2 shows a time-span reduction; the top musical staff shows the melody and the staves below show the heads for successively larger and larger time-spans. At each level, the less important event(s) of each time-span are eliminated, and a 'skeleton' of the melody emerges. The tree above the top musical staff combines the information conveyed by the skeletal melodies with the information conveyed by the time-span segmentation. Its branching structure emphasizes structural relationships between levels of the reduction: that events of lesser importance are heard as elaborations of the more important events. The tree also identifies the structural ending of the musical passage, the cadence, indicated by the ellipse 'tying' together two branches of the tree, as shown in Figure 2.

Reductionist theories can be applied to explain the perception of musical variation. Figure 3 compares the theoretical reduction of the original melody *Hush Little Baby* with a reduction of the improvised variation on this melody (from Figure 1). At the third skeletal level, the two reductions are identical. Lerdahl and Jackendoff's (1983) theory thus can be applied to predict an intermediate level of mental representation at which structural similarities are captured. These theoretical reductions can be quantified, as shown in Figure 2; the numbers correspond to the relative importance of each event described by the time-span reduction analysis. Each number is a count of the number of branch points passed in traversing the tree from

Figure 2. Analysis of *Hush Little Baby* following Lerdahl and Jackendoff (1983), showing metrical structure analysis, time-span segmentation, and time-span reduction. The original melody is shown in musical notation and the tree above it is the time-span reduction. The lower staves show the dominant events at each level of the time-span segmentation (marked in brackets). The metrical structure analysis is marked as rows of dots, and the quantifications of relative importance for each event are shown below the segmentation.

the root to the branch that projects in a straight line to the event, inclusive. For instance, to calculate importance for the first note of the melody, count 1 for the root, 1 for a left turn, 1 for a branch point passed, and 1 for a second left turn. This final branch projects in a straight line to the event, so counting stops.[2] According to this strategy, the smaller the number, the more important is the corresponding event. Metrical accents also make predictions of relative importance based on event location. These predictions can be quantified by counting the levels of beats that correspond to metrical predictions (the dots in Figure 2). The two measures are

Figure 3. The first three levels of reduction for *Hush Little Baby* and its improvised variation (from Figure 1). The reductions are identical at the third level.

usually correlated because time-span reduction is partially based on metrical accent, but the time-span reduction adds information beyond metrical structure. We will compare both quantifications of relative importance and metrical accents, computed as in Palmer and Krumhansl (1987a,b), with the measures from improvisational music performance and with predictions derived from connectionist formalisms, described next.

3. A Reductionist Mechanism

In this section we address the issue of the mechanism by which time-span reductions may be computed, given a time-span segmentation as input. One difficulty with designing a mechanism based on Lerdahl and Jackendoff's (1983) theory lies in the specification of a relative weighting scheme for the set of rules that create reductions. A scheme has not yet been proposed that will work for every musical context. For complex musical pieces, one must enlist the aid of musical 'common sense' in providing the proper weighting of musical considerations. A second problem regards learning. Reductionist theories assume that a great deal of musical knowledge is acquired as a result of experience with the musical culture or style in question. Empirical evidence suggests that a restructuring of mental representations for novel musical sequences may occur with as few as five or six exposures to a sequence (Serafine *et al.*, 1989). However, reductionist theories have not yet addressed the issue of how the musical knowledge necessary for the production of reduced descriptions is acquired.

One approach that offers a solution to these problems is the application of connectionist models, which learn internal representations in response to the statistical regularities of a training environment using general-purpose learning algorithms such as back-propagation (Rumelhart, Hinton & Williams, 1986). The solution for musical variation offered by reductionist theories requires the representation of constituent structure, however, and connectionist models have been notoriously weak at representing constituent relationships such as those in language and music (Fodor & Pylyshyn, 1988). In fact, the lack of useful compositional representations has been an important stumbling block in the application of neural networks and other pattern-recognition techniques to the problems of cognitive science in general. One solution to this problem involves learning distributed representations for compositional data structures using a recursive encoder network. This connectionist architecture, known as Recursive Auto-Associative Memory (RAAM), has been used to model the encoding of hierarchical structures found in linguistic

A. **Encoding** (Compressor)

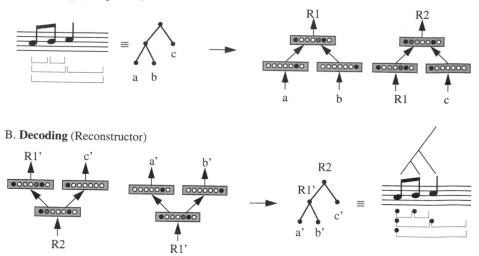

B. **Decoding** (Reconstructor)

Figure 4. Encoding and decoding of a musical sequence by a RAAM network. (a) Based on a vector representation for each event and a constituent structure analysis, the compressor combines the group (a b) into a single vector, R1, and then combines (R1 c) into a single vector R2. (b) The reconstructor decodes the vector R2 to produce the facsimile (R1′ c′). It then decodes R1′ into (a′ b′).

syntax and logical expressions (Chalmers, 1990; Chrisman, 1991; Pollack, 1988, 1990).

   To produce a memory representation for a musical sequence with the RAAM architecture, we first parse the sequence to recover a compositional data structure that captures the sequence's time-span segmentation. Thus, the network's input represents a musical sequence and its constituent structure; it does not capture the relative importance information conveyed by metrical accent or time-span reduction. We then train a RAAM network to produce a distributed representation for each time-span described by this structure. For example, the sequence of musical events in Figure 4, 'a b c', may be represented as the nested structure ((a b) c). A compressor network is trained to combine a and b into a vector R1, and then to combine the vector R1 with c into a vector R2. A reconstructor network is trained to decode the vectors produced by the compressor into facsimiles (indicated by the prime symbol) of the original sets of patterns. In the example, the reconstructor decodes R2 into R1′ and c′, and R1′ into a′ and b′. Thus, the vector R2 is a *representation* for ((a b) c) because we can apply a reconstruction algorithm to R2 to retrieve a facsimile of the original sequence. It is a *distributed* representation because it is realized as a pattern of activation. It is a *recursive* distributed representation because its construction requires the network to process recursively representations that it has produced. The representations are *reduced descriptions* of musical sequences because the vector representation for an entire pattern is equal in size to the vector representation of a single event.

   The structures that the RAAM reconstructs are facsimiles of the original structures because the construction of a recursive distributed representation is a data compression process, which necessarily loses information. The network may reconstruct some events with lowered activation and may fail to reconstruct other events entirely. The question we address regards which events will be reconstructed faithfully, and which will be lost or altered in the compression/reconstruction process. If, in the compression/reconstruction process, the network consistently loses information pertaining to less important events and retains information about more important events (i.e. as predicted by the music-theoretic analyses), then the network has also captured information that extends beyond pitch and time-span segmentation. The test is whether or not the network training procedure discovers the relative importance of events corresponding to metrical accent and time-span reduction.

If the network passes this test, then the use of recursive distributed representations to represent musical sequences may provide answers to some of the questions we have posed for reductionism. Reductions of musical sequences may be computed by a memory-coding mechanism whose purpose is to produce descriptions for musical sequences that reduce demands on memory while retaining the gist of the sequences. This implies that the culture- and style-specific musical knowledge necessary for computing reductions is realized as a set of parameters (in a RAAM network, a set of weights) in the coding mechanism. The acquisition of this set of parameters can be viewed as the acquisition of the musical knowledge relevant to computing reductions.

This view of reduced memory representations for musical sequences has a number of advantages over other possible mechanisms. The vector representations produced by a RAAM for melodic segments are reduced descriptions of the sequence, similar to the 'chunks' proposed by recoding theorists. However, the compressed representation for a sequence is more than just a label or pointer to the contents of a structure (cf. Estes, 1972); it actually *is* the description of its contents. Therefore, the numeric vectors produced by the network potentially contain as much information as the cognitive structures proposed by rule-formation theorists. Because the reduced descriptions are represented as neural vectors, they are suitable for use with association, categorization, pattern recognition and other neural-style processing mechanisms (Chrisman, 1991). Such processing mechanisms could, for example, be trained to perform sequence-extrapolation tasks (Simon & Summer, 1968).

In the next section we address issues of empirical validation. Do humans weight melodic events in terms of relative importance? Can reductionist accounts explain the phenomenon of invariant identification across musical variation? We describe an empirical study of variations on melodies improvised by skilled pianists. We extract a measure of relative importance for each melody, based on the improvisations. We compare these measures to reductionist predictions based on Lerdahl and Jackendoff's (1983) theory. In the following section, we describe a study in which we train a RAAM network to produce reduced descriptions for a set of melodies. We then test the network on the same three melodies on which pianists improvised in the empirical study. We measure the network's ability to produce representations for these melodies, including the ability to recognize melodic variation. We describe a method for determining the network's assignment of relative importance to individual events in the melodies, and compare the network findings with the empirical data and with the theoretical predictions. In the final section, we discuss the implications of reductionist theories for models of human learning and memory.

4. Empirical Investigation

Empirical evidence supporting the reductionist point of view has emerged in the literature. However, these early studies have dealt primarily with perceptual phenomena (Palmer & Krumhansl, 1987a,b; Serafine *et al.*, 1989). The reductionist hypothesis also leads to predictions concerning music performance. For example, in musical traditions that employ improvisation, performers may identify the gist of a theme in terms of its structurally important events and use techniques of variation to create coherent improvisations on that theme (Johnson-Laird, 1991; Lerdahl & Jackendoff, 1983; Pressing, 1988). Therefore, it should be possible to identify the events of greater and lesser importance in a melody by collecting improvisations on that melody and measuring the events that are retained across improvisations. We use this rationale to identify structurally important events by asking performers to improvise variations on a melody, and we examine the variations for events altered or retained from the original melody.

A number of methods have been employed to elicit the structure of listeners' mental representations for musical sequences. For example, Palmer and Krumhansl (1987a,b) asked subjects to listen to excerpts from a musical passage and rate how "good or complete" a phrase each excerpt formed. The rating was taken as a measure of the relative importance for the final event in each musical excerpt. Listeners' judgments of phrase completion at various points in a musical passage correlated well with predictions of each event's relative importance derived from Lerdahl and Jackendoff's (1983) time-span reductions (Palmer & Krumhansl, 1987a,b). The nature of the musical task, however, was somewhat unnatural, because music is usually not presented in fragments. Additionally, the application of this paradigm to longer musical works is problematic. Serafine *et al.* (1989) asked listeners to judge the similarity between related melodies. Although this paradigm does not provide measures of importance for individual musical events, it does allow the assessment of reductionist claims within an ecologically valid task. The similarity judgments among melodies corresponded to the degree of relatedness predicted by a reductionist theory (Schenker, 1979), even when radical surface differences existed (such as in the musical harmony). This agreement increased with repeated hearings, indicating a significant role of learning in determining the structure of listeners' mental representations (Serafine *et al.*, 1989). Schenker's reductionist theory, although similar in spirit to Lerdahl and Jackendoff's proposal, is less specific in its description of rules and their applications, often requiring a trained analyst (Serafine *et al.*, 1989) to make judgments regarding theoretical predictions.

The experiment reported here is based on a paradigm described earlier (Large, Palmer, & Pollack, 1991). In this paradigm, musicians are presented with notated melodies and are asked to improvise (create and perform) simple variations on them. Improvisation in Western tonal music commonly requires a performer to identify some framework of melodic and harmonic events and apply procedures to create elaborations and variants on them (Johnson-Laird, 1991; Steedman, 1982; also, see Pressing, 1988, for a review of improvisational models). Thus, improvisation of variations allows the musician freedom to determine which if any musical events should be retained from the original melody. This paradigm addresses the reductionist account by measuring musicians' intuitions about a particular melody within the context of a familiar task. This paradigm has an additional advantage in that it allows for the collection of individual ratings of importance for each event. Musical events that are viewed as structurally important should tend to be retained in improvised variations. Events viewed as less important (i.e. events that function as elaborations of important events) should be more likely to be replaced with different elaborations.

We measure the relative importance of each pitch event in the original melody by counting the number of times it was retained in the same relative temporal location across improvisations. Although this is a coarse measure of improvisation, it allows us to generalize across many aspects specific to music performance (including dynamics, phrasing, rubato, pedaling, etc.) and improvisation (including motific development, stylistic elaboration, etc.) and to concentrate instead on those factors that reflect reductionist considerations.

The primary objective of this study was to extend earlier findings (Large *et al.*, 1991) that suggested that a musician's improvisations on a tune indicated an underlying reduced representation of the melody. According to our application of the time-span reduction hypothesis to improvisation, more important events (those retained across multiple levels of the time-span reduction) should be more likely than unimportant events to be retained in variations on a melody. Therefore, the number of individual pitch events retained in the musicians' improvisations should correspond to the theoretical predictions of structural reductions.

4.1. Method

4.1.1. Subjects. Six skilled pianists from the Columbus, Ohio, community participated in the experiment. The pianists had a mean of 17 years (range of 12 to 30 years) of private instruction, and a mean of 24 years (range of 15 to 32 years) of playing experience. All of the pianists were comfortable with sight reading and improvising. All were familiar with the pieces used in this study.

4.1.2. Materials. Three children's melodies (*Mary Had a Little Lamb*, *Baa Baa Black Sheep*, and *Hush Little Baby*) were chosen as improvisational material that would be familiar (well learned) for most listeners of Western tonal music, to insure a well-established notion of relative importance for each event and to avoid learning effects. Additionally, these pieces were fairly unambiguous with regard to their time-span reductions.

4.1.3. Apparatus. Pianists performed on a computer-monitored Yamaha Disklavier acoustic upright piano. Optical sensors and solenoids in the piano allowed precise recording and playback without affecting the touch or sound of the acoustic instrument. The pitch, timing, and hammer velocity values (correlated with intensity) for each note event were recorded and analyzed on a computer.

4.1.4. Procedure. The following procedure was repeated for each piece. Pianists performed and recorded the melody, as presented in musical notation, five times. These initial recordings allowed each pianist to become acquainted with the improvisational material. With the musical notation remaining in place, the pianists were then asked to play five simple improvisations. The pianists were also asked to play five more complex improvisations, which are not discussed here. All performances were of a single-line melody only; pianists were instructed not to play harmonic accompaniment. All pianists indicated familiarity with all of the musical pieces.

4.2. Results

4.2.1. Coding improvisations.   Each improvisation was coded in terms of the number of events retained from the original melody, to develop a measure of relative importance for each event. The following procedure applied to the coding of each improvisation. First, the improvisation was transcribed by two musically trained listeners, who agreed on the transcriptions. Next, sections of the improvisation were matched to sections of the original. For most improvisations this was straightforward; for two of the improvisations, sections that repeated in the original melody (*Baa Baa Black Sheep*) were rendered only once in the improvisation, and these were doubled for purposes of analysis. Finally, individual events of the improvisation were placed into correspondence with the original. If only the pitch contents and rhythm changed (meter and mode remained the same), as in most of the improvisations, this process was straightforward: events were placed into correspondence by metrical position. In the case of mode change (e.g. the flatted third is substituted for the major third in a major to minor mode shift), substitutions were counted as altered events. In the case of a meter change, metrical structures were aligned according to the onsets of each measure and half-measure, and events were then placed into correspondence by temporal location. Those events whose pitch class was retained in the correspondence between original melody and variation were coded as 'hits' and received a score of 1; those events whose pitch class was altered (or for whom no event corresponded in the improvisation) were coded as 'misses' and received a score of 0. For example, if a quarter note, C, were replaced with four sixteenth notes, C-B-C-B, beginning at the same metrical location, the C would be coded as a hit. If, however, the C had been replaced with B-C-B-C, the C would be coded as a miss. Thus, only deletions and substitutions of events in the original melody affected the number of hits.

The number of hits for each pitch event in the original melody was summed across the five improvisations for each performer. Figure 5 shows the mean number of retained events across performers for each melody. To rule out the possibility that events in the original melody were altered at random, or that performers simply added events to create improvisations, an analysis of variance (ANOVA) on performers' mean number of retained events by event location was conducted for each melody. Each of the three ANOVAs indicated a significant effect of event location (Melody 1: $F(25, 125) = 4.02$, $p < .01$; Melody 2: $F(52, 260) = 6.64$, $p < .01$; Melody 3: $F(18, 90) = 7.76$, $p < .01$). Thus, performers were more likely to retain some melodic events than others across improvisations. The factors influencing the number of retained events at each location were further investigated in the following analyses.

4.2.2. Comparison with theoretical predictions.   Both metrical accent and time-span reduction make predictions about relative importance based on event location. Correlations between improvisation measures and both sets of theoretical predictions for each melody are summarized in Table 1. First, the correlation between the number of pitch events retained and the quantified metrical accent predictions for each event location was significant for each melody ($p < .05$). Improvisation measures were next compared with predictions from the time-span reduction analysis for each melody, obtained by quantifying the number of branch points passed in the tree, from root to terminal branch, as shown in Figure 2. Correla-

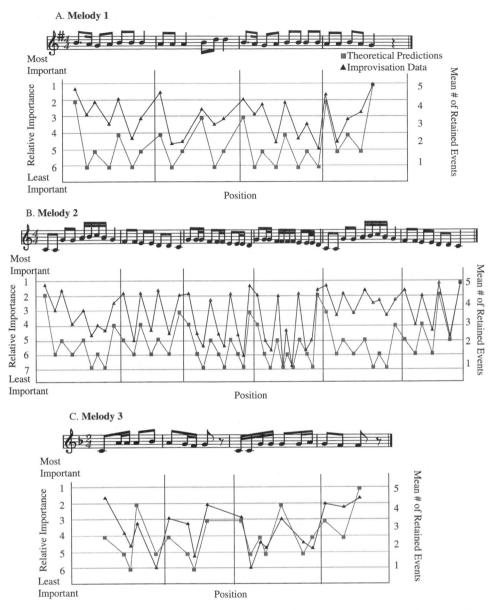

Figure 5. Theoretical and empirical measures of relative importance for melodies A (*Mary Had a Little Lamb*), B (*Baa Baa Black Sheep*), and C (*Hush Little Baby*).

Table I. Squared correlation coefficients for theoretical predictions and improvisation-based measures

	Melody 1 (Mary)	Melody 2 (Baa)	Melody 3 (Hush)
Metrical accent predictions	.63*	.80*	.78*
Time-span predictions	.76*	.79*	.67*
Semipartial (metrical accent removed)	.42*	.30*	.21

*$p < .05$

tions between the number of pitch events retained and the quantified time-span reduction predictions were also significant for each melody ($p < .05$). Figure 5 shows the time-span quantifications along with the improvisational data, indicating that those events predicted to be most important according to the time-span reduction tended to be retained across improvisations.

To insure the predictive power of the time-span reduction beyond metrical accent (on which time-span reductions are partially based), the improvisation measures were correlated with time-span reduction predictions after the effects of metrical accent were partialed out. These semipartial correlations, also shown in Table I, were significant ($p < .05$) for Melodies 1 and 2, indicating that time-span reduction did contribute information beyond metrical accent. The semipartial correlation was not significant for Melody 3 ($p = .37$), indicating that in this case correlation of improvisation measures with the time-span reduction analysis was largely due to the effects of metrical accent.

4.3. Discussion

Musicians' improvisations of variations on simple melodies provided strong support for the reductionist hypothesis. Performers tended to retain certain events in each melody and used improvisational techniques to create variations around those retained events. In addition, the music performances agreed with reductionist predictions of which events were relatively important in these simple melodies. Furthermore, the findings for two of the three melodies indicate that musical factors specific to time-span reductions played an important role in musicians' improvisation of variations.

The relatively high contribution of metrical structure to the improvisations based on the third melody (*Hush Little Baby*) may indicate a qualitative difference between the performers' intuitions and the theoretical predictions for this piece. For example, the improvisations often retained the first event of Measure 1 (as seen in Figure 5), an indicator of its relative importance, disagreeing with the theoretical weighting of this event. This may be due to the salience of the large initial pitch interval, or it may be a general primacy effect (making the first few events more likely to be retained regardless of reductionist considerations). The performances also disagreed with the predictions at the structural ending; all events in Measure 4 were retained relatively often. Alternatively, this could be accounted for as a recency effect.

These discrepancies emphasize the difficulty of providing a relative weighting for a set of rules that determine the reductionist structure of mental representations. For example, the particular order in which a subset of rules is applied can lead to different weightings of constituents. However, the improvised performances do show general agreement with the theoretical predictions of time-span reduction. This is the first demonstration, to our knowledge, that the musical factors incorporated in the reductionist theory (Lerdahl & Jackendoff, 1983) can account for the structure of performers' mental representations for musical improvisations. We next compare these measures with the reduced memory descriptions generated by a connectionist network for the same three melodies.

5. Network Model

In this section we describe an implementation of the RAAM architecture for producing reduced memory descriptions of musical sequences. A RAAM network is trained on a corpus of simple melodies and is then tested in two ways. First, we examine the network's ability to compress and reconstruct accurately a test set of three tunes. Second, we examine the structure of the representations produced by the network. The RAAM network is an example of a mechanism that applies knowledge about a musical genre to the task of producing reduced memory descriptions for specific musical sequences. This knowledge is captured as a set of weights that the network extracts directly from a training environment (the corpus of melodies), thereby accounting for learning.

The network experiment has two goals. The first is to measure the performance of the RAAM network using a *well-formedness* test (Pollack, 1990). For a given input melody, the compressor network creates a reduced description. The reconstructor network is then applied to the reduced description to retrieve its constituents. If the reconstructed sequence matches the input melody, either exactly or within some tolerance, then the reduced description is considered to be well formed. The well-formedness test can also be used to measure the ability of a RAAM network to generalize, by testing the network's performance on novel sequences. In this experiment, we examine the performance of the network on a test set of three melodies: known, variant, and novel. The *known* melody is one of the melodies presented to the network during a training phase. Performance on this melody establishes a baseline of the network's ability to encode melodies correctly. The *variant* melody is a variation of material presented to the network in the training phase, and the *novel* melody is a melodic sequence not related in any obvious way to the material presented in the training phase. If the network is able to generalize from the examples presented in the training phase, then it should be able to produce well-formed reduced descriptions for one or both of the variant and novel melodies as well as for the known melody.

The second goal is to determine the structure of the representations produced by the network. The network is provided with a time-span segmentation for each melody. The question we ask is: Will the network be able to take advantage of this information about temporal structure to preserve musical regularities that are systematically related to this structure? Our prediction is that the network's reduced descriptions will differentially weight constituent events, and furthermore, that this differential weighting will agree with both the improvisation measures and the theoretical predictions (Lerdahl & Jackendoff, 1983) regarding the relative importance of events. This prediction is based on the observation that RAAM networks learn a data compression algorithm that is tailored to the statistical regularities of a training set. If our training set is adequately representative of the statistical characteristics of simple Western tonal melodies, the network should be able to make use of this information, and we should see significant levels of agreement among network, theoretical, and empirical measures.

5.1. Network Implementation

The RAAM architecture uses a connectionist substrate of fully connected feed-forward neural networks to produce recursive distributed representations (Pollack, 1990). For example, to encode binary trees with k-bit patterns as the terminal nodes, the RAAM compressor would be a single-layer network with two k-unit input buffers and one k-unit output buffer. The RAAM reconstructor would then be a single-layer network with one k-unit input buffer and two k-unit output buffers. The input and output buffers are required to be the same size because the network is used recursively: The output of the network is fed back into the network as input. During training, the compressor and reconstructor are treated as one standard three-layer network ($2k$ inputs, k hidden units, and $2k$ outputs) and trained using an auto-associative form of back-propagation (Cottrell, Munro & Zipser, 1987; Rumelhart *et al.*, 1986), in which the desired output values are simply the input values. To create the individual training patterns for the network, the structures that make up the training set are divided into two-element groups (e.g. (a b) or (R1 R2)).

Two special issues arise in designing a RAAM network for encoding musical structure. First, we must determine a constituent structure for each musical sequence that will specify how events are presented to the network input buffers, as shown in Figure 6 (top). As discussed above, we will use the time-span segmentation, a nested constituent description that captures aspects of the sequence's rhythmic structure (Lerdahl & Jackendoff, 1983). In the simple melodies used in this study, the time-spans at smaller constituent levels (less than a measure) were 'regular' (Lerdahl & Jackendoff, 1983); that is, they were aligned with the locations of strong metrical beats. Therefore, the lower levels of time-span segmentation were determined by the metrical structure. Grouping rules (Lerdahl & Jackendoff, 1983) contributed to determining time-span segments at constituent levels larger than the single measure. Each encoding produced by the network is the representation of a time-span (and its events) at some level in the time-span segmentation. Once an encoding has been produced, temporal information is implicitly managed by the recursive structure of the decoding process, also shown in Figure 6 (bottom). As decoding proceeds, the output codes represent smaller and smaller time-spans (at lower and lower levels), until, at the termination of the decoding process, a single pitch event is output and the temporal location of that event is uniquely determined. Thus the temporal structure of each melody plays an important part in network processing; the reduced descriptions of the melody in Figure 6 capture temporal structure in a way analogous to Lerdahl and Jackendoff's (1983) hierarchically nested time-spans, shown for the same melody in Figure 2.

Second, we must specify the representation of pitch events to be encoded by the RAAM. The different pitches in each melody are represented as binary feature vectors (on or off). We chose a 'local' representation of pitch class; seven units represented the seven pitch classes of the diatonic scale in Western tonal music. We also added two units to represent melodic contour. One unit means 'up' from the previous event, the other means 'down', and turning both units off means no contour change. This representation nominally captures octave equivalence and pitch height but makes no further assumptions regarding the psychophysical components of pitch, as other connectionist researchers have done (cf. Mozer, 1991). More sophisticated encoding strategies may prove useful for certain musical applications (cf. Large *et al.*, 1991), but for the purposes of this study we sought to minimize inductive biases that would be introduced by more complex coding schemes.

Two modifications to the RAAM architecture are necessary to encode Western tonal melodies such as those in our training set. First, existing applications of the RAAM architecture have only accurately handled tree structures that are four to five levels deep. However, the 25 training melodies used in this study contain constituent structure hierarchies six to seven levels deep, which expand to more than 1000 individual training patterns. Previous experiments found that this training set

A. Encoding (Compression)

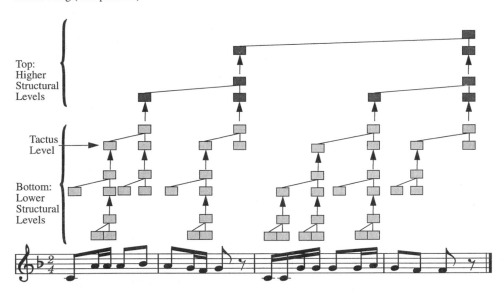

B. Decoding (Reconstruction)

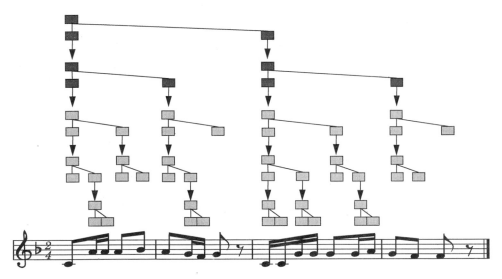

Figure 6. Simplified schematic of the modular RAAM used in the network experiment. (a) In the encoding diagram, time flows from left to right and bottom to top. (b) In the decoding diagram, time flows from top to bottom and left to right.

size outstrips the capacity of a RAAM network that contains a reasonably small number of hidden units (Large *et al.*, 1991). We adopt a method here of scaling up the basic architecture by having one RAAM network recursively encode lower levels of structure and then passing the encodings it produces to a second RAAM that encodes higher levels of structure, as shown in Figure 6. This method, known as *modular* RAAM (Angeline & Pollack, 1990; Sperdutti, 1993), allows us to build recursive encoders that can handle trees with many hierarchical levels by using multiple networks that each contain fewer hidden units. This form of training, however, violates one of the original design decisions of RAAM: that the terminals be recognizable as binary strings so that it is clear when to terminate the decoding process (Pollack, 1990). We address this problem by adding an extra unit to each RAAM module, which is trained as a terminal detector. This allows us to determine a) when to pass a code from the higher-level RAAM network module to the lower-level RAAM module during decoding, and b) when to interpret a code produced by the bottom module as a pitch event.[3]

The second modification addresses ternary groups common in Western tonal music; binary branching structures are not sufficient to capture musical groupings that often consist of three elements. To handle both pairs and triples, we might create a network with three input buffers, only two of which would be used to encode binary segments. However, this would lead to the situation shown in Figure 7(a), in which a triple with a rest in the middle is indistinguishable from a pair. Instead, a network with four input buffers can encode both duple and triple segments and distinguish among them, as shown in Figure 7(b). Here Buffer 1 corresponds to the first event of any group, Buffer 3 corresponds to the second event of a binary group, and Buffers 2 and 4 correspond to the second and third events, respectively, of a ternary group. To interpret the output of these buffers properly at decoding, we add four extra units at the output. The network is trained to turn on an output unit when the corresponding buffer's output is to be used; otherwise the contents of the buffer are ignored and trained with a don't-care condition (Jordan, 1986).

A.   B.

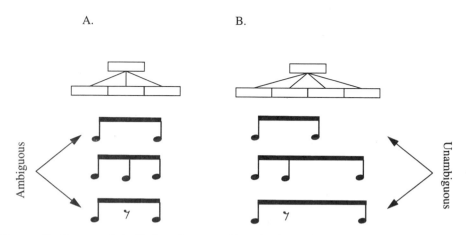

Figure 7. Proposed buffering for encoding duple and triple grouping structures. (a) Three buffers cannot discriminate between a group of two events and a group of three events in which the middle event is a rest. (b) Four input buffers can make the discrimination.

5.2. Method

5.2.1. Training the network. Twenty-five simple children's melodies (listed in the Appendix) were chosen as a training set because they provided a simple, natural musical case for study. The tunes comprised 18 unique melodies; five of these 18 melodies had variations in the training set. Each melody was between 4 and 12 measures in length, with a time-signature of 2/4, 3/4, 4/4, 6/8, or 12/8. The tunes provided constituent structures six to seven levels deep, in which either binary or ternary groups appeared at each level. Although the pitch event representations required only nine bits (7 pitch class units and 2 contour units), we used 35 units, allowing 26 extra degrees of freedom for the system to use in arranging its intermediate representations. These extra dimensions of representation were set to 0.5 on input, and trained as don't-cares (Jordan, 1986) on output. As described above, the two RAAM modules each required four input buffers, and each resulting module had 140 input units, 35 hidden units, and 148 output units.

The first module was trained on the bottom two to three levels of the trees, such that the input corresponded to metrical levels up to and including coding of the 'tactus', or beat level (see Figure 2). Therefore, the representations that emerged from the lower RAAM (the output) corresponded to time-spans with a length of one half-note for binary groups, and one dotted half-note for ternary groups (see Figure 6). The second module was trained on the upper three to four levels of the trees, corresponding to larger structural levels of the melodies. This division of labor allowed the modular architecture to balance approximately the learning load between the two modules, measured by the number of unique training patterns. The two modules were trained simultaneously, with the bottom module's output providing the input for the top module. Rather than the network being exposed to the entire training set of 25 melodies, 4 melodies were chosen randomly from the training set and forward-propagated in each training cycle; then error was back-propagated through the network (cf. Cottrell & Tsung, 1991). This method allowed a faster running time for the large training set. Because the length of the tunes in the training set (and therefore the number of individual training patterns) varied for each cycle of back-propagation, the learning rate was set to 0.7 divided by the number of training patterns seen on that cycle. Momentum was set to 0.5 and weight decay to 0.0001. Training lasted for 1300 cycles, at which point the error associated with the test set of melodies reached a minimum value.

5.2.2. Testing the network. We tested the network's performance in two ways. First, well-formedness tests assessed the ability of the network to compress and re-construct each melody accurately and thereby revealed the basic representational capacity of the network. Second, tests of representational structure assessed the relative weighting of constituents on an event-by-event basis and thereby revealed the nature of the representational strategy developed by the network.

The network was tested on a set of three melodies: a known melody, a variant melody, and a novel melody, shown in Figure 8. These were the same three melodies used in the empirical study of improvisation; the names used here denote the particular relationship of each melody to the network training set. The known melody, *Mary Had a Little Lamb*, occurred in the training set (Appendix, Melody 16(a); all melodies are shown in the key of C). The network's performance on this melody is representative of the network's performance on familiar (learned) melodies. The variant melody, *Baa Baa Black Sheep*, did not occur in the training set; however, four closely related variations of this melody (Melodies 18(a) (d)) did occur in the training set. The local structure (duration patterns and melodic contour of individual measures) of the variant melody was very similar to that of training set Melodies 18(c) and (d). The global structure (3 two-measure phrases with similar melodic and harmonic implications) of the variant melody was similar to training set Melodies 18(a) and (b). Performance on this melody indicates the ability of the network to account for simple melodic variation, because the network was required to recombine familiar local structures (individual measures) in novel global contexts (different melodies) that shared structural features with known melodies. The novel melody, *Hush Little Baby*, did not occur in the network training set, nor was it closely related to any of the melodies in the training set. Network performance on this melody indicates the ability of the network to perform a type of generalization different from that required for melodic variation: the ability to represent novel musical sequences at local levels of structure, as well as the ability to combine novel local structures in novel global contexts.

5.3. Results

5.3.1. Tests of well-formedness.
Each melody was reconstructed by the decoder network from the recursive distributed representation produced by the compressor. Errors in the reconstructed melody took the form of additions (the network reconstructed an event that was not present in the original melody), deletions (the network failed to reconstruct an event that was present in the original melody), and substitutions (the network reconstructed an event incorrectly in the same position). These errors correspond to two aspects of the network's performance. The first is whether or not the network correctly reconstructs the time-span segmentation, which determines the rhythm (duration pattern) of the output sequence. The second is whether or not the network correctly reconstructs the contents of the output vectors, which correspond to the pitch contents of the output sequence. We combined these considerations into a single measure of network performance by calculating whether the network gives the correct output for each possible temporal location. Each of the melodic sequences in the test set had a smallest durational value of a sixteenth note, and no reconstruction produced any smaller temporal values. Therefore, we based our error measure on the number of sixteenth-note locations in each piece. There were 64 (16×4) sixteenth-note locations in the known melody, 96 (16×6) in the variant melody, and 32 (8×4) in the novel melody. Given our coding scheme, the chance estimate for percentage of events correct at each location is 1/16, or 6.25%, based on 16 possible outcomes: seven pitch classes times two contour changes (up or down) plus a repeated pitch and a rest.

As an approximate measure of the network's ability to compress and reconstruct constituent structures correctly, we calculated average performance on the training set melodies. We measured performance at two points in the time-span segmentation for each melody. First, the network's ability to compress and reconstruct time-span segments with only three levels of recursive nesting—corresponding to a time-span of one half note for binary groups—was examined. Network performance in reconstructing training set melodies with three levels was 92%. Next, the network's ability to compress and reconstruct time-span segments that corre-

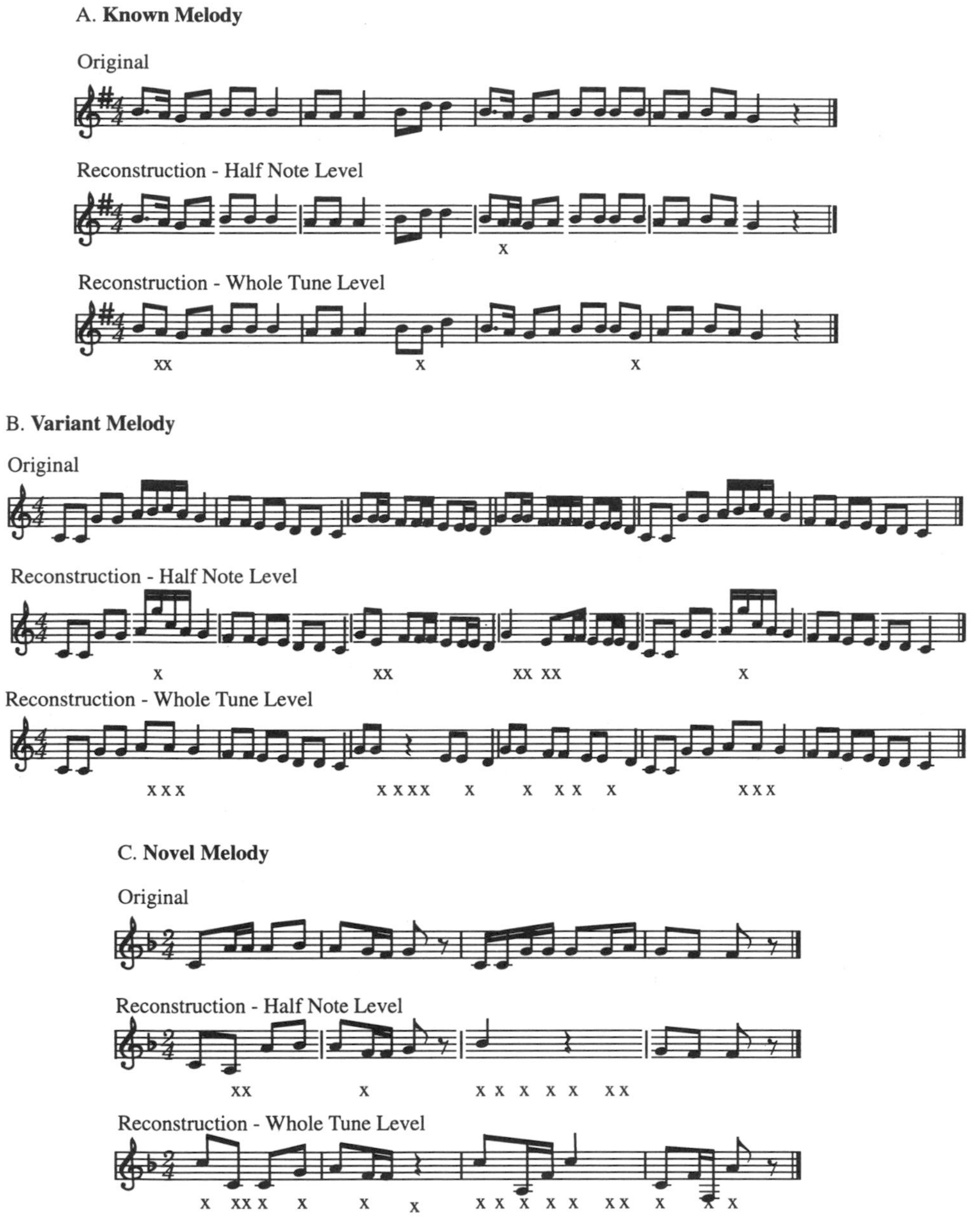

A. **Known Melody**

Original

Reconstruction - Half Note Level

Reconstruction - Whole Tune Level

B. **Variant Melody**

Original

Reconstruction - Half Note Level

Reconstruction - Whole Tune Level

C. **Novel Melody**

Original

Reconstruction - Half Note Level

Reconstruction - Whole Tune Level

Figure 8. Original melodies and network reconstructions: (a) *Mary Had a Little Lamb* (known), (b) *Baa Baa Black Sheep* (variant), (c) *Hush Little Baby* (novel). Each melody was reconstructed from several codes (the half-note level RAAM), and from a single code (the whole-tune level RAAM). Xs denote failures in network reconstructions.

sponded to entire melodies, with six to seven levels of recursive nesting, was examined. Here the network's performance was 71%. Thus, the representations captured lower-level structures quite faithfully, whereas at global levels of structure, the representations began to lose sequence details. (The network's performance at the lower levels will always be more accurate than at the global levels because more data compression at global levels results in greater susceptibility to loss of information.)

To better understand the network's performance, we examined the reconstructions for the three test melodies in detail, which are shown in Figure 8. The reconstruction of the known melody, *Mary Had a Little Lamb*, gives an indication of network performance on melodies learned in the training set. As described above, we first examined the reduced descriptions produced by the lower-level RAAM module for the known melody (subsequences of events up to the level of half notes; lowest three levels of hierarchical nesting). In this reconstruction, the network made a single error, adding an event in the third measure, for a performance of 98%. Reconstruction at the whole-tune level (all seven levels of hierarchical nesting) resulted in four errors, giving an overall performance of 94% (60/64) for this melody, which was significantly better than chance (binomial test, $p < .01$). This reconstruction was better than the average for training-set melodies, probably due to the fact that two instances of this melody (16(a) and (b)) occurred in the training set. Note also that the network's reconstruction of the first measure of this melody at the whole-tune level resembles the duration pattern of Melody 16(b); however, the reconstructions of 16(a) and 16(b) did differ (the network was able to differentiate between them).

The reconstruction of the variant melody, *Baa Baa Black Sheep*, gives an indication of the network's performance on simple variations of learned melodies. The reconstruction produced by the lower-level RAAM module for subsequences corresponding to half notes (three lowest levels of hierarchical nesting) resulted in a performance of 92% (88/96). The network successfully learned the lower-level details because most of these surface features were present in the training set (see Melodies 18(c) and (d)). The network's reconstruction at the whole-tune level (all seven levels of nesting) resulted in 15 errors, for a performance of 84% (81/96), again significantly better than chance ($p < .01$). The reconstruction of this melody at (only) the whole-tune level was the same as its reconstruction of *Twinkle Twinkle Little Star*, one of the four related melodies in the training set (18(a)), for which its performance was 98% (94/96 events). This is not a surprising result, but it is revealing to note that the network reconstructed Melody 18(a) rather than one of the other related training-set melodies (18(b)–(d)). As Figure 8 shows, the half-note level representations preserved local structure. The ability to exploit constituent structure, combined with the use of a recursive encoding strategy, allowed the network to rely upon structural similarities at the whole-tune level, rather than melodic and rhythmic features at lower levels, in determining the representation of this melody.

The reconstruction of the novel melody, *Hush Little Baby*, is indicative of the RAAM's ability to encode novel sequences. Again, we first examined the reduced descriptions produced by the lower-level RAAM module for subsequences of the original melody by encoding groups of events only up to the level of half notes (three levels of hierarchical nesting). Figure 8 shows the reconstruction from the reduced descriptions for each half note of the tune. The lower-level reconstructions produced 10 errors, for a success rate of 69% (22/32), again significantly better than chance ($p < .01$). Seven of the 10 errors occurred in the third measure, and the other three measures of the tune were reconstructed rather faithfully. At the whole-tune level there were 17 errors, for a performance of 47% (15/32), which is significantly better than chance ($p < .01$), but overall, the reconstruction is rather poor (there are only 19 events in the original tune). It is interesting to note that the rhythm was reconstructed well (27/32, or 84%), but very few pitch events were reconstructed correctly (3/19, or 16%). Thus the network's representation of this melody at the whole-tune level was not well formed, and generalization to this novel sequence was better at the lower levels of the hierarchy.

5.3.2. Test of representational structure. Next, we analyzed the structure of the distributed representations to determine the relative contributions of individual events. One method is to examine the representation vectors directly to determine the function of individual hidden units. Little information can be retrieved from recursive distributed representations of this size, however, because of their complexity (Pollack, 1990). As an alternative approach, the 'certainty' with which the network reconstructed each event of the original sequence was measured by computing the distance between the desired (d) and obtained (o) vector representations at each sequence location (i). This analysis considered only those output units that represent pitch class (ignoring contour), consistent with the analysis of the improvisations. To compensate for the fact that some events were added and others deleted in the reconstructions, we considered only the location in the reconstructions for which pitch vectors should have been output. Thus, only deletions and substitutions of events from the original melody affected this measure, as in the empirical study above. A similarity measure was defined,

$$\text{sim}(d, o) = 1 - \left(\sqrt{\sum_{i=1}^{n} (d_i - o_i)^2} \right) \Big/ n$$

that ranged from 0 (most different) to 1 (identical) and represented the probability that desired pitch events occupied the appropriate positions in the original sequence, based on the network representation. Thus, sequence locations at which this measure was smallest were locations at which the network was most likely to make a reconstruction error. These probabilities were then interpreted as predictions of relative importance for each event in the distributed representation.

The probability measures of relative importance at the whole-tune level were correlated with the musical improvisation data, as summarized in Table II. The correlations were large for the known ($p < .10$) and variant ($p < .05$) melodies, but not for the novel melody. This was not surprising because the novel melody did not have a well-formed distributed representation at the whole-tune level. However, when the novel melody was reconstructed from the reduced descriptions corresponding to the half-note level of the tune (shown on the bottom of Figure 8), the resulting correlation approached significance ($p < .10$).

Next, we compared the network measures of relative importance with the quantifications of theoretical predictions, as shown in Table II. The correlations with time-span reduction predictions were significant for the known and variant melodies and for the measure-level reconstruction of the novel melody ($p < .05$) but not for the whole-tune-level reconstruction of the novel melody. The correlations with metrical accent predictions also were significant for each melody ($p < .05$). We therefore correlated the network measure with time-span reduction predictions

Table II. Squared correlation coefficients for network reconstructions

	Known (Mary) Whole Tune	Variant (Baa) Whole Tune	Novel (Hush) Whole Tune	Novel (Hush) Half Note
Improvisation data (No. of events retained)	.35*	.64**	.10	.40*
Metrical accent predictions	.39**	.55**	.24	.45**
Time-span predictions	.39**	.64**	.25	.52**
Semipartial (metrical accent removed)	.14	.35**	.27	.29

*$p < .10$ **$p < .05$

after metrical accent was partialed out. The semipartial correlation was not significant for the known or novel melodies but was significant for the variant melody ($p < .05$), indicating some ability of the network to extract structure beyond metrical accent.

5.4. Discussion

We have demonstrated a mechanism, RAAM, that is capable of producing recursive distributed representations for musical sequences. A general learning algorithm, back-propagation, extracted sufficient information from a training set of 25 simple melodies to produce reduced descriptions of known, variant, and novel sequences. The reconstructions of melodies produced by the network were fairly accurate but did not retain all of the details. The network produced reduced memory representations that preserved the important structural features of the sequences.

We first investigated the performance of the network using the RAAM well-formedness test. In all three test cases, the network failed to reconstruct some events, reconstructed other events incorrectly, and occasionally added some that were not present in the original sequence. However, three sources of evidence suggested that the representations successfully captured the major structural features of the melodies. First, the reconstructions were faithful to the rhythm of the original melodies, even in the case of the novel melody. Second, the network correctly reconstructed most of the pitches in the original melodies. Third, the events on which the network made reconstruction errors tended to be the less important events, as shown by the correspondence of network predictions of relative importance with theoretical predictions and improvisational data.

The network performed best on familiar (learned) melodies and differentiated between subtle variations of the same melody (16(a) and (b)). We also tested the ability of the network to generalize: to represent both a variant of a learned melody and a truly novel melody (one unrelated to the learned melodies). The performance of the network in reconstructing the variant melody showed how the network handles simple melodic variation. This melody shared local structure with training set Melodies 18(c) and (d), and the network's lower-level codes (up to the half-note level) preserved this structure. At a global level, the compression/reconstruction process followed the attractor (a known path) for another melody with which the variant shared global structure (18(a)). The network also identified the important pitch events in the variant, indicated by the fact that network measures of relative importance for this melody correlated strongly with the time-span reduction predictions. Comparison with the empirical data from improvisations supported the conclusion that the network successfully identified events interpreted as major structural features by musicians. Overall, these results indicate the ability of the network to exhibit a limited but important form of generalization.

The findings for the novel melody indicated that the network still performed well at lower levels of structure in handling unlearned sequences; it produced well-formed memory representations for the three lowest levels of the constituent structure. At higher levels of structure, however, the network failed to generalize, reproducing the correct rhythm but incorrect pitches for this melody. This aspect of performance may be due to the learning environment, which may not have provided a rich enough set of patterns at higher levels of structure.

The information retained by the network in the compression/reconstruction process agreed well with music-theoretic predictions of the relative importance of musical events. The limited sizes of the training and test sets make it difficult to say precisely why the agreement occurred; however, the time-span segmentation used as input to the network was related to the music-theoretic predictions. The network used this information about rhythmic structure, coded as position in a fixed input buffer, to learn representations that retained musically important events and major structural features. For instance, the network may have learned metrical accent by weighting the first element of lower-level time-spans (which aligned with strong metrical beats) more heavily than others. The relative importance predictions, however, were based on more complex rhythmic relationships. To learn relative importance, the network may have learned other stylistic factors. For example, the RAAM network may have learned that the last event in each sequence was predictable—it is always the tonic. Thus, the network appears to have extracted some relationships beyond metrical accent, and did so strictly on the basis of the regularities in the training set. The network was forced to distill musical regularities such as these from the training set in response to two opposing pressures: a) to retain as much information about each sequence as possible, and b) to compress the information about each sequence into a pattern of activation over a small number of units.

Finally, and most importantly, we demonstrated the psychological plausibility of this approach to creating reduced memory representations for music. Certain events dominated the structure of the reduced descriptions by virtue of the fact that they had the greatest probability of being correctly reconstructed by the network. The events that dominated the network's reduced descriptions were precisely those events most important in the mental representations for these melodies measured by the musical improvisations and posited in the theoretical reductionist predictions. These findings indicate that the RAAM coding mechanism produced reduced descriptions for musical sequences that implicitly weighted events in each sequence in terms of their relative structural importance. This is a major finding because it supports the psychological plausibility of recursive distributed representations as an approach to modeling human memory. Combined with the network's overall performance in reconstruction, these findings suggest that the reduced memory representations successfully captured the structure of musical sequences in ways similar to the mental representations underlying improvisational music performance.

6. General Discussion

We began with the problem of musical variation: How do listeners and performers judge certain musical sequences to be variations of others? We have argued that musicians make such judgments based not on characteristics of the surface structure of sequences, but instead based on similarity of reduced memory representations formed from the sequences. We have provided empirical support for the reductionist account of musical memory from a study of improvisational music performance, in which pianists tended to retain structurally important events across improvisations on simple melodies. The improvisations corresponded well with predictions from a reductionist account of music perception. The link between performance and perception may be the nature of memory, which highlights the musical gist at the expense of other musical features. These reduced memory structures may be based on knowledge extracted from passive exposure to many musical patterns from the same style or culture. Evidence to support this claim was provided by a connectionist network model that learned to produce reduced memory descriptions for simple melodies. In this section, we explore the relationship between the musical improvisation findings and our reductionist approach to modeling musical memory. We discuss the problem of the recovery of rhythmic structure in music, and its relationship to the general problem of the recovery of constituent structure in sequence processing. We then compare our network model with other connectionist models that have been proposed for music processing.

6.1. Musical Improvisation and Reduced Memory Structures

The structure of memory greatly influences the content of musical improvisations. Improvisation on a theme has been described as a largely unconscious process of identifying important structural elements and applying creative procedures to elaborate on those elements (Johnson-Laird, 1991; Steedman, 1982). An important aspect of the application of the reductionist view to improvisation is that it relieves a potentially heavy burden on short-term memory. Instead of remembering each element in a musical sequence, only a reduced set of elements must be retained, from which improvisations can be generated. Johnson-Laird (1991) argues that, given an appropriate memory representation of musical structure, acceptable jazz improvisations can be generated by relatively simple computational processes, a constraint imposed by the demands of real-time processing. Thus, the relationships we have identified between the improvisational music performances, computational model, and reductionist theories of music cognition may result from similar representational requirements.

The view of musical memory that we propose is also closely related to Pressing's (1988) account of musical improvisation. In his view, the performer's mental representation for a musical sequence consists of event clusters: arrays of objects, features, and processes with associated cognitive strengths. Improvisation consists of the generation of novel sets of event clusters based on a set of improvisational goals applied to the schematic representation of a theme, given a memory of the event clusters previously generated (Pressing, 1988). Our connectionist network produced reduced memory descriptions for 'clusters' of events in which structurally important events dominated. Furthermore, the variations improvised by the performers in our experiment were related in terms of similar underlying representations of the musical theme, and events with greater cognitive strength occurred more often in the improvisations. The improvisation measures of relative importance correlated strongly with the theoretical predictions and network measures, suggesting that reductionist memory representations capture the cognitive strength of events in improvisations of musical variations.

6.2. Temporal Structure and Constituent Structure

The model of memory representation for music that we have proposed relies on constituent structure that is not computed by the network architecture but is available as input to it. Other connectionist researchers in music have assumed that knowledge about constituent structure should be extracted from a training set using general learning algorithms and then explicitly or implicitly dealt with by a network memory-coding mechanism (Mozer, 1992; Todd, 1991). Our assumption is based on the theory that the constituent structures most relevant to music cognition are closely related to rhythmic structure (Lerdahl & Jackendoff, 1983). In this section we briefly discuss the relationship between rhythmic structure and constituent structure in music, and its relationship to general issues of constituent structure in temporal sequence processing.

Typically, listeners are provided with many cues or markers to rhythmic structure in music. Musical signals contain complex forms of temporal organization, including periodic structure on multiple time scales (Cooper & Meyer, 1960; Jones & Boltz, 1989; Large & Kolen, 1994; Lerdahl & Jackendoff, 1983; Palmer & Krumhansl, 1990; Yeston, 1976) and temporal variation in expressive performance (Drake & Palmer, 1993; Palmer, 1989; Shaffer, Clarke, & Todd, 1985; Sloboda, 1983; Todd, 1985). The temporal information present in individual musical sequences affords the perception of rhythmic organization, including metrical and grouping structure. For example, mechanisms for the perception of metrical structure have been proposed that use only event inter-onset times and event accent information as input (Essens & Povel, 1985; Large & Kolen, 1994; Longuet-Higgins & Lee, 1982). Additionally, expressive timing variations in musical performance provide cues for the perception of metrical and grouping structure (Palmer, 1988; Sloboda, 1983; Todd, 1985). Thus, the perception of metrical and grouping structure may not have to rely heavily on factors such as learned knowledge of melodic regularities. The perception of these forms of rhythmic organization combine to form the basis for the time-span segmentation (Lerdahl & Jackendoff, 1983), the constituent structure that we have assumed as input to our model.

Our network made use of this input information to produce representations that captured two kinds of musical structure. First, the network represented the time-span segmentation of the musical sequences. It used the time-span segmentation to adapt its processing strategy at each level, compressing and reconstructing groups of either two or three elements, to serve as an efficient encoder of predetermined structure. This is an important result because connectionist models are notoriously deficient at representing constituent structures as rich as those found in music. Next, the reduced descriptions captured the theoretically predicted and empirically observed 'relative importance of musical events'. To accomplish this, the network used time-span segmentations to learn stylistic regularities that are systematically related to rhythmic structure. Such regularities, by definition, can only be captured by understanding a melody in relationship to knowledge of other melodies in that style.

Our assumption that constituent structure would be available as input to a memory process may be too strong. Previously learned patterns, such as cadences, can also influence listeners' perception of constituent structure (Lerdahl & Jackendoff, 1983). It seems likely that the perceptual processes responsible for segmenting a musical sequence into constituents and the representational processes responsible for encoding and/or recognizing constituents must interact. Reduced memory representations, such as those produced by RAAM networks, could mediate this interaction by facilitating the recognition of familiar patterns. The RAAM formalism provides a criterion by which we can measure the stability of any constituent's representation (the well-formedness test). In some cases, perceptual processes may simply provide the representational mechanism with groupings of events; in other cases, representational processes may effectively 'choose' groupings of events that yield stable or familiar representations. Thus, we envision mutually supporting roles for the perception of temporal organization and the formation of memory representations for melodies.

6.3. Comparison with Other Connectionist Models

Other connectionist researchers have explored issues of sequential structure in music with discrete-time recurrent network architectures (Bharucha & Todd, 1989; Mozer, 1991; Todd, 1991). Recurrent networks are often trained to predict the next event of a sequence, given a memory of past events in the same sequence (Mozer, 1993), rather than being explicitly trained to develop a representation for an entire sequence. Recurrent networks are appealing for a number of reasons. First, recurrent networks are simple; they process a sequence one event at a time and assume no complex control mechanism. Second, recurrent networks are capable in principle of capturing arbitrary sequential and/or temporal relationships, including metrical structure, grouping structure, and even time-span reduction. Third, recurrent neural networks provide natural models of musical expectations for future events (Bharucha & Todd, 1989). Finally recurrent networks can be used for musical composition. By connecting a network's output units to its input units, novel sequences are generated that reveal what has been learned about musical structure (Todd, 1991; Mozer 1991).

Recurrent networks have demonstrated some limitations in accomplishing these tasks, however. Recurrent networks have difficulty capturing relationships that span long temporal intervals, as well as relationships that involve high-order statistics (Mozer, 1993); thus they have had difficulty capturing the global structure of musical sequences (Todd, 1991; Mozer, 1991). In addition, at least one study suggests that the ability of discrete-time recurrent neural networks to learn simple temporal relationships, such as would be required to extract metrical structure, is also limited (McGraw, Montante & Chalmers, 1991). In attempts to make recurrent networks more sensitive to the global structure of music, augmented versions of recurrent architectures have been proposed. One proposal is to build recurrent networks with hidden units that have various different constants of temporal integration. This allows the network to retain memory of past events more efficiently and has resulted in networks with improved sensitivity to global structure (Mozer, 1992). Another proposal is to train hierarchically cascaded recurrent networks to extract and represent constituent structure explicitly (Todd, 1991). Neither of these proposals, however, (explicitly) uses temporal structure information to develop an emergent sensitivity to the relative importance of musical events, as our model does.

In principle, recurrent networks can represent any temporal relationships (e.g. metrical structure). In practice, however, discrete-time recurrent neural networks trained with back-propagation have not learned the temporal relationships that are most relevant for music. One reason may be because recurrent networks are not typically given material that offers much information for the recovery of temporal structure. Another reason may be that the architectures and learning algorithms employed are not biased toward discovering the temporal structures, such as metrical structure, to which humans are sensitive. For instance, the perception of rhythmic structure in music may be predicted primarily from duration and accent information present in individual musical sequences (Large & Kolen, 1994; Longuet-Higgins & Lee, 1982; Palmer & Krumhansl, 1990). If recurrent networks were biased toward making use of relevant information about temporal structure, as is our network architecture, then they may be more likely to capture temporally relevant relationships such as relative importance.

6.4. Limitations and Future Work

The approach that we have described here has some limitations that highlight the need for further work. One regards the choice of musical materials in this study. The use of musical materials as simple as nursery tunes leads to some difficulties in interpreting the network findings. For instance, it is not clear whether the network's representational capability at global structural levels was limited by the network architecture or by the choice of training materials. In addition, the use of material as multifaceted as music means the relationship between metrical accent and time-span reduction predictions of importance were not controlled; the restriction to a small set of musical materials makes it difficult to determine how the network learns relative importance measures independently of metrical structure or how one might model these structural relationships in more complex improvisational forms of music. Thus, it is difficult to say precisely what structural relationships our model is capable of learning. Further study might use training and test melodies that control for interactions among structural relationships (cf. Elman, 1990).

Another possibility for further work concerns the choice of neural network architecture. One of the constraints of the RAAM architecture is the requirement of an external stack control mechanism for handling intermediate results during encoding and decoding (Pollack, 1988, 1990). In addition, the model requires a fixed-structure input buffer to make use of relevant temporal information. Although this buffer design is sufficient for handling simple melodies, a more complex buffer design would probably be necessary for melodies in which metrical structure and grouping structure may be misaligned or 'out of phase' (Lerdahl & Jackendoff, 1983). Recurrent network architectures might be altered to exploit temporal information without necessarily entailing the restrictive design constraints of the RAAM architecture.

7. Conclusions

The phenomenon of musical variation can be explained by positing mechanisms that compute memory reductions. The reduced memory descriptions computed here for musical melodies resulted from encoding and decoding mechanisms that compressed and reconstructed the original sequences. These mechanisms led to reduced descriptions similar to those predicted by reductionist theories of music. This type of memory representation abstracts and summarizes sections of musical material, extracting what Dowling and Harwood (1986) refer to as the 'gist' of a musical sequence. The reduced representations are suitable for manipulation by other neural-style processing mechanisms and therefore may be useful for modeling musical tasks such as sequence extrapolation, structure recognition, and musical improvisation. A general learning algorithm (back-propagation) provided an example of how the knowledge relevant to computing reduced memory descriptions may be extracted from a learning environment, addressing an important challenge to reductionist theories. These findings support reductionist theories of music comprehension but suggest that the computation of musical reductions is not an end in itself; rather, it is a natural result of the construction of memory representations for musical sequences.

Most importantly, we have demonstrated the psychological plausibility of reductionist theories of music comprehension, by comparing evidence from improvisational music performance with a model of reduced memory representations and with theoretical predictions regarding the relative importance of musical events. The fact that musical events were weighted similarly in musicians' choices of events to retain in improvisations, network encodings of the same melodies, and theoretical predictions of relative importance suggests that recursive distributed representations capture relevant properties of humans' mental representations for musical melodies.

Acknowledgements

The research was partially supported by NIMH Grant 1R29-MH45764 to Caroline Palmer, and by ONR Grant N00014-92-J115 to Jordan B. Pollack. This article was completed while the second author was a fellow at the Center for Advanced Study in the Behavioral Sciences. We are grateful for financial support from NSF SES-9022192. We thank Fred Lerdahl for his comments on our stimulus materials and analyses and John Kolen, Gregory Saunders, and David Stucki for comments on an earlier draft. Reprint requests should be addressed to Edward W. Large, Department of Computer and Information Science, 3401 Walnut Street, Suite 301C, University of Pennsylvania, Philadelphia, PA 19104-6228, or to Caroline Palmer, Psychology Department, 1885 Neil Avenue, The Ohio State University, Columbus, OH 43210.

Notes

1. Beats themselves are often marked by the onset of acoustic events, but the sensation of beat can also occur when no event is physically present. When you tap your foot, or snap your fingers along with a piece of music, you are physically marking one particular level of beats from the metrical hierarchy called the tactus. According to Lerdahl and Jackendoff (1983), beats of the tactus level are always present in the perception of music. Beats marking smaller temporal levels are present only when acoustic events are present to mark them.
2. The branch leading to the first event of a cadence is not counted as a branch point because it is considered structurally to be 'part of' the final event (Lerdahl & Jackendoff, 1983). For example, to calculate importance for the first note of measure three, count 1 for the root, 1 for a branch point passed, 0 for a left turn (because this branch is tied), and 1 for a second left turn.
3. Knowing when to terminate decoding is equivalent to determining the level of the time-span segmentation to which a melodic event corresponds. In general, levels of constituent structure in the network's input will correspond to levels of time-span segmentation and metrical accent; however, the network must learn the level of constituent structure at which to end the decoding process.

References

Angeline, P.J. & Pollack, J.B. (1990) *Hierarchical RAAMs*. (Tech. Rep. 91-PA-HRAAMS). Laboratory for Artificial Intelligence Research, The Ohio State University, Columbus, OH.

Bharucha, J.J. & Todd, P.M. (1989) Modeling the perception of tonal structure with neural nets. *Computer Music Journal*, **13**, 44–53.

Chalmers, D. (1990) Syntactic transformations on distributed representations. *Connection Science*, **2**, 53–62.

Chrisman, L. (1991) Learning recursive distributed representations for holistic computation. *Connection Science*, **3**, 345–366.

Cooper, G. & Meyer, L.B. (1960) *The Rhythmic Structure of Music*. Chicago: University of Chicago Press.

Cottrell, G.W., Munro, P.W. & Zipser, D. (1987) Image compression by back propagation: A demonstration of extensional programming. In N.E. Sharkey (Ed.), *Advances in Cognitive Science* (Vol. 2, pp. 305–321). Chichester, England: Ellis Horwood.

Cottrell, G.W. & Tsung, F.S. (1991) Learning simple arithmetic procedures, In J.A. Barnden & J.B. Pollack (Eds.), *High Level Connectionist Models* (pp. 305–321). Norwood, NJ: Ablex Publishing.

Deutsch, D. & Feroe, F. (1981) Internal representation of pitch sequence in tonal music. *Psychological Review*, **88**, 503–522.

Dowling, W.J. & Harwood, D.L. (1986) *Music Cognition*. San Diego, CA: Academic Press.

Drake, C. & Palmer, C. (1993) Accent structures in music performance. *Music Perception*, **10**, 343–378.

Elman, J. (1990) Finding structure in time. *Cognitive Science*, **14**, 179–211.

Essens, P.J. & Povel, D. (1985) Metrical and nonmetrical representation of temporal patterns. *Perception and Psychophysics*, **37**, 1–7.

Estes, W.K. (1972) An associative basis for coding and organization in memory. In A.W. Melton & E. Martin (Eds.), *Coding Processes in Human Memory* (pp. 161–190). New York: Halsted.

Fodor, J.A. & Pylyshyn, Z.W. (1988) Connectionism and cognitive architecture: A critical analysis. *Cognition*, **28**, 3–71.

Garner, W.R. & Gottwald, R.L. (1968) The perception and learning of temporal patterns. *Quarterly Journal of Experimental Psychology*, **20**, 97–109.

Johnson-Laird, P.N. (1991) Jazz improvisation: A theory at the computational level. In P. Howell, R. West, & I. Cross (Eds.), *Representing Musical Structure* (pp. 35–71). London: Academic Press.

Jones, M.R. (1974) Cognitive representations of serial patterns. In B.H. Kantowitz (Ed.), *Human Information Processing* (pp. 201–233). New York: John Wiley & Sons.

Jones, M.R. (1981) Music as a stimulus for psychological motion: Part I: Some determinants of expectancies. *Psychomusicology*, **1**, 34–51.

Jones, M.R. & Boltz, M. (1989) Dynamic attending and responses to time. *Psychological Review*, **96**, 459–491.

Jones, M.R., Boltz, M. & Kidd, G. (1982) Controlled attending as a function of melodic and temporal context. *Journal of Experimental Psychology: Human Perception & Performance*, **7**, 211–218.

Jordan, M. (1986) *Serial Order*. (Tech. Rep. 8604). Institute for Cognitive Science, University of California at San Diego, La Jolla, CA.

Knopoff, L. & Hutchinson, W. (1978) An index of melodic activity. *Interface*, **7**, 205–229.

Krumhansl, C.L. (1979) The psychological representation of musical pitch in a tonal context. *Cognitive Psychology*, **11**, 346–384.

Krumhansl, C.L. (1990) *Cognitive Foundations of Musical Pitch*. New York: Oxford University Press.

Krumhansl, C.L., Bharucha, J.J. & Castellano, M.A. (1982) Key distance effects on perceived harmonic structure in music. *Perception & Psychophysics*, **32**, 96–108.

Large, E.W. & Kolen, J.F. (1994) Resonance and the perception of musical meter. *Connection Science*, **6**(1), 177–208.

Large, E.W., Palmer, C. & Pollack, J.B. (1991) A connectionist model of intermediate representations for musical structure. In *Proceedings of the Thirteenth Annual Conference of the Cognitive Science Society* (pp. 412–417). Hillsdale, NJ: Erlbaum.

Lerdahl, E. & Jackendoff, R. (1983) *A Generative Theory of Tonal Music*. Cambridge, MA: MIT Press.

Longuet-Higgins, H.C. & Lee, C.S. (1982) The perception of musical rhythms. *Perception*, **11**, 115–128.

McGraw, G., Montante, R. & Chalmers, D. (1991) *Rap-master Network: Exploring Temporal Pattern Recognition with Recurrent Networks*. (Tech. Rep. No. 336). Computer Science Department, Indiana University.

Miller, G.A. (1956) The magical number seven, plus or minus two: Some limits on our capacity for processing information. *Psychological Review*, **63**, 81–97.

Mozer, M.C. (1991) Connectionist music composition based on melodic, stylistic and psychophysical constraints. In P.M. Todd & D.G. Loy (Eds.), *Music and Connectionism* (pp. 195–211). Cambridge, MA: MIT Press.

Mozer, M.C. (1992) Induction of multiscale temporal structure. In R.P. Lippmann, J. Moody & D.S. Touretsky (Eds.), *Advances in Neural Information Processing Systems 4* (pp. 275–282). San Mateo, CA: Morgan Kaufman.

Mozer, M.C. (1993) Neural net architectures for temporal sequence processing. In A. Weigend & N. Gershenfeld (Eds.), *Predicting the Future and Understanding the Past* (pp. 243–264). Reading, MA: Addison-Wesley.

Palmer, C. (1988) Timing in skilled music performance. Unpublished doctoral dissertation, Cornell University, Ithaca, NY.

Palmer, C. (1989) Mapping musical thought to musical performance. *Journal of Experimental Psychology: Human Perception & Performance*, **15**, 331–346.

Palmer, C. & Krumhansl, C.L. (1987a) Pitch and temporal contributions to musical phrase perception: Effects of harmony, performance timing, and familiarity. *Perception and Psychophysics*, **41**, 505–518.

Palmer, C. & Krumhansl, C.L. (1987b) Independent temporal and pitch structures in determination of musical phrases. *Journal of Experimental Psychology: Human Perception & Performance*, **13**, 116–126.

Palmer, C. & Krumhansl, C.L. (1990) Mental representations of musical meter. *Journal of Experimental Psychology: Human Perception & Performance*, **16**, 728–741.

Pollack, J.B. (1988) Recursive auto-associative memory: Devising compositional distributed representations. In *Proceedings of the Tenth Annual Conference of the Cognitive Science Society* (pp. 33–39). Hillsdale, NJ: Erlbaum.

Pollack, J.B. (1990) Recursive distributed representations. *Artificial Intelligence*, **46**, 77–105.

Pressing, J. (1988) Improvisation: Methods and models. In J. Sloboda (Ed.), *Generative Processes in Music: The Psychology of Performance, Improvisation, and Composition* (pp. 129–178). New York: Oxford University Press.

Restle, F. (1970) Theory of serial pattern learning: Structural trees. *Psychological Review*, **77**, 481–495.

Rumelhart, D.E., Hinton, G.E. & Williams, R.J. (1986) Learning internal representations by error propagation. In D.E. Rumelhart & J.L. McClelland (Eds.), *Parallel Distributed Processing* (pp. 318–362). Cambridge, MA: MIT Press.

Schenker, H. (1979) *Free Composition* (E. Oster, Trans.). New York: Longman.

Serafine, M.L., Glassman, N. & Overbeeke, C. (1989) The cognitive reality of hierarchic structure in music. *Music Perception*, **6**, 347–430.

Shaffer, L.H., Clarke, E. & Todd, N.P.M. (1985) Metre and rhythm in piano playing. *Cognition*, **20**, 61–77.

Simon, H.A. & Kotovsky, K. (1963) Human acquisition of concepts for sequential patterns. *Psychological Review*, **79**, 369–382.

Simon, H.A. & Sumner, K. (1968) Pattern in music. In B. Kleinmuntz (Ed.), *Formal Representation of Human Thought* (pp. 219–250). New York: Wiley.

Sloboda, J.A. (1983) The communication of musical metre in piano performance. *Quarterly Journal of Experimental Psychology*, **35**, 377–396.

Sloboda, J.A. (1985) *The Musical Mind*. Oxford: Oxford University Press.

Sperdutti, D. (1993) Representing symbolic data structures using neural networks. Unpublished doctoral dissertation, University of Pisa, Italy.

Steedman, M. (1982) A generative grammar for jazz chord sequences. *Music Perception*, **2**, 52–77.

Todd, N.P. (1985) A model of expressive timing in tonal music. *Music Perception*, **3**, 33–59.

Todd, P.M. (1991) A connectionist approach to algorithmic composition. In P.M. Todd & D.G. Loy (Eds.), *Music and Connectionism* (pp. 173–194). Cambridge, MA: MIT Press.

Vitz, P.C. & Todd, T.C. (1969) A coded element model of the perceptual processing of sequential stimuli. *Psychological Review*, **76**, 433–449.

Yeston, M. (1976) *The Stratification of Musical Rhythm*. New Haven, CT: Yale University Press.

Appendix: Network Training Set

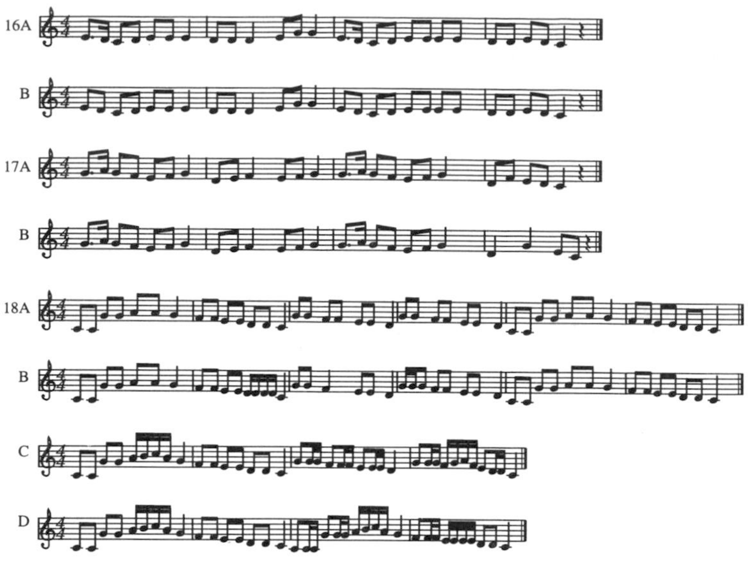
16A
B
17A
B
18A
B
C
D

Frankensteinian Methods for Evolutionary Music Composition

PETER M. TODD & GREGORY M. WERNER

Victor Frankenstein sought to create an intelligent being imbued with the rules of civilized human conduct, who could further learn how to behave and possibly even evolve through successive generations into a more perfect form. Modern human composers similarly strive to create intelligent algorithmic music composition systems that can follow prespecified rules, learn appropriate patterns from a collection of melodies, or evolve to produce output more perfectly matched to some aesthetic criteria. Here we review recent efforts aimed at each of these three types of algorithmic composition. We focus particularly on evolutionary methods and indicate how monstrous many of the results have been. We present a new method that uses coevolution to create linked artificial music critics and music composers and describe how this method can attach the separate parts of rules, learning, and evolution together into one coherent body.

KEYWORDS: Algorithmic composition, evolutionary algorithms, coevolution, learning, musical rules.

> Invention, it must be humbly admitted, does not consist in creating out of void, but out of chaos; the materials must, in the first place, be afforded. —Mary Shelley, *Frankenstein*, 1831/1993

1. Introduction: Following in Frankenstein's Footsteps

Musical composition, it must be humbly admitted, does not consist in creating out of void, but out of the accumulated individual experiences, cultural contexts, and inherited predilections swirling about within the composer. When, in the most natural instance, that composer is a member of our own species, it is easy to apprehend how these various chaotic materials will be afforded and gathered in the service of invention. But when, with Frankensteinian hubris, we dare to create an artificial system and imbue it with the spark of musical invention in our stead, how are we to assemble its constituent parts to ensure that its behavior will be on the whole pleasing and majestic, rather than filling us with aesthetic horror that "no mortal could support" (Shelley, 1818/1993, p. 87)?

In this chapter, we review a variety of approaches to the central problem of creating artificial composition systems: how to build into them the musical

This paper was written for this volume and appears here for the first time.

knowledge necessary for new compositions. Human composers, as mentioned above, come pre-equipped with an evolved auditory perception system that influences our aesthetics (e.g. Rasch & Plomp, 1982); we learn a set of examples and expectations through immersion in our aural culture as we grow (e.g. Bharucha & Todd, 1989); and in many cases we receive further formal training in the rules of composition of particular musical genres. Over the past few hundred years (and in some cases earlier—see Loy, 1991), several techniques of musical knowledge induction from these three broad categories have been explored. But increasingly within the last decade, with the spread of new computer methods of simulating learning (e.g. Rumelhart & McClelland, 1986) and evolution (Holland, 1975; Goldberg, 1989; Mitchell, 1996), novel forms of introducing musical knowledge into algorithmic composers are being developed. Many of these new creations still provide occasions for horror, as we will see; but within these techniques, or their combination, the seed of successful algorithmic composition may lie, and it is on these approaches that we concentrate here.

We conduct our rapid survey of techniques for constructing algorithmic composition systems in the order in which they were first introduced: formal rules, example learning, and evolutionary descent with modification. (Note though that this is the reverse of the order in which the corresponding natural sources of musical knowledge make their appearance during a human composer's lifetime.) In Section 2, we briefly describe the rule-based approach to encoding musical knowledge and the methods used to learn musical knowledge from collections of precomposed examples. Our coverage is limited to a mere flavor of these approaches, because much has been written about them elsewhere (e.g. Loy, 1989, 1991; Todd & Loy, 1991; see also the papers in this volume). Our main focus begins in Section 3, where we explore the newer and lesser-known ways that algorithmic composition systems can be evolved through successive generations of modification and reproduction. In evolutionary systems, it is necessary to determine which individuals are more 'fit'—that is, are better composers—and so should have more offspring. This 'fitness evaluation' is performed by a critic of some sort, and so the problem of musical knowledge induction is partly shifted to addressing how to build such knowledge into an aesthetically savvy critic. As we show, this new problem can be addressed in the same ways as the original composer's-knowledge problem: The critic can be human, or rule based, or learning based, or even evolved itself.

We take the opportunity in Section 4 to introduce a new method for developing artificial composition systems based on the last technique just mentioned: evolving both the composer and the critic simultaneously. This coevolutionary method has been applied with success in other problem-solving domains (Hillis, 1992), as well as being the wellspring of much of the natural complexity we see in the world around us (Futuyama & Slatkin, 1983; Ridley, 1993). We conclude by indicating how the three knowledge sources, rules, learning, and evolution, can be combined to create the next generation of algorithmic composition systems.

Throughout our discussion, we must repeatedly confront an issue of central importance in the construction of any behaving system: the structure/novelty tradeoff. When we start filling the void with the chaotic materials necessary for invention, the more such materials we introduce—the more structure and knowledge we add to the system—the more structure will be present in the system's output behavior. That is, more highly structured systems can produce more highly constrained output. In algorithmic composition systems, this means that more knowledge and structure allows the creation of new pieces that are more tightly matched to the desired musical genre. The flipside of more structure, though, is less novelty: The highly constrained output will be less likely to stray beyond a genre's bounds or be surprising. Thus, the highly structured composition system will be less general, able to reach less of 'music space' with its output.

Viewing this tradeoff from the other end of the amount-of-structure spectrum, we see that building less knowledge into a system means that it will be less constrained in what it produces. This in turn will increase the chance that the system will produce intriguingly unexpected output. On the other hand, this broader search through 'music space' is also more likely to produce less structured, musically uninteresting creations. Thus the tradeoff: More structure and knowledge built into the system means more reasonably structured musical output, but also more pre-dictable, unsurprising output; less structure and knowledge in the system means more novel, unexpected output, but also more unstructured musical chaff. Different approaches to algorithmic composition end up at different points on this tradeoff, as we will see. (The costs of introducing more structure into the system should also be taken into account in deciding how to make this tradeoff.)

2. "My workshop of filthy creation": Designing and Training Composition Systems

The best music composition system we know of is the mind of an artistic human. And the best way to train this kind of system to produce workable, if not beautiful, compositions is to expose it to a wide range of examples of good (and bad) music, and to teach it some particular rules to follow in extending that body of music. But suppose, like Frankenstein, we wanted to enter the "workshop of filthy creation" (Shelley, 1818/1993, p. 81) and replace the human composer with an artificial composition system—whether out of a wish to ease a composer's workload, or intellectual interest in understanding the composition process, or desire to explore unknown musical styles, or mere curiosity in the possibility. How could we proceed? As in building human composers, the standard methods of building artificial composers are using rules and examples, though usually not in combination.

The creation of a new intelligent living being, at least in the early 1800s, involved discovering and following the rules by which life operates. Probably the most intuitive means of creating an artificial composition system, particularly one to be implemented on a computer, is to come up with a set of compositional rules for the computer to follow. The rules in a musical algorithm can be very simple, as for example in the 'musical dice games' developed by Mozart and others where pre-composed phrases were merely combined in new random orders (Loy, 1991). They can also embody complex knowledge about specific musical styles, as in Ebcioglu's (1984) involved collection of rules for chorale harmonization. (In the visual arts, Harold Cohen's 'Aaron' system uses many years' worth of accumulated rule-based knowledge to produce drawings and paintings with readily interpretable content—see McCorduck, 1990.) Because the computer is constrained to follow the rules it is given, its compositions will (generally) be well formed according to those rules, and thus will attain at least some minimal level of musicality. (Indeed, Mozart's dice compositions cannot help but sound reasonable.) Thus rule-based composition systems come down squarely on one end of the structure/novelty tradeoff: incor-porating musical knowledge into the system in this way leads to properly structured artificial compositions.

On the other hand, we pay the price for this rule-following lawfulness: Compositions from rule-based systems are unlikely to be surprising, and almost certainly not genre breaking. One could hardly be shocked by the combinations produced by Mozart's dice music. Perhaps more discouragingly, coming up with the rules to put into the algorithm in the first place is no simple matter. For centuries, scholars have tried to specify fully the rules involved in particular musical styles, such as counterpoint; but whenever a set of rules is nailed down, exceptions and extensions are always discovered that necessitate more rules (Loy, 1991). This is the other price of a highly structured composition system—the cost of creating the *right* structure. Indeed, many artists question whether creativity can be captured by a set of rules at all. If not, where can we turn in our quest for an ersatz composer?

Frankenstein's monster emerged into the world with rather little going for him, behaviorally speaking. From a stumbling, inarticulate beginning, his eventual eloquence was obtained through long and patient learning, listening to examples of human speech over and over again: "I cannot describe the delight I felt when I learned the ideas appropriated to each of these sounds, and was able to pronounce them" (Shelley, 1818/1993, p. 155). Such repetitive training provides another approach to the construction of artificial composition systems: systems that can *learn* how to create a new piece of music. Rather than requiring the development of a set of musical rules, a learning composition system can simply be trained on a set of musical examples. These examples are chosen to represent the kind of music that the user would like the composition system to create new instances of (or at least mimic old instances of): For a waltz-composing system, train it on a corpus of waltzes; for a Bach/Hendrix amalgamator, train it on melodies from both composers. Thus, the big advantage of a learning composition system over a rule-based one is that, as the saying goes, users do not have to know much about music—they only have to know what they like. In this way, humans are removed a bit further from the composition process: they no longer have to be rule creators, rather now only example collectors.

Early instances of the learning approach to algorithmic composition analyzed a collected set of musical examples in terms of their overall pitch-transition probabilities (Loy, 1991; Jones, 1981). Based on how often particular pitches followed each other in the examples, new compositions could be constructed with similar statistical structure. Such Markov-process music sounds good over the short term, reflecting the note-by-note structure in the original input. Novelty is also introduced through the probabilistic nature of the composition process. This seems like the ideal point on the structure/novelty tradeoff, but the difficulty here arises when we listen to this music over the long term: There is no structure beyond the moment, and the novelty of randomness often accumulates and leads compositions to wander aimlessly.

The development of new neural network learning algorithms (Rumelhart & McClelland, 1986) led to the possibility of connectionist music composition systems (Todd, 1988, 1989; Todd & Loy, 1991; see also the papers in this volume). Feedforward and recurrent neural networks can be trained to produce successive notes or measures of melodies in a training set, given earlier notes or measures as input. Once they have learned to reproduce the training melodies, these networks can be induced to compose new melodies based on the patterns they have picked up. Neural networks can be made to learn more abstract and long-term patterns than typical Markov-process systems, allowing them to incorporate a greater amount of musical structure from the example set. In addition, networks can have further structure built into them, including psychologically motivated constraints on pitch and time representation (e.g. Mozer, 1991, 1994), that help their output to be more musically appropriate.

And yet, despite the increasingly sophisticated neural network machinery being thrown at the problem of composition, the results to date have still been rather disappointing. As Mozer commented about his own CONCERT system, the outputs are often "compositions that only their mother could love" (Mozer, 1994, p. 274). Much of the problem is that these networks are still learning and reproducing largely surface-level features of the example musical input; while neural networks should in principle be able to pick up and utilize deeper temporal structure, "experiments ... show no cause for optimism in practice" (Mozer, 1994, p. 274). In addition, by merely manipulating surface-level musical aspects of the training set, networks can come up with *new* compositions, but they will not be particularly *novel* in an interesting way. True novelty should involve manipulations of multiple levels of structure. If a learning approach to algorithmic composition is not so amenable to producing such novelty, where then can we turn for inspiration? When we consider the source and generator of the great variety of complex novelty and innovation in the natural world around us, one approach sings out seductively: evolution through modification and descent.

3. "A new species": Evolving Composition Systems

Viktor Frankenstein hoped for much more than the creation of a single superior living being—he intended his creatures to beget a whole new race that would grow in number and in goodness, generation after generation: "A new species would bless me as its creator and source; many happy and excellent natures would owe their being to me" (Shelley, 1818/1993, p. 80). Later he worried that this process might not go exactly as he planned, with the children becoming more monstrous than the parents, a realization that led him to abandon his efforts at creating a female progenitor. Though he labored several decades before the appearance of Darwin's theory of evolution (Darwin, 1859), Frankenstein's (and Shelley's) intuitive understanding of descent with modification led him to the correct conclusion that this ongoing creative process, once it was out of his hands, could as easily lead to new horrors as to hoped-for beauty.

A new generation of algorithmic composition researchers is discovering this same truth. By using simulated evolution techniques to create new composition systems, it is easy to obtain novelty—often complex novelty—but it is correspondingly difficult to rein in the direction that novelty takes. As we will see in the systems in this section, the results of this still-young approach are frequently more frightening than pleasing. This is a consequence of the structure/novelty tradeoff once again, with the balance this time shifting towards innovation. The challenge faced by the designers of evolutionary composition systems is how to bring more structure and knowledge into, while trying to take people out of, the compositional loop.

This loop is, in an evolutionary system, a rather simple one on the face of it: *generate, test, repeat*. Basically, we make a bunch of things, we test them according to some criteria and keep the ones that are better according to those criteria, and then we repeat the process by generating a new bunch of things based on the old ones. This loop continues for possibly many generations until the things we are making are good enough according to the criteria being used. The complication comes when we have to specify what we mean by 'generate' and 'test'. In natural evolution, what is being generated are individual organisms, through a process of genetic modification (usually either sexual recombination or asexual 'cloning', both with some possible mutation), and the criteria of success are the forces of natural and sexual selection (i.e. ability to survive and reproduce). (Furthermore, in natural evolution, there is no 'stopping point' when some criteria have been met—the test keeps changing as a consequence of ongoing evolution of other species as well.) What and how should we generate and test when dealing with music composition systems?

There are a few possibilities to consider. First, we can generate two different kinds of things: either the musical compositions directly, or a music composition system itself. In the former case, the whole evolutionary system is the algorithmic composition system; in the latter case, the evolutionary process *creates* composition systems, which are then used. (We will speak of direct musical representations and indirect composition generators in the following sections.) Second, the testing can be done in a few different ways. In some sense, the test criteria incorporate the majority of the musical knowledge in an evolutionary composition system, filtering out the bad generated creations and only allowing the musically good ones to make it into the next generation. Thus we need a rather smart tester or music critic in our evolutionary loop. Just as we discussed in Section 2 for composers, there are several ways to implement smart critics: Again we can use humans directly, or rule-based critics, or learning critics, or even evolving critics. We will investigate each of these possibilities in turn.

All of these evolutionary approaches do, however, share many features in common. They are all based on the general framework provided by Holland's original genetic algorithm, or GA (Holland, 1975; see also Goldberg, 1989, and Mitchell, 1996, for general introductions), either directly, or indirectly via the genetic programming paradigm of Koza (in which chunks of code are evolved—see Koza, 1993.) In nearly every case, new populations of potential solutions to some problem (here, the problem of music composition) are created, generation after generation, through three main processes. First, to make sure that better solutions to the problem will increase over time, more copies of good solutions than of bad solutions from one generation are put into the next generation (this is fitness-proportionate reproduction, because the fitter solutions get proportionally more offspring). Second, to introduce new solutions into the population, a low level of mutation operates on all acts of reproduction, so that some offspring will have randomly changed characteristics. Third, to combine good components between solutions, sexual crossover is often employed, in which the 'genes' of two parents are mixed to form offspring with aspects of both.

With these three processes in effect, the evolutionary loop can efficiently explore many points in the solution space in parallel, and good solutions can often be found quite quickly. In creative processes such as music composition, however, the goal is rarely to find a single good solution and stop; rather, an ongoing process of innovation and refinement is usually more appropriate. This is also something that evolution, and artificial evolutionary systems, often excel at (see e.g. Nitecki, 1990, regarding innovations in nature; and Sims, 1994, and Ray, 1991, for models of surprisingly elaborate evolved artificial organisms). In addition, an iterative process of generation and selection, akin to that of evolution by natural selection, has been suggested as a model of human creativity itself (Campbell, 1960; Perkins, 1994). As Dawkins (1986, p. 66) puts it, "Cumulative selection, whether artificial selection as in [a] computer model or natural selection out there in the real world, is an efficient searching procedure, and its consequences look very like creative intelligence." These factors all suggest a fruitful role for the use of evolutionary models in creating algorithmic music.

On the other hand, evolution is not often described as being fast (though it can be in some cases—see e.g. Weiner, 1994), and patience is commonly called for in artificial evolutionary systems as well. It can take many generations of potential candidates, each of which must be evaluated in a time-consuming fashion (for instance, in the cases of interest to us, by listening to the music each candidate composition system produces—what Biles, 1994, and others identify as the "fitness bottleneck"), before something interesting comes along. The main reason for this sometimes-glacial pace is that, as described above, evolution builds systems through the gradual accrual of beneficial bits and pieces, rather than through systematic design or rapid learning from the environment. Operating without foresight, evolution cannot tell if some modification added on now will prove useful or lethal when combined with other bits added on later—the best that can be done is to make changes the each contribute a small amount to the system's performance (or at least do not hurt at present).

As a further consequence of this piecemeal tinkering approach (what Wimsatt, in press, terms "evolution as a backwoods mechanic"), the designs that evolution ultimately comes up with are not intended to be clean, or simple, or easy to understand—they are just whatever worked in the particular situations encountered. The implication for artificially evolved music composition systems is that, even once they do work to a certain extent, they will likely be unfathomable in their workings. However, this need not be a problem, if a user is content just to run the composition system without understanding it (or being able to modify it readily). So far, for most of the systems described below, this has been the pragmatic approach that the programmers and users have adopted. (See Burton & Vladimirova, 1997b, for a related review of evolutionary composition systems.)

3.1. Humans as Critics

Part of the reason that evolution in nature is often slow is that the forces of selection can be very noisy and temporarily ineffectual. Weak, sickly, or just plain ugly individual organisms may still succeed in finding mates, having offspring, and passing on their sub-par genes, while organisms with a new advantageous trait may not manage to live long enough to find a mate and influence the next generation. Goldschmidt (1940) called the more extreme examples of these lonely gifted mutants—those with radically new features—"hopeful monsters". But their hope would often be in vain: The improvements they bore could appear and be lost to the process of evolution time and time again. (While it is questionable whether "hopeful monsters" really appear in nature—that is, whether or not radical macromutations can ever be beneficial, as Dawkins, 1986, chapter 9, discusses—it is possible for them to crop up in some of the artificial systems we are concerned with here because of high-level genetic representations and operators.)

One way to speed up evolution is thus to implement a more ruthless, strict, and observant selective pressure on a population. This is the principle behind artificial selection, in which humans play the major selective role, only letting those organisms (be they pet animal breeds or garden flower varieties) that meet certain phenotypic criteria produce offspring for the next generation. With such careful supervision, large changes in traits can be achieved in a few generations. Darwin, for instance, discussed how breeders have effected the more or less rapid accumulation of human-desired traits in pigeons, dogs, and cabbages, noting that such artificially selected domestic races "often have a somewhat monstrous character" (1859/1964, p. 16). This is due in part to the breeders' ability to rescue the interesting new 'hopeful monsters' (even those only slightly monstrous) from a childless fate and ensure that their desired traits are kept in the gene pool of successive generations.

This teratogenic power has been harnessed more recently by artists working with computer-based artificial selection systems to generate visual images (Sims, 1991) or objects (S. Todd & Latham, 1992; see also Dawkins, 1986, for a powerful demonstration of the effects of accumulation of small changes across generations). These systems typically operate by presenting the user with a collection of images (initially random), shown next to each other simultaneously on-screen, from which to choose the parent or parents of the next generation of images. The new generation is created by some set of genetic operators, the corresponding new images are computed, and then these images are again displayed for further choice. With only a few such generations of viewing and selection, users can follow promising visual avenues to create quite striking final images.

At about the same time, a few researchers began experimenting with the power of evolutionary methods to create interesting musical structures as well. Putnam (1994) and Takala and colleagues (Takala *et al.*, 1993) explored the use of genetic algorithms to produce individual sounds or waveforms directly. Putnam evolved simple C program subroutines that would output waveform files that were then played for a human listener acting as critic. The listener's rating of the sound was used as the fitness for that particular routine, and new routines were bred according to the methods of genetic programming (Koza, 1993). However, the results were less than successful: ". . . many of the noises produced in the early generations are very irregular, noisy, and sometimes change loudness quite suddenly. In short, they are unpleasant and irritating and the process of listening to the noises and rating them is slow" (Putnam, 1994, p. 4)—a reappearance of the fitness bottleneck mentioned earlier, here exacerbated by the painful nature of the sounds to be evaluated.

By incorporating more musical structure into the evolved entities, constraining them to be sequences of pitched notes rather than lower-level soundfiles, less un-pleasant results could be obtained. (But again the structure/novelty tradeoff takes its toll: Atonal or purely timbral compositions cannot be made with this type of representation.) Moore (1994) developed a very simple genetic algorithm system, called GAMusic, for listeners to evolve 'melodies' of 32 notes or less, each in a 16-pitch range. Because the representation of melodies in this system is a direct binary encoding of the sequence of pitches, the search space of possible melodies covered in enormous (approximately $3.4 * 10^{38}$ different sequences). But this vastness also undermines the compositional usefulness of this system, if there is nothing to guide the search in productive or desirable directions.

Ralley (1995) addressed this problem of unguided search by building a GA system to create variations on a particular starting melody, so that the possible melodies of interest would be greatly reduced. He seeded the initial population of 100 melodies in his system with variants on a user-supplied melody and then let the user evaluate a small sample of representative melodies automatically chosen by cluster analysis at each generation. In this way, he hoped to avoid the fitness bottleneck of evaluating all 100 melodies in the population. In a limited setting, with sequences of 12 notes each selected from only one octave of pitches (for a total of $8.9 * 10^{12}$ possible sequences), Ralley found that the system "was able to produce a large number of interesting melodic variations of initial material", though with a "propensity toward homogeneity". The crossover and mutation operations of the GA he employed were thus sufficient to produce reasonable new melodic fragments from the old ones with which the population started.

But when Ralley explored users' ability to evolve short sequences in a particular direction—with a particular goal in mind—he found that people were rather poor at this task. The main problem seems to be the difficulty of comparing similarity between melodies, something that is necessary when one wants to base fitness on how close a given melody is to some desired goal. Without being able to tell how quickly, or even if, this genetic algorithm *will* reach some goal, we cannot be sure how good a job at searching the musical space this technique actually does. On the other hand, natural evolution is not teleological, not aimed at some specific goal (see e.g. Dawkins, 1986), so it is reasonable not to expect our evolutionary composition systems to be goal-oriented, either. The real test for such systems should be whether or not they help composers get *somewhere* interesting.

The difference here is between knowing what you like, on the one hand, using this knowledge to guide a meandering evolutionary process in an interesting direction, and knowing what you want, on the other hand, and trying to cajole the evolving system in that particular direction. This difference is akin to the distinction between simple reinforcement learning in neural networks—providing feedback as to whether something is good or bad—and error-correction learning, in which a teacher must provide the desired goal for the learner's behavior (see Rumelhart & McClelland, 1986). The latter can yield faster learning—that is, it can result in knowledge being built into the learner more quickly—but it requires considerably more specific knowledge in the first place on the part of the teacher. This is also the case in the music evolution systems: The user with a unique goal in mind has more specific knowledge than the user with just a set of preferences. In addition, this form of learning demands the ability to compute the difference between the current and the desired behavior, which is what Ralley found caused his users difficulty.

This knowledge—musical preferences or goals—that users have is exactly the structure that trades off with novelty in composition systems. The systems described so far have mostly had too little structure already built in to make them serious compositional aids, even though they can produce rather novel output. Thywissen (1996) has developed a compositional system called GeNotator that introduces more structure into the evolutionary process by applying genetic algorithms to several aspects of a composition, at different levels of abstraction. First, a phrase-evolver can modify independently the pitch, rhythm, dynamics, and harmony of a musical sequence (all using direct representations of the note or chord characteristics). Second, a system-evolver can evolve the set of musical operators (e.g. transposition, inversion) that are hierarchically applied to the phrases to produce a complete musical work. In addition, users can define rules or grammars that will prune the phrases or system/phrase combinations before they are presented for fitness evaluation, thereby decreasing the aural workload.

Biles (1994) uses several techniques to build more musical structure into his GenJam system for evolving jazz solos. Like Thywissen (1996), he employs a hierarchically structural musical form, in which both measures of 32 eighth-notes and phrases of four of these measures evolve in two linked populations simultaneously. In fact, the populations themselves are another important hierarchical level, because GenJam's goal is not to evolve a single best measure or phrase, but rather a set of such musical elements that can be drawn upon to create pleasing solo sequences. Beyond this hierarchical structure, Biles provides a rich context in which these musical elements evolve. Measures and phrases are put together into solos that are played with a jazz accompaniment of piano, bass, and drum tracks all following a particular chord progression. Measures are represented as notes abstracted from any particular scale; the actual pitches that are played in a solo are determined by mapping those measure notes onto a particular scale determined by the current chord in the ongoing progression. Thus, as Biles says, a particular measure or phrase can "fit different harmonic contexts and will not play a 'wrong' note" (p. 134)—though clearly some note choices will be better than others. The user listens to solos and reinforces those choices that are better or worse by entering 'g' (good) or 'b' (bad) keystrokes in real time as the measures are played. This reinforcement is acquired and summed up for both the measures and phrases simultaneously and used to breed a new population of each structure. During the breeding phrase as well, Biles introduces more musical structure: He uses 'musically meaningful mutation' operators such as reverse, invert, transpose, and sort notes, rather than the usual blind random-replacement mutation of standard genetic algorithms.

The inclusion of all this musical structure pays off: The results are typically quite pleasing to listen to (see—or rather hear—Biles, 1995a). As Biles himself puts it, "After sufficient training, GenJam's playing can be characterized as competent with some nice moments" (1994, p. 136). Sufficient training seems to be about 10 generations, though the first few "are quite numbing for the mentor." But Biles acknowledges that all this extra musical structure has its downside as well, on the structure/novelty see-saw: "A clever representation that efficiently represents alternative solutions, perhaps by excluding clearly unacceptable solutions, will lead to a more efficient search. However, if a representation 'cleverly' excludes the best solution, its efficiency is irrelevant.... GA designers walk a thin line between too large a search space on one side and inadequately sampled solutions on the other" (1994, p. 132).

Between the large search space of possible musical items and the (hopefully not too inadequately sampled) set of considered items lies the dreaded fitness bottleneck. With human critics manning this bottleneck, there are two main ways of trying to keep it from getting clogged: First, just present the human critics with a small set of reasonable musical items to judge. This can be attempted by using a high-structure composition system to generate the items—the approach taken by Thywissen (1996) and Biles (1994). Or second, use a *lot* of human judges, so that each one does not face a mind-numbing listening session alone. Biles (1995b) combined these two approaches in GenJam Populi, where multiple listeners could give feedback to GenJam's evolving solos. He initially tried sequential, independent feedback, in which different critics could listen to one evolving GenJam population at different times and affect its behavior. Putnam (1994) ran a similar experiment with his system on the World Wide Web, presenting each individual critic with only a few melodies to rate so that they would not become "tired and bored". This form of multiple-critic feedback distributes (and can speed up) the evaluation of many different musical items in a large population. However, each different critic might be judging the items on different criteria, so that the evolving population is pulled in many directions at once. This may slow down the system's ability to get anywhere interesting in the search space.

Alternatively, one can use several critics simultaneously listening to and evaluating the *same* population members, and then combine the critics' ratings into a single final score for each item. This method helps to overcome the possibly noisy evaluations that one individual critic or a set of different sequential critics might make. Such better feedback should mean that the fitness function is more accurate, and therefore that fewer generations of musical items will need to be run before interesting outcomes are created—another way to overcome the bottleneck. Biles (1994) has also run multiple-critic GenJam sessions of this form, where audience members listening to GenJam's solos can hold up cards for positive or negative real-time ratings. But in practice this technique did not result in improved evolutionary performance, as Biles (personal communication) reports: "The single-mentor training sessions are typically better from a musical viewpoint (the resulting soloists tend to play better solos). . . . [T]he quality of most multi-mentor soloists is inferior mainly because there is even more noise in accumulating fitness values for the individuals, which comes from both the timing and the quality of the mentors' feedback" (the audience feedback on individual measures is usually delayed and not unanimous, in comparison to that from single critics).

But with both types of multiple-critic systems, the human bottleneck still remains: People still have to listen to and judge the musical items in a time-consuming manner. And amassing multiple simultaneous critics in particular is difficult to do. As Spector and Alpern (1994) put it, "According to some theories of art this is the best, or even the only, form of assessment by which to judge the quality of a work. . . . [But] the science of artist construction will proceed quite slowly if each iteration of each system can be assessed only by organizing a public show and by waiting for critical reviews" (p. 3). Instead, it would be faster to eliminate the human critic altogether. To do this, we can first try building an automated rule-based critic, as Spector and Alpern and others have done.

3.2. Rule-based Critics

Traditionally, computational evolutionary systems were designed with readily computable fitness functions in mind. This has meant that genetic algorithms (see Goldberg, 1989) and genetic programming methods (see Koza, 1993) have generally employed simple rules or more complex rule-based algorithms to compute the fitness of each member of the evolving population of problem solutions. It is not surprising, then, that the earliest applications of computational evolutionary methods to music also used rule-based fitness functions or critics.

In what was probably the first musical genetic algorithm, Horner and Goldberg (1991a, 1991b) used the GA to search for thematic bridges: sequences of simple operations that would transform an initial note-set into a final desired note-set within a certain number of steps. Operations included note insertion, deletion, and rotation; each member of the evolving population was a sequence of these operations. To evaluate the fitness of any such individual, first the operation sequence was applied to the beginning note-set to generate a transformed outcome note-set. The fitness function them combined the judgments of two scoring rules: The individual received higher marks the closer the outcome note set was to the desired note set, and the closer the actual number of transformation steps was to the desired duration.

Both the nature of the evolving individuals—sequences of operations that can be chopped up and mixed back together—and the specific goal of the fitness function made this musical application well suited for evolutionary search. As a consequence, the results were "musically pleasing to the authors with the usual qualifications regarding personal taste" (1991b, p. 5). But given the highly structured inputs, genetic operations, and goals, this compositional-aide system could show little unexpected novelty in its output.

Horner and colleagues have developed other musical applications of genetic algorithms with rule-based fitness functions that also put the evolutionary search process to good use. These include a system that harmonizes progressions by searching for chord sequences that meet a prespecified set of rules (Horner & Ayers, 1995; see also McIntyre, 1994, for a similar approach that uses a clever three-tiered fitness evaluation scheme to ensure that the population converges on well-formed harmonies before it proceeds to evolving harmonies that are fine-tuned for good motion and smoothness). They have also developed a genetic algorithm that looks for FM synthesis parameter combinations that come closest to matching the spectra of desired sounds (Horner, Beauchamp, & Haken, 1993). Another research team (Hörnel & Ragg, 1996) has explored the evolution of neural networks that perform harmonization of melodies in different musical styles, using network size, learning ability, and aspects of its musical behavior as fitness-rule components.

Spector and Alpern (1994) have aimed at a more general goal: the automatic construction of synthetic artists that could operate in any specified aesthetic tradition. They strove to accomplish this by segregating all aesthetic considerations into a distinct critic and then using a method that could create artists that meet those critical criteria. The method they chose is genetic programming (Koza, 1993). In this application, genetic programming evolves programs that produce artistic output, and this output is then judged by the critic acting as a fitness function. Spector and Alpern further supplied much of the culture-specific knowledge that the artificial artist could draw upon in a case-base of prior works in the particular genre of interest. In the application they describe, the case-base is a library of Bebop jazz melodies. The evolved musician programs could take examples of melodies from the case-base and alter them with a set of predetermined transformation functions, such as INVERT, AUGMENT, and COMPARE-TRANSPOSE, which are also largely culture specific.

The fitness function in this Bebop case consisted of five critical criteria gleaned from jazz improvisation techniques—rules that looked for a balance of novel tonal material and material taken from the case-base, or for rhythmic novelty balance, and so on. Musician programs that generated new Bebop melodies meeting these criteria would have more offspring in the next generation (created by reproduction and crossover alone, to scramble the existing combinations of transformation functions). Spector and Alpern ran their system with a case-base of five Charlie Parker song fragments of four bars each. After 21 generations of populations with 250 evolving composers, individuals emerged that could produce four-bar 'improvisations' that were found highly satisfying by the five-rule critic. The system's creators, though, were less impressed: "Although the response . . . pleases the critic, it does not please *us* (the authors) particularly well" (Spector & Alpern, 1994, p. 7). They do not see this, though, as a failing of the evolutionary artist construction method in general. Instead, Spector and Alpern feel that with a proper choice of critical rules, the approach can be made to succeed—and "nobody said it would be easy to raise an artist" (Spector & Alpern, 1994, p. 8).

Perhaps more worrisome for this rule-based approach was Spector and Alpern's discovery that, while their evolved musician could produce critic-pleasing snippets based on the small case-base available during evolution, it failed to produce such rule-following output when it was applied to a new set of Charlie Parker melodies.

That is, the artificial composer was not robust—it did not generalize well to new cultural input (even in the same jazz genre). Knowing how to follow the rules when dealing with one set of musical input did not translate to knowing how to follow those same rules with another set of melodies. Again, Spector and Alpern do not think this will be an insurmountable problem: They expect that the fitness landscape in which artificial composers are sought can be sculpted sufficiently by the proper fitness functions to yield suitably robust musicians. However, countless failed studies by researchers applying genetic algorithms in many fields stand in mute testimony to the ability of evolutionary processes to find sneaky, unintended shortcuts satisfying the letter of the fitness function, but not the intent—and thus rendering the evolved results useless in even slightly different environments.

Horowitz (1994) has applied both user-as-critic and rule-based critic approaches in tandem to the evolution of rhythms, rather than melodies. His users listen to and rate a set of rhythms that have already been evolved through several generations of rule-based fitness evaluation; the user ratings affect the further evolution of the rhythms. The fitness rule used in the initial evolutionary stage is a weighted sum of how different the current rhythm is from desired levels of syncopation, density, downbeat, beat repetition, and other factors. Horowitz has explored adding a further meta-selection stage, in which the actual desired levels and weighted importance of syncopation, density, and so forth, are not prespecified but rather are also evolved—in this case, users evaluate whole families of rhythms created in accordance with a particular set of desired levels and weights. Better fitness rules, and hence better evolved rhythms, can emerge as a consequence.

But there remains a deeper problem with rule-based critic approaches in general, as people found earlier with rule-based composers. Artificial critics who go strictly by their given rules, as opposed to more forgiving (or sloppier) human critics, are generally very brittle. Rule-bound critics may rave about the technically correct but rather trite melody, while panning the inspired but slightly-off passage created by just flipping two notes. In fact, for good composers it is critical to know when to break the rules. As a consequence, for critics it is imperative to know when to *let* the composers break the rules. Rule-based systems, by definition, lack exactly this higher-level knowledge. Critics based on learning methods such as neural network models, on the other hand, can generalize their judgments sufficiently to leave (artificial) composers some much-needed rule-breaking 'wiggle room'—though this too can end in tragedy, as we will see in the next section.

3.3. Learning-based Critics

To further remove (or at least transform) the necessity of human interaction in the algorithmic composition process, the critics used in evolving artificial composers can be trained using easy-to-collect musical examples, rather than constructed using difficult-to-determine musical rules. Baluja, Pomerleau, and Jochem (1994), for instance, working in the visual domain, have trained a neural network to replace the human critic in an interactive image evolution system similar to that created by Sims (1991). (Gibson & Byrne, 1991, suggested a similar approach for very short musical fragments.) The network 'watches' the choices that a human user makes when selecting two-dimensional images from one generation to reproduce in the next generation, and over time learns to make the same kind of aesthetic evaluations as those made by a human user. When the trained network is put in place of the human critic in the evolutionary loop, interesting images can be evolved automatically. With learning critics of this sort, whether applied to images or music, even less structure will end up in the evolved artificial creators, because it must get there indirectly via the trained fitness-evaluating critic that learned its structural preferences from a user-selected training set. We can thus expect a great degree of novelty in the compositions created by this approach, but how will they sound?

Spector and Alpern (1995) extended their earlier rule-based system (described in the previous section) to find out. They expected that a neural network trained to make aesthetic evaluations of a case-base of melodies would be able to evaluate the musical output of evolving composers at a deeper structural level than their rule-based critics could. This time, their composers were to create single-measure responses to single-measure calls in a collection of Charlie Parker melodies. The composers were again evolved in the genetic programming paradigm, but using more abstract (less musically specific) functions than before. The critic neural networks were trained to return a positive evaluation of one measure of original Charlie Parker followed by the correct next measure. They were also trained to return negative evaluations of one Charlie Parker measure followed by different kinds of bad continuations: silence, random melody, or chopped-up Charlie. To evaluate a given composer program, the program was given an original Charlie Parker measure as input, and then both that input and the composer program's one-measure output were passed to the neural network critic. The critic then returned a fitness value indicating how well it thought the composed measure followed the original measure.

One advantage of a system like this is that new critical constraints can be added simply by training the neural network critic on additional musical examples, rather than constructing new rules. The problem, though, is that one can never be sure the network is learning the musical criteria one would like it to, as Spector and Alpern discovered. As in their earlier work, a composer-program with a very high fitness value was quickly found (in fact, after only a single generation of evolution). But again as before, its performance did not meet the standards of its human overseers: In response to a simple measure of eight eighth-notes, it returned a monstrosity containing 35 notes of miniscule duration (mostly triplets) jumping over three octaves. As Spector and Alpern note (1995, p. 45), "In retrospect it is clear that the network had far too small a training set to learn about many of these kinds of errors."

The problem that evolutionary search processes are so adept at exploiting weaknesses and quirks of fitness functions is exacerbated in this case by not knowing what the weaknesses and quirks of a trained neural network are. To circumvent this difficulty partly, Spector and Alpern created a hybrid fitness function by adding specific rules (similar to the ones they employed in their 1994 study) to the trained network's evaluation. This improved matters greatly (the network's response to the same input mentioned above shrank to six notes in just over an octave range), but "it still leaves much to be desired" (Spector & Alpern, 1995, p. 47), and Spector and Alpern would rather elaborate the architecture of the network critic so that it performs better, instead of resorting once more to rules.

Biles and colleagues had even less success in using a neural network critic with the GenJam system (Biles, Anderson, & Loggi, 1996). To unclog the fitness bottleneck caused by presenting a user with too many musical examples to evaluate, these researchers hoped a neural network critic could at least filter out measures that were "clearly ummusical" before they reached the user. The output of the simple three-layer network they used was a single unit whose activation represented ratings from

VERYBAD to VERYGOOD. Biles and colleagues tried various input representations for the measures to be rated. The first representations they explored consisted solely of statistical reductions of the music, including the number of new notes, the size of the maximum interval, and the number of changes of direction between successive intervals. Networks with these input representations never even managed to learn the training set sufficiently, even when large numbers of hidden units were used. Similar failure awaited an interval- and note onset-histogram representation. When the actual intervals were used, the network learned the training set but failed to generalize to the test set of measures. At this point, Biles and colleagues gave up, concluding that "the populations [of measures] that so clearly evolve for the better under the guidance of a human mentor are so much statistical mush to a neural network" (1996, p. B43).

Biles and his colleagues argue that the lack of harmonic context in the network training task hindered the network's performance—human critics are able to do a more consistent (or at least more evolutionarily useful) job of evaluating measures because they hear them after a history of other measures and with an accompanying harmonic background. Human critics are also sensitive to variety and novelty, and therefore will rate highly a rare fragment that they might pan if it were repeated every third measure. Network critics cannot cope so easily with such frequency-dependent preferences and thus become confused when trained on human preference data. Citing these difficulties, Biles and colleagues state: "It seems, then, that there are so few absolutes that there is nothing objective to tap for even the crudest determinations of musical merit. Automating fitness may well require the use of knowledge intensive artificial intelligence techniques" (1996, p. B43).

This concern over the inability of neural networks to learn anything musically merit-worthy is certainly too pessimistic—many of the chapters in this book give reason to hope otherwise. But the difficulty Biles and colleagues had in training networks to recognize special cases of measures that are acceptable in some contexts but not in others is symptomatic of a broader problem with learning-based critics. Instead of being brittle, like rule-based critics, neural networks are typically soft—they can generalize well to new circumstances. But networks can be too soft. If the space of musically useful sequences is spiky—that is, if changing one note (let alone a harmonic context) can make a melody go from good to awful—then some of the generalizations between nearby melodies that neural networks make can be erroneous. We need a system that can be soft when this is useful, but that can still make hard decisions when they are called for. Neural networks can behave this way if they are trained properly, using both positive and negative musical examples.

Another reasonable solution to this challenge may be to combine the soft generalization abilities of neural networks with the hard decision-making behavior of rule-based systems, as Spector and Alpern (1995) did with their hybrid fitness evaluator. A rather different approach is to allow a network to draw its own boundaries around musically important categories. Burton and Vladimirova (1997a) have suggested achieving this self-organization through the use of ART networks to learn appropriate clusters of useful rhythms in an unsupervised fashion. In their proposed system, newly evolved rhythms receive higher fitness the closer they are to existing (pre-trained or previously formed) clusters of rhythms, and new clusters can be formed if different-enough rhythms are encountered. Just how different is different enough, and what fitness to give to new clusters, are important aspects to define in such a self-organizing critic. And all these ways of altering the generalization ability of learning critics face the problem that once the critics have been specified and fixed (by training or coding), they will still be susceptible to exploitation by evolving creators looking for the easy way to higher fitness.

There is another problem with fixed critics as well: Once the evolving population of creators has found a way to satisfy the critics, the population will typically converge on that first solution, and no further innovations or variety will result. This can be especially true when the population quickly finds a loophole in the fitness function—the 'cheating' solutions will have such a fitness advantage over other members of the population that they will rapidly take over, killing off any other alternative approaches. This is not such a problem with human critics (as noted by Biles, Anderson, & Loggi, 1996), because their selection criteria can change over time to search for new aspects in creators and thus avoid stagnation. But how can we build such changeable criteria into artificial critics, to ensure continued evolution and generation of novel creators? We must un-fix them. We can allow the critics to evolve as well, tying both critics and creators together into a co-adapting skein.

4. "My creator ... your master": Coevolving Music Creators and Critics

Frankenstein and his monster shared an inextricably entwined existence. Though the former had created the latter through his actions, the Creature in turn defined and controlled his creator through his own relentless behavior. After repeatedly confronting and reacting to each others' desires, the monster reminded Frankenstein that they were both responsible for, and had power over, the happiness and existence of the other: "You are my creator, but I am your master—obey!" (Shelley, 1818/1993, p. 229).

In the same way, the two halves of the creative loop, creator and critic, or performer and audience, should dance around each other, shaping and being shaped by the others' behavior. This is a very general principle—essentially that of a feedback loop—that lies at the heart of a wide range of dynamic systems, whether within the psychology of a single creative mind, or between a pair of interacting individuals, or among the groups generating and responding to artifacts in a particular culture, or even among species interacting in an ecosystem. If only one side of any of these systems can change, then it will only change until it is in line with the other fixed component, and then creativity and innovation will stop. Both sides must be free to adapt to the other for continuing novelty to be generated. In the evolutionary composition systems we have already considered, however, the critic is held fixed, and only the musical creator (or creations themselves) are allowed to change over time. In this section, we take a first few steps in exploring how to capitalize on the creative power of coadapting systems for algorithmic composition—specifically, how to unchain the critic and let it (co)evolve with the creators as well.

Coevolution can help solve several of the problems we have already encountered plaguing evolutionary composition systems. First, coevolving creators and critics simultaneously can reduce the ability of creators to find easy ways to 'trick' critics into giving them high fitness. Hillis (1992) evolved simple routines for sorting lists of numbers, but found that with a fixed test set of number sequences to be sorted, the evolved programs would not generalize to all possible sequences—they used shortcuts to sort just the test cases. When Hillis made the test cases coevolve, by giving each number sequence higher fitness whenever it tricked a sorter routine, the sorters were continually challenged and ended up with the desired general sorting behavior. In a similar way, coevolving music critics along with the creators will continuously challenge the creators with new fitness criteria and prevent them from finding static fitness loopholes to exploit.

Second, coevolution can produce diversity within a population at any one time. This *synchronic diversity* can be generated, for example, through the process of sexual selection, when females choose males to mate with based on particular traits the males bear. When both the female preferences for particular traits and the male traits themselves coevolve, new species can form, splitting up the original population into subpopulations of individuals with distinct traits and preferences (see Todd & Miller, 1991a, for a simulation model of this speciation process). Coevolution's ability to generate synchronic diversity through speciation is a source of much of the variety and beauty of our natural world (Miller & Todd, 1995; Skutch, 1992), and it can also be very important for algorithmic composition systems, where diversity can all too easily be selected out of a population. David Ralley (personal communication) noted that because of the boredom involved in listening to melodies in an artificial selection system, "The listeners tended to be drawn to the mutants because of their novelty, not because they represented better solutions, and [they] pursued those lines of evolution to dead ends. That is, eventually the whole population sounds like the original mutant, [and] you've lost the genotypic richness that might allow you to go elsewhere in the search space." Biles (1994, 1995b) has been specifically interested in preserving diversity in the population of jazz solo measures he evolves—it would not be very useful if GenJam only had one solo to call upon. But he found that the necessary diversity can quickly disappear, particularly in multi-critic situations or when the population is small. To combat this, he developed a set of diversity operators that keep some variation in the population. Coevolution can achieve similar ends without the need for specific new operators.

Third, coevolution can generate diversity across time—*diachronic diversity*, in which the traits in a population continuously change, generation after generation. This pattern of constant change can be seen in arms races between different species, for instance predators and prey, where adaptations in one species—ability to chase faster, say—are countered by new adaptations in the other species—ability to change direction quickly when fleeing (Futuyama & Slatkin, 1983). In musical evolution systems, diachronic diversity is equivalent to generating a succession of new artificial composers. As mentioned in the previous section, this is something that human listeners can accomplish by changing their critical criteria over time; coevolving artificial critics allow us to take humans out of the evolutionary loop.

Thus, to generate musical diversity both across time and at any given instant—both diachronically and synchronically—we must build a system that can create a multitude of distinctly defined 'species' within one population, and that can further induce those species to move around in musical space from one generation to the next. Sexual selection through mate choice allows the former, leading a population to cluster into subpopulations with unique (musical) traits and preferences. We need some further force to push a population out of its attained stable pattern of speciation, though, the role that parasites played in Hillis's (1992) sorting system. In sexual selection, this can be achieved through directional mate preferences (Kirkpatrick, 1987; Miller & Todd, 1993, 1995), which for example cause females always to look for brighter, or more colorful, or more behaviorally complex males. These changing preferences can induce a population to continue evolving. For the evolution of musical creators, as we will see, this constant striving force can be effected through *neophilia*: females always looking for males who create musical patterns that are novel and unexpected. Our coevolutionary model thus ends up looking like (and being inspired by) the evolution of birdsong through sexual selection of critical females choosing which singing males to mate with. While this starting point for investigating coevolutionary composition systems may seem a long way from the complexities of human music composition, there are lessons to be learned that point the way beyond today's systems and toward the algorithmic composers of the future. (See Werner & Todd, 1997, for more details about our simulation methods and results with this system.)

Coevolutionary processes have not been much explored in compositional systems in the past. Horner, Assad, and Packard (1994) developed a system in which musical lines could evolve to work together in one of a number of competing strata, each of which is likened to a colony interacting in an ecology. "Working strata" receive more energy to divide up among the musical lines that form them, so it is in the best interest of any one musical line to join a stratum containing other lines that it can cooperate beneficially with. As the authors put it (p. 81), "The fitness of any given line is highly dependent on other lines near it temporally and textually; thus, successful music entails the evolution of groups of individual lines that interact in musically meaningful ways". In some sense, then, the lines will coevolve over time to complement each other within their competitive strata; this is more like mutualism, with an entire cooperating colony being a composition, than the sexually selected coevolution of individual composers and critics that we develop here.

Jacob (1995, 1996) created the *variations* system to implement his own composition process via three interacting modules. The composer module creates proposed modifications of themes or phrases through the addition of motives and then passes these phrases on to the ear module, which either accepts or rejects each modification. In this way, a set of accepted phrases is built up over time, which are finally sent to the arranger module for combination into usable structures. Both the creators—composer modules—and critics—ear modules—are evolved in Jacob's system, as in ours described in this section. But the evolution of each type of module is performed separately, through human user fitness feedback (artificial selection, as in Section 3.1), rather than coevolving through sexual selection by affecting each others' fitness. As we will now see, introducing coevolution can 'close the loop' and eliminate the need for constant human judgment in the selection process—but it can also make for some compositionally less-useful results.

4.1. Coevolving Rhythm-generating and Judging Neural Networks

In a preliminary model, we coevolved artificial 'males' who produce rhythmic 'songs' along with picky 'females' who judge those songs and use them to decide whom to mate with. Both the male song creators and female song critics use neural networks to guide their behavior, either to produce rhythms in the male case or to listen to them and rate them in the female case. It is these neural circuits that (co)evolve over time. In females, the neural network maps inputs from an 'ear' to output units that indicate her decision to mate or abstain. In males, the circuitry produces a sequence of sounds in response to the presence of a female. We define the quality of a song to be the increased chance a female will mate with a male after hearing a song.

The neural model we used was somewhat different from the standard logistic-activation feedforward network. Each unit has a threshold, as usual, but summation of activation arriving in the unit occurs over multiple time steps. If this threshold is reached, the unit fires for one time step, and its stored input is reset to zero. The output of each neuron is binary, and weights between units are small integer values. Output signals take one time step to propagate down a connection from one neuron to another, so that the firing of a neuron at time t influences the firing of other neurons at time $t + 1$. Each unit also has a baseline (bias) input value. If this bias is positive, the unit will fire at regular intervals, even lacking input from other units. For example, if a unit's bias value is $+1$, and its threshold is $+3$, this unit will function as a pacemaker unit, firing every three time steps. This behavior engenders interesting dynamics in the firing of interconnected neurons, which is important for the males producing rhythmic songs. It also allows individual neurons to detect temporal patterns, which is important for the females listening to input patterns over time.

Each individual carries genes encoding for a song-producing network as well as a song-rating network. However, male animals use only their genes for song producing and female animals only their genes for song rating. Each neuron in the network has a gene that encodes its threshold and bias activation. A number of genes encode the connections between the neurons, in terms of the source neuron, the destination neuron, and the strength of the connection. Males have a single input unit (indicating whether or not a female is listening and they should start singing), and several output units (different 'notes' that they can sing, simultaneously or individually). Females have a corresponding number of input units (one to register each possible 'note' that the males can sing) and two output units, one defined as indicating how much the female likes what she is currently hearing, and the other indicating how much she dislikes this male's song. We felt that it was necessary to include both a score-increasing (liking) unit and a score-decreasing (disliking) unit, because without an output that could reduce the score of a song, males would simply evolve to sing songs that had every possible note on at every time step. This cacophony could flood the listening females' networks with activation so that these songs would receive high scores, and nothing more interesting would appear in the population.

When this model was run, the male neural networks produced complex output patterns. The songs typically contained several concurrent, not-quite-repeating patterns that were out of phase with each other. These songs changed dramatically over evolutionary time, driven by the preferences of the female networks. However, these patterns proved to be very difficult to analyze for complexity, diversity, or change. It was clear that the songs were evolving, but not clear how. It was time to call in more rudimentary musicians.

4.2. Coevolving Hopeful Singers and Music Critics

In our latest simulation, we created 'dumbed-down' male singers, each of whom has genes that directly encode the notes of his song (rather than a song-generating network). Each male song (and hence genotype) consists of 32 notes, each of which can be a single pitch selected from a two-octave (24 pitch) range. Females' genes now encode a transition matrix that is used to rate transitions from one note to another in male songs. This matrix is an N-by-N table, where N is the number of possible pitches the males can produce (24 in these experiments). Each entry in this table represents the female's expectation of the probability of one pitch following another in a song. For instance, entry $(4, 11)$ (or C-G in our two-octave case) in a particular female's table captures how often she thinks pitch 11 will follow pitch 4, on average, in male songs. Given these expectations, females can decide how well they like a particular song in different ways, as we will see in the next subsection. Whatever method she uses, as she listens to a male, the female considers the transition from the previous note's pitch to the current note's pitch for each note in a song, gives each transition a score based on her transition table, and sums those scores to come up with her final evaluation of the male and his serenade.

Each female listens to the songs of a certain number of males who are randomly selected to be in her 'courting choir'. All females hear the same number of males, and the size of the courting choir—that is, a female's sample size—is specified for each evolutionary run. After listening to all the males in her potential-mate choir, the female selects the one that she most preferred (i.e. the one with the highest score) as her mate. This female choice process ensures that all females will have exactly one mate, but males can have a range of mates from 0 (if his song is unpopular with everyone) to something close to the courting-choir size (if he has a platinum hit that is selected by all the females who listen to him). Each female has one child per generation created via crossover and mutation with her chosen male mate (so this child will have a mix of the musical traits and preferences genetically encoded in its mother and father). This temporarily puts the population at about 50% above a specified 'carrying capacity' (target population size). We then kill off approximately a third of the individuals, bringing the population back to a predetermined carrying capacity. This whole process is repeated for some desired number of generations.

We employed three different methods for scoring the male songs using these tables. In the first method, the female simply scores each transition as it occurs in the song by immediately looking up how much she expected that particular transition and adding it to the running total score for the song. Thus, those songs that contain more of the individual transitions that the female expects (e.g. songs with many C-G transitions, if she expects C's to be followed by G's very often) will be scored higher by her, and she will prefer to mate with the males who sing these songs. We call this the *local transition preference* scoring method.

In the second method, the female listens to a whole song first, counting the number of each type of transition that occurs in the song (e.g. she might tally up G's following C's four times in the song, and other notes following C's two times). Then from these counts she constructs a transition matrix for that particular individual song (e.g. with an entry of .66 for the C-G transition, because that is what occurred two-thirds of the time after a C in this song). Finally, she compares that song's transition table with her expected (preferred) transition table, and the closer the two tables match (on an entry-by-entry basis), the higher score and preference she gives to that song.

Thus, this method means that a female will prefer songs that match the overall statistical pattern of transitions in her transition table. We call this the *global transition preference* scoring method. Continuing with our example, if the female has a value of .75 stored in her own transition table for the C-G transition, she will like songs most that have a C-G transition exactly three-fourths of the time (along with other C-x transitions, where x is any note other than G, for the other quarter of the time that C appears). In contrast, with local transition scoring, she would prefer C-G transitions after every C, because they give a higher local score than any other transition from C.

The third scoring method produced females that enjoy being surprised. The female listens to each transition in the song individually as in the first method, looks up how much she expected that transition, and subtracts this probability value from the probability she attached to the transition she most expected to hear. Consider our female from the previous paragraph again. Whenever she hears a C in a male's song, she most expects a G to follow it (75% of the time). Imagine she instead hears a C-E transition in a song. This transition is a surprise to her, because it violates the C-G transition expectation—and so she likes this song more as a consequence.

But how much of a surprise was this note, and how much does it increase her preference for this song? To find out, the female critic first looks up the C-E transition in her table, and finds she expected that transition 15% (for example) of the time. Thus, this C-E transition was not a complete surprise, because she had some previous expectation for it, but it was a reasonably large one. We quantify the surprise level with a score of $.75 - .15 = .6$ for that transition (i.e. $prob(C\text{-}G) - prob(C\text{-}E)$). This expected-minus-actual-transition-probability score is summed up for all the transitions in the current song, and the final sum registers how much surprise the female experienced, and therefore how much she preferred that song. Not surprisingly, we call this the *surprise preference* scoring method. Note that it will not result in the males singing random songs—to get a high surprise score, a song must first build up expectations, by making transitions to notes that have highly expected notes following them, and then violate those expectations, by not using the highly expected note. Thus there is a constant tug-of-war between doing what is expected and what is unexpected in each song.

The first two preference scoring methods can be considered forms of nondirectional mate preferences: Evolved male songs that match evolved female expectations most precisely (either locally or globally) will receive the most mating interest. The third surprise preference scoring method, however, is a type of directional mate preference. Rather than rewarding male songs that match female expectations, surprising songs that are some ways off from the evolved female transition tables in song space will be sought after. Thus we expected to see less movement through song space for the local and global transition preferences and more continual change—maintaining diversity over time—when surprise preferences were used.

We also expected that surprise scoring would create greater diversity within any given generation than would preferences based on matching local or global expectations, because there are more ways to violate expectations (causing surprise) than to meet them. Note that this is different from the kinds of directional preferences where only a single preferred direction was indicated (e.g. a greener vs. a bluer patch of plumage). In those cases, the population could evolve to all head in one direction in phenotype space; here, the population will be more likely to scatter in many directions in phenotype space.

We also compared cases where female expectation transition tables were fixed across time (i.e. female offspring contain exact copies of their mother's transition table) with runs where females were allowed to coevolve with the male songs. In this way we tested our expectation that coevolving preferences would allow more change (or diversity) in songs over time because the targets for the males would themselves be moving. In a system without coevolution, male songs will tend to converge on the female preferences and stay there, providing little evolutionary movement.

4.3. Resulting Song Change over Time

We ran populations of 1000 individuals for 1000 generations in six different conditions: all three preference scoring methods, with fixed or coevolving preferences.

We consider here cases where the female's courting choir contained just two males (see Werner & Todd, 1997, for further details). In each case, we initiated the male songs randomly, and the female transition tables were set in the first generation with probabilities calculated from a collection of simple folk-tune melodies. This way we could ensure that female preferences in our simulations at least started out with some resemblance to human melodic preferences; however, once evolution started moving the preferences and songs around, any hope of the population's aesthetics matching human aesthetics would quickly be lost. Thus, we could not listen to the system and readily judge its progress; we had to resort to more objective measures (which is another reason for using the simplified form of song and preference representation presented in the previous section).

To measure evolving song change over time—diachronic diversity—we used a 'progress chart' technique modified from Cliff and Miller's (1995) work on tracking coevolutionary progress in pursuit-evasion games. This method allows us to compare and visualize the difference between the modal male song (i.e. the most common note at each of the 32 positions) at any generation G and that at any previous generation G', with difference measured as the number of positions where the two songs differ (from 0 to 32).

Using this technique, we compared the rate of change of population modal songs over time for our six different conditions. Surprise scoring yielded greater change than either global or local transition scoring. Local scoring, in fact, made the population converge rather rapidly to the locally preferred song transitions, so that male songs often degenerated to repetition of a single note or alternation between two notes. (This also gave these runs very low within-generation synchronic diversity scores, so we did not analyze this type of preference further.) Finally, coevolution led to faster change than fixed female preferences, at least when surprise scoring was used—the situation is less clear with global transition scoring, and we are still investigating this particular, possibly anomalous case.

4.4. Resulting Song Diversity within Populations

To measure the synchronic diversity of songs within a population at any particular generation, we computed the set of differences (again 0–32) between every pair of males' songs in the population. This set of differences can be plotted as a histogram for any given generation, with highly converged, low-diversity populations having histograms skewed toward low values, and unconverged, high-diversity populations having histograms skewed toward high values. Furthermore, populations with two or more distinct 'species' of songs will show up as multiple peaks in the histogram (representing the distributions of between-species and within-species distances). To explore how this within-generation diversity changes across generations, we can simply line up several of these histograms next to each other.

We used this visualization method to compare the evolving synchronic diversity of songs in populations in four conditions (leaving out the degenerate hyper-converged local transition score populations). Again our expectations were mostly met: Coevolution yielded greater synchronic diversity than fixed female preferences (i.e. most songs in the population were about 18 notes different from the modal song for the coevolving-female-preference surprise population vs. about 11 notes different for the fixed-female-preference surprise population after 1000 generations). The preference scoring method (surprise vs. global transition scoring) showed little consistent effect on within-generation diversity, however.

Interestingly, when we changed the female's choir size from 2 to 20 singing males, the synchronic diversity dropped dramatically (from 10–20 notes different from the modal song on average, to just 2–3 notes different with the large choir). However, this tight clustering with a large choir size, when combined with the directional selection effects of surprise preferences, can lead new song 'species' to emerge and differentiate from each other over time. Thus, as the choir size is increased, diversity across the whole population can be replaced by diversity between speciated subpopulations.

5. "The instrument of future mischief": Conclusions, Implications, and Further Work

Frankenstein's unhappy creation took it upon himself to end the experiment that had produced so much misery: "Fear not that I shall be the instrument of future mischief. My work is nearly complete" (Shelley, 1818/1993, p. 290). Our experimental results to date are similarly unhappy, or at least somewhat unappealing to behold. Our coevolutionary system of female critics and male song creators has worked to produce the diversity and novelty we desired, but at the cost, as usual, of musical structure. As one colleague put it, "each individual male song sounds crappy—but each sounds crappy in a unique new way." We could therefore do as the wise Creature did and bring this project to a rapid and merciful conclusion. But our work is not nearly complete—there are many directions we can go to address the aesthetic problems we face, and to improve the performance of coevolutionary algorithmic composition.

Our simulations here lend strong support for the role of coevolving songs and directional (surprise-based) preferences in maintaining diversity over time, and in continuously altering that diversity as time goes by. With noncoevolving, nondirectional preferences, progress is slower and diversity collapses. This diversity could actually be increased if the female song preferences could change faster, altering within any given female's lifetime rather than just between mother and daughter. This is exactly the role that learning can play, enabling adaptations faster than evolution can accomplish (Todd & Miller, 1991b). Thus, by combining (co)evolution and learning, we may be able to further increase the novelty-generating power of our algorithmic composition systems.

The first place to explore the addition of learning to our system is in the creation of the female musical expectations: Where should their transition tables come from? In our current setup, females inherit their transition tables from their mother and father (after the females in the initial generation were loaded with transition expectations computed from real song examples, as mentioned in Section 4.3). Because of this, 'surprising' note transitions can only be surprising relative to a particular female's inherited expectations. But certainly for humans, and for other animals as well, expectations are built up through experience and learning within one's lifetime (see Bharucha & Todd, 1989). So instead we can let a female learn expectations about note transitions based on a set of songs from her current generation, or from the previous generation, as if she has heard those songs and picked up knowledge of her 'culture' from them. Then she will be surprised when she hears something new that toys with these learned expectations, building them up and then violating them. We expect that using learning to create the note transition expectations, rather than evolving them, will allow the population to 'change its tune' even more rapidly than the cases we have described in this paper, because the expectations will be able to shift just as rapidly as the songs themselves—learning operates faster than selection.

Furthermore, we could allow learning in the females to occur at an even faster time-scale, so that instead of habituating to songs heard too many times last week, for example, each female could habituate to notes and phrases heard too many times within the current male's song. In this case, females would seek novelty and expectation-violation *within* each song they hear. To sing preferred songs, males would have to balance the amount of repetition and newness in their song. We expect that this type of 'real-time' preference learning will lead to increased complexity of the internal structure of the songs themselves, not just of the population of songs.

Combining evolution and learning may increase the speed with which novelty is generated in our system, but that could just get us to bad-sounding novelty that much faster. One of the biggest problems with our coevolutionary approach is that, by removing the human influence from the critics (aside from those in the initial generation of folksong-derived transition tables), the system can rapidly evolve its own unconstrained aesthetics. After a few generations of coevolving songs and preferences, the female critics may be pleased only by musical sequences that the human user would find worthless. Unchaining critics to yield continual novelty also frees them from incorporating any particular aspects of musical structure. To rein the critics (and thus creators) back in slightly, so that they continue to incorporate at least some basic desirable elements of musical structure, we can add selected fitness rules to the coevolutionary system, creating hybrid fitness criteria similar to those discussed in Section 3.3. These rules can be used to eliminate (male) songs from the population that are in flagrant violation of the human user's encoded aesthetics. The power of sexual selection through female choice will continue to produce a variety of attractive males singing preferred songs; but now the human-provided fitness rules will act akin to natural selection, keeping the population healthy and well adapted as well as attractive.

Thus, we propose a new algorithmic composition system based on a combination of all the approaches we have described here: rule-following, learning, and evolution. By coevolving female song critics with learned musical preferences alongside the male-produced songs they choose between (which can also be honed by learning within the male's lifetime as he encounters multiple choosy females), sexual selection will produce ongoing novelty. By pruning that novelty with human-produced rules, natural selection will keep the system within appropriate musical bounds. Structure and novelty, like the effects of natural and sexual selection, can be balanced.

Frankenstein's monster was born desiring to be good, filled with the love of virtue, but his form was aesthetically repulsive. His form, rather than his intentions, caused Frankenstein to opt out of their coevolving creator-critic relationship early on, leaving the Creature to develop on his own toward his ultimately tragic condition. Many of the evolving musical examples we have considered here began their lives similarly unlovely. If Frankenstein had been more patient, had remained engaged in a guiding role for his creation, had grown with the Creature and helped him to learn about the good and bad aspects of the world, and had taught him the rules that govern proper human behavior, the outcome of their story would have been very different and almost certainly happier for all. Musicians intent on creating algorithmic composition systems with the spark of human creativity would do well to adopt this combination of coevolution, learning, and rule-following, and thereby with luck avoid the horrors that were visited upon Victor Frankenstein and his creation.

Acknowledgements

Thanks are due to Al Biles, Tony Burton, Dominik Hörnel, Andrew Horner, Bruce Jacob, David Ralley, Lee Spector, and Kurt Thywissen for helpful discussions and details about their research experiences, to Geoffrey Miller, Niall Griffith, and Anita Todd for their comments on earlier drafts, and to Imogen Todd for inspiring the metaphor of the monster.

References

Baluja, S., Pomerleau, D., & Jochem, T. (1994) Towards automated artificial evolution for computer-generated images. *Connection Science,* **6**(2–3), 325–354. (Reprinted in this volume.)

Bharucha, J.J., & Todd, P.M. (1989) Modeling the perception of tonal structure with neural nets. *Computer Music Journal,* **13**(4), 44–53. Also in P.M. Todd & D.G. Loy (Eds.), *Music and Connectionism* (pp. 128–137). Cambridge, MA: MIT Press.

Biles, J.A. (1994) GenJam: A genetic algorithm for generating jazz solos. In *Proceedings of the 1994 International Computer Music Conference* (pp. 131–137). San Francisco: International Computer Music Association.

Biles, J.A. (1995a) *The Al Biles Virtual Quintet: GenJam.* Compact disc recording DRK-CD-144. Rochester, NY: Dynamic Recording Studios.

Biles, J.A. (1995b) GenJam Populi: Training an IGA via audience-mediated performance. In *Proceedings of the 1995 International Computer Music Conference* (pp. 347–348). San Francisco: International Computer Music Association.

Biles, J.A., Anderson, P.G., & Loggi, L.W. (1996) Neural network fitness functions for a musical GA. In *Proceedings of the International ICSC Symposium on Intelligent Industrial Automation (IIA'96) and Soft Computing (SOCO'96)* (pp. B39–B44). Reading, UK: ICSC Academic Press.

Burton, A.R., & Vladimirova, T. (1997a) Genetic algorithm utilising neural network fitness evaluation for musical composition. In G.D. Smith, N.C. Steele, & R.F. Albrecht (Eds.), *Proceedings of the 1997 International Conference on Artificial Neural Networks and Genetic Algorithms* (pp. 220–224). Vienna: Springer-Verlag.

Burton, A.R., & Vladimirova, T. (1997b) *Applications of Genetic Techniques to Musical Composition.* Unpublished manuscript. Available at http://www.ee.surrey.ac.uk/Personal/A.Burton/docs/cmjcompo.prn.uue.

Campbell, D. (1960) Blind variation and selective retention in creative thought as in other knowledge processes. *Psychological Review,* **67**(6), 380–400.

Cliff, D., & Miller, G.F. (1995). Tracking the Red Queen: Measurements of adaptive progress in coevolutionary simulations. In F. Moran, A. Moreno, J.J. Merelo & P. Cachon (Eds.), *Advances in Artificial Life: Proceedings of the Third European Conference on Artificial Life* (pp. 200–218). Lecture Notes in Artificial Intelligence 929. Berlin: Springer-Verlag.

Darwin, C.R. (1859) *On the Origin of Species.* London: John Murray. (Reprinted in 1964 with an introduction by E. Mayr; Cambridge, MA: Harvard University Press.)

Dawkins, R. (1986) *The Blind Watchmaker.* New York: Norton.

Ebcioglu, K. (1984) An expert system for Schenkerian synthesis of chorales in the style of J.S. Bach. In *Proceedings of the 1984 International Computer Music Conference* (pp. 135–142). San Francisco: International Computer Music Association.

Futuyama, D., & Slatkin, M. (Eds.) (1983) *Coevolution.* Sunderland, MA: Sinauer.

Gibson, P.M., & Byrne, J.A. (1991) NEUROGEN, musical composition using genetic algorithms and cooperating neural networks. In *Proceedings of the IEE Second International Conference on Artificial Neural Networks* (pp. 309–313). London: IEE.

Goldberg, D.E. (1989) *Genetic Algorithms in Search, Optimization, and Machine Learning.* Reading, MA: Addison-Wesley.

Goldschmidt, R. (1940) *The Material Basis of Evolution.* New Haven: Yale University Press.

Hillis, W.D. (1992) Co-evolving parasites improve simulated evolution as an optimization procedure. In C. Langton, C. Taylor, J.D. Farmer, & S. Rasmussen (Eds.), *Artificial Life II* (pp. 313–324). Reading, MA: Addison-Wesley.

Holland, J.H. (1975) *Adaptation in Natural and Artificial Systems*. Ann Arbor: University of Michigan Press. (Second edition: MIT Press, 1992.)

Hörnel, D., & Ragg, T. (1996) Learning musical structure and style by recognition, prediction and evolution. In *Proceedings of the 1996 International Computer Music Conference* (pp. 59–62). San Francisco: International Computer Music Association.

Horner, A., Assad, A., & Packard, N. (1994) Artificial music: The evolution of musical strata. *Leonardo Music Journal*, **3**, 81.

Horner, A., & Ayers, L. (1995) Harmonization of musical progressions with genetic algorithms. In *Proceedings of the 1995 International Computer Music Conference* (pp. 483–484). San Francisco: International Computer Music Association.

Horner, A., Beauchamp, J., & Haken, L. (1993) Machine tongues XVI: Genetic algorithms and their application to FM matching synthesis. *Computer Music Journal*, **17**(4), 17–29.

Horner, A., & Goldberg, D.E. (1991a) Genetic algorithms and computer-assisted music composition. In *Proceedings of the 1991 International Computer Music Conference* (pp. 479–482). San Francisco: International Computer Music Association.

Horner, A., & Goldberg, D.E. (1991b) *Genetic Algorithms and Computer-assisted Music Composition*. Technical Report CCSR-91-20, University of Illinois at Urbana-Champaign, Center for Complex Systems Research, The Beckman Institute.

Horowitz, D. (1994) Generating rhythms with genetic algorithms. In *Proceedings of the 1994 International Computer Music Conference* (pp. 142–143). San Francisco: International Computer Music Association.

Jacob, B.L. (1995) Composing with genetic algorithms. In *Proceedings of the 1995 International Computer Music Conference* (pp. 452–455). San Francisco: International Computer Music Association.

Jacob, B.L. (1996) Algorithmic composition as a model of creativity. *Organised Sound*, **1**(3), 157–165.

Jones, K. (1981) Compositional applications of stochastic processes. *Computer Music Journal*, **5**(2), 45–61.

Kirkpatrick, M. (1987) The evolutionary forces acting on female preferences in polygynous animals. In J.W. Bradbury & M.B. Andersson (Eds.), *Sexual Selection: Testing the Alternatives* (pp. 67–82). New York: Wiley.

Koza, J. (1993) *Genetic Programming*. Cambridge, MA: MIT Press/Bradford Books.

Loy, D.G. (1989) Composing with computers—A survey of some compositional formalisms and music programming languages. In M.V. Mathews & J.R. Pierce (Eds.), *Current Directions in Computer Music Research* (pp. 291–396). Cambridge, MA: MIT Press.

Loy, D.G. (1991) Connectionism and musiconomy. In P.M. Todd & D.G. Loy (Eds.), *Music and Connectionism* (pp. 20–36). Cambridge, MA: MIT Press.

McCorduck, P. (1990) *Aaron's Code: Meta-art, Artificial Intelligence and the Work of Harold Cohen*. New York: W.H. Freeman.

McIntyre, R.A. (1994) Bach in a box: The evolution of four part Baroque harmony using the genetic algorithm. In *Proceedings of the First IEEE Conference on Evolutionary Computation* (pp. 852–857). New York: IEEE.

Miller, G.F., & Todd, P.M. (1993) Evolutionary wanderlust: Sexual selection with directional mate preferences. In J.-A. Meyer, H.L. Roitblat, & S.W. Wilson (Eds.), *From Animals to Animats 2: Proceedings of the Second International Conference on Simulation of Adaptive Behavior* (pp. 21–30). Cambridge, MA: MIT Press/Bradford Books.

Miller, G.F., & Todd, P.M. (1995) The role of mate choice in biocomputation: Sexual selection as a process of search, optimization, and diversification. In W. Banzhaf & F.H. Eeckman (Eds.), *Evolution and Biocomputation: Computational Models of Evolution* (pp. 169–204). Berlin: Springer-Verlag.

Mitchell, M. (1996) *An Introduction to Genetic Algorithms*. Cambridge, MA: MIT Press/Bradford Books.

Moore, J.H. (1994) *GAMusic: Genetic algorithm to evolve musical melodies*. Windows 3.1 software available at: http://www.cs.cmu.edu/afs/cs/project/ai-repository/ai/areas/genetic/ga/systems/gamusic/0.html.

Mozer, M.C. (1991) Connectionist music composition based on melodic, stylistic, and psychophysical constraints. In P.M. Todd & D.G. Loy (Eds.), *Music and Connectionism* (pp. 195–211). Cambridge, MA: MIT Press.

Mozer, M.C. (1994) Neural network music composition by prediction: Exploring the benefits of psychoacoustic constraints and multi-scale processing. *Connection Science*, **6**(2–3), 247–280. (Reprinted in this volume.)

Nitecki, M. (Ed.) (1990) *Evolutionary Innovations*. Chicago: University of Chicago Press.

Perkins, D.N. (1994) Creativity: Beyond the Darwinian paradigm. In M.A. Boden (Ed.), *Dimensions of Creativity* (pp. 119–142). Cambridge, MA: MIT Press/Bradford Books.

Putnam, J.B. (1994) *Genetic Programming of Music.* Unpublished manuscript. Socorro, NM: New Mexico Institute of Mining and Technology.

Ralley, D. (1995) Genetic algorithms as a tool for melodic development. In *Proceedings of the 1995 International Computer Music Conference* (pp. 501–502). San Francisco: International Computer Music Association.

Rasch, R.A., & Plomp, R. (1982) The perception of musical tones. In D. Deutsch (Ed.), *The Psychology of Music* (pp. 1–24). New York: Academic Press.

Ray, T.S. (1991) An approach to the synthesis of life. In C. Langton, C. Taylor, J.D. Farmer, & S. Rasmussen (Eds.), *Artificial Life II* (pp. 371–408). Reading, MA: Addison-Wesley.

Ridley, M. (1993) *The Red Queen: Sex and the Evolution of Human Nature.* New York: Macmillan.

Rumelhart, D.E., McClelland, J.L., & The PDP Research Group (1986) *Parallel Distributed Processing: Explorations in the Microstructure of Cognition.* Cambridge, MA: MIT Press/Bradford Books.

Shelley, M. (1818/1993) *Frankenstein; or, The Modern Prometheus.* In L. Wolf (Ed.), *The Essential Frankenstein.* New York: Plume/Penguin.

Shelley, M. (1831/1993) Introduction to *Frankenstein; or, The Modern Prometheus* (1831 edition). In L. Wolf (Ed.), *The Essential Frankenstein* (Appendix A). New York: Plume/Penguin.

Sims, K. (1991) Artificial evolution for computer graphics. *Computer Graphics, 25*(4), 319–328.

Sims, K. (1994) Evolving 3D morphology and behavior by competition. In R.A. Brooks & P. Maes (Eds.), *Artificial Life IV: Proceedings of the Fourth International Workshop on the Synthesis and Simulation of Living Systems* (pp. 28–39). Cambridge, MA: MIT Press/Bradford Books.

Skutch, A.F. (1992) *Origins of Nature's Beauty: Essays by Alexander F. Skutch.* Austin, TX: University of Texas Press.

Spector, L., & Alpern, A. (1994) Criticism, culture, and the automatic generation of artworks. In *Proceedings of the Twelfth National Conference on Artificial Intelligence (AAAI94)* (pp. 3–8). Menlo Park, CA, and Cambridge, MA: AAAI Press/MIT Press.

Spector, L., & Alpern, A. (1995) Induction and recapitulation of deep musical structure. In *Working Notes of the IJCAI-95 Workshop on Artificial Intelligence and Music* (pp. 41–48).

Takala, T., Hahn, J., Gritz, L., Geigel, J., & Lee, J.W. (1993) Using physically-based models and genetic algorithms for functional composition of sound signals, synchronized to animated motion. In *Proceedings of the 1993 International Computer Music Conference* (pp. 180–185). San Francisco: International Computer Music Association.

Thywissen, K. (1996) GeNotator: An environment for investigating the application of genetic algorithms in computer assisted composition. In *Proceedings of the 1996 International Computer Music Conference.* San Francisco: International Computer Music Association.

Todd, P.M. (1988) A sequential network design for musical applications. In D. Touretzky, G. Hinton, & T. Sejnowski (Eds.), *Proceedings of the 1988 Connectionist Models Summer School* (pp. 76–84). San Mateo, CA: Morgan Kaufmann.

Todd, P.M. (1989) A connectionist approach to algorithmic composition. *Computer Music Journal, 13*(4), 27–43.

Todd, P.M., & Loy, D.G. (1991) *Music and Connectionism.* Cambridge, MA: MIT Press.

Todd, P.M., & Miller, G.F. (1991a) On the sympatric origin of species: Mercurial mating in the quicksilver model. In R.K. Belew & L.B. Booker (Eds.), *Proceedings of the Fourth International Conference on Genetic Algorithms* (pp. 547–554). San Mateo, CA: Morgan Kaufmann.

Todd, P.M., & Miller, G.F. (1991b) Exploring adaptive agency II: Simulating the evolution of associative learning. In J.-A. Meyer & S.W. Wilson (Eds.), *From Animals to Animats: Proceedings of the First International Conference on Simulation of Adaptive Behavior* (pp. 306–315). Cambridge, MA: MIT Press/Bradford Books.

Todd, S., & Latham, W. (1992) *Evolutionary Art and Computers.* New York: Academic Press.

Weiner, J. (1994) *The Beak of the Finch: A Story of Evolution in Our Time.* New York: Knopf.

Werner, G.M., & Todd, P.M. (1997) Too many love songs: Sexual selection and the evolution of communication. In P. Husbands & I. Harvey (Eds.), *Fourth European Conference on Artificial Life* (pp. 434–443). Cambridge, MA: MIT Press/Bradford Books.

Wimsatt, W.C. (in press) *Re-engineering Philosophy for Limited Beings: Piecewise Approximations to Reality.* Cambridge, MA: Harvard University Press.

Towards Automated Artificial Evolution for Computer-generated Images

SHUMEET BALUJA, DEAN POMERLEAU & TODD JOCHEM

In 1991, Karl Sims presented work on artificial evolution in which he used genetic algorithms to evolve complex structures for use in computer-generated images and animations. The evolution of the computer-generated images progressed from simple, randomly generated shapes to interesting images which the users created interactively. The evolution advanced under the constant guidance and supervision of the user. This paper describes attempts to automate the process of image evolution through the use of artificial neural networks. The central objective of this study is to learn the user's preferences, and to apply this knowledge to evolve aesthetically pleasing images which are similar to those evolved through interactive sessions with the user. This paper presents a detailed performance analysis of both the successes and shortcomings encountered in the use of five artificial neural network architectures. Further possibilities for improving the performance of a fully automated system are also discussed.

KEYWORDS: Artificial neural networks, computer-generated images, genetic algorithms, genetic programming.

1. Introduction

In automating a system to produce aesthetically pleasing images, two fundamental components must interact. The first component encompasses the mechanisms to create images. The second component must evaluate the images and choose the next move. The system developed here draws from the field of genetic algorithms and genetic programming for the mechanisms used to create potentially pleasing images. The tool used to evaluate the images produced by the genetic procedures is an artificial neural network.

Genetic algorithms were chosen as the method for creating images because they are general-purpose tools designed to explore irregular, poorly characterized function spaces. One such function space is the space of possible pixel images. With the aid of a genetic algorithm, a user can explore the space of images. This exploration, although dependent upon the user, is aided by the mechanisms inherent to the genetic algorithm. Karl Sims showed this to be a very effective method of creating aesthetically pleasing images (Sims, 1991). In viewing genetic algorithms as a search

This article appeared originally in *Connection Science*, 1994, **6**, 325–354, and is reprinted with permission.

tool, perhaps a better explanation of the role of the genetic algorithm is to emphasize their ability to 'find' appealing images rather than to create appealing images. This distinction will become apparent throughout this paper. The goal of this work is to automate the process of finding aesthetically pleasing images—to simulate the constant interaction of the user.

Artificial neural networks (ANNs) are the principal tool used in automating the evaluation of images. There were several reasons for choosing ANNs over other potential methods for addressing this problem. Perhaps the most important motivation was that the desired computation can be 'programmed' into the ANN by repeatedly presenting examples of the desired behavior. This property allows ANNs to perform tasks for which creating explicit rules may either be an overwhelming or an extremely time-consuming endeavor. This property also maps well to the requirement of the task. It is often the case that a user will be able to decide whether or not a particular image is appealing, but will find it difficult to express what particular characteristic, or set of characteristics, makes it appealing. For many rule-based systems, this constraint would make the task of automating the user's role extremely difficult. However, as ANNs only require examples of desired behavior, this small amount of information may be enough. This ability must also be considered in light of the drawbacks it presents. If the ANN is able to perform the task on which it is trained, in other than the simplest of tasks, it becomes a very difficult undertaking to determine what the ANN has 'learned', and an even harder task to translate the knowledge embedded in the ANN into understandable rules.

In order to ensure that there is as little bias as possible in the ANN, the raw two-dimensional image is used as the input into the ANN. This ensures that the ANN is not limited to the features which the experimenters deem to be important; rather, the ANN can develop the features necessary for accomplishing the task.

The remainder of this section gives an introduction to image evolution. In Section 2, image evolution is explored in depth, through the perspective of the genetic algorithm. Section 3 describes how the user can create images using the genetic algorithm's search mechanisms. Section 4 describes several attempts to automate the user's role with artificial neural networks. Section 5 compares the ANN architectures explored in Section 4 on a sample test set. Section 6 describes how the trained ANNs can be used to automate image evolution, and presents six automatically evolved images. Finally, Section 7 presents methods of improving the automation of future systems.

1.1. Image Evolution

In 1991, Sims presented a novel approach for combining genetic algorithms with computer graphics (Sims, 1991). The system which Sims designed allows users to evolve complex figures without concern for the mathematics used to generate the images. The interface is simple: given a number of initially random figures, the users select the two which are the most interesting. These figures are used as 'parents' to produce a subsequent population of 'offspring'. The offspring possess some attributes of both parent images. From the new population of images, two parents are selected, and the cycle continues. Through this iterated process of interactive selection, the images, which may have started out as simple, uninteresting lines, can become interesting images which the users have evolved under their guidance.

Sims extended his work beyond the production of figures; he also explored the evolution of solid textures, three-dimensional plant structures and animations. One of the most attractive aspects of this style of interactive graphics development is that it abstracts many of the cumbersome details of image production away from the users. The users are not required to know how the graphics are generated, how offspring are produced from two parent images or how the images are internally represented.

The power of this method lies in the ability to direct the progress of evolution. Perhaps the easiest way to describe both how and why this process works is by analogy. By selecting some images to be the parents of the next generation, and not selecting others, the users create a bias in the evolution based upon their own likes and dislikes. The figures which are 'strong', with respect to the users' tastes, are more likely to be selected as the parents of the next generation. Assuming that the parent 'chromosomes' (the internal representation of the images) have a means to pass their 'qualities' to their children, the characteristics found in the parent images are also found in varying degrees in members of the subsequent populations. Continuing this analogy, Darwin's theory of survival of the fittest plays an integral role in explaining how subsequent populations become closer to the users' preferences. The users' preferences are the basis of the fitness function. Through a number of generations, the characteristics which the users do not find interesting will not be selected for recombination. Only the images which contain characteristics which the users find interesting will be selected; therefore, only these will influence the composition of subsequent populations.

The image evolution employed in this study, and in Sims' work, uses symbolic expressions in prefix form to specify images. These expressions specify how to calculate a color value for each pixel coordinate on a two-dimensional plane. Upon selection of two parent images, the images are recombined through the use of genetic cross-over and mutation operators. Details of these operators and the primitives which comprise the defining expressions are given in Section 2. From the two parents, a new population of children is produced, and the cycle is continued.

1.2. Background Information

One of the most attractive features of the type of evolution described in the previous section is the simplicity of the users' role; users only have to select the images which they find interesting. Although Sims used this basic idea for evolution in a variety of domains, the scope of this study is limited to two-dimensional images. The ideas presented here can be extended to the other domains examined by Sims, as the principles underlying each are very similar.

The central objective of this study is to learn the user's preferences and to apply this knowledge to evolve images which are similar to those evolved through interactive sessions with the user. In the system described to this point, the user must remain an active participant throughout the entire evolution, continuously selecting two images to be the parents of the subsequent generation's population. To attempt to learn a user's preferences, the user is asked to rate interest in each image in a set of collected sample images. These ratings are used to train an artificial neural network, which receives as training examples an image and the user's rating of the image. It is hoped that the artificial neural network will be able to generalize user preferences to images not in the initial sample, thereby making possible an automation of the selection process. This has the potential to reduce participation of a user to only judging a small set of images, rather than supervising the entire evolution.

2. Simulating Evolution with Genetic Algorithms

2.1. An Introduction to Genetic Algorithms

The genetic algorithm (GA) is established upon the foundations of natural selection and genetic recombination. A GA combines the principles of survival of the fittest with a randomized information exchange (Goldberg, 1989). Although the information exchange is randomized, the GA is far different from a simple random walk. A GA has the ability to recognize trends towards optimal solutions, and to exploit such information by guiding the search toward them.

A genetic algorithm maintains a population of potential solutions to the objective function being optimized. The initial group of potential solutions is determined randomly. These potential solutions, called 'chromosomes', are allowed to evolve over a number of generations. At every generation, the fitness of each chromosome is calculated. The fitness is a measure of how well the potential solution optimizes the objective function. The subsequent generation is created by recombining pairs of chromosomes in the current generation. Recombination between two chromosomes is the method through which the populations 'evolve' better solutions. The solutions are probabilistically chosen for recombination based upon their fitness. Although the chromosomes with high fitness values will have a higher probability of being selected for recombination than those which do not, they are not guaranteed to appear in the next generation. The 'children' chromosomes produced by the genetic recombination are not necessarily better than their 'parent' chromosomes. Nevertheless, because of the selective pressure applied through a number of generations, the overall trend is towards better chromosomes.

In most applications which employ genetic algorithms, the objective function is well defined. However, for this application it is not easy to define a clear objective. Although it is simple to say that the objective is to search for 'interesting' shapes and figures, this leads to further complications. Not only does 'interesting' vary from person to person, it also varies in an individual from instance to instance. In this system, the user has an integral role in deciding which images are interesting, and therefore serves the role of the objective function. This will be explored in greater detail in Section 2.4. Once the user has supplied the evaluations, the genetic algorithm can proceed in the same way as a standard genetic algorithm using a clearly defined objective function.

In order to perform extensive search, genetic diversity must be maintained. When diversity is lost, it is possible for the GA to settle into a local optimum. The basic GA uses two fundamental mechanisms to maintain diversity. The first, mentioned above, is a probabilistic scheme for selecting which chromosomes to recombine. This ensures that information other than that which is represented in the best chromosomes appears in the subsequent generation. Recombining only good chromosomes will cause the population to converge very quickly without extensive exploration, thereby increasing the possibility of finding only a local optimum. The second mechanism is mutation, which helps to preserve diversity and to escape from local optima. Mutations introduce random changes into the population.

The GA is typically allowed to continue for a fixed number of generations. At the conclusion of the specified number of generations, the best chromosome in the final population, or the best chromosome ever found, is returned. Unlike the majority of other search heuristics, GAs do not work from a single point in the function space. Many methods which use only a single point to explore the function space are very susceptible to local optima. GAs continually maintain a population of points from which the function space is explored; this aids in finding global optima (Baluja, 1992).

2.2. The Composition of Chromosomes

In many optimization problems for which GAs are used, the chromosomes are represented as bit strings. Although such a representation is possible for this task, a more natural representation is symbolic prefix-order expressions. The set of 19 primitives from which the symbolic expressions are composed is shown below. The set of primitives used in this study is smaller and simpler than that chosen by Sims. If interesting images are to evolve, the GA must combine only these simple primitives in novel ways. The primitives are categorized into two classes, those which take one argument, and those which take two.

One argument: reciprocal (1/argument), natural log, log (base 10), exponent, square, square root, sine, hyperbolic sine, cosine, hyperbolic cosine.

Two arguments: average, minimum, maximum, addition, subtraction, multiplication, division, modulo, random (randomly choose either argument 1 or argument 2).

Using these simple primitives, a sample equation might be

   subtract (log(x), avg(sqrt(y), log(x)))

where x and y represent coordinates on the pixel plane. One method of increasing the diversity in the images produced is to add new primitives. For example, with the primitives which Sims allowed, such as iterative statements, fractal images can also be evolved. Some of the other primitives which Sims included were noise generators, blur operators and bandpass convolutions. Several of these primitives rely upon neighboring pixel values; the primitives chosen for this study do not. Further, each of the primitives are functions of x and/or y only. For simplicity, no explicit constants are used in the equations. The next section will show how these equations are used in genetic recombination.

2.3. Recombination of Chromosomes

The effectiveness of GAs lies in their ability to recombine good solutions to produce potentially better solutions. As chromosomes are, in many GA tasks, represented as fixed-size bit strings, cross-over operators are usually straightforward: a randomly chosen section of bits from the two parent chromosomes are swapped, and the two resulting chromosomes are the offspring. However, as the potential 'solutions' used here are not bit strings, this simple form of cross-over is not appropriate for two reasons. First, restricting the growth of equations to a fixed size may be detrimental to the production of interesting images, as larger equations may result in more interesting images. Simple swapping may not work, as a long expression may not have corresponding counterparts in shorter expressions. Second, it is not evident how such a simple cross-over can be implemented, since two equations may have different structures, as shown in Figure 1.

In order to provide a general cross-over mechanism, a cross-over operator

sin
|
cos
|
avg
/ \
x   log
|
y

sin (cos (avg (x, log (y))))

subtract
/ \
log avg
| / \
x sqrt log
| |
y   x

subtract (log(x), avg (sqrt(y), log(x)))

Figure 1. Two unique chromosomes structures which may be 'bred' together to produce 'children' chromosomes.

commonly employed in 'genetic programming' tasks is used (Koza, 1992). It designates one parent to be a 'receiver', and the second to be a 'donator'. Once the roles have been assigned, the cross-over procedure is as follows.

(1) Randomly choose a node in the donator's tree structure.
(2) Randomly choose a node in the receiver's tree structure.
(3) Delete everything at, and below, the chosen node in the receiver's tree.
(4) Copy everything at and below the donator's chosen node to the receiver's chosen node.

Figure 2 shows five of the possible children of the two equations shown in Figure 1.

2.4. Assessing the Fitness of a Chromosome

The objective of the GA is to find 'interesting' shapes and figures. In order to avoid the complexities involved with attempting to quantify the quality of being 'interesting', the issue is not addressed directly. In this system, as well as Sims' system, the user plays an active role in deciding what is interesting: the user's

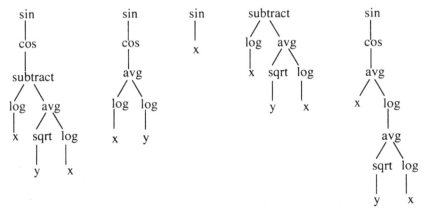

Figure 2. Five potential children of *sin(cos(avg(x,log(y))))* and *subtract (log(x), avg(sqrt(y),log(x)))*. For these examples, the first equation is defined as the receiver and the second as donator.

preferences are the objective function. If an image in the current population satisfies a user's objective in evolving images, its chances of being chosen increase above the others. This not only avoids the problems associated with quantifying interest, it also does not limit the program to one interpretation of 'interesting'. The drawback to this method is that it requires the constant interaction of the user. In Section 4, methods for automating the interaction are presented.

2.5. *The Need for Preserving Diversity in Genetic Search*

Maintaining diversity is crucial to performing productive genetic search. If diversity is not maintained, premature convergence of genetic search can lead to non-optimal solutions. In the context of GAs used for function optimization, premature convergence can correspond to finding a strong local optima. In the context of image production, loss of diversity may cause the images produced after convergence to be very similar to each other. Unless the user is satisfied with the types of images produced, further attempts at search may be unproductive.

Three mechanisms are used to preserve diversity. The first is the alternating of roles between the two parents as receiver and donator. The second is inherent to the system: the users are free to choose images which are to their liking or which are simply 'different' from the other images on the screen. As a brief observation of users has shown, users will often choose an image because it is different from the other images on the screen. The third mechanism is mutation, which is described below.

2.5.1. *Mutation.*

Recombining similar chromosomes over a number of generations can cause subsequent populations to converge very quickly. Mutation is a mechanism used to avoid stagnation in genetic search. In genetic algorithms which use chromosomes represented as bit strings, mutation is usually implemented as a random bit flip. In this system, the mutation operator selects a random node within the equation, and randomly changes its contents. If the function at the node has only one parameter, the new function is randomly chosen from the set of one-parameter functions, and similarly for two-parameter functions. If the node contains an 'x', it is changed to 'y', and vice versa. The mutation rate used in this study is a constant one mutation per chromosome per generation.

3. Interactively Evolving Computer-generated Images

The description of the user interface is not critical in understanding the methods used to automate the system. It is included to provide a description of the role of the user, and therefore of the task which will be automated.

3.1. *The User Interface*

When the program is initialized, nine images are displayed on the screen. These images correspond to nine randomly generated expression trees (chromosomes), using the primitives described in Section 2.2. Two of these images are selected by the user to be the parents of the next generation. From the chosen parents, nine new children are produced which replace the previous nine images displayed. This process is repeated until the user has found an image which is satisfactory.

The images are composed of 256 colors. There were two motivations for using only 256 colors. The first was that by the use of only a few colors, the emphasis in the images is shifted away from the colors in the image to the structures produced. Secondly, and more importantly, 256 colors allowed an easier implementation of the training phase of the ANN. This will be discussed in greater detail in Section 4.

Unlike Sims' work, the possible colors were determined before the evolutionary process was started. However, this could easily be modified to allow the color selection to also be evolved. The color scheme chosen was 128 shades of grey, followed by 128 shades of red. We found that this gives pleasing results, partially because of the simplicity in the color scheme, and partially because it creates an artificial boundary between the bright white and very dark red colors.

3.1.1. Using the image repository.   In addition to the nine images with which the user is presented, the user may, at any time, also store and recall images from the image repository. If the user decides that the population has become too homogeneous, as in Figure 3, the user has the option to save the image repository to disk for later use, and to load previously saved images into the repository for immediate use. With this facility, it is possible to combine images from different sessions (see Figure 4). Because of the random nature of genetic algorithms, the evolutions at each session will be different, and unique images will evolve. Using the image repository as a way to recombine previously stored images with the current images can be considered analogous to using several subpopulations to evolve chromosomes in parallel (Cohoon *et al.*, 1988).

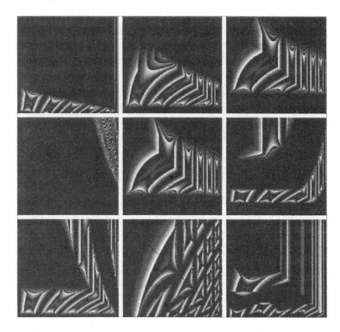

Figure 3. The nine images shown in this figure are children of the same parents. The images are very similar; heterogeneity in the population is lost. It is likely that any two parents chosen from this set of nine will lead to children which are very similar to the images seen here.

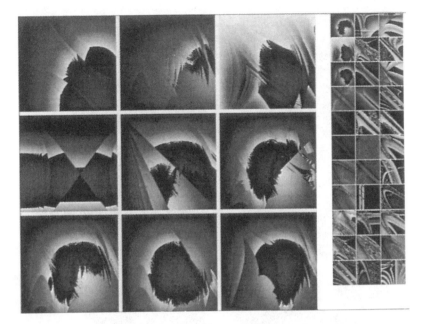

Figure 4. The user interface. The nine large images on the left represent the children of the previously selected parents. The images on the right are in the image repository. These images can be used for recombination in subsequent generations. The top three images in the first column of the repository are smaller copies of three of the images found in the larger squares. The defining equations for the three images on the bottom row of the nine large images are shown in the appendix.

3.2. Selected Images

Six images which were produced through several interactive evolution sessions are shown in Figure 5. Although these images used the red and grey color map described previously, the color map could have easily been chosen differently. For printing purposes, the images are presented in grey-scale.

4. Towards Automation

4.1. Motivation and Overview

To this point, the mechanisms for interactively evolving computer-generated images have been described. The users do not need to know any of the underlying mathematics or the mechanisms used to recombine the equations which the images represent. Although this provides a simple interface with which to interact, it is quite a challenging task to automate the user's decisions. The rest of this paper presents descriptions and analysis of the attempts to automate the process of parent selection, and the various successes and failures encountered in the pursuit of this goal.

The mechanism employed to learn the user's preferences is an ANN. The ANN is trained to give an evaluation to each image it is presented, without respect to any other image which may also be on the screen. The evaluation is on the scale of −1 to +1, with larger numbers representing greater preference. The network is

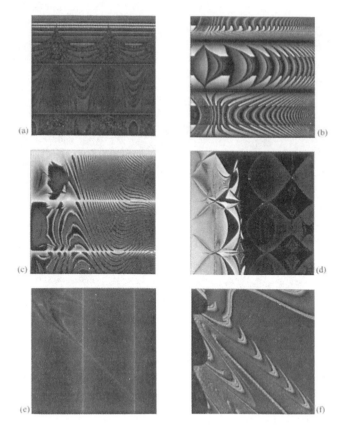

Figure 5. Six images, produced through several interactive evolution sessions, are shown in Figure 5. Although these images used the color map described previously, the color map could have easily been chosen differently.

trained on a large set of images which the user has previously graded on a similar scale.

ANNs were chosen as the learning tool because of their ability to generalize. If ANNs are not over-trained and are sufficiently large, they hold the potential for generalization to images which have not yet been encountered. Unlike many other non-learning techniques which may fail catastrophically if presented with images which have not yet been encountered, ANNs show a slower degradation of performance. The accuracy of the ANN's prediction degrades with the presentation of images which have decreasing similarity with the training images. Therefore, in training the ANN, it is important to get a diverse enough sample group to give a good representation of the input space. This is a particularly hard task for this domain, as the set of all possible functions which can be evolved is infinite.

The attempts to teach the ANN a user's preferences are conducted with raw two-dimensional pixels as the inputs to the ANN. The hope is that the ANN will develop the feature detectors and internal representations which are required to simulate accurately the preferences of the user. Pixel-based inputs have been used successfully in a variety of other tasks, such as autonomous road following (Pomerleau, 1992), gaze tracking (Baluja & Pomerleau, 1994) and recognizing handwritten ZIP codes (Le Cun *et al.*, 1989). However, in comparison to this task, the aforementioned applications have had a much more structured input. The variety of inputs the ANN is likely to encounter in this study is much larger than in the other domains; therefore, the internal representations needed may be substantially more complex.

One possible alternative to using only the image pixels is to pre-process the image with traditional vision-based techniques in order to extract features such as circles, lines, noise, etc., and use these high-level features as inputs into the ANN. However, the goal of this study is to perform the task with as little a *priori* knowledge of salient image features embedded in the ANN as possible. By building few assumptions about the basis of the user's preferences into the network, the system maintains the maximum amount of flexibility.

4.2. The Training Set

To train the ANN, a set of 400 unique 48×48 pixel images was used. The process used to obtain these images was as follows. Through several interactive evolutions, the two images the subject chose as parents of the next generation, as well as two randomly selected images from the selection of nine images present on the screen, became candidates for the training set. Several hundred images were collected in total. From this collection, 400 images were randomly chosen for the final training set. The subject was asked to rank these images individually on a scale of 0.1 to 1.0, in increments of 0.1, to gauge preference towards each image. To train the ANN, the subject's ranking was scaled to the range -1 to $+1$. Although collecting only randomly generated images would have been easier than selecting images from interactive evolutions, randomly created images are generally not very interesting or pleasing. Therefore, in order to provide the ANN with examples of images which were ranked high as well as low, images which were selected by the user further into the interactive evolution were required.

The training set was developed using the above method to ensure that the included images uniformly spanned the set of possible rankings. The measures taken only partially accomplished this task. One of the difficulties inherent to the task of automation is that the relative availability of images which the user is likely to find uninteresting is very high in comparison to the images which the user is likely to find interesting. In order to show the distribution of the rankings of images obtained in a readily accessible format, the evaluations are divided into three categories, 'low', 'medium' and 'high'. The range of these categories is shown below. One of the peculiarities about this division is that although the 'low' region begins at 0.0, the users only graded images between 0.1 and 1.0, in increments of 0.1.

$0.0 \leq Low \leq 0.4$

$0.4 < Medium \leq 0.7$

$0.7 < High \leq 1.0$

Given this ranking, the distribution of the images into these three categories in the training and testing set is given in Table I. The majority of the images are classified by the user into the 'low' region. As will be seen in the next section, the skewed distribution of the images is a potential cause of degraded performance in classifying images in the 'medium' and 'high' ranges. In order to eliminate the effects of a training set with a skewed distribution of training points, the performance of ANNs

Table I. User classification of training and testing images

Image set	Number of images in set	Percentage of 'low' images	Percentage of 'medium' images	Percentage of 'high' images
Training	2000	64	19	17
Testing	1200	61	22	17

trained on uniformly distributed training sets was also measured. In several of the tests performed, a large number of the images ranked in the 'low' region were removed from the training set in order to make the number of images in each region more uniform. These tests will be described in greater detail throughout the remainder of this section.

A simplifying assumption made in the process of automation was that the user's preference of an image was based upon the structures present in the image. Further, it was assumed that the user would like the same structures in any degree of rotation. To achieve a small amount of rotation tolerance, each image in the training set was rotated three times by 90°. As the role of color was de-emphasized, while the role of shape was given more importance, the inverses of the original and each of the three rotated images were also captured. Because the color scheme only used 256 colors, the inverse of each image was calculated by subtracting the pixel's value from 256. This resulted in seven additional images for each original image; these additional images were assigned the same rating as the original image. Each image was composed of pixels with values in the range of 0–255, linearly scaled to values between −1 to +1. A total of 3200 images were produced in this manner. From the 3200 images, 2000 images were randomly chosen for use in training the ANN; the remaining 1200 images were used in the test set. It should be noted that the images within the training set and the testing set are correlated as they may be rotations or inverses of each other. No duplicate chromosomes (the equations which the image represent) were allowed in the set of 400 original chromosomes. However, because many images are taken from each sequence of evolutions, it is possible that different chromosomes may represent similar images. The ramifications of these limitations on the test set will be discussed in greater detail in Section 5.

4.3. Preliminary Trials and Improvements

The first ANN architecture explored was a simple one hidden-layer network, as shown in Figure 6. The input layer is arranged as a 48×48 grid, each coordinate corresponding to a pixel in the image. The input layer is fully connected to the hidden unit layer, which contains nine units. The hidden layer is fully connected to the output layer, which consists of a single output neuron. The output is a single value, which corresponded to the 'estimated preference value' of the image. The output neuron yields a value between −1 and +1, where −1 indicates a poor image according to its training set, and +1 indicates a good image. Although not shown, a bias input unit, a unit with its value permanently clamped to 1, is also present. The bias unit is connected to the hidden and output layers (Hertz *et al.*, 1991).

The single hidden-layer ANN, as well as all of the other ANNs mentioned throughout this paper, was trained using the standard error back-propagation algorithm. Although this network's error decreased rapidly through the training

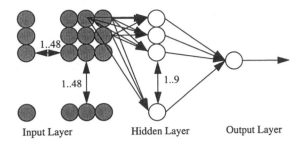

Input Layer   Hidden Layer   Output Layer

Figure 6. The first ANN architecture attempted. In this model, there are a total of $((48 \times 48 + 1) \times 9 + 9 \times 1 + 1) = 20\ 755$ connections, including the bias unit's connections.

process, the network was unable to make reasonable selections on the training or test sets. For example, the network sometimes chose almost blank images to be parent chromosomes. Although this sometimes led to interesting 'children', as blank images may be the result of complex equations, the choices did not correspond to the choices a human user would be likely to make. To improve the performance on subsequent attempts, both the network architecture and the presentation of the training and testing images was modified. The modifications are described below.

The first modification was to alter the red features to appear as grey. One difficulty with using pixel values as inputs into the ANN is that although the user sees a great distinction between the pixel values of 127 (white) and 128 (very dark red), the neural network cannot place the correct emphasis on this 'color cliff'. The values which are given to train the neural network (127 and 128) are very close to each other, yet form a much more pronounced visual jump than the values from 126 to 127 or 128 to 129. The relative closeness of the color values does not adequately represent the great difference in actual appearance. To address this, all of the images were pre-processed to reduce both of the red and grey scales to only grey scale. This was accomplished by subtracting 128 from all pixels with a value greater than 127. Many of the important features of the image were still kept, although sudden discontinuities between bright red and bright grey in the original pictures were sometimes lost. However, the discontinuities which occurred between white and dark red were still prominent in the pre-processed image. This modification placed a larger emphasis on features rather than colors, and effectively reduced the color space to 128 shades of gray. Each pixel was again scaled to the range -1 to $+1$.

The second modification was the introduction of weight yoking, or weight sharing, in the ANN, to achieve some degree of shift invariance. Shift invariance is necessary, as a user who finds an interesting feature in one portion of the image may also find the same feature interesting in a different region of the image. Weight yoking is a technique used to find features regardless of where they appear in the image. LeCun *et al.* (1989) have used it successfully in their attempts to recognize hand-written Zip Codes. The technique of weight yoking in a spatial dimension is also commonly used outside of the visual domain. For example, similar techniques are frequently used in speech-recognition tasks (Waibel, 1990). As speech is fundamentally a process which occurs through time, one way of designing an ANN to learn patterns over time is to map the patterns into an ordered spatial dimension. As Todd points out, by performing this mapping, the problem of learning patterns over time becomes one of learning spatial patterns (Todd, 1989). Although Todd opts for a different technique for using connectionist architectures to learn structures in music, he also points out that the problem is decomposable in a similar manner.

Training a standard ANN on pixel images will not encourage the recognition of features in locations other than those in which they appeared in the images of the training set. With weight yoking, groups of weights work as templates, or feature detectors, which are uniformly used in many locations throughout the input array. In networks that do not use weight sharing, when feature detectors are developed through training, they are only sensitive to locating features in the regions in which they occurred in the images of the training set. Weight sharing allows the developed feature detectors to be applied in many other locations. A more detailed description of weight yoking is given in LeCun *et al.* (1989).

Figure 7 provides a pictorial description of weight yoking. For this large

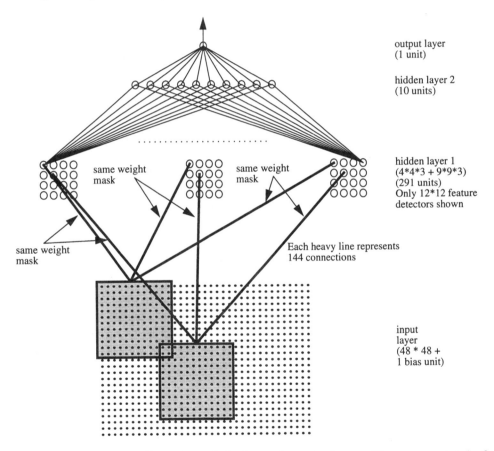

Figure 7. Only a small portion of the input layer is shown. There are a total of 9×9 (81) 6×6 input groups and a total of 4×4 (16) 12×12 input groups. Each 6×6 group is connected to three units in hidden layer 1. Each 12×12 group is also connected to three units in hidden layer 1. Only the 12×12 feature detectors are shown. The bias unit (not shown) is connected to each of the hidden units (in hidden layer 1 and in hidden layer 2) and the output layer. The total number of connections is $(81 \times (36 + 1) \times 3) + (16 \times (144 + 1) \times 3) + ((291 + 1) \times 10) + (10 + 1) = 18\ 822$.

architecture, there were a total of six yoked groups, three which covered an area of the image 6×6 pixels in area, and three which were 12×12 pixels. Each yoked group has the same weight templates, which were applied to many regions across the image. For the tests presented here, the spacing between applications of the weight template was 5×5 pixels for the 6×6 groups, and 10×10 pixels for the 12×12 groups; the templates overlapped each other. The second hidden layer consisted of 10 fully connected neurons. The final output was a single unit.

4.4. Gauging Network Performance

The network was trained with the 2000-image training set previously described. In order to gauge the ability of the system to classify images as the user would classify them, a set of 1200 test images was used. Table II gives the total error in classifying the images. The error is computed as follows:

$$Sum\ of\ Errors = \sum_{i=0}^{1200} |(UserPreference_i - NetworkEstimatedPreference_i)|$$

User Preference and *NetworkEstimatedPreference* are normalized between 0 and 1.

The error in classifying the images decreases through the training period. Each epoch represents a presentation of the 2000 training images to the ANN. In order to create a point of reference from which to compare the performance of the ANN, four other simple measurements are given. Three of the measurements output constant values of 0.3, 0.5 and 0.7 for the evaluation of each image. The fourth measurement randomly selects a value between 0.0 and 1.0. Of these four measurements, the constant value of 0.3 should perform the best as the majority of the images were placed into the 'low' region by the user. Although the ANN classification's were better than these four simple measurements, consistently producing an output of 0.3 does comparably well with the ANN outputs between 75 and 300 epochs.

In order to ensure that the ANN is learning more than the simple probability distribution of the user's responses, the performance of a biased random number generator is examined. The random number generator was tested with two settings, the first which generates numbers with the distribution the ANN predicts at epoch 600, and the second in which the random numbers are generated in the actual distribution of the testing data. The results of this simulation revealed that the errors

Table II. Performance measurements—sum of errors (1200-image test set)

Method of classification	Sum of errors	Average error per image
ANN output (epoch 0)	371.71	0.31
ANN output (epoch 75)	298.00	0.25
ANN output (epoch 150)	288.74	0.24
ANN output (epoch 300)	287.50	0.24
ANN output (epoch 450)	271.58	0.23
ANN output (epoch 600)	269.78	0.22
Constant output of 0.30	292.90	0.24
Constant output of 0.50	324.50	0.27
Constant output of 0.70	443.90	0.37
Random output	402.94	0.34

Table III. Error per region—'Large' ANN architecture (1200-image test set)

Description	Error from classifying each region's images (% of total error)		
	Low	Medium	High
Random	64	17	19
Epoch 0	78	05	17
Epoch 75	49	16	35
Epoch 150	50	15	35
Epoch 300	50	18	32
Epoch 450	48	22	30
Epoch 600	48	22	30

of using a biased random number output to be close to those of the ANN between epochs 0 and 75 (Baluja *et al.*, 1993).

In order to improve the performance of the ANN, it is first important to discover where the errors are occurring. Table III provides a breakdown of the occurrences of errors by region. During the beginning of training, at epoch 0, although the classifications are essentially random, they are largely within the medium range, as the network is initialized with intermediate range weights. As almost all of the images are classified within the 'medium' range, the images actually in the 'medium' range contribute very little to the total error. As training progresses, the performance on the 'low' range images continues to improve at the expense of correct classification of both the 'medium' and 'high' range images. Because of the disproportionate number of images placed in the 'low' region by the user, the degradation in performance of two of the three regions still allows the overall classification error to be reduced. By epoch 600, the total error contributions of the 'low' region is 48%, and the 'high' region is 30%. However, the images ranked into the 'low' region by the user comprise 61% of the total number of images in the testing set, while the images in the 'high' region comprise only 17%.

Because of the skewed distribution of images in each region, correct classification of images in the 'low' region has the potential for greater error reduction than the correct classification of images in the 'high' range. During the early stages of training, the ANN reduces the total error by improving the classification of 'low' region images. After epoch 75, the errors in classifying the images in the 'high' region are also reduced. As the initial classification placed all of the images into the 'medium' range, adding further discrimination decreases the tendency to classify images into this range, and thereby increases the errors associated with classifying 'medium' range images. Figure 8 shows graphically the average error of the three regions as a function of epochs.

In analyzing the distribution of correctly classified images, it was found that by epoch 600, 35% of all the images are classified within an error of 0.1. Only 26% of the images in the 'medium' range and 9% of the images in the 'high' range fall into this category. The remaining images in this category constitute 45% of the images in the 'low' range. It is evident, therefore, that if the test set included no 'low' images, the ANN would not perform well; the errors of the 'medium' and 'high' ranges would not be offset by the effects of correctly classifying 'low' images. As it is usually assumed that the training and testing sets have similar distributions, perhaps this result is expected.

Average Error By Region and Epoch
Large Architecture, 2000 Image Training Set

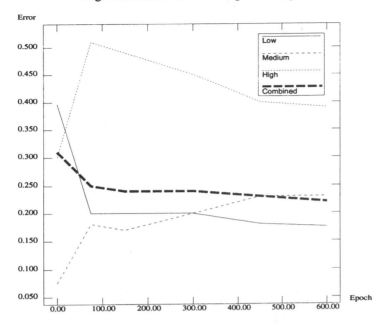

Figure 8. The average errors with classifying each region's images are shown as a function of epochs. The results for the 'Large' ANN, trained with the 2000-image training set, are shown. The performance is measured on the 1200-image test set.

The results given in this section accord very well with our intuitive expectations: training with a non-uniformly distributed training set will hurt performance in the classes which are not represented well. The question arises of what the ANN can learn from a uniformly distributed training set; one which contains approximately equal numbers of 'low', 'medium' and 'high' images. The first motivation for this test is determining whether the large number of training examples in the 'low' region made it possible to do well in classifying images in the 'low' region, or whether it was the features inherent to the images classified within the 'low' region. The second motivation is the hope that once the ANN is trained on a uniformly distributed training set, there will be less reliance on the distribution of images, and the ANN will be able to perform well on uniformly distributed test sets, as well as non-uniformly distributed test sets, which are likely to be generated by human users.

In order to rectify the problems associated with a skewed distribution of images in the training set, a smaller, uniformly distributed training set was created. This smaller training set comprised 1120 images. Of the 2000 images which were present in the previous training set, 880 randomly selected 'low' ranked images were removed. After removal of these images, the distribution of the smaller training set was 'low': 36%, 'medium': 33%, 'high': 31%. In order to gauge performance to the previous results, the same test set, of 1200 images, was used.

The first problem encountered with a reduced-size training set was that the ANN described in the previous section was able to memorize a large portion of the training data, thereby making generalization impossible. To reduce the probability of memorization, three variations of reduced-size ANNs were tested. Each is based

Table IV. Original and three smaller ANN architectures

Architecture	12 × 12 retina grids	6 × 6 retina grids	Total hidden units	Total connections
Original, Large ANN	3	3	301	18882
Small ANN 1	3	0	58	7461
Small ANN 2	1	1	107	6308
Small ANN 3	0	2	172	7635

upon the yoked-weight architecture described previously, and shown in Figure 7. The primary difference between these architectures and the previously described 'Large' ANN is a reduction in the number of feature detectors. The difference between the three smaller architectures is the number and types of feature detectors each contains. As only the size and number of feature detectors vary in the three small ANNs, the performance of each architecture will reflect the usefulness of its feature detectors in this domain. The number of connections was kept approximately equal in each of three smaller architectures. Table IV gives a brief description of the three smaller ANN architectures.

Each architecture was trained on the 1120-image set multiple times, with slightly different parameter settings. The performance of Small ANN 3 on both the training and testing sets was much worse than that of Small ANN 1 and 2. The failure of Small ANN 3 lends support to the hypothesis that the 6 × 6 retina grids are too small to pick up important features. It should also be considered that when the 6 × 6 retina grid is used in conjunction to the 12 × 12 retina grids (Small ANN 2), the performance of the network was comparable to using additional 12 × 12 grids (Small ANN 1). Due to Small ANN 3's inability to match the performance of the other ANNs, this architecture is not explored further in this paper.

The performances of Small ANN 1 and 2, trained with the 1120-image set, were comparable. A detailed examination of Small ANN 1 is presented in the next section. In the interest of space, the same detail is not devoted to Small ANN 2; however, it should be noted that the behaviors of both networks were very similar. The performance of Small ANN 2 is briefly returned to in Section 5; more details on this architecture can be found in Baluja *et al.* (1993).

4.5. Using a Smaller Architecture: Small ANN 1

This ANN architecture consisted of three 12 × 12 yoked groups. The performance of this ANN, trained on the 1120-image set, is measured on the 1200-image test

Table V. Distribution of error—Small ANN 1
(1200-image test set)

Epoch	Summed error	Error from classifying each region's images (% of total error)		
		Low	Medium	High
0	340.52	73	14	13
75	343.28	73	05	22
150	298.58	67	14	20
300	279.69	64	19	17
600	287.83	62	21	17
1200	297.67	61	22	17

Average Error by Region & Epoch
Small Architecture #1, 1120 Image Training Set

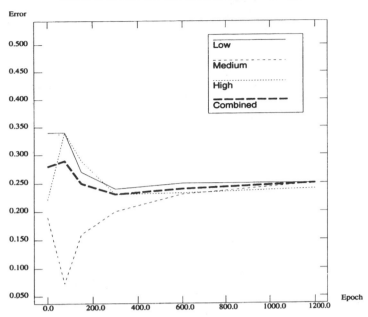

Figure 9. The average errors with classifying each region's images are shown as a function of epochs. The results for Small ANN 1, trained with the 1120-image training set, are shown. The performance is measured on the 1200-image test set.

set. Table V shows the distribution of errors at six points during training. By epoch 300, the error contribution from each region closely matches the percentage of images actually in each region of the test set. Unlike the original architecture examined, there is no bias towards better classification of 'low' images. Figure 9 shoes graphically the average errors for the three regions as a function of epochs.

In order to complete the comparison between the smaller architectures described above with that of the original 'Large' ANN described earlier in this section, one additional test needs to be performed. In the original test performed with the 'Large' ANN, there were more feature detectors and a larger training set than in the tests performed with Small ANN 1. In order to discern which of these two differences accounts for the difference in performances, Small ANN 1 needs to be trained with the larger, 2000 image, training set. It should be noted that the difference in performance was small, the 'Large' ANN was able to decrease the error to 269.78 (Table II), and the Small ANN 1 to 279.69 (Table V).

In this test, the 2000-image training set used was the same biased one used to train the large network. The testing set used is the same 1200 images used for testing the previous architectures. The lowest error reached with Small ANN 1 was at epoch 600. The summed error was 224.30, considerably lower than the lowest error, 269.78, achieved by the large network (Table II). This error is also smaller than the lowest errors achieved by any of the smaller architectures using a uniformly distributed training set.

The distribution of the errors among the three regions was most similar to the original, large, architecture. The distribution of errors across the regions was: 'low':

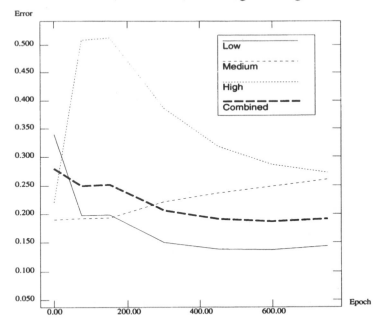

Average Error by Region & Epoch
Small Architecture #1, 2000 Image Training Set

Figure 10. The average errors with classifying each region's images are shown as a function of epochs. The results for Small ANN 1, trained with the 2000-image training set, are shown. The performance is measured on the 1200-image test set.

47%, 'medium': 29%, 'high': 26%. The skewed distribution of training images had the same effect on this architecture as the original 'Large' ANN; the images in the 'low' region were classified more accurately than those in the other regions. Figure 10 shows the average error of the three regions, using the Small ANN 1 and the full 2000-image training set, as a function of epochs. The average errors in classifications for Small ANN 1 were slightly higher with the larger training set than with the small training set for the 'medium' and 'high' range images (Figure 9, epoch 300 & Figure 10, epoch 600). However, the classification of 'low' images was more accurate using the larger training set. In comparison with the 'Large' ANN, which was also trained with the 2000-image set, this architecture classified the images more accurately. This indicates that this architecture may be more suited to this task than the original 'Large' ANN.

Figure 11 shows the distribution of the ANN's predicted classification and the human user's actual classification for the 1200-image test set. While the network underestimates the number of images in the lowest bin, the overall distribution matches the human's fairly closely.

There are at least three potential reasons why the presentation of the 2000-image training set leads to improved performance in comparison to the 1120-image training set. The first is the most intuitive—by giving an ANN more examples to train with, the ANN will be able to provide more accurate classifications. The second is that the correlation between the training and testing sets has increased. By examining the overlap between the 2000-image training set with the 1200-image

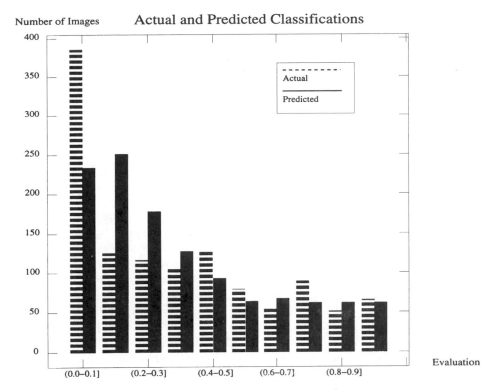

Figure 11. A histogram showing the distribution of responses from the user and the network on the 1200-image test set. The network's responses are taken from epoch 600.

testing set, 3.4% of the images were found in both the test set and the training set. In the smaller training set, consisting of 1120 images, 3.0% of the images in the test set were in the training set. Although there is an increase in the number of identical images in the larger training set, the increase is very small. The overlap in the training and testing sets occurs because different defining equations for the images may represent the same pixel image. In addition, because the images in the training and testing sets may be rotations or inverses of each other, the extra 880 images in the larger training set provide a much fuller, and more correlated, training set for the test set used. The third contributing factor is that by providing the network with many more 'low' images, the relative importance of correctly classify images in the 'low' region increases above the correct classification of images in the other two regions. In order to determine which of these factors contributed to the improved performance, an additional test was conducted with a new test set. The results are reported in the next section.

5. A Comparison of Architectures

In order to eliminate some of the biases in the training and testing sets mentioned in the previous section, an entirely new test set was gathered. It was chosen in a similar manner to the previous set, through several interactive evolution sessions. The new test set comprised a total of 100 images. From the set of 100 images, the

Table VI. Performance of ANNs on test set 2 (100-image test set)

ANN architecture	Number of image in training set	Summed error	Distribution of error (% of total)		
			Low	Medium	High
Large ANN	2000	34.05	63.3	32.2	4.4
Small ANN 1	1120	23.09	49.5	41.5	9.0
Small ANN 2	1120	20.99	47.8	43.9	8.2
Small ANN 1	2000	20.50	47.5	47.2	5.3
Random	N/A	31.64	68.8	28.8	2.3
Biased Random	N/A	24.28	53.7	42.0	4.2

user ranked 64 in the 'low' region, 32 in the 'medium' region and 4 in the 'high' region. The performance of the architectures which have performed well on the 1200-image test was measured at the epoch in which their error was minimized for the 1200-image test set. The performance of these architectures on the 100-image test set is shown in Table VI. Also shown is the performance of random classifications and biased random classifications. The biased random classifier outputs a classification in the 'low', 'medium' and 'high' regions with probabilities 0.64, 0.32 and 0.04, respectively. Although the results of the biased random classifier are included for comparison, the exact distribution of images would, of course, not be available when using the ANN to simulate the human user.

The results in Table VI are somewhat disappointing. The 'Large' ANN, which had delivered good results on the original 1200-image test set, did significantly worse than all the smaller ANN architectures. Further, it did worse than both the random and biased random outputs. Due to the correlation between training and testing sets, perhaps the most likely explanation of the success of the 'Large' ANN on the original testing set may be its greater potential for memorization of features required to do well in both the training and testing sets.

The best result came from Small ANN 1 and 2. Small ANN 1, with the large training set, and Small ANN 2, with the small training set, performed comparably. It is suspected that a larger training set could have also improved the performance of Small ANN 2. On the 100-image test set, both smaller architectures were able to classify images within the 'low' region much more accurately than the other regions, whether trained with the original training set or with the smaller, uniformly distributed training set.

In the previous section, it was shown that training Small ANN 1 with the larger set resulted in improved performance when tested on the 1200-image test set. This trend is again seen here with the 100-image test set. However, the results reported also suggest that the disproportionately large number of 'low' images in the training set may not be the only reason which makes them easier to classify (Table VI). Perhaps another reason for the more accurate classification of images in the 'low' range is that a large portion of the 'low' region's images may be similar. These images may be blank, or very simple horizontal or vertical lines. The possible uniformity and simplicity of the features contained in images which are classified by the user as 'low' may make them easier for the ANN to identify accurately. In contrast, attempting to classify images in the 'medium' and 'high' ranges is much more difficult as this requires a much deeper knowledge of the preferences of the user.

6. Discussion and Pictorial Results

Many factors make the process of automation difficult. First, there is the large task of collecting a diverse set of images from all the regions on the evaluation scale. This is an inherent difficulty for this task, as most images produced will probably not be interesting. It is only through the process of evolution that interesting images are found. A possible solution, which was explored in this paper, is to collect images while repeatedly simulating the process of manual evolution. The importance of using images from several evolution sessions is two-fold. First, using evolutions, rather than randomly generated images, increases the chances of obtaining a larger range in the user's rankings of images. Second, using several sessions ensures that the images produced will be diverse, as each simulation evolves unique images.

Another factor which makes this problem difficult is the desire to accomplish the task while embedding as little *a priori* knowledge as possible of the features which contribute to a user's preferences. Although some knowledge is inherent in an ANN architecture which implements weight sharing, the amount of knowledge is kept relatively small. The space in which this work was done, that of two-dimensional pixel images, was certainly not the easiest with which to train an ANN. Using two-dimensional pixels made the size of the networks very large, as multiple connections are constructed for each input pixel. Further, as the 'image space' defined by pixels is very large in comparison to the number of samples obtainable, generalization based upon the pixel representation is difficult. Other feature spaces could have been chosen, in which the input to the network is not the pixel values, but a more abstract representation of the image. Perhaps these inputs could be based on more traditional image features, as described before.

Other applications such as road following (Pomerleau, 1992) and gaze tracking (Baluja & Pomerleau, 1994) have had success with pixel input representations, and one reason for this is that spatial location and variation play an important role in determining the final outcome. In this application, both rotation and spatial invariance must be achieved, which is a much harder task. Additionally, as mentioned before, the range of images which are likely to be encountered in this task is much larger than in other tasks using pixel input representations.

Other factors which make this problem difficult arise not only in the ANN techniques for classification but also in the user's ranking of images. In the set of 400 images originally collected, several images which were exactly the same were ranked differently when given to the user to rank twice, indicating inconsistencies in the user's rankings. To make the problem harder, the user's preferences may be based upon small features in the image. For example, the image in Figure 5(e) would very rarely be picked for recombination by a fully trained ANN, as it is very similar to a simple blank screen.

All of the exploration of architectures and training sets described in the previous sections was done to develop an ANN to simulate a human user's behavior and preferences with respect to a genetic image generation system. In the automated system, the ANN is allowed to direct the genetic search. Several methods of implementing the automation were considered. The first method simply chose the two images to which the ANN gave the highest evaluation to be the parents of the next generation. However, the need for maintaining diversity in subsequent populations weighed heavily against this idea. As discussed previously, GAs need to preserve diversity in order to perform extensive exploration. If only the best candidate chromosomes are selected for recombination, the chromosomes produced rapidly become very homogenous; this can severely limit the potential for further genetic search. In order to avoid stagnation, an alternative method was adopted. In this implementation, the value the ANN returned for each image was used as a 'fitness' value. This fitness value was used to determine the image's probability for recombination. Images classified with higher fitness values had a higher probability of being chosen for recombination than those classified with lower ones. However, the best are not guaranteed to be chosen. Standard GAs also use similar probabilistic methods of selection.

Although the probabilistic method yielded good results, the automated system did not as yet incorporate the image repository. In order to provide a small mechanism to escape from very homogenous populations, the automated system selected images from the repository randomly, with a small probability, every generation. The repository was initialized with random images during system start-up. Using the repository allowed for more exploration to be conducted and provided an escape from too homogenous populations. The image repository has not yet been used to store images in the automated system.

The success of this project must finally be judged by the system's ability to create aesthetically pleasing images with minimal interaction of the user. Given this criterion, the results achieved are mixed and very difficult to quantify. The system is able to prune out bad images successfully. However, the judgements on the better images are not as accurate, and some of the better images are also mistakenly pruned away. Throughout this paper, the system has been evaluated on its ability to predict the user's preferences on a static image set. Although this is straightforward, in simulating evolutions, evaluation is much more difficult since the underlying process of evolution is stochastic. The decisions the ANN makes are combined with the random factors from the GA before the final product is produced. For example, the evaluations provided by the ANN are used as fitness values—they are used to select *probabilistically* the images from the population.

Further, other relevant characteristics of a human user are also hard to implement. In general, users have a very low patience when the current population converges to very similar images, and are apt to restart the program quickly, or to load alternative image libraries. However, the ANN has neither a notion of population convergence, nor the ability to reinitialize the population. The ANN provides an evaluation for each image based solely upon the image, and not on the population in which the image is contained. These are severe constraints in simulating a user. Nevertheless, in a more limited context, that of providing evaluations of the images to the GA so that it can continue its search process, the user's task can be automated by this project. The goal of this project was to create an end-to-end system which can automatically create pleasing images. Although a few of the automated evolutions have failed, as they converged very quickly and were unable to perform sufficient exploration to find pleasing images, other evolutions, in which convergence occurred much more slowly, revealed complex and interesting images.

An important question, which should be considered along with these results, is how important it is to have a learning agent trying to simulate the user. Would it be possible to get equally good results just using a random selection process? In the experiments attempted in this study, the ANN, in comparison to a random process which has a uniform probability of selecting any image, typically produces much more complex images, and maintains diversity in the population longer than simple random selection. One of the reasons that random selection performs poorly is that once a population loses diversity, it is difficult to regain it, given the cross-over and mutation operators used. For example, if two images which are each represented by small equations are recombined, the children produced are likely to be similar. The ANN-based selection method has the advantage of not generally selecting these images, because in its training set such images were usually given low evaluations by the user. As the ANNs used in this study have been given an extensive amount of training data with images which are not considered pleasing, the ANN is more likely to avoid selecting images which are represented by smaller equations, and thereby more likely to avoid convergence. Nonetheless, because the ANN makes errors in its judgements and because of the stochastic nature of the GA and the small population size used, the populations evolved in this study all eventually converge, whether they are evolved automatically, or manually. The success or failure of a particular evolution must be judged by the amount of useful exploration that is conducted before the population converges.

In order to show how the automated evolution typically progresses, Figure 12 presents two evolutions of 24 generations each. The figures show the two parents chosen for recombination in each generation. Figure 12(a) shows a typical evolution using uniform random selection for the images. As can be seen, the exploration is very limited and largely uninteresting. Because of the small probability of choosing randomly from the image repository, sometimes images from outside the population are chosen as parents. However, as the selection process is entirely random, the interesting children produced by the novel parent image may not be chosen again for recombination. Therefore, the population will again quickly converge to uninteresting images. The second set of images, Figure 12(b), shows a typical evolution which is controlled by the ANN. Immediately, a vast difference between Figure 12(a) and Figure 12(b) is apparent. The majority of the images chosen are more complex than those which appear in Figure 12(a). However, as can be seen, the network makes mistakes in its selection procedure. Towards the end, these mistakes happen in consecutive generations, the population loses its interesting properties, and quickly becomes too homogenous to perform further interesting search until an image from the repository is randomly selected.

Figure 13 presents 6 images which do not appear in Figure 12. These images were also selected for recombination by the ANN. These images were hand-picked from the results of several automated evolution sessions. In comparison to the images shown in Figure 5, which were manually evolved through many hours of interactive time with the system, the images in Figure 13 were selected by the authors in only a few minutes of interactive time with the automated system. One of the potential methods of using this system is to prune away the large number of images which the user will probably dislike, and to present only images which the user is likely to find interesting. Such methods of extending the ability to learn about the user's preferences to work in conjunction with the user is an area for future research. This concept is expanded upon in the next section.

7. Conclusions and Future Directions

The idea of hiding the details of how the mathematical functions are generated, recombined and stored, provides users with the ability to concentrate on the aspect of the algorithm with which they are concerned: the images. By simply selecting images which the users find interesting, it is possible to evolve subsequent populations of images which are closer to individual conceptions of 'interesting'.

Evolution is a powerful method for creating images (Sims, 1991; Todd &

(a)

(b)

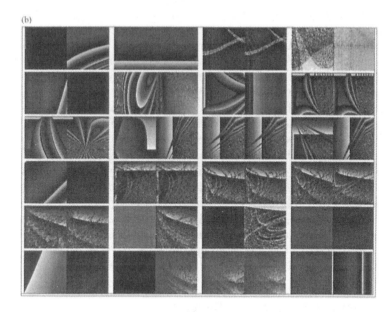

Figure 12. Two automated evolutions. The first is directed by a uniform random selection process. The second is directed by a trained ANN. The parents of 24 consecutive generations are shown. The parents of generations 1 are shown in the upper-left corner of the image. The sequence of consecutive generations proceeds from left to right. The lower-right corner images are the parents of generation 24.

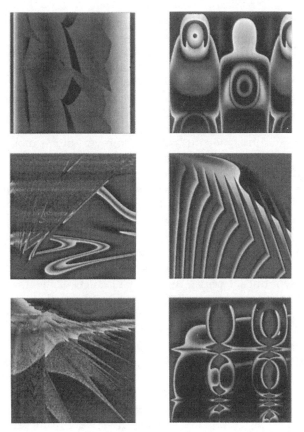

Figure 13. Shown here are six images which the ANN selected for recombination through several different evolutions.

Latham, 1992). Although there exists a large random factor in the images which are created, through a number of generations, images will be produced which are closer to the user's desires. Sims stated concisely the role of evolution in this process:

> Evolution is a method for creating and exploring complexity that does not require human understanding of the specific process involved. This process of artificial evolution could be considered as a system for helping the user with creative explorations, or it might be considered as a system which attempts to 'learn' about human aesthetics from the user. In either case, it allows the user and computer to interactively work together in a new way to produce results that neither could easily produce alone. (Sims, 1991).

With the addition of ANNs, we hoped to increase the ability for the system to learn and automatically create aesthetically pleasing images which are focused upon the individual tastes of a specific user. Although we cannot claim to have taught the system to understand human aesthetic values, we have made a step in the direction of teaching the system how to simulate an individual user's aesthetic preferences.

Although ANNs hold the promise of being able to generalize from examples, the examples must be carefully chosen. To illustrate this point, consider giving only the raw image to the system without the appropriate corrections made for the large color cliff between white and red. Although it is theoretically possible for the ANN to find the distinction, practically, it is helpful to accentuate the differences. This feature, although visually striking, may be lost in other features of the pixel image. Second, consider giving only the sequence of images from a single evolution. Even if the training set contains good and bad images, the images will probably not be heterogeneous enough to allow the ANN to generalize to images from another evolutionary sequence. Instead, the ANN must be trained on a variety of images taken from several evolutions.

The GA is a good basis for the system; however, much more can be done to improve the ability of automating the evolutionary process. Further exploration should be divided into at least five areas. The first is that of the neural network architecture. As can be witnessed in the several attempts shown here, different architectures have the potential to lead to very different success rates. However, larger architectures also become increasingly difficult to train, as the need for larger training sets becomes more pronounced. Another architecture which should be considered is an unsupervised learning model in which the similar features are first ascertained, and the images placed into groups based upon similarity. With the formation of these groups, learning the user's rankings of the images may prove to be an easier task.

The second area for possible future attention is creating a fuller, more representative, training set. As has been addressed throughout the paper, it is difficult to get a large set of images which are in the 'medium' and 'high' range. The training set used in these experiments was derived from several manual evolutions. As the ANN is very sensitive to the input data used for training, a larger training set, with many more images classified in the higher regions, may greatly improve performance.

The third area for research requires relaxing the constraint of imbedding no *a priori* knowledge into the ANN, and training the system using other characteristics of the image in addition to the pixel image, or as a replacement for the pixel image. These additional features may yield more accurate classifications. Such features might include those commonly used in traditional machine vision techniques; they include clusters, edges, circles, regions of noise, etc. The human eye can easily gauge many of these features automatically and incorporate them into decision-making processes. Giving these features explicitly to an ANN may also prove to be beneficial.

The fourth area of future research is examining the effects of using a larger population size. The population size was limited to the nine images in the user interface to make the role of the user easier. However, in an automated system, this is not a concern, and a larger population can be employed. Additionally, more traditional GA techniques may be used for generating subsequent populations. For example, in this study, only one set of parents was chosen to create all of the children of the next generation. A more effective means of ensuring diversity is to select different pairs of parents probabilistically to contribute a single 'child' image to the next generation. In this way, multiple parents are allowed to contribute to the subsequent populations. This should have a tremendous beneficial impact in preserving diversity.

Finally, methods for tying the learning mechanisms more closely with the user interface should be explored. One can imagine a system which can work with the user by proposing images which the user may find interesting, while pruning away images which the user will probably dislike. This task would fit well with the abilities of the current system. In addition, the system could also suggest its choice for recombination. If the user disagrees with the system's selection, the user can select an alternative image. If an alternative image is chosen, the learning mechanisms can revise its knowledge to better model the user's preferences. As an extension, perhaps this system can run in the background, periodically querying the user for feedback, and continuing with its defaults when no feedback is given.

Acknowledgements

Profuse thanks are extended to Henry Rowley for his comments and discussions. The authors would also like to thank Kaari Flagstad, Dayne Freitag and Robert Driskill for their aid in revising this paper. Thanks are due to Dr Joseph Bates who introduced us to Karl Sims' work, and provided valuable discussions and ideas. The authors would also like to thank the reviewers and editors for providing suggestions and extensions to the system.

Shumeet Baluja is supported by a National Science Foundation Graduate Fellowship. Todd Jochem is partially supported by a ARPA Research Assistantship in High Performance Computing administered by the Institute for Advanced Computer Studies, University of Maryland. This research was supported by the Department of the Navy, Office of Naval Research under Grant No. N00014-93-1-0806.

The views and conclusions contained in this document are those of the authors and should not be interpreted as representing the official policies, either expressed or implied, of the National Science Foundation, ARPA, or the US government.

References

Baluja, S. (1992) *A Massively Distributed Parallel Genetic Algorithm.* CMU-CS-92-196R. School of Computer Science, Carnegie Mellon University.

Baluja, S. & Pomerleau, D.A. (1994) Non-intrusive gaze tracking using artificial neural networks. In J.D. Cowan, G. Tesauro & J. Alspector (Eds), *Advances in Neural Information Processing Systems (NIPS) 6.* San Francisco, CA: Morgan Kaufmann.

Baluja, S., Pomerleau, D.A. & Jochem, T. (1993) *Simulating a User's Preferences: Towards Automated Artificial Evolution for Computer Generated Images.* CMU-CS-93-198, School of Computer Science, Carnegie Mellon University, 1993.

Cohoon, J.P., Hedge, S.U., Martin, W.N. & Richards, D. (1988) *Distributed Genetic Algorithms for the Floor Plan Design Problem.* TR-88-12, School of Engineering and Applied Science, Computer Science Department, University of Virginia.

Goldberg, D.E. (1989) *Genetic Algorithms in Search, Optimization, and Machine Learning.* Reading, MA. Addison-Wesley.

Hertz, J., Krogh, A. & Palmer, R. (1991) *Introduction to the Theory of Neural Computation.* Reading, MA: Addison-Wesley.

Koza, J.R. (1992) *Genetic Programming: On the Programming of Computers by Means of Natural Selection.* Cambridge, MA: The MIT Press.

LeCun, Y., *et al.* (1989) Backpropagation applied to handwritten zip code recognition. *Neural Computation,* **1,** 541–551, Massachusetts Institute of Technology.

Pomerleau, D.A. (1992) *Neural Network Perception for Mobile Robot Guidance.* PhD Thesis, CMU-CS-92-115. School of Computer Science, Carnegie Mellon University.

Sims, K. (1991) Artificial evolution for computer graphics. *SIGGRAPH '91 Conference Proceedings,* **25,** 319–328.

Todd, P. (1989) A connectionist approach to algorithmic composition. *Computer Music Journal,* **13,** 27–43.

Todd, S. & Latham, W. (1992) *Evolutionary Art and Computers.* Academic Press, London.

Waibel, A. *et al.* (1989) Phoneme recognition using time-delay neural networks. In A. Waibel & K.F. Lee (Eds), *Readings in Speech Recognition,* pp. 393–404. San Mateo, CA: Morgan Kaufmann.

Appendix: Typical Image Equations

The equations for the images grow large very quickly. Understanding the contributions of each element within the context of the equation rapidly becomes cumbersome. It is also interesting to note that many of the sub-expressions either do nothing, or may easily be replaced by constants. The equations for the images in the bottom row of the 9 squares in Figure 5 are, respectively:

avg(mod(x,x),mul(sin(x),mul(sin(y),add(sin(x),sub(sin(y),mod(sin(y),mul(sub(x,sub(sqr(x),mod(sin(x),mod(sin(x),min(sin(x),sub(y,x)))))),sub(x,add(y,add(sin(x),mod(sin(sin(x)),add(sin(x),sub(sin(y),x)))))))))))))))

avg(mod(x,x),mul(sin(x),mul(sin(y),add(sin(x),sub(sin(y),mod(sin(y),mul(sub(x,sub(sqr(x),mod(sin(x),mod(sin(x),min(sin(x),sub(y,x)))))),sub(x,add(y,add(sin(mod(x,x)),mod(sin(x),add(sin(x),sub(sin(y),x))))))))))))))

avg(mod(x,x),mul(sin(x),mul(sin(y),add(sin(x),sub(sin(y),mod(sin(y),mul(sub(x,sub(hsn(x),mod(sin(x),x))),sub(x,add(y,add(sin(x),mod(sin(x),add(sin(x),sub(sin(y),x))))))))))))))

The Connectionist Air Guitar: A Dream Come True

GARRISON W. COTTRELL

A major problem faced by many Cognitive Scientists has been the latent desire to be a rock'n'roll star, without the requisite talent.[1] Recent advances in connectionist learning mechanisms (Sutton, 1987) have obviated this need. In this work we present the design for the *connectionist air guitar*[2]—the first air guitar to actually produce the notes played.

This work was motivated by the observation that it is not hard for people to play the songs of their favorite groups on their *internal phonograph*[3] (Kosslyn, 1977). Thus the problem may simply be one of poor mapping hardware. This suggests that augmentation by cognitive models may be useful. PDP models are the obvious candidate for this task, given that they are 'neurally-inspired', or 'brain-like'.[4] In this talk we present the first true augmentation of the mind by a connectionist model, called Neuro-acoustic Programming.

We use a three-layer system as follows: Electrodes are placed on the subject's scalp using the International 10–20 system and amplified by Grass 7P511 pre-amplifiers.[5] These are the inputs to the hidden units. The output layer is simply a localist representation of the notes. These are then interfaced with a standard guitar synthesizer.

In training, the subject listens to Springsteen while 'air guitaring' the lead. The EEG drives the network, resulting in a set of outputs. This result is then compared to the correct output (the *music teacher* signal) at small Δts using Sutton's temporal difference method, and the errors are back-propagated in the usual way. After two albums, the network learns to produce the desired notes from the EEG. Of note here is that the hidden units develop a distributed encoding of the *qualia* of the notes, including coarsely-coded features sufficient to distinguish Jerry Garcia from Conway Twitty.[6] However, electromyographic noise in the EEG often leads to noise in the output, so it appears necessary to implant arrays of silicon electrodes (developed by Jim Bower at CalTech) directly into the temporal lobes, eliminating interference from muscle signals. In this case, the network must actually be borne to run.

Notes

1. One approach is to ignore this and form a band anyway. People who took this tack started the punk movement.
2. An *air guitar* is a conceptual representation of a guitar, played in synchrony with actual music. A cult has formed around this endeavor, with many contests currently being held in local bars.

This article appeared originally in *Connection Science*, 1989, **1**, 413, and is reprinted with permission.

3. Some people claim that they actually *can't* play the songs internally as well as they hear them. This is the 'bad cognitive needle' problem, or, in the case of Kosslyn's more advanced *internal cassette player* model, 'air heads'. As long as the signal uniquely specifies the song, it still maps to the right notes, so this technique is useful for the hard of thinking.
4. This is to be contrasted with 'neurally-expired' or 'brain-dead' models.
5. Other types of Grass amplifiers produce a more 'sixties-like' sound.
6. Some hidden units convert six into nine, the so-called *Jimi Hendrix* units (Easy Rider, 1969).

Bibliography

[Note: We intend to maintain this bibliography in an updated form on-line. Please visit http://mitpress.mit.edu/book-home.tcl?isbn=0262071819 for the latest version, and to submit additional references.]

Akarte, N.J. (1992) *Music Composition Using Neural Networks*. Master's thesis, University of Nevada, Reno.

Alpaydin, R. & Akin, H. (1992) A connectionist approach to improvisation on the guitar. In *Proceedings of the International Symposium on Computer and Information Sciences VII* (pp. 573–576). Paris: Ecole des Hautes Etudes Informatiques.

Anderson, S. (1994) *A Computational Model of Auditory Pattern Recognition*. Research Report 112, Indiana University, Dept. of Cognitive Science.

Anderson, S. & Port, R. (1990) *A Network Model of Auditory Pattern Recognition*. Research Report 11, Indiana University, Dept. of Cognitive Science.

Baggi, D.L. (1992) NeurSwing: An intelligent workbench for the investigation of swing in jazz. In D. Baggi (Ed.), *Readings in Computer-Generated Music* (pp. 79–94). Los Alamitos, CA: IEEE Computer Society Press, IEEE Computer Society Readings.

Barnard, E., Cole, R.A., Vea, M.P. & Alleva, F.A. (1991) Pitch detection with a neural-net classifier. *IEEE Transactions on Signal Processing*, **39**(2), 298–307.

Battel, G.U. & Bresin, R. (1994) Analysis by synthesis in piano performance: A study on the theme of Brahms' "Variations on a theme of Paganini" op. 35. In *Proceedings of the 1993 Stockholm Music Acoustic Conference* (pp. 69–73). Stockholm: Royal Swedish Academy of Music.

Battel, G.U., Bresin, R., De Poli, G. & Vidolin, A. (1993) Automatic performance of musical scores by means of artificial neural networks: Evaluation with listening tests. In G. Haus & I. Pighi (Eds.), *Proceedings of X Colloquium on Musical Informatics* (pp. 97–101). Milan: AIMI.

Battel, G.U., Bresin, R., De Poli, G. & Vidolin, A. (1994) Neural networks vs. rule systems: Evaluation tests of automatic performance of musical scores. In *Proceedings of the 1994 International Computer Music Conference* (pp. 109–113). San Francisco: International Computer Music Association.

Bellgard, M.I. & Tsang, C.P. (1992) Harmonizing music using a network of Boltzmann machines. In *Proceedings of the Fifth Annual Conference of Artificial Neural Networks and Their Applications* (Neuro-Nimes) (pp. 321–332).

Bellgard, M.I. & Tsang, C.P. (1995) Using an effective Boltzmann machine to learn context dependencies of a sequence. In *Proceedings of the 1995 IEEE International Conference on Neural Networks* (pp. 2841–2846). IEEE.

Bellgard, M.I. & Tsang, C.P. (1996) On the use of an effective Boltzmann machine for musical style recognition and harmonization. In *Proceedings of the 1996 International Computer Music Conference* (pp. 461–464). San Francisco: International Computer Music Association.

Berger, J. & Gang, D. (1996) Modeling musical expectations: A neural network model of dynamic changes of expectation in the audition of functional tonal music. In *Proceedings of the Fourth International Conference on Music Perception and Cognition* (pp. 373–378). Montreal: McGill University, Faculty of Music.

Berger, J. & Gang, D. (1997) A neural network model of metric perception and cognition in the audition of functional tonal music. In *Proceedings of the 1997 International Computer Music Conference* (pp. 23–26). San Francisco: International Computer Music Association.

Berkley, S. (1993) A neural network model of sound localization in binaural fusion. In *Proceedings of the 1993 International Computer Music Conference* (pp. 256–259). San Francisco: International Computer Music Association.

Bertoni, A. & Bresin, R. (1995) Real-time musical rhythm tapping: A neural networks-numerical algorithms hybrid system. In *Atti XI Colloquio di Informatica Musicale* (pp. 185–188). Venice: Associazione di Informatica Musicale Italiana.

Bharucha, J. (1987) A connectionist model of musical harmony: Evidence from priming. *Bulletin of the Psychonomic Society*, **25**(5), 329.

Bharucha, J. (1987) MUSACT: A connectionist model of musical harmony. In *Proceedings of the Ninth Annual Meeting of the Cognitive Science Society* (pp. 508–517). Hillsdale, NJ: Erlbaum Associates.

Bharucha, J. (1987) Music cognition and perceptual facilitation: A connectionist framework. *Music Perception*, **5**(1), 1–30.

Bharucha, J. (1988) Neural net modeling of music. In *Proceedings of the First Workshop on Artificial Intelligence and Music* (pp. 173–182). Menlo Park. CA: American Association for Artificial Intelligence.

Bharucha, J.J. (1989) Neural networks and perceptual learning of tonal expectancies. In *Proceedings of the First International Conference on Music Perception and Cognition* (pp. 81–86). Kyoto: Kyoto City University of Arts, Faculty of Music.

Bharucha, J.J. (1991) Pitch, harmony and neual nets: A psychological perspecitve. In P.M. Todd & D.G. Loy (Eds.), *Music and Connectionism* (pp. 84–99). Cambridge, MA: MIT Press.

Bharucha, J.J. (1994) Tonality and expectation. In R. Aiello (Ed.), *Musical Perceptions* (pp. 213–239). New York: Oxford University Press.

Bharucha, J.J. & Olney, K.L. (1989) Tonal cognition, artificial intelligence and neural nets. *Contemporary Music Review*, **4**, 341–356.

Bharucha, J.J. & Todd, P.M. (1988) Connectionist learning of schematic musical expectancies. *Bulletin of the Psychonomic Society*, **26**(6), 496.

Bharucha, J.J. & Todd, P.M. (1989) Modeling the perception of tonal structure with neural nets. *Computer Music Journal*, **13**(4), 44–53. Also in P.M. Todd & D.G. Loy (Eds.) (1991) *Music and Connectionism* (pp. 128–137). Cambridge, MA: MIT Press.

Brecht, B. & Aiken, J. (1995) A lot of nerve: Introducing neural network computing, a powerful resource for intelligent accompaniment, additive synthesis control, real-time gesture mapping and a whole lot more. *Keyboard Magazine*, **21**(6), 39–42.

Bresin, R. (1993) MELODIA: A program for performance rules testing, teaching, and piano score performance. In G. Haus & I. Pighi (Eds.), *Atti X Colloquio di Informatica Musicale* (pp. 325–327). Venice: Associazione di Informatica Musicale Italiana.

Bresin, R. (1994) Performance of musical scores by means of neural networks: Progress and status report. In *Symposium on Generative Grammars for Musical Performance* (pp. 3–6). Stockholm: Royal Institute of Technology, Dept. of Speech Communication and Music Acoustics.

Bresin, R., De Poli, G. & Ghetta, R. (1995) A fuzzy approach to performance rules. *Atti XI Colloquio di Informatica Musicale* (pp. 163–168). Venice: Associazione di Informatica Musicale Italiana.

Bresin, R., De Poli, G. & Vidolin, A. (1991) A connectionist approach to timing deviation control in musical performance. *Atti del Secondo Convegno Europeo di Analisi Musicale* (pp. 635–638). Universite degli Studi di Trento.

Bresin, R., De Poli, G. & Vidolin, A. (1992) Symbolic and sub-symbolic rules system for real time score performance. In *Proceedings of the 1992 International Computer Music Conference* (pp. 211–214). San Francisco: International Computer Music Association.

Bresin, R., De Poli, G. & Vidolin, A. (1994) A neural networks based system for automatic performance of musical scores. In *Proceedings of the 1993 Stockholm Music Acoustic Conference* (pp. 74–78). Stockholm: Royal Swedish Academy of Music.

Bresin, R. & Vecchio, C. (1994) Analysis and synthesis of the performing action of a real pianist by means of artificial neural networks. In *Proceedings of the Third International Conference for Music Perception and Cognition* (pp. 353–354). Liege: European Society for the Cognitive Sciences of Music.

Bresin, R. & Vecchio, C. (1995) Neural networks play Schumann: Analysis and synthesis of the performing action of a real pianist. In *Proceedings of the Symposium on Grammars for Music Performance* (pp. 5–14). Stockholm: Royal Institute of Technology.

Bresin, R. & Vedovetto, A. (1994) Neural networks for a simpler control of synthesis algorithm of musical tones and for their compression. In *Proceedings of the Fifth International Conference on Signal Processing Applications and Technology.*

Bresin, R. & Vedovetto, A. (1994) Neural networks for musical tones compression, control, and synthesis. In *Proceedings of the 1994 International Computer Music Conference* (pp. 368–371). San Francisco: International Computer Music Association.

Bresin, R. & Vedovetto, A. (1994) Neural networks for the compression of musical tones and for the control of their resynthesis. In *Proceedings of the IEEE-SP International Symposium on Time-Frequency and Time-Scale Analysis*.

Brubeck, D. & McNamara, N. (1994) *The Intelligent Drum Machine*. Technical Report, University of California, Berkeley, Center for New Music and Audio Technology.

Bryson, J. (1992) *The Subsumption Strategy Development of a Music Modeling System*. Master's thesis, University of Edinburgh, Dept. of Artificial Intelligence.

Bryson, J. (1995) The reactive accompanist: Adaptation and behaviour decomposition in a music system. In L. Steels (Ed.), *The Biology and Technology of Intelligent Autonomous Agents*. London: Springer Verlag.

Bryson, J., Smaill, A. & Wiggans, G. (1992) *The Reactive Accompanist: Applying Subsumption Architecture to Software Design*. Research Paper 606, University of Edinburgh, Dept. of Artificial Intelligence.

Calvert, D. & Stacey, D. (1991) Neural based methods for music composition. In *International Joint Conference on Neural Networks* (Vol. 2, p. 918). New York: IEEE.

Camurri, A. (1997) Network models in motor control and music. In P. Morasso & V. Sanguineti (Eds.), *Self-Organization, Computational Maps and Motor Control*. Amsterdam: North Holland Elsevier.

Camurri, A., Capocaccia, M. & Zaccaria, R. (1990) ENA: Experimental neural accompanist. In *International Neural Network Conference* (Vol. 1, p. 159).

Camurri, A., Haus, G. & Zaccaria, R. (1986) Describing and performing musical processes by means of Petri nets. *Interface*, **15**(1), 1–23.

Cariani, P. (1996) Temporal coding of musical form. In *Proceedings of the Fourth International Conference on Music Perception and Cognition* (pp. 425–430). Montreal: Faculty of Music, McGill University.

Carpinteiro, O. (1995) A neural model to segment musical pieces. In E. Miranda (Ed.), *Proceedings of the Second Brazilian Symposium on Computer Music, Fifteenth Congress of the Brazilian Computer Society* (pp. 114–120). Brazilian Computer Society.

Carpinteiro, O. (1996) *A Connectionist Approach in Music Perception*. Unpublished doctoral dissertation, University of Sussex, School of Cognitive and Computing Sciences. CSRP 426.

Carpinteiro, O. & Barrow, H. (1996) *A Self-Organizing Map Model for Sequence Classification*. Technical Report CSRP 424, University of Sussex, School of Cognitive and Computing Sciences.

Casey, M.A. (1993) Distal learning of musical instrument control parameters. In *Proceedings of the 1993 International Computer Music Conference* (pp. 240–243). San Francisco: International Computer Music Association.

Casey, M.A. (1996) A model-based representation for musical timbre. In *Proceedings of the Fourth International Conference on Music Perception and Cognition* (pp. 215–216). Montreal: McGill University.

Casey, M.A. & Smaragdis, P. (1996) Netsound: Realtime audio from semantic descriptions. In D. Rossiter (Ed.), *Proceedings of the 1996 International Computer Music Conference* (p. 143). San Francisco: International Computer Music Association.

Ciaccia, P., Lugli, F. & Maio, D. (1992) Using neural networks to perform harmonic analysis in music. In *The Fifth Italian Workshop on Neural Nets, WIRN VIETRI-92* (pp. 273–279). Singapore: World Scientific.

Cohen, M.A., Grossberg, S. & Wyse, L.L. (1995) A spectral network model of pitch perception. *Journal of the Acoustical Society of America*, **498**(2), 862–879.

Cosi, P., DePoli, G. & Lauzzana, G. (1994) Auditory modeling and self-organizing neural networks for timbre classification. *Journal of New Music Research*, **23**(1), 71–98.

Cosi, P., DePoli, G. & Prandoni, P. (1994) Timbre characterization with mel-cepstrum and neural nets. In *Proceedings of the 1994 International Computer Music Conference* (pp. 42–45). San Francisco: International Computer Music Association.

Covey, E., Hawkins, H. & Port, R. (1996) *Neural Representation of Temporal Patterns*. New York: Plenum Publishing.

D'Autilia, R. & Guerra, F. (1991) Qualitative aspects of signal processing through dynamical neural networks. In G. DePoli, A. Piccialli & C. Roads (Eds.), *Representations of Musical Signals*. Cambridge, MA: MIT Press.

DePoli, G., Prandoni, P. & Tonella, P. (1993) Timbre clustering by self-organizing neural networks. In G. Haus & I. Pighi (Eds.), *Proceedings of the Tenth Colloquium on Musical Informatics* (pp. 102–107). Milan: AIMI.

DePoli, G. & Tonella, P. (1993) Self-organizing neural network and Grey's timbre space. In *Proceedings of the 1993 International Computer Music Conference* (pp. 260–263). San Francisco: International Computer Music Association.

Desain, P. (1992) A connectionist and a traditional AI quantizer, symbolic versus sub-symbolic models of rhythm perception. In P. Desain & H. Honing (Eds.), *Music, Mind and Machine* (pp. 101–118). Amsterdam: Thesis Publishers.

Desain, P. & Honing, H. (1989) The quantization of musical time: A connectionist approach. *Computer Music Journal*, **13**(3), 56–66. Also in P.M. Todd & D.G. Loy (Eds.) (1991) *Music and Connectionism* (pp. 150–160). Cambridge, MA: MIT Press.

Desain, P. & Honing, H. (Eds.) (1992) *Music, Mind and Machine: Studies in Computer Music, Music Cognition and Artificial Intelligence*. Amsterdam: Thesis Publishers.

Dirst, M. & Weigend, A.S. (1994) Baroque forecasting: On completing J.S. Bach's last fugue. In A.S. Weigend & N.A. Gershenfeld (Eds.), *Time Series Prediction: Forecasting the Future and Understanding the Past* (pp. 151–172). Reading, MA: Addison-Wesley.

Dolson, M. (1989) Machine Tongues XII: Neural networks. *Computer Music Journal*, **13**(3), 28–40. Also in P.M. Todd & D.G. Loy (Eds.) (1991) *Music and Connectionism* (pp. 3–15). Cambridge, MA: MIT Press.

Drago, G.P., Martini, C., Morando, M. & Ridella, S. (1992) A high performance music composer based on a modified Jordan network. In *The Fifth Italian Workshop on Neural Nets, WIRN VIETRI-92* (pp. 280–285). Singapore: World Scientific.

Drago, G.P., Martini, C., Morando, M. & Ridella, S. (1992) A neural network for music composition. In M.H. Hamza (Ed.), *Proceedings of the Tenth IASTED International Conference* (pp. 211–214). Zurich: Acta Press.

Duff. M.O. (1989) Backpropagation and Bach's 5th cello suite (Sarabande). In *International Joint Conference on Neural Networks* (Vol. 2, p. 575). New York: IEEE.

Elsberry, W.R. (1989) *Integration and Hybridization in Neural Network Modeling (Network Modeling)*. Master's thesis, University of Texas at Arlington.

Fedor, P. (1977) Principles of the design of D-neuronal networks I: A neural model for pragmatic analysis of simple melodies. *Biological Cybernetics*, **27**, 129–146.

Fedor, P. (1992) Principles of the design of D-neuronal networks I: Net representation for computer simulation of a melody compositional process. *International Journal of Neural Systems*, **3**(1), 65–73.

Fedor, P. (1992) Principles of the design of D-neuronal networks I: Composing simple melodies. *International Journal of Neural Systems*, **3**(1), 75–82.

Fedor, P. & Breznen, B. (1989) A deterministic neural network for processing of temporal sequences. In *International Joint Conference on Neural Networks* (Vol. 2, p. 611). New York: IEEE.

Feiten, B. & Behles, G. (1994) Organizing the parameter space of physical models with sound feature maps. In *Proceedings of the 1994 International Computer Music Conference* (pp. 398–401). San Francisco: International Computer Music Association.

Feiten, B., Frank, R. & Ungvary, T. (1991) Organization of sounds with neural nets. In *Proceedings of the 1991 International Computer Music Conference* (pp. 441–443). San Francisco: International Computer Music Association.

Feiten, B. & Guenzel, S. (1994) Automatic indexing of a sound data base using self-organizing neural nets. *Computer Music Journal*, **18**(3), 53–65.

Feulner, J. (1992) Learning the harmonies of western tonal music using neural networks. In E. Gelenbe, U. Halici & N. Yalabik (Eds.), *Proceedings of the International Symposium on Computer and Information Sciences VII* (pp. 303–307). Paris: EHEI Press.

Feulner, J. (1993) Neural networks that learn and reproduce various styles of harmonization. In *Proceedings of the 1993 International Computer Music Conference* (pp. 236–239). San Francisco: International Computer Music Association.

Feulner, J. & Hörnel, D. (1994) MELONET: Neural networks that learn harmony-based melodic variations. In *Proceedings of the 1994 International Computer Music Conference* (pp. 121–124). San Francisco: International Computer Music Association.

Freisleben, B. (1992) The neural composer: A network for musical applications. In *Proceedings of the 1992 International Conference on Artificial Neural Networks* (Vol. 2, pp. 1663–1666). Amsterdam: Elsevier.

Gang, D. & Berger, J. (1996) Modeling the degree of realized expectation in functional tonal music: A study of perceptual and cognitive modeling using neural networks. In D. Rossiter (Ed.), *Proceedings of the 1996 International Computer Music Conference* (pp. 454–457). San Francisco: International Computer Music Association.

Gang, D. & Lehmann, D. (1995) An artificial neural net for harmonizing melodies. In E. Michie (Ed.), *Proceedings of the 1995 International Computer Music Conference* (pp. 440–447). San Francisco: International Computer Music Association.

Gang, D., Lehmann, D. & Wagner, N. (1997) Harmonizing melodies in real-time: The connectionist approach. In *Proceedings of the 1997 International Computer Music Conference* (pp. 27–31). San Francisco: International Computer Music Association.

Gasser, M. & Eck, D. (1996) Representing rhythmic patterns in a network of oscillators. In *Proceedings of the Fourth International Conference on Music Perception and Cognition* (pp. 367–372). Montreal: McGill University, Faculty of Music.

Gasser, M., Eck, D. & Port, R. (1997) Meter as mechanism: A neural network that learns metrical patterns. In M. Lynch (Ed.), *The Cognitive Science of Prosody*, North-Holland/Elsevier.

Geake, E. (1991) Neural networks bring harmony to hummers. *New Scientist*, 132(1794), 19.

Gibson, P.M. & Byrne, J.A. (1991) NEUROGEN: Musical composition using genetic algorithms and cooperating neural networks. In *Proceedings of the Second International Conference on Artificial Neural Networks* (pp. 309–313). IEE.

Gjerdingen, R.O. (1989) Meter as a mode of attending: A network simulation of attentional rhythmicity in music. *Integral*, 3, 67–92.

Gjerdingen, R.O. (1989) Using connectionist models to explore complex musical patterns. *Computer Music Journal*, 13(3), 67–75. Also in P.M. Todd & D.G. Loy (Eds.) (1991) *Music and Connectionism* (pp. 138–146). Cambridge, MA: MIT Press.

Gjerdingen, R.O. (1990) Categorization of musical patterns by self-organizing neuronlike networks. *Music Perception*, 7(4), 339–370.

Gjerdingen, R.O. (1992) Learning syntactically significant temporal patterns of chords: A masking field embedded in an ART3 architecture. *Neural Networks*, 5, 551–564.

Gjerdingen, R.O. (1994) Apparent motion in music? *Music Perception*, 11, 335–370.

Goldman, C., Gang, D., Rosenschein, J. & Lehmann, D. (1996) NETNEG: A hybrid interactive architecture for composing polyphonic music in real time. In D. Rossiter (Ed.), *Proceedings of the 1996 International Computer Music Conference* (pp. 133–140). San Francisco: International Computer Music Association.

Goto, K. & Yokota, M. (1992) Musical interval extraction by neural networks. *Transactions of the Institute of Electronics, Information and Communication Engineers A*, J75-A(3), 618–623. (In Japanese)

Govindarajan, K.K., Grossberg, S., Wyse, L.L. & Cohen, M.A. (1994) *A Neural Network Model of Auditory Scene Analysis and Source Segregation*. Technical Report CAS/CNS-TR-94-039, Boston University, Dept. of Cognitive and Neural Systems.

Griffith, N.J.L. (1993) Representing the tonality of musical sequences usng neural nets. In *Proceedings of the First International Conference on Cognitive Musicology* (pp. 109–132). Jyväskylä, Finland: University of Jyväskylä.

Griffith, N.J.L. (1994) *Modeling the Acquisition and Representation of Musical Tonality as a Function of Pitch-Use through Self-Organizing Artificial Neural Networks*. Unpublished doctoral thesis, University of Exeter, Dept. of Computer Science.

Griffith, N.J.L. (1994) Modeling the influence of pitch duration on the induction of tonality from pitch-use. In *Proceedings of the 1994 International Computer Music Conference* (pp. 35–37). San Francisco: International Computer Music Association.

Griffith, N.J.L. (1995) Connectionist visualization of tonal structure. *AI Review*, 8, 393–408.

Griffith, N.J.L. (1995) Using complementary streams in a computer model of the abstraction of diatonic pitch. In L. Smith & P. Hancock (Eds.), *Proceedings of the Third Neural Computation in Psychology Workshop* (pp. 137–146). London: Springer Verlag.

Hild, H., Feulner, J. & Menzel, D. (1992) HARMONET: A neural net for harmonizing chorals in the style of J.S. Bach. In R. Lippmann, J. Moody & D. Touretzky (Eds.), *Advances in Neural Information Processing 4* (pp. 267–274). San Francisco: Morgan Kaufmann.

Hipfinger, G. & Linster, C. (1990) Preprocessing of musical information and applications for neural networks. In *Proceedings of the Tenth European Meeting on Cybernetics and Systems Research*.

Hiraga, Y. (1997) Structural recognition of music by pattern matching. In *Proceedings of the 1997 International Computer Music Conference* (pp. 426–429). San Francisco: International Computer Music Association.

Hörnel, D. & Degenhardt, P. (1997) A neural organist improvising baroque-style melodic variations. In *Proceedings of the 1997 International Computer Music Conference* (pp. 430–434). San Francisco: International Computer Music Association.

Hörnel, D. & Ragg, T. (1996) A connectionist model for the evolution of styles of harmonization. In *Proceedings of the Fourth International Conference on Music Perception and Cognition* (pp. 219–224).

Hörnel, D. & Ragg, T. (1996) Learning musical structure and style by recognition, prediction and evolution. In D. Rossiter (Ed.), *Proceedings of the 1996 International Computer Music Conference* (pp. 59–62). San Francisco: International Computer Music Association.

Horner, A. & Goldberg, D.E. (1991) Genetic algorithms and computer-assisted music composition. In B. Alphonce & B. Pennycook (Eds.), *Proceedings of the 1991 International Computer Music Conference* (pp. 479–482). San Francisco: International Computer Music Association.

Incerti, E. (1997) Modeling methods for sound synthesis. Network combinations and complex models for physical modeling: Applications to modes clustering. In *Proceedings of the 1997 International Computer Music Conference* (pp. 160–163). San Francisco: International Computer Music Association.

Jakobsson, M. (1992) Machine-generated music with themes. In *Proceedings of the 1992 International Conference on Artificial Neural Networks* (Vol. 2, pp. 1645–1646). Amsterdam: Elsevier.

Kaipainen, M., Toiviainen, P. & Louhivuori, J. (1995) A self-organizing map that recognizes and generates melodies. In P. Pylkkänen & P. Pylkkö (Eds.), *New Directions in Cognitive Science* (pp. 286–315). Finnish Artificial Intelligence Society.

Kohonen, T. (1989) A self-learning musical grammar, or "Associative memory of the second kind". In *Proceedings of the International Joint Conference on Neural Networks* (pp. 1–5). New York: IEEE.

Kohonen, T., Laine, P., Tiits, K. & Torkkola, K. (1991) A nonheuristic automatic composing method. In P.M. Todd & D.G. Loy (Eds.), *Music and Connectionism* (pp. 229–242). Cambridge, MA: MIT Press.

Laden, B. (1990) Representation of pitch input to neural network models of music perception. *Journal of the Acoustic Society of America*, **87**, S18. (abstract)

Laden, B. (1994) A parallel learning model for pitch perception. *Journal of New Music Research*, **23**(2), 133–144.

Laden, B. & Keefe, B.H. (1989) The representation of pitch in a neural net model of pitch classification. *Computer Music Journal*, **13**(4), 12–26. Also in P.M. Todd & D.G. Loy (Eds.) (1991) *Music and Connectionism* (pp. 64–78). Cambridge, MA: MIT Press.

Laine, P. (1997) Generating musical patterns using mutually inhibited artificial neurons. In *Proceedings of the 1997 International Computer Music Conference* (pp. 422–425). San Francisco: International Computer Music Association.

Large, E.W., Palmer, C. & Pollack, J.B. (1991) Connectionist representation of intermediate music structure. In *Proceedings of the 13th Annual Cognitive Science Conference* (pp. 412–417). Hillsdale, NJ: Erlbaum.

Laske, O. (1990) Letter: Connectionist composition. *Computer Music Journal*, **14**(2), 11–12. Also in P.M. Todd & D.G. Loy (Eds.) (1991) *Music and Connectionism* (p. 260). Cambridge, MA: MIT Press.

Lee, M., Freed, A. & Wessel, D. (1991) Real-time neural network processing of gestural and acoustic signals. In B. Alphonce & B. Pennycook (Eds.), *Proceedings of the 1991 International Computer Music Conference* (pp. 277–280). San Francisco: International Computer Music Association.

Lee, M. & Wessel, D. (1992) Connectionist models for real-time control of synthesis and compositional algorithms. In *Proceedings of the 1992 International Computer Music Conference* (pp. 277–280). San Francisco: International Computer Music Association.

Lee, M. & Wessel, D. (1993) Real-time neuro-fuzzy systems for adaptive control of musical processes. In *Proceedings of the 1993 International Computer Music Conference* (pp. 172–175). San Francisco: International Computer Music Association.

Lee, S.K. & Shin, J.W. (1994) Recognition of music scores using neural networks. *Journal of the Korean Information Science Society*, **21**(7), 1358–1366. (In Korean)

Leman, M. (1988) Sequential (musical) information processing with PDP-networks. In *Proceedings of the First Workshop on AI and Music* (pp. 163–172). American Association for Artificial Intelligence.

Leman, M. (1990) Emergent properties of tonality functions by self-organization. *Interface*, **19**, 85–106.

Leman, M. (1991) Artificial neural networks in music research. In A. Marsden & A. Pople (Eds.), *Computer Representations and Models in Music* (pp. 265–301). London: Academic Press.

Leman, M. (1991) The ontogenesis of tonal semantics: Results of a computer study. In P.M. Todd & D.G. Loy (Eds.), *Music and Connectionism* (pp. 100–127). Cambridge, MA: MIT Press.

Leman, M. (1992) The theory of tone semantics: Concept, foundation, and application. *Minds and Machines*, **2**(4), 345–363.

Leman, M. (1992) Tone context by pattern integration over time. In D. Baggi (Ed.), *Readings in Computer Generated Music* (pp. 79–94). Los Alamitos: CA: IEEE Computer Society Press. IEEE Computer Society Readings.

Leman, M. (1993) Symbolic and subsymbolic description of music. In G. Haus (Ed.), *Music Processing* (pp. 119–164). New York: Oxford University Press.

Leman, M. (1994) Schema-based tone center recognition of musical signals. *Journal of New Music Research*, **23**, 169–204.

Leman, M. (1996) *Music and Schema Theory: Cognitive Foundations of Systematic Musicology.* London: Springer Verlag.

Leman, M. & Van Renterghem, P. (1989) Transputer implementation of the Kohonen feature map for a music recognition task. In *Proceedings of the Second International Transputer Conference: Transputers for Industrial Applications II.* Antwerp: BIRA.

Leng, X.D., Shaw, G.L. & Wright, E.L. (1990) Coding of musical structure and the trion model of cortex. *Music Perception,* 8(1), 49–62.

Lewis, J.P. (1988) Creation by refinement: A creativity paradigm for gradient descent learning networks. In *Proceedings of the International Conference on Neural Networks* (Vol. 2, pp. 229–233). San Diego: IEEE/SOS Printing.

Lewis, J.P. (1989) Algorithms for music composition by neural nets: Improved CBR paradigms. In *Proceedings of the 1989 International Computer Music Conference* (pp. 180–183). San Francisco: International Computer Music Association.

Lewis, J.P. (1991) Creation by refinement and the problem of algorithmic music composition. In P.M Todd & D.G. Loy (Eds.), *Music and Connectionism* (pp. 212–228). Cambridge, MA: MIT Press.

Linster, C. (1989) *"Get rhythm", A Musical Application for Neural Networks.* Arbeitspapiere der GMD 365, Gesellschaft für Mathematik und Datenverarbeitung MBH.

Linster, C. (1989) Rhythm analysis with backpropagation. In R. Pfeifer, Z. Schreter, F. Fogelman-Soulie & L. Steels (Eds.), *Connectionism in Perspective* (pp. 385–393). North-Holland: Elsevier Science Publishers B.V.

Linster, C. (1990) A neural network that learns to play in different styles. In *Proceedings of the 1990 International Computer Music Conference* (pp. 311–313). San Francisco: International Computer Music Association.

Lischka, C. (1987) Connectionist models of musical thinking. In *Proceedings of the 1987 International Computer Music Conference* (p. 90). San Francisco: International Computer Music Association.

Lischka, C. (1991) Understanding music cognition: A connectionist view. In G. De Poli, A. Piccialli & C. Roads (Eds.), *Representations of Musical Signals* (pp. 417–445). Cambridge, MA: MIT Press.

Loy, D.G. (1991) Connectionism and musiconomy. In P.M. Todd & D.G. Loy (Eds.), *Music and Connectionism* (pp. 20–38). Cambridge, MA: MIT Press.

Marsden, A. & Pople, A. (1989) Towards a connected distributed model of musical listening. *Interface,* 18, 61–72.

Martin, P. & Bellissant, C. (1992) Neural networks for the recognition of engraved musical scores. *International Journal of Pattern Recognition and Artificial Intelligence,* 6(1), 193–208.

McAuley, J.D. (1995) *On the Perception of Time as Phase: Toward an Adaptive-Oscillator Model of Rhythm.* Research Report 137, Indiana University, Dept. of Cognitive Science.

McAuley, J.D. (1995) *Perception of Time as Phase: Toward an Adaptive-Oscillator Model of Rhythmic Pattern Processing.* Research Report 151, Indiana University, Dept. of Cognitive Science.

McGraw, G., Montante, R. & Chalmers, D. (1991) *Rap-Master Network: Exploring Temporal Pattern Recognition with Recurrent Networks.* Technical Report 336, Indiana University, Dept. of Computer Science.

McIlwain, P. (1995) The Yuri program: Computer generated music for multi-speaker sound systems. In *Proceedings of the ACMA 1995 Conference* (pp. 150–151). Melbourne: Australian Computer Music Association.

McIlwain, P. & Pietsch, A. (1996) Spatio-temporal patterning in computer-generated music: A nodal network approach. In D. Rossiter (Ed.), *Proceedings of the 1996 International Computer Music Conference* (pp. 312–315). San Francisco: International Computer Music Association.

Mencl, W.E. (1996) Effects of tuning sharpness on tone categorization by self-organizing neural networks. In *Proceedings of the Fourth International Conference on Music Perception and Cognition* (pp. 217–218). Montreal: McGill University, Faculty of Music.

Miller, M.H., Harpster, J.L. & Howard, J.H. (1991) An artificial neural-network simulation of auditory intensity perception and profile analysis. *Journal of the Washington Academy of Sciences,* 81(1), 1–21.

Mourjopoulos, J.N. & Tsoukalas, D.E. (1992) Neural network mapping to subjective spectra of music sounds. *Journal of the Audio Engineering Society,* 40(4), 253–259.

Mozer, M.C. (1991) Connectionist music composition based on melodic, stylistic, and psychophysical constraints. In P.M. Todd & D.G. Loy (Eds.), *Music and Connectionism* (pp. 195–211). Cambridge, MA: MIT Press.

Mozer, M.C. & Soukup, T. (1991) Connectionist music composition based on melodic and stylistic constraints. In R. Lippmann, J. Moody & D. Touretzky (Eds.), *Advances in Neural Information Processing Systems 3* (pp. 789–796). San Mateo, CA: Morgan Kaufmann.

Nishijima, M. (1990) Teaching musical style to a neural network. In *International Symposium Computer World '90. Multimedia Technology and Artificial Intelligence Program and Abstracts* (pp. 195–201). Osaka: Kansai Institute for Information Systems. (In Japanese)

Nishijima, M. & Watanabe, K. (1992) Interactive music composer based on neural networks. In *Proceedings of the 1992 International Computer Music Conference* (pp. 53–56). San Francisco: International Computer Music Association.

Nishijima, M. & Watanabe, K. (1993) Interactive music composer based on neural networks. *Fujitsu Scientific Technical Journal*, 29(2), 189–192. (In Japanese)

Ohya, K. (1995) A sound synthesis by recurrent neural network. In E. Michie (Ed.), *Proceedings of the 1995 International Computer Music Conference* (pp. 420–423). San Francisco: International Computer Music Association.

Page, M. (1991) The musical expectations of self-organizing neural networks. In B. Alphonce & B. Pennycook (Eds.), *Proceedings of the 1991 International Computer Music Conference* (pp. 206–209). San Francisco: International Computer Music Association.

Page, M.P.A. (1993) *Modeling Aspects of Music Perception Using Self-Organizing Neural Networks.* Unpublished doctoral thesis, University of Wales, College of Cardiff, Dept. of Physics.

Palmieri, F., et al. (1991) Learning binaural sound localization through a neural network. In *Proceedings of the 1991 IEEE Seventeenth Annual Northeast Bioengineering Conference* (pp. 13–14).

Patel, A.D., Gibson, E., Ratner, J., Besson, M. & Holcomb, P.J. (1996) Processing grammatical relations in music and language: An event-related potential (ERP) study. In *Proceedings of the Fourth International Conference on Music Perception and Cognition* (pp. 337–342). Montreal: McGill University, Faculty of Music.

Port, R. & Anderson, S. (1989) Recognition of melody fragments in continuously performed music. In *Proceedings of the Eleventh Annual Conference of the Cognitive Science Society* (pp. 820–827). Hillsdale, NJ: Erlbaum Associates.

Port, R., Anderson, S. & McAuley, J.D. (1994) *Towards Simulated Audition in Open Environments.* Research Report 138, Indiana University, Dept. of Cognitive Science.

Richard, D.M. (1989) *A Connectionist Model for Automatic Polyphonic Music Recognition Using a Cultural Code.* Unpublished doctoral thesis, University of Pennsylvania, Dept. of Computer Science. Vol. 50/09-B of Dissertation Abstracts International, p. 4199.

Röbel, A. (1993) *Neuronale Modelle nichtlinearer dynamischer Systeme mit Anwendung auf Musiksignale.* Unpublished doctoral thesis, Technische Universität Berlin.

Röbel, A. (1995) Neural networks for modeling time series of musical instruments. In E. Michie (Ed.), *Proceedings of the 1995 International Computer Music Conference* (pp. 424–428). San Francisco: International Computer Music Association.

Röbel, A. (1995) RBF networks for snythesis of speech and music signals. In *Third Workshop Fuzzy-Neuro Systeme '95* (pp. 165–172). Bonn: Deutsche Gesellschaft für Informatik E.V., Gesellschaft für Informatik.

Röbel, A. (1996) Scaling properties of neural networks for the prediction of time series. In *Proceedings of the 1996 IEEE Workshop on Neural Networks for Signal Processing VI* (pp. 190–199). Piscataway, NJ: IEEE.

Röbel, A. (1997) Neural network modeling of speech and music signals. In M.C. Mozer, M.I. Jordan & T. Petsche (Eds.), *Advances in Neural Information Processing Systems 9.* Cambridge, MA: MIT Press.

Roberts, S.C. & Greenhough, M. (1995) Rhythmic pattern processing using a self-organising neural network. In E. Michie (Ed.), *Proceedings of the 1995 International Computer Music Conference* (pp. 412–419). San Francisco: International Computer Music Association.

Sano, H. & Jenkins, K.B. (1989) A neural network model for pitch perception. *Computer Music Journal*, 13(3), 41–48. Also in P.M. Todd & D.G. Loy (Eds.) (1991) *Music and Connectionism* (pp. 42–49). Cambridge, MA: MIT Press.

Sayegh, S.I. (1989) Fingering for string instruments with the optimum path paradigm. *Computer Music Journal*, 13(3), 76–84. Also in P.M. Todd & D.G. Loy (Eds.) (1991) *Music and Connectionism* (pp. 243–251). Cambridge, MA: MIT Press.

Sayegh, S.I. & Tenorio, M.F. (1988) Inverse Viterbi algorithm as learning procedure and application to optimization in the string instrument fingering problem. In *IEEE International Conference on Neural Networks* (Vol. 2, pp. 491–497). New York: IEEE.

Scarborough, D.L., Miller, B.O. & Jones, J.A. (1989) Connectionist models for tonal analysis. *Computer Music Journal*, 13(3), 49–55. Also in P.M. Todd & D.G. Loy (Eds.) (1991) *Music and Connectionism* (pp. 54–60). Cambridge, MA: MIT Press.

Scarborough, D.L., Miller, B.O. & Jones, J.A. (1990) PDP models for meter perception. In *Proceedings of the Twelfth Annual Conference of the Cognitive Science Society* (pp. 892–899). Hillsdale, NJ: Erlbaum.

Scarborough, D.L., Miller, B.O. & Jones, J.A. (1992) On the perception of meter. In M. Balaban, K. Ebcioglu & O. Laske (Eds.), *Understanding Music with AI: Perspectives in Music Cognition* (pp. 427–447). Cambridge, MA: MIT Press.

Sergent, J. (1993) Mapping the musician brain. *Human Brain Mapping*, 1, 20–38.

Sergent, J., Zuck, E. & Terriah, S. (1992) Distributed neural network underlying musical sight-reading and keyboard performance. *Science*, 257, 106–109.

Shibata, N. (1991) A neural network-based method for chord/note scale association with melodies. *NEC Research and Development*, 32(3), 453–459.

Shibata, N., Shimazu, M. & Takashima, Y. (1990) A method for neural network based melody harmonizing. In M. Caudill (Ed.), *Proceedings of the International Joint Conference on Neural Networks* (Vol. 2, pp. 695–698). Hillsdale, NJ: Erlbaum.

Shuttleworth, T. & Wilson, R. (1995) A neural network for triad classification. In E. Michie (Ed.), *Proceedings of the 1995 International Computer Music Conference* (pp. 428–431). San Francisco: International Computer Music Association.

Stevens, C. (1992) Connectionist models of musical pattern recognition. In *Proceedings of the Third Australian Conference on Neural Networks* (pp. 17–20).

Stevens, C. & Latimer, C. (1992) A comparison of connectionist models of music recognition and human performance. *Minds and Machines*, 2(4), 379–400.

Stevens, C. & Wiles, J. (1993) Representations of tonal music: A case study in the development of temporal relationships. In M.C. Mozer, P. Smolensky, D.S. Touretzky, J.E. Elman & A.S. Weigend (Eds.), *Proceedings of the 1993 Connectionist Models Summer School* (pp. 228–235). Hillsdale, NJ: Erlbaum.

Su, A. (1997) On searching the model parameters of digital waveguide filters by using error back-propagation methods. In *Proceedings of the 1997 International Computer Music Conference* (pp. 192–195). San Francisco: International Computer Music Association.

Szilas, N. & Cadoz, C. (1993) Physical models that learn. In *Proceedings of the 1993 International Computer Music Conference* (pp. 72–75). San Francisco: International Computer Music Association.

Taylor, I. (1994) *Artificial Neural Network Types for the Determination of Musical Pitch*. Unpublished doctoral thesis, University of Wales, College of Cardiff, Dept. of Physics.

Taylor, I. & Greenhough, M. (1993) An object oriented ARTMAP system for classifying pitch. *Proceedings of the 1993 International Computer Music Conference* (pp. 244–247). San Francisco: International Computer Music Association.

Taylor, I.J. & Greenhough, M. (1995) Neural network pitch tracking over the pitch continuum. In E. Michie (Ed.), *Proceedings of the 1995 International Computer Music Conference* (pp. 432–435). San Francisco: International Computer Music Association.

Taylor, I., Page, M. & Greenhough, M. (1993) Neural networks for processing musical signals and structures. *Acoustics Bulletin*, 18, 5–9.

Thorson, M., Warthman, F. & Holler, M. (1993) A neural-network audio synthesizer: Generating natural and space-age sounds in hardware. *Dr. Dobb's Journal*, 18(2), 50–58.

Thywissen, K. (1997) Evolutionary based algorithmic composition: A demonstration of recent developments in genotator. In *Proceedings of the 1997 International Computer Music Conference* (pp. 368–371). San Francisco: International Computer Music Association.

Todd, P.M. (1984) *Abstracting Musical Features Using a Parallel Distributed Processing Approach*. Master's thesis, University of California, San Diego, Institute for Cognitive Science.

Todd, P.M. (1988) A sequential network design for musical applications. In D. Touretzky, G. Hinton & T. Sejnowski (Eds.), *Proceedings of the 1988 Connectionist Models Summer School* (pp. 76–84). Menlo Park, CA: Morgan Kaufmann.

Todd, P.M. (1989) Review of T. Kohonen, "A self-learning musical grammar, or 'Associative memory of the second kind'". *Neural Network Review*, 3, 114–116.

Todd, P.M. (1991) A connectionist approach to algorithmic composition. *Computer Music Journal*, 13(4), 27–43. Also in P.M. Todd & D.G. Loy (Eds.) (1991) *Music and Connectionism* (pp. 173–189). Cambridge, MA: MIT Press.

Todd, P.M. (1991) Further research and directions. In P.M. Todd & D.G. Loy (Eds.), *Music and Connectionism* (pp. 263–266). Cambridge, MA: MIT Press.

Todd, P.M. (1991) Neural networks for applications in the arts. In M. Scott (Ed.), *Proceedings of the Eleventh Annual Symposium on Small Computers in the Arts* (pp. 3–8). Philadelphia, PA: Small Computers in the Arts Network, Inc.

Todd, P.M. (1992) A connectionist system for exploring melody space. In *Proceedings of the 1992 International Computer Music Conference* (pp. 65–68). San Francisco: International Computer Music Association.

Todd, P.M. & Loy, D.G. (1990) Responses to Laske. *Computer Music Journal*, 14(2), 12–13. Also in P.M. Todd & D.G. Loy (Eds.) (1991) *Music and Connectionism* (pp. 261–262). Cambridge, MA: MIT Press.

Todd, P.M. & Loy, D.G. (Eds.) (1991) *Music and Connectionism*. Cambridge, MA: MIT Press.

Toiviainen, P. (1993) An artificial neural network approach for modeling harmony-based jazz improvisation. In *International Workshop on Knowledge Technology in the Arts* (pp. 79–88). Osaka: Laboratories of Image Information Science and Technology.

Toiviainen, P. (1995) Modeling the target-note technique of bebop-style jazz improvisation: An artificial neural network approach. *Music Perception*, 12(4), 399–413.

Toiviainen, P. (1996) Modeling musical cognition with artificial neural networks. In *Jyväskylä Studies in the Arts 51*. University of Jyväskylä, Finland.

Toiviainen, P., Kaipainen, M. & Louhivuori, J. (1995) Musical timbre: Similarity ratings correlate with computational feature space distances. *Journal of New Music Research*, 24(3), 282–298.

Tramo, M.J., Bharucha, J.J. & Musiek, F.E. (1990) Music perception and cognition following bilateral lesions of auditory cortex. *Journal of Cognitive Neuroscience*, 2, 195–212.

Trubitt, D.R. & Todd, P.M. (1991) The computer musician: Neural networks and computer music. *Electronic Musician*, 7(1), 20–24.

Uno, Y. & Mozer, M.C. (1997) Neural net architectures in modeling compositional syntax: Prediction and perception of continuity in minimalist works by Phillip Glass & Louis Andriessen. In *Proceedings of the 1997 International Computer Music Conference* (pp. 129–132). San Francisco: International Computer Music Association.

Vercoe, B. (1988) Hearing polyphonic music with the connection machine. In *Proceedings of the First Workshop on AI and Music* (pp. 183–194). American Association of Artificial Intelligence.

Vercoe, B. & Cumming, D. (1988) Connection machine tracking of polyphonic audio. In *Proceedings of the 1988 International Computer Music Conference* (pp. 65–68). San Francisco: International Computer Music Association.

Vidyamurthy, G. & Chakrapani, J. (1992) Cognition of tonal centers: A fuzzy approach. *Computer Music Journal*, 16(2), 45–50.

Weigend, A.S. (1994) Connectionism for music and audition. In J. Cowan, G. Tesauro & J. Alspector (Eds.), *Advances in Neural Information Processing Systems 6* (pp. 1163–1164). San Francisco: Morgan Kaufmann.

Yadid, O., Brutman, E., Dvir, L., Gerner, M. & Shimon, U. (1992) RAMIT: A neural network for recognition of musical notes. In *Proceedings of the 1992 International Computer Music Conference* (pp. 128–131). San Francisco: International Computer Music Association.

Yadid-Pecht, O., Dvir, L., Brutman, E., Gerner, M. & Shimon, U. (1996) Handwritten musical note recognition via a modified neocognitron. *Machine Vision and Applications*, 9(1).

Yeo, S., Han, M. & Lee, C. (1997) A new connectionist model for associative retrieval of harmonic tunes. In *Proceedings of the 1997 International Computer Music Conference* (pp. 434–437). San Francisco: International Computer Music Association.

Contributors

Shumeet Baluja
Justsystem Pittsburgh Research Center
4616 Henry Street
Pittsburgh, Pennsylvania 15213
USA
baluja@jprc.com

Matthew I. Bellgard
Department of Information Technology
Murdoch University
Murdoch, Western Australia 6150
Australia
m.bellgard@murdoch.edu.au

Michael A. Casey
Machine Listening Group
MIT Media Laboratory
E15 401c
20 Ames Street
Cambridge, Massachusetts 02139
USA
mkc@media.mit.edu

Garrison W. Cottrell
Deparament of Air Science
Condominium Community College of
    Southern California

Peter Desain
NICI, University of Nijmegen
P.O. Box 9104
NL-6500 HE Nijmegen
The Netherlands
desain@nici.kun.nl

Robert O. Gjerdingen
The School of Music
Northwestern University
Evanston, Illinois 60208-1200
USA
r-gjerdingen@nwu.edu

Mike Greenhough
Department of Physics and Astronomy
University of Wales, College of Cardiff
P.O. Box 913
Cardiff, CF2 3YB, Wales
UK
greenhough@cardiff.ac.uk

Niall Griffith
Department of Computer Science and
    Information Systems
University of Limerick
Limerick, Ireland
niall.griffith@ul.ie

Stephen Grossberg
Department of Cognitive and Neural
    Systems
Center for Adaptive Systems
Boston University
677 Beacon Street
Boston, Massachusetts 02215
USA
steve@cns.bu.edu

Henkjan Honing
NICI, University of Nijmegen
P.O. Box 9104
NL-6500 HE Nijmegen
The Netherlands
honing@nici.kun.nl

Todd Jochem
Smith Hall 216—Robotics
Carnegie Mellon University
5000 Forbes Avenue
Pittsburgh, Pennsylvania 15213
USA
tjochem@ri.cmu.edu

Bruce F. Katz
School of Cognitive and Computing
   Sciences
University of Sussex
Falmer, Brighton, BN1 9QH
UK
brucek@cogs.susx.ac.uk

John F. Kolen
Computer Science Department
The University of West Florida
11000 University Parkway
Pensacola, Florida 32514
USA
jkolen@ai.uwf.edu

Edward W. Large
Institute for Research in Cognitive
   Science
University of Pennsylvania
3401 Walnut Street, Suite 301C
Philadelphia, Pennsylvania 19104-6228
USA
large@grip.cis.upenn.edu

Michael C. Mozer
Department of Computer Science
University of Colorado
Boulder, Colorado 80309-0430
USA
mozer@cs.colorado.edu

Michael P. A. Page
M.R.C. Applied Psychology Unit
15 Chaucer Road
Cambridge, CB2 2EF
UK
page@mrc-apu.cam.ac.uk

Caroline Palmer
Department of Psychology
Ohio State University
1885 Neil Avenue
Columbus, Ohio 43210-1277
USA
cpalmer@magnus.acs.ohio-state.edu

Jordan B. Pollack
Computer Science Department
Brandeis University
Waltham, Massachusetts 02254
USA
pollack@cs.brandeis.edu

Dean Pomerleau
Department of Computer Science
Carnegie Mellon University
5000 Forbes Avenue
Pittsburgh, Pennsylvania 15213
USA
pomerleau@cs.cmu.edu

Stephen W. Smoliar
FX Palo Alto Laboratory
3400 Hillview Avenue
Building 4
Palo Alto, California 94304
USA
smoliar@pal.xerox.com

Ian Taylor
Department of Physics and Astronomy
University of Wales, College of Cardiff
P.O. Box 913
Cardiff, CF2 3YB, Wales
UK
ijt@cm.cf.ac.uk

Peter M. Todd
Max Planck Institute for Human
   Development
Center for Adapive Behavior and
   Cognition
Lentzeallee 94
14195 Berlin
Germany
ptodd@mpib-berlin.mpg.de

C.P. Tsang
Logic & AI Laboratory
Department of Computer Science
The University of Western Australia
Nedlands, Western Australia 6009
Australia
tsang@cs.uwa.edu.au

Gregory M. Werner
School of Cognitive and Computing
    Sciences
University of Sussex
Falmer, Brighton, BN1 9QH
UK
gwerner@ix.netcom.com